S0-AEM-724

STRUCTURED COBOL PROGRAMMING

STRUCTURED COBOL PROGRAMMING

NANCY STERN
Hofstra University

ROBERT A. STERN
Nassau Community College

THIRD EDITION

JOHN WILEY & SONS
New York   Chichester
Brisbane   Toronto
Singapore

This book was set in Times Roman by Waldman Graphics.
It was printed and bound by Semline.
The designer was Fern Logan. The drawings were designed and executed by John Balbalis with the assistance of the Wiley Illustration Department. The copyeditor was Rosemary Wellner. Claire Egielski supervised production.

Copyright © 1970, **1975,1980** , by John Wiley & Sons, Inc.

All rights reserved. Published simultaneously in Canada.

Reproduction or translation of any part of
this work beyond that permitted by Sections
107 and 108 of the 1976 United States Copyright
Act without the permission of the copyright
owner is unlawful. Requests for permission
or further information should be addressed to
the Permissions Department, John Wiley & Sons.

Library of Congress Cataloging in Publication Data:

Stern, Nancy B
   Structured COBOL Programming
   Second ed. published in 1975 under title: COBOL
programming.

   Includes index.
   1. COBOL (Computer program language) 2. Structured
programming. I. Stern, Robert A., joint author.
II. Title.

QA76.73.C25S75   1980   001.6′424   79-18434
ISBN 0-471-04913-1

Printed in the United States of America

20 19 18 17 16 15 14 13 12

TO LORI AND MELANIE

PREFACE

OBJECTIVES OF THE BOOK

This book has been written with three primary objectives. We wish to provide the beginner in data processing with (1) the ability to write efficient ANS COBOL programs using the structured approach, (2) an understanding of how COBOL is used effectively in commercial applications, and (3) the most efficient logical approach necessary for writing sophisticated programs. The approach used in this textbook differs from others on COBOL in the following ways.

1. This is neither a reference manual nor a programmed instruction textbook. Instead, it combines the advantages of both, while minimizing the disadvantages. This results in a combined text-workbook approach. Thorough explanations of each topic are contained here, with illustrations, questions, and answers immediately following. (For the exercises, the student should use a sheet of paper to cover up the answers. The asterisks indicate where the answers begin.) Several topics are presented with many illustrations and questions, so that the reader can relate the information and better understand the logical approach necessary for structured programming in ANS COBOL.

2. The organization of the text is most beneficial to the student. Most books on COBOL are fragmented, generally commencing with a discussion of the PROCEDURE DIVISION and leaving the rest for a later explanation. This makes it extremely difficult for beginners to understand how to organize a COBOL program effectively. They may understand each segment, but the relationship of one to another is difficult to conceptualize. To effectively utilize COBOL as a programming language, the programmer must understand this interrelationship. Therefore, with this book, the reader is able to write complete COBOL programs, however simple, after the first few lessons. Not only are segments of programs provided in the various explanations and illustrations, but previous learning is reinforced at all points. By giving complete illustrations and programs as answers to problems, the reader's conceptual understanding of COBOL is enhanced as is the ability to program in the language.

3. Illustrations, questions, and programs to be written by the reader are totally applicable to the commercial field. Most books in this field supply examples and questions that, although relevant to the particular points being explained, do not relate effectively to the business environment. As a result, the beginner does not fully understand the total applicability of ANS COBOL to business. We have overcome this problem by providing examples and programs that are realistic, in a business sense.

CHANGES IN THE NEW EDITION

STRUCTURED PROGRAMMING

The structured approach to COBOL programming has been introduced in a simple and straightforward manner. That is, instead of beginning with verbose justifications and explanations of why structuring is so popular and why it has been instituted to replace previous techniques, we simply present it as the programming method used in the book. In this way, students are given a thorough exposure to this method and come to recognize its intrinsic characteristics by themselves. Only in later chapters is structured programming given as an alternative to other techniques. Thus the student learns this efficient and effective technique from the start.

ADDITIONAL TOPICS

Several topics have been added to the book. These include:

1. Sequential file processing techniques, including control breaks, and tape updates.
2. The SORT feature.
3. The SEARCH statement as a method of table handling.
4. Validity Checking Routines.

Several topics have been expanded:

1. Disk processing
2. Appendixes
   a. Pseudocode as a method for representing logical control
   b. Job control

This added material must be understood if the student is to write intermediate-level as well as elementary-level programs. Since many COBOL courses are now two semesters these additions and expansions can be used for enhancing the student's appreciation and understanding of COBOL for these courses. The additional material is frequently useful for one-semester courses where advanced students are eager to go beyond the standard material presented.

COMPUTER PRINTOUTS

Computer printouts have been added for several reasons:

1. They make programs and program excerpts more readable.
2. They ensure the accuracy of illustrative material.
3. They familiarize the student with program listings and computer output.

FORMAT AND PEDAGOGIC APPROACH

There have been several reorganizations of sections within chapters, based on reviewers' comments and suggestions from our students. The COMPUTE section, for example, is now part of the arithmetic chapter.

The basic structure of the book, however, remains fundamentally the same. Summaries of each topic are provided as boxed units within each chapter. True-False review questions have been added to each chapter and some problems have been changed. In general, we firmly believe that the pedagogic approach presented here is well suited for college students and will provide a solid foundation for understanding the COBOL language.

ORGANIZATION OF THE BOOK

The book is now divided into six main units:

UNIT I: AN OVERVIEW OF COBOL

This unit introduces the student to structured programming in ANS COBOL. At the end of this first unit the student can write simplified COBOL programs. We believe the best way to learn the language is to write complete programs, however simple, from the beginning.

UNIT TWO: BASIC COBOL OPERATIONS

This unit contains a thorough discussion of the most frequently used COBOL verbs. It provides a thorough discussion of transfer of control and decision statements. After reading this unit, the student should be able to program elementary business applications with relative ease.

UNIT THREE: BASIC PRINT AND EDIT OPTIONS

Because printing reports is such an integral part of business applications and since COBOL provides so many options, an entire unit is devoted to this topic. After reading this unit, the student should be able to produce complex, management-level reports.

UNIT IV: ADVANCED LOGIC CONSIDERATIONS AND TABLE HANDLING ROUTINES

This unit includes a thorough discussion of all the methods that may be used to transfer control in a COBOL program. The rationale for using the structured approach is explained. Table handling, including the SEARCH statement, is presented in detail. This unit focuses on intermediate-level logic problems.

UNIT V: TAPE AND DISK PROCESSING

This unit concentrates on tape and disk processing. It has been significantly expanded from previous editions. Tape updates, merges, sorts, and control breaks are presented in detail. Disk processing is also emphasized. This unit is designed for the intermediate-level COBOL programmer.

UNIT VI: ADDITIONAL COBOL OPTIONS

This unit provides an overview of topics that are not necessary for intermediate-level COBOL programming but may facilitate such programming. It describes methods that may be used to simplify coding.

The Appendixes include standard COBOL entries such as reserved words, collating sequences, and formats. In addition, they provide a summary of three topics the student may or may not be familiar with: magnetic tape features, flowcharts and pseudocode, and job control. Students who have learned about these topics need not read these Appendixes; those with no previous exposure are encouraged to read them.

**THE USE OF
THE BOOK**

This book is intended primarily for junior-college and four-year college students and requires no prior exposure to programming languages. We have provided no introduction to computer equipment because this equipment varies greatly among computer centers. In addition, COBOL is designed to be basically computer independent.

We express special appreciation to Burroughs, Honeywell, and IBM for their cooperation in supplying specifications, illustrations, examples, and photographs.

We would like to thank our editor, Gene Davenport, for his support, Ellen and Ilene Goldberg for their editorial assistance, Diane Zaremba for her help in preparing the instructor's manual, and Melanie and Lori Stern for preparing the index.

NANCY STERN
ROBERT A. STERN

ACKNOWLEDGMENT

The following acknowledgment has been reproduced from COBOL Edition, U.S. Department of Defense, at the request of the Conference on Data Systems Languages.

"Any organization interested in reproducing the COBOL report and specifications in whole or in part, using ideas taken from this report as the basis for an instruction manual or for any other purpose is free to do so. However, all such organizations are requested to reproduce this section as part of the introduction to the document. Those using a short passage, as in a book review, are requested to mention 'COBOL' in acknowledgment of the source, but need not quote this entire section.

"COBOL is an industry language and is not the property of any compnay or group of companies, or of any organization or group of organizations.

"No warranty, expressed or implied, is made by any contributor or by the COBOL Committee as to the accuracy and functioning of the programming system and language. Moreover, no responsibility is assumed by any contributor, or by the committee, in connection therewith.

"Procedures have been established for the maintenance of COBOL. Inquiries concerning the procedures for proposing changes should be directed to the Executive Committee of the Conference on Data Systems Languages.

"The authors and copyright holders of the copyrighted material used herein

FLOW-MATIC (Trademark of Sperry Rand Corporation), Programming for the Univac (R) I and II, Data Automation Systems copyrighted 1958, 1959, by Sperry Rand Corporation: IBM Commercial Translator Form No. F28-8013, copyrighted 1959 by IBM; FACT, DSI 27A5260-2760, copyrighted 1960 by Minneapolis-Honeywell

have specifically authorized the use of this material in whole or in part, in the COBOL specifications. Such authorization extends to the reproduction and use of COBOL specifications in programming manuals or similar publications."

N.S.
R.A.S.

CONTENTS

UNIT TWO: BASIC COBOL OPERATIONS

UNIT THREE: BASIC PRINT AND EDIT OPTIONS

UNIT FOUR: ADVANCED LOGIC CONSIDERATIONS AND TABLE HANDLING ROUTINES

UNIT FIVE: TAPE AND DISK PROCESSING

UNIT SIX: ADDITIONAL COBOL OPTIONS

APPENDIX

PRINTER SPACING CHARTS

STRUCTURED COBOL PROGRAMMING

1 AN OVERVIEW OF COBOL

CHAPTER 1 INTRODUCTION TO COBOL PROGRAMMING

A. COMPUTER PROGRAMMING

No matter how complex a computer may be, its actions are directed by individual computer instructions designed and tested by a computer **programmer.** The program consists of a set of instructions that will operate on input data and convert it to output. A computer, then, can operate only as efficiently and effectively as it is programmed.

All instructions to be operated on must be in machine language. For the programmer to code instructions in this form is very tedious and cumbersome. Memory addresses must be remembered, and complex numerical computer codes must be utilized.

Since programming in a machine language is so difficult, advances in programming technology were developed to enable the programmer to write Englishlike instructions. These instructions, however, must be translated or **compiled** into machine language before they can be executed. The computer itself performs this translation into machine language with the use of a control program.

Among the numerous **programming languages** that can be translated into machine form is COBOL, which is the one used most often for commercial applications.

The programmer, then, writes a set of instructions, called the **source program,** in one of the programming languages. It **cannot** be executed or operated on by the computer until it has been translated into machine language.

The source program is generally punched into cards by a keypunch machine. This **source deck** enters the computer and must be translated into a machine language program called the **object program** before execution can occur. A special program called a **compiler** translates source programs into object programs.

While the computer is performing this translation, any errors detected by the compiler will be listed. That is, any violation of a programming rule is denoted as an error. This type of error is sometimes referred to as a **syntax**

1

error. For example, if the instruction to add two numbers is spelled AD instead of ADD, the computer will print an error message. If errors are of considerable magnitude, translation will be terminated. Note that the errors detected during a compilation are **not** of a logical nature. A logic error is one in which the **sequence** of programming steps is not executed properly. The machine generally has no way of judging the logic in a program, but this may be tested by executing the program in a "trial run."

If errors are not present in the source program or only minor violations of rules occur, the translation process will continue until all instructions are in machine language form. The program can then be executed, or tested, at this point. If, however, execution is not desirable at this time, the object program may be saved by punching it into cards to obtain an object deck or by storing it on some other medium. Thus, this object program may be used to execute the instructions without the necessity to recompile. Figure 1.1 illustrates the steps involved in programming.

A program, therefore, specifies the logical sequence of computer instructions. When the logic of a program becomes complex, pictorial representations called **flowcharts** are drawn **prior to** the coding of the program. These pictorial representations illustrate program logic in a less complex manner, thus facilitating the writing of the program.

Such flowcharts will be illustrated throughout. For the beginner in data processing with no previous exposure to flowcharting, Appendix C provides an introduction to the basic concepts. This appendix also provides an introduction to **pseudocode,** which is another technique used to facilitate program coding.

SELF-EVALUATING QUIZ

Each question in the exercises will be followed by an asterisk which signals that the solution will follow. Use a sheet of paper to cover the solution when testing yourself.

1. The major task of a computer programmer is to _____.
   *****
   write and test computer instructions
2. A set of instructions that will operate on input data and convert it to output is called a _____.
   *****
   program
3. To be executed by the computer, all instructions must be in _____ language.
   *****
   machine
4. Programs are written in _____ language. Why?
   *****
   symbolic programming
   Machine language coding is cumbersome and tedious.
5. Programs written in a language other than machine language must be _____ before execution can occur.
   *****
   translated or compiled

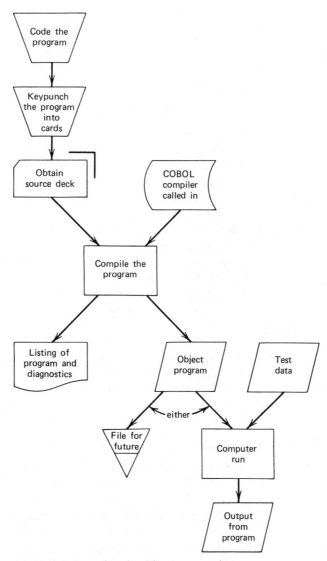

Figure 1.1 Steps involved in programming a computer.

6. _____ is an example of an Englishlike programming language.
   *****
   COBOL
7. _____ is the process of converting a COBOL program into machine language.
   *****
   Compilation
8. The program written in a language such as COBOL is called the _____ program.
   *****
   source
9. The source deck is the _____.
   *****

set of instructions in a language such as COBOL that has been punched into cards

10. The object program is the _____.
    *****
    set of instructions that has been converted into machine language

11. A _____ converts a _____ program into a(n) _____ program.
    *****
    compiler
    source
    object

12. The errors that are detected during compilation denote _____, and are usually referred to as _____ errors.
    *****
    any violation of programming rules in the use of the symbolic programming language; syntax

13. The logic of a program can be checked by _____.
    *****
    testing it or executing it in a "trial run"

14. After a program has been compiled, it may be _____ or _____.
    *****
    executed
    saved in translated form for future processing

B. THE NATURE OF COBOL

COBOL is the most widespread commercial programming language in use today. The reasons for its vast success are discussed in this section.

The word COBOL is an abbreviation for **CO**mmon **B**usiness **O**riented **L**anguage. It is a **B**usiness **O**riented computer language designed for commercial applications. The rules governing the use of the language make it applicable for commercial problems. Thus, applications of a scientific nature cannot be adequately handled by COBOL; a scientific computer language such as FORTRAN would be more appropriate.

COBOL is a computer language that is common to many computers. That is, most computer manufacturers have designed their machines to accept a COBOL compiler, so that the same COBOL program may be compiled on a variety of different computers such as an IBM s/370 and a UNIVAC 1100 with only minor variations.

The universality of COBOL, therefore, allows computer users greater flexibility. A company is free to use computers of different manufacturers while retaining a single programming language. Similarly, conversion from one model computer to a more advanced or newer one presents no great problem. Computers of a future generation will also be equipped to use COBOL.

Since its creation in 1959, the COBOL language has undergone extensive refinement in an effort to make it more standardized. The American National Standards Institute (ANSI), an association of computer manufacturers and users, has developed an industry-wide standard COBOL called ANS COBOL. Since most users have adopted this standard of COBOL, we utilize this version throughout this book. Where differences exist between ANS COBOL and other versions, we use footnotes to describe these differences. This text is based on the 1974 ANS COBOL standard. It also places emphasis on the features that have been proposed for the 1980 standard.[1]

Thus the meaning of the word COBOL suggests two of its basic advantages. It is common to most computers, and it is commercially oriented. There are, however, additional reasons why it is such a popular language.

COBOL is an Englishlike language. All instructions are coded using English words rather than complex codes. To add two numbers together, for example, we use the word ADD. Similarly, the rules for programming in COBOL conform to many of the rules for writing in English, making it a relatively simple language to learn. It therefore becomes significantly easier to train programmers. In addition, COBOL programs are written and tested in far less time than programs written in other computer languages.

Thus the Englishlike quality of COBOL makes it easy to **write** programs. Similarly, this quality makes COBOL programs easier to **read.** Such programs can generally be understood by nondata processing personnel. The business executive who knows little about computers can better understand the nature of a programming job simply by reading a COBOL program.

SELF-EVALUATING QUIZ

1. The word COBOL is an abbreviation for _____ _____ _____ _____.
   *****
   COmmon **B**usiness **O**riented **L**anguage
2. COBOL is a common language in the sense that _____.
   *****
   it may be used on many different makes and models of computers
3. COBOL is a business-oriented language in the sense that _____.
   *****
   it makes use of ordinary business terminology
4. COBOL generally (would, would not) be used for scientific applications.
   *****
   would not
5. An additional feature of COBOL is that it is _____.
   *****
   Englishlike
6. ANS is an abbreviation for _____.
   *****
   American National Standards

C. STRUCTURED PROGRAMMING

INTRODUCTION

Structured programming is a coding technique that has become exceedingly popular in recent years. It involves the designing of programs with a limited number of branching functions. This type of program design results in a more efficient program regardless of the language utilized.

---

[1]For those students who may be using the 1968 ANS COBOL standard, you may find that minor adjustments to your program are necessary. See Appendix F for a description of 1968 language features that are not consistent with the 1974 standard.

When programmers code their programs using the structured technique, they **modularize** or segment their programs into independent sections or **modules.** The following is a list of some of the objectives of this technique.

OBJECTIVES OF STRUCTURED PROGRAMMING
1. To simplify debugging
2. To facilitate the coding of long and complex problems
3. To make programs more efficient
4. To make programs easier to read and understand

TECHNIQUES USED IN STRUCTURED PROGRAMMING

Most nonstructured programs include numerous branch points that often make it difficult to follow the logic and to debug a program when an error occurs. One major purpose of structured programming is to simplify debugging by reducing the number of entry and exit points in a program. For that reason, structured programming is sometimes referred to as GO TO-LESS programming, where a GO TO statement is the COBOL code for a branch. Using the techniques of structured programming, the GO TO or branch statement becomes unnecessary. In COBOL, this means writing programs where sequences are controlled by PERFORM statements. (In FORTRAN, this would mean writing programs where sequences are controlled by DO statements and subroutines.)

Using this technique, each section of a program can be handled independently without too much concern for where it enters the logic flow and what must be coded after that section has been completed. Thus, the programmer codes one main routine, and when some other routine is required, a PERFORM statement indicates that this routine will appear elsewhere in the program. With such a modularized concept, it is possible for different programmers to code different sections of a large and complex program. The main routine simply calls for the execution of these modules or sections as needed.

TOP-DOWN APPROACH

A more descriptive term used to indicate a program that is structured is "top-down" programming. The term implies that efficient programs are read and written by reading from top to bottom. The first series of instructions represents the main routine followed by intermediate and then minor routines. With this top-down approach, it is not necessary to skip all over the listing to follow the logic. When GO TO statements are used, this neat, top-down approach cannot easily be achieved.

In short, we avoid the use of GO TO statements in our programs. Moreover, we focus on the coding of efficient top-down programs that conform to this modular approach.

D. A SAMPLE PROGRAM

Every COBOL program consists of four separate **divisions.** Each division is written in an Englishlike manner designed to decrease programming effort and to facilitate the understanding of a program by nondata processing personnel. Each of the four divisions has a specific function.

THE FOUR DIVISIONS	
Name	**Purpose**
IDENTIFICATION DIVISION	Serves to identify the program to the computer. It also provides documentation that is extremely useful to nondata processing personnel analyzing or reading the program.
ENVIRONMENT DIVISION	Describes the computer equipment that will be utilized by the specific program.
DATA DIVISION	Describes the input and output formats to be processed by the program. It also defines any constants or work areas necessary for the processing of data.
PROCEDURE DIVISION	Contains the actual instructions necessary for reading input, processing it, and creating output.

The structure and organization of a COBOL program can best be explained by an illustration.

DEFINITION OF THE PROBLEM

A computer center of a large company is assigned the task of calculating weekly wages (Gross Pay) for all nonsalaried personnel. The hourly rate and number of hours worked are supplied for each employee, and the weekly wages figure is computed as follows:

WEEKLY-WAGES = HOURS-WORKED × HOURLY-RATE

For processing, the incoming data or **input,** must be in a form that is "readable" or understandable to the computer. Punched cards, magnetic tape, magnetic disk, terminals, and floppy disk are common forms of input to a computer system.

INPUT-LAYOUT AND DEFINITION

Thus the employee data, consisting of EMPLOYEE-NAME, HOURS-WORKED, and HOURLY-RATE, will be transcribed or **keypunched** onto a punched card so that it may be accepted as input to the data processing system. These data items are called **fields** of information. Specific columns of the card must be set aside to hold each field. The data will be entered on the card as shown in Figure 1.2. Card Columns 1–20 are **reserved** for EMPLOYEE-NAME. If any

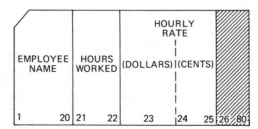

Figure 1.2

name contains less than 20 characters, the **low-order,** or rightmost, positions are left blank. Similarly, HOURS-WORKED will be placed in Columns 21–22 and HOURLY-RATE in Columns 23–25. The HOURLY-RATE figure, as a dollars and cents amount, is to be interpreted as a field with two decimal positions. That is, 125 in columns 23–25 is to be interpreted by the computer as 1.25. The decimal point is **not** punched into the card, since it would waste a storage position. We will see that this method of **implying** decimal points is easily handled in COBOL.

OUTPUT-LAYOUT AND DEFINITION

A deck of employee cards, with the above format, will be read as input to the computer. WEEKLY-WAGES will be calculated by the computer as HOURS-WORKED multiplied by HOURLY-RATE. The computed figure, however, **cannot** be added directly to the input data. That is, we cannot create output data on an input record. Input and output must ordinarily utilize separate devices.[2]

In this way, we will create an output file that contains all input data **in addition to** the computed wage figure. The output PAYROLL-FILE will be placed on a magnetic tape with the record format shown in Figure 1.3.

Thus the input to the system will be called EMPLOYEE-CARDS. The computer will calculate WEEKLY-WAGES from the two input fields HOURS-WORKED and HOURLY-RATE. The input data along with the computed figure will be used to create the output tape called PAYROLL-FILE.

THE PROGRAM

Once the input and output record formats have been clearly and precisely defined as in Figures 1.2 and 1.3, the program may be written. You will recall that a program is a set of instructions and specifications that operate on input to produce output. Figure 1.4 is a simplified COBOL program that will operate on employee cards to create a payroll tape file with the computed wages.

Note that the number zero is distinguished from the letter O by slashing all zeros. This convention will be used throughout the book. Note also that the program is divided into four major divisions. The IDENTIFICATION, ENVIRONMENT, DATA, and PROCEDURE DIVISIONS are coded on lines 01, 03, 07, and 22, respectively. Every COBOL program **must** contain these four divisions in the above order.

The IDENTIFICATION DIVISION has, as its only entry, the PROGRAM-ID. That is, the IDENTIFICATION DIVISION of this program merely serves to identify the program.

The ENVIRONMENT DIVISION assigns the input and output files to specific devices in the INPUT-OUTPUT SECTION. EMPLOYEE-CARDS, the name as-

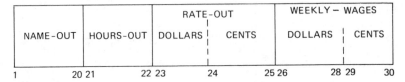

Figure 1.3

[2]An exception to this is **disk** processing, which will be discussed in Chapter 22.

IBM   COBOL Coding Form

SYSTEM

PROGRAM *FIRST SAMPLE PROGRAM*   PAGE   OF

PROGRAMMER *N. STERN*   DATE

GX28-1464-5 U/M 050*
Printed in U.S.A.

PUNCHING INSTRUCTIONS
GRAPHIC
PUNCH
CARD FORM #

SEQUENCE			COBOL STATEMENT
(PAGE)	(LINE)	A	B
ØØ1	Ø1	IDENTIFICATION DIVISION.
ØØ1	Ø2	PROGRAM-ID. SAMPLE.
ØØ1	Ø3	ENVIRONMENT DIVISION.
ØØ1	Ø4	INPUT-OUTPUT SECTION.
ØØ1	Ø5	FILE-CONTROL. SELECT EMPLOYEE-CARDS ASSIGN TO READER.
ØØ1	Ø6	SELECT PAYROLL-FILE ASSIGN TO TAPE-1.
ØØ1	Ø7	DATA DIVISION.
ØØ1	Ø8	FILE SECTION.
ØØ1	Ø9	FD EMPLOYEE-CARDS LABEL RECORDS ARE OMITTED.
ØØ1	1Ø	Ø1 EMPLOYEE-RECORD.
ØØ1	11	Ø2 EMPLOYEE-NAME PICTURE A(2Ø).
ØØ1	12	Ø2 HOURS-WORKED PICTURE 9(2).
ØØ1	13	Ø2 HOURLY-RATE PICTURE 9V99.
ØØ1	14	FD PAYROLL-FILE LABEL RECORDS ARE OMITTED.
ØØ1	15	Ø1 PAYROLL-RECORD.
ØØ1	16	Ø2 NAME-OUT PICTURE A(2Ø).
ØØ1	17	Ø2 HOURS-OUT PICTURE 9(2).
ØØ1	18	Ø2 RATE-OUT PICTURE 9V99.
ØØ1	19	Ø2 WEEKLY-WAGES PICTURE 999V99.
ØØ1	2Ø	WORKING-STORAGE SECTION.
ØØ1	21	Ø1 EOF PICTURE 9 VALUE Ø.
ØØ1	22	PROCEDURE DIVISION.
ØØ1	23	OPEN INPUT EMPLOYEE-CARDS, OUTPUT PAYROLL-FILE.
ØØ1	24	READ EMPLOYEE-CARDS AT END MOVE 1 TO EOF.
ØØ1	25	PERFORM WAGE-ROUTINE UNTIL EOF = 1.
ØØ1	26	CLOSE EMPLOYEE-CARDS, PAYROLL-FILE.
ØØ1	27	STOP RUN.
ØØ1	28	WAGE-ROUTINE.
ØØ1	29	MOVE EMPLOYEE-NAME TO NAME-OUT.
ØØ1	3Ø	MOVE HOURS-WORKED TO HOURS-OUT.
ØØ1	31	MOVE HOURLY-RATE TO RATE-OUT.
ØØ1	32	MULTIPLY HOURS-WORKED BY HOURLY-RATE GIVING WEEKLY-WAGES.
ØØ1	33	WRITE PAYROLL-RECORD.
ØØ1	34	READ EMPLOYEE-CARDS AT END MOVE 1 TO EOF.

IDENTIFICATION

*A standard card form, IBM Electro 081989Z, is available for punching source statements from this form.
Instructions for using this form are given in any IBM COBOL reference manual.
Address comments concerning this form to IBM Corporation, Programming Publications, 1271 Avenue of the Americas, New York, New York 10020.

*No. of sheets per pad may vary slightly

Figure 1.4

signed to the input file, will be processed by a card reader. Similarly, PAY-ROLL-FILE is the output file assigned to a specific tape drive.

The DATA DIVISION describes, in detail, the field designations of the two files. The input and output areas in memory are fully described in the DATA DIVISION, in the FILE SECTION. The File Description, or FD, for EMPLOYEE-CARDS describes the card file, which has no identifying labels (LABEL REC-ORDS ARE OMITTED).

The **record** format is called EMPLOYEE-RECORD. It has three input fields, EMPLOYEE-NAME, HOURS-WORKED, and HOURLY-RATE. Each field has a corresponding PICTURE clause denoting the size and type of data that will appear in the field.

The EMPLOYEE-NAME field is an alphabetic data field containing 20 characters. PICTURE A(20) indicates the **size** of the field (20 characters) and the **type** of data, A denoting alphabetic information. Similarly, HOURS-WORKED is a two-position numeric field. PICTURE 9(2) indicates the type and size of data: 9 denoting numeric information, and (2) denoting a two-position area. HOURLY-RATE is a three-position numeric field with an **implied** decimal point. PICTURE 9V99 indicates a three-position numeric field with an implied or assumed decimal point after the first position. Thus 125 in this field will be interpreted by the computer as 1.25. The decimal point does **not** appear on the input record but is nonetheless implied.

Similarly, the output file called PAYROLL-FILE has no labels. It has a record format called PAYROLL-RECORD, which is subdivided into four fields, each with an appropriate PICTURE clause. The first three fields, NAME-OUT, HOURS-OUT, and RATE-OUT will be taken directly from each input record. The last field, WEEKLY-WAGES, must be computed.

The constant EOF is defined in the WORKING-STORAGE SECTION of the DATA DIVISION. This field is initialized with a value of zero. It will be used in the PROCEDURE DIVISION as a special, coded field. That is, it will have a value of zero until the last data card has been read and processed, at which time a "1" will be moved into it. EOF, then, is an abbreviation for **End of File** since it will be used to indicate when the last data card has been read and processed.

The PROCEDURE DIVISION contains the set of instructions or operations to be performed by the computer. Each instruction is executed in the order in which it appears.

The first PROCEDURE DIVISION entry is the following:

```
OPEN INPUT EMPLOYEE-CARDS, OUTPUT PAYROLL-FILE.
```

This instruction accesses the files and indicates to the computer which file is input and which is output.

The next instruction in the PROCEDURE DIVISION is:

```
READ EMPLOYEE-CARDS AT END MOVE 1 TO EOF.
```

This is an instruction that causes the computer to read **one** data card into storage. If there are no more cards to be read when this statement is executed, a "1" will be moved to the field called EOF; otherwise EOF remains unchanged. In most instances, the first attempt to read a card causes data to be transmitted from a single card to storage and the next instruction to be executed.

The next instruction is the following:

```
PERFORM WAGE-ROUTINE UNTIL EOF = 1.
```

This instruction will cause all the statements specified within the paragraph labelled WAGE-ROUTINE (beginning on line 28) to be executed repeatedly until EOF = 1. A quick glance at the statements within WAGE-ROUTINE indicates that the instructions will be executed until there are no more cards, at which time a "1" is moved to EOF.

Once EOF = 1, the statement to be executed next is the one immediately following the PERFORM. That is, PERFORM WAGE-ROUTINE UNTIL EOF = 1 causes execution of WAGE-ROUTINE until there are no more cards, at which point control returns to the statement following the PERFORM. The instructions on lines 26 and 27, CLOSE and STOP RUN, are executed only after all cards have been processed at WAGE-ROUTINE.

The first instruction, OPEN, activates the files. The next instruction, READ, reads a single record. At WAGE-ROUTINE, the first record is processed and subsequent records are read and processed until there are no more input records. Then the CLOSE, which deactivates the files, and the STOP RUN are executed and the program is terminated. The five steps—OPEN, READ, PERFORM, CLOSE, and STOP—represent the main body of the PROCEDURE DIVISION.

Let us look more closely at the instructions to be executed at the WAGE-ROUTINE paragraph. First, EMPLOYEE-NAME of the **first** card, which was read with the READ statement on line 24, is moved to NAME-OUT of the output area. HOURS-WORKED and HOURLY-RATE of this first card are also moved to the output area. WEEKLY-WAGES, an output field, is then calculated by multiplying HOURS-WORKED by HOURLY-RATE.

After the data has been moved to the output area, a WRITE command is executed. This WRITE command takes the information in the output area and places it on magnetic tape.

The above set of instructions will process the **first** card and create one tape record. The READ statement is then executed and data from another card is transmitted to storage.

The sequence of instructions within WAGE-ROUTINE is executed under the control of the PERFORM statement on line 25. That is, execution of WAGE-ROUTINE instructions will be repeated until EOF = 1, which will only occur after all cards have been processed. Hence, after the second card has been read, WAGE-ROUTINE will be executed again, the input data moved, the calculation performed, a tape record written, and a third card read. This continues until there are no additional cards available for processing, at which point the instruction on line 26, the CLOSE, is executed.

Figure 1.4, then, represents a sample COBOL program. It is a complete program that will run on any system. Figure 1.5 is the computer listing of the same program.

An analysis of the program reveals two essential points. The Englishlike manner and the structural organization of a COBOL program make it comparatively easy to learn. Similarly, the ease with which a COBOL program may be read by nondata processing personnel makes it a distinct asset to most computer installations.

```
00101   IDENTIFICATION DIVISION.
00102   PROGRAM-ID. SAMPLE.
00103   ENVIRONMENT DIVISION.
00104   INPUT-OUTPUT SECTION.
00105   FILE-CONTROL. SELECT EMPLOYEE-CARDS ASSIGN TO READER.
00106              SELECT PAYROLL-FILE ASSIGN TO TAPE-1.
00107   DATA DIVISION.
00108   FILE SECTION.
00109   FD  EMPLOYEE-CARDS LABEL RECORDS ARE OMITTED.
00110   01  EMPLOYEE-RECORD.
00111       02  EMPLOYEE-NAME        PICTURE A(20).
00112       02  HOURS-WORKED         PICTURE 9(2).
00113       02  HOURLY-RATE          PICTURE 9V99.
00114   FD  PAYROLL-FILE    LABEL RECORDS ARE OMITTED.
00115   01  PAYROLL-RECORD.
00116       02  NAME-OUT            PICTURE A(20).
00117       02  HOURS-OUT           PICTURE 9(2).
00118       02  RATE-OUT            PICTURE 9V99.
00119       02  WEEKLY-WAGES        PICTURE 999V99.
00120   WORKING-STORAGE SECTION.
00121   01  EOF                     PICTURE 9 VALUE 0.
00122   PROCEDURE DIVISION.
00123       OPEN INPUT EMPLOYEE-CARDS, OUTPUT PAYROLL-FILE.
00124       READ EMPLOYEE-CARDS AT END MOVE 1 TO EOF.
00125       PERFORM WAGE-ROUTINE UNTIL EOF = 1.
00126       CLOSE EMPLOYEE-CARDS, PAYROLL-FILE.
00127       STOP RUN.
00128   WAGE-ROUTINE.
00129       MOVE EMPLOYEE-NAME TO NAME-OUT.
00130       MOVE HOURS-WORKED TO HOURS-OUT.
00131       MOVE HOURLY-RATE TO RATE-OUT.
00132       MULTIPLY HOURS-WORKED BY HOURLY-RATE GIVING WEEKLY-WAGES.
00133       WRITE PAYROLL-RECORD.
00134       READ EMPLOYEE-CARDS AT END MOVE 1 TO EOF.
```

Figure 1.5

SELF-EVALUATING QUIZ

1. All COBOL programs are composed of (no.) divisions.
   *****
   four
2. The names of these four divisions are _____, _____, _____, and
   _____.
   *****
   IDENTIFICATION
   ENVIRONMENT
   DATA
   PROCEDURE
3. The function of the IDENTIFICATION DIVISION is to _____.
   *****
   identify the program

4. The function of the ENVIRONMENT DIVISION is to _____.
   *****
   describe the equipment to be used in the program
5. The function of the DATA DIVISION is to _____.
   *****
   describe the input, output, constants, and work areas used in the program
6. The function of the PROCEDURE DIVISION is to _____.
   *****
   define the instructions and operations necessary to convert input data into output
7. Incoming data is called _____.
   *****
   input
8. Outgoing information is called _____.
   *****
   output
9. _____, _____, and _____ are examples of forms of computer input.
   *****
   Punched cards
   magnetic tape
   magnetic disk
10. A technique for simplifying the design of a COBOL program and facilitating debugging is called _____.
    *****
    structured programming
11. (T or F) Structured programs are designed by segmenting the program into modules.
    *****
    T
12. Another term for structured programming is _____.
    *****
    top-down programming
    or modular programming
13. Structured COBOL programs avoid the use of _____ instructions.
    *****
    GO TO or branch

REVIEW QUESTIONS

I. True-False Questions

True False

☐ ☐   1. A COBOL program that compiles without any errors will always run properly.

☐ ☐   2. Programs written in COBOL need not be compiled.
☐ ☐   3. COBOL programs must be converted into machine language before execution can occur.

☐ ☐   4. Although COBOL is a commercial programming language, it contains basic mathematical functions that can be used for high–level mathematical problems.

☐ ☐   5. COBOL may be used only on a small number of commercial computers.
☐ ☐   6. A COBOL program must contain four divisions.

☐ ☐   7. The sequence in which the divisions are written is IDENTIFICATION, DATA, ENVIRONMENT, PROCEDURE.

☐ ☐   8. The division that changes depending on the computer equipment utilized is the DATA DIVISION.

☐ ☐   9. The division that seems to require the least programming effort is the IDENTIFICATION DIVISION.

☐ ☐   10. Instructions are coded in the PROCEDURE DIVISION.

II. General Questions
1. Define the following terms:
   (a) Program.
   (b) Compiler.
   (c) Source program.
   (d) Object program.
2. State the differences between a high-level programming language and a machine language.
3. State the major reasons why COBOL is such a popular language.
4. What is the meaning of structured programming?
5. What is the meaning of ANS COBOL?
6. Indicate the purpose of each of the following:
   a. IDENTIFICATION DIVISION
   b. ENVIRONMENT DIVISION
   c. DATA DIVISION
   d. PROCEDURE DIVISION
7. What is the meaning of diagnostics?
8. What is the purpose of the PICTURE clause?
9. What is the purpose of the SELECT statement?
10. What is the purpose of the WORKING-STORAGE SECTION?

PROBLEMS   1. Figure 1.6 is an illustration of a sample COBOL program.
   (a) Define the input.
   (b) Define the output.
   (c) Describe the type of processing that converts input data into output.
   (d) Draw a flowchart of the procedures utilized.

IBM

COBOL Coding Form

SYSTEM

PROGRAM PROBLEM #1

PROGRAMMER R. STERN

PUNCHING INSTRUCTIONS

SEQUENCE	CONT	A	B	COBOL STATEMENT
ØØ1Ø1			IDENTIFICATION DIVISION.	
ØØ1Ø2			PROGRAM-ID. PROBLEM1.	
ØØ1Ø3			ENVIRONMENT DIVISION.	
ØØ1Ø4			INPUT-OUTPUT SECTION.	
ØØ1Ø5			FILE-CONTROL. SELECT FILE-1 ASSIGN TO READER.	
ØØ1Ø6			SELECT FILE-2 ASSIGN TO TAPE-1.	
ØØ1Ø7			DATA DIVISION.	
ØØ1Ø8			FILE SECTION.	
ØØ1Ø9			FD FILE-1 LABEL RECORDS ARE OMITTED.	
ØØ11Ø			Ø1 SALES-REC.	
ØØ111			Ø2 CUSTOMER-NAME-IN PICTURE A(2Ø).	
ØØ112			Ø2 UNIT-PRICE PICTURE 99V99.	
ØØ113			Ø2 QUANTITY PICTURE 999.	
ØØ114			Ø2 DISCOUNT-AMOUNT PICTURE 999V99.	
ØØ115			FD FILE-2 LABEL RECORDS ARE OMITTED.	
ØØ116			Ø1 RECORD-OUT.	
ØØ117			Ø2 CUSTOMER-NAME-OUT PICTURE A(2Ø).	
ØØ118			Ø2 TRANSACTION-AMOUNT PICTURE 99999V99.	
ØØ119			WORKING-STORAGE SECTION.	
ØØ12Ø			Ø1 EOF PICTURE 9 VALUE Ø.	
ØØ121			PROCEDURE DIVISION.	
ØØ122			OPEN INPUT FILE-1, OUTPUT FILE-2.	
ØØ123			READ FILE-1 AT END MOVE 1 TO EOF.	
ØØ124			PERFORM CALC-RTN UNTIL EOF = 1.	
ØØ125			CLOSE FILE-1, FILE-2.	
ØØ126			STOP RUN.	
ØØ127			CALC-RTN.	
ØØ128			MOVE CUSTOMER-NAME-IN TO CUSTOMER-NAME-OUT.	
ØØ129			MULTIPLY UNIT-PRICE BY QUANTITY GIVING TRANSACTION-AMOUNT.	
ØØ13Ø			SUBTRACT DISCOUNT-AMOUNT FROM TRANSACTION-AMOUNT.	
ØØ131			WRITE RECORD-OUT.	
ØØ132			READ FILE-1 AT END MOVE 1 TO EOF.	

GX28-1464-5 U/M 050*
Printed in U.S.A.

Figure 1.6

2. Figure 1.7 is an illustration of a sample COBOL program.
   (a) Define the input.
   (b) Define the output.
   (c) Describe the type of processing that converts input data into output.
   (d) Draw a flowchart of the procedures utilized.

```
00101   IDENTIFICATION DIVISION.
00102   PROGRAM-ID. PROBLEM2.
00103   ENVIRONMENT DIVISION.
00104   INPUT-OUTPUT SECTION.
00105   FILE-CONTROL.   SELECT SALES-FILE ASSIGN TO TAPE-1.
00106                   SELECT PRINT-FILE ASSIGN TO PRINTER.
00107   DATA DIVISION.
00108   FILE SECTION.
00109   FD  SALES-FILE  LABEL RECORDS ARE OMITTED.
00110   01  SALES-REC.
00111       02  NAME                PICTURE A(15).
00112       02  AMOUNT-OF-SALES     PICTURE 999V99.
00113   FD  PRINT-FILE  LABEL RECORDS ARE OMITTED.
00114   01  PRINT-REC.
00115       02  NAME-OUT            PICTURE A(15).
00116       02  AMT-COMMISSION      PICTURE 99V99.
00117   WORKING-STORAGE SECTION.
00118   01  EOF                     PICTURE 9   VALUE 0.
00119   PROCEDURE DIVISION.
00120       OPEN INPUT SALES-FILE OUTPUT PRINT-FILE.
00121       READ SALES-FILE AT END MOVE 1 TO EOF.
00122       PERFORM COMMISSION-ROUTINE UNTIL EOF = 1.
00123       CLOSE SALES-FILE, PRINT-FILE.
00124       STOP RUN.
00125   COMMISSION-ROUTINE.
00126       MOVE NAME TO NAME-OUT.
00127       IF AMOUNT-OF-SALES IS GREATER THAN 100.00
00128           MULTIPLY .03 BY AMOUNT-OF-SALES GIVING AMT-COMMISSION
00129       ELSE MULTIPLY .02 BY AMOUNT-OF-SALES GIVING AMT-COMMISSION.
00130       WRITE PRINT-REC.
00131       READ SALES-FILE AT END MOVE 1 TO EOF.
```

Figure 1.7

CHAPTER

2 DATA ORGANIZATION

A. DESCRIPTION OF FILES, RECORDS, AND FIELDS

As we have seen from the program illustration, data is processed by the computer in an organized pattern. Areas are reserved in memory for **files, records, and fields.** Each of these terms has special significance in COBOL and must be fully understood before programs may be written.

This section explains the above terms and their relation to each other. As we will see later, every field, record, or file used in a COBOL program must be assigned a **data-name.** The rules for forming such names are also discussed here.

FILES A **file** is the overall classification of data pertaining to a specific category. In a business environment, the term has a broad meaning. Company ABC, for example, has an inventory file, which contains **all** inventory information. Employee X's medical file contains **all** medical data on employee X.

In an electronic data processing context, a file has similar significance. It is the **major** grouping of data containing information of a specific nature. Files are generally considered the **input** and **output** to a data processing system. A file enters the computer flow as input, is processed, and an output file is produced.

A payroll card file, an accounts receivable tape file, and a transaction print file are examples of often-used data processing files.

A file, then, is the major classification of data in a data processing environment. If an application uses payroll cards as input and prints a salary report as output, we say that **two** files are processed. A card file, consisting of payroll data, and a print file, containing computed salaries, constitute the two files for the application.

Most COBOL programs utilize at least one input and one output file. Except for disk[1] applications, data cannot ordinarily be updated within the same file.

---

[1]Disk applications employ unique concepts in data processing and are discussed in Chapter 22 independently.

17

That is, the input must be distinct from the output. Suppose, for example, a sales-ticket file is entered as card input to the system. Price and quantity appear on each ticket and sales amount is to be computed as price × quantity. The extended sales amount figure cannot be placed on the input cards in most cases. We cannot create output data on input cards. Output data must be created independently on an output device. A new file containing the input data **and** the extended sales amount figure must then be created. Thus the card punch unit will duplicate input information and add the extended output results. Two files exist for this application—the input and the output files.

For **each** form of input and output used in a data processing application, we have **one** file. If weekly transaction **cards** from week 1 and a weekly transaction **tape** from week 2 are entered as input to a system, and a master **tape** file, combining the two, is created as output, we say we have **three** files. Transactions from week 1, transactions from week 2, and master transactions each constitute an independent file. Three devices are used: a card reader and two magnetic tape drives.

RECORDS   **A record** is a unit of grouped data **within** a file that contains information of a specific nature. Consider an accounts receivable file, entered as card input to a data processing system. The file is subdivided into records. Each record contains data of a specific nature. The accounts receivable file, for example, contains **two** records, a **credit** and a **debit** record. The credit record has the following card format:

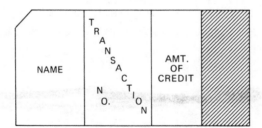

The debit record has the following card format:

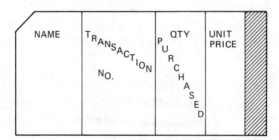

All cards within the accounts receivable file will be credit or debit records. Thus, we say that the file contains two record formats.

A record, then, is a specific kind of data within a file. We have one file for each form of input and output that the program employs. We have one record for each format within the file.

Consider the following magnetic tape layout containing payroll data:

| NAME | PRESENT SALARY | PAST SALARY | ▨ | NAME | SALARY | NO. OF DEPEN- DENTS | LIFE INSURANCE PREMIUMS | HEALTH INSURANCE PREMIUMS | ▨ | NAME | FEDERAL TAX | STATE TAX | CITY TAX |

├─────SALARY HISTORY RECORD─────┤ ├──────CURRENT PAYROLL RECORD──────┤ ├──────TAX RECORD──────┤

Note that three types of records exist within the file: a salary history record, a current payroll record, and a tax record. Since the magnetic tape file contains **three** formats of data, we say that three records exist within the payroll file.

Usually, however, we have only **one** record within a file. That is, all data within the file is of the same format. An inventory card file, for example, where all cards have the following form:

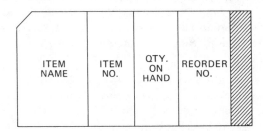

is said to contain only one record format.

GROUP ITEMS AND ELEMENTARY ITEMS   Consider the credit record described below:

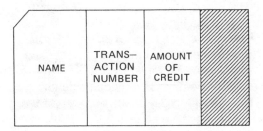

It contains the following **data fields:**

NAME, TRANSACTION-NUMBER, AMOUNT-OF-CREDIT

You will recall that a **field** of data is a group of consecutive storage positions reserved for a specific kind of data.

Fields, in COBOL, fall into two major categories: **group items** and **elementary items.** A **group item** is a data field that is further subdivided. That is, a group item is a major field consisting of minor fields. A NAME field, for example, which contains three minor fields (LAST-NAME, FIRST-INITIAL, SECOND-IN-

ITIAL) is considered a group item. An ADDRESS field that consists of CITY and STATE is a group item. The following record format consists of three group items:

DATE		NAME	IDENTITY	
MO YR	INIT	LAST-NAME	LEVEL	POSITION

DATE, NAME, and IDENTITY are group items.

A data field not further subdivided is called an **elementary item.** MO (for month), YR (for year), INIT (for initial), LAST-NAME, LEVEL, and POSITION are elementary items in the above example.

In the credit records above, **all** fields are elementary items, since none are further subdivided. Thus group items need not exist within a record format.

The hierarchy of data may be defined as follows: **Files** contain **records.** Records contain **data fields.** Fields are described as **group items,** if they are further subdivided, and as **elementary items,** if they are not. Group items are always further subdivided into elementary items.

RULES FOR FORMING DATA-NAMES

Files, records, group items, and elementary items are data groupings defined in a COBOL program. They must be given **data-names.** A data-name is a programmer-supplied name for any unit of data used in a COBOL program. The programmer must supply the names used for items of information. Programmer-supplied data-names must conform to certain rules.

RULES FOR FORMING DATA-NAMES

1. 1 to 30 characters
2. Letters, digits, and hyphens (-) only
3. May not begin or end with a hyphen
4. No embedded blanks (blanks within the data-name)
5. Must contain at least one alphabetic character
6. May not be a COBOL reserved word, which is a word that has special significance to the COBOL compiler. These words are listed in Appendix A.

EXAMPLES OF VALID DATA-NAMES

DATE-IN
NAME
LAST-NAME
AMOUNT1
AMOUNT-OF-TRANSACTION

EXAMPLES OF INVALID DATA NAMES

Data-Name	Reason Invalid
EMPLOYEE NAME	Embedded blank between EMPLOYEE and NAME. EMPLOYEE-NAME is OK.
DISCOUNT-%	%, as a special character, is invalid.
INPUT	INPUT is a COBOL reserved word.
123	Data-name must contain at least one alphabetic character.

Consider the following record layout within a card file:

The data fields may be named as follows:

```
DATE-OF-TRANS
AMOUNT
INVOICE-NO
CUSTOMER-NAME
```

Note that hyphens are used in place of embedded blanks.

Each file, record, and data field must be assigned a name in the COBOL program. Once a name is assigned within the program, the **same** name must be used throughout when referring to the specific unit of data. CREDIT-AMT, defined as a data-name in the DATA DIVISION may **not** be referred to as CR-AMT in the PROCEDURE DIVISION. The same name must be used throughout the program.

Note that the data-names used in the examples suggest the type of data field. DATE-OF-TRANS is a more meaningful data-name than perhaps A7, although both names are valid. In general, use data-names that suggest the meaning of the field. This facilitates the writing of the PROCEDURE DIVISION and also enables noncomputer personnel to better understand the meaning of the program.

COBOL programs make extensive use of organized data. Files are assigned to specific input-output devices. Each record format within a file must be fully described by assigning data-names to the group items and to the elementary items within the file. The rules for forming programmer-supplied data-names must be utilized when assigning names to files, records, and fields.

Let us consider the following program excerpt that illustrates the DATA DIVISION of a COBOL program:

```
DATA  DIVISION.
FILE  SECTION.
FD    PAYROLL-FILE
      DATA  RECORDS  ARE  SALARY-REC,
      DEDUCTIONS-REC.
Ø1    SALARY-REC.
      Ø2    NAME
      Ø2    JOB-TITLE
      Ø2    NO-OF-DEPENDENTS
      Ø2    SALARY
Ø1    DEDUCTIONS-REC.                    .
      Ø2    FICA
      Ø2    FED-TAX
      Ø2    STATE-TAX
      Ø2    HEALTH-INSUR-PREMIUM
      Ø2    LIFE-INSUR-PREMIUM
```

You will recall that we slash numeric zeros to distinguish them from the letter O. Data-names are defined within the DATA DIVISION in the above example. The FD entry defines the file name. PAYROLL-FILE, which consists of two record formats, is the name assigned to the file. SALARY-REC and DEDUCTIONS-REC are the record names. Each is subdivided into data fields. NAME, JOB-TITLE, NO-OF-DEPENDENTS, and SALARY are elementary data fields within SALARY-REC. Note that the names assigned conform to the rules for forming programmer-supplied data-names. Similarly, DEDUCTIONS-REC is subdivided into five fields, FICA, FED-TAX, STATE-TAX, HEALTH-INSUR-PREMIUM, and LIFE-INSUR-PREMIUM. In Chapter 5 you will learn the specific format of the DATA DIVISION. Any name that must be assigned to files, records, group items, and elementary items in this division must conform to the rules described above.

DATA ORGANIZATION

1. **File**—An overall classification of data pertaining to a specific category
2. **Record**—A unit of data within a file that contains information of a specific nature
3. **Field**—A group of consecutive columns or positions reserved for a specific kind of data
   a. **Group item**—A field that is subdivided
   b. **Elementary item**—A field that is not subdivided

NOTE: files, records, and fields are all defined in a COBOL program by data-names

4. Illustration

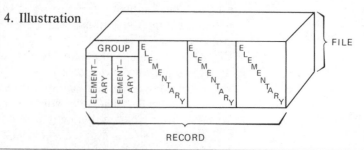

SELF-EVALUATING
QUIZ

1. A file is defined as _____.
   *****
   the major grouping of data in a COBOL program
2. A record is defined as a _____.
   *****
   grouping of data within a file
3. The input and output in a COBOL program are assigned _____ names.
   *****
   file
4. Each format within a file is assigned a _____ name.
   *****
   record
5. The two types of fields within a record are _____ and _____.
   *****
   group items
   elementary items
6. A group item is defined as a _____.
   *****
   field that is further subdivided into subordinate fields
7. An elementary item is defined as a _____.
   *****
   field that is not further subdivided
8. If an amount field contains a code and a price, then the amount is called a(n) _____ item and code is a(n) _____ item.
   *****
   group
   elementary
9. Files, records, group items, and elementary items must be given _____-names in a COBOL program.
   *****
   data
10. State what, if anything, is wrong with the following data-names:

    (a)   DATA

    (b)   RECORD 1

    (c)   AMT-IN-$

    (d)   ABC-123

    *****
    (a) DATA is a COBOL reserved word.
    (b) No embedded blanks: RECORD-1 may be used.
    (c) No special characters: $ is a special character.
    (d) OK.

B. TYPES OF DATA

Thus far, we have discussed the organization of data as it appears in a COBOL program. Input and output files are described by record formats. Each record has field descriptions classified as group items or elementary items.

By defining files, records, and fields and assigning corresponding data-names in the DATA DIVISION we reserve storage for data. The File Description entry, as illustrated in the previous section, reserves storage for input and output files. The area described by the File Description entry is said to contain **variable** data.

Variable data is that data which changes within the program. The contents of data fields in the input area change with each READ command. READ PAYROLL-FILE results in input data being stored in the area defined by the File Description for PAYROLL-FILE. This data is considered variable since it will change with each card that is read. After input fields are processed, results are placed in the output area, which is defined by another File Description. Thus we say that the contents of output fields are also variable.

By defining a data field with a data-name, we say nothing about the **contents** of the field. AMT, for example, is a data field within RECORD-1; the content of AMT, however, is variable. It depends on the input record being processed, and thus changes within the program. Any field described within an input or output file contains variable data.

A **constant** is a form of data required for processing that is **not** dependent on the input to the system. A constant, as opposed to variable data, remains unchanged in the program. Suppose, for example, we wish to multiply each amount field of the input records by .05, the tax rate. The tax rate, .05, is **not** a value on the input record but is nevertheless required for processing. We call .05 a **constant,** since it is a form of data required for processing that is not dependent on the input to the system.

Similarly, suppose we wish to edit input cards and print the message 'INVALID RECORD' for any erroneous card. The message 'INVALID RECORD' will be part of the output, but is not entered as input to the system. It is a constant, required for processing and not part of input.

A constant may be defined directly in the PROCEDURE DIVISION of a COBOL program. AMT, a field within the input file, is to be multiplied by the tax rate, .05, to produce TAX-AMT, a field within the output file. The PROCEDURE DIVISION entry to perform this operation is as follows:

```
MULTIPLY AMT BY .05 GIVING TAX-AMT.
```

The two data fields, AMT and TAX-AMT, are described in the DATA DIVISION. The constant .05 is defined directly in the above PROCEDURE DIVISION entry and need **not** be described in the DATA DIVISION.

Three types of constants may be defined in the PROCEDURE DIVISION of a COBOL program: numeric literals, nonnumeric literals, and figurative constants. These are discussed in detail.

NUMERIC LITERAL   A **numeric literal** is a constant defined in the PROCEDURE DIVISION and **used** for arithmetic operations.

> **RULES FOR FORMING NUMERIC LITERALS**
> 1. A maximum of 18 digits.
> 2. A plus or minus sign to the **left** of the number.
> 3. A decimal point **within** the literal. The decimal point, however, may not be the last character of the literal.

Note that an operational plus or minus sign is **not** required within the literal but **may** be included. If it is included, it must appear to the left of the number. That is, +16 or −12 are valid numeric literals but 16+ or 12− are not. If no sign is used, the number is assumed positive. Since a decimal point may not appear as the last character in a numeric literal, 18.2 is a valid literal but 16. is not; however, 16.0 is valid.

The following are valid numeric literals that may be used in the PROCEDURE DIVISION of a COBOL program:

> **VALID NUMERIC LITERALS**
> +15.8
> −387.58
>   42
>   .05
> −.97

Suppose we wish to add 10.3 to an output data field, TOTAL, defined in a File Description entry in the DATA DIVISION. The following is a valid instruction:

> ADD 10.3 TO TOTAL.

The numeric literal 10.3 may be used in the PROCEDURE DIVISION for arithmetic operations.

The following are **not** valid numeric literals for the reasons noted:

> **INVALID NUMERIC LITERALS**
>
> | Literal | Error |
> |---------|-------|
> | 1,000 | Commas are **not** permitted |
> | 15. | A decimal point is not valid as the last character |
> | $100.00 | Dollar signs are not valid |
> | 38J | Letters are not permitted |
> | 17.45− | Operational signs must appear to the left of the number |

A numeric literal, then, is a constant that may be used in the PROCEDURE DIVISION of a COBOL program. Numeric literals are numeric constants that are used for arithmetic operations. The above rules must be employed when defining a numeric literal.

NONNUMERIC LITERAL   A **nonnumeric literal** is a constant used in the PROCEDURE DIVISION for all operations **except** arithmetic operations. The following rules must be employed when defining a nonnumeric or alphanumeric literal.

RULES FOR FORMING NONNUMERIC LITERALS
1. The literal must be enclosed in quotation marks.[2]
2. A maximum of 120 characters, including spaces, may be used.
3. Any character in the COBOL Character Set[3] may be used except the quotation mark.

The following are valid nonnumeric literals:

VALID NONNUMERIC LITERALS
'CODE'
'ABC 123'
'1,000'
'INPUT'
'$100.00'
'MESSAGE'

Printing any of the above literals results in the printing of those characters **within** the quotation marks; that is CODE, ABC 123, 1,000, etc. will print. Note that a nonnumeric literal may contain **all** numbers. '123' is a valid non-numeric literal. It is to be distinguished from the numeric literal 123, which is used for arithmetic operations.

Suppose we wish to move the message INVALID RECORD to an output field, MESSAGE-FIELD, before we write an output record. The following is a valid COBOL instruction:

MOVE 'INVALID RECORD' TO MESSAGE-FIELD.

Note that 'INVALID RECORD' is a nonnumeric literal. It is defined in the PROCEDURE DIVISION and does not appear in the DATA DIVISION. MES-SAGE-FIELD is not a literal but a data-name. It conforms to the rules for forming programmer-supplied words. It could not be a nonnumeric literal, since it is not enclosed in quotation marks. All data-names, such as MESSAGE-FIELD, must be defined in the DATA DIVISION.

In summary, a nonnumeric literal is any constant defined directly in a PRO-CEDURE DIVISION statement that is not used for arithmetic operations. It must conform to the rules specified above.

FIGURATIVE CONSTANT   A **figurative constant** is a COBOL reserved word that has special significance to the compiler. We discuss in this chapter two such figurative constants: ZEROS and SPACES.

---

[2]We have adopted the notation of a single quotation mark or apostrophe. Some compilers, however, require the double quotation marks(''). Check your specifications manual.
[3]Characters in the COBOL character set are those characters that are permitted within a COBOL program. Appendix A lists these characters.

Consider the figurative constant ZEROS. It is a COBOL reserved word meaning all zeros. To say, for example,

```
MOVE ZEROS TO TOTAL.
```

results in the data field, TOTAL, being filled with all zeros. ZEROS is a figurative constant having the **value** of all zeros. ZERO, ZEROES, and ZEROS are equivalent figurative constants having the same value. They may be used interchangeably in the PROCEDURE DIVISION of a COBOL program.

SPACES is another figurative constant meaning all blanks. To say, for example,

```
MOVE SPACES TO CODE-OUT.
```

results in blanks being placed in CODE-OUT. The word SPACES is a COBOL reserved word having the value of all blanks. It may be used interchangeably with the figurative constant SPACE.

ZEROS and SPACES are the two figurative constants most frequently used. There are, however, other figurative constants that are discussed later in this book.

Thus, three types of data may be defined in the PROCEDURE DIVISION. A numeric literal, a nonnumeric literal, and a figurative constant may be defined directly in any instruction in the PROCEDURE DIVISION. Variable data fields that appear in PROCEDURE DIVISION entries must be described in the DATA DIVISION.

In future discussions of PROCEDURE DIVISION entries, the use of constants will become clearer. At this juncture, the reader should be able to recognize literals and to distinguish them from data fields. The specific formats of ADD and MOVE statements, in which these literals were illustrated, are discussed more fully later.

TYPES OF DATA

1. **Variable Data**

   Definition: Data that changes within the program

   Files
   Records   } defined by data-names
   Fields

2. **Constant or Literal**

   Definition: Data that remains fixed within the program; fixed data required for processing that is **not** dependent on the input to the system

   a. Numeric Literal—A constant used in the PROCEDURE DIVISION for arithmetic operations

   b. Nonnumeric Literal—A constant used in the PROCEDURE DIVISION for all operations except arithmetic operations

   c. Figurative Constant—A COBOL reserved word with special significance to the COBOL compiler, that is:

   ZERO or ZEROES or ZEROS
   SPACE or SPACES

1. The contents of fields defined within input and output files are (fixed, variable).
*****
variable

2. A constant is defined as _____.
*****
a form of data necessary for processing but not dependent on the input to the system

3. A constant may be used directly in the _____ DIVISION.
*****
PROCEDURE

4. Data fields that appear in PROCEDURE DIVISION statements must be defined in the _____ DIVISION.
*****
DATA

5. The three types of constants are _____, _____, and _____.
*****
numeric literals
nonnumeric literals
figurative constants

6. What types of constants are the following?
'ABC'
'123'
123.5
ZERO
'SPACE'
*****
Nonnumeric literal.
Nonnumeric literal.
Numeric literal.
Figurative constant.
Nonnumeric literal (any group of characters enclosed in quotes is a nonnumeric literal).

7. What, if anything, is wrong with the following numeric literals?
123.
15.8−
1,000,000.00
$38.90
58
*****
Decimal point may not be the last character.
Minus sign must be to the left of the number.
Commas not permitted.
Dollar sign not permitted.
OK.

8. What, if anything, is wrong with the following nonnumeric literals?
'THE MESSAGE 'CODE' MUST BE PRINTED'
'INPUT'
'ZERO'

'123'
'   '

*****
Single quotation marks may not be used within a nonnumeric literal.
OK.
OK.
OK.
OK.

9. The literal ' ', if printed, would result in the printing of _____.
*****
two blanks

10. Quotation marks (are, are not) part of the literal.
*****
are not (they merely define the limits of the nonnumeric literal)

11. Two examples of figurative constants are _____ and _____.
*****
ZERO, ZEROES, ZEROS
SPACE, SPACES

12. A figurative constant is defined as a _____.
*****
COBOL reserved word that represents a specific value

13. Consider the following instruction:
    MOVE '1' TO FLD1
'1' is a _____.
FLD1 is a _____ and must be defined in the _____ DIVISION.
*****
nonnumeric literal—enclosed in quotes
data-name—not enclosed in quotes
DATA

14. To print the _____ 'ZEROS' results in _____ printing.
    To print the _____ ZEROS results in _____ printing.
*****
nonnumeric literal
the word ZEROS
figurative constant
the value 0000

REVIEW QUESTIONS

I. True-False Questions

True	False	
☐	☐	1. A field is a collection of data records.
☐	☐	2. Files are collections of data records.
☐	☐	3. Fields are generally described by PICTURE clauses in the record description entries.
☐	☐	4. Numeric literals utilize quotation marks.
☐	☐	5. Numeric literals may not exceed 9 characters.
☐	☐	6. A comma may not be used in a numeric literal.
☐	☐	7. Data-names are names assigned to fields.
☐	☐	8. SPACE is a figurative constant.

9. A field may not exceed 30 characters.

10. MOVE SPACES TO FLD1 is a valid statement regardless of the size of FLD1.

II. General Questions

1. Make necessary corrections to the following data-names:
   (a) CUSTOMER NAME
   (b) AMOUNT-
   (c) INVOICE-NO.
   (d) PROCEDURE
   (e) TAX-%
   (f) QUANTITY-OF-PRODUCT-ABC-ON-HAND
   (g) AMT-OF-SALES

2. Make necessary corrections to the following literals:
   (a) '123'
   (b) 123
   (c) 'ABC'
   (d) ABC
   (e) $100.00
   (f) '$100.00'
   (g) 1,000
   (h) 100.7−
   (i) 54

In each of the following cases, state the contents of the data field, FIELDA, after the MOVE operation:

```
3.     MOVE 'ABC' TO FIELDA.

4.     MOVE ABC TO FIELDA.

5.     MOVE 100.00 TO FIELDA.

6.     MOVE 'SPACES' TO FIELDA.

7.     MOVE SPACES TO FIELDA.
```

PROBLEMS

1. Using Figure 1.4 in the previous chapter, indicate which elements in the program are:
   (a) Files.
   (b) Records.
   (c) Fields.
   (d) Numeric literals.
   (e) Nonnumeric literals.
   (f) Figurative constants.

2. Using Figure 1.6, indicate which elements in the program are:
   (a) Files.
   (b) Records.
   (c) Fields.
   (d) Numeric literals.
   (e) Nonnumeric literals.
   (f) Figurative constants.

3. Using Figure 1.7, indicate which elements in the program are:
   (a) Files.
   (b) Records.
   (c) Fields.
   (d) Numeric literals.
   (e) Nonnumeric literals.
   (f) Figurative constants.

3 THE IDENTIFICATION DIVISION

You will recall that **all** COBOL programs consist of **four divisions.** In the next four chapters, we discuss each division in detail. At the end of this discussion, the reader should be able to write elementary COBOL programs with no difficulty.

Before we begin, however, some basic rules for coding these programs must be understood.

A. BASIC STRUCTURE OF A COBOL PROGRAM

COBOL programs are generally written on **coding** or **program sheets** (Fig. 3.1). The coding sheet has space for 80 columns of information. Each **line** of a program sheet will be keypunched into **one** punched card. Usually the standard COBOL card is used for this purpose (Fig. 3.2).

Thus, for every line written on the coding sheet, we will obtain one punched card. The entire deck of cards keypunched from the coding sheets is called the **COBOL source program.**

Let us examine the COBOL program sheet more closely. The body of the form is subdivided into 72 positions, or columns. These positions, when coded, will be keypunched into Card Columns 1–72, respectively. On the righthand side there is provision for the program identification number, labeled positions 73–80. The identification number will be entered into Columns 73–80 of all cards keypunched from this form.

The data recorded on the top of the form is **not** keypunched into cards. It supplies identifying information only. Figure 3.3 illustrates the conversion of COBOL program sheets to punched cards.

The identification number, positions 73–80, and the page and serial number, positions 1–6, are optional entries in a COBOL program. Both, however, can be extremely useful.

Page and serial numbers on each line and, therefore, on each punched card are advisable, since cards are sometimes inadvertently dropped. In such cases,

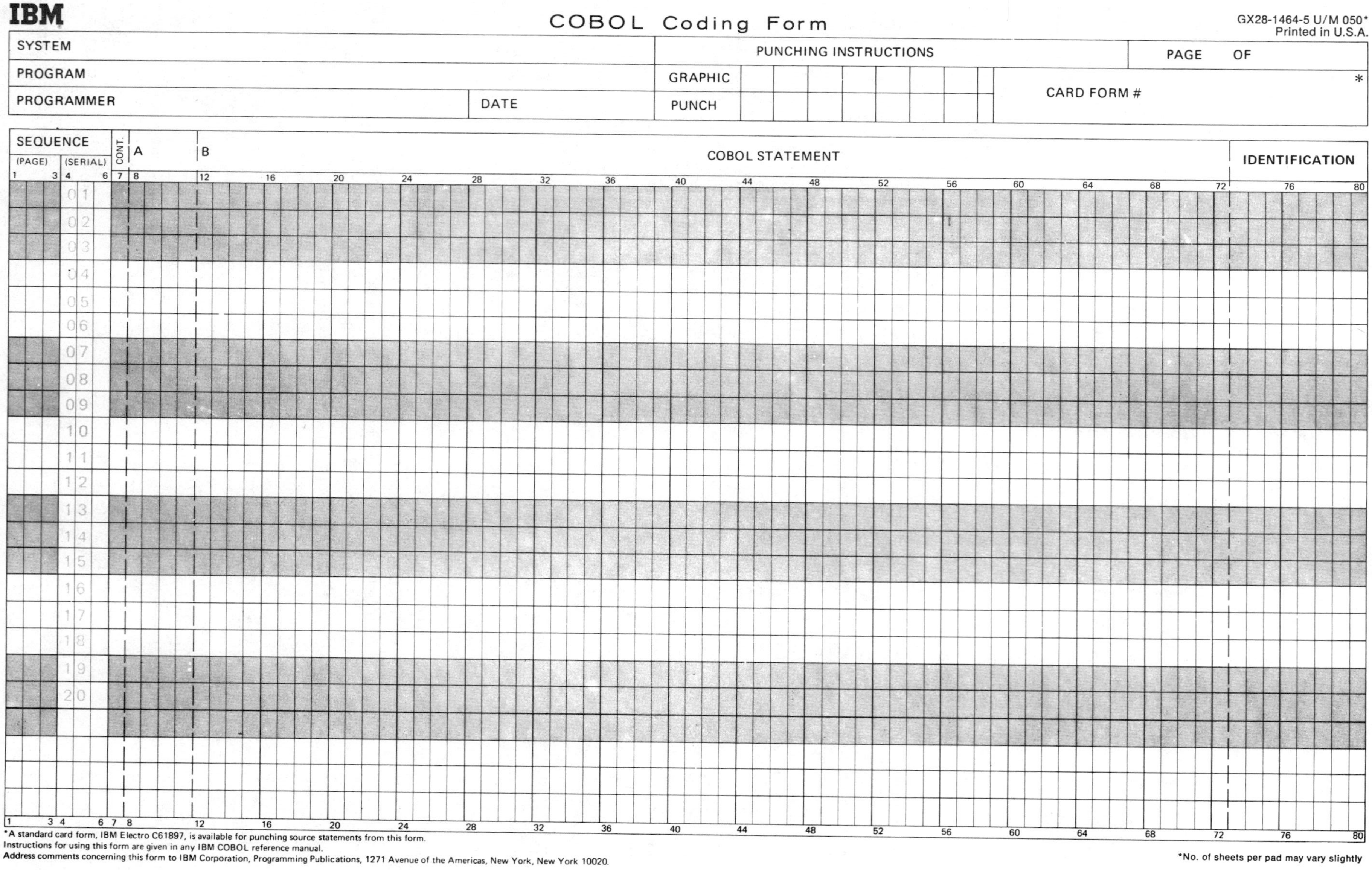

IBM

COBOL Coding Form

GX28-1464-5 U/M 050*
Printed in U.S.A.

SYSTEM

PROGRAM

PROGRAMMER

DATE

PUNCHING INSTRUCTIONS

GRAPHIC

PUNCH

PAGE OF

CARD FORM # *

SEQUENCE (PAGE) 1 3 (SERIAL) 4 6 | CONT. 7 | A 8 | B 12 | COBOL STATEMENT | IDENTIFICATION 76 80

12 16 20 24 28 32 36 40 44 48 52 56 60 64 68 72

01 02 03 04 05 06 07 08 09 10 11 12 13 14 15 16 17 18 19 20

1 3 4 6 7 8 12 16 20 24 28 32 36 40 44 48 52 56 60 64 68 72 76 80

*A standard card form, IBM Electro C61897, is available for punching source statements from this form.
Instructions for using this form are given in any IBM COBOL reference manual.
Address comments concerning this form to IBM Corporation, Programming Publications, 1271 Avenue of the Americas, New York, New York 10020.

*No. of sheets per pad may vary slightly

Figure 3.1

COBOL SOURCE PROGRAM CARD
PAGE SERIAL A B COBOL STATEMENT IDENT.

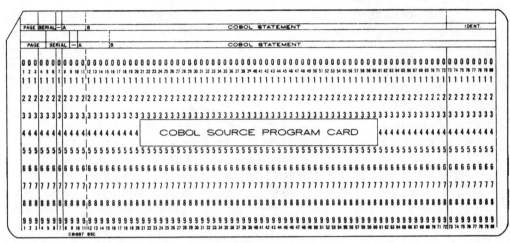

Figure 3.2

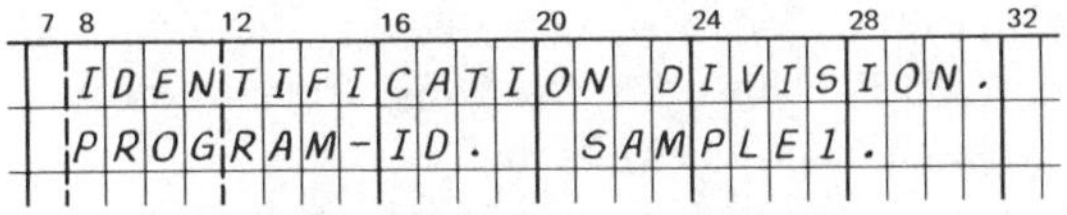

7 8 12 16 20 24 28 32
IDENTIFICATION DIVISION.
PROGRAM-ID. SAMPLE1.

IDENTIFICATION DIVISION.
PROGRAM-ID. SAMPLE1.
COBOL SOURCE PROGRAM CARD

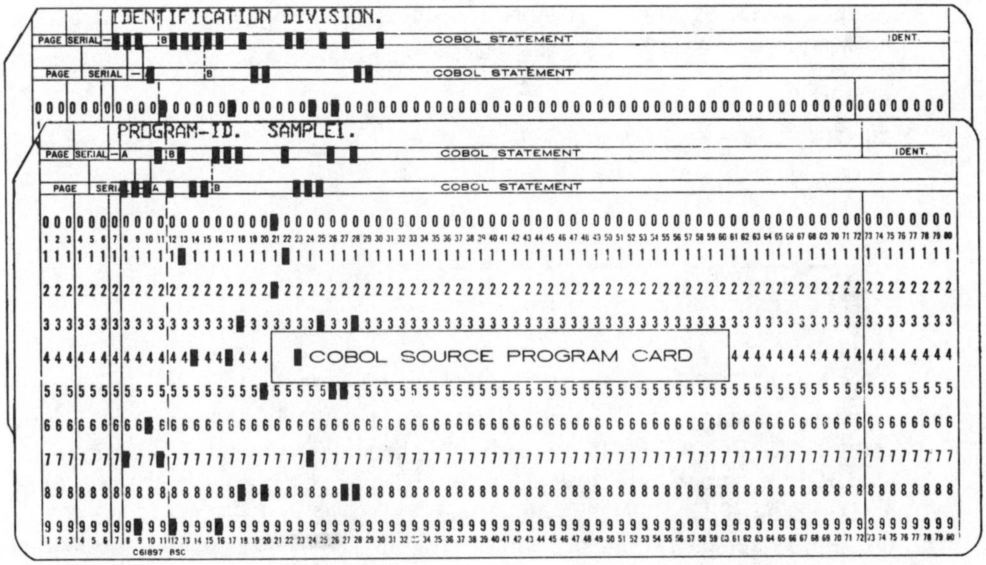

Figure 3.3

resequencing is necessary. If page and serial numbers are supplied, it is an easy task to insert cards in their proper place.

Page number generally refers to the number of the coding sheet. The first page is usually numbered 001, the second 002, and so on. Serial number refers to the line number. The first card generally has serial number 010, the second 020, and so on. They are numbered by tens, so that insertions may easily be made. If an entry is accidentally omitted and must then be inserted between serial numbers 030 and 040, for example, it may be sequenced as 031. Thus 002060 will signify page 002, line 060. This method is used for sequencing of most program decks. It is, however, only a suggested method, as some applications may require other entries.

Identification numbers are also optional but are quite useful. They make it easy to distinguish one program from another.

Column 7 of the program sheet is a **continuation position.** It is used primarily for the continuation of nonnumeric literals. Continuation positions are discussed in detail in Chapter 8.

COMMENTS   An asterisk (*) in column 7 may also be used to designate the entire line as a comment. Such comment lines are useful for providing documentary information on how the program will process data.

Positions 8–72 are used for all program entries. Note, however, that Column 8 is labeled A, and Column 12 is labeled B. These are **Margins.** Certain entries must begin in Margin A and others must begin in Margin B.

If an entry is to be coded in Margin A, it may begin in position 8, 9, 10, or 11. Most often, A margin entries are coded beginning in position 8. If an entry is to be coded in Margin B, it may begin anywhere after position 11. That is, it may begin in position 12, 13, 14, etc. Note that margin rules specify the **beginning** point of entries. A word that must **begin** in Margin A may **extend** into Margin B.

Example 1

AUTHOR., a paragraph name, must begin in Margin A. Any statement may then follow in Margin B.

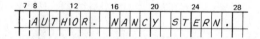

The A of AUTHOR may be placed in Column 8, or Margin A. The word itself extends into Margin B. The next entry must begin in Margin B or in any position after Column 11. In our example, the statement begins in position 16.

COBOL programs are divided into **divisions.** The divisions have fixed names—IDENTIFICATION, ENVIRONMENT, DATA, and PROCEDURE. They must **always** appear in that order in a program. Divisions may be subdivided into **sections.** The DATA DIVISION, for example, which describes all storage areas needed in the program, is divided into two sections: the FILE SECTION and the WORKING-STORAGE SECTION. The FILE SECTION of the DATA DIVISION describes the input and output areas, and the WORKING-STORAGE

SECTION of the DATA DIVISION describes the intermediate work areas necessary for processing. Each section may be further subdivided into **paragraphs.** All other entries in the program are considered COBOL **statements.**

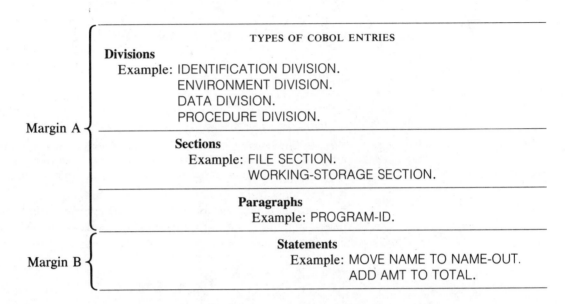

Margin A

TYPES OF COBOL ENTRIES

Divisions
   Example: IDENTIFICATION DIVISION.
             ENVIRONMENT DIVISION.
             DATA DIVISION.
             PROCEDURE DIVISION.

Sections
   Example: FILE SECTION.
             WORKING-STORAGE SECTION.

Paragraphs
   Example: PROGRAM-ID.

Margin B

Statements
   Example: MOVE NAME TO NAME-OUT.
             ADD AMT TO TOTAL.

MARGIN RULES
1. Division, section, and paragraph names begin in Margin A.
2. All other statements and clauses begin in Margin B.

It will be seen that the great majority of COBOL entries begin in Margin B.

   Figure 3.4 illustrates the above margin rules. The ENVIRONMENT DIVISION begins in Margin A, as does the CONFIGURATION SECTION. SOURCE-COMPUTER and OBJECT-COMPUTER are **paragraph** names and, as such, must begin in Margin A. SOURCE-COMPUTER and OBJECT-COMPUTER must have COBOL statements following them.

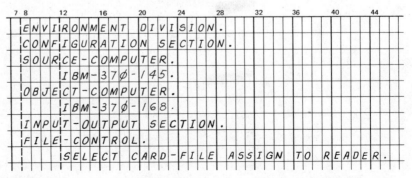

Figure 3.4

Each entry is followed by a period. Note that ENVIRONMENT DIVISION, CONFIGURATION SECTION, and SOURCE-COMPUTER are each followed by a period. Statements, as well, must end with a period. Where several entries appear on one line, each period will be directly followed by at least one space. In the PROCEDURE DIVISION, for example, where several statements may appear on one line, the following is permissible:

```
PROCEDURE DIVISION.
     MOVE TAX TO TOTAL.  WRITE TAPE-1.  ADD 1 TO COUNTER.
```

We will, however, use the convention of coding one statement per line for the sake of clarity.

Division and section names **must** appear on a line with no other entry. That is, they must occupy independent lines. Paragraph names, however, may appear on the same line as statements, keeping in mind, however, that each period must be followed by at least one space. The following is acceptable:

7 8	12	16	20	24	28	32	36	40	44	48	52	56
ENVIRONMENT DIVISION.												
CONFIGURATION SECTION.												
SOURCE-COMPUTER. UNIVAC-SERIES-90 90-60.												
OBJECT-COMPUTER. UNIVAC-SERIES-90 90-60.												
INPUT-OUTPUT SECTION.												
FILE-CONTROL. SELECT CARD-FILE ASSIGN TO READER.												

REVIEW OF COBOL CODING FORM

Columns	Use	Explanation
1–6	Sequence numbers (optional)	Used as a method for ensuring that cards are sequenced properly
7	Continuation or comment	Used to continue nonnumeric literals (see Chapter 8) or to denote line as comment (* in col 7)
8–11	Margin A	Specific entries such as DIVISION, SECTION, and paragraph names must be coded in Margin A
12–72	Margin B	Most COBOL entries, particularly those in the PROCEDURE DIVISION, are coded in Margin B
73–80	Program identification (optional)	Used to identify program

> REVIEW OF CODING RULES
> 1. Division and Section names:
>   a. Begin in Margin A
>   b. End with a period
>   c. Must appear on a line with no other entries
> 2. Paragraph name:
>   a. Begins in Margin A
>   b. Ends with a period
>   c. May appear on a line by itself or with other entries; must always be followed by at least one space
> 3. Statement:
>   a. Begins in Margin B
>   b. May end with a period if it represents a sentence
>   c. May appear on a line by itself or with other entries; must always be followed by at least one space

SELF-EVALUATING
QUIZ

1. COBOL programs are written on _____.
   *****
   coding or program sheets
2. Each line of the coding sheet corresponds to one _____ in the program deck.
   *****
   card
3. The deck of cards keypunched from the coding sheets is called the _____.
   *****
   COBOL source deck
4. The optional entries on the coding sheet are _____ and _____.
   *****
   identification (positions 73–80)
   page and serial number (positions 1–6)
5. Margin A begins in position _____.
   Margin B begins in position _____.
   *****
   8
   12
6. If an entry must begin in Margin A, it _____; if an entry must begin in Margin B, it _____.
   *****
   may begin in position 8, 9, 10 or 11
   may begin in position 12, 13, 14, etc.
7. COBOL programs are divided into (no.) divisions.
   *****
   four
8. In the order in which they must appear, these divisions are _____, _____, _____, and _____.
   *****

IDENTIFICATION
ENVIRONMENT
DATA
PROCEDURE

9. All _____, _____, and _____ names must be coded in Margin A.
   *****
   division
   section
   paragraph

10. Most entries are coded in Margin _____.
    *****
    B

11. All entries must be followed by a _____.
    *****
    period

12. Each period must be directly followed by a _____.
    *****
    space

13. _____ and _____ must each appear on a separate line. All other entries
    may have several statements on the same line.
    *****
    Divisions
    sections

B. CODING REQUIREMENTS OF THE IDENTIFICATION DIVISION

The IDENTIFICATION DIVISION is the smallest, simplest, and least significant division of a COBOL program. As the name indicates, it supplies identifying data about the program.

The IDENTIFICATION DIVISION has **no** effect on the execution of the program but is, nevertheless, **required** as a means of identifying the job to the computer.

The IDENTIFICATION DIVISION is **not** divided into sections. Instead, it may consist of the following paragraphs:

PROGRAM-ID.
AUTHOR.
INSTALLATION.
DATE-WRITTEN.
DATE-COMPILED.
SECURITY.

As a division name the IDENTIFICATION DIVISION is coded in Margin A. The above entries, as paragraph names, are also coded in Margin A, and each is followed by a period.

The only entry **required** within the IDENTIFICATION DIVISION is the PROGRAM-ID. That is, all programs must be identified by a name. The name that follows PROGRAM-ID is an external-name, and must be coded in Margin B. External-names can consist of letters, digits, and hyphens, and can contain a maximum of 30 characters, but the first eight characters must be unique in the program. That is, the first eight characters of the external-name actually identify the program for the computer.

Thus the first two entries of a program must be IDENTIFICATION DIVISION and PROGRAM-ID:

```
IDENTIFICATION DIVISION.
PROGRAM-ID. SAMPLE1.
```

PROGRAM-ID is followed by a period and then a space. The external-name is coded in Margin B and must conform to the rules specified above. Note that the two entries may also be coded:

```
IDENTIFICATION DIVISION.
PROGRAM-ID.
    SAMPLE1.
```

Since PROGRAM-ID is a paragraph name, the external-name SAMPLE1 may appear on the same line or on the next one. In either case, PROGRAM-ID and the name must each be followed by a period.

The other paragraph names listed above are optional. They are useful items that provide significant facts about the nature of the program, but are not required.

For ANS COBOL users, the DATE-COMPILED paragraph can be coded simply as:

> DATE-COMPILED.

The computer-generated listing will include the actual run date. Thus if the program is compiled three different times on three separate dates, it is not necessary to keep revising this entry. The computer itself will list the actual run date.

Any, or all, of these paragraphs may be included in the IDENTIFICATION DIVISION. As paragraph names, these entries are coded in Margin A. Each paragraph name is generally followed by a statement, which may contain **any** character. The only requirement is that each statement be followed by a period.

The illustration below will indicate the coding of the IDENTIFICATION DIVISION. Recall that an * in column 7 may be used to designate any line as a comment line.

```
6 7 8      12      16      20      24      28      32      36      40
  IDENTIFICATION DIVISION.
  PROGRAM-ID. EXHIBIT1.
  AUTHOR. R. A. STERN.
  INSTALLATION. COMPANY ABC
                ACCOUNTING DEPT.
  DATE-WRITTEN. JAN. 1, 1980.
  DATE-COMPILED.
  SECURITY. TOP SECRET.
 *    THIS PROGRAM WILL CREATE        *
 *    A MASTER PAYROLL SYSTEM,        *
 *    EDITING THE INPUT DATA AND      *
 *    PRODUCING AN ERROR LIST.        *
```

Note that INSTALLATION, as well as the other entries, may extend to several lines. Each entry within a paragraph must, however, be coded in Margin B. The last character must be a period.

SUMMARY OF IDENTIFICATION DIVISION ENTRIES

1. Paragraphs within the IDENTIFICATION DIVISION inform the reader about the nature of the program.
2. The IDENTIFICATION DIVISION and its paragraphs do not affect the execution of the program.
3. The first item to be coded in a program is:
   IDENTIFICATION DIVISION.
4. The second item to be coded in a program is:
   PROGRAM-ID. external-name.
5. The external name can contain letters, digits, and hyphens only, can consist of a maximum of 30 characters, but only the first 8 are used by the computer and must therefore be unique.
6. All other paragraphs and identifying information in this division are optional. Paragraphs that may be included are:
   AUTHOR.
   INSTALLATION.
   DATE-WRITTEN.
   DATE-COMPILED.
   SECURITY.
   If no entry follows the DATE-COMPILED paragraph, the computer will then insert the date of run on the listing.

SELF-EVALUATING QUIZ

1. The first two entries of a COBOL program must always be _____ and _____.
   *****

   ```
   IDENTIFICATION DIVISION.
   PROGRAM-ID.
   ```

2. Each of these entries must be followed by a _____, which, in turn, must be followed by a _____.
   *****
   period
   space or blank
3. The above entries are both coded beginning in _____.
   *****
   Margin A
4. The name that follows PROGRAM-ID is an _____-name.
   *****
   external
5. Code the IDENTIFICATION DIVISION for a program called EXPENSES for a corporation, Dynamic Data Devices, Inc., written July 15, 1981. This

program has a security classification and is available to authorized personnel only. It produces a weekly listing by department of all operating expenses.
*****
The following is a **suggested** solution:

6 7 8	12	16	20	24	28	32	36	40	44	48	52	56	60	64
IDENTIFICATION DIVISION.
PROGRAM-ID. EXPENSES.
AUTHOR. N. B. STERN.
INSTALLATION. DYNAMIC DATA DEVICES, INC.
DATE-WRITTEN. 7/15/81.
SECURITY. AUTHORIZED PERSONNEL ONLY.
* THIS PROGRAM PRODUCES A WEEKLY LIST BY DEPARTMENT *
* OF ALL OPERATING EXPENSES. *

NOTE: Only the IDENTIFICATION DIVISION and PROGRAM-ID are required.
6. The DATE-COMPILED paragraph usually does not include an entry since

_____.

*****

the computer itself generates the date of the run on the program listing

REVIEW QUESTIONS

I. True-False Questions

True False

1. Only one statement is permitted on a coding line.
2. IDENTIFICATION DIVISION, PROGRAM-ID, and AUTHOR are the three required entries of the division.
3. SAMPLE 12 is a valid external-name.
4. A division name must appear as an independent item on a separate line.
5. The IDENTIFICATION DIVISION contains instructions that significantly affect execution of the program.
6. Information supplied in the IDENTIFICATION DIVISION makes it easier for a nondata processing employee to understand the nature of the program.
7. COBOL programs are designed to be self-documenting.
8. DATE-COMPILED is a paragraph-name that requires no additional entries.
9. Every period in a COBOL program must be followed by at least one space.
10. The INSTALLATION paragraph is restricted to one line.

II. General Questions

Make necessary corrections to each of the following (1-5):

1.
```
IDENTIFICATION DIVISION
PROGRAM-ID SAMPLE1.
```

2.
```
IDENTIFICATION DIVISION.
PROGRAM ID. SAMPLE2
```

3.
```
ENVIRONMENT DIVISION.
    CONFIGURATION SECTION.
```

4.
```
IDENTIFICATION DIVISION.
AUTHOR.MARY DOE.
PROGRAM-ID. SAMPLE4.
```

5.
```
DATA DIVISION. FILE SECTION.
```

6. State which of the following entries are coded in Margin A:
   a. IDENTIFICATION DIVISION
   b. PROGRAM-ID
   c. (name of author)
   d. FILE SECTION
   e. (COBOL Statement) ADD TAX TO TOTAL
7. Indicate the rules for forming external-names.
8. What is the difference between the DATE-WRITTEN and the DATE-COM-PILED paragraph?

PROBLEMS   1. Code the IDENTIFICATION DIVISION for a program called UPDATE for the United Accounting Corp. The program must be written by 8/25/81 and completed by 10/25/81, and it has a top secret security classification. The program will create a new master tape each month from the previous master tape and selected detail cards.
2. Code the IDENTIFICATION DIVISION for a program that will punch out billing cards for the American Utility Co.

4 THE ENVIRONMENT DIVISION

The ENVIRONMENT DIVISION of a COBOL program supplies information concerning the **equipment** to be used in the program. The ENVIRONMENT DIVISION entries are **machine-dependent.** Unlike the other divisions of a COBOL program, the entries in this division will be dependent on (1) the computer, and (2) the specific devices used in the program.

The ENVIRONMENT DIVISION is composed of two sections:

SECTIONS OF THE ENVIRONMENT DIVISION

CONFIGURATION SECTION.
INPUT-OUTPUT SECTION.

CONFIGURATION SECTION supplies data concerning the computer on which the COBOL program will be compiled and executed. The INPUT-OUTPUT SECTION supplies information concerning the specific devices used in the program. The card reader, printer, card punch, tape drives, and mass storage units are devices that may be referred to in the INPUT-OUTPUT SECTION of the ENVIRONMENT DIVISION.

The ENVIRONMENT DIVISION is the only division of a COBOL program that will change significantly if the program is to be run on different computers. Since computer users have varied models and equipment, each data processing installation has unique ENVIRONMENT DIVISION specifications. The entries required in the ENVIRONMENT DIVISION are generally supplied to the programmer by the installation. Throughout this discussion, we will use some **sample** statements, keeping in mind that such entries are dependent on the actual computer used, and the devices available with that computer.

A. CONFIGURATION
SECTION (optional)

The CONFIGURATION SECTION of the ENVIRONMENT DIVISION is an optional section that indicates: (1) the SOURCE-COMPUTER—the computer that will be used for **compiling** the program and (2) the OBJECT-COMPUTER—the computer that will be used for executing or running the program. SOURCE-COMPUTER and OBJECT-COMPUTER are optional entries within the CONFIGURATION SECTION.

You will recall that all section names, in addition to division names, are coded in Margin A. Thus the CONFIGURATION SECTION will follow the ENVIRONMENT DIVISION entry, in Margin A. SOURCE-COMPUTER and OBJECT-COMPUTER, as paragraph names, are also coded in Margin A.

The SOURCE- and OBJECT-COMPUTER entries must specify:

ENTRIES FOR SOURCE-COMPUTER AND OBJECT-COMPUTER PARAGRAPHS

1. The computer manufacturer
2. The computer number
3. The computer model number (optional)

Observe the following sample entries:

```
ENVIRONMENT DIVISION.
CONFIGURATION SECTION.
SOURCE-COMPUTER.  NCR-200.
OBJECT-COMPUTER.  NCR-200.
```

Note that each paragraph name is directly followed by a period and then a space. The designated computer, NCR-200, is also followed by a period.

In the example, the source and object computers are the same. In general, this will be the case, since compilation and execution are usually performed on the same computer. If, however, the program will be compiled on one model computer and executed, at some future time, on another model computer, these entries will differ:

Example

ENVIRONMENT DIVISION.
CONFIGURATION SECTION.
SOURCE-COMPUTER. IBM-370.
OBJECT-COMPUTER. UNIVAC-SERIES-90 90-60.

In the above illustration, the program will be compiled on an IBM 370 and executed on a UNIVAC series 90, model 60. The computer number and model is generally supplied by the installation since it will remain the same for **all** COBOL programs run at a computer center.

In Chapter 13, we discuss the SPECIAL-NAMES paragraph of the CONFIGURATION SECTION that can be used in conjunction with the printing of reports.

B. INPUT-OUTPUT SECTION

The INPUT-OUTPUT SECTION of the ENVIRONMENT DIVISION follows the CONFIGURATION SECTION and supplies information concerning the devices used in the program. In this chapter, we will discuss the FILE-CONTROL paragraph of the INPUT-OUTPUT SECTION. In the FILE-CONTROL paragraph a file name is assigned to each device to be used by the program.

Thus far, we have the following entries that may be coded in the ENVIRONMENT DIVISION:

```
ENVIRONMENT DIVISION.
CONFIGURATION SECTION.
SOURCE-COMPUTER.
     (computer and model number supplied by the manufacturer)
OBJECT-COMPUTER.
     (computer and model number supplied by the manufacturer)
INPUT-OUTPUT SECTION.
FILE-CONTROL.
     (entries which assign each file name to a device)
```

The FILE-CONTROL paragraph consists of SELECT clauses. Each SELECT clause defines a file name and assigns an input or output device to that file. The format may be as follows:

> SELECT (file name) ASSIGN TO (device specification)

FILE NAME

The file name assigned to each device must conform to the rules for forming programmer-supplied names:

> **RULES FOR FORMING PROGRAMMER-SUPPLIED NAMES**
>
> 1. 1 to 30 characters.
> 2. No special characters except a dash.
> 3. No embedded blanks.
> 4. At least one alphabetic character.
> 5. Names should be meaningful.

In addition to conforming to these rules, the file name must be **unique:** that is, the name may not be assigned to any other data element in the program.

For each device used in the program, a SELECT clause must be specified. If a program requires cards as input and produces a printed report as output, two SELECT clauses will be specified. One file name will be assigned to the card file, and another to the print file.

DEVICE SPECIFICATIONS   The device specifications vary among computer manufacturers.

(1) SIMPLIFIED VERSIONS OF THE DEVICE SPECIFICATION

Most systems enable the programmer to access frequently used devices by special device names. The following are common short-hand device specifications:

Card Reader	SYSIPT, SYSRDR, or SYSIN
Card Punch	SYSPCH or SYSPUNCH
Printer	SYSLST or SYSOUT

Hence for most systems,[1] the following entries would be valid for a program that utilizes cards as input and a printed report as output.

Example 1

      FILE-CONTROL. SELECT FILE-1 ASSIGN TO SYSIPT.
                          SELECT FILE-2 ASSIGN TO SYSLST.

   Similarly, a program that utilizes card input and punched card output might have the following ENVIRONMENT DIVISION entries:

      FILE-CONTROL. SELECT FILE-A ASSIGN TO SYSRDR.
                          SELECT FILE-B ASSIGN TO SYSPCH.

(2) FORMAL DEVICE SPECIFICATIONS

In general, the device specifications vary among computer manufacturers. The following format of a SELECT clause is standard for ANS compilers:

$$\text{SELECT}\begin{pmatrix}\text{file}\\\text{name}\end{pmatrix}\text{ASSIGN TO}\overset{①}{\begin{pmatrix}\text{system}\\\text{number}\end{pmatrix}}-\overset{②}{\begin{Bmatrix}\text{UR}\\\text{UT}\\\text{DA}\end{Bmatrix}}-\overset{③}{\begin{pmatrix}\text{device}\\\text{number}\end{pmatrix}}-\overset{④}{\begin{Bmatrix}\text{S}\\\text{D}\\\text{I}\end{Bmatrix}}\overset{⑤}{\begin{bmatrix}-&\text{external}\\&\text{name}\end{bmatrix}}.$$

The [external name] entry is optional.

Examples

   IBM
      SELECT CARD-IN ASSIGN TO SYS005-UR-2540R-S.
      SELECT TAPE-OUT ASSIGN TO SYS006-UT-2400-S.
   UNIVAC
      SELECT TAPE-1 ASSIGN TO SYSO10-UT-590-5.

   The FILE-CONTROL paragraph may seem unnecessarily complex at this point. The entries, however, are standard for a particular installation. The only programmer-supplied term is the file name.

   Let us define each of the five entries for the device specification and then discuss each in detail.

---

[1]Consult your computer's specification manual to determine if these device specifications are utilized.

DEVICE SPECIFICATIONS

1. System number
   supplied by computer center that assigns a number to each device

2. Classification
$\left\{ \begin{array}{l} UR \\ UT \\ DA \end{array} \right\}$

   UR—unit record
   UT—utility (tape)
   DA—direct access[3]

3. Device number
   supplied by computer manufacturer

4. Access mode
   S for sequential
   $\left. \begin{array}{l} D \\ I \end{array} \right\}$ for direct-access files[2]

5. External name (optional)

---

1. System Number. The **system number** is dependent on the particular installation. The item will vary among data processing centers and must therefore be supplied by each particular computer center. Each physical device in a computer facility will have a unique system number. The system number used may be an external-name or may have the format SYSnnn, where nnn is a number from 001-256.

2. Classification. The **classifications** that may be used are standard entries. There are three types of device classifications: UNIT-RECORD, UTILITY, and DIRECT-ACCESS. The printer, card punch, and card reader are UNIT-RECORD devices. That is each record associated with any of these devices is of **fixed length.** A card, for example, is a UNIT-RECORD document, since it **always** consists of 80 positions of data. A printed form is similarly a UNIT-RECORD document since each line **always** consists of the same number of print positions. Thus card and print files will always have a classification of UR for UNIT-RECORD.

Tape is not a UNIT-RECORD document since tape records can be any size. Tape is classified as UT for a UTILITY device. Mass storage units such as disk, drum, and data cells are classified as DA for DIRECT-ACCESS devices.

3. Device Number. The **device number** is designated by the computer manufacturer. IBM, for example, most often uses the following device numbers for the S/370 units:

TAPE	2400
READER	2540R
PRINTER	1403
PUNCH	2540P

---

[2]Direct-access entries are discussed in Chapter 22.

4. *Access Mode.* The **access mode** will always be S, for card, tape or print files, since these file types are always accessed sequentially. The D and I access modes are discussed in Chapter 22 since they pertain only to disk processing.

Note that the entire device specification clause following ASSIGN TO contains separate entries connected by hyphens. The omission of these hyphens in coding will cause errors in the program.

5. *External Name.* This entry is optional. It is used by some operating systems to access the file. It is the name used by the job control cards for data definition purposes. See Appendix D. If used, the external name must be 1–8 characters, letters and digits and hyphens only.

Using arbitrary system numbers, since these will depend on the installation, let us examine the following illustrations.

Example 1

A card file, consisting of transaction data, may be assigned as follows for an IBM System:

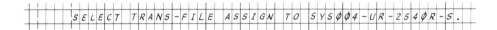

The name, TRANS-FILE, is supplied by the programmer. The remaining data in the statement is necessary when utilizing the reader. The reader is a UNIT-RECORD device with number 2540R, and assigned to SYS004, for this installation.

Note that SELECT clauses are coded in Margin B.

Example 2

A tape file, consisting of employee data, may be assigned as follows for a UNIVAC System:

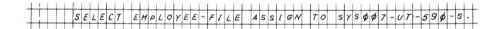

EMPLOYEE-FILE is the name assigned to the tape file. All entries after the words ASSIGN TO are supplied by the installation to indicate a specific tape drive.

Note that the important entry in the SELECT clause is the file name assigned. This name is utilized in the DATA DIVISION to reserve the input or output area to be used by the file. It is again denoted in the PROCEDURE DIVISION to access the file. The other entries in the SELECT clause are computer dependent. The system numbers, however, must be obtained from the particular installation. Any system numbers used in this book are arbitrary assignments.

Problem

Code the IDENTIFICATION and ENVIRONMENT DIVISION entries for the following system:

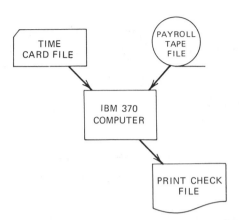

All SELECT clauses are coded in Margin B. The order in which the files are specified is not significant.

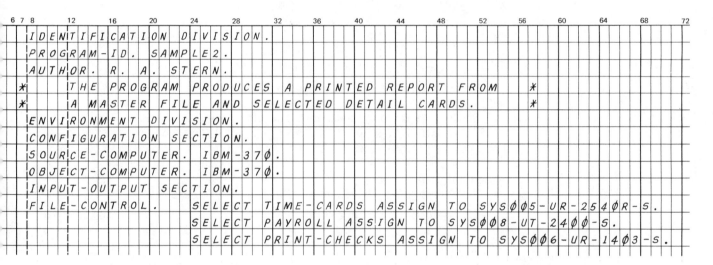

A common alternative method for coding SELECT statements has the following format:

SELECT (file-name) ASSIGN TO $\begin{bmatrix} \text{UR} \\ \text{UT} \end{bmatrix}$ -(device)-S-(external-name)

Using this format, the system number is omitted and the external name, which will be supplied by the computer installation, must be used.

Example

```
SELECT CARD-IN ASSIGN TO UR-2540R-S-INFILE.
SELECT PRINT-OUT ASSIGN TO UR-1403-S-OUTPRT.
SELECT TAPE-1 ASSIGN TO UT-2400-S-OUTTAPE.
SELECT CARD-OUT ASSIGN TO UR-2540P-S-OUTFILE.
```

The external name must be 1 to 8 characters in length and is used in place of the system number to identify the file for purposes of job control.

Consult your specifications manual or the programming manager for the requirements of the SELECT statements at your computer center.

1. The ENVIRONMENT DIVISION of a COBOL program supplies information about _____.
   *****
   equipment to be used
2. The entries in the ENVIRONMENT DIVISION are dependent on _____ and _____.
   *****
   the computer
   the specific devices used
3. The two sections of the ENVIRONMENT DIVISION are the _____ SECTION and the _____ SECTION.
   *****
   CONFIGURATION
   INPUT-OUTPUT
4. The entries in the ENVIRONMENT DIVISION (will, will not) change significantly if the program is run on a different computer.
   *****
   will—it is the only division that would change significantly
5. The two paragraphs required in the CONFIGURATION SECTION are _____ and _____.
   *****
   SOURCE-COMPUTER
   OBJECT-COMPUTER
6. The above entries are coded in Margin _____ and are followed by a _____.
   *****
   A
   period
7. The INPUT-OUTPUT SECTION of the COBOL program supplies information about the _____.
   *****
   devices being used
8. Files are defined and assigned in the _____ paragraph of the INPUT-OUTPUT SECTION.
   *****
   FILE-CONTROL
9. FILE-CONTROL consists of a series of _____ clauses.
   *****
   SELECT
10. For every device used in the program, a _____ name must be specified.
    *****
    file
11. The file name used in the SELECT clause must conform to the rules for forming _____.

*****
programmer-supplied names

12. The SELECT clause assigns the file to a device having five specifications: _____, _____, _____, _____, and _____.
*****
system number
classification
device number
access mode
external name

13. The three types of device classifications are _____, _____, and _____.
*****
UR for UNIT-RECORD
UT for UTILITY
DA for DIRECT-ACCESS

14. A UNIT-RECORD device is one that _____.
*****
consists of records of a fixed length

15. A card reader and a printer are examples of _____ devices.
*****
UNIT-RECORD

16. A tape drive is a _____ device.
*****
UTILITY

17. The device and system number are _____-dependent entries.
*****
machine

18. SELECT clauses are coded in Margin _____.
*****
B

19. Code the IDENTIFICATION and ENVIRONMENT DIVISION entries for a program that edits input transaction cards, creates an error listing for all erroneous cards, and creates a master tape.
*****

```
IDENTIFICATION DIVISION.
PROGRAM-ID. EDIT1.
AUTHOR. N. B. STERN.
*    THIS PROGRAM EDITS INPUT CARDS, CREATES
*    A TAPE AND AN ERROR LISTING.
ENVIRONMENT DIVISION.
CONFIGURATION SECTION.
SOURCE-COMPUTER. IBM-370.
OBJECT-COMPUTER. IBM-370.
INPUT-OUTPUT SECTION.
FILE-CONTROL.
     SELECT TRANSACTION-CARDS ASSIGN TO SYS005-UR-2540R-S.
     SELECT ERROR-FILE ASSIGN TO SYS006-UR-1404-S.
     SELECT MASTER-TAPE ASSIGN TO SYS007-UT-2400-S.
```

REVIEW QUESTIONS

True False   **I. True-False Questions**

☐ ☐   1. The ENVIRONMENT DIVISION of a COBOL program, like the other three divisions, is generally the same regardless of the computer on which it is run.

☐ ☐   2. A UTILITY device is one that may have fixed length records or variable length records.

☐ ☐   3. A magnetic tape may sometimes be considered a UNIT-RECORD device.

☐ ☐   4. The INPUT-OUTPUT SECTION of the ENVIRONMENT DIVISION assigns the file names.

☐ ☐   5. The CONFIGURATION-SECTION is an optional entry in the ENVIRONMENT DIVISION.

☐ ☐   6. FILE-CONTROL is an optional entry in the ENVIRONMENT DIVISION.

☐ ☐   7. The SOURCE-COMPUTER and OBJECT-COMPUTER entries must be exactly the same.

☐ ☐   8. S in an ASSIGN clause denotes standard.

☐ ☐   9. The rules for forming file names are the same as those for forming data-names.

☐ ☐   10. A maximum of three files may be defined in the INPUT-OUTPUT SECTION.

II. General Questions

1. Indicate which entries are coded in Margin A:
   (a) ENVIRONMENT DIVISION.
   (b) CONFIGURATION SECTION.
   (c) SOURCE-COMPUTER.
   (d) FILE-CONTROL.
   (e) SELECT clause.

2. Define each of the following:
   (a) OBJECT-COMPUTER.
   (b) UTILITY.
   (c) UNIT-RECORD.
   (d) File name.
   (e) CONFIGURATION SECTION.

3. Which entries of the ENVIRONMENT DIVISION are coded in Margin A and which are coded in Margin B?

   Make the necessary corrections to each of the following and assume that device specification, where noted, is correct (4–7):

4.
```
ENVIRONMENT DIVISION
CONFIGURATION SECTION.
SOURCE COMPUTER. MODEL-120.
```

5.
```
ENVIROMENT DIVISION.
   .
   .
   .
INPUT OUTPUT SECTION
```

6.
```
SELECT FILE A ASSIGN TO SYS002-UR-2540R-S.
```

7.
```
FILE CONTROL.
   SELECT FILEA ASSIGN TO PRINTER.
```

PROBLEMS   1. Code the IDENTIFICATION DIVISION and the ENVIRONMENT DIVISION for a COBOL update program that uses a detail card file and a previous master inventory tape file to create a current master inventory tape file.
2. Code the IDENTIFICATION DIVISION and the ENVIRONMENT DIVISION for a COBOL program that will use a master billing tape to punch gas-bill cards and electric-bill cards.

NOTE: Code these programs for the computer used at your installation.

5 THE DATA DIVISION

The DATA DIVISION is that part of a COBOL program that defines and describes data fields in storage. Any area of storage that is required for the processing of data must be established in the DATA DIVISION in either the FILE SECTION or the WORKING-STORAGE SECTION.

Any program that (1) reads data as input or (2) produces output data requires a FILE SECTION to describe the input and output. Since all programs read in data, operate on it, and produce output, the FILE SECTION will be an essential part of every program.

We will see that the WORKING-STORAGE SECTION is used for defining fields that are not part of input or output.

A. FILE SECTION

The FILE SECTION, as the name implies, describes all input and output files used in the program. Such files have already been defined in the ENVIRONMENT DIVISION, in a SELECT clause, where the file name is designated and an input-output device is assigned. Let us use the following sample statements as examples:

```
FILE-CONTROL.
    SELECT FILE-1 ASSIGN TO SYS005-UR-2540R-S.
    SELECT FILE-2 ASSIGN TO SYS007-UR-1403-S.
    SELECT FILE-3 ASSIGN TO SYS008-UT-2400-S.
```

The DATA DIVISION can consist of three sections:

---

1. FILE SECTION—defines all data areas that are part of input or output files.
2. WORKING-STORAGE SECTION—sets up memory for fields not part of input or output but nonetheless required for processing. These include constants, work areas, hold areas, etc.
3. REPORT SECTION—describes the specific format of reports that are generated by the Report Writer Feature. This section is used only for specific types of report processing and is not generally used in the majority of COBOL programs. It is not discussed in this text.

The sections included in the DATA DIVISION of a program must appear in the above sequence. This chapter will discuss the FILE SECTION, the first section of the DATA DIVISION. The WORKING-STORAGE SECTION that follows the FILE SECTION, if required in a program, is discussed at the end of this chapter, but also in Chapter 8 in more detail. Most COBOL programs make use of these two sections.

For every SELECT clause written in the ENVIRONMENT DIVISION, a file name is denoted. Thus, for every SELECT clause, we will have one file to describe in the FILE SECTION of the DATA DIVISION.

The FILE SECTION, as mentioned, describes the input and output areas used in the program. An **input area** is storage reserved for an incoming file. A READ instruction, in the PROCEDURE DIVISION, will transmit data to this input area. Similarly, an **output area** is storage reserved for an outgoing file. When a WRITE statement is executed, any data stored in this output area is transmitted to the specified output device. The devices and file names are **assigned** in the ENVIRONMENT DIVISION in a SELECT clause. The input or output area for each file is **described** in the FILE SECTION of the DATA DIVISION.

FILE DESCRIPTION   The FILE SECTION describes each file with an FD entry. FD denotes **File Description.** Each FD entry will describe a file established by a SELECT clause in the ENVIRONMENT DIVISION. Thus, for the above example, we have:

```
DATA DIVISION.
FILE SECTION.
FD  FILE-1
          .
          .
FD  FILE-2
          .
          .
FD  FILE-3
          .
          .
```

Each FD entry will be followed by a file name and certain clauses, to be discussed. Since there are three SELECT clauses in our example, there must be three FD level entries in the FILE SECTION.

The two entries, DATA DIVISION and FILE SECTION, are coded in Margin A. FD is also coded in Margin A. The file name, however, is coded in Margin

B. **No period follows the file name.** FD PUNCH-FILE, for example, signals the compiler that PUNCH-FILE is **about to be** described. Several entries are used to describe a file. These will follow FD (file name), and no period will be written until the last clause is specified. Observe the following examples:

```
FD   CARD-FILE
     LABEL RECORDS ARE OMITTED
     RECORD CONTAINS 80 CHARACTERS
     DATA RECORD IS EMPLOYEE-REC.
                    .
                    .
                    .
                    .
FD   TAPE-FILE
     LABEL RECORDS ARE STANDARD
     RECORD CONTAINS 50 CHARACTERS
     BLOCK CONTAINS 20 RECORDS
     DATA RECORD IS TRANSACTION-REC.
```

1. LABEL RECORDS CLAUSE—REQUIRED

$$\text{LABEL RECORDS ARE} \begin{Bmatrix} \text{OMITTED} \\ \text{STANDARD} \end{Bmatrix}$$

Data on a disk or a tape cannot be "read" as one reads a book or a punched card; that is, data is stored as magnetized bits that cannot be seen by the naked eye.

Label records, then, are usually created as the first and last records of a tape or disk to provide identifying information. Since the data on a tape or disk is not visible, these label records will provide a check to see if the correct file is present. Labels are created on output files so that, when the same file is later read as input, the labels may be checked. That is, labels are **created** on output files and **checked** on input files. The COBOL compiler will supply the routine for writing labels on output files or for checking labels on input files if the following entry is denoted as part of the File Description:

LABEL RECORDS ARE STANDARD

This clause signifies two things:

(a) The first record on the file is **not** a data record but a standard 80-position **header label** and, similarly, that the last record is a **trailer label.**
(b) With input files, these labels will be computer-checked and, with output files, they will be computer-created.

Although no further COBOL statements are necessary to perform the label routines, a control card must be supplied when executing a program. This control card contains the information desired on the labels.[1]

The clause LABEL RECORDS ARE STANDARD is permitted **only** for tape or direct-access files. Unit-record devices do **not** utilize label records. Such identifying information is unnecessary on devices where data is visible, such as on punched cards or printed data. For unit-record files, the entry LABEL RECORDS ARE OMITTED is required.

Similarly, a tape or direct-access file sometimes requires LABEL RECORDS ARE OMITTED as the entry when there is some assurance that checking for correct files is unnecessary. In that case, label records will be neither created nor checked.

The LABEL RECORDS clause is a **required** entry for each File Description. We will generally indicate STANDARD labels for tape or disk files. The clause LABEL RECORDS ARE OMITTED **must** be used for unit-record files.

Example 1

Card files or print files may have the following entries:

```
FD    FILE-NAME-1
      LABEL RECORDS ARE OMITTED
```

Example 2

Tape or direct-access files usually have the following entries:

```
FD    FILE-NAME-2
      LABEL RECORDS ARE STANDARD
```

2. RECORD CONTAINS CLAUSE—OPTIONAL

RECORD CONTAINS (integer) CHARACTERS

The RECORD CONTAINS clause indicates the size of each record. A print file, for example, may have the following entry:

RECORD CONTAINS 133 CHARACTERS

In our discussions, the print files will have 133 position records. You will recall that the usual size of a printed line is 132 characters. We establish our records as 133, however, to allow for carriage control, or the spacing of the form. The **first** position in these 133 position print records is the carriage con-

---

[1]See Appendix D.

trol position and is not printed. Thus positions 2-133 of the record represent the actual data to be printed.

A card file will have the following entry:

> RECORD CONTAINS 80 CHARACTERS

For tape or direct-access files, the RECORD CONTAINS clause varies. One of the advantages of these files is that records can be any size.

The RECORD CONTAINS clause in the File Description entry is **optional.** However, it is advisable to include it, since it provides a check on record size.

Example 3

FD entry for a card file:

```
FD   CARD-FILE
     LABEL RECORDS ARE OMITTED
     RECORD CONTAINS 80 CHARACTERS
```

Example 4

FD entry for a disk file **may** be, for example:

```
FD   DISK-FILE
     LABEL RECORDS ARE STANDARD
     RECORD CONTAINS 150 CHARACTERS
```

3. BLOCK CONTAINS CLAUSE—OPTIONAL[2]

> BLOCK CONTAINS (integer) RECORDS

This clause is only included in the File Description entry for tapes or disk.

Tape or disk files often have blocked records for efficiency of operations. A specific number of logical records are included within one block to make maximum use of a tape or disk area. Note that the programmer generally does not ascertain the most beneficial block size or **blocking factor** but obtains this data from a systems analyst.

By indicating a BLOCK CONTAINS clause for an input tape or disk, the computer is able to read the correct block. By indicating BLOCK CONTAINS for an output tape or disk, the computer is able to create the correct block of records.

Thus the BLOCK CONTAINS clause of a tape or disk file is the **only** entry

---

[2]The BLOCK CONTAINS entry is frequently unnecessary since the job control statements can be used for indicating a blocking factor.

required to perform operations on blocked data. **No** additional COBOL statements are necessary.

When blocking of records is not specified, as on unit-record devices, the BLOCK CONTAINS clause is **omitted.**

4. DATA RECORD(S) CLAUSE—OPTIONAL

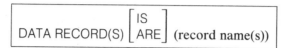

The DATA RECORD clause defines the record or records within the file. If there is only one record layout, DATA RECORD IS (record name) is used. Any record name may be specified. The name, however, must conform to the rules for forming programmer-supplied names. It must also be unique. Any name that appears as a file or record name may not be used for something else in the program.

If more than one record format exists for a file, specify DATA RECORDS ARE (record-1, record-2, . . .). Note that while DATA RECORDS ARE specifies more than one format for the file, it does **not** reserve additional storage. To use several record descriptions within one file does **not** set up additional I-O areas; it merely redefines a **single** input or output area in several ways.

The DATA RECORD(S) clause is an optional entry for all File Descriptions and is followed by a period, since this is the last entry to be discussed. Note that no other period has appeared in the FD.

Example 5

Description of a card file that contains employee records:

```
FD  CARD-FILE
    LABEL RECORDS ARE OMITTED
    RECORD CONTAINS 80 CHARACTERS
    DATA RECORD IS EMPLOYEE-REC.
```

Example 6

Description of a tape file containing transaction credit records and transaction debit records. Record size is 50, block size is 20:

```
FD  TAPE-FILE
    LABEL RECORDS ARE STANDARD
    RECORD CONTAINS 50 CHARACTERS
    BLOCK CONTAINS 20 RECORDS
    DATA RECORDS ARE TRANS-DEBIT, TRANS-CREDIT.
```

The above four clauses in the FD entry are the most commonly used statements but not the only ones.[3] For most applications in COBOL, they are quite adequate. Table 5.1 provides a summary of these clauses.

[3]The RECORDING MODE clause, for example, is an optional entry for IBM and other systems. See the specifications manual for the computer you are using for further details.

TABLE 5.1

Clause	Entries	Optional or Required	Use
LABEL RECORDS ARE	$\begin{Bmatrix} \text{OMITTED} \\ \text{STANDARD} \end{Bmatrix}$	required	Indicates if header and trailer labels are used on tape or disk; OMITTED is used for unit-record files
RECORD CONTAINS	(integer) CHARACTERS	optional	Indicates the number of characters in the record
BLOCK CONTAINS	(integer) RECORDS	optional	Indicates blocking factor for tape or disk
DATA RECORD(S)	$\begin{bmatrix} \text{IS} \\ \text{ARE} \end{bmatrix}$ (record-name(s))	optional	Indicates the name of each record in the file

---

RULES FOR CODING FILE DESCRIPTION ENTRIES

1. FD is coded in Margin A.
2. All other entries are coded in Margin B.
3. No period is coded until the last clause has been specified.
4. Commas are optional anywhere in a COBOL program to separate clauses.
5. If commas are used they must be followed by at least one blank.
6. Each clause may appear on a separate line or the clauses may be coded in paragraph form. (See Figure 5.1.) Note, however, that we will continue to use one clause per line for the sake of clarity.

```
     FD   CARD-FILE, LABEL RECORDS ARE OMITTED, RECORD CONTAINS
          80 CHARACTERS, DATA RECORD IS EMPLOYEE-REC.



     FD   TAPE-FILE, LABEL RECORDS ARE STANDARD, RECORD CONTAINS 50
          CHARACTERS, BLOCK CONTAINS 20 RECORDS, DATA RECORDS ARE
          TRANS-DEBIT, TRANS-CREDIT.
```

Figure 5.1

The word IS or ARE in any COBOL statement may be omitted. To say, LABEL RECORDS STANDARD, for example, is entirely appropriate.

Last, the **order** of these entries is **not** significant. Any clause may appear first in an FD entry.

Example 7

The following is a correctly coded File Description:

SELF-EVALUATING
QUIZ

1. The DATA DIVISION is that part of a COBOL program that _____.
   *****
   defines and describes data fields in storage
2. The two primary sections of a DATA DIVISION are the _____ and the
   _____.
   *****
   FILE SECTION
   WORKING-STORAGE SECTION
3. The FILE SECTION defines all data areas _____.
   *****
   that are part of input or output
4. The first time a file name appears in a COBOL program is in a _____
   clause of the _____ DIVISION.
   *****
   SELECT
   ENVIRONMENT
5. File names must be one to (no.) characters in length, contain at least one
   _____, and have no _____.
   *****
   30
   alphabetic character
   special characters (except -)
6. FILE 1 is not a valid file name because it _____.
   *****
   contains an embedded blank
7. File names (must, need not) be unique.
   *****
   must
8. For every file defined in a SELECT clause, there will be one _____ entry
   in the FILE SECTION.
   *****
   FD
9. The four clauses that may be used with an FD entry are _____,
   _____, _____, and _____.
   *****
   LABEL RECORDS
   RECORD CONTAINS
   BLOCK CONTAINS
   DATA RECORD(S)

10. For unit-record devices, LABEL RECORDS ARE _____.
    *****
    OMITTED
11. When LABEL RECORDS ARE STANDARD is specified, header and trailer labels will be _____ on input files and _____ on output files.
    *****
    checked
    created
12. The LABEL RECORDS clause is (optional, required).
    *****
    required
13. The RECORD CONTAINS clause is (optional, required).
    *****
    optional
14. The BLOCK CONTAINS clause is only used for _____.
    *****
    blocked tape or disk files
15. The DATA RECORD(S) clause is (optional, required) and defines the _____.
    *****
    optional
    records within the file
16. Write an FD entry for a tape file blocked 20 with 100 position records and standard labels; one record format exists.
    *****

```
FD   TAPE-FILE LABEL RECORDS ARE STANDARD RECORD CONTAINS 100
     CHARACTERS BLOCK CONTAINS 20 RECORDS DATA RECORD IS
     REC-1.
```

17. Write an FD entry for a print file with header and detail records.
    *****

```
FD   PRINT-FILE
     LABEL RECORDS ARE OMITTED
     RECORD CONTAINS 133 CHARACTERS
     DATA RECORDS ARE HEADER1, DETAIL-LINE.
```

Make any necessary corrections to the following DATA DIVISION entries (18,19):

18.

```
DATA DIVISION.
FILE-SECTION
FD   CARD-FILE.
     LABELS ARE OMITTED
     DATA RECORD IS REC-IN
```

*****
No dash between FILE and SECTION; period after all Section names.
No period after FD CARD-FILE.

LABEL clause should read LABEL RECORDS ARE OMITTED (assuming it is a card file).

Period is required after last clause.

Corrected entry:

```
DATA DIVISION.
FILE SECTION.
FD  CARD-FILE
      LABEL RECORDS ARE OMITTED
      DATA RECORD IS REC-IN.
```

19.

```
FD  PRINT-FILE
      RECORD CONTAINS 133 CHARACTERS
      DATA RECORD IS PRINT REC
```

*****

PRINT REC may not have an embedded blank. File Description entries must end with period. Must have a LABEL RECORDS clause.

Corrected entry:

```
FD  PRINT-FILE
      LABEL RECORDS ARE OMITTED
      RECORD CONTAINS 133 CHARACTERS
      DATA RECORD IS PRINT-REC.
```

20. Which entry is required in an FD?

*****

LABEL RECORDS

RECORD DESCRIPTION

LEVEL INDICATORS

After a file is described by an FD, **record description** entries for each record within the file follow. A record description is required for each record named in the File Description clause to illustrate the **structure** of a record. It will indicate what items appear in the record, the order in which they appear, and how these items are related to each other. Just as the file name is specified on the FD level, a record name is coded on the 01 level. (See Figure 5.2.)

Examine the following illustrations.

Example 1

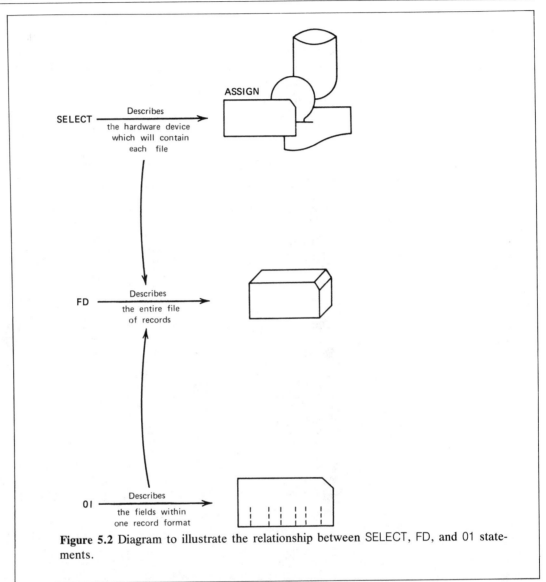

Figure 5.2 Diagram to illustrate the relationship between SELECT, FD, and 01 statements.

Example 2

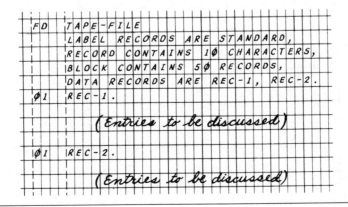

Each FD must be followed by record description entries for the file. We have observed that records are defined on the 01 level. Now we must indicate just what is contained in each record of the file and how the items are organized.

Data is grouped in COBOL around the **level** concept. Records are considered the **highest level of data** and thus are coded on the 01 level. Any field of data within the record is coded on a level **subordinate to** 01, that is, 02, 03, and so on. Any level number between 02 and 49 may be used to describe data fields within a record.

Let us examine the following card layout:

NAME	ANNUAL SALARY	JOB DESCRIPTION

The record description entries within the FD are as follows:

Example 3

```
Ø1    EMPLOYEE-REC.
      Ø2    NAME
      Ø2    ANN-SALARY
      Ø2    JOB-DESCRIPTION
```

The name of the record, EMPLOYEE-REC, is coded on the 01 level in Margin A. All fields within the record are coded on any level between 02 and 49, anywhere in Margin B. By specifying the above fields on the 02 level, two facts are established.

1. All fields on the 02 level are **subordinate to,** or part of, the 01 level entry.
2. All fields that are coded on the same level are **independent** items.

Thus NAME, ANN-SALARY, and JOB-DESCRIPTION are fields within EMPLOYEE-REC, and each is independent of the other.

Let us redefine the above input:

NAME				JOB DESCRIPTION		
				TITLE		
INITIAL 1	INITIAL 2	LAST NAME	ANNUAL SALARY	LEVEL	POSITION	DUTIES

Sometimes fields are **not** independent of one another, as in the preceding redefined input; that is, a field may be subordinate to, or contained in, **another** field within a record. MONTH and YEAR, for example, may be fields within DATE-OF-HIRE, which itself is contained within a record. MONTH and YEAR, then, would be coded on a level subordinate to DATE-OF-HIRE. If DATE-OF-HIRE were specified on level 02, MONTH and YEAR could each be specified on level 03.

Example 4

Record description for redefined input:

```
 7 8    12      16      20      24      28      32      36
  Ø1    EMPLOYEE-REC.
        Ø2    NAME
              Ø3    INITIAL1
              Ø3    INITIAL2
              Ø3    LAST-NAME
        Ø2    ANN-SALARY
        Ø2    JOB-DESCRIPTION
              Ø3    JOB-TITLE
                    Ø4    LEVEL
                    Ø4    JOB-POSITION
              Ø3    DUTIES
```

There are three **major** fields within the record: NAME, ANN-SALARY, and JOB-DESCRIPTION, which are still independent and coded on the 02 level. The NAME field, however, is further subdivided into INITIAL1, INITIAL2, and LAST-NAME. These 03 level items are independent of each other, but contained within NAME. Similarly, JOB-TITLE and DUTIES are independent items within JOB-DESCRIPTION. JOB-TITLE is further subdivided into LEVEL and JOB-POSITION.

Note that all fields are coded in Margin B. Only the highest level of organization, the record, is coded in Margin A. Note also the indentation of subordinate levels. While this indentation is not required, it does make the line easier to read. Using this method, the fact that INITIAL1, INITIAL2, and LAST-NAME are contained within NAME is quite clear.

The names of fields (data-names), like the names of records and files, must conform to the rules for forming programmer-supplied words:

PROGRAMMER-SUPPLIED WORDS
One to 30 characters
No special characters except a hyphen
No embedded blanks
At least one alphabetic character
No COBOL reserved words

Level numbers may vary from 02 to 49 for fields of data. Level numbers, however, need not be consecutive. The following are valid entries:

```
   7 8      12      16      20      24      28
    Ø1    REC-A.
          Ø3    DATE-OF-HIRE
                Ø7    MONTH
                Ø7    YEAR
          Ø3    REMAINDERS
```

This is an illustration of a FILE SECTION where level numbers are not consecutive. Note that MONTH and YEAR, on the 07 level, are contained within
DATE-OF-HIRE, on the 03 level.

Observe the following illustration:

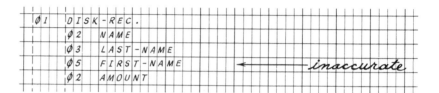

```
Ø1    DISK-REC.
      Ø2    NAME
      Ø3    LAST-NAME
      Ø5    FIRST-NAME        ←————————— inaccurate
      Ø2    AMOUNT
```

This entry is **not** correct. It implies that FIRST-NAME, as an 05 level item,
is contained in LAST-NAME, an 03 level item. To indicate that LAST-NAME
and FIRST-NAME have equal but independent status, they both must be coded
on the same level. To place them both on the 03, 04, or 05 level would be
accurate.

The **order** in which fields are placed within the record is crucial. If NAME
is the first 02 level within DISK-REC, this implies that NAME is the first data
field in the record.

An item that is **not** further subdivided is called an **elementary item.** An item
that **is** further subdivided is called a **group item.** In Example 4, NAME is a
group item that is subdivided into three elementary items, INITIAL1, INITIAL2,
and LAST-NAME. ANN-SALARY, on the same level as NAME, is an elementary
item since it is not further subdivided.

All elementary items must be additionally described by indicating **size** and
type of the field. A group item needs no further specification. Thus we have,
for example:

```
Ø1    TAPE-REC.
      Ø2    CUSTOMER-NAME.
            Ø3    LAST-NAME              (entry required)
            Ø3    FIRST-NAME            (entry required)
      Ø2    TRANSACTION-NUMBER          (entry required)
      Ø2    DATE-OF-TRANSACTION.
            Ø3    MONTH                  (entry required)
            Ø3    YEAR                   (entry required)
```

Note that there is a period at the end of each group item. Elementary items
require further description. We treat the record entry, on the 01 level, as a
group item, since it is, in fact, a data element that is further subdivided.

SELF-EVALUATING
QUIZ

1. All records are coded on the _____ level.
*****
01

2. Levels _____ to _____ may be used to represent fields within a record.
*****
02
49

3. An 03 level item may be subordinate to an _____ level item if it exists.
*****
02

4. What, if anything, is wrong with the following data-names:
(a) CUSTOMER NAME
(b) TAX%
(c) DATA
*****
No embedded blanks allowed.
No special characters (%).
DATA is a COBOL reserved word.

5. An elementary item is defined as _____, and a group item is defined as

_____.
*****
one which is not further subdivided
one which is further subdivided

6. 01 level is coded in Margin _____, 02 to 49 levels are coded in Margin

_____.
*****
A
B

7. Write record description entries for the following:

TRANSACTION RECORD

	LOCATION			PRODUCT DESCRIPTION		
				NO. OF ITEM		ITEM NAME
INVOICE NUMBER	WARE-HOUSE	CITY	JOB LOT	SIZE	MODEL	

*****

```
01  TRANSACTION-REC.
    02  INVOICE-NO
    02  LOCATION.
        03  WAREHOUSE
        03  CITY
        03  JOB-LOT
    02  PRODUCT-DESCRIPTION.
        03  NO-OF-ITEM.
            04  SIZE-X
            04  MODEL
        03  ITEM-NAME
```

NOTE: Periods follow group items only.

PICTURE CLAUSES

Group items are defined by a level indicator and end with a period. Elementary items are those fields that are not further subdivided, and they must be described in detail:

PICTURE CLAUSES
1. Specify the **type** of data contained within an elementary item.
2. Indicate the **size** of the field.

A PICTURE **clause** associated with **each** elementary item will provide the above information about a field.

There are **three** types of data fields.

TYPES OF DATA FIELDS
1. ALPHABETIC. A field that may consist of letters or blanks is classified as alphabetic. A name field or a heading field will generally be considered alphabetic.
2. ALPHANUMERIC. A field that may contain **any** valid character is considered alphanumeric. An address field, for example, would be classified as alphanumeric, since it may contain combinations of letters, digits, or even special characters.
3. NUMERIC. Any field that will contain digits and plus or minus signs **only** is considered numeric.

To denote the type of data within an elementary field, a PICTURE clause will contain:

CHARACTERS USED IN PICTURE CLAUSES

A for alphabetic
X for alphanumeric
9 for numeric

A field will contain a PICTURE of all A's, for example, if it is alphabetic. We denote the **size** of the field by the **number** of A's, X's, or 9's used in the PICTURE. For example, consider the following:

---
02 AMT PICTURE IS 99999.

The above field is an elementary item consisting of five positions of numeric data.

The entry:

---
02 ITEM1 PICTURE AAAA.
---

defines a four-position storage area called ITEM1 that will contain only alpha-betic data or blanks. Observe the following entries:

```
01   REC-1.
     02 ITEM1    PICTURE AAAA.
     02 AMT      PICTURE 99999.
     02 CDE      PICTURE XX.
```

ITEM1 is the first data field in the record. If REC-1, for example, defined a card record, Columns 1–4 would represent the field called ITEM1. AMT, as the second entry specified, would be describing the next field of data, or Columns 5–9. That is, the five positions directly following ITEM1 would represent the field called AMT.

If a field is numeric, its PICTURE clause may contain only 9's; if a field is alphabetic, its PICTURE clause may contain only A's; if a field may contain any character or combination of digits and letters, it is defined with a PICTURE of X's. Numeric fields may contain a maximum of 18 digits. Thus a PICTURE clause of 9(20), for example, is invalid.[4]

The following notation is acceptable to indicate a 10-position alphabetic field:

```
04 NAME PICTURE A(10).
```

Parentheses may be used to designate the size of the field rather than 10 A's. The word IS in the PICTURE clause is optional, as in all COBOL statements, and may always be omitted. A period will follow each PICTURE clause in the FILE SECTION. The abbreviation PIC may be used in place of PICTURE. Thus the above field may be defined as:

```
04 NAME PIC A(10).
```

Thus group items are those fields that are further subdivided and contain **no** PICTURE clause. Only elementary items require a PICTURE clause, which denotes the size of a field and its mode, that is, the type of data it will contain.

The record description entry for the following card layout is:

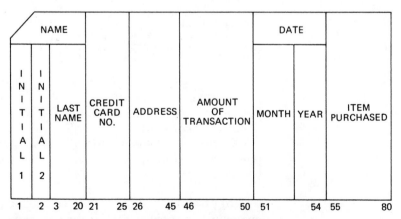

[4]There is no such limitation in the 1968 version of ANS COBOL.

```
01  CREDIT-CARD-ACCT.
    02  NAME.
        03    INIT1            PICTURE  A.
        03    INIT2            PICTURE  A.
        03    LAST-NAME        PICTURE  A(18).
    02  CREDIT-CARD-NO         PICTURE  9(5).
    02  ADDRESS-I              PICTURE  X(20).
    02  AMT-OF-TRANS           PICTURE  9(5).
    02  DATE-OF-TRANS.
        03    MONTH            PICTURE  99.
        03    YEAR             PICTURE  99.
    02  ITEM-PURCHASED         PICTURE  X(26).
```

The PICTURE clause may appear **anywhere** on the line. For purposes of clarity, each PICTURE clause was placed in the same position; this is not, however, required. At least one space must follow the word PICTURE. All A's, X's, or 9's must appear consecutively with no spaces between these characters. Similarly, if parentheses are used to denote the size of a field, no spaces may appear within the clause. The following entries are illegal:

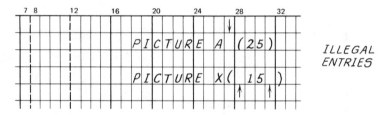

ILLEGAL
ENTRIES

The PICTURE clauses in a record description entry must, in total, yield the number of characters in the record. Thus, if CREDIT-CARD-ACCT is a card record, all PICTURE clauses on the elementary level must total 80 positions of storage.

In actual practice, the A specification is rarely used. The X specification can encompass alphabetic data and is usually used to represent all nonnumeric data.

USE OF FILLERS

Examine the following card layout:

SAMPLE CARD LAYOUT	
cc1-25	EMPLOYEE-NAME
cc26-30	not used
cc31-35	HOURS-WORKED
cc36-80	not used

Card Columns 26–30 and 36–80 contain no pertinent data. These areas, however, must be noted as fields in the record description entry. To say **incorrectly:**

```
01   TIME-CARD.
     02 EMPLOYEE-NAME PICTURE A(25).
     02 HOURS-WORKED  PICTURE 9(5).
```

causes two major errors:

1. The computer will assume that HOURS-WORKED immediately follows EM-PLOYEE-NAME, since it is the next designated field. A READ command, then, would place card Columns 26–30 in the storage area called HOURS-WORKED.
2. The PICTURE clause should result in 80 positions of storage. Instead, only 30 positions have been defined.

The following would then be correct:

```
Ø1    TIME-CARD.
         Ø2    EMPLOYEE-NAME      PIC  A(25).
         Ø2    WASTE1             PIC  X(5).
         Ø2    HOURS-WORKED       PIC  9(5).
         Ø2    WASTE2             PIC  X(45).
```

To denote a nonsignificant field of data, one that will not be utilized in the program, the COBOL reserved word FILLER may be used instead of creating data-names. A FILLER with an appropriate PICTURE clause designates an area set aside for some part of a record. As a COBOL reserved word specifying an unused area, it may not be accessed in the PROCEDURE DIVISION. To say: MOVE FILLER TO OUT-AREA, for example, is invalid. Our record description entry would usually be coded as:

```
Ø1    TIME-CARD.
         Ø2    EMPLOYEE-NAME      PIC  A(25).
         Ø2    FILLER             PIC  X(5).
         Ø2    HOURS-WORKED       PIC  9(5).
         Ø2    FILLER             PIC  X(45).
```

Except for the COBOL reserved word FILLER, we will keep all other data-names unique for now; that is, we will not use the same name for different fields. A record or a file name must **never** be used more than once in the DATA DIVISION. We will see in Chapter 11 that one data-name may, if coded properly, be used to define several fields.

In general, a field is denoted as numeric, with PICTURE of 9's, when an arithmetic operation is to be performed. When a field is so designated, the data in the area may consist of digits and a sign only. A space, for example, is not a valid character in a numeric field. Thus, if a field is denoted as numeric, it must contain only valid numeric characters.

Note that an alphanumeric field may contain any data, including all numbers. Thus 123 in FLDA, where FLDA has PICTURE XXX, is entirely acceptable. FLDA, however, may not be used in an **arithmetic** operation. Only fields with **numeric** PICTURE clauses may be specified in computations. In short, then, fields that are to be used in calculations must be defined with PICTURE of 9's. If there is any doubt about the type of data contained in a field, define it as alphanumeric, since such fields can contain any character.

IMPLIED DECIMAL POINT

Because numeric fields may be used in arithmetic operations, their PICTURE clauses may utilize entries in addition to the basic 9. Most of these will be discussed later, since they are necessary only in higher-level COBOL programs. The symbol V, however, to denote an implied decimal, will be discussed here because of its widespread use and importance.

Suppose a five-position amount field, with contents 10000, is to be interpreted as 100.00. That is, the computer is to "assume" that a decimal point exists. The data is five positions, and there is no decimal point within the field; but we want the computer to assume its existence. When any calculations are performed on the amount field, the computer is to consider the data as having three integer positions and two decimal positions. Its PICTURE clause, then, is

```
02 AMT PICTURE 999V99.
```

Note that V does **not** occupy a storage position. The field is five positions. We have merely indicated that data entering the field is to have three integer and two decimal positions. If 38726 is read into the area, it will be interpreted as 387.26, when the program is executed.

We have completed record description entries for the coding of elementary COBOL programs. For **every** record specified in the DATA RECORDS clause, an 01 level and its corresponding entries must be included.

All records within an FD are described before the next FD is defined. The DATA DIVISION in Figure 5.3 indicates the sequence in which entries are coded.

Note that the input file called INPUT-FILE has two records. Assume that the debit record has a 1 in cc80, and the credit record has a 2 in cc80. The computer establishes only **one** input area for this file. When a record is read, the computer must be instructed as to whether it is a debit or credit record. That is, do we move AMT-OF-DEBIT to the output record or AMT-OF-CREDIT? We must check card column 80 to determine if the record is a credit or a debit. If, for example, CODE-1 (card column 80 of the incoming card) is equal to 1, then we can assume that this is a debit record and move AMT-OF-DEBIT to the output area. This test and data transfer operation is performed in the PROCEDURE DIVISION, as follows:

COBOL Coding Form

IBM

SYSTEM								PAGE	OF	GX28-1464-5 U/M 050* Printed in U.S.A.
PROGRAM				PUNCHING INSTRUCTIONS				CARD FORM #		*
PROGRAMMER		DATE		GRAPHIC						
				PUNCH						

SEQUENCE		CONT.	A	B	COBOL STATEMENT					IDENTIFICATION
(PAGE)	(SERIAL)									

```
01    DATA DIVISION.
02    FILE SECTION.
03    FD  INPUT-FILE
04        LABEL RECORDS ARE OMITTED,
05        RECORD CONTAINS 80 CHARACTERS,
06        DATA RECORDS ARE REC-1, REC-2.
07    01  REC-1.
08        02  CUSTOMER-NAME      PIC X(20).
09        02  ADDRESS-1          PIC X(15).
10        02  AMT-OF-DEBIT       PIC 999V99.
11        02  FILLER             PIC X(39).
12        02  CODE-1             PIC 9.
13    01  REC-2.
14        02  NAME               PIC X(20).
15        02  AMT-OF-CREDIT      PIC 999V99.
16        02  FILLER             PIC X(54).
17        02  CODE-2             PIC 9.
18    FD  OUTPUT-FILE
19        LABEL RECORDS ARE STANDARD,
20        RECORD CONTAINS 25 CHARACTERS,
          DATA RECORD IS REC-OUT.
      01  REC-OUT.
          02  NAME-OUT           PIC X(20).
          02  AMT-OF-TRANS       PIC 999V99.
```

*A standard card form, IBM Electro C61897, is available for punching source statements from this form.
Instructions for using this form are given in any IBM COBOL reference manual.
Address comments concerning this form to IBM Corporation, Programming Publications, 1271 Avenue of the Americas, New York, New York 10020.

*No. of sheets per pad may vary slightly

Figure 5.3

IF CODE-1 = 1 MOVE AMT-OF-DEBIT TO AMT-OF-TRANS.

IF CODE-1 (card column 80) is not equal to 1, then CODE-2 (card column **80 of the same card**) should equal 2 to make this a credit record.

Thus we can see that the input record is placed in an input area. The field designations of that input area will be determined by what type of record it is. It is always best to establish a code to specify the type of record being processed and, thus, the field designations required.

SUMMARY OF RECORD DESCRIPTION ENTRIES

1. Record names are coded on the 01 level.
2. Field names are coded on levels 02–49.
3. Level 01 is coded in Margin A; all other levels are coded in Margin B.
4. Items with higher level numbers are considered subordinate to, or contained within, items with lower level numbers. In the following, DEPT is contained within JOB-DESCRIPTION:
   02 JOB-DESCRIPTION
   03 DEPT
5. Group items are further subdivided; elementary items are not.
6. Only elementary items have PICTURE or PIC clauses to describe the data:
   X—alphanumeric
   A—alphabetic
   9—numeric
   V—implied decimal position (used only with numeric fields)
7. Items must be defined in the DATA DIVISION in the same sequence as they appear in the record.
8. FILLER is a COBOL reserved word used to define areas within a record that will not be used for processing.
9. A period must follow a PICTURE clause; a period directly follows a group item as well.

B. THE WORKING-STORAGE SECTION

You will recall that the DATA DIVISION is divided into two sections: the FILE SECTION and the WORKING-STORAGE SECTION. The following discussion provides a preliminary introduction to the WORKING-STORAGE SECTION. Chapter 8 gives a more detailed account.

Any field necessary for processing that is not part of input or output may be defined in the WORKING-STORAGE SECTION. For example, if a field is to be initialized with a value of zero and incremented by one only when the last card has been read, we can define that field in the WORKING-STORAGE SECTION. If some intermediate total areas are necessary for processing, they too may be defined in this section.

RULES FOR USING THE WORKING-STORAGE SECTION

1. The WORKING-STORAGE SECTION **follows** all entries in the FILE SECTION.
2. WORKING-STORAGE SECTION is coded on a line by itself beginning in Margin A and ending with a period:

7 8	12	16	20	24	28	32
W O R K I N G - S T O R A G E S E C T I O N .						

3. A group item that will be subdivided into individual storage areas as needed is then defined. For example:

```
WORKING-STORAGE SECTION.
01 STORED-AREAS.
```

4. All necessary fields are then defined within this 01-level entry:

```
WORKING-STORAGE SECTION.
01   STORED-AREAS.
       02   END-OF-FILE-SWITCH
       02   GROSS-AMT
```

5. Names associated with group items and with elementary items must conform to the rules for forming data-names.
6. Each independent elementary item must contain a PIC clause:

```
WORKING-STORAGE SECTION.
01   STORED-AREAS.
       02   END-OF-FILE-SWITCH          PIC 9.
       02   GROSS-AMT                   PIC 999V99.
```

7. Each independent elementary item may contain an initial value, if one is desired:

```
WORKING-STORAGE SECTION.
01   STORED-AREAS.
       02   END-OF-FILE-SWITCH          PIC 9          VALUE ZERO.
       02   GROSS-AMT                   PIC 999V99     VALUE ZERO.
```

If the field called END-OF-FILE-SWITCH is to be used for signaling when no more cards exist, it may be used in the PROCEDURE DIVISION as follows:

```
READ CARD-FILE AT END MOVE 1 TO END-OF-FILE-SWITCH.
```

Thus END-OF-FILE-SWITCH is initialized at zero in the WORKING-STORAGE SECTION. It remains at zero until there are no more cards to be processed, at which point a 1 is moved into the field.

GROSS-AMT is another item that may be defined in WORKING-STORAGE. WORKING-STORAGE entries may have VALUE clauses, but these are not required.

SELF-EVALUATING
QUIZ

1. A PICTURE clause must be used in conjunction with each _____ in a record description.
   *****
   elementary item
2. A PICTURE clause specifies the _____ and the _____ of a data field.
   *****
   size
   type
3. The three types of data fields are _____, _____, and _____.
   *****
   alphabetic
   numeric
   alphanumeric
4. The characters that may be included in an alphabetic field are _____.
   *****
   letters and blanks
5. The characters that may be included in an alphanumeric field are

   _____.
   *****
   any characters in the COBOL character set
6. The characters that may be included in a numeric data field are _____.
   *****
   digits and plus or minus sign
7. An alphanumeric PICTURE clause contains _____; an alphabetic PICTURE clause contains _____; a numeric PICTURE clause contains

   _____.
   *****
   X's
   A's
   9's

   What, if anything, is wrong with the following entries (8–10):
8. 01   CARD-REC.
       02   DATE-OF-SALE PICTURE 9999.
           03   MONTH PICTURE 99.
           03   YEAR PICTURE 99.
   *****
   Group items, such as DATE-OF-SALE, should not have PICTURE clauses.
9. 03 FIELDA PICTURE XX.
   *****
   OK
10. 04 FIELDB PICTURE X (22).
    *****
    Should be: 04 FIELDB PICTURE X(22). There is no space between X and (.

11. The PICTURE clauses in a record description must, in total, indicate
    _____.
    *****
    the number of positions in the record
12. The word _____ is used to denote an area of a record that will not be
    used for processing.
    *****
    FILLER
13. The symbol _____ is used to denote an implied decimal point in an
    arithmetic field.
    *****
    V
14. A PICTURE clause of 9V9 indicates a (no.)-position data field.
    *****
    two
15. If a three-position tax field is to be interpreted as .xxx, its PICTURE clause
    should be _____.
    *****
    V999.
16. The _____ SECTION of the DATA DIVISION usually follows the FILE
    SECTION.
    *****
    WORKING-STORAGE
17. WORKING-STORAGE entries may contain _____ clauses to indicate the
    initial contents of fields.
    *****
    VALUE

REVIEW QUESTIONS

True False

☐ ☐
☐ ☐

☐ ☐
☐ ☐
☐ ☐

☐ ☐
☐ ☐
☐ ☐
☐ ☐
☐ ☐

I. True-False Questions
1. There may be only one 01 level for a specific file.
2. The order in which fields are specified in a record description is not significant.
3. Group items must not have PICTURE clauses.
4. Elementary items may or may not have PICTURE clauses.
5. A FILLER is a COBOL reserved word that may be used in the DATA and PROCEDURE DIVISIONS.
6. A record name is assigned in the ENVIRONMENT DIVISION.
7. Two files may be assigned the same names.
8. Levels 03, 08, 75 may be subordinate to a record level.
9. The WORKING-STORAGE SECTION follows the FILE SECTION.
10. Independent entries not part of input or output but necessary for processing are coded in the WORKING-STORAGE SECTION.

II. General Questions
1. Which of the following entries are coded in Margin A?
   (a) FD
   (b) FILE SECTION
   (c) 01

(d) 03

(e) LABEL RECORDS ARE OMITTED

2. Name the clauses that are required within an FD.

3. Name the clauses that are optional within an FD.

4. How many FD entries are required in a COBOL program?

5. Under what conditions is the BLOCK CONTAINS clause required?

6. State exactly what is meant by the PICTURE clause 9999V9999.

7. Which entries are coded in the FILE SECTION? Which are coded in the WORKING-STORAGE SECTION?

8. What are the rules for forming data-names?

9. How many characters must be included in the PICTURE clauses used to describe a card record?

10. Correct the following DATA DIVISION:

```
DATA DIVISION.
FILE-SECTION.
FD   TAPE FILE.
     DATA RECORD IS INPUT.
01   INPUT.
     02   TRANS.NO           PICTURE 9999.
     02   TRANSACTION-NAME    PICTURE 20X.
     02   ADDRESS
          03   NUMBER         PICTURE XXXX.
          03   STREET         PICTURE A(15).
          03   CITY           PICTURE AAA.
     02   CREDIT-RATING       PICTURE XX.
          03   CREDIT-CODE    PICTURE X.
          03   LIMIT OF PURCHASE  PICTURE X.
     02   UNIT-PRICE          PICTURE 99.9.
     02   QTY-PURCHASED       PICTURE 9(5).
     02   DISCOUNT-%          PICTURE V99.
```

PROBLEMS   1. Write the FD and record description entries necessary for an inventory file with the following record format:

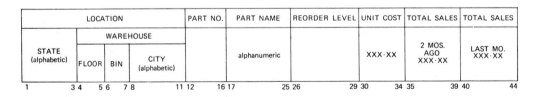

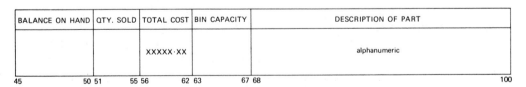

(UNLESS OTHERWISE NOTED, FIELDS ARE NUMERIC)
XXX.XX denotes a PICTURE clause of 999V99

The inventory file will be on magnetic tape with standard labels and blocked 20.

2. Write the FD and record description entries for the following purchase record:

Item Description	Field Type	Field Size	Positions to Right of Decimal Point
Name of item	Alphabetic	20	—
Date of order (month, day, year)	Numeric	6	0
Purchase order number	Numeric	5	0
Inventory group	Alphanumeric	10	—
Number of units	Numeric	5	0
Cost/unit	Numeric	4	0
Freight charge	Numeric	4	0
Tax percent	Numeric	2	2

3. Write FD entries for the following card format:

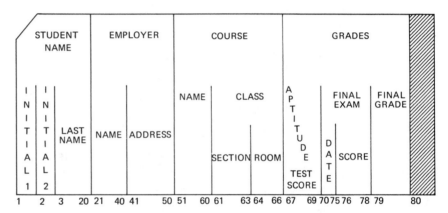

4. Write FD entries for a master transaction tape file with the following **two** record formats:

The master tape has standard labels and is blocked 10.

5. Write FD entries for the following file of records:

Account Identification	[Type of Account	↔	Alphanumeric 5 positions
	[Customer Name	↔	Alphabetic 20 positions
	Acct. No. [Store No.	↔	Numeric 5 positions
	[File No.	↔	Numeric 3 positions
Account History	[Yr. Began	↔	Numeric 2 positions
	[Highest Balance	↔	Numeric 6 positions (4 integer 2 fractional)
	[Date of Last Transaction	↔	Numeric 6 positions
Last Month	[Trans. No.	↔	Numeric 5 positions
	[Balance	↔	Numeric 6 positions (4 integer 2 fractional)
This Month	[Trans. No.	↔	Numeric 5 positions
	[Balance	↔	Numeric 6 positions (4 integer 2 fractional)
Last Payment	[Date	↔	Numeric 6 positions
	[Amount	↔	Numeric 6 positions (4 integer 2 fractional)

The file is on magnetic tape. The tape has standard labels and is blocked 50.

6 THE PROCEDURE DIVISION

Thus far, three of the four divisions of a COBOL program have been discussed. The PROCEDURE DIVISION, the last to be studied, is unquestionably the most important. The PROCEDURE DIVISION contains all the instructions to be executed by the computer. All the logic of the program is contained within these instructions.

The IDENTIFICATION and ENVIRONMENT DIVISIONS supply information about the nature of the program and the specific equipment that will be used. The FILE SECTION of the DATA DIVISION defines, in detail, the input and output areas. The input area is storage reserved for an incoming file. The output area is storage reserved for the accumulation of data to be produced as output by the computer. The WORKING-STORAGE SECTION of the DATA DIVISION is used for defining any areas not part of input and output but nonetheless required for processing. It is in the PROCEDURE DIVISION, however, that data is read and processed and output information is produced.

All instructions are written in the PROCEDURE DIVISION. The majority of chapters in this book concern themselves with executable instructions. The coding of the first three divisions is fairly straightforward; it is the manipulation of data in the PROCEDURE DIVISION that is the core of programming.

In this chapter, we will learn to:

1. Access input and output files.
2. Read and write information.
3. Perform simple move-and-transfer operations.
4. Perform specific end-of-job operations.

Knowledge of these types of instructions will be sufficient for writing elementary COBOL programs in their entirety. The PROCEDURE DIVISION incorporated in this book will emphasize the **structured** approach to writing COBOL programs.

The PROCEDURE DIVISION is divided into **paragraphs.** Each paragraph defines an independent **routine,** or series of instructions, designed to perform a specific function.

Each paragraph is further subdivided into statements or sentences. A **statement** is a COBOL instruction to the computer. A **sentence** is a statement or group of statements within a paragraph. Each statement, unless it tests a condition, begins with a verb or operation. READ, MOVE, and WRITE are examples of COBOL operations.

A statement usually ends with a period, which must be followed by at least one space. Several statements may be written on one line of a COBOL coding sheet, but words should not be subdivided when the end of a line is reached. Figure 6.1 illustrates a correct coding of instructions in free-form. Figure 6.2 shows the correct coding of instructions in a neater and more systematic fashion. We will use the latter format in our coding.

All statements are executed in the order written unless a PERFORM instruction transfers control to some other part of the program. For example, consider the following:

```
MOVE NAME TO NAME-OUT.
MOVE AMT TO AMT-OUT.
WRITE DATA-REC.
```

In the above routine, the MOVE statements will be executed first and then the WRITE statement will be performed.

All statements in the PROCEDURE DIVISION are coded in Margin B. Only paragraph names are written in Margin A. Rules for forming paragraph names are the same as for data-names except that a paragraph name need not contain any alphabetic characters.

Figure 6.2 illustrates a paragraph labelled BEGIN. It contains instructions that are normally incorporated in the main routine of all programs. It is frequently referred to as the **main module.** The actual processing to be performed by each program depends on what is coded in the paragraph labelled CALC-RTN.

Let us begin by discussing all the instructions indicated in the BEGIN paragraph. These instructions will be coded in all our subsequent programs. The only changes that will be necessary will be in the file and paragraph names used.

After this main module has been explained in detail, we discuss sample entries that can be coded in CALC-RTN.

A. OPEN STATEMENT

Before an input or output file can be read or written, we must first OPEN the file. We instruct the computer to **access** a file by an OPEN statement.

An OPEN statement in COBOL has the following format:

```
OPEN [INPUT (file name(s))] [OUTPUT (file name(s))]
```

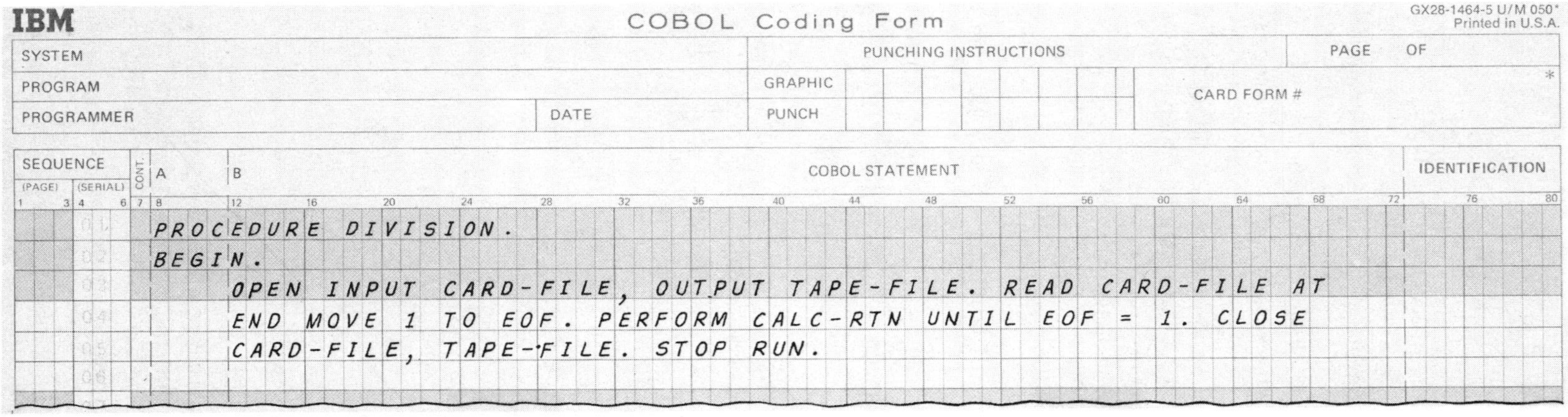

IBM COBOL Coding Form

```
       PROCEDURE DIVISION.
       BEGIN.
           OPEN INPUT CARD-FILE, OUTPUT TAPE-FILE. READ CARD-FILE AT
           END MOVE 1 TO EOF. PERFORM CALC-RTN UNTIL EOF = 1. CLOSE
           CARD-FILE, TAPE-FILE. STOP RUN.
```

Figure 6.1 PROCEDURE DIVISION excerpt written in free-form style.

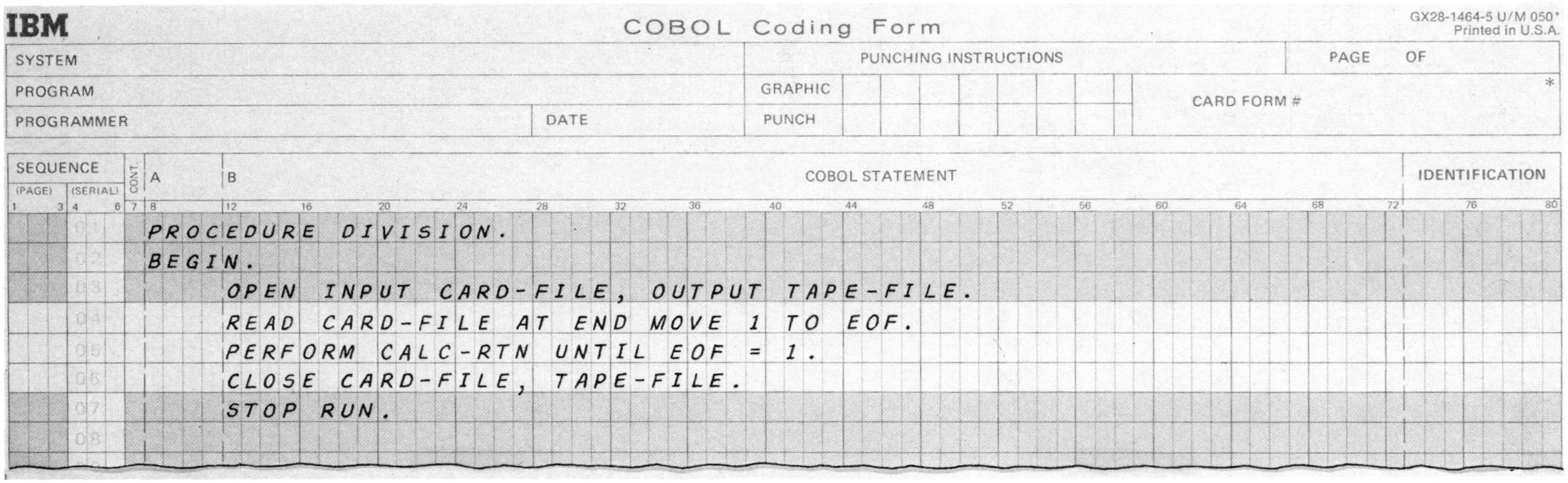

IBM COBOL Coding Form

```
       PROCEDURE DIVISION.
       BEGIN.
           OPEN INPUT CARD-FILE, OUTPUT TAPE-FILE.
           READ CARD-FILE AT END MOVE 1 TO EOF.
           PERFORM CALC-RTN UNTIL EOF = 1.
           CLOSE CARD-FILE, TAPE-FILE.
           STOP RUN.
```

Figure 6.2 PROCEDURE DIVISION excerpt written in a more systematic fashion.

FORMAT SPECIFICATIONS   The format for COBOL statements as denoted in the boxed entry above will
follow a particular pattern throughout this book.

✓   FORMAT SPECIFICATIONS
1. All capitalized words are COBOL reserved words.
2. All underlined words are required elements in the statement or option
   specified.
3. All lowercase words are programmer-supplied. The symbol 's' after a
   programmer-supplied word denotes that several such words are permissible.
4. The braces { } denote that one of the enclosed items is required.
5. The brackets [ ] denote that the enclosed item may be either used or
   omitted, depending on the requirements of the program.
6. Punctuation, when included in the format, is required.

Thus the above OPEN format specifies that:

(a) OPEN, INPUT, and OUTPUT are required COBOL reserved words, since
    they are capitalized and underlined.
(b) All input file names and output file names are programmer-supplied words.

For every SELECT clause in the ENVIRONMENT DIVISION, a file name is
defined and a device is assigned.

Example

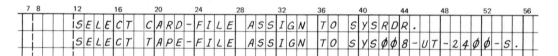

The file name CARD-FILE is assigned to the card reader by the SELECT
clause. For each file name specified, a file description entry in the DATA DI-
VISION is required. Thus CARD-FILE and TAPE-FILE must each be described
by an FD entry.

Thus far, devices are assigned and files are described. At no point, however,
have we indicated which files are input and which are output. This is accomplished by the OPEN statement:

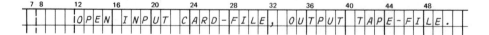

This instructs the computer that the storage positions assigned to CARD-
FILE will serve as an input area, and the storage positions assigned to TAPE-
FILE will serve as an output area. Data from CARD-FILE will be read by the
computer and data from TAPE-FILE will be written by the computer.

An OPEN statement designates files as either input or output. It also accesses
the specific devices. If TAPE-IN, for example, were an input file in a program,
the OPEN statement would access the specific tape drive to determine if it is

ready to read data. If not, execution would be suspended until the operator readies the device.

In addition to distinguishing input files from output files and accessing specified devices, an OPEN statement performs certain checking functions. If label records for an input tape file are indicated as STANDARD, for example, an OPEN statement checks the header label to determine if the correct tape is mounted. If label records for an output tape file are designated as STANDARD, the OPEN statement will create the header label. Header information must, however, be entered on a Job Control Card (see Appendix D).

In summary, two basic functions are performed by the OPEN statement:

OPEN STATEMENT FUNCTIONS
1. Indicates which files will serve as input and which will serve as output.
2. Makes files available for processing.

Programs are often written using several input and output files. An **update** program, for example, may merge two input files, TAPE-1 and TAPE-2, into one master output file, TAPE-3, and also create an error listing, PRINT-FILE. The OPEN statement for such a program would read:

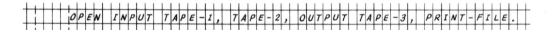

All input files follow the COBOL reserved word INPUT and, similarly, all output files follow the COBOL word OUTPUT. The word INPUT need not be repeated for each incoming file. The word OUTPUT may also be omitted after the first output file is noted.

The above statement, however, may also be written as four distinct sentences:

```
OPEN  INPUT   TAPE-1.
OPEN  INPUT   TAPE-2.
OPEN  OUTPUT  TAPE-3.
OPEN  OUTPUT  PRINT-FILE.
```

When separate statements are used, the words INPUT or OUTPUT must be indicated for each file that is opened. This method is often used when files are to be opened at varying intervals throughout the program; that is, the program processes one file before it accesses the next. Unless periodic intervals are required for the opening of files, it is considered inefficient and somewhat cumbersome to issue an independent OPEN statement for each file.

The order in which files are opened is not significant. The only restriction is that a file must be opened before it may be read or written; a file must be **accessed** before it may be **processed.** Since the OPEN statement allows the accessing of files, it is generally the first instruction issued to the computer in the PROCEDURE DIVISION.

1. The PROCEDURE DIVISION contains all _____ to be executed.
   *****
   instructions
2. The PROCEDURE DIVISION is divided into _____.
   *****
   paragraphs
3. Each paragraph defines a _____.
   *****
   routine
4. A routine is a _____.
   *****
   series of instructions designed to perform a specific function
5. Paragraphs are divided into _____.
   *****
   statements or sentences
6. Statements are executed in the order _____ unless a _____ occurs.
   *****
   in which they appear
   PERFORM
7. An OPEN statement indicates _____, and it also _____ the files.
   *****
   which files are input and which are output
   accesses
8. Before a file may be read, it must be _____.
   *****
   opened
9. The OPEN statement is coded in Margin _____.
   *****
   B
10. The file name indicated in the OPEN statement also appears in a
    _____ clause and on the _____ level.
    *****
    SELECT
    FD

B. READ STATEMENT

After an input file has been opened, it may be read. A READ statement transmits data from the input device, assigned in the ENVIRONMENT DIVISION, to
the input storage area, defined in the FILE SECTION of the DATA DIVISION.
   The following is the format for a READ statement:

READ (file name) AT END (statement).

   The file name specified in the READ statement appears in three previous
places in the program:

1. The SELECT clause, indicating the name and the device assigned to the file.
   If the card reader is the device assigned, for example, a READ operation
   transmits data from an input card to the input area.
2. The FD entry, describing the file.

3. The OPEN statement, accessing the file.

The primary function of the READ statement is to transmit one data record to storage. That is, each time a READ statement is executed, **one** record is read. It has, however, several other functions. Like the OPEN statement, it performs certain checks. It checks the length of each input record to ensure that it corresponds to the length specified in the DATA DIVISION. If a discrepancy exists, a wrong length record error has occurred and execution of the program is terminated. The READ statement will also use the BLOCK CONTAINS clause, if specified, to perform a check on the blocking factor. Although the primary function of the READ command is the transmission of data, these checking routines are essential for proper execution of the program.

The AT END clause in the READ expression tests to determine if there is any more input. An AT END clause together with a COBOL READ statement instructs the computer what to do if there is no more data to be read. The READ instruction is generally written in the form:

```
READ (file name) AT END MOVE 1 TO EOF.
```

MOVE 1 TO EOF is executed only when there are no more cards to process. EOF is a special WORKING-STORAGE item that will always contain a zero except when an end-of-file condition occurs, at which point a 1 will be moved into the field.

Example

```
READ CARD-FILE AT END MOVE 1 TO EOF.
```

A card will be read from the specified input device and the next sequential instruction in the program will be executed **unless there are no more cards.** If, in fact, there are no more input cards, 1 is moved to EOF. If, for example, ten cards constitute the input data, the **eleventh** attempt to read a card will cause a 1 to be moved to EOF.

On most third-generation computers, a card with a /* (slash-asterisk) in the first two columns is placed at the end of data. In this case, the /* card causes an AT END condition to be executed.

An AT END clause **must be** specified for every READ statement.[1] The computer must be instructed what to do when there is no more data.

Examine the following DATA DIVISION entry:

```
FD  TAPE-FILE
    LABEL RECORDS ARE OMITTED,
    RECORD CONTAINS 20 CHARACTERS,
    BLOCK CONTAINS 10 RECORDS,
    DATA RECORD IS TAPE-REC.
01  TAPE-REC.
    02  NAME          PIC X(15).
    02  AMT-OF-TRANS      PIC 9(5).
```

[1]The AT END clause may be omitted when input is on disk. This is discussed in Chapter 22, which describes disk operations.

Suppose the statement READ TAPE-FILE AT END MOVE 1 TO EOF is executed. The first 15 positions of data from the tape will be placed in storage in the field called NAME. The next five tape positions will be placed in the field called AMT-OF-TRANS. The sequence in which entries are denoted in the DATA DIVISION is crucial; data is placed in the fields in the order in which the data names are specified. The READ command will also perform a checking function. The length of the tape block will be compared to 200 positions, or 10 records, when a block is read. Any discrepancy constitutes a wrong length record error, which would cause execution to be terminated.

Similarly, if data is read from cards, the first card columns would be placed in the first data field specified in the DATA DIVISION. A less elaborate checking routine would be performed, since there is no blocking of cards.

C. PERFORM . . . UNTIL STATEMENT

The format of this statement is as follows:

```
PERFORM (paragraph name) UNTIL (condition)
```

This statement is the critical one for implementing the structured programming approach. First, it transfers control to the paragraph named. This named paragraph is executed continually until the condition specified is met. When the condition is met, control returns to the statement **directly following** the PERFORM.

Example

```
PERFORM CALC-RTN UNTIL EOF = 1.
```

The instructions in CALC-RTN will be executed repeatedly until EOF = 1. EOF is the special WORKING-STORAGE item that is initialized at zero and will contain a 1 only when an AT END condition is met. Hence, the PERFORM statement is really indicating that all instructions in CALC-RTN are to be executed until there are no more cards to process, at which point control will return to the statement **following** the PERFORM.

The sequence of steps appears as follows:

```
BEGIN.
    OPEN
    READ
    PERFORM
    CLOSE
    STOP
CALC-RTN.
    {processing steps}
    READ CARD-FILE AT END MOVE 1 TO EOF.
```

After a file is opened, a card is read. The PERFORM statement then transfers control to CALC-RTN where

> SEQUENCE AT CALC-RTN
> 1. The first card is processed.
> 2. The next card is read.
> 3. A test is performed to see if EOF = 1. It will only be a 1 if the AT END condition has been met.
> 4. If EOF is not equal to 1, CALC-RTN is executed again. That is, the next card is processed and another card is read.
> 5. This sequence continues until there are no more cards to process, at which point EOF = 1. When EOF = 1, control returns to the statement following the PERFORM, in this case the CLOSE statement.

Note that if there are 10 cards to process, the 11th attempt to read a card is the one that causes an AT END condition to be executed. We need not worry, therefore, about the last data card—it will be processed because it does **not** cause an AT END condition to be executed; the next READ will result in an AT END condition.

Note that with the use of the PERFORM . . . UNTIL, the first paragraph labelled BEGIN may be treated as an independent module—in fact the main module. CALC-RTN is also a separate module that processes the card data.

The PERFORM statement executes all instructions within the named paragraph. Consider the following:

```
PERFORM RTN1 UNTIL EOF = 1.
           .
           .
           .

           .
RTN1.
       —
       —

       —
RTN2.
```

Only those four instructions that follow RTN1 and precede RTN2 will be executed by the PERFORM. The **range** of the PERFORM includes all instructions within the named paragraph until another paragraph name is sensed or until no more instructions are indicated.

The PERFORM . . . UNTIL involves a computer test. That is, a condition must be met in order for control to return to the statement following the PERFORM. The point at which that test is made is a critical fact. It is important to note that the test is made initially and then again each time the named paragraph has been executed in its entirety. The schematic for this is as follows.

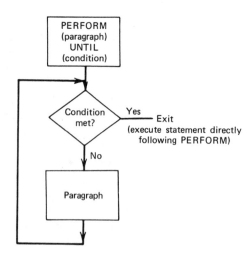

With this sequencing in mind, examine the following and see if you can determine why it is **not** an adequate alternative for the previous example:

```
OPEN
PERFORM
            .
            .
            .
CALC-RTN.
      READ
      {processing}
```

In the previous example, a data card was read in the main module and then control was transferred to the CALC-RTN module, where that first card was processed, another card read, and so on. Here the main module does not contain a READ. Instead, CALC-RTN reads a card and processes it each time.

The sequence of steps in both these procedures are exactly the same **except** for the processing of the **last** card. We have seen in the previous example that when an effort is made to read a data card and there are no more such cards, an AT END condition occurs. At that point (since the READ is the last statement), a test is made to determine if EOF = 1. When it is equal to 1, control would return to the main module.

What happens in the above case when an effort is made to read a card and there are no more? The AT END condition is executed and EOF is set equal to 1. **But** the test to return control is not performed **until after the entire paragraph is executed.** This means that processing will continue even though there are no more cards. After this processing is completed, control will return to the main module. What usually results if the above is coded is that the last actual data card is processed twice.

In short, when using the

```
PERFORM (paragraph name) UNTIL EOF = 1
```

as we will in our programs, the paragraph named should contain **as its last instruction** a READ statement. In this way, an AT END condition will always result in the immediate transfer of control to the main module.

Thus, all our programs will have the following form:

```
OPEN
READ
PERFORM (paragraph name) UNTIL EOF = 1.
        .
        .
        .
        .
        .
        .
```

(paragraph name)

```
        .
        .
        .


READ . . . AT END MOVE 1 TO EOF.
```

SELF-EVALUATING QUIZ

Consider the following statement for Questions 1–4.

    READ IN-CARD AT END MOVE 1 TO END-OF-IT.

1. IN-CARD must be defined on the _____ level of the DATA DIVISION.
   *****
   FD
2. (T or F) IN-CARD is defined in a SELECT statement.
   *****
   T
3. (T or F) READ IN-CARD AT END MOVE 1 TO END-OF-IT is a valid statement.
   *****
   True—END-OF-IT is a valid data name
4. Where must END-OF-IT be defined?
   *****
   as an elementary item in the WORKING-STORAGE SECTION
5. The PERFORM (paragraph name) UNTIL (condition) transfers control to the _____. When the condition specified is met, control returns to the

   _____.
   *****
   named paragraph
   statement directly following the PERFORM
6. In the statement PERFORM RTN1 UNTIL EOF = 1, EOF should be initialized at _____. Where is EOF defined and initialized? Provide the required WORKING-STORAGE entries.
   *****
   0—actually any other value but 1
   in the WORKING-STORAGE SECTION

```
WORKING-STORAGE SECTION.
01   STORED-AREAS.
     02   EOF     PIC 9 VALUE 0.
```

7. Write the first three instructions that would normally be coded in a simple structured COBOL program.
   *****
   ```
   OPEN
   READ
   PERFORM (paragraph name) UNTIL (condition)
   ```

8. (T or F) In Question 7 the paragraph named in the PERFORM statement will normally have a READ command as its first instruction.
   *****
   False—the first card read has not yet been processed. The named paragraph should begin with a set of instructions for processing that first card.

9. Consider the following statement:
   ```
   PERFORM CALC-RTN UNTIL ABC = 1.
   ```
   Code the **last** instruction that should be included within CALC-RTN.
   *****
   READ (file name) AT END MOVE 1 TO ABC. (ABC is simply a data name.)

10. Why should the last statement in the paragraph include a READ command?
    *****
    The condition in the PERFORM statement is tested initially and then **after** the paragraph has been executed. Once the AT END is executed, when there are no more cards, we want to **immediately** transfer control to the main module. This can only be accomplished if the READ is the last statement in the paragraph.

11. If there are 15 cards to be read, the _____ attempt to read a card causes an AT END condition because _____.
    *****
    16th

    the 16th card is a special /* card that signals the end of the data

12. When a PERFORM (paragraph name) UNTIL (condition) is executed, how does the computer know when the paragraph to be executed is completed?
    *****
    when it senses another paragraph name or when it reaches the end of the program.

D. CLOSE AND STOP RUN STATEMENTS

Let us continue with the main module of our previous example before considering options to be included in CALC-RTN.

CALC-RTN will be performed until EOF = 1, that is, until there are no more cards to process. At that point, control will return to the instruction directly following the PERFORM statement in the main module. After all cards have been processed, we will want to execute end-of-job functions. This usually includes releasing all files and terminating the processing. (See Figure 6.2.)

There are **two** statements that are a necessary part of every end-of-job routine. We must first CLOSE all files to indicate that they are no longer needed for processing, and we must instruct the computer to STOP.

CLOSE STATEMENT

Files must be accessed by an OPEN statement before data may be read or written. A CLOSE statement is necessary at the end of the job after all records have been processed to release these files. We say:

> CLOSE (file name(s))

All files that have been opened must be closed at the end of a job. The CLOSE statement, like the OPEN instruction, will perform additional functions. When creating tape records, for example, CLOSE TAPE-OUT will automatically create trailer labels and rewind the tape.

Note that a CLOSE statement, unlike an OPEN command, does **not** denote which files are input and which are output. We say, for example, OPEN INPUT CARD-FILE OUTPUT TAPE-FILE to access the files but, to release them, we say CLOSE CARD-FILE, TAPE-FILE. Distinguishing between input and output files is essential **before** processing commences but is not meaningful when the job is being terminated.

As with an OPEN statement, the following two routines are equivalent:

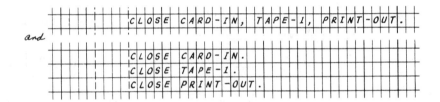

and

```
CLOSE CARD-IN, TAPE-1, PRINT-OUT.

CLOSE CARD-IN.
CLOSE TAPE-1.
CLOSE PRINT-OUT.
```

Unless files are closed at different points in the program, the latter method is considered inefficient.

STOP RUN STATEMENT

The STOP RUN command instructs the computer to terminate the job. All programs should end with a STOP RUN statement. This instruction will cause the computer to discontinue the processing of the current program and to automatically read in the next program.

You will note that we have discussed the following main module in detail:

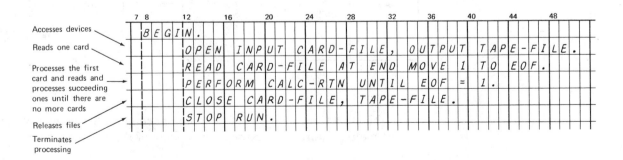

```
BEGIN.
    OPEN INPUT CARD-FILE, OUTPUT TAPE-FILE.
    READ CARD-FILE AT END MOVE 1 TO EOF.
    PERFORM CALC-RTN UNTIL EOF = 1.
    CLOSE CARD-FILE, TAPE-FILE.
    STOP RUN.
```

Accesses devices
Reads one card
Processes the first card and reads and processes succeeding ones until there are no more cards
Releases files
Terminates processing

The instructions specified at CALC-RTN will include:

1. The processing for a card.
2. A READ command to read succeeding cards.
3. An AT END condition that instructs the computer to MOVE 1 TO EOF.

Example

CALC-RTN.

.

.

READ CARD-FILE AT END MOVE 1 TO EOF.

Presumably at CALC-RTN we will want to manipulate data in some way and then produce output records. Most of this book is devoted to methods used to process or manipulate data. For now, let us concentrate on the simplest form— the MOVE operation.

Now that we are able to OPEN files and READ files, it will be necessary to store data in the output area so that when we issue a WRITE command, there will be some information to be created as output.

E. SIMPLIFIED MOVE STATEMENT

A MOVE statement has the following format:

MOVE (data-name-1) TO (data-name-2)

Any field in storage may be moved to another field by the MOVE instruction.

Example Problem

To produce output tape records from input cards in the following manner:

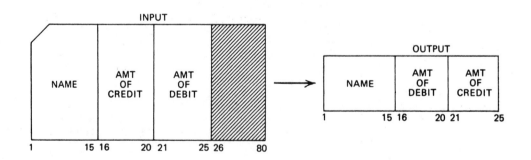

The first three divisions of the program conform to the rules of the last three chapters. Figure 6.3 illustrates the coding of these DIVISIONS.[2]

---

[2]As in all illustrations, the ENVIRONMENT DIVISION entries are samples. The ENVIRONMENT DIVISION is a machine-dependent division and will, therefore, vary from computer to computer.

COBOL Coding Form

GX28-1464-5 U/M 050*
Printed in U.S.A.

SYSTEM		PUNCHING INSTRUCTIONS		PAGE	OF	
PROGRAM		GRAPHIC		CARD FORM #		
PROGRAMMER	DATE	PUNCH				

```
IDENTIFICATION DIVISION.
PROGRAM-ID. SAMPLE.
ENVIRONMENT DIVISION.
INPUT-OUTPUT SECTION.
FILE-CONTROL.
    SELECT CARD-FILE ASSIGN TO SYSØØ5-UR-254ØR-S.
    SELECT TAPE-FILE ASSIGN TO SYSØØ8-UT-24ØØ-S.
DATA DIVISION.
FILE SECTION.
FD  CARD-FILE
    LABEL RECORDS ARE OMITTED
    RECORD CONTAINS 8Ø CHARACTERS
    DATA RECORD IS CARD-REC.
Ø1  CARD-REC.
    Ø2  NAME-IN                PIC X(15).
    Ø2  AMT-OF-CREDIT-IN       PIC 9(5).
    Ø2  AMT-OF-DEBIT-IN        PIC 9(5).
    Ø2  FILLER                 PIC X(55).
FD  TAPE-FILE
    LABEL RECORDS ARE OMITTED
    RECORD CONTAINS 25 CHARACTERS
    DATA RECORD IS TAPE-REC.
Ø1  TAPE-REC.
    Ø2  NAME-OUT               PIC X(15).
    Ø2  AMT-OF-DEBIT-OUT       PIC 9(5).
    Ø2  AMT-OF-CREDIT-OUT      PIC 9(5).
WORKING-STORAGE SECTION.
Ø1  STORED-AREAS.
    Ø2  EOF                    PIC 9 VALUE Ø.
```

*A standard card form, IBM Electro C61897, is available for punching source statements from this form.
Instructions for using this form are given in any IBM COBOL reference manual.
Address comments concerning this form to IBM Corporation, Programming Publications, 1271 Avenue of the American, New York, New York 10020.

*No. of sheets per pad may vary slightly

Figure 6.3

The PROCEDURE DIVISION may be coded thus far as follows:

```
PROCEDURE DIVISION.
BEGIN.
    OPEN INPUT CARD-FILE, OUTPUT TAPE-FILE.
    READ CARD-FILE AT END MOVE 1 TO EOF.
    PERFORM CALC-RTN UNTIL EOF = 1.
    CLOSE CARD-FILE, TAPE-FILE.
    STOP RUN.
CALC-RTN.
    MOVE NAME-IN TO NAME-OUT.
    MOVE AMT-OF-CREDIT-IN TO AMT-OF-CREDIT-OUT.
    MOVE AMT-OF-DEBIT-IN TO AMT-OF-DEBIT-OUT.
```

Assuming the PICTURE clause of the output field is the same as the PICTURE clause of the input field, a MOVE operation **duplicates** input data at the output area. Note that the technique of using the same base name for different fields while altering only the prefix or suffix is considered good programming form. That is, the distinction between AMT-OF-CREDIT-IN, as an input field, and AMT-OF-CREDIT-OUT, as the same field for the output, is clear.

Note, again, that CALC-RTN is a **separate** module. It is only executed when under the control of the PERFORM statement. To complete CALC-RTN, we will need to WRITE the record accumulated at the output area and then READ the next card.

F WRITE STATEMENT

The WRITE instruction takes data accumulated in the output area of the DATA DIVISION and transmits it to the device specified in the ENVIRONMENT DIVISION.

The WRITE statement has the following format:

> WRITE (record name)

One important point must be noted. Although **files** are **read,** we **write records.** The record name appears on the 01 level and is generally subdivided into fields. The record describes the **format** of the output. With each WRITE command, we instruct the computer to write data according to the format noted:

```
FD TAPE-FILE    LABEL RECORDS ARE OMITTED, RECORD CONTAINS
   25 CHARACTERS, DATA RECORD IS TAPE-REC.
01 TAPE-REC.
   02 NAME-OUT              PIC X(15).
   02 AMT-OF-DEBIT-OUT      PIC 9(5).
   02 AMT-OF-CREDIT-OUT     PIC 9(5).
```

To write information stored in the DATA DIVISION, the appropriate command is WRITE TAPE-REC, **not** WRITE TAPE-FILE. When we **write** or produce information, we use the 01 **level-name;** when we read from a file, we use the FD name.

To say WRITE TAPE-REC transmits data to the output device according to the format specified in the TAPE-REC record. If more than one record format were specified for TAPE-FILE, then the one to be created would be indicated in the WRITE statement. For example, consider the following:

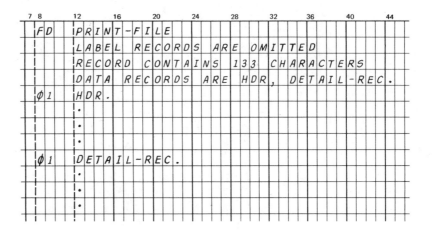

```
 7 8    12      16      20      24      28      32      36      40      44
   FD  PRINT-FILE
       LABEL  RECORDS  ARE  OMITTED
       RECORD  CONTAINS  133  CHARACTERS
       DATA  RECORDS  ARE  HDR,  DETAIL-REC.
   Ø1  HDR.
        .
        .
        .
   Ø1  DETAIL-REC.
        .
        .
        .
```

Depending on the format desired, we would code **either** WRITE HDR or WRITE DETAIL-REC.

We may now code our sample program in its entirety keeping in mind that after a complete record has been processed and an output record created, we want to read another input record:

```
 7 8    12      16      20      24      28      32      36      40      44      48      52      56
 PROCEDURE  DIVISION.
 BEGIN.
       OPEN  INPUT  CARD-FILE,  OUTPUT  TAPE-FILE.
       READ  CARD-FILE  AT  END  MOVE  1  TO  EOF.
       PERFORM  CALC-RTN  UNTIL  EOF  =  1.
       CLOSE  CARD-FILE,  TAPE-FILE.
       STOP  RUN.
 CALC-RTN.
       MOVE  NAME-IN  TO  NAME-OUT.
       MOVE  AMT-OF-DEBIT-IN  TO  AMT-OF-DEBIT-OUT.
       MOVE  AMT-OF-CREDIT-IN  TO  AMT-OF-CREDIT-OUT.
       WRITE  TAPE-REC.
       READ  CARD-FILE  AT  END  MOVE  1  TO  EOF.
```

As a review, most programs illustrated or required in this text will utilize the following structure:

```
                          PROCEDURE DIVISION.
                      ⎧      OPEN . . .
       Main           ⎪      READ . . . AT END MOVE 1 TO EOF.
       module         ⎨      PERFORM (paragraph name) UNTIL EOF = 1.
                      ⎪      CLOSE . . .
                      ⎩      STOP RUN.
                          (paragraph name)
                      ⎧            .
       Processing     ⎪            .
       steps          ⎨            .
                      ⎪      WRITE . . .
                      ⎩      READ . . . AT END MOVE 1 TO EOF.
```

SUMMARY OF PROCEDURE DIVISION ENTRIES

1. Paragraph names are coded in Margin A.
2. All statements are coded in Margin B, either in paragraph form or one statement per line.
3. Instructions are executed in the order in which they appear unless a PERFORM statement transfers control.
4. The following main module is usually coded for most structured programs:

   ```
   OPEN INPUT (file) OUTPUT (file).
   READ (file) AT END MOVE 1 TO EOF.
   PERFORM (paragraph) UNTIL EOF = 1.
   CLOSE (files).
   STOP RUN.
   ```
5. The paragraph specified in the PERFORM is executed repeatedly until there are no more input records.
6. The last statement in the paragraph specified by the PERFORM is usually a READ statement:

   ```
   CALC-RTN.
        —
        —
        —
   READ (file) AT END MOVE 1 TO EOF.
   ```

REVIEW OF COMMENTS IN COBOL

There is a method that may be used for inserting comments in a COBOL program:

COMMENTS IN COBOL

An asterisk (*) in column 7 (the continuation position) of any line makes the entire line a comment.

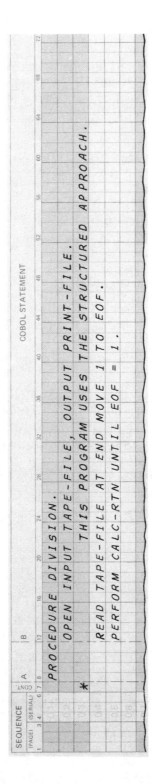

The coding form contains the following COBOL statements:

```
PROCEDURE DIVISION.
    OPEN INPUT TAPE-FILE, OUTPUT PRINT-FILE.
*       THIS PROGRAM USES THE STRUCTURED APPROACH.
    READ TAPE-FILE AT END MOVE 1 TO EOF.
    PERFORM CALC-RTN UNTIL EOF = 1.
```

Example of a program excerpt with a comment.

SELF-EVALUATING QUIZ

1. Before a file may be read it must be _____.
   *****
   opened

2. Consider the following instruction: READ FILEA AT END MOVE 1 TO EOF. FILEA appears in a _____ clause of the _____ DIVISION, an _____ level of the _____ DIVISION, and an _____ statement of the _____ DIVISION.
   *****
   SELECT
   ENVIRONMENT
   FD
   DATA
   OPEN
   PROCEDURE

3. With every READ statement, an _____ clause must be specified.
   *****
   AT END

4. READ instructions _____ data to the input area and also perform _____ functions.
   *****
   transmit
   checking

5. The AT END clause tells the computer what to do if _____.
   *****
   there is no more input data

6. In the instruction READ TAPE-IN AT END MOVE 1 TO EOF, if there are 20 tape records, the (no.) attempt to read a record will cause a 1 to be moved to the field called EOF.
   *****
   21st

7. Unlike READ statements in which _____ are read, a WRITE statement writes _____.
   *****
   files
   records

8. The record level specifies the _____.
   *****
   layout or record format

9. What is wrong with the following?
   (a) WRITE REC-1 AT END MOVE 1 TO EOF.
   (b) PUNCH REC-2.
   *****
   (a) AT END clause is only specified with a READ statement.
   (b) WRITE command should be used, not PUNCH.

10. To transmit data from one field of storage to another, the _____ statement is used.
    *****
    MOVE

11. To obtain *exactly* the same data at the output area that appears in the input

area, the _____ clause of both fields should be identical.
*****
PICTURE or PIC

12. The instruction used to transfer control from the main module to some other part of the program is a _____ instruction.
*****
PERFORM . . . UNTIL

13. If PERFORM STEP-5 UNTIL EOF = 1 is a statement in the program, STEP-5 is a _____ that must appear somewhere in the program in Margin _____.
*****
paragraph name
A

14. Paragraph names (must, need not) be unique within a program.
*****
must

15. In general, execution will proceed to the _____ unless a _____ statement is coded.
*****
next sequential step
PERFORM

16. Two statements that are a required part of the end-of-job routine are _____ and _____.
*****
CLOSE
STOP RUN

17. For every file that is opened, a _____ statement must appear in the end-of-job routine.
*****
CLOSE

18. CLOSE INPUT CARD-IN (is, is not) valid.
*****
is not (NOTE: INPUT or OUTPUT is **not** specified with CLOSE statements.)

19. A STOP RUN operation _____.
*****
terminates the job

20. If PERFORM STEP-1 UNTIL EOF = 1 is a coded statement in the main module, the last instruction of STEP-1 should be a _____.
*****
READ (file name) AT END MOVE 1 TO EOF

| SAMPLE PROBLEM— WITH SOLUTION | From this point on, each chapter includes one sample problem with a suggested solution provided to assist you in reviewing the material and in coding the problems that follow. Make every effort to code the program on your own. Then check your solution against the one provided. |

Write a program to punch output salary cards from the following input employee record card:

ccs	1-20	Employee name
	21-25	Salary
	26	Number of dependents
	27-31	F.I.C.A. (xxx.xx)
	32-37	State tax (xxxx.xx)
	38-43	Federal tax (xxxx.xx)
	44-80	Unused

The output contains only employee name and salary as its first two fields. The remainder of the output card should be blank. (**Hint.** You must move SPACES to the output record to ensure that the FILLER in the last 55 positions is blank.)

```
IDENTIFICATION DIVISION.
PROGRAM-ID.  CHAPT6.
ENVIRONMENT DIVISION.
CONFIGURATION SECTION.
SOURCE-COMPUTER. IBM-370.
OBJECT-COMPUTER. IBM-370.
INPUT-OUTPUT SECTION.
FILE-CONTROL.
     SELECT EMPLOYEE-CARDS ASSIGN TO UR-S-SYSIN.
     SELECT SALARY-CARDS ASSIGN TO UR-S-SYSPUNCH.
DATA DIVISION.
FILE SECTION.
FD  EMPLOYEE-CARDS
    LABEL RECORDS ARE OMITTED
    RECORD CONTAINS 80 CHARACTERS
    DATA RECORD IS EMPLOYEE-REC.
01  EMPLOYEE-REC.
    02   EMPLOYEE-NAME-IN             PIC X(20).
    02   SALARY-IN                    PIC 9(5).
    02   NO-OF-DEPENDENTS             PIC 9.
    02   FICA                         PIC 999V99.
    02   STATE-TAX                    PIC 9(4)V99.
    02   FED-TAX                      PIC 9(4)V99.
    02   FILLER                       PIC X(37).
FD  SALARY-CARDS
    LABEL RECORDS ARE OMITTED
    RECORD CONTAINS 80 CHARACTERS
    DATA RECORD IS SALARY-REC.
01  SALARY-REC.
    02   EMPLOYEE-NAME-OUT            PIC X(20).
    02   SALARY-OUT                   PIC 9(5).
    02   FILLER                       PIC X(55).
WORKING-STORAGE SECTION.
01  WORK-AREAS.
    02   EOF                          PIC 9.
PROCEDURE DIVISION.
    OPEN INPUT EMPLOYEE-CARDS, OUTPUT SALARY-CARDS.
    MOVE 0 TO EOF.
    MOVE SPACES TO SALARY-REC.
    READ EMPLOYEE-CARDS AT END MOVE 1 TO EOF.
    PERFORM CALC-RTN UNTIL EOF = 1.
    CLOSE EMPLOYEE-CARDS, SALARY-CARDS.
    STOP RUN.
CALC-RTN.
    MOVE  EMPLOYEE-NAME-IN TO EMPLOYEE-NAME-OUT.
    MOVE SALARY-IN TO SALARY-OUT.
    WRITE SALARY-REC.
    READ EMPLOYEE-CARDS AT END MOVE 1 TO EOF.
```

Figure 6.4

REVIEW QUESTIONS

True False   **I. True-False Questions**

☐ ☐   1. Paragraph names are coded in Margin A of the PROCEDURE DIVISION.

☐ ☐   2. An OPEN statement must be executed before a file is read.

☐ ☐   3. Files must be opened in the order in which they are read or written.

☐ ☐   4. Structured programming enables each section of a program to be treated as an independent module.

☐ ☐   5. The range of a PERFORM includes all instructions within a named paragraph.

☐ ☐   6. For the statement
PERFORM CALC-RTN UNTIL EOF = 1
EOF must be defined in the FILE SECTION.

☐ ☐   7. Suppose EOF were initialized at 1. It would be correct to use the following as an end-of-file test:
READ CARD-IN AT END MOVE 0 TO EOF.

☐ ☐   8. Consider the following statement:
PERFORM CALC-RTN UNTIL EOF = 1.
The last statement in CALC-RTN would usually be a WRITE statement.

☐ ☐   9. The last instruction to be executed in a COBOL program should be a STOP RUN.

☐ ☐   10. It is unnecessary to close files at an end of job.

II. Indicate the DIVISION in which each of the following may be found and the purpose of each:

(a) DATE-COMPILED
(b) WORKING-STORAGE SECTION
(c) paragraph names
(d) CONFIGURATION SECTION
(e) FD
(f) level numbers
(g) LABEL RECORDS
(h) FILE SECTION
(i) SELECT
(j) AUTHOR
(k) STOP RUN
(l) AT END clause
(m) INPUT-OUTPUT SECTION
(n) VALUE
(o) PICTURE
(p) FILE-CONTROL
(q) FILLER
(r) OPEN

III. General Questions

1. When the computer encounters a READ command in the PROCEDURE DIVISION, how does it know which of its input units to activate?

2. Give two functions of the OPEN statement.

3. When are paragraph names assigned in the PROCEDURE DIVISION?

4. State which of the following, if any, are invalid paragraph names:

(a) INPUT-RTN

(b) MOVE

(c) 123

(d) %-RTN

5. If a READ statement is used for a sequential file, what clause is required? Why?

Make necessary corrections to each of the following (6-10). Assume that spacing and margin use are correct:

6. OPEN MASTER-IN, MASTER-OUT.

7.

```
PROCEDURE DIVISION
BEGIN
        OPEN INPUT OLD-FILE, OUTPUT NEW-FILE
        READ OLD-REC AT END MOVE 1 TO FINALLY-OVER.
        PERFORM UPDATE-RTN UNTIL FINALLY-OVER = 1.
        CLOSE OLD-FILE, NEW FILE.
        STOP THE RUN.
UPDATE-RTN
        MOVE OLD-REC TO NEW-REC.
        WRITE NEW-FILE.
        READ OLD-REC AT END MOVE 1 TO FINALLY-OVER.
```

8.

```
PROCEDURE DIVISION
        OPEN INPUT OLD-FILE OUTPUT NEW-FILE
        PERFORM UPDATE-RTN UNTIL EOF = 1.
        CLOSE OLD-FILE, NEW-FILE.
        STOP RUN.
UPDATE-RTN.
        READ OLD-FILE AT END MOVE 1 TO EOF.
        MOVE OLD-REC TO NEW-REC.
        WRITE NEW-REC.
```

9. CLOSE INPUT FILE-A, OUTPUT FILE-B.

10. WRITE REC-A AT END MOVE 0 TO EOF.

PROBLEMS   1. Write a program to create a master tape file from input sales records. The input is on punched cards in the following format:

SALESMAN NAME	SALESMAN CODE			YEAR TO DATE FIGURES			CURRENT			
	REGION NO.	OFFICE NO.	BADGE NO.	QUOTA xxxx.xx	SALES xxxx.xx	Commission xxxx.xx	QUOTA	SALES	COMM.	

1   20 21   22 23   24 25   26 27   32 33   38 39   44 45   50 51   56 57   62 63   80

The output is on magnetic tape that contains standard labels and is blocked 20. The output format is exactly the same as the input.

2. Write a program to print all information from the following sales card:

SALESMAN NAME	SALESMAN CODE			YEAR TO DATE FIG.			CURRENT FIGURES			
	REGION NO.	OFFICE NO.	BADGE NO.	QUOTA	SALES	COMMISSION	QUOTA	SALES	COMMISSION	

1   20 21   22 23   24 25   26 27   31 32   36 37   41 42   46 47   51 52   56 57   80

The printed form should contain blank spaces between fields for "readability." You may position fields in any way you choose on the output.

3. Write a program to create one master tape record for every group of two input data cards. The input consists of two types of records:

Credit Record		Debit Record	
1-20	Customer name	1-20	Customer name
21-25	Amount of credit	21-40	Address
	xxx.xx	41-45	Amount of debit
26-80	Not used		xxx.xx
		46-80	Not used

Each transaction will have both records as input. The credit record for a customer will **always** be followed by a debit record for the customer. One output record will be created from the two input records. The output format is as follows:

  1-20   Customer name
21-40   Address
41-45   Amount of debit
          xxx.xx
46-50   Amount of credit
          xxx.xx

The output tape is blocked 25 and has standard labels.

HINT: The DATA RECORD clause for the input cards must include **two** record formats. You may code, for example, DATA RECORDS ARE CR-REC, DB-REC for the input file. The sequence of instructions at CALC-RTN after a card has been read would be: MOVE, READ, MOVE, WRITE, READ—two read instructions for every write instruction.

4. XYZ Utility Company has the following master tape records:

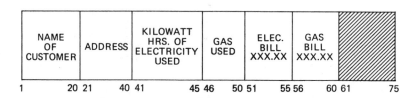

The records are blocked 10 and have standard labels. Write a program to create two punched cards (bills) for each input record. The format of the two output cards is as follows:

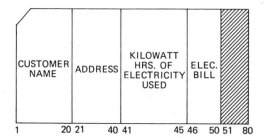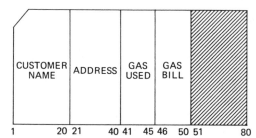

HINT: The DATA RECORD clause for the output cards must include **two** record formats. You may code, for example, DATA RECORDS ARE GAS-BILL, ELEC-BILL for the punch file. The sequence of instructions at CALC-RTN after a tape record has been read would be: MOVE, WRITE, MOVE, WRITE, READ. That is, there will be two write commands for every read command.

5. Two input tape files are used to create one output master tape file. The format for the two input files is as follows:

File 1		File 2	
1-20	Employee name	1-20	Employee name
21-40	Address	21-40	Address
41-43	Hours worked	41-45	Salary
44-46	Wages x.xx	46	No. of dependents
47	No. of dependents	47-51	F.I.C.A. xxx.xx
48-52	F.I.C.A. xxx.xx	52-57	Fed. tax xxxx.xx
53-58	Fed. tax xxxx.xx	58-63	State tax xxxx.xx
59-64	State tax xxxx.xx	64	Unused

The format for the output file is the same as the input files.

Write a program to write on the output file all records from file 1 and **then** all records from file 2. All files have standard labels. Blocking factor = 30.

6. Modify Problem 5 to write on tape **first** a record from file 1 and then a record from file 2. Alternate this way until records from both files are all processed. Assume that file 1 and file 2 have the same number of records.

2 BASIC COBOL OPERATIONS

CHAPTER

7 THE MOVE STATEMENT

A. A BASIC APPROACH

A basic format for the MOVE statement is

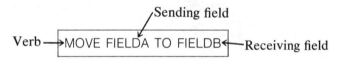

In the above COBOL sentence or statement, MOVE is called the **verb.** Every COBOL statement that appears in the PROCEDURE DIVISION, like every English sentence, must contain a verb. The data-name FIELDA is called the **sending field.** The contents of FIELDA will be transmitted, copied, or sent, to another field (FIELDB) as a result of the MOVE operation. The data-name FIELDB is called the **receiving field.** The contents of FIELDB will be replaced by another field (FIELDA) as a result of the MOVE operation.

The result of the MOVE operation is obvious. The information, or contents, stored at the sending field, FIELDA, will be moved to the receiving field, FIELDB.

Note that the MOVE statement like all COBOL operational verbs, appears only in the PROCEDURE DIVISION. FIELDA and FIELDB, however, are data-names and as such must be defined in the DATA DIVISION. You will recall that data-names in the DATA DIVISION are referenced by PICTURE clauses to indicate the kind of data in the field (numeric, alphanumeric, or alphabetic), and the size of the field. To perform a MOVE operation that replaces FIELDB with the **very same contents** as FIELDA, the PICTURE clauses of both fields must be identical.

Example 1

TAXA   PICTURE 999
       (numeric—three positions)
       Contents 123

TAXB   PICTURE 999
       Contents 456

If the statement MOVE TAXA TO TAXB is performed, TAXB will be replaced by 123, the contents of TAXA. This will occur only if TAXA and TAXB have the identical PICTURE clause (in this case, 999). The original content of TAXB, 456, is lost during the MOVE operation. When moving a sending field to a receiving field, the original content of the receiving field is always destroyed.

Note also that data is not physically moved from the sending to the receiving field but, instead, is **transmitted** from one field to the other; that is, the content of the sending field, TAXA, in the above case, is duplicated at the receiving field, TAXB. At the end of the operation, both fields will have the same contents. Thus the content of TAXA is **not** erased during the operation. TAXA remains unchanged; its content is transmitted, or duplicated, at TAXB.

Example 2

FIELDA   PICTURE XXXX
         (alphanumeric—four positions)
         Contents ABCD

FIELDB   PICTURE XXXX
         Contents EFGH

If the operation MOVE FIELDA TO FIELDB is performed, FIELDB has ABCD as its contents and, also, FIELDA remains with ABCD. Since both fields have the same PICTURE clause, they are identical at the end of the operation.

SELF-EVALUATING QUIZ

Use the following statement to answer Questions 1–6:

MOVE FIELD1 TO FIELD2

1. MOVE is called the _____.
   FIELD1 is called the _____.
   FIELD2 is called the _____.
   *****
   verb or operation
   sending field
   receiving field

2. The MOVE statement appears only in the _____ DIVISION while FIELD1 and FIELD2 must be defined in the _____ DIVISION, with corresponding _____ clauses.
   *****
   PROCEDURE
   DATA
   PICTURE

3. To duplicate the exact information of FIELD1 at FIELD2, both fields must have the same _____ clauses.
   *****
   PICTURE

4. A PICTURE clause indicates numeric data by _____, alphanumeric data by _____, and alphabetic data by _____.

*****
9's
X's
A's

5. The number of 9's, X's or A's in a PICTURE clause indicates the _____ of a data-field.

*****
size

6. Assume FIELD1 has contents of 128, FIELD2 has contents of 736, and both fields have the same PICTURE clause. At the end of the MOVE operation, FIELD2 has _____ as its contents and FIELD1 has _____ as its contents.

*****
128

128 (NOTE: The contents of a sending field remain unchanged in a MOVE operation.)

B. THE FORMATS OF THE MOVE STATEMENT

We have thus far discussed one form of the MOVE statement:

Format 1

> MOVE (data-name-1) TO (data-name-2)

In this case, data-name-1 and data-name-2 must be given specifications in the DATA DIVISION. To obtain in data-name-2 the same contents as in data-name-1, the PICTURE clauses of both fields are assumed to be the same.

A second form of the MOVE statement is as follows:

Format 2

> MOVE (literal) TO (data-name)

Recall that there are two kinds of literals, numeric and nonnumeric:

REVIEW OF LITERALS

Numeric literals
   1 to 18 digits
   decimal point (optional)
   sign (optional)

Nonnumeric or alphanumeric literals
   1 to 120 characters
   any characters may be used (except the quote mark)
   literal is enclosed in quotes

Example 1

7	8			12			16			20			24			28	
				M	O	V	E		1	2	3		T	O		D	E	P	T	.	

Example 2

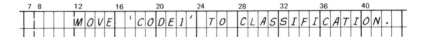

Although data-names must be defined in the DATA DIVISION, literals need not be defined elsewhere in the COBOL program. Assuming correct PICTURE clauses in the receiving field, the exact form of the literal will be placed in that field. Keep in mind that the receiving field is **always** a data-name. In Example 1, the literal 123 is a numeric literal. We know that it is a literal and not a data-name because it contains all numbers, while data-names must have at least one alphabetic character. To move a numeric literal to a data-field, we require that the field have the same format as the literal, namely that it be a numeric field. Thus, in Example 1, DEPT must have a PICTURE of 9's. To obtain exactly 123 in DEPT, DEPT should have a PICTURE of 999, to indicate that it is a three-position numeric field.

In Example 2, 'CODE1' is a nonnumeric literal. We know that it is not a data-name because it is enclosed in quotation marks. To move this literal to a data-field, the data-field must have the same format as the literal, namely, it must be an alphanumeric field. Thus, in Example 2, CLASSIFICATION must have a PICTURE of X's to indicate that it is alphanumeric. To obtain exactly 'CODE1' as the contents of CLASSIFICATION, CLASSIFICATION must have a PICTURE clause of X(5) to specify a five-position alphanumeric field.

To say: MOVE 123 to ADDRESS-1 would be considered poor form if ADDRESS-1 had a PICTURE of XXX, because the literal is not in the same mode as the receiving field. If ADDRESS-1 has a PICTURE of X(3), the literal should be nonnumeric. Thus we should code MOVE '123' to ADDRESS-1.

A third form of the MOVE statement is as follows:

Format 3

> MOVE (figurative constant) TO (data-name)

You will recall that a figurative constant is a COBOL reserved word, such as SPACES or ZERO, having a specific value.

Example 3

MOVE ZEROS TO TOTAL.

Example 4

MOVE SPACES TO HDR.

In Example 3, ZEROS is a figurative constant, meaning all 0's. Since 0 is a valid numeric character and also a valid alphanumeric character, TOTAL may be numeric, having a PICTURE of 9's, or alphanumeric, having a PICTURE of X's. In either case, TOTAL will be replaced with all zeros. The size of TOTAL is unimportant; all zeros will be placed in that field regardless of its size.

In Example 4, SPACES is a figurative constant meaning all blanks. Since blanks are not valid numeric characters, the PICTURE clause of HDR must be X's, indicating an alphanumeric field, or A's, indicating an alphabetic field. Again, the size of HDR is unimportant since all blanks will be placed in it regardless of its length.

Thus, there are three formats for the MOVE statement:

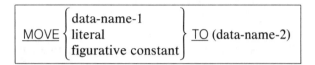

The braces indicate that any one of the three elements may be used as sending fields. The receiving field must always be a data-name.

Note that **any** nonnumeric literal may be moved to an alphanumeric field. However, only those nonnumeric literals with alphabetic data or spaces may be moved to an alphabetic field.

SELF-EVALUATING QUIZ

1. In a MOVE operation, the sending field may be a _____ or a _____ or a _____.
   *****
   literal
   data-name
   figurative constant
2. The two kinds of literals are _____ and _____.
   *****
   numeric
   nonnumeric or alphanumeric
3. The receiving field in a MOVE operation is always a _____.
   *****
   data-name

Use the statement below to answer Questions 4–6:

MOVE A12 TO FIELD3

4. A12 is a _____.
   *****
   data-name
5. A12 cannot be a nonnumeric literal since it is not _____. A12 is not a numeric literal since it _____.
   *****
   enclosed in quotation marks
   has an alphabetic character
6. If the data-name A12 has contents of 453, _____ will be moved to FIELD3 and A12 will have _____ as its contents at the end of the operation.
   *****
   453
   453

Use the statement below to answer Questions 7–11:

MOVE 'AB1' TO FIELD6

7. The sending field is a _____.
   *****
   nonnumeric literal
8. The sending field cannot be a data-name since it is _____.
   *****
   enclosed in quotation marks
9. Assuming a correct PICTURE clause in FIELD6, the contents of FIELD6 will contain _____ at the end of the operation.
   *****
   AB1
10. To obtain exactly AB1 in FIELD6, the PICTURE clause of the receiving field should be _____.
   *****
   XXX or X(3)
11. 'AB1' (is, is not) defined in the DATA DIVISION.
    *****
    is not (NOTE: Literals appearing in the PROCEDURE DIVISION need not be defined elsewhere in the program.)

Use the statement below to answer Questions 12–15:

MOVE 12384 TO SAM

12. The sending field is a _____.
    *****
    numeric literal
13. The sending field must be a numeric literal and not a data-name since it _____.
    *****
    contains no alphabetic character
14. Assuming SAM has the correct PICTURE clause to accept the sending field, the contents of SAM at the end of the operation will be _____.
    *****
    12384
15. To obtain exactly 12384 in SAM, its PICTURE clause must be _____.
    *****
    99999 or 9(5)
16. In the operation MOVE SPACES TO FIELDA, SPACES is a _____, and FIELDA must have an _____ PICTURE clause. The contents of FIELDA will be replaced with _____ at the end of the operation.
    *****
    figurative constant

alphanumeric or alphabetic
blanks or spaces

17. In the operation MOVE ZEROS TO FIELDA, FIELDA may have a(n)
    _____ PICTURE clause. FIELDA will be replaced with _____.
    *****
    alphanumeric or numeric (NOTE: Zero is a valid numeric and alphanumeric
    character.)
    0's

18. In the operation MOVE 'SPACES' TO FIELDA, FIELDA having a PICTURE
    of X(6), 'SPACES' is a _____. The contents of FIELDA will be _____
    at the end of the operation.
    *****
    nonnumeric literal (NOTE: It is enclosed in quotes.)
    the word SPACES

C. NUMERIC MOVE

The relative complexity of the MOVE statement necessitates two classifications: numeric MOVE operations and alphanumeric MOVE operations.[1] We will leave the discussion of the alphanumeric MOVE until the next section.

A numeric MOVE operation may be defined in two ways:

1. Movement of a numeric field, with a PICTURE of 9's, to another numeric field.
2. Movement of a numeric literal to a numeric field.

Consider the following:

MOVE (data-name-1) TO (data-name-2)

Both fields have numeric PICTURE clauses.

Assuming the size of both fields to be identical, data-name-2 will be replaced with the contents of data-name-1, without changing the sending field.

Example 1

FIELDA   PICTURE 999
         Contents 123

FIELDB   PICTURE 999
         Contents 456

Operation: MOVE FIELDA TO FIELDB
---

[1]We will not discuss the **alphabetic** moves, since they conform to the same rules as alphanumeric move operations. The only distinction is that, in an alphabetic move, only letters or blanks should be transmitted and not special characters.

Example 2

FIELDC   PICTURE 99V99   (implied decimal point after first two digits)
            Contents 12.34   (to be interpreted as 12.34)
FIELDD   PICTURE 99V99
            Contents 45.67

Operation: MOVE FIELDC TO FIELDD

The first example, as illustrated in the previous section, places the same contents of FIELDA, 123, in FIELDB.

Although it is not quite as obvious in Example 2, the receiving field again acquires the very same contents as the sending field, 1234, to be interpreted as 12.34. (You will recall that the decimal point does not actually appear in memory.) In other words, the MOVE operation maintains decimal alignment.

Often in a COBOL program, it will be necessary to move one numeric field to another, where the sizes of the two fields differ. You might want to move a field to a larger one to perform an arithmetic operation on it, or to move a work area with precision of three decimal places (V999) to an output area, which requires precision of only two decimal places (V99). In both these cases, the MOVE operation will **not** produce in the receiving field the same contents as the sending field, since the sizes of the two fields differ.

Two rules will apply in all numeric MOVE operations—one for the movement of the integer portion of a number, and one for the decimal or fractional portion.

Rule 1: When moving an integer sending field or an integer **portion** of the sending field to the receiving field, movement is from **right** to **left.** All nonfilled high-order (leftmost) integer positions of the receiving field are filled with zeros.

Example 3

FIELD1 PICTURE 999
            Contents 123
FIELD2 PICTURE 9(4)
            Contents 4567

Operation: MOVE FIELD1 TO FIELD2

According to Rule 1, movement is from right to left:

(a) The 3 in FIELD1 replaces the 7 in FIELD2.
(b) The 2 in FIELD1 replaces the 6 in FIELD2.
(c) The 1 in FIELD1 replaces the 5 in FIELD2.

and all nonfilled high-order positions are filled with zeros:

(d) 0 replaces the 4 in FIELD2.

Thus we obtain 0123 in FIELD2. No portion of the original contents of the receiving field is maintained after the MOVE is performed:

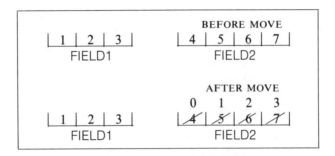

Example 4

FIELD3	PICTURE 999
	Contents 012
FIELD4	PICTURE 99
	Contents 34

> **Operation:** MOVE FIELD3 TO FIELD4.

(a) The 2 of FIELD3 will replace the 4 of FIELD4.
(b) The 1 of FIELD3 will replace the 3 of FIELD4.

The operation will terminate at this point, since the receiving field is thus filled. FIELD4 will have contents of 12, while FIELD3 will remain unchanged:

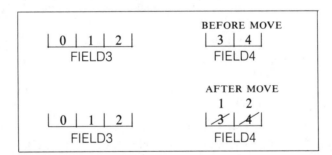

A good rule-of-thumb to follow in numeric MOVE operations is to be sure that the receiving field has at least as many whole number (integer) positions as the sending field. If the receiving field is **larger** than the sending field, the high-order positions of the former will be replaced with zeros, which do not affect the result. If, however, the receiving field is **smaller** than the sending field, you may inadvertently truncate the most significant digits.

Example 5

TAKE-HOME-PAY	PICTURE 9(4)
	Contents 1000
AMT-OF-CHECK	PICTURE 999

> **Operation:** MOVE TAKE-HOME-PAY TO AMT-OF-CHECK

In the above example, the receiving field is only three positions long. Since movement of integer positions is from right to left, 000 will be placed in AMT-OF-CHECK. It is clear that the check's recipient will not be pleased. To avoid such difficulties, be sure that the receiving field is at least as large as the sending field.

We will now consider the movement of fields that have fractional components, that is, numeric fields with implied decimal positions.

> **Rule 2:** When moving a decimal or fractional portion of the sending field to the receiving field movement is from left to right, beginning at the implied decimal point. Low-order (rightmost) nonfilled decimal positions are filled with zeros.

Example 6

```
FLDA   PICTURE 99V99
       Contents 1234
FLDB   PICTURE 99V999
       Contents 56789
```

> **Operation:** MOVE FLDA TO FLDB

The integer portion of FLDA replaces the integer portion of FLDB, according to Rule 1. The decimal portion of each field is as follows:

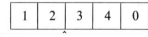

FLDA   FLDB

According to Rule 2, movement from the implied decimal point on is from left to right:

(a) The 3 of FLDA replaces the 7 of FLDB.
(b) The 4 of FLDA replaces the 8 of FLDB.

Low-order nonfilled decimal positions of the receiving field are zero-filled:

(c) 0 replaces the 9 of FLDB.

Thus we have

1	2	3	4	0

FLDB

Example 7

```
FLDC   PICTURE V99
       Contents 12
```

```
FLDD   PICTURE V9
       Contents .3
```

> **Operation:** MOVE FLDC TO FLDD

In Example 7, movement, from the implied decimal point on, is from left to right. Thus the 1 of FLDC replaces the 3 of FLDD. The operation is terminated at this point since FLDD is only one position.

Example 8

```
FLDE   PICTURE 999V9
       Contents 1234
FLDF   PICTURE 99
       Contents 00
```

> **Operation:** MOVE FLDE TO FLDF

Since integer movement is from right to left, the 3 of FLDE replaces the low-order 0, and 2 of FLDE replaces the high-order zero. Since there are no more integer positions in the receiving field, that portion is terminated. The operation itself is terminated at this point, since there are no decimal positions in FLDF. Thus the content of FLDF is 23.

The second form of a numeric MOVE is as follows:

> MOVE (literal) TO (data-name)

where the **literal** and the data-name are both numeric.
The two rules specified above apply in this type of numeric move:

Example 9

```
FLD1   PICTURE 9(4)
```

> **Operation:** MOVE 123 TO FLD1

Since we are concerned with integers in Example 9, movement is from right to left and high-order positions of the receiving field are replaced with zeros. Thus we obtain 0123 in FLD1. Treat the literal 123 as if it were FLDZ with a PICTURE of 999, contents 123, and proceed as in Case 1; that is, MOVE FLDZ TO FLD1 is performed. This can be applied to movement of all numeric literals.

Example 10

```
FLD2   PICTURE 99
```

> **Operation:** MOVE 123 TO FLD2

In this case, truncation occurs because the receiving field cannot accommodate the entire sending field. Since movement is from right to left, FLD2 becomes 23. This would be the same result if the operation were MOVE FLDZ TO FLD2, where FLDZ had a PICTURE of 999, contents 123. The truncation that occurs is undesirable since the most significant digit, the hundreds place, is not transmitted to the receiving field.

Example 11

    FLD3   PICTURE 99V999

> **Operation:** MOVE 12.34 TO FLD3

Note that a numeric literal is expressed with a decimal point where intended, while it is only implied in the data-field (FLD3). The integer positions of the sending field are transmitted with a result of 12 in those positions of FLD3. Movement from the implied decimal point on is from left to right, the result being 34 in the first two decimal positions of FLD3. Nonfilled low-order decimal positions of FLD3 are zero-filled. Thus we obtain | 1 | 2 | 3 | 4 | 0 | in FLD3. Note again that the result is the same as if we had performed the operation MOVE FLDZ TO FLD3, where FLDZ had a PICTURE of 99V99, and contents 1234.

It should be clear at this point that the numeric MOVE operation functions exactly the same whether the sending field is a literal or a data-name. Treat a numeric literal as if it were a data field in storage, and proceed according to Rules 1 and 2.

SELF-EVALUATING QUIZ

1. When moving integer portions of sending fields to receiving fields, movement is from _____ to _____. High-order integer positions, which are not filled, are replaced with _____.
   *****
   right
   left
   zero

2. When moving decimal portions of sending fields to receiving fields, movement is from _____ to _____. Low-order decimal positions of the receiving fields are replaced with _____.
   *****
   left
   right
   zero

Use the following statement to complete Questions 3–8:

> MOVE TAX TO TOTAL

	TAX		TOTAL	
	PICTURE	**Contents**	PICTURE	**Contents** (after MOVE)
3.	99V99	10.35	999V999	_____
4.	99V9	37.2	999	_____
5.	9(4)	1234	999	_____
6.	V99	.12	V9	_____
7.	99V99	02.34	9V9	_____
8.	9V9	1.2	_____	.20

*****
010350
037
234
.1
2.3
V99

9. The particular statement or question from the above group that might give undesirable results is _____.

*****

5—truncation of the high-order or most significant digit occurs

10. The operation MOVE 12.487 TO WORK is performed. To obtain the **exact** form of the literal in the field called WORK, its PICTURE clause must be

_____.

*****

99V999

Use the following statement to complete Questions 11–16:

> MOVE 12.35 TO AREA-1

	AREA-1	
	PICTURE	**Contents**
11.	999V99	_____
12.	999V9	_____
13.	999V999	_____
14.	9V9	_____
15.	V999	_____
16.	_____	012.3

*****
012.35
012.3
012.350
2.3
.350
999V9

17. In a numeric MOVE operation, there (are, are not) instances when some **significant** portion of the receiving field is retained and not replaced with something else.

*****

are **not** (**Note: All** positions of the receiving field are replaced either with positions of the sending field or with zeros.)

D. ALPHANUMERIC MOVE

You will recall that the MOVE operation was separated into two categories: **numeric** MOVE and **alphanumeric** MOVE. The latter is discussed in this section.

By an alphanumeric MOVE operation, we mean:

ALPHANUMERIC MOVE
1. Movement of an alphanumeric field, defined by a PICTURE of X's to another alphanumeric field.
2. Movement of an alphanumeric literal to an alphanumeric field.
3. Movement of a numeric field to an alphanumeric field.

Rule: In an alphanumeric move, data is transmitted from the sending field to the receiving field from **left** to **right.** Low-order or rightmost positions of the receiving field, which are not filled, are replaced with spaces or blanks.

Example 1

```
FLDA    PICTURE XXX
        Contents ABC
FLDB    PICTURE X(5)
        Contents DEFGH
```

Operation: MOVE FLDA TO FLDB

According to the rule, data is transmitted from left to right. Thus:

(a) The A of FLDA replaces the D of FLDB.
(b) The B of FLDA replaces the E of FLDB.
(c) The C of FLDA replaces the F of FLDB.

Low-order positions of FLDB are replaced with spaces. Thus:

(d) A blank replaces the G of FLDB.
(e) A blank replaces the H of FLDB.

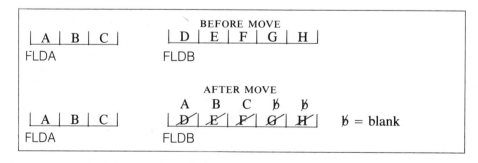

We are left with ⌐A│B│C│   │   ⌐ in FLDB. Again, no portion of the receiving field is retained after the move.

The effect of the above operation would have been the same if the following were performed: MOVE 'ABC' TO FLDB. We have replaced a data-name with a nonnumeric literal having the same contents, and the result is identical.

Example 2

```
CDE        PICTURE X(4)
           Contents NAME
OUT-AREA   PICTURE XXX
           Contents (spaces)
```

> **Operation:** MOVE CDE TO OUT-AREA.

In this case:

(a) The N of CDE replaces the leftmost blank of OUT-AREA.
(b) The A of CDE replaces the middle blank of OUT-AREA.
(c) The M of CDE replaces the rightmost blank of OUT-AREA:

```
                        BEFORE MOVE
 | N | A | M | E |     | Ƀ | Ƀ | Ƀ |        Ƀ = blank
 CDE                  OUT-AREA
                        AFTER MOVE
 | N | A | M | E |     | N | A | M |
 CDE                  OUT-AREA
```

The operation is terminated at this point, since the entire receiving field is filled. Again we experience truncation, but of **rightmost** characters. As in the case of numeric moves, truncation will be avoided if the receiving field is at least as large as the sending field. The result would have been the same if the following were performed: MOVE 'NAME' TO OUT-AREA.

Example 3

```
FLDA   PICTURE 999
       Contents 321

FLDB   PICTURE XXXX
       Contents DCBA
```

> **Operation:** MOVE FLDA TO FLDB

Note that although FLDA is numeric, this is considered to be an alphanumeric MOVE operation. The resultant field determines the type of move.

(a) The 3 of FLDA replaces the D of FLDB.
(b) The 2 of FLDA replaces the C of FLDB.
(c) The 1 of FLDA replaces the B of FLDB.
(d) A space replaces the A of FLDB.

You may have observed that, although alphanumeric MOVE instructions encompass the movement of data from **numeric** to **alphanumeric** fields, no mention has been made of the reverse situation, the movement of alphanumeric to numeric fields. Suppose you know that FLDC, which has a PICTURE of X's, has numeric data. Can FLDC be moved to a numeric field? Similarly, can MOVE '123' TO FLDD be performed if FLDD has a picture of 9's? The question can be simplified: Is it permissible to move alphanumeric fields or literals to numeric receiving fields? The answer is **no**. If you know that a field is numeric, define it with a PICTURE of 9's. **Never try to move alphanumeric fields to numeric fields.** The move will be performed by the computer, but the results will sometimes cause an abnormal end or termination of the job.

GROUP ITEMS   A matter of some importance in alphanumeric MOVE operations is the treatment of group items, or fields, that are further subdivided. It should be noted that **all** group items, even those with numeric subfields, are treated as alphanumeric fields.

Example

```
02   DATE1.
     03   MONTH PICTURE 99.
     03   YEAR    PICTURE 99.
```

If MONTH or YEAR is moved to some other field, the movement is numeric. If, however, the programmer attempts to move DATE1 to some field, it will be treated as an alphanumeric MOVE.

Below is a chart outlining the various MOVE operations. A check (✔) denotes that the move is permissible; an X denotes that it is not.

Sending fields, you will note, are of six types. Numeric, alphabetic, and alphanumeric sending fields can be either data-names **or** literals. A numeric data field is moved in precisely the same manner as a numeric literal. The receiving fields are only of four types: numeric, alphabetic, alphanumeric, and group. These refer only to data fields. A literal or a figurative constant cannot serve as a receiving field.

Note that, when mixed formats appear, the MOVE operation, if permissible, is always performed in the mode of the receiving field.

Sending Field	Receiving Field			
	Numeric	Alphabetic	Alphanumeric	Group
Numeric	✔	x	✔	✔
Alphabetic	x	✔	✔	✔
Alphanumeric	x	✔[a]	✔	✔
ZEROS	✔	x	✔	✔
SPACES	x	✔	✔	✔
Group	x	✔	✔	✔

[a]Transmitting a group or alphanumeric field to an alphabetic field may produce undefined results and is **not** recommended.

1. In an alphanumeric move, information is transmitted from _____ to _____.
   *****
   left
   right

2. In an alphanumeric move, if the receiving field is larger than the sending field, (right-, left-) most positions are replaced with _____.
   *****
   right-
   spaces or blanks

Use the following statement to complete Questions 3–5:

> MOVE FLD1 TO FLD2

		FLD1		FLD2
	PICTURE	**Contents**	PICTURE	**Contents**
3.	X(4)	AB12	X(6)	_____
4.	X(4)	AB12	X(3)	_____
5.	XXX	ABC	_____	AB

*****
AB12ØØ (Ø denotes a blank)
AB1
XX

E. MOVE CORRESPONDING STATEMENT

The MOVE CORRESPONDING statement is an option of the simple MOVE command. The format is as follows:

> MOVE $\begin{bmatrix} \underline{CORRESPONDING} \\ \underline{CORR} \end{bmatrix}$ (group-item-1) $\underline{TO}$ (group-item-2)

You will recall that a group item is a data field or record that is further subdivided into elementary entries. In the format statement above, all items within group-item-1 that have the **same names** as corresponding items in group-item-2 are moved.

Example 1

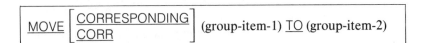

With this option of the MOVE command, all data fields in RECORD-1 that have the same names as data fields in RECORD-2 are moved. The same named data fields in RECORD-2 need not be in any specific order. Any fields of the sending record, RECORD-1, not matched by the same named fields in the receiving record, RECORD-2, are ignored. Sending fields, as in all MOVE operations, remain unchanged.

There will be further discussion on the "same name" idea in Chapter 11, in the Qualification of Names Section. Up to this point, we have been using unique names for different fields. When using the MOVE CORRESPONDING statement, we can establish fields within two different records with the **same name.**

01 RECORD-1.			Contents before MOVE	Contents after MOVE	01 RECORD-2.			Contents before MOVE	Contents after MOVE
02	NAME	PIC X(6).	ARNOLD		02	NAME	PIC X(6).	PETERS	ARNOLD
02	AMT	PIC 999V99.	10000		02	DATEX	PIC 9(4).	0579	0680
02	TRANS	PIC X(5).	12345		02	AMT	PIC 999V99.	000,00	100,00
02	DATEX	PIC 9(4).	0680		02	DISC	PIC V99.	10	10

(UNCHANGED)

Thus we see that the MOVE CORRESPONDING performs a series of simple moves. All fields in RECORD-1 that have the same name as fields in RECORD-2 are moved.

NAME, AMT, and DATEX of RECORD-2 are not in the same order as they appear in RECORD-1. The contents of these fields in RECORD-1 are, nevertheless, transmitted to RECORD-2, regardless of the order in which they appear.

Entries in RECORD-2 for which there are no corresponding items in RECORD-1 are unaffected by the MOVE CORRESPONDING statement. DISC, a field in RECORD-2, retains its original contents, since there is no corresponding DISC field in RECORD-1.

Entries in RECORD-1 for which there are no corresponding items in RE-CORD-2 are not transmitted. TRANS, a field in RECORD-1, is not moved, since there is no corresponding TRANS field in RECORD-2. In all cases, sending field items remain unchanged after the MOVE.

All rules for MOVE operations apply to MOVE CORRESPONDING statements. For numeric MOVE operations:

NUMERIC MOVE

1. Data is right-justified in the receiving field:
   For example, 075 moved to a two-position numeric field is transmitted as 75.
2. If the receiving field is larger than the sending field, high-order positions are replaced with zeros:
   For example, 524 moved to a four-position numeric field is transmitted as 0524.

For nonnumeric (alphabetic and alphanumeric) MOVE operations:

NONNUMERIC MOVE

1. Data is left-justified in the receiving field:
   For example, ABC moved to a two-position nonnumeric field is transmitted as AB.
2. If the receiving field is larger than the sending field, low-order positions are replaced with spaces:
   For example, ABC moved to a four-position nonnumeric field is transmitted as ABCb.

A numeric field may be moved to an alphanumeric field, but the reverse is not valid.

Example 2

```
MOVE CORR IN-REC TO OUT-REC.
```

```
                                                                            Contents
                                                                            after
01   IN-REC.                      Contents                                  MOVE
     02   DATEX PIC X(15).        JANUARY 15, 1980   01   OUT-REC.          JANUARY 15, 1980
     02   AMT    PIC 999.         023                     02   DATEX PIC X(15).   23
     02   HRS    PIC 99.          40                      02   AMT   PIC 99.      040
                                                          02   HRS   PIC 999.
```

We will see in Chapter 13 that the MOVE CORRESPONDING option is most often used to **edit** incoming fields.

Note that when using the MOVE CORRESPONDING option, all data-names that will be transmitted from the sending field must have the same name as corresponding items in the receiving field.

Consider the following input and output areas:

```
01   RECORD-A.                         01   RECORD-B.
     02 NAME       PICTURE X(10).           02 NAME       PICTURE X(10).
     02 DB-AMT     PICTURE 99.              02 DB-AMT     PICTURE 99.
     02 CR-AMT     PICTURE 99.              02 CR-AMT     PICTURE 99.
```

In this case, it would be inefficient to use the MOVE CORRESPONDING option. It is more advantageous to simply say:

MOVE RECORD-A TO RECORD-B

since **all** items in RECORD-A are identical in size and relative location to items in RECORD-B.

The MOVE CORRESPONDING option is used to replace a series of simple MOVE instructions. All fields in the sending area are moved to the same named fields in the receiving area. All rules for MOVE operations hold when using the MOVE CORRESPONDING option. Note, however, that fields to be moved **must** have the same name in the sending and receiving areas.

SUMMARY OF MOVE CORRESPONDING

1. **Purpose:** To replace a series of simple MOVE instructions
2. **Result:**   1. All fields in the sending area are moved to **the same named fields** in the receiving area.
                 2. Field names in the receiving area that do not have the same names in the sending area remain unchanged.
3. **Rules:**   All rules for MOVE operations apply.

```
                      SUMMARY OF MOVE OPERATIONS
        1. Numeric Move
           Sending and receiving fields are both numeric.
           Rules
           a. Integer Portion
                right to left
                nonfilled high-order positions are replaced with zeros
           b. Decimal Portion
                left to right
                nonfilled low-order positions are replaced with zeros
        2. Nonnumeric Move
           Receiving field is nonnumeric.
           Rules
           left to right
           low-order nonfilled positions are replaced with spaces
```

SELF-EVALUATING 1. With a MOVE CORRESPONDING statement, all fields in the sending area
         QUIZ   that _____ will be moved to the receiving area.
                     *****
                     have the same name as items in the receiving area
                  2. The items in both areas (need not, must) be in the same order.
                     *****
                     need not
                  3. Any item of the sending record or field that is not matched by the same
                     named item in the receiving area is _____.
                     *****
                     ignored
                  4. The contents of the sending fields are _____ after the MOVE operation.
                     *****
                     unchanged
                  5. Fill in the missing entries:

          MOVE CORRESPONDING RECORDA TO RECORDB.
```
                                Contents  Contents                              Contents
                                before    after                                 after
                                MOVE      MOVE                                   MOVE
01   RECORDA.                                        01   RECORDB.
     02 FLDA    PICTURE XX.     AB        _____          02 FLDA    PICTURE XXX.  _____
     02 AMT     PICTURE 9(5).   02345     _____          02 DATEX   PICTURE 99.   _____
     02 DATEX   PICTURE 9(4).   0181      _____          02 AMT     PICTURE 9(6). _____
     02 NAME    PICTURE X(5).   MARIE     _____          02 NAME    PICTURE XXX.  _____
     *****                                AB                                       ABØ
                                          02345                                    81
                                          0181                                     002345
                                          MARIE                                    MAR
```

PRACTICE PROBLEM
WITH SOLUTION
Using the following card record as input, print all fields on a single line. Spacing will be determined by the programmer. For readability, place a period between initials of the name, and a / between month and year of the date. Also print field headings at the top of the page. That is, print the word NAME above where the name fields will be printed, etc. Solution appears as Figure 7.1.

NOTE: Chapters 12 and 13 will illustrate easier methods for aligning and printing data.

REVIEW QUESTIONS

True False

I. True-False Questions

1. Elementary numeric items within a group item are treated as alphanumeric fields.
2. Group items, although they contain elementary numeric items, are treated as alphanumeric fields.
3. ABCØØ will be moved to a three-position alphabetic field as CØØ.
4. 95300 will be moved to a three-position numeric field as 300.
5. 92.17 will be moved to a field with a PICTURE of 999V999 as 092017.
6. The statement MOVE ZEROS TO FLD1 is only valid if FLD1 is numeric.
7. A MOVE CORRESPONDING statement requires fields in both records to have unique names.
8. Blanks in a numeric field are valid characters.
9. Data items are always left-justified in a field.
10. Group items never contain PICTURE clauses.

II. General Questions

In each of the following, determine the contents of the resultant field:

| | **Sending Field** | | **Receiving Field** | |
	PICTURE	Contents	PICTURE	Contents
1.	9(5)	12345	9(6)	
2.	99V99	1234	9(3)V9(3)	
3.	9V99	789	9V9	
4.	999V9	6789	99V99	
5.	99	56	XX	
6.	99	56	XXX	
7.	XX	AB	XXX	
8.	X(4)	CODE	XXX	
9.	XXX	124	999	
10.	AAA	ABC	XXX	
11.	AAA	ABC	A(5)	

```
            IDENTIFICATION DIVISION.
            PROGRAM-ID. CHAPT7.
            ENVIRONMENT DIVISION.
            CONFIGURATION SECTION.
            SOURCE-COMPUTER. IBM-370.
            OBJECT-COMPUTER. IBM-370.
            INPUT-OUTPUT SECTION.
            FILE-CONTROL.
                SELECT CARD-FILE ASSIGN TO UR-S-SYSIN.
                SELECT PRINT-FILE ASSIGN TO UR-S-SYSOUT.
            DATA DIVISION.
            FILE SECTION.
            FD  CARD-FILE
                LABEL RECORDS ARE OMITTED
                RECORD CONTAINS 80 CHARACTERS
                DATA RECORD IS CARD-REC.
            01  CARD-REC.
                02  CUSTOMER-NAME.
                    03  INITIAL-1              PIC X.
                    03  INITIAL-2              PIC X.
                    03  LAST-NAME              PIC X(18).
                02  DATE-OF-TRANSACTION.
                    03  MONTH                  PIC 99.
                    03  YEAR                   PIC 99.
                02  AMOUNT-OF-TRANSACTION      PIC 9(6).
                02  FILLER                     PIC X(50).
            FD  PRINT-FILE
                LABEL RECORDS ARE OMITTED
                RECORD CONTAINS 133 CHARACTERS
                DATA RECORDS ARE HEADER, DETAIL-LINE.
            01  HEADER.
                02  FILLER            PIC X(21).
                02  LITERAL1          PIC X(4).
                02  FILLER            PIC X(25).
                02  LITERAL2          PIC X(19).
                02  FILLER            PIC X(25).
                02  LITERAL3          PIC X(21).
                02  FILLER            PIC X(18).
            01  DETAIL-LINE.
                02  FILLER            PIC X(16).
                02  INIT1-OUT         PIC X.
                02  POINT1            PIC X.
                02  INIT2-OUT         PIC X.
                02  POINT2            PIC X.
                02  LAST-NAME-OUT     PIC X(18).
                02  FILLER            PIC X(19).
                02  MONTH-OUT         PIC 99.
                02  DASH              PIC X.
                02  YEAR-OUT          PIC 99.
                02  FILLER            PIC X(39).
                02  AMOUNT-OUT        PIC 9(6).
                02  FILLER            PIC X(26).
            WORKING-STORAGE SECTION.
            01  WORK-AREAS.
                02  EOF                         PIC 9 VALUE 0.
            PROCEDURE DIVISION.
                OPEN INPUT CARD-FILE, OUTPUT PRINT-FILE.
                MOVE SPACES TO HEADER.
                MOVE 'NAME' TO LITERAL1.
                MOVE 'DATE OF TRANSACTION' TO LITERAL2.
                MOVE 'AMOUNT OF TRANSACTION' TO LITERAL3.
                WRITE HEADER.
                MOVE SPACES TO DETAIL-LINE.
                MOVE '.' TO POINT1.
                MOVE '.' TO POINT2.
                MOVE '/' TO DASH.
                READ CARD-FILE AT END MOVE 1 TO EOF.
                PERFORM CALC-RTN UNTIL EOF = 1.
                CLOSE CARD-FILE, PRINT-FILE.
                STOP RUN.
            CALC-RTN.
                MOVE INITIAL-1 TO INIT1-OUT.
                MOVE INITIAL-2 TO INIT2-OUT.
                MOVE LAST-NAME TO LAST-NAME-OUT.
                MOVE MONTH TO MONTH-OUT.
                MOVE YEAR TO YEAR-OUT.
                MOVE AMOUNT-OF-TRANSACTION TO AMOUNT-OUT.
                WRITE DETAIL-LINE.
                READ CARD-FILE AT END MOVE 1 TO EOF.
```

Figure 7.1

In each of the following, determine the contents of FLDX if the operation performed is:

MOVE 13.579 TO FLDX

FLDX

	PICTURE	**Contents**
12.	99V999	
13.	999V9(4)	
14.	9V99	
15.	99V9	

In each of the following determine the contents of FLDY after the following operation is performed:

MOVE 'NAME' TO FLDY

FLDY

	PICTURE	**Contents**
16.	XXXX	
17.	AAAA	
18.	AAA	
19.	A(5)	
20.	9999	

PROBLEMS

1. Write a program to print data from a magnetic tape. The input is as follows:

> 1–15 Customer name
> 16–20 Customer number
> 21–25 Amount of purchase (in dollars)

Output should contain all input fields spaced across the line. Print heading on top of page: PURCHASE REPORT. The heading should also be spaced in the center of the form. In addition to the tape fields, print today's date (literal) on each line. The input contains standard labels and 15 records/block.

2. Write a program to create one master tape record for every group of two input data cards. The input consists of two types of records:

Credit record:
> 1–20 Customer name
> 21–25 Amount of credit xxx.xx
> 26–80 Not used

Debit record:
> 1–20 Customer name
> 21–40 Address
> 41–45 Amount of debit xxx.xx
> 46–80 Not used

Each transaction will have both records as input. The credit record is always followed by a debit record. One output record will be created from two input records. The output format is as follows:

> 1–25 Customer name
> 25–50 Address
> 51–60 Amount of debit (4 positions after implied decimal)
> 61–70 Amount of credit (4 positions after implied decimal)

8 THE WORKING-STORAGE SECTION

A. INDEPENDENT ITEMS AND VALUE CLAUSES

You will recall that the DATA DIVISION is divided into two sections: the FILE SECTION and the WORKING-STORAGE SECTION.

The DATA DIVISION, as a whole, contains **all defined storage areas** to be set aside for the processing of data. The FILE SECTION is where all input and output files must be described in detail. The WORKING-STORAGE SECTION contains all fields not part of input or output that are necessary for the processing of data. Any constants, intermediate totals, or work areas not part of the files but which are necessary for processing are placed in the WORKING-STORAGE SECTION. This section may contain two categories of data fields:

1. Independent data items on the 77-level.
2. Group items—subdivided into independent elementary items.

77-level items are not used very frequently. Hence, we will emphasize the use of group items that may be subdivided into individual, elementary items as in the following example:

```
WORKING-STORAGE SECTION.
01   WORK-AREAS.
     02   EOF         PIC 9      VALUE 0.
     02   GROSS-AMT   PIC 999V99 VALUE 0.
```

THE USE OF INDEPENDENT ITEMS IN WORKING-STORAGE

Independent data items, defined in the WORKING-STORAGE SECTION, are individual fields, each performing a separate function and not related to any other data item. The use of independent data items will be illustrated by the following examples.

---

¹The REPORT SECTION is a special section of this DIVISION and will be discussed in Chapter 23.

Example 1

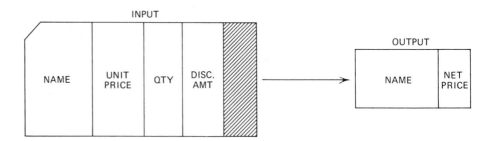

NET-PRICE is equal to UNIT-PRICE multiplied by QTY minus DISC-AMT.

Two steps are required to obtain NET-PRICE:

Multiplication

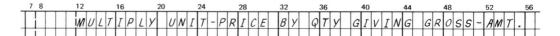

GROSS-AMT must be an independent item defined in WORKING-STORAGE. It is not part of the input and is only an intermediate result necessary for calculating NET-PRICE.

Subtraction

The independent item GROSS-AMT is then an intermediate resultant field that eventually produces an output result.

Example 2

Suppose we wish to count the number of cards that are contained within a file. The following serves as a program excerpt.

```
        MOVE ZERO TO CTR.
        PERFORM BEGIN UNTIL EOF = 1.
        MOVE CTR TO PRINT-A.
        WRITE PRINT-REC.
BEGIN.
        READ CARD-FILE AT END MOVE 1 TO EOF.
        ADD 1 TO CTR.
```

CTR is also a field that is not part of the input but is required for processing. It can be defined as an independent item that must be specified in the WORK-ING-STORAGE SECTION.

Note that EOF must be an independent item in the WORKING-STORAGE SECTION.

> **RULES FOR CODING INDEPENDENT ITEMS**
> 1. The WORKING-STORAGE SECTION, like all sections, is coded in Margin A.
> 2. The WORKING-STORAGE SECTION must follow the FILE SECTION.
> 3. Independent data items may be coded as part of a group item (or as special 77-level items).
> 4. The group item is coded on the 01 level in Margin A; the independent items would then be coded on some level subordinate to 01.
> 5. Names given to items in this section conform to the rules for forming data-names.
> 6. All independent items must have PICTURE or PIC clauses:
>   X denotes alphanumeric
>   A denotes alphabetic
>   9 denotes numeric

Example

```
WORKING-STORAGE SECTION.
01  WORK-AREAS.
      02   INTERMEDIATE-TOTAL      PIC 9(5)V99.
      02   CONSTANT-1              PIC X(4).
      02   FLDA                    PIC XXX.
```

VALUE CLAUSES As in the FILE SECTION, the size of the field is indicated by the number of X's, 9's, or A's.

Independent items in the WORKING-STORAGE SECTION are generally **initialized;** that is, they are given initial contents by a VALUE clause. It is important to recall that most computers **do not automatically clear storage** when reading in new programs. An area that is specified in the DATA DIVISION has an undefined quantity when a program begins execution. Unless the programmer indicates an initial value for a field, it cannot be assumed that the field is cleared with blanks or zeros.

To ensure that output records or fields specified in the FILE SECTION are blank at the beginning of a program, we move SPACES to these areas in the PROCEDURE DIVISION before any processing is performed. In the WORKING-STORAGE SECTION, however, we may initialize an independent item by using a VALUE clause.

Examples

```
WORKING-STORAGE SECTION.
01  WORK-AREAS.
      02   TOTAL          PIC 999 VALUE ZEROS.
      02   CONSTANT-1     PIC XXXX VALUE SPACES.
```

A VALUE clause need not be specified for an independent item. If it is omitted, however, no assumption can be made about the initial contents of the field. If no VALUE clause is indicated, it is best to use a MOVE instruction in the PROCEDURE DIVISION to obtain an initial value in the field.

Four entries, then (the first three are required), are used to denote independent items in the WORKING-STORAGE SECTION.

INDEPENDENT ITEMS IN WORKING-STORAGE

1. Level 01 coded in Margin A, signals the computer that a group data item is about to be defined. Independent items are coded on a level subordinate to 01.
2. The programmer-supplied name defines the field.
3. The size of a field and its format or mode are defined by the PICTURE clause.
4. An initial value may be stored in the field by a VALUE clause.

The VALUE clause will contain a literal or figurative constant to be placed in the field. It must be in the same mode as the PICTURE clause. If the PICTURE denotes a numeric field, the value must be a numeric literal or ZERO.

Examples:

```
WORKING-STORAGE SECTION.
01   WORK-AREAS.
     02   FICA           PIC V9999      VALUE .0617.
     02   CONSTANT-1     PIC 9(5)       VALUE 07600.
     02   TOTAL          PIC 9999       VALUE ZERO.
```

Notice that to say 02 TOTAL PICTURE 9999 VALUE ZERO is the same as setting up the 02 level item **without** the VALUE clause and issuing the following instruction in the PROCEDURE DIVISION: MOVE ZERO TO TOTAL. Similarly, the entry 02 FICA PICTURE V9999 VALUE .0617 is identical to MOVE .0617 TO FICA where FICA has no VALUE clause.

Since the VALUE clause performs the same operation as a MOVE instruction, all rules for MOVE operations apply.

Example

This is the same as moving 12 to FLDA. According to the rules for numeric MOVE operations (see Chapter 7), 012 will be placed in FLDA. In general, to obtain in the receiving field the same contents as the literal, use a PICTURE clause with the same specifications. To obtain exactly 12 in FLDA, FLDA should have PICTURE 99.

The rules for alphanumeric fields also apply to independent items in WORKING-STORAGE. If a field contains an alphanumeric or alphabetic PICTURE clause, its VALUE clause, if used, must contain a nonnumeric literal:

Examples

```
WORKING-STORAGE SECTION.
01   WORK-AREAS.
     02   DATEX          PIC X(5) VALUE 'APRIL'.
     02   FLDB           PIC XXX  VALUE SPACES.
```

It is poor form to say, for example, 02 FLD1 PICTURE X, VALUE 3. If a field is defined with PICTURE X, the VALUE should contain a nonnumeric literal. The value 3 is a numeric literal. The entry, therefore must read 02 FLD1 PICTURE X, VALUE '3'. Similarly, we should **not** say 02 TOTAL PICTURE 99, VALUE SPACES. **A space is not a valid numeric character.** Digits 0–9, decimal points, and plus or minus signs are the only characters that may be used in a numeric literal. To clear a numeric field, we fill it with zeros and not blanks. The above entry should read 02 TOTAL PICTURE 99, VALUE ZERO. You will recall that commas may be used anywhere in the program but they must be followed by at least one blank.

Note that VALUE clauses for initializing fields may **not** be used in the FILE SECTION of the DATA DIVISION. Only WORKING-STORAGE entries may have such VALUE clauses.

To place ZEROS in TOTAL at the onset of execution results in the initializing of the field. If information is then accumulated in TOTAL, it will no longer have value zero:

```
WORKING-STORAGE SECTION.
01   WORK-AREAS.
     02  TOTAL     PIC 9(5)    VALUE ZERO.
     .
     .
     .
PROCEDURE DIVISION.
     .
     .
     .
     ADD 5800 TO TOTAL.
```

At this point, TOTAL has a value of 05800 and **not** zero. If, however, we did not initialize TOTAL, its contents after the ADD would be unpredictable. When a field is not initialized, its content is unknown.

Note that we may substitute an independent data item for a literal used in the PROCEDURE DIVISION:

is the same as

where CREDIT is an independent item defined as follows:

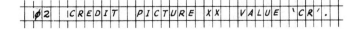

The programmer decides which of the above methods to use. As a general rule, however, any literal that will be used more than once in the PROCEDURE DIVISION should, instead, be given an assigned storage area and a data-name in WORKING-STORAGE. It is more efficient to use this name several times in the program than to redefine the same literal again and again.

The VALUE clause of a numeric field will contain a numeric literal:

12.34 is a numeric literal. You will recall that numeric literals and numeric fields may not exceed 18 digits in length. Thus the VALUE and PICTURE clauses of a numeric item in the WORKING-STORAGE SECTION may not exceed 18 digits.

NONNUMERIC VALUES

A nonnumeric VALUE clause, however, may contain up to 120 characters. A nonnumeric VALUE clause, like a nonnumeric literal, is enclosed in quotes and contains a maximum of 120 characters.

CONTINUATION OF LITERALS

Since the VALUE clause for an alphanumeric field in the WORKING-STORAGE SECTION may contain a maximum of 120 characters, it is sometimes necessary to continue a VALUE clause from one line of the coding sheet to another. The continuation of nonnumeric literals to two or more lines conforms to the following rules.

RULES FOR CONTINUATION OF LITERALS
1. Begin the literal with a quotation mark.
2. Continue the literal until the end of the line is reached (do not close with quotation mark).
3. Place a dash (—) in the position marked CONTINUATION of the **next line** (position 7).
4. Continue the literal in Margin B of this next line, beginning with a quotation mark.
5. End literal with a quotation mark.

Example

```
CONT.
8   12
Ø1  HEADING   PICTURE X(36) VALUE 'MONTHLY TRANSACTIONS FOR APRI
-      'L, 1981'.
```

Figure 8-1 illustrates the continuation of a nonnumeric literal to three lines.

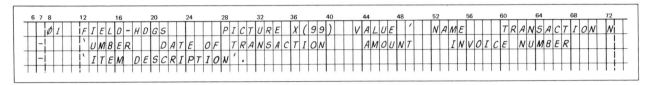

Figure 8.1

Note that a nonnumeric literal may encompass more than one line when defined in the PROCEDURE DIVISION as well. Consider the following WORK-ING-STORAGE entry:

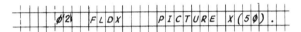

The rules for continuation of literals in the PROCEDURE DIVISION are the same. See Figure 8.2 on page 144 for an illustration.

Independent WORKING-STORAGE items are an essential part of most COBOL programs. Constants, intermediate totals, and work areas are generally required within a program. It is not always possible, however, to forecast their need before the PROCEDURE DIVISION is written. As instructions are coded, a need for additional storage areas often arises. It is general practice, therefore, to allow space on the coding sheet for WORKING-STORAGE entries **prior** to beginning the PROCEDURE DIVISION. As independent items are needed, they may be assigned in the space provided.

SELF-EVALUATING
QUIZ

1. The two sections of the DATA DIVISION are the _____ SECTION and the _____ SECTION.
   *****
   FILE
   WORKING-STORAGE

2. Independent data items are _____, _____, or _____ defined in WORKING-STORAGE.
   *****
   constants
   intermediate totals
   work areas

3. Independent items in WORKING-STORAGE are usually coded as part of a _____ item.
   *****
   group

4. WORKING-STORAGE SECTION is coded in Margin _____.
   *****
   A

5. WORKING-STORAGE SECTION and its entries follow the _____ _____ and precede the _____ _____ in a COBOL program.
   *****

Figure 8.2 Illustration of continuation of literals in the PROCEDURE DIVISION.

FILE SECTION
PROCEDURE DIVISION

6. Independent items in WORKING-STORAGE **must** have a _____, a _____, a _____, and **may** have a _____.

     *****

     level number
     programmer-supplied name
     PICTURE clause
     VALUE clause

7. VALUE clauses to initialize fields may only be used in the _____ _____ _____.

     *****

     WORKING-STORAGE SECTION

8. Values should be assigned to all WORKING-STORAGE entries because _____.

     *****

     the computer is not automatically cleared at execution time

9. The VALUE clause may contain a _____ or a _____.

     *****

     literal
     figurative constant

10. The VALUE specified for a field must be in the same format or mode as the _____ clause.

     *****

     PICTURE

     Make any necessary corrections to the following (11–16):

11. WORKING STORAGE SECTION
12. 02 FLD 1 PICTURE X VALUE SPACE.
13. 02 FLDA PICTURE X VALUE 4.
14. 02 FLDB PICTURE X VALUE ZERO.
15. 02 FLDC PICTURE 99 VALUE SPACES.
16. 02 FLDD PICTURE 99V99 VALUE 12.34.

     *****

11. WORKING-STORAGE SECTION. (Note the hyphen)
12. FLD-1 or FLD1
13. 02 FLDA PICTURE X VALUE '4'. (Mode of literal should be the same as the PIC clause.)
14. Nothing wrong.
15. Numeric fields cannot have a value of spaces.
16. Nothing wrong.

B. GROUP ITEMS SUBDIVIDED INTO RELATED FIELDS

The DATA DIVISION as emphasized in the last section, contains **all** defined storage areas necessary for the processing of data. The WORKING-STORAGE SECTION of the DATA DIVISION contains all those storage areas that are not part of input or output.

Thus far, we have discussed independent items defined in WORKING-S~~?~~AGE as part of a group item we arbitrarily called WORK-AREAS. An~~?~~

tary or independent item that requires definition in the WORKING-STORAGE SECTION can be specified as a data field within WORK-AREAS. Such items may be assigned VALUE clauses, if we wish to initialize them.

In addition to using a group item subdivided into independent elementary items, we may use group items to define storage areas that are subdivided into two or more **related** entries. A NAME field, subdivided into FIRST-NAME and LAST-NAME, and a DATE-OF-RUN field, subdivided into MONTH, DAY-OF-RUN, and YEAR, are examples of group items containing related entries.

All group items in the WORKING-STORAGE SECTION are coded on the 01 level, in MARGIN A. The following is an illustration of a sample WORKING-STORAGE SECTION that contains a WORK-AREAS group and related data entries within group items as well:

```
WORKING-STORAGE SECTION.
01   WORK-AREAS.
     02   TOTAL              PIC 9(5)   VALUE ZERO.
     02   CONST              PIC X(4)   VALUE 'CODE'.
     02   SAVE-AREA          PIC XXX    VALUE SPACES.
01   ADDRESS-1.
     02   NUMB               PIC 9999.
     02   STREET             PIC X(20).
     02   CITY               PIC X(25).
     02   STATE              PIC XXX.
01   DATEX.
     02   MONTH              PIC 99     VALUE 06.
     02   YEAR               PIC 99     VALUE 80.
```

Group items are thus used for two purposes in the WORKING-STORAGE SECTION: (1) as a field called WORK-AREAS that contains independent storage fields necessary for processing; and (2) as fields that are subdivided into related entries.

If fields within group items do not have specified values, data will be **moved** into that area. We may assume that data will be moved into the group item, ADDRESS-1, for example, since it has no VALUE clauses. Group items may also have corresponding VALUE clauses that initialize the fields, as DATEX did in the above example.

Let us examine some COBOL programs that require group items in the WORKING-STORAGE SECTION.

Example 1

Suppose a card file consists of two records, a date card and detail transaction cards. The FILE SECTION entry for the card file is shown on the next page.

The date card will be the first card read. All succeeding cards will contain transaction data, which must be compared against the date card to determine if they are within the current period. If the date on the detail transaction card is not within the current period, an error must be indicated.

The first READ command will transmit the information from the date card to the input area. Unless the date is moved to some other area of storage, a second READ operation will **overlay** the date in the input area with the second card's data. Computers perform **destructive** READ operations. In other words, previous data in the input area is destroyed with each READ command.

```
FD  CARD-FILE
    LABEL RECORDS ARE OMITTED
    RECORD CONTAINS 80 CHARACTERS
    DATA RECORDS ARE DATE-REC, TRANS-REC.
01  DATE-REC.
    02  DATEX.
        03    MONTH              PICTURE 99.
        03    YEAR               PICTURE 99.
    02  FILLER                   PICTURE X(76).
01  TRANS-REC.
    02  CUSTOMER-NAME            PICTURE X(20).
    02  TRANS-NO                 PICTURE 9(5).
    02  AMT                      PICTURE 999V99.
    02  FILLER                   PICTURE X(46).
    02  DATE-OF-TRANS.
        03    MONTHX             PICTURE 99.
        03    YEARX              PICTURE 99.
```

The date on the first card must be moved to some area of storage that is not part of input or output. We must move DATEX to a WORKING-STORAGE entry for future processing.

We establish the WORKING-STORAGE entry as follows:

```
01  STORED-DATE.
    02  MONTHY                   PICTURE 99.
    02  YEARY                    PICTURE 99.
```

The instruction to store the date in WORKING-STORAGE is coded in the PROCEDURE DIVISION as a MOVE statement:

```
MOVE DATEX TO STORED-DATE.
```

Note that STORED-DATE is a group item further subdivided into two elementary fields: MONTHY and YEARY. After the date is moved to STORED-DATE, it is **always** available for processing unless an instruction is issued to clear it.

Example 2

Employee record cards contain salary information. Using an appropriate tax rate, which is based on salary, annual take-home pay will be computed. Since tax rates change fairly often, the **tax rate table** will be read into the computer as the first card instead of being created with a VALUE clause. The tax table will be subdivided into five 5-position tax percentages.

Thus the FD entry for the card file is as follows:

```
FD  CARD-IN
    LABEL RECORDS ARE OMITTED
    RECORD CONTAINS 80 CHARACTERS
    DATA RECORDS ARE TAX-CHART, EMPLOYEE-REC.
01  TAX-CHART.
    02  TAX-PERCNT-FOR-SAL-BELOW-4000              PICTURE 9(5).
    02  TAX-PERCNT-FOR-SAL-BET-4001-8000           PICTURE 9(5).
    02  TAX-PERCNT-FOR-SAL-BET-8001-10000          PICTURE 9(5).
    02  TAX-PERCNT-FOR-SAL-BET-10001-20000         PICTURE 9(5).
    02  TAX-PERCNT-FOR-SAL-OVER-20000              PICTURE 9(5).
    02  FILLER                                     PICTURE X(55).
01  EMPLOYEE-REC.
    02  NAME                                       PICTURE X(20).
    02  SAL                                        PICTURE 9(5).
    02  FILLER                                     PICTURE X(55).
```

Since the tax data will be the **first** input card, a READ command will transmit the information to the input area. Unless the tax data is moved to storage, it will be destroyed by the next READ command. Thus a WORKING-STORAGE SECTION entry may appear as follows:

```
01  STORED-TAX-RATES.
    02  TAX1                   PICTURE 9(5).
    02  TAX2                   PICTURE 9(5).
    02  TAX3                   PICTURE 9(5).
    02  TAX4                   PICTURE 9(5).
    02  TAX5                   PICTURE 9(5).
```

To obtain the information in WORKING-STORAGE for future processing, the TAX-CHART will be read and the **first** 25 positions of the card will be moved:

```
    READ CARD-IN AT END MOVE 1 TO EOF.
    MOVE TAX-CHART TO STORED-TAX-RATES.
```

Note that the MOVE statement denotes a group MOVE, which is always considered nonnumeric (see Chapter 7 on MOVE statements). Data in TAX-CHART is moved from left to right; since STORED-TAX-RATES is 25 positions, only the first 25 columns of card data are moved. The first 25 columns of the tax card, however, contain the desired tax data.

A major use, then, of group items in the WORKING-STORAGE SECTION is for the storage of groups of input fields that must be saved for future processing. Table data and date cards are examples of entries that generally must be stored for further processing. In Chapter 17, we will see that group items in WORKING-STORAGE are essential for storing **tables**.

A second major use of group items in the WORKING-STORAGE SECTION is for the **accumulation of output data**. Thus far, we have written programs where output data has been accumulated in the output area of the FILE SECTION. A WRITE (record-name) instruction will transmit the stored data to the corresponding output device.

Output data may, however, be stored in WORKING-STORAGE. It must then be **moved** to the output area before a WRITE instruction may be executed.

One might question, at this point, why output data would be accumulated in WORKING-STORAGE. The answer is that **values** may be assigned to specific fields in the WORKING-STORAGE SECTION, whereas VALUE clauses cannot be used in the FILE SECTION.

Consider the following print record:

```
FD   PRINT-FILE
     LABEL RECORDS ARE OMITTED
     RECORD CONTAINS 133 CHARACTERS
     DATA RECORD IS PRINT-REC.
01   PRINT-REC.
     02   FILLER            PIC X.
     02   INITIAL1          PIC X.
     02   CONST1            PIC X.
     02   INITIAL2          PIC X.
     02   CONST2            PIC X.
     02   LAST-NAME         PIC X(18).
     02   FILLER            PIC XXXX.
     02   MONTH             PIC 99.
     02   CONST3            PIC X
     02   YEAR              PIC 99.
     02   FILLER            PIC X(101).
```

In addition to reading the first initial, the second initial, last name, month, and year from an input document and moving them to PRINT-REC, the following MOVE operations are necessary for maintaining a neat and "readable" report:

```
     MOVE SPACES TO PRINT-REC.
     MOVE '.'    TO CONST1.
     MOVE '.'    TO CONST2.
     MOVE '/'    TO CONST3.
```

The output report would then have the appropriate constants:

```
J.E.SMITH      07/44
R.A.JONES      05/41
```

If, however, STORED-PRINT-LINE were defined in WORKING-STORAGE as follows, the above MOVE operations would be unnecessary:

```
01   STORED-PRINT-LINE.
     02   FILLER            PIC X, VALUE SPACES.
     02   INITIAL1          PIC X.
     02   CONST1            PIC X, VALUE '.'.
     02   INITIAL2          PIC X.
     02   CONST2            PIC X, VALUE '.'.
     02   LAST-NM           PIC X(18).
     02   FILLER            PIC XXXX, VALUE SPACES.
     02   MONTH             PIC 99.
     02   CONST3            PIC X, VALUE '/'.
     02   YEAR              PIC 99.
     02   FILLER            PIC X(101), VALUE SPACES.
```

Since VALUE clauses are permitted in the WORKING-STORAGE SECTION, the constants may be given initial values rather than moving the appropriate literals to these fields in the PROCEDURE DIVISION.

To print the data in STORED-PRINT-LINE after the input fields are moved to the record, we say:

Thus, when specified values are required in an output record, a WORKING-STORAGE group item may be established with the appropriate value clauses. This entry may then be moved to the output area before a record is written. The method discussed above is considered more efficient than setting up fields in the FILE SECTION and performing independent MOVE operations for each literal desired.

The technique of establishing group items in WORKING-STORAGE to store output data is even more useful when creating header records on the printer. This topic is discussed more fully in Chapter 13, which treats **printed output.**

C. USE OF 77-LEVEL ITEMS IN WORKING-STORAGE

A 77-level item in the WORKING-STORAGE SECTION may be used to define an **independent data field.** It may contain a VALUE clause and, if used, it must be coded in Margin A. Hence, the following two methods of coding may be used in a COBOL program:

Method 1—Preferred

```
WORKING-STORAGE SECTION.
01   WORK-AREAS.
     02   EOF     PIC 9         VALUE 0.
     02   TOTAL   PIC 999       VALUE 0.
     02   CTR     PIC 99        VALUE 0.
```

Method 2

```
WORKING-STORAGE SECTION.
77   EOF      PIC 9         VALUE 0.
77   TOTAL    PIC 999       VALUE 0.
77   CTR      PIC 99        VALUE 0.
```

Note that 77-level items may **not** be subdivided. [1]

You can see from the above illustrations that it is not necessary to use 77-level items in a program at all. By defining a group item on the 01 level, which we have called WORK-AREAS, all independent items can simply be coded as part of that entry. For purposes of documentation and debugging, it is preferable to use an 01 entry (typically called WORK-AREAS) followed by independent data fields instead of using 77-level items.

Note, too, that the following produces the same results as above:

[1]For users of the 1968 version of ANS COBOL, note that if 77-level items are used in the WORKING-STORAGE SECTION they must **precede** any group items that are defined on the 01 level.

Method 3

```
WORKING-STORAGE SECTION.
01   WORK-AREAS     VALUE ZERO.
     02   EOF         PIC 9.
     02   TOTAL       PIC 999.
     02   CTR         PIC 99.
```

SELF-EVALUATING
QUIZ

1. A group item is _____.
   *****
   one which is further subdivided into elementary items

2. A group item (does, does not) have a PICTURE clause.
   *****
   does not (only elementary items have PICTURE clauses)

3. (T or F) Independent items in WORKING-STORAGE must have VALUE clauses.
   *****
   F

4. Group items are coded on the _____ level in Margin _____.
   *****
   01
   A

5. When input data is _____, it may be stored as a group item in WORKING-STORAGE.
   *****
   necessary for future processing

6. Two examples of input data which must be stored for future processing are _____ and _____.
   *****
   date cards
   table data

7. When output data utilizes fields _____, it may be stored as a group item in WORKING-STORAGE.
   *****
   with specified values

8. To print data that is accumulated in WORKING-STORAGE, it must be _____ to the output area before a WRITE statement is executed.
   *****
   moved

REVIEW QUESTIONS

True	False	
☐	☐	**I. True-False Questions**

I. True-False Questions

1. WORKING-STORAGE entries consist of independent items and group items. ☐ ☐

2. VALUE clauses may be used in the WORKING-STORAGE SECTION and the FILE SECTION. ☐ ☐

3. A field called EOF may be initialized by giving it a VALUE in WORKING-STORAGE. ☐ ☐

□ □ 4. A VALUE clause is frequently used in an input area.

□ □ 5. The WORKING-STORAGE SECTION may either precede or follow the FILE SECTION.

□ □ 6. VALUE clauses are restricted to 132 characters.

□ □ 7. The VALUE clause may precede the PICTURE clause in a WORKING-STORAGE item.

□ □ 8. Nonnumeric literals may be continued from one line to the next with the use of the continuation column.

□ □ 9. 01-level items may or may not be subdivided.

□ □ 10. WORKING-STORAGE entries are sometimes used for the accumulation of output data.

II. General Questions

Make necessary corrections to each of the following (1–8). Assume that margin use and spacing are correct.

1. 02 CONSTANTA PICTURE X VALUE 2.
2. 01 DATE-OUT.
       02 MONTH   PICTURE 99.
       02 YEAR   PICTURE 99
      77 TOTAL   PICTURE 9(5).
3. 02 CONSTANTB   PICTURE X VALUE A.
4. 02 SUM-IT   PICTURE 999 VALUE SPACES.
5. 77 HEADER.
       02 FLDA PICTURE X(4).
       02 FLDB PICTURE X(4).
6. WORKING STORAGE SECTION
     01 FLD1 PICTURE X VALUE ZERO.
7. 02 FLD2 VALUE 3.
8. 02 FIELDA PICTURE X(132) VALUE SPACES.
9. Write a WORKING-STORAGE description of a three-position alphanumeric field called BOB with an initial value of zero.
10. Which of the following are coded in Margin A?
    a. WORKING-STORAGE SECTION
    b. 77 level
    c. 01 level
    d. 02 level
11. Write a WORKING-STORAGE description of a 120-position independent field with the following contents:

    THIS REPORT IS RUN MONTHLY TO DETERMINE THE NAMES OF ALL EMPLOYEES WHO HAVE BEEN PROMOTED

PROBLEMS   This chapter will not include any practice problems. Chapter 10 includes an extended series of problems so that more meaningful WORKING-STORAGE exercises can be programmed.

9 ARITHMETIC OPERATIONS

A. ADD STATEMENT

A simple ADD statement has the following two formats:

Format 1

Format 2

$$\underline{\text{ADD}} \quad \left\{ \begin{array}{l} \text{data-name-1} \\ \text{literal-1} \end{array} \right\} , \left\{ \begin{array}{l} \text{data-name-2} \\ \text{literal-2} \end{array} \right\} \quad \underline{\text{GIVING}} \text{ (data-name-3)}$$

Examples

```
ADD TAX TO DEDUCTIONS.
ADD 15.80 TO TAX.
ADD 1.20, AMOUNT GIVING TOTAL.
ADD AMT1, AMT2 GIVING NET.
```

It is important to note that all specified operands (an operand is a data-field or a literal) must be numeric when used in an arithmetic statement. The computer will not perform an arithmetic operation on a nonnumeric field. Thus, in the examples above, all literals are numeric, and it is assumed that all data-names, when specified in the DATA DIVISION, have numeric PICTURE clauses.

The result, or sum, of an ADD operation is always placed in the last field mentioned. The **only** operand that is altered as a result of the ADD operation is this last field, which is the one directly following the word TO, when using Format 1, or GIVING, when using Format 2. Thus, in Example 1, the sum of TAX and DEDUCTIONS is placed in DEDUCTIONS. TAX remains with its original contents.

It is important to note at this point that **the resultant field must be a data-name.** It cannot be a literal. The statement ADD HOURS-WORKED TO 40 is incorrect, since 40, which is the operand immediately following the word TO and therefore the resultant field, has an incorrect format. The word directly after TO or GIVING must be a data-name.

When using the TO format in an ADD statement, **all** the data-names and literals are added together, and the result is placed in the last field. When using the GIVING format, all fields and literals preceding the word GIVING are added together and the sum is placed in the field following the word GIVING. Note that, when using the GIVING format, the last data-field is **not** part of the ADD operation.

Example 5

Both fields are added together; the sum is placed in WEEKLY-HOURS; HOURS-WORKED remains unchanged.

Example 6

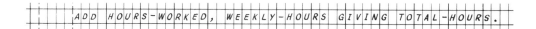

The same addition is performed as in Example 5: HOURS-WORKED and WEEKLY-HOURS are summed. In this case, however, the result is placed in TOTAL-HOURS. The original contents of TOTAL-HOURS, preceding the ADD, are destroyed and do not in any way affect the operation.

Keep in mind that the data-names specified in any arithmetic statements may appear in an input or output area of the FILE SECTION, or in the WORKING-STORAGE SECTION.

Note that the COBOL words TO and GIVING may **not** be used in the same ADD operation. To say ADD TAX TO NET GIVING TOTAL is incorrect. The statement may be ADD TAX TO NET, in which case the result is placed in NET; or the statement may be ADD TAX, NET GIVING TOTAL, in which case the result is placed in TOTAL.

The commas specified in the above statement, as all commas in a COBOL program, may be used for clarity of expression but are not required. Thus ADD TAX NET GIVING TOTAL is also correct.

A rule-of-thumb to follow when using an ADD statement is to use the GIVING format when the contents of operands are to be retained. When you will no longer need the original contents of an operand after the addition, the TO format may be used.

Format 1 and Format 2, then, may be expanded:

Format 1—Expanded Version

$$\underline{ADD} \quad \begin{Bmatrix} \text{data-name-1} \\ \text{literal-1} \end{Bmatrix}, \begin{bmatrix} \text{data-name-2} \\ \text{literal-2} \end{bmatrix} , \ldots \underline{TO} \text{ (data-name-n)}$$

Format 2—Expanded Version

$$\underline{\text{ADD}} \quad \begin{Bmatrix} \text{data-name-1} \\ \text{literal-1} \end{Bmatrix} , \quad \begin{Bmatrix} \text{data-name-2} \\ \text{literal-2} \end{Bmatrix} \quad , \ldots \underline{\text{GIVING}} \text{ (data-name-n)}$$

Thus far, we have restricted ourselves to simple ADD statements, with a limited number of operands. However, the number of operands that may be specified in an ADD operation is considered to be relatively limitless, being a function only of the size of the computer and the level of the COBOL compiler.

The rules specified thus far are as follows:

RULES FOR ADDITION

1. All literals and data-fields must be numeric.
2. The resultant field, following the word TO or the word GIVING, must be a data-name and may not be a literal.[1]
3. When using the TO format, all fields including data-name-n, are added together.
4. When using the GIVING format, data-name-n is **not** part of the ADD operation and only serves as a field in which to place the sum.
5. In no case may the words TO and GIVING be specified in the same statement.

Example 7

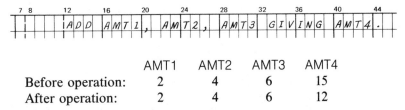

	AMT1	AMT2	AMT3	AMT4
Before operation:	2	4	6	15
After operation:	2	4	6	12

Note that the original content of AMT4, the resultant field, is destroyed and has no effect on the ADD operation. The three operands AMT1, AMT2, and AMT3 are unchanged.

Example 8

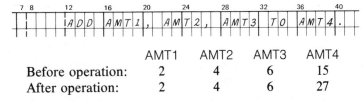

	AMT1	AMT2	AMT3	AMT4
Before operation:	2	4	6	15
After operation:	2	4	6	27

Note that the other three fields are added to the original content of AMT4. The result is again placed in AMT4, while AMT1, AMT2, AMT3 remain unaltered.

---

[1]The last data field when using the GIVING format may be a report–item that permits edit symbols. Report–items are explained in detail in Chapter 13.

It is also possible, under ANS COBOL, to perform **several** ADD operations with a single statement, using the TO format. That is, the following is a valid statement:

The above results in the same series of operations as:

```
  7 8     12      16      20      24      28      32      36
| |  |  |A|D|D| |A|M|T|1|,| |A|M|T|2| |T|O| |T|O|T|A|L|1|.| | | | | |
| |  |  |A|D|D| |A|M|T|1|,| |A|M|T|2| |T|O| |T|O|T|A|L|2|.| | | | | |
```

Thus Format 1 of the ADD statement may be expanded as follows:

$$
\underline{ADD} \quad \left\{ \begin{matrix} \text{data-name-1} \\ \text{literal-1} \end{matrix} \right\}, \left[\begin{matrix} \text{data-name-2} \\ \text{literal-2} \end{matrix} \right]
$$

$$
\underline{TO} \ (\text{data-name-n}), (\text{data-name-n} + 1), \ldots
$$

SELF-EVALUATING QUIZ

Indicate the errors, if any, in Statements 1–3.

1. ADD '12' TO FLDA.
   *****
   '12' is not a numeric literal.
2. ADD TAX TO 15.8.
   *****
   The resultant field must be a data-name.
3. ADD TAX TO TOTAL GIVING AMT.
   *****
   The words TO and GIVING may not appear in the same ADD statement.
4. If ADD 1, 15, 3 TO COUNTER is performed and COUNTER is initialized at 10, the sum of _____ will be placed in _____ at the end of the operation. All other fields will _____.
   *****
   29
   COUNTER
   remain unchanged
5. Without using the word TO, write a statement equivalent to the one in Question 4.
   *****
   ADD 1, 15, 3, COUNTER GIVING FIELDX.
6. The commas used in an ADD statement are _____.
   *****
   optional
7. When using a TO format, the last data-field (is, is not) part of the ADD operation. When using a GIVING format, the last data-field (is, is not) part of the ADD operation.

*****
is
is not
8. If ADD 1, 15, 3 GIVING COUNTER is performed, _____ will be the result in _____.
*****
19
COUNTER

B. SUBTRACT STATEMENT

The SUBTRACT operation has the following two formats:

Format 1

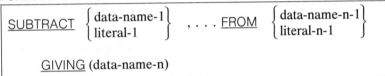

$$\underline{\text{SUBTRACT}} \begin{Bmatrix} \text{data-name-1} \\ \text{literal-1} \end{Bmatrix}, \begin{bmatrix} \text{data-name-2} \\ \text{literal-2} \end{bmatrix}, \ldots$$

$$\underline{\text{FROM}} \text{ (data-name-n)}$$

Format 2

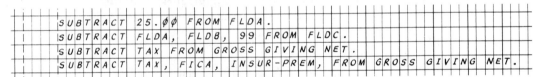

$$\underline{\text{SUBTRACT}} \begin{Bmatrix} \text{data-name-1} \\ \text{literal-1} \end{Bmatrix}, \ldots \underline{\text{FROM}} \begin{Bmatrix} \text{data-name-n-1} \\ \text{literal-n-1} \end{Bmatrix}$$

$$\underline{\text{GIVING}} \text{ (data-name-n)}$$

Examples

```
SUBTRACT  25.00  FROM  FLDA.
SUBTRACT  FLDA,  FLDB,  99  FROM  FLDC.
SUBTRACT  TAX  FROM  GROSS  GIVING  NET.
SUBTRACT  TAX,  FICA,  INSUR-PREM,  FROM  GROSS  GIVING  NET.
```

You will note that the rules specified for addition have their counterpart in a SUBTRACT operation:

RULES FOR SUBTRACTION

1. All literals and data-names must be numeric.
2. The word directly following FROM in Format 1 or GIVING in Format 2 must be a data-name and not a literal.
    The following statement is incorrect: SUBTRACT TAX FROM 100.00. If you want to subtract a quantity from a constant (100.00), you must use the GIVING format: SUBTRACT TAX FROM 100.00 GIVING NET.
3. When using Format 1, all data-fields and literals preceding the word FROM will be added together and the sum subtracted from the last data-field. The result, or difference, will be placed in this last field. All other fields will remain unchanged.
4. When using the GIVING format, Format 2, the operation performed is the same as in Rule 3 but the answer, or difference, is placed in the field following the word GIVING.

Example 5

			S	U	B	T	R	A	C	T		1	5	.	4	Ø	,		T	A	X	,		T	O	T	A	L		F	R	O	M		A	M	T	.

	TAX	TOTAL	AMT
Before operation:	3000	1000	10000
After operation:	3000	1000	04460

Example 6

| | | | S | U | B | T | R | A | C | T | | 1 | 5 | . | 4 | Ø | , | | T | A | X | , | | T | O | T | A | L | | F | R | O | M | | A | M | T | | G | I | V | I | N | G | | N | E | T | . |

	TAX	TOTAL	AMT	NET
Before operation:	3000	1000	10000	8700
After operation:	3000	1000	10000	4460

The contents of NET before the operation are destroyed and do **not** enter into the calculation.

When the contents of an operand are not needed after the SUBTRACT operation, then Format 1 may be used. When the contents of operands are to be retained, use Format 2.

As in ADD operations, all commas are optional and are only used for clarity of expression. A space must, however, follow each comma.

It is also possible, under ANS COBOL, to perform several SUBTRACT operations with a single statement using Format 1. That is, the following is a valid statement:

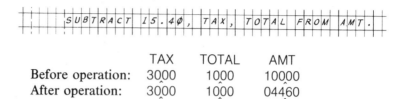

The above results in the same series of operations as:

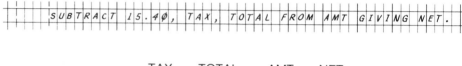

Thus Format 1 of the SUBTRACT statement may be expanded as follows:

$$
\text{SUBTRACT} \begin{bmatrix} \text{data-name-1} \\ \text{literal-1} \end{bmatrix}, \begin{bmatrix} \text{data-name-2} \\ \text{literal-2} \end{bmatrix} \ldots
$$

$$
\text{FROM} \qquad \text{(data-name-n), (data-name-n + 1), } \ldots
$$

SELF-EVALUATING
QUIZ

1. In the operation SUBTRACT 1500 FROM X GIVING Z, the result, or difference, is placed in _____. The original contents of X _____. If X has an original value of 8500, and Z has an original value of 2000, the result in Z would be _____.

*****

Z

remains unchanged

7000

What is wrong with the following statements (2 and 3)?

2. SUBTRACT $23.00 FROM AMOUNT.

*****

$23.00 is an invalid numeric literal—numeric literals may not contain dollar signs.

3. SUBTRACT AMT FROM 900.00.

*****

The resultant field of a SUBTRACT operation may not be a literal.

4. Change the above statement to make it valid.

*****

SUBTRACT AMT FROM 900.00 GIVING TOTAL.

5. Use one SUBTRACT statement to subtract three fields, TAX, CREDIT, DISCOUNT, from TOTAL placing the answer in AMT.

*****

SUBTRACT TAX, CREDIT, DISCOUNT FROM TOTAL GIVING AMT

6. If SUBTRACT A, B, C, 15.80 FROM D is performed, the PICTURE clauses of A, B, C, and D are assumed to be _____.

*****

numeric

C. MULTIPLY AND DIVIDE STATEMENTS

Because of their similarities, the MULTIPLY and DIVIDE statements are covered together.

The MULTIPLY statement has the following two formats:

Format 1

MULTIPLY $\begin{Bmatrix} \text{data-name-1} \\ \text{literal-1} \end{Bmatrix}$ BY (data-name-2)

Format 2

MULTIPLY $\begin{Bmatrix} \text{data-name-1} \\ \text{literal-1} \end{Bmatrix}$ BY $\begin{Bmatrix} \text{data-name-2} \\ \text{literal-2} \end{Bmatrix}$ GIVING (data-name-3)

Examples

```
MULTIPLY 100 BY QTY-ON-HAND.
MULTIPLY QTY BY PRICE.
MULTIPLY TAX BY GROSS GIVING DEDUCTIONS.
MULTIPLY 750 BY DEPENDENTS GIVING STD-DED.
```

The DIVIDE statement has the following two formats:

Format 1

$$\underline{\text{DIVIDE}}\quad \begin{Bmatrix} \text{data-name-1} \\ \text{literal-1} \end{Bmatrix} \quad \underline{\text{INTO}}\ (\text{data-name-2})$$

Format 2

$$\underline{\text{DIVIDE}}\begin{Bmatrix} \text{data-name-1} \\ \text{literal-1} \end{Bmatrix}\begin{Bmatrix} \underline{\text{INTO}} \\ \underline{\text{BY}} \end{Bmatrix}\begin{Bmatrix} \text{data-name-2} \\ \text{literal-2} \end{Bmatrix}\underline{\text{GIVING}}\ (\text{data-name-3})$$

Examples

```
DIVIDE 12 INTO ANN-SAL.
DIVIDE N INTO SUM.
DIVIDE 12 INTO ANN-SAL GIVING MONTHLY-SAL.
DIVIDE N INTO SUM GIVING AVERAGE.
DIVIDE ANN-SAL BY 12 GIVING MO-SAL.
```

At this point, you know that all arithmetic statements have two basic formats. When operands are not to be destroyed during an arithmetic operation, you will always use Format 2, which specifies the GIVING option. If operands need not be retained, you may use Format 1. When using either format, for all arithmetic operations, the last field mentioned is the resultant field—it must always be a data-name and never a literal.

Unlike ADD and SUBTRACT operations, MULTIPLY and DIVIDE are limited in the number of operands that may be specified. With these verbs, we may perform only **one** simple multiplication or division for each statement. For example, suppose the desired product were PRICE × QTY × DISCT. **Two** operations would be necessary to perform this multiplication: (1) MULTIPLY PRICE BY QTY. The result, or product, is placed in QTY. (2) MULTIPLY QTY BY DISCT. The product of the three numbers is now in DISCT. Hence, with each MULTIPLY or DIVIDE statement specified, **two operands only** will be multiplied or divided.

The preposition used with the MULTIPLY verb is always BY. To say: MULTIPLY PRICE TIMES QTY is incorrect. You will note that, in the DIVIDE operation, the preposition is either BY or INTO. To say DIVIDE QTY INTO TOTAL places in the resultant field, TOTAL, the quotient of TOTAL / QTY. In the example DIVIDE 3 INTO 6 GIVING AMT, the result in AMT will be 6/3 or 2. Note that this is the same as saying:

DIVIDE 6 BY 3 GIVING AMT

Let us now employ these arithmetic rules in performing some operations. We will assume that all data fields used in the following examples have the proper numeric PICTURE clauses in the DATA DIVISION. Keep in mind that the solution indicated for each example is only **one** method for solving the problem.

Example 1

Celsius temperatures are to be converted to Fahrenheit temperatures according to the following formula:

$$F = (9/5) C + 32$$

C is a data field in the input area and F is a data field in the output area. Both have numeric PICTURE clauses in the DATA DIVISION.

Solution

```
      MULTIPLY 9 BY C.
      DIVIDE 5 INTO C.
      ADD 32, C GIVING F.
```

If C had an initial value of 20, its value at the end of the operation would be 36 (9/5 × C) and F would have 68.

The routine may be reduced to two steps: (9/5C = 1.8C).

```
      MULTIPLY 1.8 BY C.
      ADD 32, C GIVING F.
```

Example 2

Compute the average of three fields: HRS-WEEK1, HRS-WEEK2, HRS-WEEK3. Place the answer in AVERAGE, and do not alter the contents of the three data fields.

Solution

```
      ADD HRS-WEEK1, HRS-WEEK2, HRS-WEEK3 GIVING AVERAGE.
      DIVIDE 3 INTO AVERAGE.
```

Example 3

$$\text{Find } C = A^2 + B^2.$$

Again, it is assumed that A, B, and C are data fields defined in the DATA DIVISION.

Solution

```
      MULTIPLY A BY A.
      MULTIPLY B BY B.
      ADD A, B GIVING C.
```

Note that to multiply A by itself places A × A or A^2 in the field A.

Observe that the following is **not** a correct solution:

The ADD operation places in B the sum of A + B. The multiplication would then result in the product of $(A + B) \times (A + B)$, which is **not** $A^2 + B^2$.

REMAINDER   When performing a division operation, the result will be placed in the receiving field according to the specifications of that field.

Example 4

> DIVIDE 130 BY 40 GIVING ITEM-A.
>
> ITEM-A has a PICTURE of 99.
>
> **Result:** 03 is placed in ITEM-A.
>
> $$\begin{array}{r} 3 \\ 40\overline{)130} \\ 120 \\ \hline 10 \leftarrow \text{Remainder} \end{array}$$

It is sometimes useful to retain the remainder of a division operation for testing or for future processing. The DIVIDE operation itself can be used for this purpose:

> DIVIDE $\left\{\begin{array}{l}\text{date-name-1}\\\text{literal-1}\end{array}\right\}$ $\left\{\begin{array}{l}\underline{\text{INTO}}\\\underline{\text{BY}}\end{array}\right\}$ $\left\{\begin{array}{l}\text{data-name-2}\\\text{literal-2}\end{array}\right\}$
>
> GIVING data-name-3 [REMAINDER data-name-4]

Hence, to retain the remainder for future processing in the above example, we have:

```
WORKING-STORAGE SECTION.
01   WORK-AREAS.
     02   REMAIN-1        PIC 99.
          .
          .
          .

PROCEDURE DIVISION.
          .
          .

     DIVIDE 130 BY 40 GIVING ITEM-A
          REMAINDER REMAIN-1.
```

Note that the use of the REMAINDER clause is optional. Note too that including it does **not** change, in any way, the results of the original divide operation.

Table 9-1 illustrates the arithmetic operations and how they are performed.

TABLE 9.1

Arithmetic Statement	Value *After* Execution of the Statement			
	A	B	C	D
ADD A TO B	A	A+B		
ADD A, B, C TO D	A	B	C	A+B+C+D
ADD A, B, C GIVING D	A	B	C	A+B+C
SUBTRACT A FROM B	A	(B−A)		
SUBTRACT A, B FROM C	A	B	[C−(A+B)]	
SUBTRACT A, B FROM C GIVING D	A	B	C	C−(A+B)
MULTIPLY A BY B	A	(A×B)		
MULTIPLY A BY B GIVING C	A	B	A×B	
DIVIDE A INTO B	A	(B/A)		
DIVIDE A INTO B GIVING C	A	B	(B/A)	
DIVIDE A BY B GIVING C	A	B	(A/B)	

SELF-EVALUATING QUIZ

1. Using MULTIPLY and DIVIDE verbs, compute A × B/C.
   *****

```
MULTIPLY A BY B.
DIVIDE C INTO B GIVING ANS.
```

2. Using MULTIPLY and DIVIDE verbs, compute (C/B + E/F) × S.
   *****

```
DIVIDE B INTO C.
DIVIDE F INTO E.
ADD C, E GIVING HOLD1.
MULTIPLY HOLD1 BY S GIVING ANS.
```

What, if anything, is wrong with the following four statements?

3.

```
DIVIDE $45.00 INTO A GIVING B.
```

   *****
   Dollar sign makes literal an invalid numeric field.

4.

```
DIVIDE -35 INTO A.
```

   *****
   Nothing.

5.

```
MULTIPLY A TIMES B GIVING C.
```

*****

Preposition must be BY in the MULTIPLY operation.

6.

```
MULTIPLY A BY B BY C GIVING D.
```

*****

Only two operands may be multiplied together with one MULTIPLY verb.

D. ROUNDED OPTION

Consider the following example:

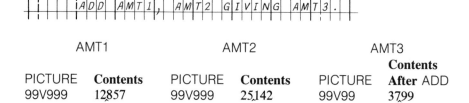

	AMT1		AMT2		AMT3
					Contents
PICTURE	**Contents**	PICTURE	**Contents**	PICTURE	**After** ADD
99V999	12857	99V999	25142	99V99	3799

This situation is not uncommon in programming. Two fields, each with three decimal positions, are added together, and the answer desired is only valid to two decimal places. In the above example, the computer adds the two fields AMT1 and AMT2, and obtains the sum 37999 in an accumulator. It attempts to place this result into AMT3, a field with two decimal positions. The effect is the same as performing the following MOVE operation: MOVE 37.999 TO AMT3. The low-order decimal position is truncated. Thus AMT3 is replaced with 3799.

It should be clear that a more desirable result would be 3800. Generally, we consider results more accurate if answers are ROUNDED to the nearest decimal position.

To obtain rounding of results, the ROUNDED option may be specified with any arithmetic statement. The following examples serve as illustrations:

It is also possible to use the ROUNDED option with the GIVING format of the above verbs. The word ROUNDED directly follows the resultant data-name in all cases.

Example 5a and 5b

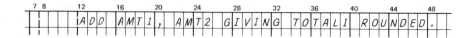

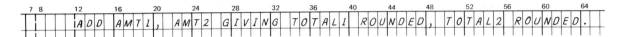

If AMT1 and AMT2 have the same quantities as specified above, the computer will round the answer to 3800.

Note that using ROUNDED with any arithmetic operator is an option only and need not be utilized. If the ROUNDED option is not specified, truncation of decimal positions, or fractional components, will occur if the resultant field cannot accommodate the decimal positions in the answer. With the ROUNDED option, the computer will always round the result to the PICTURE specification of the receiving field.

Example 6

DISCOUNT		TOTAL		AMT	
PICTURE	**Contents**	PICTURE	**Contents**	PICTURE	**Contents**
99V99	87.23	99V99	99.98	99	00

Operation A:

In this case, 87.23 is subtracted from 99.98 and the result, 12.75, is placed in an accumulator. The computer moves this result to AMT. Since AMT does not allow for fractional components, truncation occurs and 12 is placed in AMT.

Operation B:

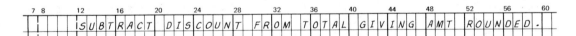

In this case 12.75 is to be rounded to the PICTURE specification of the receiving field; that is, rounding to the nearest integer position will occur. 12.75 rounded to the nearest integer is 13, and thus, 13 is placed in AMT.

If ROUNDED and REMAINDER are to be used in the same DIVIDE statement, ROUNDED must appear first:

The REMAINDER of the DIVIDE operation will be placed in (data-name-4).

SELF-EVALUATING   1. When the COBOL word ROUNDED is not specified, _____ may occur.
QUIZ   *****
             truncation

2. ROUNDED is an _____ and therefore need only be used at the programmer's discretion.
*****
option

3. State the result in the following cases.

	A PIC	A Contents	B PIC	B Contents	C PIC	C Contents	D PIC	D Contents
SUBTRACT A, B FROM C GIVING D	99V9	123	99V9	456	999V9	1568	999	_____
DIVIDE A INTO B GIVING C	9V9	51	9V9	80	9	_____		
DIVIDE A INTO B GIVING C ROUNDED	9V9	51	9V9	80	9	_____		
DIVIDE A INTO B GIVING C ROUNDED REMAINDER D	99	20	99	50	99	_____	99	_____

*****
098
1
2
C = 03, D = 10

E. ON SIZE ERROR OPTION

Let us suppose that the following operations were performed:

The fields before the operation look like this:

	AMT1		AMT2		AMT3
PICTURE	Contents	PICTURE	Contents	PICTURE	Contents
999	800	999	150	999	050

The computer will add 800, 150, 050 in an accumulator. It will attempt to place the sum, 1000, into a three-position field. The effect would be the same as an internal MOVE operation: MOVE 1000 TO AMT3. Since numeric MOVE operations move integer data from right to left, 000 will be placed in AMT3. In such a case, where the resultant field is not large enough to store the accumulated sum, we say that an **overflow** or **size error** condition has occurred. It is important to note that the computer will not stop or abort the run because of a size error condition. It will merely truncate high-order positions of the field. In our example, 000 will remain in AMT3.

The best way to avoid a size error condition is to be absolutely certain that the receiving field is large enough to accommodate any possible result. Sometimes, however, the programmer, who must be concerned with many details, forgets to account for the rare occasion when an overflow might occur. COBOL has a built-in solution. Each time **any** arithmetic operation is performed, use an ON SIZE ERROR option as follows:

$$\left\{ \begin{array}{l} \text{arithmetic} \\ \text{statement} \end{array} \right\} \quad [\text{ON \underline{SIZE} \underline{ERROR}}] \quad \left\{ \begin{array}{l} \text{imperative} \\ \text{statement} \end{array} \right\}$$

Examples

```
 6 7 8    12    16    20    24    28    32    36    40    44    48    52    56    60    64    68    72
         ADD  A,  B  TO  C  ON  SIZE  ERROR  MOVE  ØØØ  TO  C.
         MULTIPLY  A  BY  B  ON  SIZE  ERROR  PERFORM  ERROR-RTN.
         DIVIDE  A  INTO  C  ON  SIZE  ERROR  MOVE  'INVALID  DIVIDE'  TO  CDE.
```

It is clear that **any** arithmetic statement, using either Format 1 or Format 2 may be tested for an overflow, or size error, condition. By an imperative statement, we mean any COBOL statement that gives a direct command and does not perform a test. Statements beginning with the COBOL word IF, or conditional statements, are not considered imperative statements. This concept will become clearer in the next chapter. When an imperative statement is specified, the computer will perform the operation indicated if a size error condition is met. In Example 1, the computer will move zeros to C only if C does not contain enough integer positions to accommodate the sum of A, B, and C. If C is large enough for the result, zeros will **not** be moved to C and execution will continue with the next statement.

A size error, then, for all arithmetic operations, is a condition in which the receiving field cannot accommodate the entire result. In a divide operation, however, the size error condition has additional significance. If an attempt is made to divide by zero, a size error condition will occur.

Example 4

```
 7 8    12    16    20    24    28    32    36    40    44    48    52    56    60    64
         DIVIDE  QTY  INTO  TOTAL  ON  SIZE  ERROR  MOVE  Ø  TO  TOTAL.
```

Here are the fields before the operation:

	QTY		TOTAL
PICTURE	**Contents**	PICTURE	**Contents**
9999	0000	99	10

Because of the size error condition being met, TOTAL becomes zero. If the first operand specified in a DIVIDE statement contains 0, the computer will attempt to divide by zero, an impossible feat. The result of such a division is unpredictable. If ON SIZE ERROR is specified, the programmer does not have to worry about improper divide operations.

If the ON SIZE ERROR option is employed along with the ROUNDED option, the following format is applicable:

$$\begin{bmatrix} \text{arithmetic} \\ \text{statement} \end{bmatrix} \quad \underline{\text{ROUNDED}} \text{ ON } \underline{\text{SIZE}} \text{ } \underline{\text{ERROR}} \quad \begin{bmatrix} \text{imperative} \\ \text{statement} \end{bmatrix}$$

Hence the word ROUNDED will always precede ON SIZE ERROR in an arithmetic statement if both options are used.

When using a REMAINDER in a DIVIDE operation, we have:

$$\underline{\text{DIVIDE}} \text{ . . . . } [\underline{\text{ROUNDED}}] \text{ } [\underline{\text{REMAINDER}} \text{ (data-name)}] \text{ } [\text{ON } \underline{\text{SIZE}} \\ \underline{\text{ERROR}} \text{ (imperative statement)}]$$

SELF-EVALUATING QUIZ

1. An ON SIZE ERROR condition occurs when _____.
   *****
   the resultant field is not large enough to store the answer
2. An ON SIZE ERROR condition also occurs when _____.
   *****
   an attempt is made to divide by zero
3. The word ROUNDED (precedes, follows) the ON SIZE ERROR clause in an arithmetic statement.
   *****
   precedes
4. DIVIDE 0 INTO A GIVING B (will, will not) result in an ON SIZE ERROR condition.
   *****
   will
5. DIVIDE 0 BY A GIVING B (will, will not) result in an ON SIZE ERROR condition.
   *****
   will not (0 divided by any number = 0)
6. ADD 50, 60 TO FLDA ON SIZE ERROR GO TO RTN-2 results in _____ if FLDA has a PICTURE of 99.
   *****
   a branch to RTN-2
7. ADD 50, 60 TO FLDA ON SIZE ERROR GO TO RTN-2 results in _____ if FLDA has a PICTURE of 999.
   *****
   110 added to FLDA or a branch to RTN-2 if FLDA is greater than 889

F COMPUTE STATEMENT

Many business applications of programming require a relatively small number of arithmetic operations. Such applications operate on large volumes of input-output with little emphasis on numeric calculations. For this type of processing, the four arithmetic verbs discussed above are adequate.

If, however, complex or extensive arithmetic operations are required in a program, the use of the four arithmetic statements may prove cumbersome.

The COMPUTE verb provides a compact method of performing arithmetic operations.

The COMPUTE statement uses arithmetic **symbols** rather than arithmetic **verbs.** The following symbols may be utilized in a COMPUTE statement:

SYMBOLS USED IN A COMPUTE
+ corresponds to ADD
− corresponds to SUBTRACT
* corresponds to MULTIPLY
/ corresponds to DIVIDE
** exponentiation (no corresponding COBOL verb exists)

The following examples illustrate the use of the COMPUTE verb.

Examples

(1) COMPUTE TAX = .05 * AMT
(2) COMPUTE A = B * C / D
(3) COMPUTE NET = AMT − .05 * AMT

Note that the COMPUTE statement has a data-name to the left of, or preceding, the equal sign. The value computed from the arithmetic expression to the right of the equal sign **is made equal to** the data field.

Thus, if AMT = 200 in Example 1, TAX will equal .05 × 200, or 10, at the end of the operation. The original content of TAX before the COMPUTE is executed is not retained. The fields specified to the right of the equal sign remain unchanged.

Example 4

COMPUTE TOTAL = AMT1 + AMT2 − AMT3.

	Contents before operation	Contents after operation
TOTAL	100	95
AMT1	80	80
AMT2	20	20
AMT3	5	5

The fields employed in the arithmetic expression, AMT1, AMT2, and AMT3, remain unchanged after the COMPUTE is performed. TOTAL is made equal to the result of AMT1 + AMT2 − AMT3. The previous contents of TOTAL do not affect the operation. 95 is moved to TOTAL.

The fields specified after the equal sign in a COMPUTE statement may be literals or data-names. Literals need not be defined anywhere else in the program, but data fields must be given specifications in the DATA DIVISION. All fields and literals in a COMPUTE statement must be numeric.

Note that the COMPUTE statement may call for more than one operation. In Example 2, both multiplication and division operations are performed. The following **two** statements are equivalent to the single COMPUTE statement in Example 2:

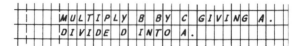

The COMPUTE statement therefore has the advantage of performing more than one arithmetic operation with a single statement. For this reason, it is often less cumbersome to use COMPUTE statements to code complex arithmetic functions.

Thus ADD, SUBTRACT, MULTIPLY, and DIVIDE correspond to the arithmetic symbols, $+$, $-$, $*$, and $/$, respectively. We may exponentiate a number, or raise it to a power, with the use of the arithmetic symbol $**$. No COBOL verb corresponds to this operation. Thus A $**$ 2 is identical to the mathematical expression A^2 or $A \times A$. A $**$ 3 is the same as A^3 or $A \times A \times A$. To find B^4 and place the results in C, we have COMPUTE C = B $**$ 4.

COBOL rules for spacing are crucial when using the COMPUTE statement. All arithmetic symbols must be **preceded and followed** by a space. This rule applies to the equal sign as well. Thus the formula $A = B + C + D^2$ corresponds to the following COMPUTE statement:

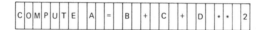

So far, we have used arithmetic expressions to the right of the equal sign. We may also have literals or data-names as the **only** entry to the right of the equal sign. To say COMPUTE A = 10.3 is the same as saying MOVE 10.3 TO A. We are placing the literal 10.3 in the field A. Similarly, to say COMPUTE B = A places the contents of A in the field called B. This is the same as saying MOVE A TO B. Thus, in a COMPUTE statement, we may have one of the three entries below following the equal sign.

1. An arithmetic expression
   for example,

2. A literal
   for example,

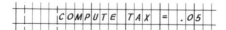

3. A data-name
   for example,

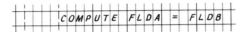

The ROUNDED and ON SIZE ERROR options may be used with the COM-PUTE statement. The rules governing the use of these clauses in ADD, SUB-TRACT, MULTIPLY, and DIVIDE operations apply to COMPUTE statements as well.

To round the results in a COMPUTE statement to the specifications of the receiving field, we use the ROUNDED option as follows:

$$\text{COMPUTE (data-name) [ROUNDED]} = \begin{cases} \text{arithmetic expression} \\ \text{literal} \\ \text{data-name} \end{cases}$$

Example 5

(a)
(b)

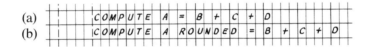

	B		C		D	
	PICTURE	**Contents**	PICTURE	**Contents**	PICTURE	**Contents**
	9V99	1.05	9V99	2.10	9V99	6.84

Result in A

	PICTURE	**Contents**
Example 5 (a)	99V9	09.9
Example 5 (b)	99V9	10.0

To test for an arithmetic overflow which will occur if the receiving field lacks enough integer positions for the result, we use an ON SIZE ERROR test. It is used in conjunction with a COMPUTE statement as follows:

$$\text{COMPUTE (data-name)} = \begin{cases} \text{literal} \\ \text{arithmetic expression} \\ \text{data-name} \end{cases}$$

$$\text{[ON \underline{SIZE} \underline{ERROR} (imperative statement)]}$$

Example 6

The COMPUTE statement results in an overflow condition if A has a PICTURE of 99. The computed result is 102. To place 102 in A, a two-position numeric field, results in the truncation of the most significant digit, the hundreds position. Thus 02 will be placed in A. To protect against truncation of high-order integer positions, we use an ON SIZE ERROR test:

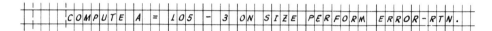

Thus the complete format for a COMPUTE statement is:

$$\underline{\text{COMPUTE}} \text{ (data-name) } [\underline{\text{ROUNDED}}] = \begin{Bmatrix} \text{literal} \\ \text{arithmetic expression} \\ \text{data-name} \end{Bmatrix}$$

$$[\text{ON } \underline{\text{SIZE}} \ \underline{\text{ERROR}} \text{ (imperative statement)}]$$

The primary advantage of a COMPUTE statement is that several arithmetic operations may be performed with one command.

The data-name preceding the equal sign is made equal to the literal, data field, or arithmetic expression to the right of the equal sign. Thus the following two arithmetic expressions are identical:

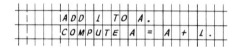

COMPUTE statements are easily written to express formulae. While the formula: $C = A^2 + B^2$ will result in several arithmetic operations, only one COMPUTE statement is required:

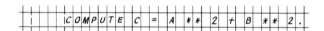

There is no COBOL arithmetic symbol to perform a **square root** operation. Mathematically, however, the square root of any number is that number raised to the 1/2 or .5 power. Thus $\sqrt{25} = 25^{.5} = 5$.

Since we cannot use square root symbols in COBOL, the square root of any number will be represented as the number raised to the .5 power, or exponentiated by .5.

Formula: $C = \sqrt{A}$
COBOL Equivalent:

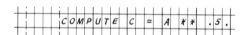

ORDER OF EVALUATION   The order of evaluation of arithmetic operations is crucial in a COMPUTE statement. Consider the following example.

Example 7

Depending on the order of evaluation of arithmetic operations, one of the following is the mathematical equivalent of the above:

(a) $D = \dfrac{A + B}{C}$ (b) $D = A + \dfrac{B}{C}$

Note that (a) and (b) are **not** identical. If A = 3, B = 6, and C = 3, the result of the COMPUTE statement evaluated according to the formula in (a) is 3 and, according to the formula in (b), is 5.

The hierarchy of arithmetic operations is as follows:

```
                    HIERARCHY OF OPERATIONS
     1. **
     2. * or / (whichever appears first from left to right)
     3. + or − (whichever appears first from left to right)
```

Exponentiation operations are evaluated, or performed, first. Multiplication and division operations follow any exponentiation and precede addition or subtraction operations. If there is more than one multiplication or division operation, they are evaluated from left to right. Addition and subtraction are evaluated last, also reading from left to right.

Thus, COMPUTE A = C + D ** 2 results in the following order of evaluation.

1. D ** 2   Exponentiation
2. C + (D ** 2)   Addition

The formula, then, is A = C + D², **not** A = (C + D)².

The statement, COMPUTE S = T * D + E / F, results in the following order of evaluation:

1. T * D   Multiplication
2. E / F   Division
3. (T * D) + (E / F)   Addition

The formula, then, is $A = T \times D + \dfrac{E}{F}$.

Thus, in Example 7, COMPUTE D = A + B / C is calculated as follows:

1. B / C
2. A + B / C

The formula, then, is $D = A + \dfrac{B}{C}$ or formula (b).

To alter the order of evaluation in a COMPUTE statement, parentheses are used. Parentheses supersede all hierarchy rules.

To compute $C = \dfrac{A + B}{3}$ is **not** performed by COMPUTE C = A + B / 3. The result of the latter operation is $C = A + \dfrac{B}{3}$. To divide the **sum** of A and B by 3, we must use parentheses:

$$\text{COMPUTE C} = (A + B) / 3$$

All operations within parentheses are evaluated first. Thus we have:
1. A + B
2. (A + B) / 3

Example 8

Suppose A, B, and C are three sides of a right triangle, C being the hypotenuse (side opposite the right angle). A and B have assigned values. We wish to compute C, according to the Pythagorean Theorem, as follows:

$$C = \sqrt{A^2 + B^2}$$

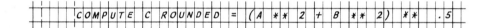

Example 9

We wish to obtain NET = GROSS − DISCOUNT where DISCOUNT = .03 × GROSS:

No parentheses are needed to alter the hierarchy, but including them for clarity, as above, is not incorrect. The following is also correct:

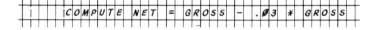

A simpler method of obtaining the correct result is:

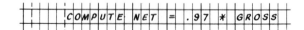

SUMMARY OF COMPUTE

1. **Format:**

   COMPUTE (data-name) [ROUNDED] =

   $$\left\{ \begin{array}{l} \text{arithmetic expression} \\ \text{data-name} \\ \text{literal} \end{array} \right\}$$

   [ON SIZE ERROR (imperative statement)]

2. **Purpose:**   To perform several arithmetic operations with one statement

   OPERATIONS

+	Addition
−	Subtraction
*	Multiplication
/	Division
**	Exponentiation

3. **Order of**   If several operations are performed with one
   evaluation: COMPUTE statement, the sequence is as follows:
   1. **
   2. * or / in sequence left to right
   3. + or − in sequence left to right

   Note: Parentheses ( ) override normal hierarchy rules

4. **Restrictions:**   Each operator (**, *, /, +, −) must be preceded and
   followed by a blank

---

1. The COMPUTE statement uses arithmetic _____ rather than arithmetic verbs.
   *****
   symbols

2. The one symbol that may be used in a COMPUTE statement for which there is no corresponding arithmetic verb in COBOL is _____, which denotes the operation of _____.
   *****
   **
   exponentiation

3. The word directly following the verb COMPUTE must be a _____.
   *****
   data-name

4. The result of the arithmetic expression to the right of the equal sign is _____ to the above data-name.
   *****
   made equal

5. The most important advantage of a COMPUTE statement is that it may _____ .

*****

perform more than one arithmetic operation with a single command

6. What, if anything, is wrong with the following COMPUTE statements.

```
(a)   COMPUTE A = B + C ROUNDED
(b)   COMPUTE A = 10.5
(c)   COMPUTE OVERTIME-PAY = (HOURS - 40.) * 1.5
(d)   COMPUTE E = A * B /* C + D
(e)   COMPUTE X = (4/3) * PI * (R ** 3)
(f)   COMPUTE X + Y = A
(g)   COMPUTE 3.14 = PI
```

*****

(a) ROUNDED follows the receiving field: COMPUTE A ROUNDED = B + C

(b) Okay.

(c) 40. is not a valid numeric literal; numeric literals may not end with a decimal point.

(d) /* may not appear together; each symbol must be preceded by and followed by a data field or a numeric literal.

(e) / must be preceded and followed by a space.

(f) Arithmetic expressions must follow the equal sign and not precede it: COMPUTE A = X + Y.

(g) Data-names, not literals, must follow the word COMPUTE: COMPUTE PI = 3.14.

7. Do the following pairs of operations perform the same function?

```
(a)   COMPUTE SUM = 0.
      MOVE ZEROS TO SUM.

(b)   COMPUTE A = A - 2.
      SUBTRACT 2 FROM A.

(c)   COMPUTE X = A * B - C * D.
      COMPUTE X = (A * B) - (C * D).

(d)   COMPUTE Y = A - B * C - D.
      COMPUTE Y = (A - B) * (C -D).
```

*****

(a) Same.

(b) Same.

(c) Same.

(d) First = A − (B × C) − D
Second = (A − B) × (C − D)
Not equivalent

8. Using a COMPUTE statement, find the average of A, B, and C.

*****

COMPUTE AVERAGE = (A + B + C) / 3

9. Using a COMPUTE statement, find total wages = rate × regular hours + (1.5 × rate × overtime hours). **Two** fields are supplied: RATE and HRS-WORKED. Overtime hours is hours worked in excess of 40 hours. (Assume everyone works at least 40 hours.)

*****

COMPUTE WAGES = RATE * 40 + 1.5 * RATE * (HRS-WORKED − 40)

PRACTICE PROBLEM—
WITH SOLUTION

Write a program to create a salary tape file. Input is on punched cards with the following format:

1–15 Employee name
16–18 Hours worked
19–21 Rate x.xx
22–80 Not used

Output is a tape with the following format:

positions 6–20 Name
          31–36 Gross pay xxxx.xx
          41–45 Social security tax xxx.xx
          51–56 Net pay xxxx.xx

The output has standard labels, 15 records per block, and 75 characters per record.

NOTES:

a. Gross pay = Hours worked × Rate
b. Social security tax = 6.13% of Gross pay
c. Net pay = Gross pay − Social security tax

See Figure 9.1 for the solution.

REVIEW QUESTIONS

I. True-False Questions

True	False	
☐	☐	1. The GIVING option may be used with all four arithmetic verbs.
☐	☐	2. The purpose of the COMPUTE is to reduce the number of arithmetic statements necessary to obtain a result.
☐	☐	3. Anything that can be coded with a COMPUTE statement can be coded with the use of the four arithmetic verbs as well.
☐	☐	4. The ON SIZE ERROR has a single use, which is to perform some operation if an overflow occurs.
☐	☐	5. The DIVIDE operation can be used to produce a remainder as well as a quotient.
☐	☐	6. The word ROUNDED may be used with a COMPUTE statement.
☐	☐	7. It is possible to multiply three fields together with a single MULTIPLY operation.
☐	☐	8. A literal may not appear as the receiving field in an arithmetic operation.
☐	☐	9. Several fields may be added together with a single ADD operation.
☐	☐	10. If both the ROUNDED and ON SIZE ERROR options are used, the ROUNDED always appears first.

II. General Questions

Fill in the missing columns (1–5):

COBOL Statement	Result at	Result if A = 3, B = 2, X = 5
1. SUBTRACT A FROM B		
2. DIVIDE A INTO B		

3. ADD A, B GIVING X

4. ADD A, B, TO X
   ON SIZE ERROR
   MOVE ZERO TO X

5. DIVIDE A INTO B ROUNDED

6. Write a routine to find $X = A + B/3$.

7. Write a routine to find $Y = (A + B)^2/X$.

```
IDENTIFICATION DIVISION.
PROGRAM-ID. CHAPT9.
ENVIRONMENT DIVISION.
CONFIGURATION SECTION.
SOURCE-COMPUTER. IBM-370.
OBJECT-COMPUTER. IBM-370.
INPUT-OUTPUT SECTION.
FILE-CONTROL.
     SELECT EMPLOYEE-CARDS ASSIGN TO UR-S-SYSIN.
     SELECT SALARY-FILE ASSIGN TO UT-S-SYS004.
DATA DIVISION.
FILE SECTION.
FD   EMPLOYEE-CARDS
     LABEL RECORDS ARE OMITTED
     RECORD CONTAINS 80 CHARACTERS
     DATA RECORD IS EMPLOYEE-REC.
01   EMPLOYEE-REC.
     02   NAME              PIC X(15).
     02   HOURS             PIC 999.
     02   RATE              PIC 9V99.
     02   FILLER            PIC X(59).
FD   SALARY-FILE
     LABEL RECORDS ARE STANDARD
     RECORD CONTAINS 75 CHARACTERS
     BLOCK CONTAINS 15 RECORDS
     DATA RECORD IS SALARY-REC.
01   SALARY-REC.
     02   FILLER            PIC X(5).
     02   NAME-OUT          PIC X(15).
     02   FILLER            PIC X(10).
     02   GROSS-PAY         PIC 9(4)V99.
     02   FILLER            PIC XXXX.
     02   SOC-SEC-TAX       PIC 999V99.
     02   FILLER            PIC X(5).
     02   NET-PAY           PIC 9(4)V99.
     02   FILLER            PIC X(19).
WORKING-STORAGE SECTION.
01   WORK-AREAS.
     02   EOF               PIC 9 VALUE 0.
PROCEDURE DIVISION.
     OPEN INPUT EMPLOYEE-CARDS, OUTPUT SALARY-FILE.
     MOVE SPACES TO SALARY-REC.
     READ EMPLOYEE-CARDS AT END MOVE 1 TO EOF.
     PERFORM CALC-RTN UNTIL EOF = 1.
     CLOSE EMPLOYEE-CARDS, SALARY-FILE.
     STOP RUN.
CALC-RTN.
     MOVE NAME TO NAME-OUT.
     MULTIPLY HOURS BY RATE GIVING GROSS-PAY.
     MULTIPLY .0613 BY GROSS-PAY GIVING SOC-SEC-TAX.
     SUBTRACT SOC-SEC-TAX FROM GROSS-PAY GIVING NET-PAY.
     WRITE SALARY-REC.
     READ EMPLOYEE-CARDS AT END MOVE 1 TO EOF.
```

Figure 9.1

In the following questions (8–10), determine the contents of the resultant field:

		A		B
Operation	PICTURE	**Contents**	PICTURE	**Contents**
8. ADD A TO B	9V9	12	9V99	835
9. DIVIDE B INTO A	99V99	1325	9	2
10. DIVIDE B INTO A ROUNDED	99V99	1325	9	2

Determine what, if anything, is wrong with the following statements:

11. SUBTRACT A FROM 87.3 GIVING B.
12. ADD A, 10.98, B TO 100.3.
13. ADD AMT. TO TOTAL GIVING TAX.
14. DIVIDE A BY B AND MULTIPLY B BY C.

Make necessary corrections to each of the following (15–16):

15. COMPUTE X = Y + Z ROUNDED.
16. COMPUTE Z ROUNDING = A + 7 ON SIZE ERROR GO TO ERR-RTN.
17. Write a statement to calculate

$$X = \frac{(M \times N)^2}{T}$$

18. Use a COMPUTE statement to add one to A.

Write a single statement to carry out the following operations (19–26):
   (a) Using the COMPUTE verb
   (b) Using the four arithmetic verbs
19. Add the values of FIELD1 and FIELD2, with the sum replacing the value of FIELD2.
20. Determine the number of feet in X inches, placing the quotient in FEET and the remainder in INCHES.
21. Decrease the value of ITEMA by 15.3.
22. Add the values of FRI, SAT, and SUN, and place the sum in WEEK-END.
23. Add the values of AMT1, AMT2, and AMT3, and place the result in TOTAL.
24. Add the values of AMT1, AMT2, and AMT3 to TOTAL.
25. Decrease the value of AMT-X by 47.5.
26. Divide the TOTAL-TUITION by 15 to determine TUITION-PER-CREDIT.

PROBLEMS   Round all the results and stop the run on a size error condition.

1. Write a program to create a master sales file from input sales records (cards) with the following format:

   1–5   Salesman number
   6–11 Net price   xxxx.xx (i.e., PICTURE 9999V99)
   12–80 Unused

The output file is created on magnetic tape with the following data fields:

1–5   Salesman number
6–11 Sales price   xxxx.xx
12–17 Commission   xxxx.xx
18–50 Unused

Notes:

a. The output tape records are blocked 20 and have standard labels.
b. Output Sales price is equal to the input Net price with an added 5% Sales Tax.
c. Commission is 20% of the price **exclusive** of the tax.

2. Write a program to convert British pounds to dollars and cents. The card input has the following format:

1–25 Name of British Agency
26–30 Number of pounds
31–80 Not used

Output cards are to be punched with the following format:

1–25 British Agency
26–31 Number of U.S. dollars
32–41 Unused
42–43 Number of U.S. cents
44–80 Not used

NOTES:

a. 1 pound = $1.90
b. Dollars and cents are two **separate** data fields.

   Extra Assignment: Redo this problem allowing for a variable conversion rate that is to be read in as card input. That is, the first three columns of the first card will indicate the dollar amount equivalent to one pound.

3. Write a program to print out each student's class average. The input records are student class cards with the following format:

1–20 Student name
21–23 Exam 1 score
24–26 Exam 2 score
27–29 Exam 3 score
30–32 Exam 4 score
33–80 Not used

Each output line should contain Student name and Class average, spaced anywhere on the line.

NOTES:

a. Class average should be rounded to nearest integer (i.e., 89.5 = 90).
b. First line should include heading: CLASS GRADES.

4. Write a program to create a tape file from the following transaction card records:

  1–5   Transaction number
  6–20 Customer name
  21–25 Amount 1 xxx.xx
  26–30 Amount 2 xxx.xx
  31–35 Amount of discount xxx.xx
  36–80 Not used

The output tape records are blocked 10 and contain standard labels. The format for the output tape is as follows:

  1–15 Customer name
  16–20 Transaction number
  21–25 Total xxx.xx
  26–30 Amount due xxx.xx
  31–34 Date (month & year)
  35–50 Not used

NOTES:
a. Total = Amount 1 + Amount 2.
b. Amount due = Total − Amount of discount.
c. If, through an error, Amount 1 + Amount 2 is too large for the Total field, stop the run.
d. Place today's date in the Date field. (HINT: Use a literal.)

10 CONDITIONAL STATEMENTS

A. SIMPLE CONDITION

We will define a **conditional statement** as any sentence that performs an operation dependent on the occurrence of some condition. Such statements, in COBOL, generally begin with the word IF and, as such, are performing a specific test.

The basic format for all conditional statements is as follows:[1]

IF (condition)	(imperative statement(s))
[ELSE	(imperative statement(s))]

An **imperative statement,** as opposed to a conditional statement, is a COBOL expression which issues a **direct** command to the computer, regardless of any existing conditions. ADD A TO B, MOVE C TO D, OPEN INPUT MASTER-TAPE are examples of imperative statements that do not test for values but perform direct operations. Hence we say that COBOL statements are divided into two broad categories: **imperative,** which perform direct operations, and **conditional,** which test for specific conditions.

A **condition,** as indicated in the above format, tests for a specific relation. A **simple condition,** which is the topic discussed in this section, is a single relational test of the following form:

SIMPLE CONDITIONS

(a) IF A IS EQUAL TO B
(b) IF A IS LESS THAN B
(c) IF A IS GREATER THAN B

---

[1]The word OTHERWISE may be used on **IBM** computers in place of ELSE.

These three tests are considered simple conditions.

An illustration of a simple conditional statement is as follows:

> IF A IS EQUAL TO B DIVIDE C INTO D
> ELSE ADD A TO TOTAL

There are really two tests performed by the above statement:

(a) IF A IS EQUAL TO B
(b) IF A IS NOT EQUAL TO B

(a) If A is equal to B, the DIVIDE operation is performed. The remainder of the statement, beginning with the ELSE option, is ignored. The program will continue execution with the very next sentence, disregarding the expression beginning with the word ELSE.

(b) If the equality, in fact, does not hold, then clearly the DIVIDE operation is not performed. Only the ELSE portion of the statement, the ADD operation, is performed. The next sentence, in either case, will be executed.

Hence with the use of the ELSE option, two tests are performed: by using the word IF, we test the initial condition and perform the instruction specified; by using ELSE, we perform an operation if the initial condition is not met.

The ELSE option is bracketed [ ], which means that it may be omitted from the conditional statement. If some operation is required **only if** a condition is present and nothing different need be done if the condition is absent, the entire ELSE clause may be omitted:

```
MOVE  NAME  TO  NAME-OUT.
MOVE  AMOUNT  TO  AMOUNT-OUT.
IF  AMOUNT  IS  EQUAL  TO  ZEROS  MOVE  'NO  TRANSACTION  THIS  MONTH'
     TO  OUT-AREA.
WRITE  PRINT-REC.
```

In this case, a message "NO TRANSACTION THIS MONTH" is printed only if AMOUNT is zero. If not, the normal flow is continued and nothing else need be performed. Since no special operation is required if AMOUNT is not zero, the ELSE clause is unnecessary.

The mathematical notation for the three simple conditions is valid within a COBOL statement:

Notation	Meaning
<	IS LESS THAN
>	IS GREATER THAN
=	IS EQUAL TO

A COBOL conditional, then, may have the following form:

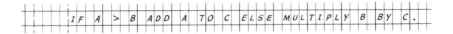

or

B is multiplied by C only if the relation does not hold, that is, if A equals B or A is less than B. Most COBOL compilers require a blank on each side of the relationals <, >, =. In coding, then, be sure you include this space.

Keep in mind that conditional statements must utilize data-fields with the same modes, in order to obtain proper execution. In the statement, IF A = '123' MOVE C TO D, it is assumed that A is an alphanumeric field, since it is compared to a nonnumeric literal. As in MOVE operations, the literal should be the same form as the data-name. If B is a numeric field, with a PICTURE clause of 9's, the following conditional would be appropriate: IF B = 123 MOVE E TO F.

In the case where data-fields are compared to one another, both fields should be numeric, alphabetic, or alphanumeric to ensure correct results. In the statement, IF A = B PERFORM RTN1, both A and B should be either numeric, alphabetic, or alphanumeric.

Regarding the comparisons of numeric fields, the following are considered equal:

$$012$$
$$12.00$$
$$12$$
$$+12$$

This implies that comparisons are performed **logically.** Although 12.00 does not have the same configuration as 012, their numeric values are known to be equal.

Similarly, when comparing alphanumeric or alphabetic fields, the following are considered equivalent:

ABC
ABC⁄b   (⁄b denotes a blank space)

Blanks, or spaces, will not upset the balance of equivalence. Only significant positions are compared.

When performing an alphanumeric comparison, the hierarchy or collating sequence is as follows for most computers:

⁄bABC. . . .Z0123. . .9

Thus A is less than B which is less than C, and so on. Any letter is considered less than any digit. The comparisons are performed from left to right. Thus:

ABCD < BBCD
BBCD < ZBCD
ZBCD < 1BCD
ABCD < ACCD

ƀBCD < ABCD
ABCD < ABCE

If an alphanumeric field is compared to a numeric field, the numeric field is treated as if it were moved to an alphanumeric field of the same size and then compared.[2] For the sake of clarity and to ensure proper results, IF statements should be used to compare fields of the same type.

Note that several imperative statements may appear within one conditional and that the use of indented entries may clarify the routine:

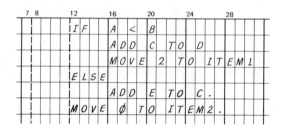

This statement may be flowcharted as follows:

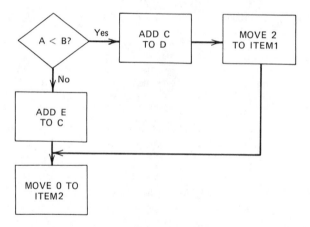

There are times when you might want to perform a series of steps only if a certain condition does **not** exist. There is a COBOL expression, NEXT SENTENCE, which will enable you to avoid performing any operation if a condition exists.

Example

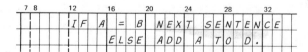

---

[2]For 1968 ANS COBOL users; comparing a numeric field to an alphanumeric field can cause a program interrupt.

If A = B **no** operation is performed and the computer continues execution with the next sentence. If A is not equal to B, A is added to D and the next sentence is executed.

Note that the following two statements produce identical results:

```
(1)        IF C = D ADD A TO B ELSE NEXT SENTENCE.

(2)        IF C = D ADD A TO B.
```

The phrase ELSE NEXT SENTENCE in the first example is unnecessary; if C is not equal to B, the computer will proceed to the next sentence anyway.

In short, the ELSE clause is only used when a specific operation is to be performed if a condition does **not** exist.

USING THE PERFORM .... UNTIL as a CONDITIONAL STATEMENT

Thus far, we have seen how the IF statement is used to test certain conditions. A conditional statement is also necessary when we wish to perform a series of steps until a certain condition exists. This procedure is called a **loop** and can be programmed with the use of a PERFORM .... UNTIL.

Example

Suppose we want each input card of information punched into five output cards:

```
PROCEDURE DIVISION.
     OPEN INPUT CARD-FILE OUTPUT PUNCH-FILE.
     READ CARD-FILE AT END MOVE 1 TO EOF.
     PERFORM CALC-RTN UNTIL EOF = 1.
     CLOSE CARD-FILE PUNCH-FILE.
     STOP RUN.
CALC-RTN.
     MOVE ZEROS TO CTR1.
     MOVE CARD-IN TO CARD-OUT.
     PERFORM WRITE-RTN UNTIL CTR1 = 5.
     READ CARD-FILE AT END MOVE 1 TO EOF.
WRITE-RTN.
     WRITE CARD-OUT.
     ADD 1 TO CTR1.
```

CALC-RTN SEGMENT

The PERFORM ... UNTIL determines if the routine is to be repeated or the job terminated. CTR1 is initialized at zero. Data from CARD-IN is moved to CARD-OUT. The PERFORM causes WRITE-RTN to be executed. A card is punched and one is added to CTR1. Thus CTR1 = 1 after a card is punched. Since CTR1 is not equal to 5, WRITE-RTN is executed again. The second card is punched and one is added to CTR1 giving CTR1 a value of 2. This process is repeated until a fifth card is punched and CTR1 contains a value of 5. At that point, CTR1 is compared to 5; since CTR1 now equals 5, control returns to the statement after the PERFORM, which causes another card to be read.

Note that CTR1 would normally be coded in the WORKING-STORAGE SECTION.

This series of steps may be flowcharted as:

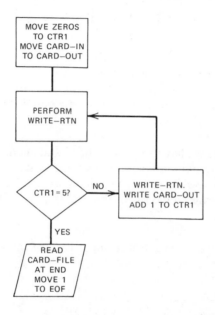

Since CTR1 begins at zero, the steps at WRITE-RTN will be repeated 5 times, that is, until CTR1 = 5.

THE MAIN MODULE OR SEGMENT

Note that, in the above, the PERFORM . . . UNTIL is itself under the control of a PERFORM. That is, the main routine or segment executes CALC-RTN until EOF = 1. Thus CALC-RTN which incorporates a PERFORM statement is itself under the control of a PERFORM. This use of PERFORMs within PERFORMs is a common programming technique.

The following operations are generally used for looping:

PROCEDURES USED IN LOOPING
1. Initialize field to be tested.
2. Code PERFORM (paragraph-name) UNTIL (condition).
3. After the PERFORM, there should be some instruction that transfers control.
4. Code paragraph to be performed with steps required.
5. Increment the field to be tested.

Consider the following program excerpt and see if you can determine the logic error that results.

> **Purpose:** to add FIELDA to SUM-TOTAL 10 times

```
    MOVE 0 TO CTRA.
    PERFORM ADD-RTN UNTIL CTRA = 10.
    WRITE TOTAL-REC.
        .
        .
        .
ADD-RTN.
    ADD FIELDA TO SUM-TOTAL.
```

You should have realized that ADD-RTN does not include a step that increments CTRA. Thus, CTRA is initialized at 0 and will remain at zero. ADD-RTN will be executed, after which a test to determine if CTRA = 10 will be performed. This will occur many more times than the required number, 10. Since ADD-RTN does not include ADD 1 TO CTRA, the PERFORM statement will cause ADD-RTN to be executed indefinitely. This is referred to as an **infinite loop.** What will actually happen is that the computer's built-in timer will sense that ADD-RTN is being executed more times than would normally be required by any program and will then automatically terminate the job.

Suppose we are attempting to multiply A by B using a series of successive additions. If three is added to itself four times, for example, the result is 12, which is the product of 3 × 4. Using a PERFORM . . . UNTIL we can code this as follows:

```
    MOVE ZEROS TO TOTAL.
    PERFORM RTN1 UNTIL A = 0.
    WRITE ANS-REC.
        .
        .
        .
RTN1.
    ADD B TO TOTAL.
    SUBTRACT 1 FROM A.
```

Suppose A = 3, and B = 4, let us see if TOTAL = 12.

	Results
MOVE ZEROS TO TOTAL.	[TOTAL = 0
PERFORM RTN1 UNTIL A = 0	
WRITE ANS-REC.	
.	
.	

RTN1.	**Results**
ADD B TO TOTAL.	1. TOTAL = 4
SUBTRACT 1 FROM A.	A = 2
	2. TOTAL = 8
	A = 1
	3. TOTAL = 12
	A = 0
	Return control to statement after PERFORM

This will work properly for all positive, integer values for B.

Note that if B were equal to 0, then RTN1 would simply not be executed. In a PERFORM (paragraph-name) UNTIL (condition), if the condition is met initially, the paragraph-name is simply not executed.

SIMPLE PERFORM
STATEMENT

Sometimes it is necessary to perform a sequence of steps from two or more points in a program. For example, we may want to execute an error routine depending on one of several conditions.

A simple PERFORM statement permits execution of a specified routine from one or more points in a program. The format is as follows:

> PERFORM (paragraph-name)

The PERFORM statement will:

1. Execute all instructions in the named paragraph
2. Transfer control to the next sequential step following the PERFORM statement.

Examples

```
COMP-RTN.
    IF   CODE-X = 1 PERFORM CREDIT-RTN ELSE PERFORM DEBIT-RTN.
    WRITE   DETAIL-REC.
    READ   CARD-FILE AT END MOVE 1 TO EOF.
```

```
COMP-RTN.
    IF AMT1 = ZERO   PERFORM ERR-RTN1.
    IF AMT2 IS NEGATIVE   PERFORM ERR-RTN2.
```

Figure 10-1 indicates the path a program takes after a PERFORM is executed.

Note, too, that the following sequences produce identical results:

Sequence 1
```
MOVE 1 TO CTR1.
PERFORM WRITE-RTN 3 TIMES.

        .

        .

        .
WRITE-RTN.
    WRITE CARD-REC.
    ADD 1 TO CTR1.
```

Sequence 2
```
MOVE 1 TO CTR1.
PERFORM WRITE-RTN.
PERFORM WRITE-RTN.
PERFORM WRITE-RTN.

        .

        .

        .
```

WRITE-RTN.
  WRITE CARD-REC.
  ADD 1 TO CTR1.

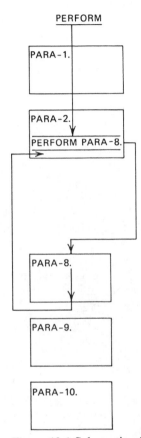

Figure 10.1 Schematic of PERFORM.

Consider the following two routines:

1. IF A = B MOVE 0 TO CODE-1 PERFORM RTN2
    ELSE PERFORM RTN2.
2. IF A = B MOVE 0 TO CODE-1. PERFORM RTN2.

Observe that the two routines above perform the same operations. In the first, if the condition does or does not exist, the program will execute RTN2. The point of this illustration is to indicate that a conditional may be written several ways and still perform the same series of operations.

SELF-EVALUATING QUIZ

What is wrong with the following statements (1–6)?

1. IF A IS LESS THAN B GO TO NEXT SENTENCE ELSE ADD 1 TO XX.
 *****
 You cannot say: GO TO NEXT SENTENCE: IF A IS LESS THAN B NEXT SENTENCE ELSE ADD 1 TO XX.

2. IF A = '127' ADD A TO B.
   *****
   Since A is compared to a nonnumeric literal, it is assumed that A is an alphanumeric field. But A is **added** to another field, which implies that it is numeric. Hence a contradiction of modes exists. While this may, in fact, produce the correct comparison (depending on the size of A), it is an inadvisable technique.

3. IF A > B ADD A TO B ELSE ADD C TO D.
   *****
   OK

4. IF A EQUALS B MOVE 1 TO A.
   *****
   This should be: IF A IS EQUAL TO B . . . .

5. ADD 6 TO XX IF A = C
   *****
   The conditional phrase must precede the imperative phrase:

   IF A = C ADD 6 TO XX.

6. IF A IS LESS THEN B MOVE 2 TO CODE1.
   *****
   With the words GREATER and LESS, the COBOL word that follows is THAN and not THEN—this is a **grammar** rule.

.7. Is the following pair of statements the same or different?
   IF A IS EQUAL TO C MOVE 1 TO C ELSE NEXT SENTENCE.
   IF A = C MOVE 1 TO C.
   *****
   Same.

8. Code the following routine:

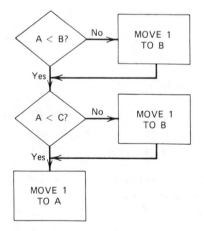

   *****
   IF A < B NEXT SENTENCE ELSE MOVE 1 TO B.
   IF A < C MOVE 1 TO A ELSE MOVE 1 TO B. MOVE 1 TO A.

9. Write a routine to move the smallest of three numbers A, B, C to PRINT-SMALL.
   *****

```
MOVE A TO PRINT-SMALL.
IF B < PRINT-SMALL
    MOVE B TO PRINT-SMALL.
IF C < PRINT-SMALL
    MOVE C TO PRINT-SMALL.
```

(Note: This is **not** the only way to write this routine.)

B. SIGN, CLASS TESTS, AND NEGATED CONDITIONALS

There are other types of conditions, besides the simple relational test, which are often used in COBOL.

SIGN TEST   We can test a data-field as to its relative position to zero:

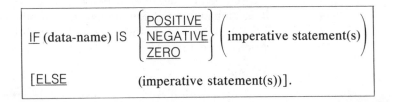

Notice that saying IF A = ZERO is the same as saying IF A IS ZERO. If a numeric field contains an amount less than zero, it is considered negative. If it has an amount greater than zero, then it is considered positive:

−387 is negative
 382 is positive
+382 is positive

0 is neither negative nor positive in this context, unless it is indicated as −0 or +0, respectively.

Example

Suppose we want to compute the distance of FIELDA from zero, regardless of its sign. For instance, if FIELDA = 2, its distance from zero is 2. If FIELDA = −2, its distance from zero is also 2, since we do not consider the sign. We call this quantity the **absolute value** of FIELDA, denoted mathematically as | FIELDA | . It is formulated as follows:

If FIELDA is greater than or equal to ($\geq$) 0, | FIELDA | = FIELDA
If FIELDA is less than (<) 0, | FIELDA | = −FIELDA

In other words, if FIELDA is greater than or equal to zero the absolute value of FIELDA is simply the value of FIELDA. If FIELDA is less than zero, the absolute value of FIELDA is equal to −1 times the value of FIELDA. Let us find the absolute value of FIELDA, using COBOL:

```
MOVE ZERO TO ABSA.
IF FIELDA IS POSITIVE MOVE FIELDA TO ABSA.
IF FIELDA IS NEGATIVE, MULTIPLY -1 BY FIELDA GIVING ABSA.
```

Note that saying IF A IS NEGATIVE is equivalent to saying IF A < 0, and IF A IS POSITIVE is the same as IF A > 0. If A is 0, the contents of ABSA remain unchanged; that is, it contains zero.

CLASS TEST   We can test the format of a field as follows:

$$
\text{\underline{IF} (data-name) IS} \left\{ \begin{array}{l} \underline{\text{NUMERIC}} \\ \underline{\text{ALPHABETIC}} \end{array} \right\} \left(\text{imperative statement(s)} \right)
$$
$$
[\underline{\text{ELSE}} \text{ (imperative statement(s))}].
$$

If the ELSE option is performed with the NUMERIC **class test,** this implies that the data-field is either strictly alphabetic, containing only letters or a space, or it is alphanumeric, containing any possible character. If the field contains 123AB, for example, the ELSE option will be performed since the field is not strictly numeric.

Example

A one-position field in a card contains the number of dependents an employee claims. To obtain the standard deduction, we multiply the number of dependents by 750. If, however, the employee claims 10 dependents, an A is placed in the field; if he or she claims 11, a B is placed in the field, and so forth. We can only perform the multiplication if the field does not contain a letter:

7 8	12	16	20	24	28	32	36	40	44
	IF	NO-OF-DEPTS	IS	ALPHABETIC					
		PERFORM	EXCEPTION-RTN						
	ELSE	PERFORM	CALC-RTN.						

NEGATED   All simple relational, class, or sign tests may be performed using a negated
CONDITIONALS   conditional as follows:

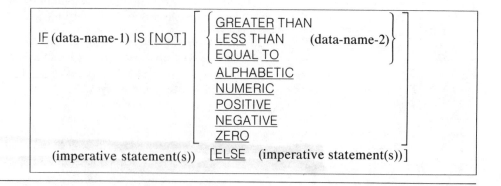

$$
\text{\underline{IF} (data-name-1) IS [\underline{NOT}]} \left[\begin{array}{l} \left\{ \begin{array}{l} \underline{\text{GREATER}} \text{ THAN} \\ \underline{\text{LESS}} \text{ THAN} \quad \text{(data-name-2)} \\ \underline{\text{EQUAL}} \underline{\text{TO}} \end{array} \right\} \\ \underline{\text{ALPHABETIC}} \\ \underline{\text{NUMERIC}} \\ \underline{\text{POSITIVE}} \\ \underline{\text{NEGATIVE}} \\ \underline{\text{ZERO}} \end{array} \right]
$$
$$
\text{(imperative statement(s))} \quad [\underline{\text{ELSE}} \text{ (imperative statement(s))}]
$$

Examples

7 8		12		16		20		24		28		32		36		40		44		48		52		56		60		64
IF	A	=	B	PERFORM	RTNX	ELSE	PERFORM	RTNY.			
IF	A	IS	NOT	EQUAL	TO	B	PERFORM	RTNY	ELSE	PERFORM	RTNX.

The two statements above are equivalent.

To say, however, IF A IS NOT NEGATIVE, is **not** the same as saying A is positive. If A is zero, it falls into **neither** category. Thus the following two statements are **not** identical.

7 8		12		16		20		24		28		32		36		40		44		48		52		56		60		64
IF	B	IS	NEGATIVE	PERFORM	RTNZ	ELSE	PERFORM	RTNQ.
IF	B	IS	NOT	POSITIVE	PERFORM	RTNZ	ELSE	PERFORM	RTNQ.

Suppose B = 0. In Case 1, RTNQ is executed; in Case 2, RTNZ is executed. Similarly, to say IF A IS NOT ALPHABETIC, is **not** the same as saying IF A IS NUMERIC. If A is alphanumeric, containing combinations of letters, digits, and special characters, then it is neither. Thus the following two statements are **not** equivalent.

7 8		12		16		20		24		28		32		36		40		44		48		52		56		60		64
IF	C	IS	NOT	ALPHABETIC	PERFORM	RTNP	ELSE	PERFORM	RTNV.
IF	C	IS	NUMERIC	PERFORM	RTNP	ELSE	PERFORM	RTNV.

C. COMPOUND CONDITIONAL

To be an efficient programmer, it is not enough simply to learn the rules of a programming language. We must be able to apply these rules to difficult logic problems. The **conditional statement,** as illustrated, is of prime importance in solving these logic problems. The **compound conditional** greatly extends the significance of IF statements. It enables the programmer to test for several conditions within one statement, and thus eases the difficulties in logic.

To perform an operation or a series of operations if **any one of several conditions exists,** the compound conditional may be utilized. Each condition within the statement is separated by the COBOL word OR, to imply that any one of the conditions so stated will cause execution of the imperative statement:

IF (condition-1) OR (condition-2) . . . (imperative statement(s))
    [ELSE (imperative statement(s))]

Examples

7 8		12		16		20		24		28		32		36		40		44		48		52		56		60
IF	A	=	B	OR	B	>	C	PERFORM	RTN5.
IF	A	<	C	OR	A	=	D	MOVE	A	TO	B	ELSE	PERFORM	ERR-RTN.

The number of conditions that may be specified in one statement is relatively limitless, depending only on the physical limitations of the computer.

The above format for a compound conditional illustrates that the word IF, the singular COBOL word that signals the compiler of an impending test, is needed **only once** in the statement.

The following is invalid:

IF A = B OR IF B = C PERFORM PARA-5.

The compound conditional is **one** test, requiring one IF, although it appears as a compound grouping.

For all compound conditionals, both operands within each condition need not be specified, since most COBOL compilers will accept **implied** operands. To say IF A = 7 OR 8 PERFORM RTN5 tests two simple conditions: (1) A = 7 and (1) A = 8. Since the data-name A is omitted from the second condition test, we say that it is implied. Such statements, then, are valid. Both operands need not be indicated for each condition. Thus the above statement can also read:

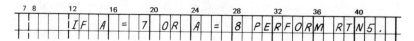

By using OR in a compound conditional, any of the conditions specified will cause execution of the imperative statement. If none of the conditions is met, either the ELSE option, if used, or the next sentence will be performed. Consider the following example:

The branch to ERR-RTN occurs only if A is greater than or equal to D **and** A is unequal to E. If either condition is met, A is added to B.

Example

Assume A is a two-position numeric field. We want to PERFORM TENS-RTN only if A is a multiple of 10. To program this loop, we may use a PERFORM . . . UNTIL statement:

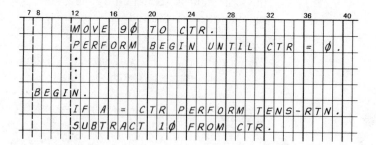

A and CTR are data-names defined in the DATA DIVISION, either in the FILE SECTION or the WORKING-STORAGE SECTION.

To program the above routine, we may also use a compound conditional:

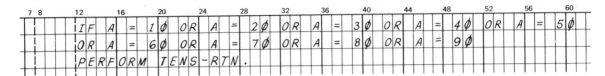

If a statement is to be executed only when **all** of several conditions are met, then the COBOL word AND must be used in the compound conditional:

> IF (condition-1) AND (condition-2) . . . (imperative statement(s))
>
> [ELSE (imperative statement(s))]

Note that the ELSE option will be performed if any of the stated conditions is not met.

Example

Suppose we wanted to perform PRINT-RTN if all of the following conditions are met:

A = B
C = D
E = F

otherwise we wish to perform STAR-1. That is, if one or more of these conditions are **not** met we wish to perform STAR-1. We may use a compound conditional for this:

> IF A = B AND C = D AND E = F PERFORM PRINT-RTN
>   ELSE PERFORM STAR-1.

If all conditions are met, PRINT-RTN is executed. If any condition is not met, STAR-1 is executed.

There are times when **both** the AND and OR are required within the same compound conditional.

Example

Write a routine to perform CALC-RTN if A is between 10 and 20, inclusive of the endpoints (including 10 and 20). Assume A is an independent item in WORKING-STORAGE.

On first sight, we might be inclined to use a compound conditional as follows:

```
IF A = 10 OR A = 11 OR A = 12 ... OR A = 20
    PERFORM CALC-RTN.
```

This statement, however, will function properly **only if** A **is an integer.** The number 10.3, for instance, is between 10 and 20, but it will not pass the above tests. For the same reason, we cannot say IF A > 9 AND A < 21 PERFORM CALC-RTN. If A is 9.8, it is **not** between 10 and 20 but it passes both tests. We want to branch to CALC-RTN if:

	(1)	A = 10
OR	(2)	A > 10 AND A < 20
OR	(3)	A = 20

Hence the statement: IF A = 10 OR A > 10 AND A < 20 OR A = 20 PERFORM CALC-RTN.

ORDER OF EVALUATION
OF COMPOUND
CONDITIONALS

When using both AND and OR in the same compound conditional, the order of evaluation of each condition becomes extremely important. For example, look at the following illustration:

> IF A = B OR C = D AND E = F PERFORM PARA-1.

Suppose A = 2, B = 2, C = 3, D = 4, E = 5, F = 6. Depending on the order of evaluation of the above conditions, PARA-1 may or may not be executed. Suppose the statement is evaluated as follows:

I.		(a) IF A = B OR C = D
	AND	(b) E = F

If this is the order of evaluation, there are two ways that PARA-1 will be executed: (1) A = B and E = F or (2) C = D and E = F. Since E does not equal F this evaluation indicates that no branch will occur.

II.		(a) A = B
	OR	(b) C = D AND E = F

If this is the order of evaluation, there are two ways that PARA-1 will be executed: (1) A = B or (2) C = D and E = F. Since the first condition, A = B, is met, this evaluation indicates that the PERFORM will occur.

Hence, with one interpretation PARA-1 is executed, and with another, it is not. It should be clear, at this point, that only one of these evaluations will prove to be accurate.

Now that the significance of the order of evaluation is clear, the hierarchy rule is as follows:

HIERARCHY RULE

1. Conditions surrounding the word AND are evaluated first.
2. Conditions surrounding the word OR are evaluated last.
3. When there are several AND connectors or OR connectors, the AND conditions are evaluated first, as they appear in the statement, from left to right. Then the OR conditions are evaluated, also from left to right.

In the above example, the conditions are evaluated as follows:

      (a) IF C = D AND E = F

OR   (b) A = B

Thus, with the given contents in the fields, PARA-1 will be executed, since A = B.

Example

We want to print A if A is between 10 and 100, inclusive. This is often written mathematically as $10 \leq A \leq 100$; if 10 is less than or equal to A and, at the same time, A is less than or equal to 100, then we wish to print A.

The problem is to determine if the following statement will perform the proper test:

> IF A < 100 OR A = 100 AND A = 10 OR A > 10 PERFORM PRINT-RTN.

Using the hierarchy rule for evaluating compound conditionals, the first conditions to be considered are those surrounding the AND. Then, from left to right, those surrounding the OR groupings are evaluated. Thus, we have:

      (1) IF A = 100 AND A = 10

OR   (2) A < 100

OR   (3) A > 10

We see that the compound expression in (1) is an impossibility; the value for A can never equal 10 and, at the same time, be equal to 100. Since the first expression will never cause a branch, it can be eliminated from the statement, which reduces to:

```
 7 8      12      16      20      24      28      32      36      40      44      48
         I F   A   <   1 Ø Ø   O R   A   >   1 Ø   P E R F O R M   P R I N T - R T N .
```

This, obviously, is not the solution to the original problem. In fact, **all** values for A will cause PRINT-RTN to be executed. If A > 100 it will cause PRINT-RTN to be performed since it passes the test: A > 10. If A < 10 it will cause PRINT-RTN to be executed since it passes the test: A < 100.

The original statement would have been correct if we could change the order of evaluation. If the following hierarchy were utilized, the statement would be correct:

      (1) IF A < 100 OR A = 100

AND (2) A = 10 OR A > 10

To change the normal order of evaluation, place parentheses around the conditions you want to be evaluated together. **Parentheses supersede the hierarchy rule**—all conditions within parentheses are evaluated together. Thus the following statement is correct:

```
 7 8      12      16      20      24      28      32      36      40      44      48      52      56
         I F   ( A   <   1 Ø Ø   O R   A   =   1 Ø Ø )   A N D   ( A   =   1 Ø   O R   A   >   1 Ø )
               P E R F O R M   P R I N T - R T N .
```

When in doubt about the normal sequence of evaluation, make use of the parentheses.

NEGATING COMPOUND CONDITIONALS

A common pitfall, which is to be avoided, arises in negating compound conditionals.

Example

Write a routine to perform SOUTH if A is not equal to 7 or 8; otherwise perform NORTH. We can write this as follows:

```
        IF A IS EQUAL TO 7 OR A IS EQUAL TO 8
           PERFORM NORTH ELSE PERFORM SOUTH.
```

But suppose we want to use the negative situation. On first thought, the following may seem appropriate:

```
     IF A IS NOT EQUAL TO 7 OR A IS NOT EQUAL TO 8
        PERFORM SOUTH ELSE PERFORM NORTH.
```

An evaluation of this statement will show that it is **not** correct. One of two conditions must exist for SOUTH to be executed:

(a) A IS NOT EQUAL TO 7
OR (b) A IS NOT EQUAL TO 8

Suppose A is 6; SOUTH will be executed, which is what we want. If A = 7, however, we wish NORTH to be executed. In the above conditional, condition (a) is not met since A does equal 7. However, condition (b) **is** met since A **is not equal to 8,** but is equal to 7. Only one condition needs to be satisfied for SOUTH to be executed, and since condition (b) is satisfied, SOUTH will be executed. Similarly, suppose A = 8. We want NORTH to be executed, but again we will see that SOUTH is executed. Condition (a) is satisfied, A is not equal to 7 (it is equal to 8). Since one condition is satisfied, SOUTH is executed. In fact, you can now see that the statement will always cause SOUTH to be executed, regardless of the contents of A.

The "moral" of this illustration is a lesson in **Boolean algebra,** which must be understood in negating compound conditionals. When negating conditions separated by OR: IF NOT (CONDITION1 OR CONDITION2 . . .), the stated conditions become: IF NOT CONDITION1 **AND** NOT CONDITION2 . . .
Hence, the IF statement could read as IF NOT (A = 7 OR A = 8) or as:

```
     IF A IS NOT EQUAL TO 7 AND A IS NOT EQUAL TO 8
        PERFORM SOUTH ELSE PERFORM NORTH.
```

Note that the IF statement can be written in sentence form extending from one line to another. A preferred form, which is used for the sake of clarity, follows:

IF   (condition)
              [statements—one per line, indented]
      ELSE
              [statements—one per line, indented].

Example

```
IF GROSS-PAY > TOTAL
    ADD 50.00 TO COMMISSION
    MULTIPLY GROSS-PAY BY TAX GIVING TOT1
ELSE
    ADD 25.00 TO COMMISSION.
```

PREFERRED FORMAT

SELF-EVALUATING QUIZ

What, if anything, is wrong with the following entries (1–5)? Correct all errors.

1. IF A = B OR IF A = C PERFORM RTN-X.
   *****
   The word IF should appear only once in the statement:
   IF A = B OR A = C PERFORM RTN-X.
2. IF B = 3 OR 4 PERFORM RTN-X.
   *****
   Nothing—implied operands are permitted. The above is the same as: IF B = 3 OR B = 4 PERFORM RTN-X.
3. If C < A + B PERFORM STEP-5.
   *****
   Each element in a condition must be a data name. A + B is an arithmetic expression. This should be: ADD A TO B. IF C < B PERFORM STEP-5.
4. If A < 21 OR A = 21 AND A = 5 OR A > 5 PERFORM RTN-1.
   *****
   There should be parentheses around elements to make the statement logical: IF (A < 21 OR A = 21) AND (A = 5 OR A > 5) PERFORM RTN-1.
5. IF A IS NOT EQUAL TO 3 OR A IS NOT EQUAL TO 4 PERFORM RTN-X.
   *****
   A branch to RTN-X will always occur. This should read:
   IF A IS NOT EQUAL TO 3 **AND** A IS NOT EQUAL TO 4
   PERFORM RTN-X.
6. The hierarchy rule for evaluating compound conditionals states that conditions surrounding the word _____ are evaluated first, followed by the conditions surrounding the word _____.
   *****
   AND
   OR
7. Indicate whether the following two statements are equivalent:
(a) IF A < 3 OR A > 4 PERFORM ERR-RTN.
(b) IF A IS NOT EQUAL TO 3 AND A IS NOT EQUAL TO 4
    PERFORM ERR-RTN.
   *****
   Only if A is an integer field.

8. Write a single statement to PERFORM PARA-5 if A is between 3 and 13, inclusive.

*****

IF A = 13 OR A < 13 AND A > 3 OR A = 3 PERFORM PARA-5.

(*NOTE*: This is **not** the only way to write the statement. Note, too, that there is no need for parentheses, but including them would be OK.)

9. Write a single statement to execute PARA-5 if A is between 3 and 13, exclusive of endpoints.

*****

IF A > 3 AND A < 13 PERFORM PARA-5.

10. Write a single statement to code the following steps: If the conditions below are met, perform PARA-3, otherwise perform PARA-2:

A = B
C = D
E = F

*****

IF A = B AND C = D AND E = F PERFORM PARA-3 ELSE PERFORM PARA-2.

PRACTICE PROBLEM— WITH SOLUTION

Write a program to print out patient name and diagnosis for each of the following input medical cards:

1–20 Patient name

21 Lung infection	{ 1-if found
	0-if not found
22 Temperature	{ 1-high
	0-normal
23 Sniffles	{ 1-present
	0-absent
24 Sore throat	{ 1-present
	0-absent

25–80 Not used

NOTES:

(a) Output is a printed report with heading: DIAGNOSIS REPORT.
(b) If patient has lung infection and temperature, diagnosis is PNEUMONIA.
(c) If the patient has a combination of two or more symptoms (except the combination of lung infection and temperature), the diagnosis is COLD.
(d) If the patient has any single symptom, the diagnosis is PHONY.

See Figure 10.2 for solution.

REVIEW QUESTIONS

True False

I. True-False Questions

☐ ☐ 1. In a compound conditional, statements surrounding the word AND are evaluated first.

☐ ☐ 2. The phrase ELSE NEXT SENTENCE can always be eliminated from conditional statements without changing the meaning.

☐ ☐ 3. The clause IF A IS POSITIVE is the converse of the clause IF A IS NEGATIVE.

```
IDENTIFICATION DIVISION.
PROGRAM-ID. CHAPT10.
ENVIRONMENT DIVISION.
CONFIGURATION SECTION.
SOURCE-COMPUTER. IBM-370.
OBJECT-COMPUTER. IBM-370.
INPUT-OUTPUT SECTION.
FILE-CONTROL.
    SELECT MEDICAL-FILE ASSIGN TO UR-S-SYSIN.
    SELECT DIAGNOSIS-REPORT ASSIGN TO UR-S-SYSOUT.
DATA DIVISION.
FILE SECTION.
FD  MEDICAL-FILE
    LABEL RECORDS ARE OMITTED
    RECORD CONTAINS 80 CHARACTERS
    DATA RECORD IS REC-IN.
01  REC-IN.
    02   PATIENT-NAME          PIC X(20).
    02   LUNG-INFECTION        PIC 9.
    02   TEMPERATURE           PIC 9.
    02   SNIFFLES              PIC 9.
    02   SORE-THROAT           PIC 9.
    02   FILLER                PIC X(56).
FD  DIAGNOSIS-REPORT
    LABEL RECORDS ARE OMITTED
    RECORD CONTAINS 133 CHARACTERS
    DATA RECORDS ARE HEADER, DETAIL-LINE.
01  HEADER.
    02   FILLER                PIC X(59).
    02   LITERAL1              PIC X(16).
    02   FILLER                PIC X(58).
01  DETAIL-LINE.
    02   FILLER                PIC X(26).
    02   NAME                  PIC X(20).
    02   FILLER                PIC X(20).
    02   DIAGNOSIS             PIC X(20).
    02   FILLER                PIC X(47).
WORKING-STORAGE SECTION.
01  WORK-AREAS.
    02   EOF                   PIC 9 VALUE 0.
PROCEDURE DIVISION.
    OPEN INPUT MEDICAL-FILE, OUTPUT DIAGNOSIS-REPORT.
    MOVE SPACES TO HEADER.
    MOVE 'DIAGNOSIS REPORT' TO LITERAL1.
    WRITE HEADER.
    MOVE SPACES TO DETAIL-LINE.
    READ MEDICAL-FILE AT END MOVE 1 TO EOF.
    PERFORM CALC-RTN UNTIL EOF = 1.
    CLOSE MEDICAL-FILE, DIAGNOSIS-REPORT.
    STOP RUN.
CALC-RTN.
    ADD LUNG-INFECTION, TEMPERATURE, SNIFFLES TO SORE-THROAT.
    IF SORE-THROAT > 1
            MOVE 'COLD' TO DIAGNOSIS
    ELSE
            MOVE 'PHONY' TO DIAGNOSIS.
    IF TEMPERATURE = 1 AND LUNG-INFECTION = 1
            MOVE 'PNEUMONIA' TO DIAGNOSIS.
    MOVE PATIENT-NAME TO NAME.
    WRITE DETAIL-LINE.
    READ MEDICAL-FILE AT END MOVE 1 TO EOF.
```

Figure 10.2

☐ ☐   4. The clause IF A IS NUMERIC is the converse of the clause IF A IS ALPHA-
            BETIC.

☐ ☐   5. Data fields being compared in an IF statement must always be the same
            size.

☐ ☐ 6. At least one space must precede and follow every symbol such as <, >, =.

☐ ☐ 7. Comparing numeric fields to nonnumeric literals can cause erroneous results.

☐ ☐ 8. The class test is frequently used before an arithmetic operation to ensure the validity of numeric data.

☐ ☐ 9. The hierarchy of operations in a compound conditional can be overridden by parentheses.

☐ ☐ 10. The symbol < may be used in place of 'IS GREATER THAN' in a conditional.

II. General Questions

Code the following flowchart exercises with a single statement (1–3).

1.
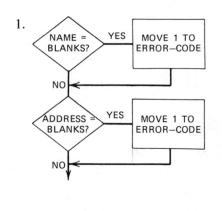

2.
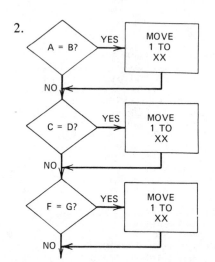

3.
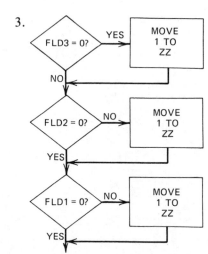

State whether FIELDA is equal to, greater than, or less than FIELDB (4–8):

	FIELDA	FIELDB
4.	012	12
5.	12.0	12
6.	−89.0	89.0
7.	ABC	ABCb
8.	43	+43

9. Write a routine for determining FICA where a field called SALARY is given. FICA is equal to 6.13% of SALARY up to $25,900. Salary in excess of $25,900 is not taxed.

10. Find the largest of four numbers A, B, C, and D and place it in the field called HOLD-IT.

Are the following groups of statements equivalent (11–14)?

11. (a) IF A = B ADD C TO D ELSE ADD E TO F. PERFORM RTN-1.
    (b) IF A = B ADD C TO D PERFORM RTN-1 ELSE ADD E TO F.

12. (a) IF A IS POSITIVE PERFORM RTN-X ELSE PERFORM RTN-Y.
    (b) IF A IS NOT NEGATIVE PERFORM RTN-X ELSE PERFORM RTN-Y.
13. (a) IF DISCOUNT IS GREATER THAN TOTAL PERFORM ERR-RTN ELSE SUBTRACT DISCOUNT FROM TOTAL.
    (b) IF TOTAL IS GREATER THAN DISCOUNT OR TOTAL = DISCOUNT NEXT SENTENCE ELSE PERFORM ERR-RTN. SUBTRACT DISCOUNT FROM TOTAL.
14. (a) IF A = B ADD C TO D PERFORM RTN-5 ELSE PERFORM RTN-5.
    (b) IF A = B ADD C TO D. PERFORM RTN-5.

What, if anything, is wrong with the following statements (15–20)?

15. IF A IS GREATER THAN OR EQUAL TO B PERFORM RTN-3.
16. IF A IS NOT EQUAL TO B OR A IS NOT EQUAL TO C PERFORM RTN-4.
17. IF A DOES NOT EQUAL 5 PERFORM STEP-3.
18. IF A = 3 OR IF A = 4 PERFORM RTN-2.
19. IF A = '123' PERFORM BEGIN.
20. IF B = '123' OR B = 21 PERFORM END1.
21. Write a routine to execute a paragraph called NO-TEMP if C is between 98.6 and 100.2 inclusive.

PROBLEMS Because of the importance of conditional statements, an extended list of problems has been included.

1. Write a program to create output tape records from the following input tape:

   1–34 Identifying data
   35–39 Sales amount xxx.xx
      40 Not used

   The output record format is as follows:

   1–34 Same as input
   35–39 Sales amount xxx.xx
   40–41 Discount % .xx
   42–46 Discount amount xxx.xx
   47–51 Net xxx.xx
   52–75 Not used

   NOTES:
   (a) Both files have standard labels and are blocked 10.
   (b) If sales exceed $100.00, allow 3% discount.
       If sales are $100.00 or less, allow 2% discount.
   (c) Discount amount = Sales × Discount %.
   (d) Net = Sales − Discount amount.

2. Write a program for a dating service that uses the following format for its input data:

Card Input

1–20 Name
21–23 Weight (in lbs.)
24–25 Height (in inches)
  26 Color of eyes: 1-Blue, 2-Brown, 3-Other
  27 Color of hair: 1-Blonde, 2-Brown, 3-Other
28–79 Not used
  80 Sex: M-male, F-female

Output is on punched cards with the names of all:

(a) Blonde hair, blue-eyed males over 6 feet tall and weighing between 185 and 200 lbs.
(d) Brown eyed, brown hair females between 5 feet 2 inches and 5 feet 6 inches and weighing less than 120 lbs.

All other combinations should **not** be printed.

3. Write a program to generate, in effect, a compiler program. Input shall be punched cards with the following format:

ccs 1–2 Operation code
   3–12 First operand (field to be operated upon)
  13–22 Second operand
  23–80 Not used

Operation Codes

10 corresponds to ADD
20 corresponds to SUBTRACT
30 corresponds to MULTIPLY
40 corresponds to DIVIDE
50 corresponds to STOP RUN

Program should read in each input card, perform the required operation, and print the result. For example, an input card with 20 0000080000 0000010000 as its first 22 positions should result in the printing of 0000070000. (80000 − 10000)

(HINT: Make sure that the output field is large enough to accommodate the answer.)

4. Write a program to accept, as input, cards that have a date in Columns 1–6 in the form of month/day/year, i.e., 022580 refers to Feb. 25, 1980. If the date is valid, convert it to Julian date (year/day of year). (In the above example, the Julian date would be 80056.) Punch an output card with the resultant Julian date.

(HINT: Assume the program will be used for **20** years only, beginning with 1980. Leap years 1980, 1984, 1988, etc. have 29 days in FEB. All others have 28 days in FEB.)

5. Write a program to read a detail Bank Transaction Tape with the following format:

1–19 Name of depositor
  20 Type: 1-Previous balance, 2-Deposit, 3-Withdrawal
21–25 Account number
26–30 Amount xxxxx
31–50 Not used

The tape records are blocked 50 and have standard labels. The tape is in sequence by account number. Type 1 records exist for each account number followed by Types 2 and 3, if they exist. Types 2 and 3 may be present for a given account number and may appear in any sequence.

Print out the name of the depositor and his or her current balance (Previous Balance + Deposits − Withdrawals). Also print the heading BANK REPORT.

6. Write a program to print an inventory reorder form for each specified card input. Information on the inventory reorder form is obtained from the card record and its corresponding tape record. Input, then, consists of a detail card record and a master inventory tape record:

Card Input

ccs 1–10 Product name
      11–15 Product number
      16–80 Not used

Master Tape Input

 1–5 Product number
 6–15 Product name
16–20 Unit price xxx.xx
21–35 Name of vendor
block size is 10, standard labels

If an input card for a specific product exists, find the corresponding tape record and print PRODUCT NUMBER, PRODUCT NAME and NAME OF VENDOR. When there are no more cards, stop the run. Cards and tape are in product number sequence. Print the heading: INVENTORY REORDER FORM.

(HINT: A flowchart may be helpful before attempting to code the program.)

7. Write a program for a college bursar to compute for each semester:
(a) Tuition of each student.
(b) Total tuition for all students.

If a student is taking 12 credits or less, tuition is $75/credit.
If a student is taking more than 12 credits, the cost is $900.

Input: Student cards
 1–20 Student name
21–22 Number of credits
23–80 Not used

Output: Magnetic tape
       Blocking factor = 50

Record size = 40
Standard labels

1–20 Student name
21–22 Number of credits
23–25 Tuition
26–40 Not used

Print message TOTAL TUITION and the computed figure.

8. Write a program to summarize accident records to obtain the following information:

   (a) Percentage of drivers under 25.
   (b) Percentage of drivers who are female.
   (c) Percentage of drivers from New York.

   There is one tape record for each driver involved in an accident in the past year:

   1–4 Driver number
   5   State code (1 for New York)
   6–9 Birth date (Month and Year)
   10   Sex (M for male, F for female)
   Blocking factor = 50, standard labels

   Results should be printed with constants:

   % OF DRIVERS UNDER 25
   % OF DRIVERS WHO ARE FEMALE
   % OF DRIVERS FROM NY

9. Write a program to compute the number of $20, $10, $5, and $1 bills that an employee should be paid when his or her salary is provided as input.

   Input: Cards
   1–20 Employee name
   21–25 Salary
   26–80 Not used

   Output: Printed report with name and above data (also print messages, i.e, NO. OF 20's, etc.).

   (NOTE: Employee should be paid in **largest** denominations possible.)

10. Write a program to create a magnetic tape file from the following input card records:

    1–20 Employee name
    21–22 Hours worked
    23–25 Rate x.xx
    26–80 Not used

    Output: Blocked 10, standard labels
    1–20 Employee name
    21–25 Gross pay xxx.xx
    26–50 Not used

Gross pay = Regular hours × Rate + Overtime hours × 1.5 × Rate. Overtime hours are those hours exceeding 40.

11. Write a program to compute the arithmetic mean for an input file with the following format:

Card 1 for group:	1–5 Account number
	6–7 Number of cards in group
Remainder of cards for group:	1–5 Account number
	6–10 Amount xxx.xx

Print. Account number and arithmetic mean for each group.
Amount should be rounded to nearest integer.

12. Write a program to compute compound interest from the following input tape records:

1–20 Name of depositor		blocking factor = 20, standard
21–25 Principal	p_o	labels
26–27 Interest rate .xx	r	
28–29 Period	n	
30–35 Not used		

Output is a punched card with name of depositor and principal amount after n periods of investment (p_n).

Formula: $p_n = p_o (1 + r)^n$

$$\left[\text{HINT: } (1 + r)^n = \underbrace{(1 + r) \times (1 + r) \times (1 + r) \ldots \times (1 + r)}_{n \text{ times}} \right]$$

3 BASIC PRINT AND EDIT OPTIONS

CHAPTER 11

ADDITIONAL DATA DIVISION ENTRIES AND VALIDITY CHECKING ROUTINES

Thus far, we have discussed the basic entries of the DATA DIVISION, which would suffice for elementary level COBOL programs. There are, however, additional techniques that may be used in the DATA DIVISION to make coding easier and more efficient.

A. QUALIFICATION OF NAMES

You will recall that file names and record names must be unique within a COBOL program. If XXX is the name of a file defined in the SELECT clause of the ENVIRONMENT DIVISION, and described by an FD entry in the DATA DIVISION, then the same name, XXX, may **not** be used to define fields, work areas, or paragraph names. Similarly, independent WORKING-STORAGE items must be given unique names.

Programmer-supplied names, however, that define data fields within records need **not** be unique. The following DATA DIVISION entries, for example, are correct:

```
FD   CARD-IN
     LABEL RECORDS ARE OMITTED
     DATA RECORD IS CARD-REC.
01   CARD-REC.
     02   NAME            PIC  A(10).
     02   AMT             PIC  9(5).
     02   CDE             PIC  X(5).
     02   FILLER          PIC  X(60).
FD   TAPE-OUT
     LABEL RECORDS ARE STANDARD
     DATA RECORD IS TAPE-REC.
01   TAPE-REC.
     02   NAME            PIC  A(10).
     02   AMT             PIC  9(5).
     02   CDE             PIC  X(5).
```

CARD-IN and TAPE-OUT, as file names, must be unique. Similarly, CARD-REC and TAPE-REC, as record names, must also be unique. Note, however, that NAME, AMT and CDE, as data fields within records, need not be unique; that is, they may be used to define more than one area of storage.

In the PROCEDURE DIVISION, when accessing a data-name that is not unique, the name must be **qualified.** We must indicate which record is to be accessed. We cannot say, for example ADD AMT TO TOTAL, since AMT is the name of two different data fields and it is unclear which is to be added.

When more than one field in storage has the same name, we qualify the name in the PROCEDURE DIVISION as follows:

Examples

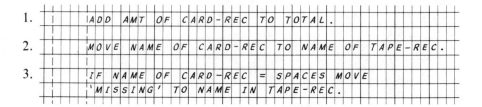

Whenever a name is used more than once in the DATA DIVISION, it must be qualified when it is processed in the PROCEDURE DIVISION. The words OF or IN may be used interchangeably to qualify a name.

The method of using the same data-name to define several fields in separate records is a useful programming tool. PROCEDURE DIVISION entries are easier to understand for someone reading the program, and easier to debug for the programmer, when qualification of names is utilized. To say MOVE AMT OF REC-IN TO AMT OF REC-OUT is relatively simple to understand. To say MOVE AMT1 TO AMT2, where AMT1 and AMT2 are uniquely defined fields in the input and output areas, respectively, is less clear. Although the latter involves less coding, the reader must consult the DATA DIVISION entries to determine what area of storage is being transmitted and which field will receive the data. That is, the location of AMT1 and AMT2 in storage is unclear. With the use of qualifiers, it is quite obvious that the amount fields are part of the input and output records.

Where a record contains several fields that are to be moved to another record, we can use the same field names along with the MOVE CORRESPOND-ING statement, as outlined in Chapter 7. In this way, qualification of names in the PROCEDURE DIVISION is unnecessary.

It is sometimes difficult to follow the logic of a program if its analysis requires constant reference to the DATA DIVISION. With the use of qualification of names, entries in the PROCEDURE DIVISION are often easier to follow.

A field may be qualified by using OF or IN with the record name **or** any group item:

```
01  REC-1.
    02  CODEX.
        03  SEX              PIC X.
        03  MARITAL-STATUS   PIC X.
        03  AGE              PIC 99.
```

If the data-name SEX is multiply defined in the DATA DIVISION, the SEX field described above may be accessed as:

SEX OF REC-1

or

SEX OF CODEX

> **SUMMARY**
> 1. File names, record names, and 77-level WORKING-STORAGE data-names must be unique.
> 2. Names that define data fields within records need not be unique.
> 3. The same name may define several different areas in the DATA DIVISION.
> 4. Each time these fields are accessed in the PROCEDURE DIVISION, however, they must be qualified.
> 5. The format used to qualify a field is:
>
> data-name $\left[\dfrac{OF}{IN} \right] \left\{ \begin{matrix} \text{record-name} \\ \text{group-item} \end{matrix} \right\}$

B. JUSTIFIED RIGHT CLAUSE

Suppose we define a field in the WORKING-STORAGE SECTION as follows:

```
01  WORK-AREAS.
    02  CODE-1  PIC X(8) VALUE 'ABC'.
```

This entry performs the same operation as MOVE 'ABC' TO CODE-1, where CODE-1 has no VALUE clause. Since the literal is three positions long and the field is defined as eight positions, 'ABC' will be **left justified** in the field. You will recall that when sending fields or literals are smaller than receiving fields in alphanumeric move operations, data is left justified in the receiving field and low-order positions are filled with spaces. Thus CODE-1 will have contents of  .

For specific applications, it is sometimes desirable to **right justify** data within a field. That is, we wish to obtain in CODE-1 | | | | | | A | B | C | .

A JUSTIFIED RIGHT clause, used in the DATA DIVISION, will produce the desired result. CODE-1 may be defined as follows:

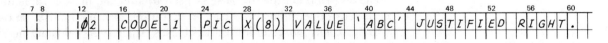

Thus JUSTIFIED RIGHT may be used in the DATA DIVISION to alter the normal rules for alphanumeric move operations. Normally alphanumeric fields are left justified; the above clause, used in an alphanumeric field, will cause data, which contains fewer characters than the receiving field, to be placed in the rightmost positions of a field, and all nonfilled high-order positions to be replaced with blanks or spaces.

The JUSTIFIED RIGHT clause may be specified for any elementary, **nonnumeric** data field. The clause is placed after the PICTURE is defined, and the VALUE, if any, assigned.

To say MOVE 'C' TO FLD1, where FLD1 is defined as

02 FLD1 PICTURE XXX JUSTIFIED RIGHT.

will result in [| | C] being placed in FLD1. Thus a JUSTIFIED RIGHT clause implies that any VALUE given to the field or any data moved into the field will **not** conform to the normal alphanumeric rules. All data placed in the field will, instead, be right justified.

The JUSTIFIED RIGHT clause is often used in a print area. Let us define a print record as follows:

```
01  PRINT-REC.
    02    FILLER        PICTURE X(61).
    02    HEADER        PICTURE X(12).
    02    FILLER        PICTURE X(60).
```

In the PROCEDURE DIVISION, the following instructions are coded:

```
    MOVE SPACES TO PRINT-REC.
    MOVE 'COMPANY ABCD' TO HEADER.
    WRITE PRINT-REC.
```

In this way, we obtain the heading 'COMPANY ABCD' in the center of the form with 60 spaces on each side of it. We can, however, simplify the DATA DIVISION entries as follows:

```
01  PRINT-REC.
    02    HEADER        PICTURE X(73)    JUSTIFIED RIGHT.
    02    FILLER        PICTURE X(60).
```

Using the same PROCEDURE DIVISION as above, we obtain the identical results. 'COMPANY ABCD' will be placed in the 12 rightmost positions of HEADER, leaving 60 high-order, or leftmost, blanks. Thus we have defined our record with two fields instead of three.

The JUSTIFIED RIGHT clause is used to alter the normal rules for alphanumeric move operations. The clause, therefore, may **not** be used in conjunction with fields with numeric PICTURE clauses, since such fields are normally right justified.

SELF-EVALUATING
QUIZ

1. Qualification of names is required in the PROCEDURE DIVISION when _____.
   *****
   the same name is used to define two or more areas of storage
2. Record names and file names must be _____ but _____ need not be unique.
   *****
   unique
   field or data-names
3. The words _____ and _____ may be used interchangeably to qualify a data-name.
   *****
   OF
   IN
4. If an alphanumeric sending field contains fewer characters than an alphanumeric receiving field, the data is ordinarily _____ justified in the field and remaining positions are filled with _____.
   *****
   left
   blanks
5. To alter the normal rules for alphanumeric move operations, a _____ clause may be used.
   *****
   JUSTIFIED RIGHT
6. The JUSTIFIED RIGHT clause may not be used with _____ fields.
   *****
   numeric
7. The JUSTIFIED RIGHT clause follows the _____ clause and the _____ clause, if any, in the _____ DIVISION.
   *****
   PICTURE
   VALUE
   DATA
8. 02 FLDA PICTURE XXXX VALUE 'ABC' will result in _____ in FLDA.
   *****
   ABCⱶ
9. To cause ⱶABC to be placed in the above field, _____ will be the DATA DIVISION entry.
   *****
   02 FLDA PICTURE XXXX VALUE 'ABC' JUSTIFIED RIGHT.
10. 02 FLDB PICTURE XXXXX VALUE '123' JUSTIFIED RIGHT will result in _____ in FLDB.
    *****
    ⱶⱶ123

C. REDEFINES CLAUSE

It is sometimes necessary to define a single field in the DATA DIVISION in **two** or more distinct ways. If the same area is to be used for different purposes, it must be **redefined** in the DATA DIVISION.

Suppose a card record has the following format:

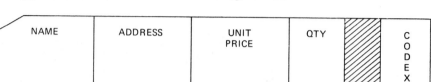

where CODE-X = 1, designating a debit record. For cards with CODE-X = 0, designating a credit record, the following format applies:

To describe these records we could establish two distinct record formats in the FD as follows:

```
FD   CARD-FILE
     LABEL RECORDS ARE OMITTED,
     DATA RECORDS ARE DB-REC, CR-REC.
01   DB-REC.
     02   NAME              PIC X(10).
     02   ADDRESS-1         PIC X(15).
     02   UNIT-PRICE        PIC 9(5).
     02   QTY               PIC 9(5).
     02   FILLER            PIC X(44).
     02   CODE-X            PIC 9.
01   CR-REC.
     02   NAME              PIC X(10).
     02   ADDRESS-1         PIC X(15).
     02   AMT-OF-CREDIT     PIC 999V99.
     02   QTY               PIC 9(5).
     02   FILLER            PIC X(44).
     02   CODE-X            PIC 9.
```

Note that the two records occupy the **same** 80-position storage area. The first record specifies the characteristics of the fields; the second record merely redefines this same area using its own specifications. In the PROCEDURE DIVISION, we can test CODE-X; if it is a 1, we use the format of DB-REC; if it is 0, we use the format of CR-REC. In COBOL, it is possible to simplify the above File Description by specifying a **single** record format and merely **redefining** the one area that differs depending on the code.

```
FD   CARD-FILE
     LABEL RECORDS ARE OMITTED,
     DATA RECORD IS IN-REC.
01   IN-REC.
     02   NAME              PIC X(10).
     02   ADDRESS-1         PIC X(15).
     02   UNIT-PRICE        PIC 9(5).
     02   AMT-OF-CREDIT REDEFINES UNIT-PRICE PIC 999V99.
     02   QTY               PIC 9(5).
     02   FILLER            PIC X(44).
     02   CODE-X            PIC 9.
```

A REDEFINES clause in the DATA DIVISION allows the programmer to employ different specifications in defining a single field of storage:

(level-no) (data-name-1)   (PICTURE clause).
(same level-no) (data-name-2) REDEFINES (data-name-1) (PICTURE clause).

In the above, UNIT-PRICE and AMT-OF-CREDIT both refer to the **same** five positions of storage. In the PROCEDURE DIVISION, we will test CODE-X. If CODE-X = 0, we will use UNIT-PRICE as the field name with a five-position integer specification. If CODE-X = 0, we will use AMT-OF-CREDIT as the field name with three integer and two decimal positions.

```
IF CODE-X = 1 MULTIPLY UNIT-PRICE BY QTY
    GIVING TOTAL OF OUT-REC.
IF CODE-X = 0 MOVE AMT-OF-CREDIT TO TOTAL OF OUT-REC.
```

A REDEFINES clause may be used on any level 02-49. It may not be used on the 01 level in the FILE SECTION since records within a file are said to provide implicit redefinition. It may, however, be used on the 01 level in the WORKING-STORAGE SECTION.

If a specific level item is to be redefined, the second specification must be on the same level. The entry 03 FLD1 PIC X may be redefined only on the 03 level. Subdivision of entries being redefined is, however, permissible. The following, then, are valid representations:

Example 1

```
02   FLD1.
     03   FLD1A     PIC X(5).
     03   FLD1B     PIC 99.
02   FLD2  REDEFINES  FLD1,   PIC X(7).
```

Example 2

```
02   FLDX        PIC X(7).
02   FLDY   REDEFINES FLDX.
     03   FLDY1   PIC X(5).
     03   FLDY2   PIC 99.
```

In Example 1, we see that an entry to be redefined may be a group item with elementary subfields. Similarly, as is indicated in Example 2, an entry that redefines another field may contain subfield breakdowns. The only requirement is that if one field redefines another field, they must both be on the same level. In addition, the redefining field must **immediately** follow the field to be redefined with no intervening entries that define storage areas.

One last restriction on REDEFINES must be specified. A redefining entry may **not** contain a VALUE clause. For this reason, if initial values are desired in a storage area, they must be assigned in the **first** entry, **not** the entry that redefines it. Thus, the following is invalid:

Invalid

```
02   ITEM1    PIC 99.
02   ITEM-X   REDEFINES ITEM1   PIC XX   VALUE '12'.
```

Note, however, that the original 02-level entry may contain a VALUE:

Valid

```
02  ITEM1     PIC 99     VALUE 12.
02  ITEM-X    REDEFINES ITEM1 PIC XX.
```

As we have indicated, another important use of REDEFINES clauses is in describing a record that may have different field specifications. Consider the following record layouts:

DEBIT	CREDIT
1–20 NAME	1–20 NAME
21–25 AMT1	21–23 TOT1
26–30 AMT2	24–26 TOT2
80 CODE-1	27–30 TOT3
	80 CODE-1

We may define our FD for the card file as having two distinct record layouts:

```
FD  CARD-FILE
    LABEL RECORDS ARE OMITTED
    RECORD CONTAINS 80 CHARACTERS
    DATA RECORDS ARE DEBIT-REC, CREDIT-REC.
01  DEBIT-REC.
    02  NAME        PICTURE A(20).
    02  AMTS.
        03  AMT1    PICTURE 999V99.
        03  AMT2    PICTURE 999V99.
    02  FILLER      PICTURE X(49).
    02  CODE-1      PICTURE X.
01  CREDIT-REC.
    02  NAME        PICTURE X(20).
    02  TOTALS.
        03  TOT1    PICTURE 999.
        03  TOT2    PICTURE 999.
        03  TOT3    PICTURE 9999.
    02  FILLER      PICTURE X(49).
    02  CODE-1      PICTURE X.
```

With the use of a REDEFINES clause, however, it is also possible to code only **one** record layout:

```
FD  CARD-FILE
    LABEL RECORDS ARE OMITTED
    RECORD CONTAINS 80 CHARACTERS
    DATA RECORD IS REC-IN.
01  REC-IN.
    02  NAME        PICTURE A(20).
    02  AMTS.
        03  AMT1    PICTURE 999V99.
        03  AMT2    PICTURE 999V99.
    02  TOTAL REDEFINES AMTS.
        03  TOT1    PICTURE 999.
        03  TOT2    PICTURE 999.
        03  TOT3    PICTURE 9999.
    02  FILLER      PICTURE X(49).
    02  CODE-1      PICTURE X.
```

In this way, only **one** record description is required. AMTS, within the record, is subdivided into two amount fields. We will consider that the record contains this two subfield breakdown when CODE-1 = 1. If CODE-1 = 0, the record contains TOTAL, which occupies the same storage area and is broken down into three total fields. Thus with a REDEFINES clause, only one record layout is required.

When the same area of storage is used for different purposes, a REDEFINES clause is necessary. We may redefine a field in two basic ways:

1. When specifying the mode or type of field in two different ways (a field may be defined numerically for one purpose and alphanumerically for another).
2. When specifying the subfields or elementary-level items in distinct ways (a group item may consist of three elementary items for one purpose and four elementary items for another).

D. ADDITIONAL PICTURE SPECIFICATIONS FOR NUMERIC FIELDS

Thus far, PICTURE specifications for numeric fields may contain (1) 9's to denote numeric data and (2) V to denote implied decimal points. With the above two specifications only, all numeric data will be considered **unsigned**. Unless the computer is instructed to maintain an operational sign on a field, that field will be considered unsigned and thus negative numbers may not be recognized as such.

OPERATIONAL SIGNS

When the possibility exists that negative numbers may be placed in a field, we must instruct the computer to maintain a sign on the field. We do this by including an S in the PICTURE clause of numeric fields. The S, which instructs the computer to retain the sign of all numbers, is always the **first** character in a PICTURE clause and does **not** add to the size of the field. 02 AMT PICTURE S999V99 is a **five**-position numeric field which will be considered signed, and which has an implied decimal point after the first three digits.

An S in the PICTURE clause of a numeric field is essential when data may contain signed numbers. Without the S, the operational sign of the number is dropped. Consider the following example:

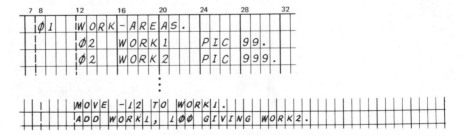

Since WORK1 is not signed, **12** and not −12 is placed in the field. The negative sign is not transmitted unless an S exists in the PICTURE clause of the receiving field. Thus the ADD operation will result in 112 in WORK2. If WORK1 were defined to include the sign as:

```
        Ø2    WORK1      PIC  S99.
```

the ADD operation would then correctly result in 088 in WORK2.

Similarly, to say, IF (data-name) IS NEGATIVE . . . is a valid conditional only if the data-name specified is numeric and allows for a sign in its PICTURE clause. If no S exists in the PICTURE clause, the number will always be considered unsigned and the condition will never be met. Unsigned numbers are always considered to contain positive quantities. In the following:

7 8		12	16	20	24	28	32	36	40	44
		MOVE	-10	TO	FLDX.					
		IF FLDX	IS	NEGATIVE	PERFORM	RTN-1.				

FLDX will be negative only if it has an S in its PICTURE clause.

Numeric quantities on punched cards are signed by having **zone** punches over the units, or rightmost, position of the field. To denote a minus sign on a card field, an 11-zone is placed over the units position of the field. 28J, punched in a numeric card field, will be interpreted as 28$\overline{1}$ (11-zone and a 1-punch in units positions). A 12-zone over the units position of a field denotes a plus sign. 28D will be interpreted as 28$\overset{+}{4}$ (12-zone and 4-punch in units position). If a numeric field on a card contains a sign in the units position, an S must be employed in the PICTURE clause of that field to retain the sign.

Suppose input card data has an amount field in card columns 1-5 that may contain a sign. It would be written as:

7 8		12	16	20	24	28	32	36
	01	CARD-REC.						
		02	AMT	PICTURE	S9(5).			

The field will occupy the first **five** positions of the card record. Without the S, 3821K would be transmitted as 38212. With the S, 3821K would be transmitted as 3821$\overline{2}$.

SUMMARY—S IN PICTURE CLAUSE

1. An S in the PICTURE clause of a numeric field must be used to denote signed numbers.
2. Without an S in the PICTURE clause, a numeric field will be considered unsigned.
3. The S does not add to the size of the field—that is, PICTURE S99 denotes a two-position signed field.
4. It is generally more efficient to include an S in the PICTURE clause of all numeric fields.

ASSUMED ZEROS   The character P in a PICTURE clause of a numeric field represents a digit position that is treated as if it contained a zero. Each P in the PICTURE clause denotes an assumed zero.

P's are used to position the assumed decimal point a fixed number of positions from the actual number. Suppose we wish the computer to interpret 25 as 25000; the PICTURE clause would be as follows:

```
  12      16      20      24      28      32      36
|Ø|2| |A|M|T| | | | |P|I|C|T|U|R|E| |9|9|P|P|.| | |
```

To say MOVE 25 TO AMT results in 25000 in the AMT field.

Note that the above field will accept only **two** positions of numeric data. The number of 9's in a PICTURE clause of a numeric field denotes the number of characters that may be placed in that field. Since there are two 9's in the field, only two positions of data will be accepted. The computer will substitute a zero for each P in the PICTURE. Thus AMT will be assumed by the computer to contain 25000.

To say DIVIDE 250 INTO AMT GIVING TOTAL, where TOTAL has a PICTURE of 999, will result in 100 in the latter field.

Consider the following PICTURE clause:

```
7 8     12      16      20      24      28      32      36      40
| | | | |Ø|2| |A|M|T|-|2| | |P|I|C|T|U|R|E| |V|P|P|P|9|9|.| | |
```

To move .25 to AMT-2 would result in AMT-2 being interpreted as containing .00025. Note that P's are used to position the assumed decimal point a fixed number of positions from the actual number being transmitted.

Example

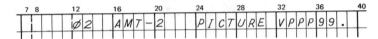

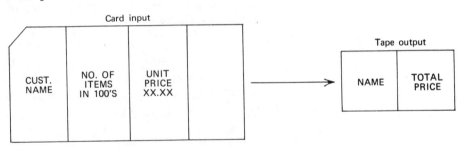

The DATA DIVISION entries are as follows:

```
DATA DIVISION.
FILE SECTION.
FD  CARD-FILE
    LABEL RECORDS OMITTED
    DATA RECORD IS CARD-REC.
Ø1  CARD-REC.
    Ø2  CUST-NAME      PICTURE A(2Ø).
    Ø2  NO-OF-ITEMS    PICTURE 99PP.
    Ø2  UNIT-PRICE     PICTURE 99V99.
    Ø2  FILLER         PICTURE X(54).
FD  TAPE-FILE
    LABEL RECORDS ARE STANDARD
    DATA RECORD IS TAPE-REC.
Ø1  TAPE-REC.
    Ø2  NAME           PICTURE A(2Ø).
    Ø2  TOTAL-PRICE    PICTURE 9(6).
```

Note that NO-OF-ITEMS contains two assumed zeros. If the two-position field on the card contains 35, for example, the computer will interpret this as 3500. Since the card field denotes hundreds of items, this would be a correct interpretation.

The arithmetic operation in the PROCEDURE DIVISION would be as follows:

SUMMARY—P IN PICTURE CLAUSE

1. Each P in a PICTURE clause establishes an assumed position in the data field.
2. P's can be used to assume integer positions. For example, PIC 99PPP will accept two integers, 25, and represent them as 1000's—25000.
3. P's can be used to assume decimal positions. For example, PIC VPPP99 will accept two decimal positions, 25, and represent them as .00025.

E. CONDITION-NAMES

Condition-names are programmer-supplied names established in the DATA DIVISION that may facilitate processing in the PROCEDURE DIVISION. A condition-name gives a name to a specific value that a data item can assume. In the DATA DIVISION, it is coded on the special level, 88. All 88-level entries are condition-names that denote values of specific data items. Consider the following example:

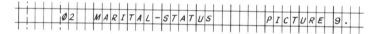

Suppose that 1 in the field called MARITAL-STATUS denotes single status. We may use a condition-name SINGLE to indicate this value:

When the field called MARITAL-STATUS is equal to 1, we will call that condition SINGLE. The 88-level item is not the name of a **field** but the name of a **condition.** The 88-level item refers only to the elementary item directly preceding it. SINGLE is a condition-name applied to the field called MARITAL-STATUS, since MARITAL-STATUS directly precedes the 88-level item. The condition SINGLE exists if MARITAL-STATUS = 1.

A condition-name conforms to the rules for forming programmer-supplied names. It is always coded on the 88 level and has only a VALUE clause associated with it. Since a condition-name is **not** the name of a data field, it will **not** contain a PICTURE clause.

The following is the format for 88-level items:

---

88 (condition-name) <u>VALUE</u> (literal).

The condition-name refers only to the elementary item preceding it and must therefore be unique. The VALUE of the condition-name must be a literal consistent with the data type of the preceding field:

The above is a **valid** statement since the value is a **nonnumeric** literal and the field is defined alphanumerically. An **incorrect** form is:

Invalid:

```
02    FLDX            PICTURE XX.
88    CONDITIONA      VALUE 12.
```

Condition-names refer only to **elementary** items in the DATA DIVISION. The data item to which the condition-name refers must contain a PICTURE clause. 77 and 01-49 level items in the WORKING-STORAGE SECTION may have condition-names associated with them.

Condition-names are defined in the DATA DIVISION to facilitate processing in the PROCEDURE DIVISION. A condition-name test is an alternative method of expressing a simple relational in the PROCEDURE DIVISION. Using the following DATA DIVISION entries:

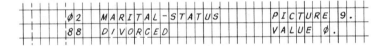

we may use **either** of the following tests in the PROCEDURE DIVISION:

or

The condition-name DIVORCED will test to determine if MARITAL-STATUS does, in fact, have a value of 0.

We may use several condition names for one data field:

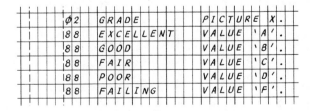

Assuming that the above values are the only valid ones, a PROCEDURE

DIVISION test may be as follows:

7 8	12	16	20	24	28	32	36	40	44	48	52	56	60
	IF	EXCELLENT	OR	GOOD	OR	FAIR	OR	POOR					
	OR	FAILING	NEXT	SENTENCE	ELSE	PERFORM	ERROR-RTN.						

Note that we may also say, IF NOT FAILING PERFORM PASS-RTN.

Condition-names may be used in the PROCEDURE DIVISION, at the discretion of the programmer, for ease of programming. There are some instances, however, where the use of condition-names is required. An overflow condition that tests for the end of a page, for example, may only be tested with a condition-name. This is discussed more fully in Chapter 13.

Condition-names are frequently used in coding PERFORM . . . UNTIL instructions:

Example

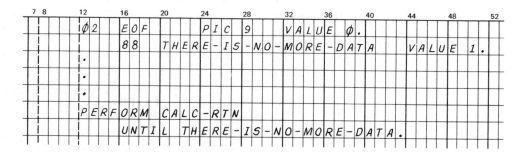

7 8	12	16	20	24	28	32	36	40	44	48	52
	Ø2	EOF		PIC	9	VALUE	Ø.				
		88	THERE-IS-NO-MORE-DATA				VALUE	1.			
	.										
	.										
	.										
	PERFORM	CALC-RTN									
		UNTIL	THERE-IS-NO-MORE-DATA.								

Using the condition-name THERE-IS-NO-MORE-DATA is more meaningful than simply comparing EOF to 1.

SUMMARY—CONDITION-NAMES
1. 88-level items are used to represent condition-names.
2. A condition-name specifies the value that a data item can assume.
3. The format is as follows:

> 88 (condition-name) <u>VALUE</u> (literal).

4. The 88-level item refers only to the elementary item directly preceding it:

    02   ITEM1   PIC 9.
    88   ABC   VALUE 8.

    .

    .

    .

    IF ABC PERFORM NEXT-RTN.

F. VALIDITY CHECKS

One of the major problem areas in computer processing is the handling of erroneous input data. Most programs are required to have some built-in checking routine to determine if important input fields contain valid data. It is not usually possible to determine if an input record contains **correct** data, but we can determine if the data meets certain prescribed criteria. COBOL programs, then, are frequently required to include **validity checks,** which are routines (1) to ensure that the data entered conforms to certain requirements, and (2) to minimize the processing of erroneous input.

Typical validity checks include the following:

TYPICAL VALIDITY CHECKS

1. Determine if numeric data fields do, in fact, contain numeric data. The CLASS test is used:

   ```
   IF (data-name) IS NUMERIC . . .
   ```

2. Determine if alphabetic data fields do, in fact, contain alphabetic data. The CLASS test is used:

   ```
   IF (data-name) IS ALPHABETIC . . . .
   ```

3. Determine if specified fields are within established limits—this is called a limit test.
   Example: SALARY field will satisfy a limit if it is between 05000 and 95000, for example. That is, if $5000 is the lowest salary and $95000 is the highest salary at the specific company, no salary should be outside these limits.

4. Determine if specified fields contain valid codes or values. Usually a condition-code is used to help document such routines.
   Example:

   ```
   02   MODEL-CAR        PIC 9.
        88   COUPE        VALUE 1.
        88   SEDAN        VALUE 2.
        88   CONVERTIBLE  VALUE 3.
             .
             .

   IF COUPE OR SEDAN OR CONVERTIBLE
        NEXT SENTENCE
   ELSE
        PERFORM ERROR-RTN.
   ```

5. Determine if specified fields are reasonable.
   Example: If employee birth date is entered as MO/YR (month/year), YR would normally be invalid if less than 01 or greater than 65, for example. A person born before 01 (1901) would be more than 79 years old; a person born after 65 (1965) would be under 15 years old, if the current year is 80.

Note that we may be as sophisticated as we like in checking for errors, but there is **no** way of being absolutely certain that data is error-free. The main objective of validity checking is to catch obvious errors and to reduce the probability of errors being processed as valid data.

If errors are detected by the validity check procedures, we may include a routine to:

TYPICAL ERROR ROUTINES

1. Abort the job entirely. (If the integrity of the data is of primary concern.)
2. Print the erroneous input with an appropriate error message. (In this case, we may wish to abort the job only if an excessive number of such errors occurs.)
3. Clear out all erroneous fields.

ILLUSTRATION OF
VALIDITY CHECKING

Suppose we are writing an edit program for a dating service where we are asked to ensure, insofar as we are able, the integrity of the data; that is, we must make certain that input errors are minimized.

The input appears as follows:

1-20	Name
21	Sex (Male = 1; Female = 2)
22	Marital status (M = married
	S = single
	D = divorced
	T = separated
	W = widowed)
23-25	Weight (in lbs)
26-27	Height (in inches)
28	Color of eyes (1 = Brown
	2 = Blue
	3 = Hazel
	4 = Other)
29	Color of hair (1 = Red
	2 = Brown
	3 = Black
	4 = Blonde
	5 = Grey
	6 = Other)
30-33	Birth date (Mo/Yr)

Note that there is no way to prevent errors entirely. If a card for John Smith is entered that has a WEIGHT field of 157 when John Smith actually weighs 257 lbs, there is no way we can easily determine that. If, however, John Smith's weight is entered as 025 or 750, we can surmise that this field is probably incorrect and indicate that there is an input error. This would be a reasonableness test.

In general, the fields indicated could be checked as follows:

FIELD	VALIDITY CHECK
1. Name	Alphabetic
2. Sex	Test for 1 or 2
3. Marital status	Test for M, S, D, T, W
4. Weight	Test for reasonableness with limits 090–300 lbs, for example
5. Height	Test for reasonableness with limits 48–84 inches, for example
6. Color of eyes	Test for 1, 2, 3, or 4
7. Color of hair	Test for 1, 2, 3, 4, 5, or 6
8. Birth date	Limit check: Month: 01–12
	Reasonableness: Year between 01 and 65

The DATA DIVISION entries for the input in this type of program would normally include many condition-names that are useful for documentation purposes. Consider the following input area:

```
DATA DIVISION.
FILE SECTION.
FD  DATING-FILE
    LABEL RECORDS ARE OMITTED
    RECORD CONTAINS 80 CHARACTERS
    DATA RECORD IS DATING-REC.
01  DATING-REC.
    02   NAME                        PIC X(20).
    02   SEX                         PIC 9.
         88 MALE          VALUE 1.
         88 FEMALE        VALUE 2.
    02   MARITAL-STATUS              PIC X.
         88   MARRIED     VALUE 'M'.
         88   SINGLE      VALUE 'S'.
         88   DIVORCED    VALUE 'D'.
         88   SEPARATED   VALUE 'T'.
         88   WIDOWED     VALUE 'W'.
    02   WEIGHT                      PIC 9(3).
    02   HEIGHT                      PIC 99.
    02   EYE-COLOR                   PIC 9.
         88   BROWN-EYES  VALUE 1.
         88   BLUE        VALUE 2.
         88   HAZEL       VALUE 3.
         88   OTHER-EYE   VALUE 4.
    02   HAIR-COLOR                  PIC 9.
         88   RED         VALUE 1.
         88   BROWN-HAIR  VALUE 2.
         88   BLACK       VALUE 3.
         88   BLONDE      VALUE 4.
         88   GREY        VALUE 5.
         88   OTHER-HAIR  VALUE 6.
    02   BIRTH-DATE.
         03   MONTH                  PIC 99.
         03   YEAR                   PIC 99.
    02   FILLER                      PIC X(47).
```

Consider, too, the following output area:

```
FD  PRINT-ERROR
    LABEL RECORDS ARE OMITTED
    RECORD CONTAINS 133 CHARACTERS
    DATA RECORD IS ERROR-LINE.
01  ERROR-LINE.
    02  FILLER                  PIC X(20).
    02  NAME-OUT                PIC X(20).
    02  FILLER                  PIC X(10).
    02  ERROR-MESSAGE           PIC X(50).
    02  FILLER                  PIC X(33).
```

Assume that we wish to print all input fields for an erroneous record with a message that indicates the type of error that has occurred. The PROCEDURE DIVISION could then be coded as follows:

```
PROCEDURE DIVISION.
    OPEN INPUT DATING-FILE, OUTPUT PRINT-ERROR.
    MOVE SPACES TO ERROR-LINE.
    READ DATING-FILE AT END MOVE 1 TO EOF.
    PERFORM ERROR-CHECK UNTIL EOF = 1.
    CLOSE DATING-FILE, PRINT-ERROR.
    STOP RUN.
ERROR-CHECK.
    IF NOT MALE AND NOT FEMALE
            MOVE 'ERROR IN SEX' TO ERROR-MESSAGE
            PERFORM WRITE-ERROR.
    IF NOT MARRIED AND NOT SINGLE
                    AND NOT DIVORCED AND NOT SEPARATED
                    AND NOT WIDOWED
            MOVE 'ERROR IN MARITAL STATUS' TO ERROR-MESSAGE
            PERFORM WRITE-ERROR.
    IF WEIGHT < 90 OR > 300
            MOVE 'ERROR IN WEIGHT' TO ERROR-MESSAGE
            PERFORM WRITE-ERROR.
    IF HEIGHT < 48 OR > 84
            MOVE 'ERROR IN HEIGHT' TO ERROR-MESSAGE
            PERFORM WRITE-ERROR.
    IF NOT BROWN-EYES AND NOT BLUE AND NOT HAZEL AND
                    NOT OTHER-EYE
            MOVE 'ERROR IN EYE COLOR' TO ERROR-MESSAGE
            PERFORM WRITE-ERROR.
    IF NOT RED AND NOT BROWN-HAIR AND NOT BLACK AND NOT BLONDE
                    AND NOT GREY AND NOT OTHER-HAIR
            MOVE 'ERROR IN HAIR COLOR' TO ERROR-MESSAGE
            PERFORM WRITE-ERROR.
    IF MONTH < 01 OR > 12
            MOVE 'ERROR IN MONTH OF BIRTH' TO ERROR-MESSAGE
            PERFORM WRITE-ERROR.
    IF YEAR < 01 OR > 65
            MOVE 'ERROR IN YEAR OF BIRTH' TO ERROR-MESSAGE
            PERFORM WRITE-ERROR.
    READ DATING-FILE AT END MOVE 1 TO EOF.
WRITE-ERROR.
    MOVE NAME TO NAME-OUT.
    WRITE ERROR-LINE.
```

We will consider validity checks again in Chapter 23, when we discuss the INSPECT statement.

SELF-EVALUATING
QUIZ

1. If the same storage area is to be used for different purposes, it must be _____ in the DATA DIVISION.
*****
redefined

2. Consider the following DATA DIVISION entry:
    02 AMOUNT-FIELD PICTURE 999.
Write a DATA DIVISION entry that will define the above storage area as alphanumeric.
*****
    02   AMOUNT-FIELD-X REDEFINES AMOUNT-FIELD PICTURE XXX.

3. A REDEFINES clause may not be used on the _____ level in the FILE SECTION.
*****
01

Make the necessary corrections to each of the following (4–5):

4. 02   ITEM-1 PICTURE XXX.
    03   ITEM-X REDEFINES ITEM-1 PICTURE 999.
*****
should be:
    02   ITEM-X REDEFINES ITEM-1 PICTURE 999.

5. 04   FLDA PICTURE XX.
    04   FLDB REDEFINES FLDA PICTURE 99, VALUE 12.
*****
cannot have a VALUE clause in a redefining entry

6. To retain the sign of a numeric field, an _____ must be the _____ character in the PICTURE clause.
*****
S
first

7. The following is a PROCEDURE DIVISION entry: IF A IS NEGATIVE PERFORM RTN-1. Write the PICTURE clause for A if it is a two-position numeric field with one decimal position.
*****
PICTURE S9V9

8. +125 would be punched into a data card as _____.
*****
12E

9. −564 would be punched into a data card as _____.
*****
56M

10. S99V9 denotes a (no.)-position field.
*****
three

11. S99PPPP denotes a (no.)-position field.
*****
two

12. The P in the above field is called an _____ _____.
*****
assumed zero

13. 34 placed in the above field is interpreted by the computer as _____.
    *****
    (+) 340000

14. .68 placed in a field with PICTURE VPP99 is interpreted by the computer
    as _____.
    *****
    .0068

15. Condition-names are assigned in the _____ DIVISION.
    *****
    DATA

16. A condition-name must have a _____ clause associated with it.
    *****
    VALUE

17. A condition-name is always coded on the (no.) level.
    *****
    88

18. A condition-name always refers to the data field _____.
    *****
    directly preceding it

19. If the following is a DATA DIVISION entry, write the PROCEDURE DIVI-
    SION entry (in two ways) to test the condition implied:

    02 SALARY   PICTURE 9(5).
    88 HIGHEST-SALARY   VALUE 99999.
    *****
    IF SALARY = 99999 PERFORM . . .
    IF HIGHEST-SALARY PERFORM . . .

20. In the following statement, TYPE1 must be a _____.
    IF TYPE1 PERFORM DEBIT-RTN.
    *****
    condition-name

21. (T or F) Validity checks are used to ensure the accuracy of input data.
    *****
    F—validity checks minimize the risk of errors, but no programming tech-
    nique can **ensure** error-free data.

22. A _____ check is used to ensure that data is within an established range.
    *****
    limit

23. Making certain that a field called HEIGHT contains a value, in inches, less
    than 84 is referred to as a test for _____.
    *****
    reasonableness

24. If the accuracy of input must be absolutely assured, then any validity
    check that produces an error should result in a _____.
    *****
    halt

25. When performing validity checks, it is normally sufficient to _____ when
    an error occurs.
    *****
    print an error message

PRACTICE PROBLEM—
WITH SOLUTION

A card file containing employee records is used to create tape files containing the first 20 positions of card data. One tape file is to be created for all females between 20 and 30 years old, under 5 feet 6 inches but over 5 feet tall, who weigh less than 120 lbs. A second tape file is to be created for all male employees over 50, between 5 feet 6 inches and 6 feet tall who weigh more than 185 lbs. and are bald. Both tape files will be blocked 20 and have standard labels. The card format is as follows:

1–15 Name
    16 Sex   M—male, F—female
    17 Age   Y—20, M—between 20 and 30, G—between 30 and 50, E—over 50
    18 Height   X—over 6 feet, M—between 5 feet 6 inches and 6 feet,
             A—between 5 feet and 5 feet 6 inches
    19 Weight   H—over 185, M—between 120 and 185, N—under 120
    20   Hair   B—bald, N—not bald
21–80 Not used

Use condition-names.

See Figure 11.1 for solution.

REVIEW QUESTIONS

True False

I. True-False Questions

1. A numeric field normally contains some SPACES.
2. A limit test checks to see if the contents of a field is within a specified range.
3. Condition-names must be unique within a COBOL program.
4. A REDEFINES clause may be used with either group or elementary data items.
5. To obtain numeric data so that is is justified right, we must use a JUSTIFIED RIGHT clause.
6. A data field with a VALUE clause may not be redefined.
7. There are instances in which 88-level items are required in a COBOL program.
8. The size of a field is increased by one position when an S is used in the PICTURE clause.
9. Without the use of an S in a PICTURE clause, an arithmetic procedure may produce erroneous results.
10. The use of a P in a PICTURE clause increases the size of the field.

II. General Questions

1. In a statement like IF MARRIED PERFORM RTNX, how does the compiler know that MARRIED is a condition-name and not a data-name?
2. An independent WORKING-STORAGE item may have a code of 1 to denote MALE and a code of 2 to denote FEMALE. Write the entry and the corresponding condition-names.
3. Write a PROCEDURE DIVISION entry to perform an error routine if the field specified above does not denote male or female (use the condition-names).

```
              IDENTIFICATION DIVISION.
              PROGRAM-ID. CHAPT11.
              ENVIRONMENT DIVISION.
              CONFIGURATION SECTION.
              SOURCE-COMPUTER. IBM-370.
              OBJECT-COMPUTER. IBM-370.
              INPUT-OUTPUT SECTION.
              FILE-CONTROL.
                  SELECT EMPLOYEE-CARDS ASSIGN TO UR-S-SYSIN.
                  SELECT FEMALE-TAPE ASSIGN TO UT-S-SYS004.
                  SELECT MALE-TAPE ASSIGN TO UT-S-SYS005.
              DATA DIVISION.
              FILE SECTION.
              FD  EMPLOYEE-CARDS
                  LABEL RECORDS ARE OMITTED
                  RECORD CONTAINS 80 CHARACTERS
                  DATA RECORD IS CARD-REC.
              01  CARD-REC.
                  02  MAJOR.
                      03  NAME          PIC X(15).
                      03  SEX           PIC X.
                          88  MALE                    VALUE 'M'.
                          88  FEMALE                  VALUE 'F'.
                      03  AGE           PIC X.
                          88  AGE-20                  VALUE 'Y'.
                          88  AGE-30                  VALUE 'M'.
                          88  AGE-50                  VALUE 'G'.
                          88  AGE-OVER-50             VALUE 'E'.
                      03  HEIGHT        PIC X.
                          88  OVER-6-FT               VALUE 'X'.
                          88  BET-66-72               VALUE 'M'.
                          88  BET-60-66               VALUE 'A'.
                      03  WEIGHT        PIC X.
                          88  OVER-185                VALUE 'H'.
                          88  BET-120-185             VALUE 'M'.
                          88  UNDER-120               VALUE 'N'.
                      03  HAIR          PIC X.
                          88  BALD                    VALUE 'B'.
                          88  NOT-BALD                VALUE 'N'.
                  02  FILLER            PIC X(60).
              FD  FEMALE-TAPE
                  LABEL RECORDS ARE STANDARD
                  RECORD CONTAINS 20 CHARACTERS
                  BLOCK CONTAINS 20 RECORDS
                  DATA RECORD IS FEMALE-REC.
              01  FEMALE-REC            PIC X(20).
              FD  MALE-TAPE
                  LABEL RECORDS ARE STANDARD
                  RECORD CONTAINS 20 CHARACTERS
                  BLOCK CONTAINS 20 RECORDS
                  DATA RECORD IS MALE-REC.
              01  MALE-REC             PIC X(20).
              WORKING-STORAGE SECTION.
              01  WORK-AREAS.
                  02  EOF          PIC 9 VALUE 0.
              PROCEDURE DIVISION.
                  OPEN INPUT EMPLOYEE-CARDS
                          OUTPUT FEMALE-TAPE, MALE-TAPE.
                  READ EMPLOYEE-CARDS AT END MOVE 1 TO EOF.
                  PERFORM CALC-RTN  UNTIL EOF = 1.
                  CLOSE EMPLOYEE-CARDS, FEMALE-TAPE, MALE-TAPE.
                  STOP RUN.
              CALC-RTN.
                  IF FEMALE AND AGE-30 AND BET-60-66 AND UNDER-120
                          MOVE MAJOR TO FEMALE-REC
                          WRITE FEMALE-REC.
                  IF MALE AND AGE-OVER-50 AND BET-66-72 AND OVER-185 AND BALD
                          MOVE MAJOR TO MALE-REC
                          WRITE MALE-REC.
                  READ EMPLOYEE-CARDS AT END MOVE 1 TO EOF.
```

Figure 11.1

4. Write the above routine without the use of condition-names.
5. How are the following fields represented on a data card?
    (a) −358
    (b) +245
    (c) 267
6. How will the computer interpret −56 read into a field with the following PICTURE clause:
    (a) PICTURE 99.
    (b) PICTURE S99.
    (c) PICTURE 99PP.
    (d) PICTURE SVPP99.
7. Suppose ABCD is read into a 7-position alphanumeric field. Indicate the two different ways ABCD may be placed in the field. (**Hint.** Explain JUSTIFIED RIGHT.)

Make the necessary corrections to the following entries (8–17):

8. 02 AMT-1   PICTURE 99.
   88 NAME-1   VALUE ZERO.
   02 AMT-2   PICTURE 99.
   88 NAME-1   VALUE ZERO.
9. 01   ITEM-X   PICTURE X(50).
   01   ITEM-Y   REDEFINES ITEM-X PICTURE 9(50).
10. 02 SUB-1   PICTURE 99 VALUE ZERO.
    02 SUB-2   REDEFINES SUB-1 PICTURE XX.
11. 02 FLDX   PICTURE S99.
    02 FLDY   REDEFINES FLDX PICTURE XXX.
12. 02 X   PICTURE XX.
    88 X-ON   VALUE 12.
13. 02   SWITCHA   PICTURE 99.
    88   A-OFF   VALUE SPACES.
14. 02 TOTAL PICTURE 9(5)V9(3)S.
15. 02 FIELDA PICTURE 9999 JUSTIFIED RIGHT.
16. MOVE A TO B JUSTIFIED RIGHT.
17. 05 HEADER JUSTIFIED RIGHT PICTURE XX.
18. Indicate the types of validity checks that may be performed on input data.
19. Indicate the procedures that may be followed if an error occurs during a validity check.

PROBLEMS

1. **Input:** Card

    1–5 Customer Number
    6–7 Number of Items Bought (in 100's)
    8–10 Cost of Each Item x.xx
    11–80 Not used

    Output: Magnetic tape; standard labels, blocked 35

    1–5 Customer Number
    6–12 Total Charge xxxxx.xx

    NOTES:
    1. Total Charge = Number of Items (total) × Cost/Item

   2. If Customer Number is a multiple of 10's (i.e., 00010, 00150), then customer has credit rating of A—allow 2% discount on Total Charge

   3. Perform Validity Checks on all input data

HINT: Customer number must be redefined to test for a multiple of 10.

2. **Input:** tape; blocking factor = 25, standard labels

   1–20 Name of Employee
     21 Code   1—Wages, 2—Salary, 3—Commission
  22–26 Amt1   xxx.xx
  27–31 Amt2   xxx.xx

Output: Print name and earned amount (xxxxxx).

NOTES:

   1. Perform Validity Checks on all input data.

   2. If Wages (Code = 1) multiply Amt1 by Amt2 to obtain earned amount

   3. If Salary (Code = 2) earned amount is equal to Amt1

   4. If Commission (Code = 3) multiply Amt1 by Amt2 and add on an additional 8%.

Use condition-names.

3. Write a program to print the name and total of all amount fields from a tape record. Before totalling the amount fields, however, make sure that they contain only numeric data.

Input: Standard labels, no blocking factor

   1–10 Name
  11–40 six amount fields each xxxxx

Print

   5–14 Name
  21–26 Total; print 'ERROR' if any input amount field is not numeric

12 EDITING PRINTED OUTPUT

Because of the unique characteristics of printed output, we will treat it as a separate topic. Most importantly, the printed form as the primary type of computer output is used **exclusively** as an end product. It is the final result of a computer run, often to be viewed by high-level management.

Tape, disk, and punched card output are generally intermediate products, having the ultimate function of being reentered into the computer flow as input to another job. These types of output are created for efficiency. Fields and records of this type are condensed to make maximum use of the computer and its storage capabilities. The printed report, however, is written with business-people in mind. Since many computer-generated reports are read by company executives, such forms must be clear, neat, and easy to interpret. Several characteristics, not applicable to other forms of output, must be considered when preparing reports.

EDITING OF PRINTED DATA

A punched card may have two amount fields with the following data: 00450, 3872658. Although these fields are acceptable on cards or other forms of output, the printed report must contain this information in edited form to make it more meaningful. $450.00 and $38,726.58, for example, are clearer methods of presenting the data.

Editing will be considered the manipulation of fields of data to make them clearer and neater for their specific purpose. The editing of input data is of prime consideration when printing information.

SPACING OF FORMS

Forms, unlike other kinds of output, must be properly spaced for ease of reading. Certain entries must be single spaced, others double spaced. The printed output must have adequate margins at both the top and bottom of the form. This requires the computer to be programmed to sense the end of a form and thus to transmit the next line of information to a new page.

ALIGNMENT OF DATA   Reports do not have fields of information adjacent to one another as is the practice with other forms of output. Printed output is more easily interpreted when data is spaced neatly and evenly across the page.

PRINTING OF HEADERS   Header information, which generally supplies job name, date, and field designations, is essential for clearness of presentation, when creating printed output.

Figure 12.1 provides a schematic of how input data may actually be printed. All the items named above, each presenting unique programming problems, will be treated individually. For that reason, we will study the printed report as a separate, and rather special, topic. The first item, editing, will be considered now. The other three items will be discussed in the next chapter.

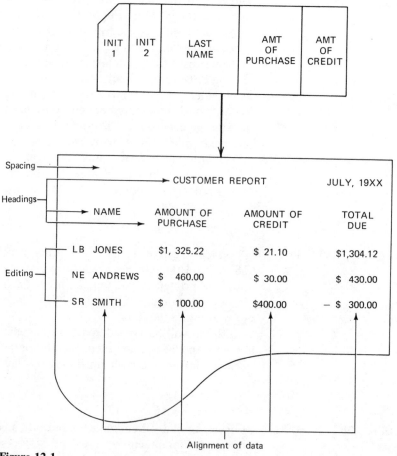

Figure 12.1

A. THE EDITING FUNCTION

The following will be considered editing functions:

> **EDITING FUNCTIONS**
> 1. Suppression of leading zeros.
> 2. Printing of decimal points where decimal alignment is implied.
> 3. Printing of dollar signs and commas.
> 4. Printing of asterisks for check protection.
> 5. Printing of plus or minus signs to reflect the value of a field.
> 6. Printing of debit or credit symbols for accounting applications.
> 7. Printing of spaces or zeros as separators within a field.

The first six editing functions may only be performed on **numeric** fields, or fields with PICTURE clauses consisting of 9's. The last editing function, the printing of zeros or spaces as separators, may be performed on any data field.

All editing is performed by moving an elementary item to a **report-item.** An elementary item, you will recall, is a field with a PICTURE clause; that is, it is a data item that is not further subdivided. A **report-item** is an elementary item that has the appropriate PICTURE clause to perform editing functions. Note that it is the PICTURE clause of the receiving field, the report-item, that causes editing. The actual operation of editing can be performed by a MOVE instruction.

To perform an editing function, the PICTURE clauses of the output area, which is the print area, must contain the appropriate symbols. Data is moved from input or work areas to these output areas. When a WRITE statement is executed, the information to be printed is in edited form. As in **all** move operations, the sending fields remain unchanged after the data has been transmitted to the report-item.

In addition, the GIVING option of the arithmetic verbs ADD, SUBTRACT, MULTIPLY, DIVIDE permits the last data field specified to be a report item. Thus, in the statement;

```
ADD AMT1, AMT2, AMT3, GIVING RESULT
```

RESULT may be a report-item. Thus we can obtain editing by performing an arithmetic operation using the GIVING option and placing the result in a report-item.

SELF-EVALUATING QUIZ

1. Editing is performed by a _____ operation or by using the _____ option of an arithmetic verb.
   *****
   MOVE
   GIVING

2. Editing is performed by moving _____ to _____.
   *****
   elementary numeric items
   report-items
3. A receiving field that has the appropriate PICTURE clause to perform editing is called a _____.
   *****
   report-item
4. Most editing is performed on _____ fields.
   *****
   numeric
5. When moving the contents of a data item to a report-item to perform editing, the contents of the data item _____ after the operation.
   *****
   remain unchanged

B. INTERPRETING EDIT CHARACTERS

SUPPRESSION OF LEADING ZEROS

Nonsignificant or leading zeros are zeros appearing in the leftmost positions of a field and having no significant value. For example, 00387 has two leading zeros. Nonsignificant zeros should generally be omitted when printing. 00387 should print as 387, since the two are numerically equivalent and the latter is considered better form. The operation to perform this type of editing is called **suppression of leading zeros.** Note that the number 10000 has **no** leading zeros. All zeros have numeric significance and none appear in the leftmost positions of the field. Under no circumstances would we want to suppress the printing of the zeros in 10000, since each adds value to the number.

The edit symbol $\boxed{Z}$ is used to suppress leading zeros and to replace them with blanks or spaces. FIELDA, with PICTURE 999, might be edited by moving it to EDIT1, with PICTURE ZZZ:

```
    .
    .
    .
01  PRINT-REC.
    02  FILLER    PIC X.
    02  EDIT1     PIC ZZZ.
    .
    .
    .
WORKING-STORAGE SECTION.
01  WORK-AREAS.
    02  FIELDA    PIC 999.
    .
    .
    .
    MOVE FIELDA TO EDIT1.
```

Each Z represents one storage position that may accept data from a sending field. In addition, any nonsignificant zeros encountered in the sending field will be replaced with blanks. (Note that a blank is represented in the following examples by a slash through a lower-case b.)

038   will print as ƀ38
003   will print as ƀƀ3
000   will print as ƀƀƀ

Any number that does not have leading zeros, such as 108, will print as is.

When suppressing leading zeros, the sending field must be defined as numeric. The receiving field should be the same size as the sending field. ZZZ indicates a three-position storage area that may accept three characters of input data, and that will suppress all leading zeros.

Often it is desirable to suppress only **some** leading zeros of a sending field. Consider the case where the contents of four sending fields denoting Charity Deductions are 0020, 4325, 0003, and 0000 respectively. The output may be as follows:

NAME	SALARY	DEDUCTIONS FOR CHARITY
A. LINCOLN	13872	20
W. WILSON	40873	4325
F. ROOSEVELT	10287	3
G. WASHINGTON	25382	

High-order zeros have been suppressed. The PICTURE clause in the output area is ZZZZ or Z(4).

As may be evident from this illustration, it is sometimes not advisable to leave fields blank when a zero balance is implied. Business people who question, at times, the accuracy of computer output, tend to regard blank fields as an indication that the computer erred or that it stopped and was restarted improperly. Perhaps G. WASHINGTON did, in fact, make a contribution but the computer, through an electronic error, failed to indicate it.

For this reason, it is sometimes good practice to print a **single** zero where a zero balance exists. In this way, the report will leave no doubt about the charitable inclinations of G. WASHINGTON.

Thus if the four-position charity field has contents 0000, we want it to print as 0. That is, we want only the three left-most positions of the field to be zero suppressed and the last position to print **without** suppressing the zero. The PICTURE clause of the report-item would then be ZZZ9. Z's indicate numeric characters to be zero suppressed and 9's indicate numeric characters to print without zero suppression. Hence 0000 will print as 0.

The combined use of Z's and 9's in a report-item is permissible as long as all Z's **precede** any 9's. Zeros may be suppressed only if they precede significant digits.

The following examples may clarify editing with the use of zero suppression. Note that edited results are obtained by the operation: MOVE SENDING-FIELD TO REPORT-ITEM (or by using the GIVING option of an arithmetic statement).

Sending-Field		Report-Item	
PICTURE	Contents	PICTURE	Edited Results
9(3)	109	ZZZ	109
9(3)	007	Z(3)	7
9(3)	000	ZZZ	
9(3)	007	Z99	07
9(4)	0082	Z999	082

PRINTING OF DECIMAL POINTS WHERE DECIMAL ALIGNMENT IS IMPLIED

TAX, with PICTURE 99V99 and CONTENTS of 1235, should print as 12.35 when edited. The implied decimal point must, through editing, be replaced with an actual decimal point. The appropriate report-item that will print a decimal point will have a PICTURE of 99.99. The decimal point, which may **never** appear in the PICTURE clause of a numeric item, instructs the computer to place an actual decimal point where it is assumed to be in the sending field. If a sending field had PICTURE of 999V999; its report-item would have a PICTURE clause of 999.999.

Note that a sending field with PICTURE 99V99 takes **four** storage positions since implied decimal points do not use storage, while the resultant field takes **five** positions, since a real decimal point does, in fact, use a position. The number 12.35, when printed, utilizes five print positions.

We can combine the two editing functions thus far discussed so that we zero suppress **and** place decimal points in the edited field. Consider the following examples:

Sending-Field		Report-Item	
PICTURE	Contents	PICTURE	Edited Results
99V99	0238	ZZ.99	2.38
99V99	0003	ZZ.99	.03
99V99	0005	Z9.99	0.05

Since numeric positions to the right of a decimal point have significance when they are zero, we will not perform zero suppression on these quantities. That is, .01 should **not** be edited to read .1, since the two numbers are not numerically equivalent. As a rule, then, we will not zero suppress characters to the right of a decimal point in a number.

There is one exception to this rule. It is permissible in COBOL to use a report-item with PICTURE ZZ.ZZ. This will suppress zeros to the right of the decimal point only if the entire field is zero, in which case all spaces will print. Thus 0003 will print as .03 but 0000 will print as blanks. Because such a PICTURE clause may be confusing, we will not, in general, use this convention.

PRINTING OF DOLLAR SIGNS AND COMMAS

The printing of dollar signs and commas are frequent editing functions performed in conjunction with the suppression of leading zeros and the printing of decimal points, since many numeric quantities eventually appear on printed reports as dollars and cents figures. The dollar sign and comma are merely placed in the positions in which they are desired, as is the case with printing decimal points. If FLDA, with PICTURE 9999V99, is to be edited as a dollars and cents figure, the dollar sign will be the first character, a digit from the sending field will follow, then a comma, three more digits, a decimal point, and two decimal positions. Thus the report-item will have a PICTURE of $9,999.99. The following examples will illustrate this point.

	Sending-Field		Report-Item	
	PICTURE	Contents	PICTURE	Edited Results
1.	9(4)V99	381234	$9,999.99	$3,812.34
2.	99V99	0500	$ZZ.99	$5.00
3.	999V99	00005	$ZZZ.99	$.05
4.	9(4)V99	000382	$Z,ZZZ.99	$3.82
5.	9(7)V99	003826845	$Z,ZZZ,ZZZ.99	$38,268.45

Note that in Example 1, the sending field takes six storage positions, while the receiving field uses nine. Dollar signs, commas, and decimal points each utilize one position of storage. A frequent result of editing is this increased use of storage for the output area. When defining the print output record in the DATA DIVISION be sure that nine positions are included for the report-item.

Examples 2 through 4 illustrate the use of zero suppression in conjunction with other forms of editing. In Example 2, one leading zero is suppressed and replaced with a space. Thus there is a single blank between the inserted dollar sign and the first significant digit. Example 4 indicates that the zero suppression character Z will also eliminate or suppress leading commas. Note that the result of the edit was **not** $, 3.82 but $ 3.82 . The Z will suppress both zeros and commas until it encounters the first significant digit of a field. Thus a comma will be appropriately suppressed if no significant digit precedes it. In Example 4, **four** spaces will appear between the dollar sign and the first significant digit, three for the suppressed zeros, and one for the suppressed comma.

At this point, it should be mentioned that the sending field must allow for the same number of integer positions as the report-item but can include additional decimal positions if desired. FLDA, with PICTURE 99 and contents 40, may be edited by moving it to EDIT1, with PICTURE $ZZ.99. As in the case of numeric move operations, the two decimal places will be filled with zeros. The result, then, in EDIT1 will be $40.00.

THE PRINTING OF ASTERISKS AS A CHECK PROTECTION CHARACTER

The suppression of zeros, by the use of Z, in conjunction with the printing of dollar signs may, at times, prove unwise.

Suppose we are using the computer to print checks. To print $ .05, as in Example 3 above, may not be advisable since the blanks between the dollar sign and the decimal point may easily be filled in by a typewriter. Some dishonest person could conceivably collect $999.05 on what should be a five cent check.

To prevent such occurrences, a check protection symbol, the asterisk (*), is used in place of blanks when leading zeros are to be suppressed. Using the correct report-item, the above would print as $***.05. In this way, it is almost impossible to revise the intended figure.

To print an asterisk in place of a blank when zero suppression is to be performed, use an * instead of a Z in each position. Asterisks are zero-suppression characters that replace nonsignificant zeros and commas with * instead of spaces.

Sending-Field		Report-Item	
PICTURE	Contents	PICTURE	Edited Results
9(3)V99	12345	$***.99	$123.45
9(3)V99	01234	$***.99	$*12.34
9(2)V99	0012	$**.99	$**.12
9(5)V99	0023456	$**,***.99	$***234.56

The asterisk is used most often for the printing of checks or when resultant amount fields may be tampered with. Under other conditions, the use of Z's for normal zero suppression is sufficient.

THE PRINTING OF PLUS OR MINUS SIGNS TO REFLECT THE VALUE OF A FIELD

Unless the computer is instructed to do otherwise, numeric quantities will print without a sign. When reports are printed, it is customary to interpret the absence of a sign as an indication of a positive quantity.

If an amount is negative and no sign instructions are issued to the computer, it will print without a sign, which will cause it to be interpreted as positive. We must instruct the computer, with the use of editing, to print a minus sign when a negative number is read. You will recall from the previous chapter, that the PICTURE clause of a numeric sending field must contain an S if quantities are to be retained as negative or positive. Without the S, all quantities are considered unsigned.

The edit symbol, $\boxed{-}$, may be placed **either** to the right **or** the left of the report-item. By placing the minus sign in one of these two positions, the computer is instructed to store the minus sign in the corresponding position if the sending field is negative, and to omit a sign when the sending field is signed positive or unsigned.

You will recall that the sign of a number is indicated by placing it above the quantity. Examine the following illustrations.

Sending-Field		Report-Item	
PICTURE	Contents	PICTURE	Edited Results
1. S999	12$\bar{3}$	−999	−123
2. S999	12$\bar{3}$	999−	123−
3. 999	123	−999	123
4. S999	12$\overset{+}{3}$	−999	123
5. S99V99	02$\bar{3}$4	ZZ.99−	2.34−

Examples 1 and 2 illustrate the positioning of the minus sign within the report-item. It may appear to the right or the left of a field and will, then, print in the corresponding position. If the sending field is negative, the edited results print with the negative sign. Examples 3 and 4 illustrate that **no** sign will print if the sending field is signed positive or unsigned. Example 5 illustrates the use of the minus sign in conjunction with other editing symbols.

There are occasions when a sign is required for both positive and negative quantities. That is, a + sign is required when the field is unsigned or signed positive, and a − sign is required when the field is signed negative. This will not be performed properly by using the edit symbol −, which generates only the minus sign if the quantity is negative and omits a sign for all other quantities.

To perform the printing of a plus sign or a minus sign for **all** fields, the edit symbol $\boxed{+}$ is used. To edit a sending field by moving it to a report-item with a + in its PICTURE clause will instruct the computer to generate a sign for each move: a + sign will be generated for positive or unsigned quantities, and a − sign will be generated for negative quantities.

Like the minus sign, the plus sign may be made to appear either to the left or to the right of a field. Examine the following illustrations.

Sending-Field		Report-Item	
PICTURE	Contents	PICTURE	Edited Results
1. S999	12$\overset{+}{3}$	+999	+123
2. S999	12$\overset{+}{3}$	999+	123+
3. S999	12$\bar{3}$	+999	−123
4. 999	123	+999	+123
5. S9999V99	0387$\underset{+}{2}$5	+Z,ZZZ.99	− 387.25

THE PRINTING OF DEBIT AND CREDIT SYMBOLS FOR ACCOUNTING APPLICATIONS

For most applications, a generated plus or minus sign to indicate positive or negative quantities is sufficient. For accountants, however, minus signs often indicate either debits or credits to particular accounts.

To facilitate the interpretation of fields specified for accounting functions, the edit symbols DB, for debit, and CR, for credit, may be used in place of the minus sign. If an amount is to be **debited** to a specific account when it is negative, DB will be used. If a quantity is to be **credited** to a specific account when it is negative, CR will be used.

These symbols must be specified to the right of the report-item. Unlike the minus sign itself, these symbols may **not** be used to the left of a field. If the amount is negative and CR or DB is used, then CR or DB will print, respectively. If the field is unsigned or signed positive, neither symbol will print.

It is important to note that, while a minus sign uses **one** storage position, the CR and DB symbols use **two** each.

The following examples will illustrate the use of the two symbols.

	Sending-Field		Report-Item	
	PICTURE	Contents	PICTURE	Edited Results
1.	S999	12$\bar{3}$	999CR	123CR
2.	S999	12$\bar{3}$	999DB	123DB
3.	S999	12$\overset{+}{3}$	999CR	123
4.	S999	123	999DB	123
5.	S9(5)V99	01234$\bar{5}$6	$ZZ,ZZZ.99CR	$ 1,234.56CR

THE PRINTING OF SPACES OR ZEROS AS SEPARATORS WITHIN A FIELD

Suppose the first nine columns of a card contain a social security number. If the field is printed without editing, it would appear as: 080749263. For ease of reading, 080 74 9263 would be a better representation. A space between the numbers, then, would add clarity.

Any field, whether alphabetic, alphanumeric, or numeric may be edited by placing blanks as separators within the field. The edit symbol B in a PICTURE clause of a report-item will cause a space to be inserted in the corresponding position.

Zeros may also be inserted into fields for editing purposes. The edit symbol 0 in a PICTURE clause will cause a 0 to be inserted in the corresponding position of the receiving field without loss of characters from the sending field.

The following examples will illustrate the use of spaces or zeros in report-items.

	Sending-Field		Report-Item	
Data-Name	PICTURE	Contents	PICTURE	Edited Results
SSNO	9(9)	089743456	999BB99BB9999	089 74 3456
NAME	A(10)	PASMITH	ABABA(8)	P A SMITH
DATE1	9(4)	0280	99BB99	02 80
QTY-IN-100	999	153	99900	15300

You will note that most editing is performed on numeric data. Only this last category of edit operations, the use of blanks or zeros within a field, will accept data that is not numeric. For all other editing, the sending field must be numeric—it must have a PICTURE clause of 9's.

Furthermore, only **elementary** numeric items may be utilized in these operations. You will recall that group items, even if they are subdivided into numeric fields, are treated as alphanumeric items by the computer. Thus, to obtain a valid numeric edit, only elementary items may be used.

It is important to understand that editing is performed by **moving** a field to a report-item, with an appropriate PICTURE clause, or by using the GIVING option of an arithmetic statement where the last data field is a report-item. It is the PICTURE clause itself that determines what type of editing is to be performed.

To say, however,

ADD TAX, TOTAL TO EDIT1.

where EDIT1 is a report-item, will result in an error. The computer performs ADD instructions, and any other arithmetic operation, on numeric fields only. EDIT1, as a report-item, is **not** a numeric field.

The MOVE CORRESPONDING option can be used to **edit** incoming fields. We edit input data by moving it to a report-item in the receiving field.

Example

```
MOVE CORRESPONDING REC-IN TO PRINT-OUT.
```

01	REC-IN.		**Contents**	01	PRINT-OUT.		**Contents**
	02 NAME	PICTURE X(6).	JEADAM		02 FILLER	PICTURE X.	b
	02 AMT	PICTURE 999V99.	575̲24		02 NAME	PICTURE XBXBXXXX.	J E ADAM
					02 AMT	PICTURE $ZZZ.99.	$575.24

Table 12.1 will serve as a review of edit operations.

Table 12.2 reviews all the symbols discussed that may be used in a PICTURE clause.

TABLE 12.1

Sending Field		Report-Item	
PICTURE	**Contents**	PICTURE	**Edited Results**
9(6)	123456	$ZZZ,ZZZ.99	$123,456.00
9999V99	0012̲34	$Z,ZZZ.99	$ 12.34
9(5)V99	000012̲3	$**,***.99	$*****1.23
S9(6)	01234̄5	+Z(6)	− 12345
S9(6)	12345̊6	−Z(6)	123456
S9999V99	1234̊56	+Z(4).99	+1234.56
S999	12̄3	ZZZ−	123−
9(6)	123456	99BBBB9999	12 3456
S99	05̄	$ZZ.99DB	$ 5.00DB
999	123	999000	123000
S99V99	123̄4	$ZZ.99CR	$12.34CR

TABLE 12.2 SYMBOLS THAT MAY BE USED IN A PICTURE CLAUSE

Symbol	Meaning
X	Alphanumeric field
9	Numeric field
A	Alphabetic field
V	Assumed decimal point; used only in numeric fields
S	Operational sign; used only in numeric fields
P	Decimal scaling position; used only in numeric fields
Z	Zero suppression character
.	Decimal point
+	Plus sign
−	Minus sign
$	Dollar sign
,	Comma
CR	Credit symbol
DB	Debit symbol
*	Check protection symbol
B	Field separator—space insertion character
0	Zero insertion character

Edit Symbols (bracket spanning Z through 0)

SELF-EVALUATING QUIZ

1. The asterisk is called a _____.
   *****
   check protection edit symbol
2. The zero suppression symbol, Z, suppresses _____ and _____ up to the first significant digit.
   *****
   high-order zeros or nonsignificant zeros or leading zeros
   commas
3. The asterisk replaces all _____ with _____.
   *****
   leading zeros and leading commas
   asterisks
4. To print a minus sign when an amount is negative, use a _____ symbol.
   *****
   − (minus sign)
5. To print a plus sign or a minus sign as appropriate with an amount field, use a _____ symbol.
   *****
   + sign

6. CR and DB symbols are accounting symbols used in place of a _____ sign.
   *****
   minus

7. All editing must be performed on _____ fields except editing using _____.
   *****
   numeric
   zeros or blanks as field separators

8. To say MULTIPLY A BY B GIVING C (is, is not) correct if C is a report-item.
   *****
   is

9. A report-item is _____.
   *****
   an output field which contains the appropriate symbols to perform editing

10. A plus or minus sign may be placed either to the _____ or to the _____ of a field but CR and DB must be placed to the _____ of a field.
    *****
    left
    right
    right

11. How many storage positions in the output area must be allotted for a report-item with PICTURE $*,***.99?
    *****
    Nine

12. How many integer positions should appear in the sending field?
    *****
    Four

For Questions 13–28, fill in the edited results.

	Sending-Field		Receiving-Field	
	PICTURE	Contents	PICTURE	Edited Results
13.	9(6)	000123	ZZZ,999	
14.	9(6)	000008	ZZZ,999	
15.	9(6)	123456	ZZZ,999.99	
16.	9(4)V99	123456	$Z,ZZZ.99	
17.	9(4)V99	000078	$Z,ZZ9.99	
18.	S9(4)V99	000078	$Z,ZZZ.99CR	
19.	S9(4)V99	000078	$Z,ZZZ.99CR	
20.	S9(6)	123456	−999,999	
21.	9(6)	123456	−999,999	
22.	S999	123	−999	
23.	999	123	+999	
24.	S999	123	+999	
25.	S999	123	−999	
26.	9(6)	000092	Z(6)00	
27.	X(6)	123456	XXXBBXXX	
28.	9(4)V99	001234	$*,***.99	

*****

13. 123
14. 008
15. 123,456.00
16. $1,234.56
17. $ 0.78
18. $ .78
19. $ .78CR
20. −123,456
21. 123,456
22. 123
23. +123
24. +123
25. −123
26. 9200
27. 123   456
28. $***12.34

29. NAME-FIELD PICTURE X(15) is part of an input document, with the first two positions of the field being INITIAL1 and INITIAL2. To edit this field so that a space appears between INITIAL1 and INITIAL2, and another space between INITIAL2 and LAST-NAME, the report-item will have the following PICTURE clause: _____.

Redefine the input area NAME-FIELD and the output area, REPORT-ITEM, and write a routine **without** using editing to perform the same function.

*****

XBXBX(13)
```
02 NAME1 REDEFINES NAME-FIELD.
    03 INIT1 PICTURE X.
    03 INIT2 PICTURE X.
    03 LAST-NAME PICTURE X(13).

02 REDEFINE1 REDEFINES REPORT-ITEM.
    03 INIT1 PICTURE X.
    03 FILLER PICTURE X.
    03 INIT2 PICTURE X.
    03 FILLER PICTURE X.
    03 LAST-NAME PICTURE X(13).
      .
      .
      .
MOVE SPACES TO REDEFINE1.
MOVE INIT1 OF NAME1 TO INIT1 OF REDEFINE1.
MOVE INIT2 OF NAME1 TO INIT2 OF REDEFINE1.
MOVE LAST-NAME OF NAME1 TO LAST-NAME OF REDEFINE1.
```

C. FLOATING STRINGS AND BLANK WHEN ZERO OPTION

FLOATING STRINGS

Examine the following sample output.

CUSTOMER NAME	QTY SOLD	AMT
J. SMITH	5,000	$38,725.67
A. JONES	− 2	$ 3.00

Although the fields are properly edited, the format is striking in one respect. The dollar sign of AMT and the minus sign of QTY SOLD for A. JONES are separated by several spaces from the numeric data. This result is a necessary consequence of the editing that we have been discussing.

The report-item must contain enough positions to accommodate the entire sending field. If the sending field, however, has many nonsignificant zeros (for example, 0000487), an appreciable number of blank positions will exist between the dollar sign and the first significant digit, or the operational sign and the first significant digit.

A leading edit character such as a plus sign, minus sign, or dollar sign may appear in the position **directly preceding** the first significant digit with the use of **floating strings.** A dollar sign or a plus or a minus sign may be made to "float" with the field; that is, to cause suppression of leading zeros and, at the same time, to force the respective floating character to appear in the position adjacent to the first significant digit.

With the proper use of floating strings in the PICTURE clause of the report-item, the following sample output may be produced.

Sending-Field Contents	Report-Item Edited Results
0012387	$123.87
0000400	$4.00
3876543	$38,765.43
0387	−387
0006	−6
010423	+10,423
000005	+5

You will note that in the above the $, −, or + sign always appears in the position directly preceding the first significant digit. Only these three edit symbols may be made to float in this way.

To perform a **floating string edit,** two steps are necessary.

1. Create the report-item PICTURE clause as in the previous section. Use the floating character of +, −, or $ in conjunction with Z's, zero suppression characters.
2. Replace all Z's with the corresponding float character.

Example 1

02 FLDA PICTURE 9(4)V99.

Problem: To edit the field using a floating dollar sign. Resultant report-item shall be called EDIT1.

In Step 1, the PICTURE clause of the report-item is created as usual: $Z,ZZZ.99.

In Step 2, replace all Z's with the floating character, a dollar sign: $$,$$$.99.

Thus EDIT1 has a PICTURE of $$,$$$.99.

Note that there are five dollar signs. The four rightmost dollar signs are zero suppression symbols. They instruct the computer to suppress leading zeros and commas, and to place the dollar sign in the position adjacent to the first significant digit. The leftmost dollar sign indicates to the computer that $ will be the first character to print. In total, there is one more dollar sign than integer positions to be edited. **Four** integer positions are edited using **five** dollar signs. In general, N characters may be edited using a floating string of $N + 1$ characters. The explanation for the extra floating character is quite logical. In case the sending field has no nonsignificant positions, the receiving field must have an additional position to put the floating character.

Example 2

02   TAX PICTURE S9(4).

Problem: To edit tax using a floating minus sign. Report-item is called EDIT2.

In Step 1, the PICTURE clause of the report-item is created according to the rules of the last section, using a minus sign and zero suppression: −ZZZZ.
In Step 2, all Z's must be replaced by the appropriate floating character: −−−−−.
Thus EDIT2 will have a PICTURE of −(5) or −−−−−.
0032̄ will print as −32
0487̄ will print as −487

Example 3

EDIT3 has a PICTURE clause of +++99.

Problem: Find the PICTURE clause of the sending field, FLD3.

Three plus signs indicate a floating-string edit that will accept **two** integer positions. The leftmost plus sign does **not** serve as a zero suppression character and is never replaced with integer data. Two characters of data will be accepted by three plus signs, and two characters of data will be accepted by two 9's. Thus the input area should have a PICTURE of S9(4).
382⁺6 will print as +3826
038̄2 will print as −382
000⁺2 will print as +02

From the above examples, it should be clear that floating-string characters may be used in conjunction with other edit symbols such as 9's, decimal points, and commas. The floating-string character, however, must be the first character in the PICTURE clause of the report-item. In addition, we may **not** use **two** floating-string characters in one report-item. If a dollar sign is to float, for example, then an operational sign may not be placed in the leftmost position of the field. You will recall, however, that signs may also appear in the rightmost position of a report-item. Thus $$,$$$.99− is a valid PICTURE clause. Only the dollar sign floats but a sign may be used in the field as well.

BLANK WHEN   At times, it is necessary to perform elaborate editing of data fields. We have
ZERO OPTION learned all the rules for performing such edits. In addition, however, it is often
desirable to print spaces when a sending field consists entirely of zeros. With
the use of complex editing, you may find that $.00 or −0 or + or − will print.
This may detract from the clarity of a report. In such cases the COBOL expression BLANK WHEN ZERO may be used **in conjunction with** the appropriate
PICTURE clause.

Example 1

    02 EDIT1 PICTURE +++.

This report-item will accept two characters of data:
03 will print as +3
7\overline{6} will print as −76
00 will print as +
To eliminate the printing of + for a zero sending field, the BLANK WHEN
ZERO option may be added:

┌───┐
│ 02 EDIT1 PICTURE +++ BLANK WHEN ZERO.   │
└───┘

When using the BLANK WHEN ZERO option in conjunction with a report-
item, the normal rules of editing will be followed, depending on the edit symbols in the PICTURE clause. If the field is zero, however, spaces will print.
Table 12.3 reviews all the rules of editing discussed here.

TABLE 12.3

Sending-Field		Report-Item	
PICTURE	**Contents**	PICTURE	**Edited Results**
999V99	00₁23	$$$$.99	$1.23
S999V99	0123\overline{4}	$$$$.99−	$12.34−
S999	12\overset{+}{3}	− − − −	123
S999	12\overline{3}	− − − −	−123
S999	00\overline{5}	− − − −	−5
99	37	+++	+37
S99	0\overline{5}	+++	−5
S99	0\overset{+}{5}	+++	+5
999	000	++++ BLANK WHEN ZERO	
999	000	++++	+
999V99	00₀00	$$$$.99	$.00
999V99	00₀00	$$$$.99 BLANK WHEN ZERO	

1. Three characters that may be used in a floating string are _____,
_____, _____.
*****
+
—
$

2. The edit character to ''float'' must be the _____ character in the field.
*****
first

3. If five minus signs appear in a floating string, (no.) characters of the sending
field may be accepted by the report-item.
*****
four

4. To print a floating dollar sign and a minus sign if a sending field with
PICTURE S999V99 is negative will require a report-item PICTURE clause
of _____.
*****
$$$$.99−

5. The BLANK WHEN ZERO option has an effect on the edited output only
if the sending field is _____.
*****
zero

For Questions 6–15, fill in the missing column.

	Sending-Field		Report-Item	
	PICTURE	Contents	PICTURE	Edited Results
6.	999V99	00005	$$$$.99	
7.	999V99	00005	$$$$.99−	
8.	S999V99	00005	$$$$.99−	
9.	9999V99	002654		26.54+
10.	9999V99	003872		+38.72
11.	S999	002	++++	
12.	S99		− − −	−4
13.	999V99	00000	$$$$.99	
14.	999V99	00000	$$$$.99 BLANK WHEN ZERO	
15.	9999V99	023875	$$,$$$.99 BLANK WHEN ZERO	

*****

6. $.05
7. $.05
8. $.05−
9. ZZZZ.99+
10. +++++.99
11. −2
12. 04
13. $.00
14.   (blanks)
15. $238.75

PRACTICE PROBLEM—
WITH SOLUTION

Write a program to print the total of the amount fields of every group of 100 tape records.

Input: Standard labels, no blocking factor
1–20 Name
21–25 Amount xxx.xx

Output: Print

11–30 Name
41–50 Total (edited with dollar sign, comma, decimal point, and check protection)

(NOTE: The name is the same for each group of 100 records. The number of tape records is a multiple of 100.)

See Figure 12.2 for solution.

REVIEW QUESTIONS

True False

I. True-False Questions

1. Editing is most often performed when output is to be printed.
2. A report-item may not be used in an arithmetic operation.
3. Dollar signs and minus signs may be used as floating characters but not in the same field.
4. A report-item may be specified in an arithmetic operation only if it follows the word GIVING.
5. A $ is called a check protection symbol.
6. The BLANK WHEN ZERO option is only permissible on fields that use floating characters.
7. DB and CR both print if the sending field is signed negative.
8. To print a sign as an edit symbol, the sending field must have an S in its PICTURE clause.
9. Without the use of edit characters, 11.55 would print as 1155.
10. A plus or minus sign most often is transmitted to the computer as an overpunch in the units position.

II. General Questions

For Questions 1–22, fill in the missing entries.

	Sending-Field PICTURE	Contents	Report-Item PICTURE	Contents
1.	99V99	0467	ZZ.99	
2.	9(4)V999	0086754	$Z,ZZZ.99	
3.	999	467	$ZZZ.99	
4.	S99V99	0098	$ZZ.99+	
5.	S99V99	0089	$ZZ.99−	
6.	S999	005	$ZZZ.99CR	
7.	S999	005	$ZZZ.99DB	
8,	S99V99	0006	$ZZ.99CR	
9.	S99V99	0005	$**.99−	
10.	9(4)	1357	$*,***.99	
11.	XXXX	CRDB	XXBBXX	

12.	9(4)	0170	99BB99	
13.	999V99	135.79	$$$$.99	
14.	999V99	000.09	$$$$.99	
15.	999V99	000.00	$$$$.99	
16.	S9(5)	00567	+++++	
17.	S99V99	00.34	$$$.99−	
18.	S99	00	+++	
19.	S99	00	−−−	
20.	9999V99	000988		$9.88
21.	9999V99	000988		$ 9.88
22.		8738		+$87.38

```
IDENTIFICATION DIVISION.
PROGRAM-ID. CHAPT12.
ENVIRONMENT DIVISION.
CONFIGURATION SECTION.
SOURCE-COMPUTER. IBM-370.
OBJECT-COMPUTER. IBM-370.
INPUT-OUTPUT SECTION.
FILE-CONTROL.
    SELECT TAPE-FILE ASSIGN TO UT-S-SYS004.
    SELECT PRINT-FILE ASSIGN TO UR-S-SYSOUT.
DATA DIVISION.
FILE SECTION.
FD  TAPE-FILE
    LABEL RECORDS ARE STANDARD
    RECORD CONTAINS 25 CHARACTERS
    BLOCK CONTAINS 25 RECORDS
    DATA RECORD IS TAPE-REC.
01  TAPE-REC.
    02  NAME              PIC X(20).
    02  AMOUNT            PIC 999V99.
FD  PRINT-FILE
    LABEL RECORDS ARE OMITTED
    RECORD CONTAINS 133 CHARACTERS
    DATA RECORD IS PRINT-REC.
01  PRINT-REC.
    02  FILLER            PIC X(11).
    02  NAME              PIC X(20).
    02  FILLER            PIC X(10).
    02  TOTAL             PIC $**,***.99.
    02  FILLER            PIC X(82).
WORKING-STORAGE SECTION.
01  WORK-AREAS.
    02  EOF               PIC 9 VALUE 0.
    02  TOTAL-AMOUNT      PIC 9(5)V99 VALUE ZEROS.
    02  CTR               PIC 9(3) VALUE ZEROS.
PROCEDURE DIVISION.
    OPEN INPUT TAPE-FILE, OUTPUT PRINT-FILE.
    READ TAPE-FILE AT END MOVE 1 TO EOF.
    PERFORM CALC-RTN UNTIL   EOF = 1.
    CLOSE TAPE-FILE, PRINT-FILE.
    STOP RUN.
CALC-RTN.
    MOVE SPACES TO PRINT-REC.
    PERFORM READ-RTN UNTIL CTR = 100.
    MOVE 0 TO CTR.
    MOVE NAME OF TAPE-REC TO NAME OF PRINT-REC.
    MOVE TOTAL-AMOUNT TO TOTAL.
    WRITE PRINT-REC.
    MOVE ZEROS TO TOTAL-AMOUNT.
READ-RTN.
    ADD AMOUNT TO TOTAL-AMOUNT.
    ADD 1 TO CTR.
    READ TAPE-FILE AT END MOVE 1 TO EOF.
```

Figure 12.2

PROBLEMS   1. Write a program to print an output report from the following card format:

1–5   Product Number
6–8   Warehouse Number
9–11 Quantity (may be negative in case of credit)
12–13 Territory Code
14–18 Unit Price xxx.xx
19–38 Product Description
39–41 Discount Percent .xxx
42–46 Customer Number
47–80 Not used

Formulas

Gross = Quantity × Unit Price
Discount Amount = Gross × Discount Percent
Net = Gross − Discount Amount

All three fields should be rounded to xxxxxx.xx specification. Print heading PRODUCT LISTING on the top of the output page.

Figure 12.3 is a Printer Spacing chart, which indicates the print positions in which data is to be written. The x's denote positions for actual data. The words in parentheses ( ) denote fields to be printed.

This chart has the same meaning as the following:

3–7	Product Number	
20–39	Product Description	
42–48	Unit Price	print decimal point; zero suppress; print dollar sign
52–55	Quantity	print minus sign, if present; zero suppress
61–72	Gross	print minus sign, if present; zero suppress; print decimal point; print $; print comma
76–87	Discount Amount	print decimal point; zero suppress; print $; print minus sign, if present; print comma
91–102	Net	zero suppress; decimal point; minus sign, if present; print $; print comma

(PRODUCT NUMBER)   (DESCRIPTION)   (UNIT PRICE) (QUANTITY)   (GROSS)   (DISCOUNT AMT)   (NET)
XXXXX   XXXXXXXXXXXXXXXXXXXX $XXX.XX   XXX- $XXX,XXX.XX- $XXX,XXX.XX- $XXX,XXX.XX-

Figure 12.3

2. Consider the following input tape format.

   1–20 Customer name (1-initial 1, 2-initial 2)
21–25 Transaction amount for week 1   xxx.xx
26–30 Transaction amount for week 2   xxx.xx
31–35 Transaction amount for week 3   xxx.xx
36–40 Transaction amount for week 4   xxx.xx
41–46 Amount of credit   xxxx.xx
47–50 Not used

Standard tape labels, no blocking factor

Problem Definition

1. Print heading MONTHLY TRANSACTIONS
2. Print each data field edited
    (a) Two spaces between initials of name.
    (b) Print decimal point, dollar sign, CR for negative transaction amount, dollar sign should float.
    (c) Print decimal point, comma, dollar sign and * for credit amount.
    (d) For each tape record, print a balance due (transaction amounts − credit), floating dollar sign, operational sign, decimal point.

13 CHAPTER SPECIAL CONSIDERATIONS FOR PRINTED OUTPUT

Thus far, we have discussed editing printed output. We have noted, however, that reports require additional programming. Let us consider first the spacing of forms.

A. SPACING OF FORMS

Issuing a WRITE (record-name) command, where the record indicated is in the file assigned to the printer, will cause **one line** of accumulated data to print. After the WRITE instruction, the paper will advance **one line;** that is, **single spacing** of forms will result.

Single spacing, however, is ordinarily not sufficient for most printing applications. Usually programs require special spacing features such as double spacing between some lines, and triple spacing between others. A simple WRITE command results in single spacing **only.**

We may achieve additional spacing of forms by issuing an AFTER or BEFORE ADVANCING option with **every** WRITE instruction for print operations:

$$\underline{\text{WRITE}} \text{ (record-name)} \left[\left\{ \begin{array}{l} \text{AFTER} \\ \underline{\text{BEFORE}} \end{array} \right\} \text{ADVANCING} \left\{ \begin{array}{l} \text{integer} \\ \text{data-name} \end{array} \right\} \text{LINES} \right]$$

The integer, if used, must be any positive integer less than 100. The data-name, if used, must contain any integer less than 100.

If a line is to print **after** the paper is spaced, the AFTER ADVANCING option is used. WRITE PRINT-REC AFTER ADVANCING 2 LINES will space two lines and **then** print. That is, after the paper advances two lines, printing will occur. If a line is to print **before** spacing occurs, the BEFORE ADVANCING option is used. WRITE HEADER-REC BEFORE ADVANCING 3 LINES will print and then advance the paper three lines.

Note that the words ADVANCING and LINES are optional. Hence, the following two statements produce the same results:

1. WRITE PRINT-REC AFTER ADVANCING 2 LINES.
2. WRITE PRINT-REC AFTER 2.

Note that the BEFORE ADVANCING option should not usually be used in the same program as the AFTER ADVANCING option. To do so may cause overprinting on the same line. That is, consider the following:

WRITE   HDR-REC AFTER ADVANCING 2 LINES.

.

.

.

WRITE   REPORT-REC BEFORE ADVANCING 2 LINES.

The first WRITE command causes two lines to be spaced and then the HDR-REC to be printed. The subsequent WRITE command prints **first** and then spaces. This means that REPORT-REC would print **on the same line** as HDR-REC. This overprinting would, of course, be incorrect. To avoid such problems, use either the BEFORE ADVANCING or the AFTER ADVANCING option in a single program, but not both.

Most computers enable the paper to be spaced a maximum of 100 lines. Check your Specifications Manual for the upper limit on this option for your computer.

To advance the paper one line and then print one line, the following instruction is issued:

Note that, even though the integer '1' denotes a **single** line, the plural LINES may be used. Although the English is not quite accurate, the notation **is** acceptable in COBOL. The word LINE would be acceptable as well for 1974 ANS COBOL users.

Using the ADVANCING option will perform special spacing operations. The computer uses the **first position** in the print area for controlling the spacing of forms. Thus we must always provide the print area with one **extra** position, which the computer will use for proper spacing of forms.

As noted, we specify 133 positions for print records, rather than 132. The first position of this area is used for **carriage** control. This first position should not be accessed in the program. The print area may be defined as follows:

```
FD   PRINT-FILE
     LABEL RECORDS ARE OMITTED
     RECORD CONTAINS 133 CHARACTERS
     DATA RECORD IS PRINTOUT.
Ø1   PRINTOUT.
     Ø2     FILLER        PICTURE X.
     Ø2     REAL-REC.
            .
            .
            .
```

Note that to specify only 132 positions for a print record will cause the printing of 131 print positions; that is, the first print position would be lost.

Note, also, that once the ADVANCING option is specified for a print record in the PROCEDURE DIVISION, the ADVANCING option must be specified for **all** print records in that program. Thus, if single spacing is sufficient, use a simple WRITE statement. If single spacing is not sufficient, the ADVANCING option must be used with **all** WRITE statements for the print file.

B. TESTING FOR THE END OF A PAGE AND SKIPPING TO A NEW PAGE

Computer generated reports are printed on **continuous forms.** All forms are connected, with perforations denoting the end of each page. After they are generated, these forms must be **burst,** or separated, into single sheets.

Unless the computer is instructed to do otherwise, it will write each line and advance the paper, printing from one form to another, ignoring the fact that each is really an individual page. At times, it may even print over the perforations which, at best, makes reading difficult.

Although printing is done from one continuous form to another, the computer must be instructed to observe page delineations. Each page should generally begin with a heading. Data lines follow and, when the end of a form is reached, we wish to skip to a new page and write the heading again.

The computer controls the sensing of various print lines by the use of a **carriage control tape.** This tape, which is attached to the printer, has designated holes corresponding to the first and last line of printing. With this tape, the computer can **sense** the last print line. When the form's end is sensed, the programmer must instruct the computer to advance to a new page. The tape will sense the start of a new page, as well as the end of the previous one.

Figure 13.1 illustrates a carriage control tape. (A) indicates a standard tape that must be punched to designate first and last line of printing. (B) indicates the tape with the ends connected. When the tape is connected as in (B), it is placed in the printer. Figure 13.2 illustrates how the tape corresponds to the actual printed page. If a hole were punched in channel 1 of line 6 of the tape, for example, an instruction to skip to channel 1 would advance the paper to line 6.

Generally, a punch in Channel 01 of this tape, called C01 in our illustrations, is used to designate the start of a new page. A punch in Channel 1 must be equated to a new page indicator in a paragraph called SPECIAL-NAMES, which is part of the CONFIGURATION SECTION of the ENVIRONMENT DIVISION. Thus the CONFIGURATION SECTION can be expanded as follows:

```
CONFIGURATION SECTION.
SOURCE-COMPUTER. (programmer-supplied-name)
OBJECT-COMPUTER. (programmer-supplied-name)
SPECIAL-NAMES. CØ1 IS (mnemonic-name).
```

That is, Channel 01 can be equated to any unique mnemonic-name:

Example

```
CONFIGURATION SECTION.
SOURCE-COMPUTER. IBM-370.
OBJECT-COMPUTER. IBM-370.
SPECIAL-NAMES. C01 IS NEW-PAGE.
```

In the above, C01 or Channel 1, which designates the top of a new form, is equated to the mnemonic name NEW-PAGE. This name is then used in con-

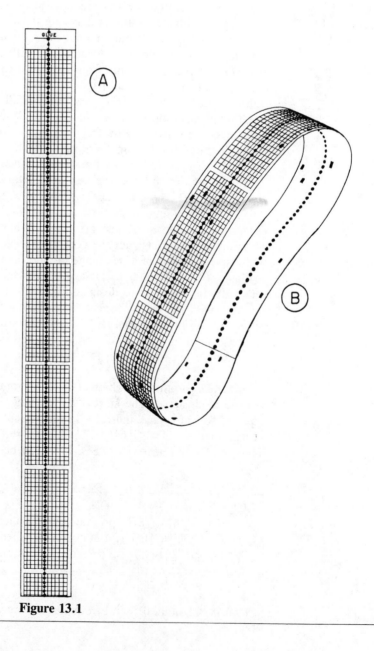

Figure 13.1

junction with the WRITE statement:

Note that the above statement will cause PRINT-REC to print on the top of a new form, since NEW-PAGE refers to Channel 01. The code C01 is applicable to IBM computers but may be different for other computers.

The mnemonic-name following the COBOL reserved word, ADVANCING, must be the **same mnemonic-name** as the one equated to Channel 01 (C01) of the SPECIAL-NAMES paragraph of the CONFIGURATION SECTION.

Channels 02 through 12 may be used in the SPECIAL-NAMES paragraph and equated to specified mnemonic-names. Keep in mind, however, that the car-

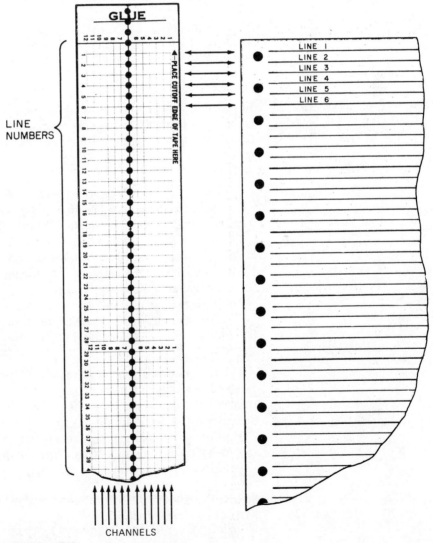

Figure 13.2

riage control tape, used in conjunction with the printed output, must contain punches in these respective channels.

We can expand the format of the WRITE statement to include **all** options of the ADVANCING clause thus far discussed:

$$\underline{\text{WRITE}} \text{ (record-name)} \left[\left\{ \begin{array}{c} \underline{\text{AFTER}} \\ \underline{\text{BEFORE}} \end{array} \right\} \text{ADVANCING} \left\{ \begin{array}{l} \text{integer LINES} \\ \text{data-name LINES} \\ \text{mnemonic-name} \end{array} \right\} \right]$$

Some compilers enable the programmer to skip to a new page without using the SPECIAL-NAMES paragraph of the CONFIGURATION SECTION. This can be performed as follows:

$$\text{WRITE (record name)} \left\{ \begin{array}{c} \text{AFTER} \\ \text{BEFORE} \end{array} \right\} \text{ADVANCING 0 LINES.}$$

The use of 0 LINES to indicate the skipping to a new page is permitted with some compilers, but not all.

END-OF-PAGE CONTROL—
WITH THE USE OF A
PROGRAMMED LINE
COUNTER

In order to ensure that information does not print over the perforations of a continuous form, from page to page, an end-of-page control routine must be coded. Using a programmed line counter to achieve end-of-page control, we must:

PROGRAMMED LINE COUNTER

1. Determine the number of lines to be printed.
2. After each WRITE command increment a WORKING-STORAGE line counter field by one. In this way, the number in the line counter field will be equal to the number of lines actually printed.
3. After each WRITE command, test the line counter to determine if it equals the number of lines we want printed. If it does, we print a heading on a new page. If it does not, we continue with the program.
4. If the line counter has reached the desired number, we perform a heading routine and reinitialize the line counter.

The programmed line counter should be employed for all programs that produce a significant number of print lines. Without such a procedure, the printer will simply print one line after another paying no attention to page delineations or perforations.

Thus we can utilize a programmed line counter that is to be incremented by one every time a line is written. When a specified number of lines have been written, we can simply instruct the computer to print a heading on a new page:

```
WRITE PRINT-REC AFTER ADVANCING 1 LINES.
ADD 1 TO LINE-COUNT.
IF LINE-COUNT = 60 WRITE HDR-REC AFTER ADVANCING NEW-PAGE
    MOVE ZEROS TO LINE-COUNT.
```

Note that LINE-COUNT must be a WORKING-STORAGE item initialized at zero. The following routine, utilizing the same method, allows for double-spacing:

```
WRITE PRINT-REC AFTER ADVANCING 2 LINES.
ADD 1 TO LINE-COUNT.
IF LINE-COUNT = 30 WRITE HDR-REC AFTER ADVANCING NEW-PAGE
   MOVE ZEROS TO LINE-COUNT.
```

Both routines allow for the printing of 60 records per page. In the first case, we print 60 records. In the second, we print 30 double-spaced records. That is, in the second routine, we have 30 print records and 30 blank records.

Note that 1974 ANS COBOL users may also use a LINAGE clause. See Appendix F.

END-OF-PAGE CONTROL—
WITH USE OF THE
EOP OPTION

The following may be used as an alternative to the above programmed line counter routine on some computers. Note that this EOP option can detect an end-of-page condition only if the printer is on-line. In most large installations, however, the output is **spooled** onto tape and then printed; in these cases, the EOP option will not work. To test for the end of a form or a page–overflow condition, the WRITE statement may be amended as follows, **but only on some computers:**

$$
\underline{\text{WRITE}} \text{ (record name)} \begin{Bmatrix} \underline{\text{BEFORE}} \\ (\text{AFTER}) \end{Bmatrix} \text{ADVANCING} \begin{bmatrix} \begin{Bmatrix} \text{integer LINES} \\ \text{data-name LINES} \\ (\text{mnemonic-name}) \end{Bmatrix} \end{bmatrix}
$$

$$
\begin{bmatrix} \underline{\text{AT}} & \begin{Bmatrix} \underline{\text{END-OF-PAGE}} \\ \underline{\text{EOP}} \end{Bmatrix} & \left(\text{imperative statement(s)} \right) \end{bmatrix}
$$

Examples

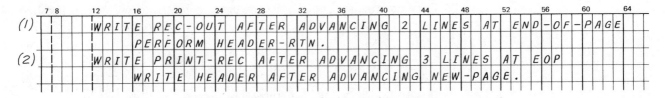

```
(1)   WRITE REC-OUT AFTER ADVANCING 2 LINES AT END-OF-PAGE
         PERFORM HEADER-RTN.
(2)   WRITE PRINT-REC AFTER ADVANCING 3 LINES AT EOP
         WRITE HEADER AFTER ADVANCING NEW-PAGE.
```

The clause beginning with AT END-OF-PAGE or AT EOP is used to test for the end of a form, usually signalled by a punch in channel 9 or 12 of the carriage control tape. The imperative statement or statements following AT $\begin{Bmatrix} \text{END-OF-PAGE} \\ \text{EOP} \end{Bmatrix}$ are executed if the end of a form has been reached.

In Example 1, a line is written after double-spacing, and HEADER-RTN is performed if the end of a form is sensed. Generally, we wish to print a heading on a new page when an end of form condition occurs. In Example 2, a line is written after triple spacing, and the HEADER record is printed at the top of a

new form if the end of a page is sensed. Note that in Example 2 the SPECIAL-
NAMES paragraph of the CONFIGURATION SECTION is required.

The COBOL reserved words EOP and END-OF-PAGE require no further
specification in the program. When using this option with the WRITE statement,
a RESERVE clause **must** be employed in conjunction with the SELECT statement for the print-file:

1968 ANS Users

> SELECT (file name) ASSIGN TO (device) <u>RESERVE</u>
> <u>NO</u> ALTERNATE AREAS.

1974 ANS Users

> SELECT (file name) ASSIGN TO (device)
> <u>RESERVE</u> 1 AREA.

Example (for 1968 users)

This RESERVE clause eliminates the buffer area established for the specific file
and is used to set up a single print area.

To summarize the entries for skipping to a new form and for sensing the end
of a form, include for the ENVIRONMENT DIVISION:

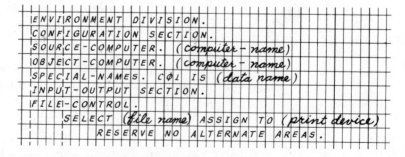

In the PROCEDURE DIVISION, the following entries may be used for testing
for end of page and skipping to a new form, assuming that the above mnemonic-
name is NEW-FORM:

```
WRITE PRINT-REC AFTER ADVANCING 2 LINES
  AT EOP WRITE HDR-REC AFTER ADVANCING
NEW-FORM.
```

Keep in mind that the COBOL reserved words EOP and END-OF-PAGE represent end of form tests for **some** compilers. Check your Specifications Manual for rules for your computer. The programmed line counter routine described above can be used with all computers.

Note, also, that a form overflow condition exists when a specific line on the form is reached. This end-of-form condition continues to exist until a new page begins. Thus if an end-of-page condition exists and the paper is then advanced two additional lines, the end-of-page condition, when tested, would still exist. It is, however, good practice to test for an end of form each time a line is written. In this way, any end-of-page condition could not be bypassed.

SELF-EVALUATING QUIZ

1. To advance the paper a specified number of lines before or after printing is called _____.
   *****
   an ADVANCING option
2. To space the paper a designated number of lines and then to print a line, the _____ clause is used as part of the WRITE statement.
   *****
   AFTER ADVANCING
3. Write a COBOL expression to advance the form two lines and then to print the record called TOTAL, which is part of the print file.
   *****
   WRITE TOTAL AFTER ADVANCING 2 LINES.
   What, if anything, is wrong with the following statements (4–5)?
4. WRITE PRINT-REC AFTER ADVANCING TWO LINES.
   *****
   Should be integer 2, unless TWO has been defined as a data-name with a value of 2.
5. WRITE PRINT-REC AFTER ADVANCING 1 LINE.
   *****
   Plural LINES must be used if you are using the 1968 ANS COBOL standard.
6. To test for the last line of printing on a form, the _____ clause may be used with the WRITE statement.
   *****
   EOP or END-OF-PAGE
7. Code a routine to write PRINT-REC, space two lines and perform a HDR-RTN if a form overflow condition exists:
   *****

```
 7 8    12    16    20    24    28    32    36    40    44    48    52
       WRITE PRINT-REC BEFORE ADVANCING 2 LINES
             AT EOP PERFORM HDR-RTN.
```

Note: a programmed line counter routine could also have been coded.

8. The _____ paragraph of the ENVIRONMENT DIVISION is required to equate a channel of the carriage control tape to a _____.
*****
SPECIAL-NAMES
mnemonic-name

9. The above mnemonic-name is then used with the _____ option of the WRITE statement.
*****
ADVANCING

10. Usually a carriage control tape has a punch in _____ to signal the start of a new page.
*****
Channel 1

11. If the following is a statement in the PROCEDURE DIVISION, code the SPECIAL-NAMES paragraph.

WRITE LINE-1 AFTER ADVANCING ONE-PAGE.
*****
SPECIAL-NAMES. C01 IS ONE-PAGE.

12. The SPECIAL-NAMES paragraph is part of the _____ SECTION and follows the _____ entries, if these are used.
*****
CONFIGURATION
SOURCE-COMPUTER and OBJECT-COMPUTER

13. If the following is the SPECIAL-NAMES paragraph of a program, code a statement to print HDR on the top of a new page:

SPECIAL-NAMES. C01 IS FORM-START.
*****
WRITE HDR AFTER ADVANCING FORM-START.

C. THE ALIGNMENT OF DATA AND THE PRINTING OF HEADER INFORMATION

The print area, you will recall, must contain 133 characters when the ADVANCING option is used for writing records. The first position of the area is used by the computer for proper spacing of forms, and should not be accessed by the programmer. Thus the second position denoted in the area is really the first **print** position. Positions 2 to 133 in the print area will be transmitted to the printer when a WRITE command is executed. Thus we set up our print area as follows:

```
01   PRINT-REC.
      02    FILLER          PICTURE X.
      02    REAL-REC.
            03    FLDA      PICTURE X.
                  .
                  .
                  .
```

The first position is called FILLER to denote that it will not be accessed in the program. When a WRITE command is issued, whatever is in FLDA will

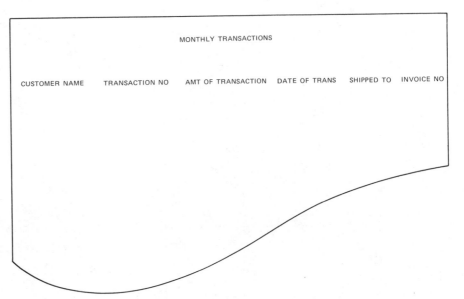

MONTHLY TRANSACTIONS

CUSTOMER NAME   TRANSACTION NO   AMT OF TRANSACTION   DATE OF TRANS   SHIPPED TO   INVOICE NO

Figure 13.3

appear in the first print position. The FILLER is not part of the print area and is used only for carriage control.

Thus 132 print positions are available. To produce clear and meaningful reports, information is ordinarily spaced on the line allowing adequate margins on each side of the paper and aligning the data so that fields are evenly distributed. In addition, headings are usually necessary to provide identifying information. Two types of headers generally appear on each page of a report:

1. Headings that identify the job, title, date, and specific application.
2. Headings that indicate field delineations.

Figure 13.3 illustrates the two types of headers. Note that line 1 of the illustration supplies data about the job and its application and line 2 designates the fields to be printed. Notice that the headings and fields are neatly spaced across the form.

The headings are essential on each page, since continuous forms are burst, or separated, after they are generated. Each page, then, must have identifying information.

PRINTER SPACING CHART   A Printer Spacing Chart, sometimes called a Print Layout Sheet, is commonly used to assist the programmer in the preparation of reports (see Figure 13.4). This chart is used for aligning data in the report so that (1) headers appear properly marginated in the middle of the page and (2) data fields are properly aligned under column headings and evenly spaced across the page.

The Printer Spacing Chart is subdivided into 132 print positions. The heading or headings are placed evenly. From the numbered positions, the programmer can then determine in which print positions he or she should place the literals, and which positions should be left blank. Figure 13.5 illustrates the Printer Spacing Chart for the report in Figure 13.3. Note that print positions 1–56 will be left blank in the print area as will positions 77–132 on the first line. The

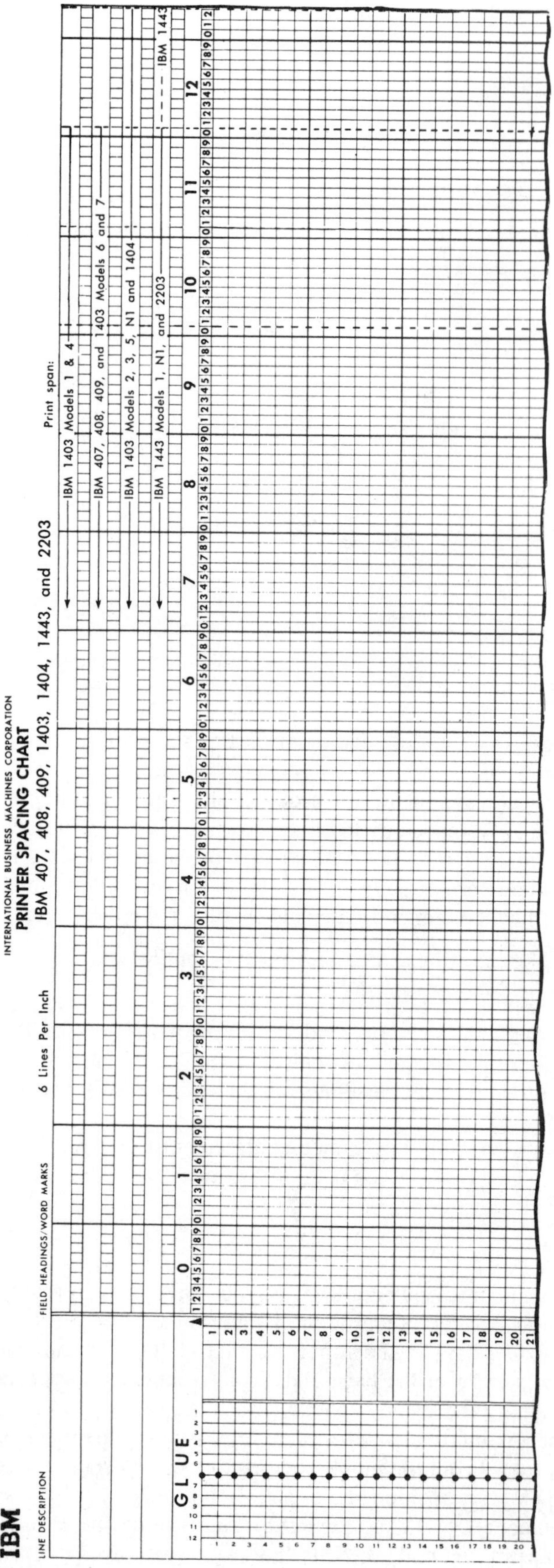

Figure 13.4

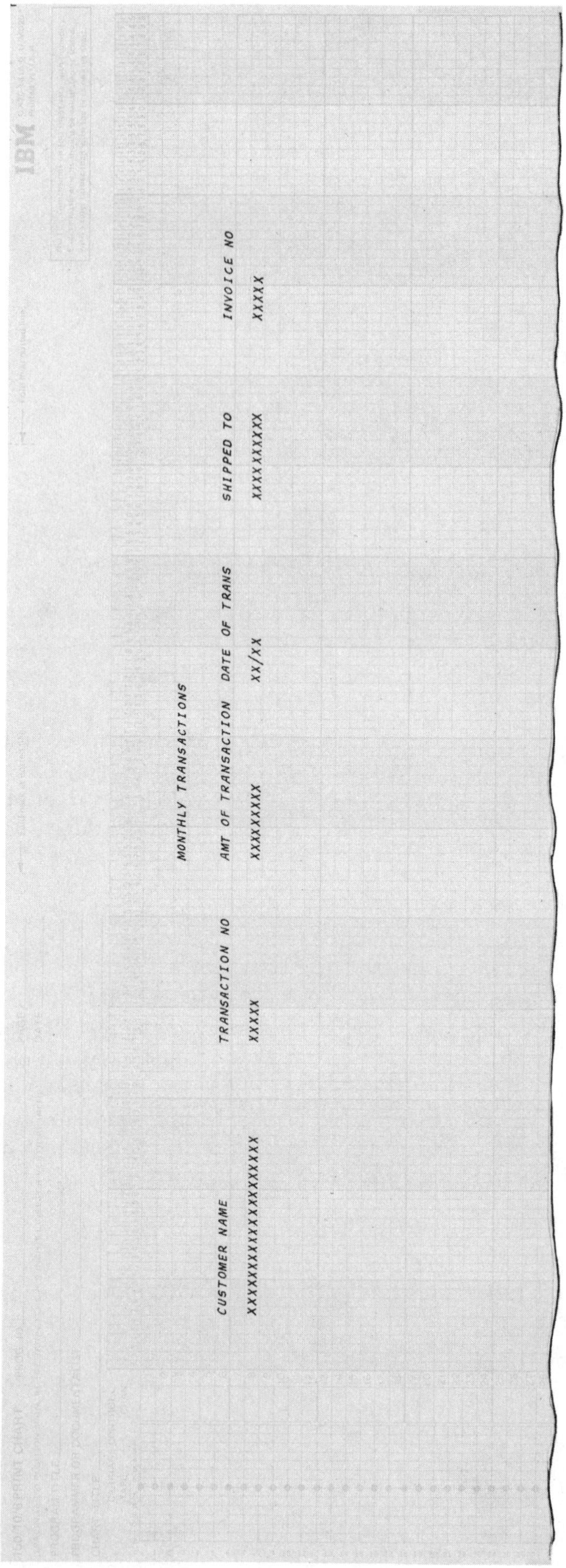

Figure 13.5

literal 'MONTHLY TRANSACTIONS' will be placed in the area between. On the Printer Spacing Chart note that X's indicate where the actual data will be placed. Twenty X's under the field delineator NAME denote that the data field contains 20 characters.

If both detail and header information are required in the report, and they generally are, then several record formats must be specified. Thus the FD entry for the print file illustrated in Figure 13.5 may be:

```
FD   PRINT-FILE
     LABEL RECORDS ARE OMITTED
     RECORD CONTAINS 133 CHARACTERS
     DATA RECORDS ARE HEADER-1,
         HEADER-2, DETAIL-LINE.
```

Each record indicated above must be described by an 01-level entry and its corresponding fields. Let us look at the headings first.

```
01   HEADER-1.
     02   FILLER        PIC X.
     02   FILLER        PIC X(56).
     02   LITERAL1      PIC X(20).
     02   FILLER        PIC X(56).
01   HEADER-2.
     02   FILLER        PIC X.
     02   FILLER        PIC X(6).
     02   LITERAL2      PIC X(13).
     02   FILLER        PIC X(17).
     02   LITERAL3      PIC X(14).
     02   FILLER        PIC X(6).
     02   LITERAL4      PIC X(18).
     02   FILLER        PIC XX.
     02   LITERAL5      PIC X(13).
     02   FILLER        PIC X(7).
     02   LITERAL6      PIC X(10).
     02   FILLER        PIC X(10).
     02   LITERAL7      PIC X(10).
     02   FILLER        PIC X(6).
```

Note that the first position of each record is a one-position FILLER, since this is the area that is used by the computer for carriage control and should not be accessed by the programmer. The fields designated as LITERAL1, LITERAL2, . . . will receive literals in the PROCEDURE DIVISION. Between each such field, there is a FILLER, since we wish spaces to appear on each side of a literal, thereby spacing the form. In the PROCEDURE DIVISION we must first clear the print area and then move the corresponding literals into each data field:

```
HEADER-RTN.
    MOVE SPACES TO HEADER-1.
    MOVE 'MONTHLY TRANSACTIONS' TO
        LITERAL1.
    WRITE HEADER-1 AFTER ADVANCING
        NEW-PAGE.
    MOVE SPACES TO HEADER-2.
    MOVE 'CUSTOMER NAME' TO LITERAL2.
    MOVE 'TRANSACTION NO' TO LITERAL3.
    MOVE 'AMT OF TRANSACTION' TO
        LITERAL4.
    MOVE 'DATE OF TRANS' TO LITERAL5.
    MOVE 'SHIPPED TO' TO LITERAL6.
    MOVE 'INVOICE NO' TO LITERAL7.
    WRITE HEADER-2 AFTER ADVANCING
        2 LINES.
```

Keep in mind that NEW-PAGE must be equated to Channel 1 in the SPECIAL-NAMES paragraph of the ENVIRONMENT DIVISION.

The print area must be initially cleared, since an output area has unpredictable contents at the onset of execution. The first heading is moved to the print area, and the line is printed on a new page. The print area must **again** be cleared before HEADER-2 is written. Note that HEADER-1 and HEADER-2 occupy the **same** 133-position print area. Thus this area must be cleared before additional information is moved in.

DETAIL-LINE, the third record of the PRINT-FILE, will also have FILLERs between each data field for proper alignment of information:

```
01  DETAIL-LINE.
    02  FILLER              PICTURE  X.
    02  FILLER              PICTURE  X(6).
    02  NAME                PICTURE  X(20).
    02  FILLER              PICTURE  X(10).
    02  TRANS-NO            PICTURE  9(5).
    02  FILLER              PICTURE  X(15).
    02  AMT-OF-TRANS        PICTURE  $$,$$$.99.
    02  FILLER              PICTURE  X(11).
    02  DATEX               PICTURE  X(5).
    02  FILLER              PICTURE  X(15).
    02  DESTINATION         PICTURE  X(10).
    02  FILLER              PICTURE  X(10).
    02  INV-NO              PICTURE  9(5).
    02  FILLER              PICTURE  X(11).
```

The DETAIL-LINE contains editing symbols in the field called AMT-OF-TRANS. Input data fields or intermediate work areas will be moved to the detail line:

```
7 8    12      16      20      24      28      32      36      40      44
DETAIL-RTN.
       MOVE SPACES TO DETAIL-LINE.
       MOVE NAME OF CARD-IN TO NAME
            OF DETAIL-LINE.
       MOVE TRANS-NO OF CARD-IN TO
            TRANS-NO OF DETAIL-LINE.
       MOVE AMT-OF-TRANS OF CARD-IN TO
            AMT-OF-TRANS OF DETAIL-LINE.
       MOVE DATEX OF CARD-IN TO DATEX OF
            DETAIL-LINE.
       MOVE DESTINATION OF CARD-IN TO
            DESTINATION OF DETAIL-LINE.
       MOVE INV-NO OF CARD-IN TO
            INV-NO OF DETAIL-LINE.
       WRITE DETAIL-LINE AFTER
            ADVANCING 2 LINES,
       AT EOP PERFORM HEADER-RTN.
       READ CARD-FILE AT END MOVE 1 TO
            EOF.
```

This method of creating output, although correct, is considered very inefficient. The two heading records and the detail line may be set up in the WORKING-STORAGE SECTION of the program. The chief reason for accumulating print information in the WORKING-STORAGE SECTION is that values may be assigned to the various fields in WORKING-STORAGE by VALUE clauses. This eliminates the necessity of moving spaces and specific literals to each area in the PROCEDURE DIVISION. Since VALUE clauses may **not** be assigned in the FILE SECTION,[1] we accumulate data in WORKING-STORAGE, move the records to the FILE SECTION, and then WRITE the information.

Thus the FILE SECTION print area is defined as 133 positions. Data from the WORKING-STORAGE SECTION will be moved into this file area. Fields need not be denoted in the FILE SECTION, since the **entire** record in WORKING-STORAGE will be moved:

```
FD  PRINT-FILE
    LABEL RECORDS ARE OMITTED
    RECORD CONTAINS 133
         CHARACTERS
    DATA RECORD IS PRINTOUT.
01  PRINTOUT    PIC X(133).
```

In the PROCEDURE DIVISION, data from WORKING-STORAGE will be moved to PRINTOUT and WRITE PRINTOUT AFTER ADVANCING 2 LINES will then be executed.

---

[1]Except for condition-names.

The two heading records and the detail line will be set up in the WORKING-STORAGE SECTION as group items:

```
WORKING-STORAGE SECTION.
01  HEADER-1.
    02  FILLER      PIC X            VALUE SPACES.
    02  FILLER      PIC X(56)        VALUE SPACES.
    02  LITERAL1    PIC X(20)        VALUE 'MONTHLY TRANSACTIONS'.
    02  FILLER      PIC X(56)        VALUE SPACES.
01  HEADER-2.
    02  FILLER      PIC X            VALUE SPACES.
    02  FILLER      PIC X(6)         VALUE SPACES.
    02  LITERAL2    PIC X(13)        VALUE 'CUSTOMER NAME'.
    02  FILLER      PIC X(17)        VALUE SPACES.
    02  LITERAL3    PIC X(14)        VALUE 'TRANSACTION NO'.
    02  FILLER      PIC X(6)         VALUE SPACES.
    02  LITERAL4    PIC X(18)        VALUE 'AMT OF TRANSACTION'.
    02  FILLER      PIC XX           VALUE SPACES.
    02  LITERAL5    PIC X(13)        VALUE 'DATE OF TRANS'.
    02  FILLER      PIC X(7)         VALUE SPACES.
    02  LITERAL6    PIC X(10)        VALUE 'SHIPPED TO'.
    02  FILLER      PIC X(10)        VALUE SPACES.
    02  LITERAL7    PIC X(10)        VALUE 'INVOICE NO'.
    02  FILLER      PIC X(6)         VALUE SPACES.
01  DETAIL-LINE.
    (Same format as specified above)
```

Note that, with the use of VALUE clauses in the WORKING-STORAGE SECTION, the movement of literals to the fields is unnecessary. Since the literal fields are not accessed by name in the PROCEDURE DIVISION, they could have been called FILLER as well. All constants and blanks are preassigned. We must still, however, move these records to the print area before a line is to be written. Thus data is accumulated in WORKING-STORAGE and then transferred to the print area:

```
HEADER-RTN.
    MOVE HEADER-1 TO PRINTOUT.
    WRITE PRINTOUT AFTER ADVANCING NEW-PAGE.
    MOVE HEADER-2 TO PRINTOUT.
    WRITE PRINTOUT AFTER ADVANCING 2 LINES.
```

Note that it is unnecessary to clear PRINTOUT. The entire 133 positions called HEADER-1, which contain appropriate blank areas, are transmitted to the PRINTOUT area. Similarly, PRINTOUT need not be cleared before HEADER-2 is moved since HEADER-2 contains the necessary blanks. The DE-TAIL-RTN remains the same as above, since data must still be moved to the various fields from the input area.

This method may appear less efficient since it sets up three additional 133 position areas in WORKING-STORAGE, which are not specified in Method 1. Note, however, that the coding of the PROCEDURE DIVISION is simplified, since VALUE clauses in the WORKING-STORAGE SECTION are somewhat easier to supply than MOVE statements. Note too that the following organization of WORKING-STORAGE entries is generally preferred because it provides better documentation.

```
WORKING-STORAGE SECTION.
Ø1  HEADINGS.
    Ø2  HEADER-1.
        Ø3  FILLER      PIC X        VALUE SPACES.
        Ø3  FILLER      PIC X(56)    VALUE SPACES.
        Ø3  LITERAL1    PIC X(2Ø)    VALUE 'MONTHLY TRANSACTIONS'.
        Ø3  FILLER      PIC X(56)    VALUE SPACES.
    Ø2  HEADER-2.
        Ø3  FILLER      PIC X        VALUE SPACES.
        Ø3  FILLER      PIC X(6)     VALUE SPACES.
        Ø3  LITERAL2    PIC X(13)    VALUE 'CUSTOMER NAME'.
        Ø3  FILLER      PIC X(17)    VALUE SPACES.
        Ø3  LITERAL3    PIC X(14)    VALUE 'TRANSACTION NO'.
        Ø3  FILLER      PIC X(6)     VALUE SPACES.
        Ø3  LITERAL4    PIC X(18)    VALUE 'AMT OF TRANSACTION'.
        Ø3  FILLER      PIC XX       VALUE SPACES.
        Ø3  LITERAL5    PIC X(13)    VALUE 'DATE OF TRANS'.
        Ø3  FILLER      PIC X(7)     VALUE SPACES.
        Ø3  LITERAL6    PIC X(1Ø)    VALUE 'SHIPPED TO'.
        Ø3  FILLER      PIC X(1Ø)    VALUE SPACES.
        Ø3  LITERAL7    PIC X(1Ø)    VALUE 'INVOICE NO'.
        Ø3  FILLER      PIC X(6)     VALUE SPACES.
Ø1  DETAIL-LINE.
        .
        .
        .
```

Several shortcuts may be used in the WORKING-STORAGE SECTION to enhance the efficiency of the program. HEADER-1, for example, may be set up as follows:

```
Ø1  HEADER-1.
    Ø2  FILLER      PICTURE X(57)    VALUE SPACES.
    Ø2  LITERAL1    PICTURE X(76)    VALUE 'MONTHLY TRANSACTIONS'.
```

The FILLER specified above will print 56 positions of blanks since the first position of the record will be used for carriage control. It is unnecessary, therefore, to set up **two** FILLER areas, one containing a single blank and one containing 56 blanks. One FILLER will serve just as well. Recall that nonnumeric literals are left justified in a field. Thus LITERAL1 will contain, in its first 20 positions (which correspond to print positions 57–76), 'MONTHLY TRANS-

IBM   COBOL Coding Form   GX28-1464-5 U/M 050*
Printed in U.S.A.

SYSTEM			PUNCHING INSTRUCTIONS						PAGE	OF	
PROGRAM			GRAPHIC					CARD FORM #			*
PROGRAMMER		DATE	PUNCH								

```
01  HEADER-2.
    02  FIELD-1      PICTURE  X(75)      VALUE '              CUSTOMER NA
-   'ME                       TRANSACTION NO       AMT OF TRANSACTION'.
    02  FIELD2       PICTURE  X(58)      VALUE '    DATE OF TRANS
-   '   SHIPPED TO        INVOICE NO       '.
```

Figure 13.6

ACTIONS'. The rest of the field will be replaced with blanks. The VALUE clause has the same effect as **moving** 'MONTHLY TRANSACTIONS' to LITERAL1.

Using the JUSTIFIED RIGHT clause, we may set up HEADER-1 slightly differently:

```
01  HEADER-1.
    02  LITERAL1     PICTURE  X(77)  VALUE
                     'MONTHLY TRANSACTIONS' JUSTIFIED RIGHT.
    02  FILLER       PICTURE  X(56)  VALUE SPACES.
```

'MONTHLY TRANSACTIONS' will be placed in positions 58–77, which correspond to **print** positions 57–76. The rest of the field will be blank.

HEADER-2 may also be coded more efficiently. We may use two literals, each containing the proper number of spaces, to incorporate the entire record. Figure 13.6 illustrates the necessary entries. Note that the rules for continuation of literals, as indicated in Chapter 11, apply. Note also that 120 positions is the maximum size of a nonnumeric literal. Thus two fields, at least, must be designated for the entire print area, which is 133 positions long.

PAGE NUMBERS   Often, when printing headers, a page number is required as part of each header record. Consider the following record described in WORKING-STORAGE:

```
01  HEAD-REC.
    02  FILLER       PIC  X(61)  VALUE SPACES.
    02  LITERALX     PIC  X(20)  VALUE 'SALARY CHANGES'.
    02  LITERALY     PIC  X(8)   VALUE 'PAGE NO.'.
    02  PAGE-CT      PIC  ZZZZ.
    02  FILLER       PIC  X(40)  VALUE SPACES.
```

A WORKING-STORAGE item, called CT1, PICTURE 9999, VALUE 0001, is set up prior to the headings. The following HEADER-RTN will print a page number on each page:

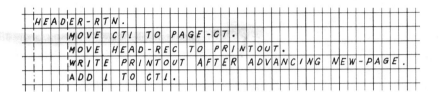

```
HEADER-RTN.
    MOVE CT1 TO PAGE-CT.
    MOVE HEAD-REC TO PRINTOUT.
    WRITE PRINTOUT AFTER ADVANCING NEW-PAGE.
    ADD 1 TO CT1.
```

HEADER-RTN would be executed, initially, right after the files are opened. To access the HEADER-RTN, CALC-RTN might be coded as follows:

CALC-RTN.

.
.
.

        MOVE DETAIL-REC TO PRINTOUT.
        WRITE PRINTOUT AFTER ADVANCING 2 LINES
                        AT EOP PERFORM HEADER-RTN.
        READ . . .

Keep in mind that NEW-PAGE must be equated to Channel 1 in the SPECIAL-NAMES paragraph of the ENVIRONMENT DIVISION.

Each time through the routine, CT1 is incremented by 1. Before each record is printed, CT1 is edited into PAGE-CT. Thus a correct page number will appear on each form. Note that the following is **not** correct.

Invalid: ADD 1 TO PAGE-CT.

PAGE-CT is a **report-item** containing editing symbols that cause zero suppression. Only **numeric** items may be used in arithmetic operations. PAGE-CT, as a report-item, is not a numeric field.

WRITE . . . FROM   A MOVE operation, in which data is transmitted to the output area, followed
STATEMENT   by a WRITE statement, may be replaced by a single WRITE . . . FROM instruction.

```
MOVE HEADING-1 TO PRINT-REC.
WRITE PRINT-REC AFTER ADVANCING NEW-PAGE.
```

may be replaced by

```
WRITE PRINT-REC FROM HEADING-1
                AFTER ADVANCING NEW-PAGE.
```

At this point, it is probably quite clear that the printing of forms requires many programming considerations that are not necessary when producing other kinds of output. The following may provide a checklist of items that ought to be considered when printing data:

CHECKLIST OF PRINT REQUIREMENTS

1. Record length must be defined as 133 characters. The first position should have initial contents of a space, and should not be accessed in the program.

2. The AFTER or BEFORE ADVANCING option should be used with each WRITE command to indicate the spacing of the form. AFTER ADVANCING 1, 2, 3 LINES, for example, will cause zero, one, or two blank lines, respectively, to appear before the next record is written.
The BEFORE or AFTER ADVANCING option can cause the paper to space up to 100 lines. Either the integers 1–99 or a data-name with corresponding integer value may be used with the ADVANCING option.

3. Print records, including headers and detail lines, should be established in WORKING-STORAGE to allow the use of VALUE clauses. These records must then be moved to the print area, and a WRITE, or a WRITE . . . FROM command issued. Spacing of data on the line may be facilitated with the use of a Printer Spacing Chart.

4. After each record is printed, a test for the end of a form should be issued so that printing of headers on each page is ensured.

5. The appropriate editing symbols should be specified in the PICTURE clauses of report-items within the detail record.

6. To skip to a new form, the SPECIAL-NAMES paragraph of the CONFIG-URATION SECTION of the ENVIRONMENT DIVISION may be used to equate channel 1 on the carriage control tape to a mnemonic-name. This mnemonic-name is then used in place of a number with the ADVANCING option to skip to a new page. The clause AFTER ADVANCING 0 LINES, available on some compilers, will also cause skipping to a new page.

7. If single spacing is sufficient, use the WRITE statement without the AD-VANCING option. If single spacing is not sufficient, the ADVANCING option must be used with **every** WRITE statement for the print file.

SELF-EVALUATING QUIZ

1. The two types of headings that may appear on a printed report are _____ and _____.
*****
job headings
fields delineators

2. A form that is often used to facilitate the spacing of data across a page is called a _____.
*****
Printer Spacing Chart

3. To facilitate PROCEDURE DIVISION coding, print records are often specified in the _____ SECTION.
*****
WORKING-STORAGE

4. Records are described in the WORKING-STORAGE SECTION because this section allows the use of _____.
   * * * * *
   VALUE clauses

5. If print records are **not** described with VALUE clauses in the WORKING-STORAGE SECTION, then numerous _____ operations are required in the _____.
   * * * * *
   MOVE
   PROCEDURE DIVISION

6. Assume print records are described in the WORKING-STORAGE SECTION with appropriate VALUE clauses. Give a sample record description entry in the FILE SECTION for the print file.
   * * * * *
   01 PRINTOUT PICTURE X(133).

GROUP PRINTING: INTRODUCTION

Thus far, we have focused our attention on the printing of individual lines for each input record read. This is called **detail printing.**

Sometimes, however, we wish to print total or summary lines for a group of records. This is called **group printing.** Group printing can be performed either in place of, or in addition to, detail printing.

GROUP PRINTING: AN ILLUSTRATION

Consider the illustration in Figure 13.7. In order to produce a report in the format indicated, input cards need to have the following data:

    1-2   DEPT-NO
    3-7   SALESMAN-NO
    8-13 AMT-OF-SALES

For this problem, each input record is to be printed; hence **detail printing** is required. In addition, **summary** lines that indicate department totals also print; hence group printing is required.

Note that for department totals to print, one for each department, the cards would be sorted into DEPT-NO sequence. That is, all salesmen cards for DEPT 01 would be read in first, followed by salesmen cards for DEPT 02, and so on.

PROGRAM REQUIREMENTS

For each card entered, a line is printed and the AMT-OF-SALES is added to a DEPT-TOTAL.

We wish to print a line, for each department, that states "TOTAL FOR DEPT IS $X,XXX.XX". This requires group printing. Note that such a group line will print only **after** an input card with a **new** DEPT-NO is entered. That is, a department total for DEPT 01 will print only after a card with DEPT 02 is read. All DEPT 01 cards are read and accumulated; after a DEPT 02 card is read, the DEPT 01 total will print.

To achieve this result, we must read in the first input card and move its DEPT-NO to a WORKING-STORAGE area, in order to save it for comparison

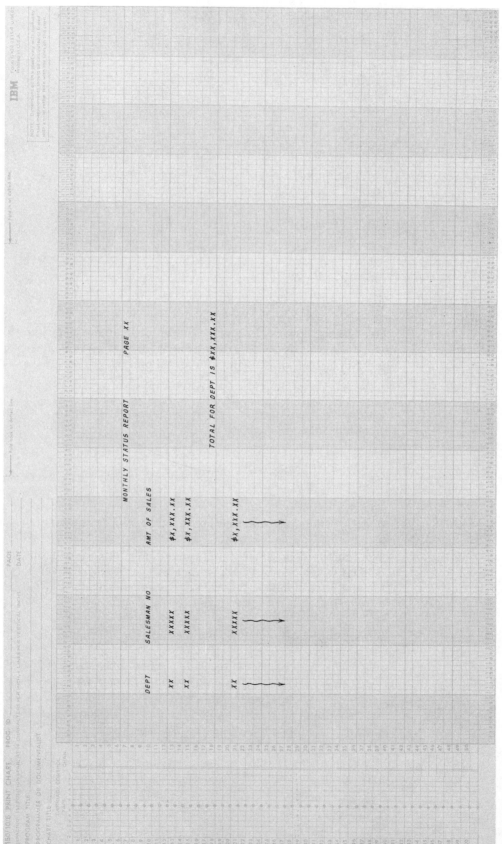

Figure 13.7

```
IDENTIFICATION DIVISION.
PROGRAM-ID. GROUP1.
ENVIRONMENT DIVISION.
INPUT-OUTPUT SECTION.
FILE-CONTROL.
    SELECT SALES-CARDS ASSIGN TO UR-S-SYSIN.
    SELECT PRINT-OUT ASSIGN TO UR-S-SYSOUT
              RESERVE NO ALTERNATE AREAS.
DATA DIVISION.
FILE SECTION.
FD  SALES-CARDS
    LABEL RECORDS ARE OMITTED
    RECORD CONTAINS 80 CHARACTERS
    DATA RECORD IS SALES-REC.
01  SALES-REC.
    02  DEPT              PIC 99.
    02  SALESMAN-NO       PIC 9(5).
    02  AMT-OF-SALES      PIC 9(4)V99.
    02  FILLER            PIC X(67).
FD  PRINT-OUT
    LABEL RECORDS ARE OMITTED
    RECORD CONTAINS 133 CHARACTERS
    DATA RECORD IS PRINT-REC.
01  PRINT-REC             PIC X(133).
WORKING-STORAGE SECTION.
01  WORK-AREAS.
    02  EOF               PIC 9 VALUE 0.
    02  HOLD-IT           PIC 99 VALUE ZERO.
    02  DEPT-TOTAL        PIC 9(5)V99 VALUE ZERO.
    02  LINE-CT           PIC 99 VALUE ZERO.
01  HEADER-1.
    02  FILLER       PIC X(50) VALUE SPACES.
    02  FILLER       PIC X(21)
                 VALUE 'MONTHLY STATUS REPORT'.
    02  FILLER       PIC X(9) VALUE SPACES.
    02  FILLER       PIC X(5) VALUE 'PAGE '.
    02  PAGE-NO      PIC 99 VALUE 01.
    02  FILLER       PIC X(46) VALUE SPACES.
01  HEADER-2.
    02  FILLER       PIC X(15) VALUE 'DEPT' JUSTIFIED RIGHT.
    02  FILLER       PIC X(17) VALUE 'SALESMAN NO'
            JUSTIFIED RIGHT.
    02  FILLER       PIC X(21) VALUE 'AMT OF SALES'
            JUSTIFIED RIGHT.
    02  FILLER       PIC X(80) VALUE SPACES.
01  DETAIL-LINE.
    02  FILLER       PIC X(12) VALUE SPACES.
    02  DEPT         PIC 99.
    02  FILLER       PIC X(9) VALUE SPACES.
    02  SALESMAN-NO PIC 9(5).
    02  FILLER       PIC X(14) VALUE SPACES.
    02  AMT-OF-SALES   PIC $Z,ZZZ.ZZ.
    02  FILLER       PIC X(82) VALUE SPACES.
01  GROUP-REC.
    02  FILLER       PIC X(61) VALUE SPACES.
    02  FILLER       PIC X(18) VALUE 'TOTAL FOR DEPT IS '.
    02  DEPT-TOTAL-OUT      PIC $ZZ,ZZZ.ZZ.
    02  FILLER       PIC X(44) VALUE SPACES.
PROCEDURE DIVISION.
    OPEN INPUT SALES-CARDS, OUTPUT PRINT-OUT.
    PERFORM HEADER-RTN.
    READ SALES-CARDS AT END MOVE 1 TO EOF.
    MOVE DEPT OF SALES-REC TO HOLD-IT.
    PERFORM CALC-RTN UNTIL EOF = 1.
    MOVE DEPT-TOTAL TO DEPT-TOTAL-OUT.
    WRITE PRINT-REC FROM GROUP-REC AFTER ADVANCING 2 LINES.
    CLOSE SALES-CARDS, PRINT-OUT.
    STOP RUN.
CALC-RTN.
    IF DEPT OF SALES-REC NOT EQUAL TO HOLD-IT PERFORM TOTAL-RTN.
    ADD AMT-OF-SALES OF SALES-REC TO DEPT-TOTAL.
    MOVE CORRESPONDING SALES-REC TO DETAIL-LINE.
    WRITE PRINT-REC FROM DETAIL-LINE AFTER ADVANCING 2 LINES.
    ADD 1 TO LINE-CT.
    IF LINE-CT > 30 PERFORM HEADER-RTN.
    READ SALES-CARDS AT END MOVE 1 TO EOF.
TOTAL-RTN.
    MOVE DEPT-TOTAL TO DEPT-TOTAL-OUT.
    WRITE PRINT-REC FROM GROUP-REC AFTER ADVANCING 2 LINES.
    ADD 1 TO LINE-CT.
    MOVE ZEROS TO DEPT-TOTAL.
    MOVE DEPT OF SALES-REC TO HOLD-IT.
HEADER-RTN.
    WRITE PRINT-REC FROM HEADER-1 AFTER ADVANCING 0 LINES.
    WRITE PRINT-REC FROM HEADER-2 AFTER ADVANCING 2 LINES.
    ADD 1 TO PAGE-NO.
    MOVE 0 TO LINE-CT.
```

Figure 13.8

purposes. Let us call this area HOLD-IT. For each succeeding record, we compare DEPT-NO to HOLD-IT. When they are equal, we:

1. Print a detail line.
2. Add AMT-OF-SALES to a DEPT-TOTAL.

When a card is entered with a DEPT-NO differing from HOLD-IT, this means that we want to print a group line that will contain the previously accumulated DEPT-TOTAL. The DEPT-TOTAL which will print is for the DEPT-NO that has been stored in HOLD-IT. Thus, when the DEPT-NO of an input record is not equal to HOLD-IT, we want to:

1. Print DEPT-TOTAL.
2. Reinitialize DEPT-TOTAL at zero, so that the next department's total can be accumulated.
3. Move the new DEPT-NO to HOLD-IT so that we can compare succeeding input records to this new DEPT-NO.
4. Continue processing the input record.

The entire program that performs both detail and group printing requires one additional entry. Note that when an AT END condition is reached, the last DEPT-TOTAL has **not** been printed. Hence, in the main module, after the CALC-RTN has been performed for all cards, we must instruct the computer to print a group line for this last DEPT-TOTAL. The entire program appears in Figure 13.8.

PRACTICE PROBLEM—
WITH SOLUTION

Write a program incorporating the following:

(a) printing of headers on each page
(b) printing of page numbers on each page
(c) double spacing between all detail lines
(d) storing of output records in WORKING-STORAGE

The program is to print the total of the amount fields of every group of 100 tape records.

Input: Standard labels
        no blocking factor
 1–20 Name
21–25 Amount xxx.xx

Output: detail line
11–30 Name
41–50 Total (edited)

NOTE: The name is the same for each group of 100 records. The number of tape records is a multiple of 100.

See Figure 13.9 for the solution.

```
                    IDENTIFICATION DIVISION.
                    PROGRAM-ID. CHAPT13.
                    ENVIRONMENT DIVISION.
                    CONFIGURATION SECTION.
                    SOURCE-COMPUTER. IBM-370.
                    OBJECT-COMPUTER. IBM-370.
                    SPECIAL-NAMES. C01 IS NEXT-PAGE.
                    INPUT-OUTPUT SECTION.
                    FILE-CONTROL.
                        SELECT TAPE-FILE ASSIGN TO UT-S-SYS004.
                        SELECT PRINT-FILE ASSIGN TO UR-S-SYSOUT
                                RESERVE NO ALTERNATE AREAS.
                    DATA DIVISION.
                    FILE SECTION.
                    FD  TAPE-FILE
                        LABEL RECORDS ARE STANDARD
                        RECORD CONTAINS 25 CHARACTERS
                        DATA RECORD IS TAPE-REC.
                    01  TAPE-REC.
                        02  NAME                PIC X(20).
                        02  AMOUNT              PIC 999V99.
                    FD  PRINT-FILE
                        LABEL RECORDS ARE OMITTED
                        RECORD CONTAINS 133 CHARACTERS
                        DATA RECORD IS PRINT-REC.
                    01  PRINT-REC               PIC X(133).
                    WORKING-STORAGE SECTION.
                    01  WORK-AREAS.
                        02  EOF             PIC 9 VALUE 0.
                        02  TOTAL-AMOUNT    PIC 9(5)V99 VALUE ZEROS.
                        02  CTR             PIC 999 VALUE ZEROS.
                        02  PAGE-NO         PIC 999 VALUE 1.
                    01  HEADER-1.
                        02  FILLER              PIC X(50) VALUE SPACES.
                        02  HDR-A               PIC X(25)
                                VALUE '100 CARD TOTALS'.
                        02  HDR-B               PIC X(9) VALUE 'PAGE NO. '.
                        02  PAGE-CT             PIC ZZZ9.
                        02  FILLER              PIC X(45) VALUE SPACES.
                    01  DETAIL-LINE.
                        02  FILLER              PIC X(11) VALUE SPACES.
                        02  NAME                PIC X(20).
                        02  FILLER              PIC X(10) VALUE SPACES.
                        02  TOTAL               PIC $**,***.99.
                        02  FILLER              PIC X(82) VALUE SPACES.
                    PROCEDURE DIVISION.
                        OPEN INPUT TAPE-FILE, OUTPUT PRINT-FILE.
                        PERFORM HDR-RTN.
                        READ TAPE-FILE AT END MOVE 1 TO EOF.
                        PERFORM CALC-RTN UNTIL EOF = 1.
                        CLOSE TAPE-FILE, PRINT-FILE.
                        STOP RUN.
                    CALC-RTN.
                        ADD 1 TO CTR.
                        ADD AMOUNT TO TOTAL-AMOUNT.
                        IF CTR = 100 PERFORM PRINT-RTN.
                        READ TAPE-FILE AT END MOVE 1 TO EOF.
                    PRINT-RTN.
                        MOVE NAME OF TAPE-REC TO NAME OF DETAIL-LINE.
                        MOVE TOTAL-AMOUNT TO TOTAL.
                        MOVE ZEROS TO CTR.
                        MOVE ZEROS TO TOTAL-AMOUNT.
                        WRITE PRINT-REC FROM DETAIL-LINE AFTER ADVANCING 2 LINES
                                AT EOP PERFORM HDR-RTN.
                    HDR-RTN.
                        MOVE PAGE-NO TO PAGE-CT.
                        ADD 1 TO PAGE-NO.
                        WRITE PRINT-REC FROM HEADER-1 AFTER ADVANCING NEXT-PAGE.
```

Figure 13.9

REVIEW QUESTIONS

True False

I. True-False Questions

1. The word LINES is optional as part of the ADVANCING option.
2. 0 LINES is used to suppress spacing.
3. The EOP routine is used for skipping to a new page when the current page has been completed.
4. The rightmost position of a 133–position print record is used for carriage control.
5. Once the ADVANCING option is used for a WRITE statement in a program, it must always be used.
6. Print records are often described in WORKING-STORAGE and then moved to the output area.
7. The SPECIAL-NAMES paragraph of the CONFIGURATION SECTION is a required part of any COBOL program that will test for form overflow.
8. The WRITE . . . FROM statement can be replaced with a MOVE and a simple WRITE.
9. Printed reports can make use of both spacing and skipping.
10. The RESERVE clause can be used to eliminate the buffer area.

II. General Questions

1. With a single WRITE statement, a maximum of (no.) spacing may be achieved.
2. Indicate why 133 positions must be denoted for the print area. What is the function of the extra position?
3. Write the ENVIRONMENT DIVISION entry necessary to test for the end of a page, and to skip to a new page.
4. Using the answer to Question 3, write the PROCEDURE DIVISION entry necessary to skip to a new page when the end of the previous page is sensed. What, if anything is wrong with the following entries (5–7)?
5. WRITE PRINT-LINE AFTER ADVANCING 110 LINES.
6. WRITE PRINT-LINE AFTER ADVANCING 1 LINE.
7. WRITE HEADER AFTER ADVANCING 0 LINES.
8. What is a carriage control tape?
9. When is a RESERVE clause required in the ENVIRONMENT DIVISION?

PROBLEMS

Code Problems 1–2 of the last chapter incorporating the following.
  (a) Print headings on each detail page.
  (b) Print page number on each page.
  (c) Double space between all detail lines.
  (d) Store output records in WORKING-STORAGE.
3. Using the following print layout sheet, write WORKING-STORAGE entries for the headers and detail line.

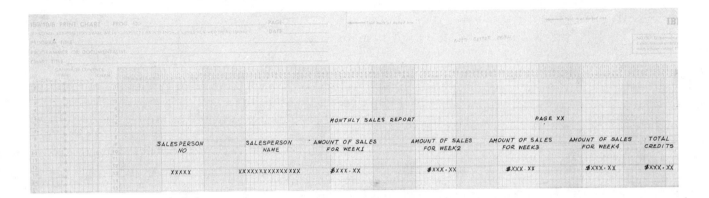

4. Data cards with the following format will be entered as input:

    1–2   TERR-NO
    3–20 EMPLOYEE-NAME
    21–25 ANNUAL-SALARY (in $)

Prepare a Printer Spacing Chart (there are some at the end of the text) and then write a program to:

1. Print each detail card (with appropriate headers).
2. Print the total salaries paid for each TERR-NO. (Assume cards have been entered in TERR-NO sequence.)
3. Print a final total of all salaries at the end of the run.

CHAPTER

14 DISPLAY AND ACCEPT STATEMENTS

A. DISPLAY STATEMENT

Thus far, we have discussed the WRITE command as the only method of producing output data. The format for a WRITE statement is:

WRITE (record-name)

The record is part of a file, assigned to a specific device in the ENVIRONMENT DIVISION, and described in the DATA DIVISION. An OPEN command must be issued before a record in the file can be written.

To produce most forms of output data, we use a WRITE statement. This is, however, not the only output operation available. The DISPLAY verb is also used to produce output. A DISPLAY statement, however, differs significantly from the WRITE operation. The format for a DISPLAY is as follows:

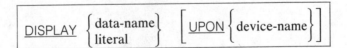

DISPLAY $\left\{\begin{array}{l}\text{data-name}\\ \text{literal}\end{array}\right\}$ $\left[\text{UPON}\left\{\text{device-name}\right\}\right]$

The UPON clause, which specifies the device, is optional. When omitted, data generally will be displayed on the printer. To say, for example, DISPLAY CODE-1 **prints** the contents of CODE-1.

When using a DISPLAY verb, **no corresponding file** need be defined in the ENVIRONMENT DIVISION. Similarly, no OPEN statement is required. We may say DISPLAY FIELDA where FIELDA is **any** field defined in the DATA DIVISION. Any item defined in the FILE SECTION or the WORKING-STORAGE SECTION may be displayed. Similarly, we may say DISPLAY 'INVALID CODE', when the specific literal or message "INVALID CODE" is required as output.

The DISPLAY verb, then, may be used in place of the WRITE statement for certain types of output. When only some fields of information are required and no record format exists, the DISPLAY verb is used.

IBM

COBOL Coding Form

SYSTEM						PUNCHING INSTRUCTIONS				PAGE	OF		GX28-1464-5 U/M 050*
PROGRAM						GRAPHIC							Printed in U.S.A.
PROGRAMMER		DATE				PUNCH				CARD FORM #		*	

SEQUENCE (PAGE) (SERIAL)	CONT	A	B	COBOL STATEMENT	IDENTIFICATION
				`PROCEDURE DIVISION.`	
				`OPEN INPUT CARD-FILE OUTPUT TAPE-FILE.`	
				`READ CARD-FILE AT END MOVE 1 TO EOF.`	
				`PERFORM CALC-RTN UNTIL EOF = 1.`	
				`CLOSE CARD-FILE, TAPE-FILE.`	
				`STOP RUN.`	
				`CALC-RTN.`	
				`ADD AMT1-IN, AMT2-IN GIVING AMT-OUT`	
				`ON SIZE ERROR PERFORM ERROR-RTN.`	
				`MULTIPLY AMT-OUT BY .06 GIVING TAX-OUT`	
				`ON SIZE ERROR PERFORM ERROR-RTN.`	
				`ADD TAX-OUT, AMT-OUT GIVING TOTAL-OUT`	
				`ON SIZE ERROR PERFORM ERROR-RTN.`	
				`WRITE TAPE-REC.`	
				`READ CARD-FILE AT END MOVE 1 TO EOF.`	
				`ERROR-RTN.`	
				`DISPLAY 'INVALID CARD DATA'.`	

Figure 14.1

A DISPLAY statement is a method of producing output data that does not require the establishment of files. We DISPLAY data fields or literals; we WRITE records.

The DISPLAY verb has a very significant use in COBOL programs. It is used to produce a **low volume of output data.** For primary output from a program, we generally establish files and WRITE records. When a field or a literal is to be displayed depending on some condition such as an error condition, or when a message is to be relayed to the computer operator, it is too cumbersome to establish files and records for these special cases. For such output operations, we use DISPLAY statements.

Consider a card-to-tape program that performs arithmetic operations on the card data to produce tape records. The tape is the major form of output; it is established as a file with a specific record format. Data is created on tape by using a WRITE operation. Let us suppose that all the arithmetic operations test for ON SIZE ERROR, or arithmetic overflow conditions. When an overflow condition exists, we wish to print the message INVALID CARD DATA. To use a WRITE statement would require the establishment of a print file and a record within the file for the message. Using a DISPLAY statement does not require files, and the message may be displayed on a printed page as a literal. See Figure 14.1 for an illustration of the DISPLAY statement.

Fields or literals may be displayed on specific devices. If a device name is not used in the DISPLAY statement, as in the above illustration, then the system logical output device is assumed. For most systems, the logical output device is the printer. Thus, to say DISPLAY TAX, where no UPON clause is specified, **prints** the data in the TAX field. Data may also be displayed on the card punch; that is, a card may be punched by the computer with the use of a DISPLAY verb. We may also display data on the console. The console is a special typewriter that may serve as input to or output from the computer. The DISPLAY verb utilizes the console as an output device.

The device, then, used in the UPON clause may denote the console or the card punch. The **names** of these devices are assigned by the manufacturer, and are thus machine-dependent. For most computers, the device names CONSOLE and SYSPUNCH are used.[1] The following indicates the options available:

DISPLAY OPTIONS		
Statement		**Result**
1. DISPLAY $\begin{Bmatrix} \text{data-name} \\ \text{literal} \end{Bmatrix}$		Prints the data on the printer
2. DISPLAY $\begin{Bmatrix} \text{data-name} \\ \text{literal} \end{Bmatrix}$ UPON CONSOLE		Prints the data on the console typewriter
3. DISPLAY $\begin{Bmatrix} \text{data-name} \\ \text{literal} \end{Bmatrix}$ UPON SYSPUNCH		Punches a card with the data

[1] Consult the reference manual for specific computer device names or for mnemonic-names which can be used with this verb.

Note that in many computer installations, where output may be routed to any one of a number of print devices, including terminals, use of the DISPLAY verb may be impractical.

SIZE OF DISPLAY

The **size** of the field or literal to be displayed is limited and depends on the device used. When information is to be printed on the printer using a DISPLAY verb, the field or literal is limited to **120** positions. To say:

DISPLAY $\begin{Bmatrix} \text{data-name} \\ \text{literal} \end{Bmatrix}$

requires that the data be no more than 120 characters.

When a field or literal is displayed upon the card punch, the size of the data must not exceed **72** positions. The maximum size for the console is 100 characters:

SIZE OF DISPLAY		
Statement		**Size Restrictions**
DISPLAY { }		120 characters
DISPLAY { }	UPON CONSOLE	100 characters (depending on size of console display)
DISPLAY { }	UPON SYSPUNCH	72 characters (cc 73–80 are punched with program identification)

EXPANDED FORMAT FOR DISPLAY

Several fields or literals may be displayed with **one** statement. Modifying the format for a DISPLAY operation, we have:

DISPLAY $\begin{Bmatrix} \text{data-name-1} \\ \text{literal-1} \end{Bmatrix}$, $\begin{Bmatrix} \text{data-name-2} \\ \text{literal-2} \end{Bmatrix}$, ... UPON (device-name)

Examples

1   DISPLAY FIELDA, FIELDB UPON CONSOLE.
2   DISPLAY 'THE MONTH OF', MONTH.

Note the difference between the following two routines:

Statements   **Printed Results**

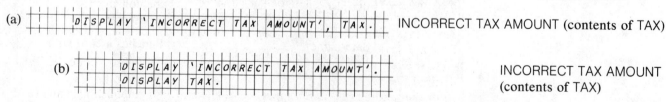

(a)   DISPLAY 'INCORRECT TAX AMOUNT', TAX.   INCORRECT TAX AMOUNT (contents of TAX)

(b)   DISPLAY 'INCORRECT TAX AMOUNT'.   INCORRECT TAX AMOUNT
       DISPLAY TAX.   (contents of TAX)

Each DISPLAY verb prints one **line** of information.

One important point must be noted. We should not WRITE and DISPLAY upon the same device. If a file is assigned to the card punch in the ENVIRON-MENT DIVISION, then we should not display upon the punch.

SUMMARY OF DISPLAY STATEMENT

1. A WRITE statement is used to produce records that are to be the primary form of output.
2. A DISPLAY statement is used to produce a low volume of output.
3. DISPLAY statements can print information on the printer or console, or punch information on cards.
4. A DISPLAY statement does not require records and files to be established.
5. Fields of data, defined in the DATA DIVISION, or literals may be displayed without opening files.
6. A DISPLAY verb is often used to give messages to the computer operator.

B. ACCEPT STATEMENT

The ACCEPT statement performs an **input** operation. It results in the **reading** of **fields** of data into some area of storage.

An ACCEPT verb is an input command that parallels the DISPLAY verb. The DISPLAY statement produces output data. It, unlike the WRITE command, does not require a device assigned in the ENVIRONMENT DIVISION, an output area defined in the DATA DIVISION, or an OPEN statement in the PROCEDURE DIVISION. It is used to produce a low volume of output data where record formats are not required.

An ACCEPT verb reads a low volume of input data into the computer. It, unlike the READ command, does not require a device assigned in the ENVI-RONMENT DIVISION, an input area defined in the DATA DIVISION, or an OPEN statement in the PROCEDURE DIVISION.

The format for an ACCEPT statement is:

ACCEPT (data-name) [FROM (device-name)]

The data-name may be any field defined in the DATA DIVISION. We may say ACCEPT (data-name-1) where data-name-1 is a work area in the WORKING-STORAGE SECTION or an 02-level item within the output record. It may be **any** field defined and described in the DATA DIVISION.

If the FROM option is not specified, data will be read from the card reader. To say ACCEPT data-name-1, where data-name-1 is a four-position numeric field, will result in the first four **card columns** of data being read.

We should not ACCEPT data from the reader if the reader is a device assigned in a SELECT clause. That is, we should not READ and ACCEPT from the same device.

The FROM option may be used with the **console.** We may code ACCEPT (data) FROM CONSOLE.

For the reading of primary input records, we always establish files and read them. For a small volume of secondary input data, the ACCEPT verb is often used. The ACCEPT statement is most often utilized to read **date** information or some form of control data into the computer. Consider the following two examples.

Example 1

A tape-to-print program is to be written. The major form of input is a tape, and thus a tape file is established in the FILE SECTION. The heading record of the output file is to contain the date of the run. The date is not part of the tape input, and will change with each monthly run.

We may read this date in a specific format from a card. The card will contain month in card columns 1 and 2, / in card column 3, and year in card columns 4 and 5. Thus 03/80 denotes MARCH, 1980.

To use a READ statement just for the one input card requires a SELECT clause in the ENVIRONMENT DIVISION, an FD in the DATA DIVISION, and an OPEN statement in the PROCEDURE DIVISION. This is rather cumbersome programming for a single input card. Instead, an ACCEPT verb may be used. We may say:

where DATE1 is a five-position data field within the heading record:

```
Ø1  HEADING-1.
    Ø2  FILLER        PICTURE X       VALUE SPACES.
    Ø2  FILLER        PICTURE X(2Ø)   VALUE 'RUN DATE IS '
                                      JUSTIFIED RIGHT.
    Ø2  DATE1         PICTURE X(5).
    Ø2  FILLER        PICTURE X(5Ø)   VALUE 'MONTHLY STATUS REPORT'
                                      JUSTIFIED RIGHT.
    Ø2  FILLER        PICTURE X(57)   VALUE SPACES.
```

Thus no file need be assigned to use the ACCEPT verb. The first five card columns of the date card are read into the field called DATE1. Note that the record shown is in WORKING-STORAGE since it contains VALUE clauses.

For 1974 ANS COBOL users, there is a special feature of the ACCEPT verb that will enable you to store an 8-position date in a field **without** having to read that date from an input record. To say:

ACCEPT (data-name) FROM DATE

stores in data-name the current date with format MO/DA/YR. DATE is a COBOL reserved word obtained from the system-generated date field.

Example 2

An input file consists of tape records. A single program is to be written to create an updated output tape biweekly and to create print records monthly. That is, with the use of some control data that denotes a biweekly or a monthly run, we will instruct the computer to create either print records or updated tape records. The routine to make certain that CODE-X is correct is as follows:

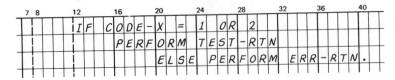

CODE-X is a control field that is read into the computer during each run. It is not a **constant**, since it changes with each computer run. We may establish CODE-X as a WORKING-STORAGE item within 01 WORK-AREAS:

We may read a 1 or 2 into CODE-X by the following:

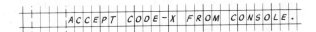

The computer operator will type a 1 for biweekly run and a 2 for monthly run. Thus we have the following routine:

| 7 8 | 12 | 16 | 20 | 24 | 28 | 32 | 36 | 40 | 44 | 4 |

```
          ACCEPT  CODE-X  FROM  CONSOLE.
      IF  CODE-X  =  1  OR  2  PERFORM  TEST-RTN
          ELSE  PERFORM  ERR-RTN.
```

Note that the computer will temporarily stop or pause after each use of the ACCEPT verb. After ACCEPT DATE1 is executed, the computer pauses. It is in the "wait state." The operator must press start before the machine will continue processing. This frequently makes the ACCEPT verb inefficient or impractical.

Thus, after ACCEPT CODE-X FROM CONSOLE is executed, the computer is in the wait state. The operator must type the required data on the console and press start before execution continues.

The ACCEPT verb is an effective tool for transmitting a small amount of input data to the computer. It does not require the establishing of files. It should not be used, however, for large volumes of input since it is a time-consuming instruction. A READ statement transmits input data from the input device to the input area and continues with the next instruction. An ACCEPT verb causes a pause in execution before data is transmitted.

C. COMBINED USE OF ACCEPT AND DISPLAY

When the computer pauses after an ACCEPT statement is issued, the computer operator must perform some function. **No** message is given to computer operators except the standard entry, 'AWAITING REPLY'. They must be familiar with the program requirements and know what a halt in execution implies. If a card is required, for example, the operator must keypunch the correct data and press start. If console data is required, the operator must type the information and press start.

It is not always feasible to expect the computer operator to remember each program's requirements. For this reason, we generally DISPLAY a message to the operator before issuing an ACCEPT command. The message informs the operator of the necessary operations. It indicates what to do when the computer pauses.

Example 1

```
|   |DISPLAY 'KEYPUNCH A CARD WITH MONTH IN CC1-2, / IN CC3, AND
|-  |'YEAR IN CC4-5, PLACE CARD IN READER AND PRESS START'.
|   |ACCEPT DATE1.
```

The above literal prints on the printer. The ACCEPT statement follows and the computer stops. The operator reads the message, performs the required operations, and presses start. The first five columns of the card in the reader are then transmitted to the DATE1 field.

Example 2

The latter routine serves as a means of communicating with the computer operator. A message or instruction is printed on the console. The operator is required to type a 1 or a 2. If a mistake has been made and a 1 or 2 has **not** been typed, the routine is performed again.

SUMMARY OF DISPLAY AND ACCEPT STATEMENTS
1. Both the DISPLAY and ACCEPT statements perform input-output functions on a low volume of data.
2. No files need to be established nor records specified when these statements are used.
3. Frequently the DISPLAY statement is used in conjunction with an ACCEPT statement. The DISPLAY prints an instruction to the operator and the ACCEPT reads in the corresponding data.

SELF-EVALUATING QUIZ

1. In addition to the WRITE statement, a _____ verb may be used to produce output.
   *****
   DISPLAY

2. If the UPON clause is omitted from a DISPLAY statement, then data will generally be displayed upon the _____.
   *****
   printer

3. We may DISPLAY _____ or _____.
   *****
   data-names
   literals

4. When displaying a data-name, it (must, need not) be part of an output record.
   *****
   need not

5. The DISPLAY verb is used to produce a (low, high) volume of computer output.
   *****
   low

6. Besides the printer, data may be displayed upon the _____ or the _____.
   *****
   console typewriter
   card punch

7. We usually (should, should not) DISPLAY and WRITE upon the same device.
   *****
   should not

8. In addition to the READ command, a(n) _____ verb may also be used to access input data.
   *****
   ACCEPT

9. If a device name is not specified in an ACCEPT statement, the _____ is generally assumed.
   *****
   card reader

PRACTICE PROBLEM—   Write a complete COBOL program that will ACCEPT your name from one
WITH SOLUTION   input card and your address from a second card and will DISPLAY the data on
a single output line.

Each of the two input cards should have an "X" in column 80; if they do
not, display an error message and restart the job. See Figure 14.2 for the
solution.

```
IDENTIFICATION DIVISION.
PROGRAM-ID. CHAPT14.
ENVIRONMENT DIVISION.
CONFIGURATION SECTION.
SOURCE-COMPUTER. IBM-370.
OBJECT-COMPUTER. IBM-370.
DATA DIVISION.
WORKING-STORAGE SECTION.
01   HDR.
     02   FILLER        PIC X(32) VALUE 'NAME'
          JUSTIFIED RIGHT.
     02   FILLER        PIC X(40) VALUE 'ADDRESS'
          JUSTIFIED RIGHT.
     02   FILLER        PIC X(48) VALUE SPACES.
01   PRINTOUT.
     02   FILLER        PIC X(20) VALUE SPACES.
     02   NAME          PIC X(20).
     02   FILLER        PIC X(20) VALUE SPACES.
     02   ADDRESS-1     PIC X(20).
     02   FILLER        PIC X(40) VALUE SPACES.
PROCEDURE DIVISION.
     ACCEPT NAME.
     ACCEPT ADDRESS-1.
     DISPLAY HDR.
     DISPLAY PRINTOUT.
     STOP RUN.
```

Figure 14.2

REVIEW QUESTIONS
True False   **I. True-False Questions**
□   □   1. A DISPLAY statement may be used for printing fields, literals, or records.
□   □   2. Data may be displayed on the console.
□   □   3. The size of the display is usually 133 characters.
□   □   4. A WRITE statement, instead of a DISPLAY statement, is used to produce
                 a low volume of output.
□   □   5. A DISPLAY statement is often used to give messages to the computer
                 operator.
□   □   6. An ACCEPT statement may be used to read a field of data into WORKING-
                 STORAGE.
□   □   7. When the ACCEPT statement is utilized, a file must be assigned and de-
                 scribed.
□   □   8. If a device is not specified in an ACCEPT statement, a tape drive is usually
                 assumed.
□   □   9. An ACCEPT statement causes a temporary pause in execution.
□   □   10. Several data fields may be displayed with one DISPLAY statement.

II. General Questions
1. Indicate the devices that can be used with a DISPLAY statement and the
   corresponding size of the display.

2. Indicate the devices that can be used with an ACCEPT statement and the corresponding size of the display.

3. Why are the ACCEPT and DISPLAY statements frequently used in place of the READ and WRITE statements?

4. A control card is the only card data in a particular program. If it has an X in Column 1, then the MONTHLY-UPDATE routine is to be performed. If it has a Y in Column 1, then the WEEKLY-UPDATE routine is to be performed. Write the control card routine, with proper edit controls, to accept and process this card.

5. When a particular error condition occurs, the program is to pause, print the message 'ERROR CONDITION X' on the console. If the operator types 'OK' in response, the program is to continue. If the operator types 'NO GO' in response, a STOP RUN instruction is to be executed. Write the routine necessary to perform the above operations.

PROBLEMS   Write a program to perform an edit test on input cards:

(a) card column 1 must have a 'C'.
(b) card columns 2–5 must contain a number between 1256 and 7826.
(c) card columns 6–20 must be alphabetic.

If any of the above conditions are not met, print a corresponding error message.

NOTE: Write this program so that the ENVIRONMENT DIVISION is not required.

UNIT 4 ADVANCED LOGIC CONSIDERATIONS AND TABLE HANDLING ROUTINES

15 THE PERFORM STATEMENT

We have discussed in detail the PERFORM . . . UNTIL statement used for structured program control. We have also discussed the simple PERFORM statement. There are additional options of this PERFORM statement that we examine in this chapter.

Let us first review the basic formats of a PERFORM.

A. THE BASIC FORMAT

I. <u>PERFORM</u> (paragraph-name).

A PERFORM statement causes execution of the series of instructions at the named paragraph. When all instructions at the indicated paragraph are executed, control is transferred to the statement directly following the PERFORM:

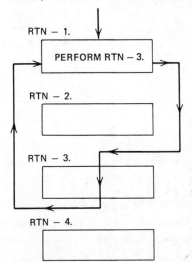

Example

```
WRITE PRINT-REC AFTER ADVANCING 2 LINES.
ADD 1 TO CTR.
IF CTR = 25
    PERFORM HDR-RTN.
READ CARD-FILE AT END MOVE 1 TO EOF.
HDR-RTN.
    WRITE HDR-REC AFTER ADVANCING NEW-PAGE.
    MOVE 0 TO CTR.
```

HDR-RTN is performed if CTR = 25. After HDR-RTN is performed, control returns to the instruction after the PERFORM statement. Note that the first four statements would themselves be under the control of a PERFORM.

PERFORM WITHIN A PERFORM   PERFORM statements are permitted within PERFORM statements. To say PERFORM PARA-1 is permissible if PARA-1 has a PERFORM statement as one of its instructions. The following is a valid routine:

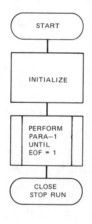
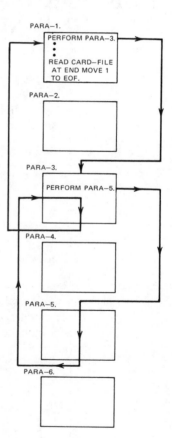

A simple PERFORM statement is used whenever a series of instructions at a particular paragraph is to be executed from different points in the program. **Several** paragraphs or routines may be executed using one PERFORM statement.

Extension of Format I:

I. <u>PERFORM</u> (paragraph-name-1) [<u>THRU</u> (paragraph-name-n)]

All statements beginning at paragraph-name-1 and terminating at the **end** of paragraph-name-n are executed. Control is then transferred to the statement after the PERFORM. The following representation illustrates the complete form of Format I:

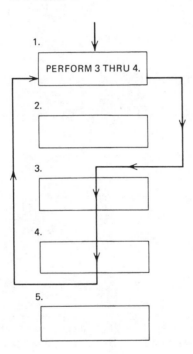

THE USE AND MISUSE OF GO TO STATEMENTS

We have so far avoided the use of any branching instructions in our COBOL programs. To transfer control to some other segment of a program, PERFORM statements are used. Structured programming form requires the elimination of a branch instruction that permanently transfers control to other parts of the program.

In COBOL, the branch instruction could be coded as

<u>GO</u> TO (paragraph-name)

Unlike the PERFORM statement that returns control to the statement following the PERFORM, the GO TO permanently transfers control; Figure 15.1 illustrates the distinction between a PERFORM and a GO TO.

In structured programming, the general approach involves the use of one main routine followed by a series of subordinate routines, all under the control

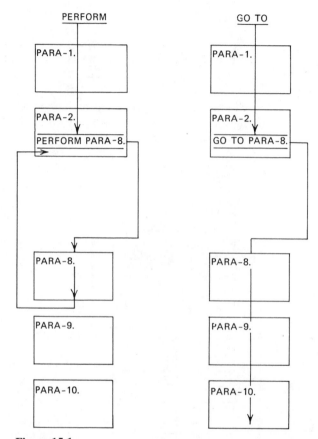

Figure 15.1

of this main routine. In this way, all the routines can be coded **independently.** This process simplifies coding and also makes debugging easier. The GO TO statement that transfers control out of statements being performed can cause unpredictable results and hence is generally avoided.

There are, however, times in which GO TO statements are permissible.

Using the THRU option, GO TO statements may appear within the named paragraphs. Consider the following routines:

```
STEP1.   ADD A TO B.
         IF C = ZERO GO TO STEP3.
STEP2.   MULTIPLY C BY C.
STEP3.   MOVE B TO EDIT1.
STEP4.   WRITE PRINTOUT AFTER ADVANCING 2 LINES.
```

To say: PERFORM STEP1 THRU STEP4 is permissible. Although a conditional branch in STEP1 transfers control to another paragraph, STEP3, the latter is included within the range of the PERFORM and, thus, is acceptable.

When using the THRU option of the PERFORM statement, branches, or GO TO statements, are permitted **within the range of the named paragraphs.** Note, however, that to say PERFORM STEP1 THRU STEP2 is **not** valid in the above illustration, since the conditional branch transfers control to STEP3, **outside** the PERFORM range. Thus control would not return to the statement directly following the PERFORM.

THE USE OF THE EXIT STATEMENT

Consider the following example.

Problem

If salary exceeds 100,000, employee is President.
If salary exceeds 50,000, employee is Vice-President.
If salary exceeds 40,000, employee is Asst-Vice-President.

The determination of an employee as PRESIDENT, VICE-PRESIDENT, or ASST-VICE-PRESIDENT is to be made from different points in the program. Thus the routine will be executed by a PERFORM statement. Note that the following is **not** a correct routine:

```
TITLE-RTN.
    IF SALARY > 100000 MOVE 'PRESIDENT' TO TITLE.
    IF SALARY > 50000  MOVE 'VICE PRESIDENT' TO TITLE.
    IF SALARY > 40000  MOVE 'ASST-VICE-PRESIDENT' TO TITLE.
```

Suppose EMPLOYEE-X earns $110,000. Since the first condition is met, 'PRESIDENT' is moved to TITLE. Note, however, that the next two conditions are **also** met. The last statement to be executed results in the literal 'ASST-VICE-PRESIDENT' in the field called TITLE.

We must alter this routine so that, if the first condition is met, (SALARY greater than 100000), no other test is performed.

The following routine will be executed properly by coding PERFORM TITLE-RTN THRU PARA-2:

```
TITLE-RTN.
    IF SALARY > 100000 MOVE 'PRESIDENT' TO TITLE GO TO PARA-2.
    IF SALARY > 50000  MOVE 'VICE-PRESIDENT' TO TITLE GO TO
       PARA-2.
    IF SALARY > 40000  MOVE 'ASST-VICE-PRESIDENT' TO TITLE GO TO
       PARA-2.
PARA-2.
    EXIT.
```

EXIT is a COBOL reserved word. It is an instruction that performs **no operation.** It allows execution simply to pass over other statements in TITLE-RTN. It is used, when necessary, as an end point in paragraphs being performed.

SELF-EVALUATING QUIZ

1. A PERFORM statement causes execution of instructions at _____. After the PERFORM is executed, control returns to _____.
   *****
   the indicated paragraph
   the statement directly following the PERFORM

2. _____ statements should not be included within paragraphs that are executed by PERFORM statements, when they _____.
   *****
   GO TO
   cause branches **outside** the range of the PERFORM

3. State the major difference between the following two routines:

   (a)   `PERFORM RTN-1 THRU RTN-3.`   (b)   `PERFORM RTN-1 THRU RTN-2.`

```
(a)    PERFORM RTN-1 THRU RTN-3.         (b)    PERFORM RTN-1 THRU RTN-2.
          .                                        .
          .                                        .
          .                                        .
       RTN-1.                                   RTN-1.
          ADD A TO B.                              ADD A TO B.
          IF B > 21 GO TO RTN-3.                   IF B > 21 GO TO RTN-3.
          MULTIPLY B BY C.                      RTN-2.
       RTN-2.                                      MULTIPLY B BY C.
          DIVIDE C INTO D.                      RTN-3.
       RTN-3.                                      MOVE C TO TOTAL.
          MOVE D TO TOTAL.
```

   *****
   a is correct. b transfers control outside the PERFORM range.

4. To execute several sequential paragraphs by a PERFORM statement, the _____ option is used. The format is _____.
   *****
   THRU
   PERFORM (paragraph-name-1) THRU (paragraph-name-n)

5. GO TO statements may be included within the named paragraphs using the THRU option as long as _____.
   *****
   control is not transferred outside the range of the indicated paragraphs

6. _____ is a COBOL reserved word that performs no operation and serves as an endpoint to paragraphs being performed.
   *****
   EXIT

B. ADDITIONAL FORMS OF THE PERFORM STATEMENT

Format II of the PERFORM statement is as follows:

> II. <u>PERFORM</u> (paragraph-name-1) [<u>THRU</u> paragraph-name-n)]
> <u>UNTIL</u> (condition).

The condition that may be specified is any relational, simple, or compound.

Examples

(a)   `PERFORM PARA-1 THRU PARA-4 UNTIL X = 2.`

```
(b)      PERFORM RTN-1 UNTIL X > 7.
(c)      PERFORM STEP-5 UNTIL A = B OR A = C.
(d)      PERFORM PARA-X UNTIL A > B AND A > C.
```

It is implicit in this option that the data-name or data-names used in the UNTIL clause be altered within the paragraph(s) being performed. To say PERFORM PARA-1 THRU PARA-8 UNTIL X = 5 implies that X will change somewhere within PARA-1 through PARA-8. If X remains as 3, for example, then these paragraphs will be performed indefinitely.

If the condition indicated in the UNTIL clause is met at the time of execution, then the named paragraph(s) will be executed 0, or no, times. If PERFORM RTN-5 UNTIL X = 3 is executed and X equals 3 initially, then RTN-5 will not be performed at all. This condition does **not** imply that an error has occurred.

PERFORM statements, in their various formats, may be used in executing **loops.** A loop, as described in Chapter 10, is a repeated execution of a routine until a specific condition is met. In Chapter 10, looping was performed by utilizing simple PERFORM or PERFORM . . . UNTIL statements. In this chapter, we will see how other options of the PERFORM statement can also be used for looping.

Example 1

Write a routine to multiply two data fields, A and B, with the use of the ADD instruction instead of the MULTIPLY.
[i.e., $4 \times 3 = 4 + 4 + 4$]

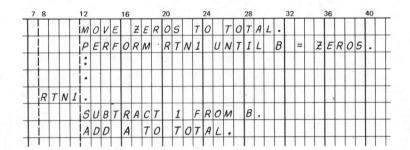

```
          MOVE ZEROS TO TOTAL.
          PERFORM RTN1 UNTIL B = ZEROS.
          :
          .
RTN1.
          SUBTRACT 1 FROM B.
          ADD A TO TOTAL.
```

Example 2

Write a routine to read a group of ten cards and print the total of the amount fields of all the cards.

```
          OPEN INPUT CARD-FILE, OUTPUT PRINT-FILE.
          MOVE ZEROS TO CTR.
          READ CARD-FILE AT END MOVE 1 TO EOF.
          PERFORM CALC-RTN UNTIL CTR = 10.
          MOVE TOTAL TO EDIT1.
          WRITE PRINT-OUT AFTER ADVANCING 2 LINES.
          CLOSE CARD-FILE, PRINT-FILE.
          STOP RUN.
CALC-RTN.
          ADD AMT TO TOTAL.
          ADD 1 TO CTR.
          READ CARD-FILE AT END MOVE 1 TO EOF.
```

CTR, a WORKING-STORAGE item, is initialized at zero. This may be accomplished in the PROCEDURE DIVISION or with a VALUE clause in WORKING-STORAGE. Each time a card is read, CTR is incremented by one. When CTR equals 10, ten cards have been read and totalled.

Suppose we wish to print totals for any multiple of 10 cards. Again, we will perform the above operations until there are no more cards. Note, however, that CTR must be initialized at zero each time and that the set of instructions is designed to work only for an exact multiple of ten cards:

```
    OPEN INPUT CARD-FILE, OUTPUT PRINT-FILE.
    READ CARD-FILE AT END MOVE 1 TO EOF.
    PERFORM COMP-RTN UNTIL EOF = 1.
    CLOSE CARD-FILE, PRINT-FILE.
    STOP RUN.
COMP-RTN.
    MOVE ZEROS TO TOTAL.
    MOVE ZEROS TO CTR.
    PERFORM READ-RTN UNTIL CTR = 10.
    PERFORM PRINT-RTN.
READ-RTN.
    ADD AMT TO TOTAL.
    ADD 1 TO CTR.
    READ CARD-FILE AT END MOVE 1 TO EOF.
PRINT-RTN.
    MOVE TOTAL TO EDIT1.
    WRITE PRINT-OUT AFTER ADVANCING 2 LINES.
```

The above is an illustration of a double loop. COMP-RTN is performed until there are no more cards. Within COMP-RTN we process ten cards at a time, print the total, and re-initialize the fields. Double loops are most efficiently coded with the use of PERFORM statements within PERFORM statements.

Example 3

Each card read has a value N. Find N!, called "N factorial." Note that N! = N × N-1 × N-2 × . . . × 1. For example, 5! = 5 × 4 × 3 × 2 × 1 = 120; 3! = 3 × 2 × 1 = 6.

```
    OPEN INPUT CARD-FILE, OUTPUT PRINT-FILE.
    READ CARD-FILE AT END MOVE 1 TO EOF.
    PERFORM CALC-RTN UNTIL EOF = 1.
    CLOSE CARD-FILE, PRINT-FILE.
    STOP RUN.
CALC-RTN.
    MOVE N TO M.
    PERFORM FACT-RTN UNTIL M = 1.
    MOVE N TO FACTORIAL OF PRINT-REC.
    WRITE PRINT-REC AFTER ADVANCING 2 LINES.
    READ CARD-FILE AT END MOVE 1 TO EOF.
FACT-RTN.
    SUBTRACT 1 FROM M.
    MULTIPLY M BY N.
```

M is a work area and assume that N is sufficiently large to be used for storing the result.

Another format for the PERFORM statement enables a paragraph or paragraphs to be executed **several times:**

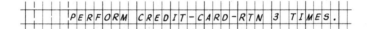

III. <u>PERFORM</u> (paragraph-name-1) [<u>THRU</u> (paragraph-name-n)]

$\left\{ \begin{matrix} \text{(integer)} \\ \text{(data-name)} \end{matrix} \right\}$ <u>TIMES</u>

Example 4

A program creates department store credit cards. Each customer is issued three cards:

```
          PERFORM  CREDIT-CARD-RTN  3  TIMES.
```

Example 5

Each customer indicates the number of credit cards desired. This data is punched into an input card in the field called NO-OF-COPIES. The card record is as follows:

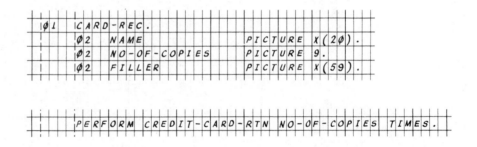

```
01   CARD-REC.
     02   NAME                PICTURE  X(20).
     02   NO-OF-COPIES        PICTURE  9.
     02   FILLER              PICTURE  X(59).
```

```
          PERFORM  CREDIT-CARD-RTN  NO-OF-COPIES  TIMES.
```

When using the format: PERFORM (paragraph-name) **data-name** TIMES, several rules are applicable. The data-name indicated must be specified in the DATA DIVISION, have a **numeric** PICTURE clause, and contain only integers or zeros. To say PERFORM RTN-1 COPY-IT TIMES is valid if COPY-IT has a numeric PICTURE clause and integer or zero contents. If COPY-IT has a zero as its value, then RTN-1 will be performed 0, or **no,** times.

Note that the word preceding TIMES may only be an integer or a data-name. It may not be an arithmetic expression. To say PERFORM PARA-1 B+1 TIMES is **invalid.**

The THRU option in Format III is not required. We may say PERFORM RTN-1 THRU RTN-8 5 TIMES, or we may say PERFORM RTN-3 5 TIMES. Both are correct instructions.

Note that the following two instructions produce the same results:

```
1.        PERFORM  STEP-1  6  TIMES.
2.        PERFORM  STEP-1  AAA  TIMES.
```

where AAA has the following description in the WORKING-STORAGE SECTION:

8	12	16	20	24	28	32	36	40
Ø1	WORK-AREAS.							
	Ø2	AAA		PIC 9		VALUE 6.		

When using the integer option for Format III, only the actual number is acceptable. We may **not** say: PERFORM RTN-1 FIVE TIMES. The integer itself must be used: PERFORM RTN-1 5 TIMES.

You will recall that in Example 1 we multiplied two data fields, A and B, with the use of the ADD instruction instead of the MULTIPLY (i.e., $4 \times 3 = 4 + 4 + 4$). The following illustrates the coding of this problem in a more complete form:

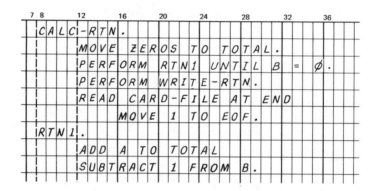

This problem may be coded with the PERFORM . . . TIMES statement as follows:

```
CALC-RTN.
    MOVE ZEROS TO TOTAL.
    PERFORM RTN1 B TIMES.
    PERFORM WRITE-RTN.
    READ CARD-FILE AT END MOVE 1 TO EOF.
RTN1.
    ADD A TO TOTAL.
```

Note that when using a PERFORM . . . TIMES statement we do **not** decrease B. B remains constant. If B = 3 and A = 4, for example, RTN1 would be executed three times; that is, A would be added to TOTAL three times. Twelve would then be the correct result in TOTAL.

All loops may be executed with the use of either PERFORM or conditional statements.

Example 2 (reading ten cards and summing the amount fields) may be coded with the TIMES option as follows:

```
        OPEN INPUT CARD-FILE, OUTPUT PRINT-FILE.
        MOVE ZEROS TO TOTAL.
        READ CARD-FILE AT END MOVE 1 TO EOF.
        PERFORM CALC-RTN 10 TIMES.
        MOVE TOTAL TO EDIT1.
        WRITE PRINT-OUT AFTER ADVANCING 2 LINES.
        CLOSE CARD-FILE, PRINT-FILE.
        STOP RUN.
    CALC-RTN.
        ADD AMT TO TOTAL.
        READ CARD-FILE AT END MOVE 1 TO EOF.
```

Note that the AT END clause and its associated MOVE 1 TO EOF in this illustration are entirely unnecessary since EOF is never tested. Nonetheless the AT END clause must be coded with every input file except disk.

The above routine is another example of a loop. CALC-RTN is executed 10 times and then TOTAL is printed.

Suppose we wish to print **five** groups of ten totals. That is, we wish to execute the above routine five times and then proceed to some other point in the program. The following addition is correct:

```
        OPEN INPUT CARD-FILE, OUTPUT PRINT-FILE.
        READ CARD-FILE AT END MOVE 1 TO EOF.
        PERFORM FIRST-RTN 5 TIMES.
        CLOSE CARD-FILE, PRINT-FILE.
        STOP RUN.
    FIRST-RTN.
        MOVE ZEROS TO TOTAL.
        PERFORM SECOND-RTN 10 TIMES.
        MOVE TOTAL TO EDIT1.
        WRITE PRINT-OUT AFTER ADVANCING 2 LINES.
    SECOND-RTN.
        ADD AMT TO TOTAL.
        READ CARD-FILE AT END MOVE 1 TO EOF.
```

The last format for a PERFORM statement is the most comprehensive and, thus, the most complicated:

$$\text{IV. } \underline{\text{PERFORM}} \text{ (paragraph-name-1) } \left[\underline{\text{THRU}} \text{ (paragraph-name-n)}\right]$$

$$\underline{\text{VARYING}} \text{ (data-name-1) } \underline{\text{FROM}} \quad \begin{Bmatrix} \text{(data-name-2)} \\ \text{(integer-1)} \end{Bmatrix} \underline{\text{BY}} \begin{Bmatrix} \text{(data-name-3)} \\ \text{(integer-2)} \end{Bmatrix}$$

$$\underline{\text{UNTIL}} \text{ (condition)}$$

Examples

```
(1)    PERFORM READ-RTN VARYING CTR FROM 0 BY 1 UNTIL CTR = 20.
(2)    PERFORM READ-RTN VARYING CTR FROM 1 BY 1 UNTIL CTR IS GREATER
          THAN 20.
```

(The two statements perform the same functions, assuming that CTR is used only as a counter and not as an arithmetic operator.)

Another example of this option is as folows:

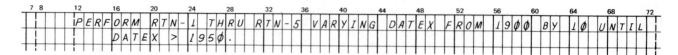

Using Format IV, the PERFORM statement itself will:

> **PERFORM . . . VARYING**
> 1. Use data-name-1 as a counter or looping indicator.
> 2. Initialize this counter at data-name-2 or integer-1.
> 3. Increment the counter by integer-2 or the contents of data-name-3.
> 4. Test the looping indicator for the condition specified. If the condition is met, no further PERFORM is executed.

Figure 15.2 illustrates the flowchart for this operation.

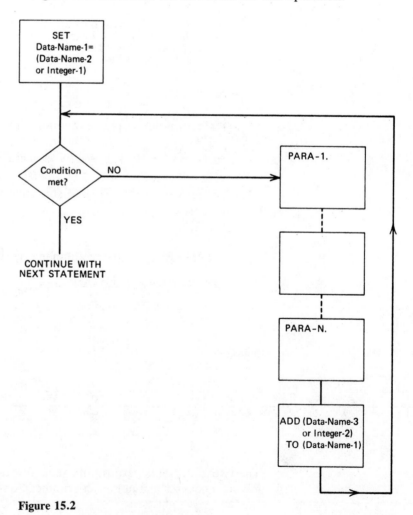

Figure 15.2

Suppose we wish to sum all odd-numbered integers from 1 to 1001. We could use Format IV of the PERFORM statement as follows:

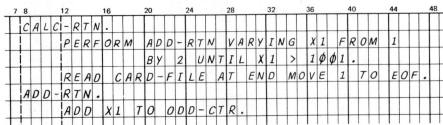

```
CALC-RTN.
        PERFORM ADD-RTN VARYING X1 FROM 1
                BY 2 UNTIL X1 > 1001.
        READ CARD-FILE AT END MOVE 1 TO EOF.
ADD-RTN.
        ADD X1 TO ODD-CTR.
```

SELF-EVALUATING QUIZ

1. After a PERFORM statement is executed, control returns to _____.
   *****
   the statement directly following the PERFORM

2. If PERFORM RTN-1 X TIMES is executed and X is equal to 0, RTN-1 will be performed _____ times.
   *****
   no

3. PERFORM PARA-1 ITEMX TIMES is valid only if ITEMX has contents of _____ or _____.
   *****
   0

   an integer

4. How many times will the paragraph named ROUTINE be executed by the following PERFORM statements?
   (a) PERFORM ROUTINE VARYING X FROM 1 BY 1 UNITL X = 10.
   (b) PERFORM ROUTINE VARYING X FROM 1 BY 1 UNTIL X > 10.
   (c) PERFORM ROUTINE VARYING X FROM 0 BY 1 UNTIL X = 10.
   *****
   9 times.
   10 times.
   10 times.

5. Write a PERFORM routine to add A to B five times.
   *****
   ```
       PERFORM BEGIN 5 TIMES.
          .
          .
          .
   BEGIN.
       ADD A TO B.
   ```
   or
   ```
       MOVE 1 TO CTR.
       PERFORM BEGIN UNTIL CTR = 6.
          .
          .
          .
   BEGIN.
       ADD A TO B.
       ADD 1 TO CTR.
   ```

What, if anything, is wrong with the following routines (6–8)?

6.   PERFORM RTNX A TIMES.

            .
            .
            .

    RTNX.
            ADD C TO B.
            ADD 1 TO A.
    *****
    A, the data-name in the PERFORM statement, may be accessed at RTNX
    but may **not** be changed. To increment A will result in improper execution.
    In this case, RTNX will be performed indefinitely.

7.   PERFORM PARA-5 8 TIMES.
            STOP RUN.
    PARA-5.
            IF A = B GO TO RTN3.
            ADD A TO B.
    RTN3.
            ADD 5 TO B.
    *****
    PARA-5, a paragraph executed by a PERFORM statement, should not have
    a GO TO statement within its range. The following is valid:

            PERFORM PARA-5 8 TIMES.
            STOP RUN.
    PARA-5.
            IF A = B ADD 5 TO B, ELSE ADD A TO B.

8.   PERFORM RTNX UNTIL CTR= 8.
            STOP RUN.
    RTNX.
            ADD A TO B.
            ADD 1 TO CTR.
            IF CTR = 8 STOP RUN.
    *****
    A PERFORM statement will internally compare CTR to 8; thus the last
    conditional is redundant, unnecessary, and incorrect.

9. Using the TIMES option of the PERFORM statement, restate the following:

            MOVE 0 TO X1.
            PERFORM RTN-X UNTIL X1 = 10.
    RTNX.

            .
            .
            .

            ADD 1 TO X1.
    *****
    PERFORM RTNX 10 TIMES.

10. Using the VARYING option of the PERFORM statement, write a routine to sum all even numbers from 2 to 100.
    *****
    PERFORM SUM-RTN VARYING X FROM 2 BY 2 UNTIL X IS GREATER THAN 100.
    .
    .
    .

SUM-RTN.
    ADD X TO EVEN-SUM.

PRACTICE PROBLEM—
WITH SOLUTION

Write a program to print one tape record from 20 card records. The input is as follows:

1–20 Customer name (same for each group of 20 cards)
21–25 Daily transaction amount xxx.xx
26–80 Not used

The output is a tape file with each record containing customer name and a total field of the 20 daily transaction amounts. The output file has standard labels and 20 records/block.

See Figure 15.3 for the solution.

REVIEW QUESTIONS

True False

I. True-False Questions

1. A PERFORM statement permanently transfers control to some other section of a program.
2. A GO TO statement must never be used in conjunction with a PERFORM statement.
3. GO TO statements are generally avoided in structured programs.
4. EXIT is a COBOL reserved word that performs no operation.
5. Using a PERFORM (paragraph) UNTIL (condition) option, the condition is tested even before the paragraph is executed.
6. PERFORM PARA-1 N TIMES is only valid if N is defined as a numeric field.
7. In the statement PERFORM PARA-1 N TIMES, N should not be altered within PARA-1.
8. It is valid to say PERFORM RTNX 0 TIMES.
9. The PERFORM and GO TO statements will cause identical branching.
10. If several paragraphs are to be executed by a PERFORM statement, we may use the THRU option.

II. General Questions

1. Using a PERFORM statement with a TIMES option, write a routine to find N factorial where N is the data item. You will recall that N factorial = N × N − 1 × N − 2 × . . . × 1; that is, 5 factorial = 5 × 4 × 3 × 2 × 1 = 120.

```
IDENTIFICATION DIVISION.
PROGRAM-ID. CHAPT15.
ENVIRONMENT DIVISION.
CONFIGURATION SECTION.
SOURCE-COMPUTER. IBM-370.
OBJECT-COMPUTER. IBM-370.
INPUT-OUTPUT SECTION.
FILE-CONTROL.
    SELECT CARD-IN ASSIGN TO UR-S-SYSIN.
    SELECT TAPE-OUT ASSIGN TO UT-S-SYS004.
DATA DIVISION.
FILE SECTION.
FD  CARD-IN
    LABEL RECORDS ARE OMITTED
    RECORD CONTAINS 80 CHARACTERS
    DATA RECORD IS CARD-REC.
01  CARD-REC.
    02  CUSTOMER-NAME               PIC X(20).
    02  TRANSACTION-AMT             PIC 999V99.
    02  FILLER                      PIC X(55).
FD  TAPE-OUT
    LABEL RECORDS ARE STANDARD
    RECORD CONTAINS 27 CHARACTERS
    BLOCK CONTAINS 20 RECORDS
    DATA RECORD IS TAPE-REC.
01  TAPE-REC.
    02  CUSTOMER-NAME               PIC X(20).
    02  TOTAL                       PIC 9(5)V99.
WORKING-STORAGE SECTION.
01  WORK-AREAS.
    02  EOF             PIC 9 VALUE 0.
PROCEDURE DIVISION.
    OPEN INPUT CARD-IN, OUTPUT TAPE-OUT.
    READ CARD-IN AT END MOVE 1 TO EOF.
    PERFORM CALC-RTN UNTIL EOF = 1.
    CLOSE CARD-IN, TAPE-OUT.
    STOP RUN.
CALC-RTN.
    MOVE ZEROS TO TOTAL.
    MOVE CUSTOMER-NAME OF CARD-REC TO CUSTOMER-NAME OF TAPE-REC.
    PERFORM READ-RTN 20 TIMES.
    WRITE TAPE-REC.
READ-RTN.
    ADD TRANSACTION-AMT TO TOTAL.
    READ CARD-IN AT END MOVE 1 TO EOF.
```

Figure 15.3

2. Assume the paragraphs in a program are called 1, 2, . . . 10 and appear in numerical sequence. Write a **single** statement to perform the following:

```
PERFORM 1.
PERFORM 2.
PERFORM 3.
```

3. Rewrite the following routine using a PERFORM statement with a TIMES option:

```
        MOVE ZEROS TO COUNTER.
        PERFORM RTN-X UNTIL COUNTER = 20.

            .
            .
            .

RTN-X.
        READ CARD-IN AT END CLOSE CARD-IN STOP RUN.
        ADD QTY OF CARD-REC TO TOTAL.
        ADD 1 TO COUNTER.
RTN-Y.

            .
            .
            .
```

4. Rewrite the TITLE-RTN in this chapter (page 301) **without** using EXIT.
5. Write a routine using the PERFORM statement with a TIMES option to sum all odd-numbered integers from 1 to 1001.
6. Write a routine using the PERFORM statement with the UNTIL option to sum all odd-numbered integers from 1 to 1001.
7. Rewrite the solution to Question 3 using the PERFORM statement with a VARYING option.

PROBLEMS   1. Write a program to compute compound interest from the following formula:

$$P_n = P_o (1 + r)^n$$

P_n = amount of principal after n periods of investment of P_o at rate r per period

The input is a card file with the following format:

```
1–6  Principal (P₀)
7–8  Rate .xx (r)
9–80 Not used
```

1–6 Principal (P_o)
7–8 Rate .xx (r)
9–80 Not used

Output is a printed report with compound interest calculated for periods 1 year to 10 years (n = 1, 2 . . 10):

PRINCIPAL — xxxxxx
RATE — .xx

PERIODS	AMOUNT
1	xxxxx.xx
2	xxxxx.xx
.	
.	
.	
10	xxxxx.xx

(HINT: $(1 + r)^3$ is the same as $(1 + r)(1 + r)(1 + r)$, that is, PERFORM MULTIPLY-RTN 3 TIMES.)

2. Write a program to print one tape record from x number of cards, where x is denoted on the first card of each group:

Input

1–2   Number of cards in group (only indicated on the first card for each group)
3–22 Salesman name—same for each card in group
23–27 Amount xxx.xx
28–80 Not used

The output is a tape file with each record consisting of salesman name and accumulated amount for x number of cards. The output file has standard labels and 50 records/block.

3. Each class in a school has exactly 20 students. The grade (0–100) for each student is punched into the first three columns of a card. Thus the first 20 cards are for the students in class 1, the second 20 cards are for students in class 2, and so on. There are exactly 25 classes. Print a report with the class average for each class:

CLASS 1   xxx.xx
CLASS 2   xxx.xx

.
.

CLASS 25 xxx.xx

16 ADDITIONAL METHODS OF ALTERING THE PATH OF A PROGRAM

A. NESTED CONDITIONALS

You will recall that the format for a simple conditional is:[1]

<u>IF</u> (condition) (statement-1) [<u>ELSE</u> (statement-2)].

In a simple conditional, statement-1 and statement-2 are **imperative.** That is, they are executable commands and do not themselves test conditions. In the conditional, IF A = B PERFORM RTN-5 ELSE ADD 5 TO B, the statements PERFORM RTN-5 and ADD 5 TO B are imperative.

In the event that statement-1 and statement-2 had themselves been conditional statements, we would have a **nested conditional.**

Example 1

7 8		12		16		20		24		28		32	
		I F		A M T	=	6							
				I F		T A X	=	1 Ø					
						P E R F O R M		R T N - 2					
				E L S E		P E R F O R M		R T N - 3					
		E L S E		P E R F O R M		R T N - 1 .							

The above example conforms to the format statement. Statement-1, however, within the format, is a conditional:

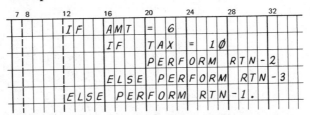

$$IF \begin{Bmatrix} \text{condition} \\ \text{AMT} = 6 \end{Bmatrix} \begin{Bmatrix} \text{(statement-1)} \\ \text{IF TAX} = 10 \text{ PERFORM RTN-2 ELSE PERFORM RTN-3} \end{Bmatrix}$$

$$ELSE \begin{Bmatrix} \text{(statement-2)} \\ \text{PERFORM RTN-1} \end{Bmatrix}$$

[1]The word OTHERWISE may be used on IBM computers in place of ELSE.

The clause (IF TAX = 10 PERFORM RTN-2 ELSE PERFORM RTN-3) is considered statement-1 in the above. The nested conditional tests several conditions with a single statement:

1. If AMT is not equal to 6, RTN-1 is performed.

   If AMT equals 6, the second condition is tested.
2. If AMT = 6 and TAX = 10, RTN-2 is performed.
3. If AMT = 6 and TAX is not equal to 10, RTN-3 is performed.

A nested conditional is a shortcut method of writing a series of simple conditionals. The nested conditional in Example 1 may be written as follows:

```
CALC-RTN.
    IF AMT IS NOT EQUAL TO 6
        PERFORM RTN-1
        GO TO CALC-RTN-EXIT.
    IF TAX = 10
        PERFORM RTN-2
    ELSE
        PERFORM RTN-3.
CALC-RTN-EXIT.
    EXIT.
```

It may also be written, using compound conditionals, in this way;

```
CALC-RTN.
    IF AMT = 6 AND TAX = 10
        PERFORM RTN-2
        GO TO CALC-RTN-EXIT.
    IF AMT = 6 AND TAX IS NOT EQUAL TO 10
        PERFORM RTN-3
        GO TO CALC-RTN-EXIT.
    PERFORM RTN-1.
CALC-RTN-EXIT.
    EXIT.
```

Note that in both cases the statement used to access either of these routines would be:

```
    PERFORM CALC-RTN THRU CALC-RTN-EXIT.
```

In addition to minimizing programming effort, nested conditionals have the added advantage of testing conditions just as they appear in a decision table or in an explanatory note.

Example 2

If A = B and C = D, perform RTN-A. If A = B and C is not equal to D, perform RTN-B.
If A is not equal to B, perform RTN-C.

Written as a nested conditional, we have:

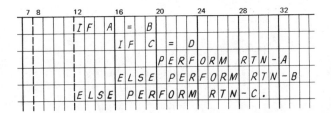

Parentheses may also be included for ease of reading. Note that in a nested IF statement, the ELSE clause refers to the conditional statement directly preceding it. If an ELSE clause follows another ELSE clause, then the last one refers to the **initial** condition. The above statement is interpreted as follows:

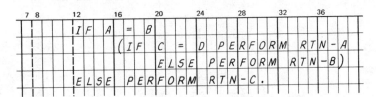

In the above, the initial condition, A = B, has the ELSE clause PERFORM RTN-C associated with it. Note, however, that ELSE clauses are optional in a conditional statement and need not be included.

Example 3

Condition	Resultant Action
1. CREDIT-AMT is not equal to DEBIT-AMT	next sentence
2. CREDIT-AMT = DEBIT-AMT and YEAR = 80	UPDATE-RTN is performed
3. CREDIT-AMT = DEBIT-AMT and YEAR is not equal to 80	INCORRECT-DATE-RTN is performed

The clause (ELSE PERFORM INCORRECT-DATE-RTN) refers to the condition directly preceding it, IF YEAR = 80. Thus, if YEAR does not equal 80, the ELSE clause is executed and INCORRECT-DATE-RTN is performed.

Since there is only one ELSE clause, the condition IF A = B has **no** ELSE clause associated with it. If A is not equal to B, execution resumes with the next sentence.

Any number of conditions may be tested in a nested conditional. The only limitations are the size of the computer and the somewhat cumbersome nature of the statement. When too many conditions are specified in a nested conditional, it becomes difficult to follow. The programmer may use as many conditions in a nested IF statement as considered feasible.

Example 4

```
IF MALE AND SINGLE ADD 1 TO SUM-1.
IF MALE AND MARRIED ADD 1 TO SUM-2.
IF FEMALE AND SINGLE ADD 1 TO SUM-3.
IF FEMALE AND MARRIED ADD 1 TO SUM-4.
```

MALE and FEMALE are condition-names referring to a sex field. SEX may contain **only** the codes for MALE and FEMALE.

SINGLE and MARRIED are condition-names referring to a marital status field. This field may contain **only** the codes for SINGLE and MARRIED.

Writing the above as a nested conditional, we have:

IF MALE IF SINGLE ADD 1 TO SUM-1 ELSE ADD 1 TO SUM-2 ELSE IF SINGLE ADD 1 TO SUM-3 ELSE ADD 1 TO SUM-4.

Nested conditionals provide a method for writing a series of simple or compound conditions in a single statement. The programmer may represent tests with nested IF or simple IF statements. Observe that the following two routines perform identical functions:

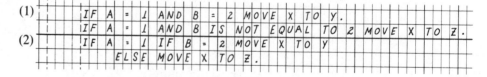

```
(1)   IF A = 1 AND B = 2 MOVE X TO Y.
      IF A = 1 AND B IS NOT EQUAL TO 2 MOVE X TO Z.
(2)   IF A = 1 IF B = 2 MOVE X TO Y
         ELSE MOVE X TO Z.
```

The nested conditional is a shortcut method for writing IF statements and is convenient for restating a series of conditions in a single statement. If not fully understood nor utilized effectively, however, it may lead to rampant logic errors. The programmer must note that **any** series of conditions may be represented by simple or compound conditionals, without the use of nested conditionals. If nested conditionals prove too cumbersome, programmers may usually use a series of simple statements.

SELF-EVALUATING
QUIZ

1. Using the following chart, write a nested conditional to perform the stated operations:

X	Y	Operation
1	1	ADD A TO B
1	Not = 1	PERFORM RTN-2
Not =1	Anything	SUBTRACT A FROM B

*****

IF X = 1 IF Y = 1 ADD A TO B ELSE PERFORM RTN-2 ELSE SUBTRACT A FROM B.

2. Using the following chart, write a nested conditional to perform the stated operations:

Y	Z	Operation
3	Not = 5	PERFORM PATHA
3	5	PERFORM PATHB
Not = 3	Anything	PERFORM PATHC

*****

IF Y = 3 IF Z IS NOT EQUAL TO 5 PERFORM PATHA ELSE PERFORM PATHB ELSE PERFORM PATHC.

3. In the following statement, if FLDX = 3 and FLDY = 4, a transfer to _____ will occur:

IF FLDX = 3 IF FLDY = 5 PERFORM Y ELSE PERFORM Z ELSE PERFORM W.

*****

Z

4. Using the above conditional, _____ will be performed if FLDX = 4 and FLDY = 5.

*****

W

5. Using the above conditional, a transfer to _____ will occur if FLDX = 3 and FLDY = 5.

*****

Y

B. GO TO . . .
DEPENDING ON . . .
STATEMENT

Examine the following illustration:

Example

```
IF  CODE-X  =  1  GO  TO  RTNA.
IF  CODE-X  =  2  GO  TO  RTNB.
IF  CODE-X  =  3  GO  TO  RTNC.
GO  TO  ERR-RTN
```

When the contents of a data field may be 1, 2, . . . n where n is any integer, and the program is to branch unconditionally to different points depending on the data field, a shortcut use of the GO TO statement may be employed:

Example

```
GO TO RTNA, RTNB, RTNC DEPENDING ON CODE-X.
GO TO ERR-RTN.
```

The computer is instructed to branch to:

The first paragraph name, RTNA, if the data-name, CODE-X, has a one (1) as its contents.

The second specified paragraph name, RTNB, if CODE-X has a two.

The third paragraph name, RTNC, will be executed only if CODE-X equals three.

If CODE-X does not equal 1, 2, or 3, a branch to ERR-RTN is performed.

In general, if there are n paragraph names specified in the GO TO . . . DEPENDING ON . . . statement, a branch to the first occurs if there is a 1 in the field, a branch to the second occurs if there is a 2 in the field, . . . a branch to the nth occurs if there is an n in the field. If the field consists of any number other than 1 to n (for example, −5, 0, n +1), the program will proceed to the next sequential step. In other words, no branch within the GO TO . . . DEPENDING ON . . . will occur. In our example, the next sequential step was an unconditional branch to ERR-RTN. The format, then, for this statement is:

<u>GO TO</u> (paragraph-name-1, paragraph-name-2, . . . paragraph-name-n)
<u>DEPENDING</u> ON (data-name).

The GO TO . . . DEPENDING ON . . . statement may only be used for **numeric** fields. The statement GO TO PARA-1, PARA-2 DEPENDING ON FLDA will execute properly only if FLDA has a PICTURE of 9's.

Any number of paragraph names may be used within the GO TO . . . DEPENDING ON . . . statement. The only limitation is the size of the computer, which in most cases allows adequate flexibility. Generally, a maximum of 2031 operands are permitted, which would be more than adequate.

Problem A

Branch to:

PARA-1 if FLDA = 3
PARA-2 if FLDA = 4
PARA-3 if FLDA = 5
otherwise branch to BEGIN.

On first inspection, it may appear that a GO TO . . . DEPENDING ON . . . statement is not applicable, since we want to proceed to different paragraphs depending on a 3, 4, or 5 in FLDA. Since the GO TO . . . DEPENDING ON . . . statement causes a branch to the first indicated paragraph if there is a 1, and not a 3, in the data field, it may seem that this statement is inappropriate. Let us consider the conditions more closely, however. Suppose FLDA = 1.

Since the field does not equal 3, 4, or 5, we wish to branch to BEGIN. Suppose FLDA = 2. Again, a branch to BEGIN is implied. Thus, if FLDA = 1, 2, 3, 4, or 5, we want to branch to BEGIN, BEGIN, PARA-1, PARA-2, PARA-3, respectively. The following would then be correct:

Solution 1 to Problem A

```
GO TO BEGIN, BEGIN, PARA-1, PARA-2, PARA-3
DEPENDING ON FLDA.
GO TO BEGIN.
```

Note that the same paragraph name may be used more than once in a GO TO ... DEPENDING ON ... statement. The only criterion for execution is that we wish to proceed to the first specified paragraph name if there is a one in the field, to the second paragraph name if there is a two in the field, and so on for all paragraph names indicated. If the field is not equal to any of these integers, the next sequential step will be executed. In our example, if FLDA is not equal to 1, 2, 3, 4, or 5, GO TO BEGIN is performed. Thus the GO TO ... DEPENDING ON ... statement is really only a shortcut method for writing a series of simple conditional statements.

The above use of the GO TO ... DEPENDING ON ... statement is not the only solution to the problem. Suppose we subtract two from FLDA. In that case, we wish to branch to PARA-1 if there is a one in FLDA, to PARA-2 if there is a two in FLDA, and to PARA-3 if there is a three in FLDA.

Solution 2 to Problem A

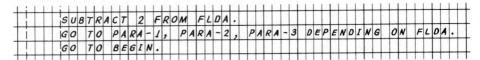

```
SUBTRACT 2 FROM FLDA.
GO TO PARA-1, PARA-2, PARA-3 DEPENDING ON FLDA.
GO TO BEGIN.
```

From the above illustraton, it should be clear that a GO TO ... DEPENDING ON ... statement is easily derived where conditions to be tested include incremental values. If the field has values of 15, 16, 17, 18, and branches to four different points occur accordingly, then merely subtract 14 from the field and proceed as if it has values 1, 2, 3, 4.

When dealing with a field that may have many values, each of which causes a specific branch, it is often advantageous to manipulate the data as above so that a GO TO ... DEPENDING ON ... command may be used. If not, a series of simple GO TO statements may prove tedious, time consuming, and inefficient. With manipulation of data, we can sometimes use this shortcut method even if the values in the field are not consecutive.

Problem B:

Branch to:

PARA-1 if FLDB = 2;
PARA-2 if FLDB = 4;
PARA-3 if FLDB = 6;
PARA-4 if FLDB = 8;
PARA-5 if FLDB = 10.

To set up five simple GO TO statements is one way to solve the problem. We can, however, use the shortcut method even though FLDB has values from 2 to 10 and is incremented by 2 instead of 1. We must first manipulate the data. Suppose we divide FLDB by 2. Then the values in the field vary from 1 to 5, with the increment being equal to 1. This is the order we are seeking. Our statements then read as follows:

Solution 1 to Problem B

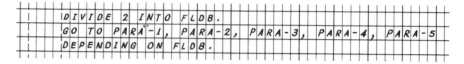

```
      DIVIDE 2 INTO FLDB.
      GO TO PARA-1,  PARA-2,  PARA-3,  PARA-4,  PARA-5
      DEPENDING ON FLDB.
```

Note that, if the original contents of FLDB were required for future processing, the above solution would require an additional step. That is, we would multiply 2 by FLDB at the end of the routine to restore its original quantity.

C. STOP STATEMENT

The STOP statement alters the path of a program by halting the run. For an end-of-job halt, we say

```
STOP   RUN.
```

This instruction **permanently** halts execution of the program. It terminates the run. The program cannot be restarted after STOP RUN is executed.

We may also instruct the computer to (1) pause and (2) print a message by issuing the following instruction:

```
STOP   (literal).
```

This statement causes the computer to stop executing. The program **may be restarted,** however, by some form of operator intervention such as depressing the START key. Thus the STOP (literal) command causes a **pause** in execution. Unlike STOP RUN, STOP (literal) is **not** a permanent halt.

Thus the combined format for a STOP statement is:

```
STOP    { RUN      }
        { (literal) }
```

The literal specified in a STOP statement will print on the printer or console as a message to the computer operator. The literal may be numeric or nonnumeric. Thus

```
      STOP 'NO DATE CARD'.
      STOP 111.
```

are valid instructions. In the first case, the message NO DATE CARD will print and the computer will pause. The message implies that a date card is required for execution and was not found. A sample date card routine follows:

```
001010 PROCEDURE DIVISION.
001020     OPEN INPUT CARD-IN, OUTPUT PRINT-OUT.
001030 DATE-CARD-RTN.
001040     READ CARD-IN AT END MOVE 1 TO EOF.
001050     IF CODE-1 IS NOT EQUAL TO 'D'
001060         PERFORM WRONG-CARD-RTN UNTIL CODE-1 = 'D'.
001070     MOVE DATE-IN TO DATE-OUT.
001080 STANDARD-STRUCTURE.
001090     READ CARD-IN AT END MOVE 1 TO EOF.
001100     PERFORM CALC-RTN UNTIL EOF = 1.
001110     CLOSE CARD-IN, PRINT-OUT.
001120     STOP RUN.
001130 WRONG-CARD-RTN.
001140     STOP 'NO DATE CARD --- ENTER DATE IN CCS 1-6,
001150-        'D IN CC 80'.
001160     READ CARD-IN AT END MOVE 1 TO EOF.
001170 CALC-RTN.
001180     .
001190     .
001200     .
```

Note that if the condition tested in a PERFORM ... UNTIL is met **initially**, then the paragraph name specified in the PERFORM statement is not executed at all. With this in mind, the statements coded on lines 001050–001060 can be simplified:

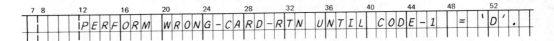

The date card contains a D in the field called CODE-1. If the date card is missing, no D will be found. In that case, the computer will print a message, stop, and read another date card after the operator inserts the correct card and depresses start.

A numeric literal is sometimes used in conjunction with a STOP statement when the computer operator is supplied with a list of numeric error codes. When STOP 111 is executed, for example, 111 will print and the computer will pause. The operator would then consult the list of codes to determine what error code 111 is, and what is to be done before the job is restarted.

SUMMARY OF STOP STATEMENT

1. STOP RUN causes permanent termination of a job.
2. STOP (literal) causes the printing of the indicated literal and a pause in execution.
3. With the STOP (literal) command, the computer operator can restart the job by depressing the start key.
4. The literal in the above may be numeric or nonnumeric.

```
                    IDENTIFICATION DIVISION.
                    PROGRAM-ID. CHAPT16.
                    ENVIRONMENT DIVISION.
                    CONFIGURATION SECTION.
                    SOURCE-COMPUTER. IBM-370.
                    OBJECT-COMPUTER. IBM-370.
                    INPUT-OUTPUT SECTION.
                    FILE-CONTROL.
                        SELECT CARD-IN ASSIGN TO UR-S-SYSIN.
                        SELECT PRINT-OUT ASSIGN TO UR-S-SYSOUT.
                    DATA DIVISION.
                    FILE SECTION.
                    FD  CARD-IN
                        LABEL RECORDS ARE OMITTED
                        RECORD CONTAINS 80 CHARACTERS
                        DATA RECORD IS CARD-REC.
                    01  CARD-REC.
                        02   CLIENT-NAME         PIC X(20).
                        02   DISTRIBUTION        PIC X.
                             88   INTERNAL-D          VALUE '1'.
                             88   EXTERNAL-D          VALUE '2'.
                        02   NO-OF-COPIES        PIC X.
                             88   LESS-THAN-10        VALUE '1'.
                             88   BET-10-AND-100      VALUE '2'.
                             88   GREATER-THAN-100 VALUE '3'.
                        02   FILLER              PIC X(58).
                    FD  PRINT-OUT
                        LABEL RECORDS ARE OMITTED
                        RECORD CONTAINS 133 CHARACTERS
                        DATA RECORD IS PRINT-REC.
                    01  PRINT-REC.
                        02   FILLER              PIC X(20).
                        02   NAME                PIC X(20).
                        02   FILLER              PIC X(20).
                        02   ACTION              PIC X(20).
                        02   FILLER              PIC X(53).
                    WORKING-STORAGE SECTION.
                    01  WORK-AREAS.
                        02   EOF                          PIC 9 VALUE 0.
                    PROCEDURE DIVISION.
                        OPEN INPUT CARD-IN, OUTPUT PRINT-OUT.
                        READ CARD-IN AT END MOVE 1 TO EOF.
                        PERFORM CALC-RTN UNTIL EOF = 1.
                        CLOSE CARD-IN, PRINT-OUT.
                        STOP RUN.
                    CALC-RTN.
                        MOVE SPACES TO PRINT-REC.
                        MOVE CLIENT-NAME TO NAME.
                        IF INTERNAL-D PERFORM INTERNAL-RTN
                                ELSE IF EXTERNAL-D PERFORM EXTERNAL-RTN
                        ELSE MOVE 'ERROR' TO ACTION.
                        WRITE PRINT-REC AFTER ADVANCING 2 LINES.
                        READ CARD-IN AT END MOVE 1 TO EOF.
                    INTERNAL-RTN.
                        IF LESS-THAN-10 MOVE 'XEROX' TO ACTION
                            ELSE IF BET-10-AND-100 MOVE 'THERMOFAX DITTO' TO ACTION
                        ELSE IF GREATER-THAN-100 MOVE 'PRINT IN PRINT SHOP' TO ACTION
                        ELSE MOVE 'ERROR' TO ACTION.
                    EXTERNAL-RTN.
                        IF LESS-THAN-10 OR BET-10-AND-100 MOVE 'XEROX' TO ACTION
                                ELSE IF GREATER-THAN-100
                                    MOVE 'PRINT IN PRINT SHOP' TO ACTION
                        ELSE MOVE 'ERROR' TO ACTION.
```

Figure 16.1

1. What, if anything, is wrong with the following paragraph names?
   (a) TOTAL-RTN
   (b) %-RTN
   (c) 1

*****

(a) Nothing wrong.
(b) No special characters permitted.
(c) Nothing wrong.

2. All paragraph names must be followed by a _____.
*****
period

3. What is wrong with the following statements?
(a) GO TO PARA-1 DEPENDING ON CODEX.
(b) GO TO RTN-1, RTN-2, DEPENDING UPON CODEX.
(c) GO TO PARA-1 DEPENDING ON CODE1, CODE2.
*****
(a) Nothing wrong—branch to PARA-1 will occur if CODEX = 1.
(b) DEPENDING ON, not UPON.
(c) Only **one** data-name may be specified.

4. Consider the following: GO TO RTN-5, RTN-6, RTN-7 DEPENDING ON FLDA. GO TO RTN-8. A branch to _____ will occur if there is a 0 in FLDA. A branch to RTN-5 will occur if there is a _____ in FLDA.
*****
RTN-8
one

5. Write a statement or statements that will cause the following branches: RTN-1 if FLDB = 3; RTN-2 if FLDB = 6; RTN-3 if FLDB = 9; otherwise branch to BEGIN.
(NOTE: Use the GO TO . . . DEPENDING ON statement.)
*****
DIVIDE 3 INTO FLDB.
GO TO RTN-1, RTN-2, RTN-3 DEPENDING ON FLDB.
GO TO BEGIN.

6. To cause the program to terminate execution, the _____ instruction is indicated.
*****
STOP RUN

7. To cause the program to pause, the _____ format is used.
*****
STOP (literal)

8. The literal in a STOP (literal) command may be a _____ or a _____ literal.
*****
numeric
nonnumeric

9. _____ is required to continue execution after STOP (literal) has been performed.
*****
Operator intervention

PRACTICE PROBLEM—   Write a series of steps to perform the following:
WITH SOLUTION

| | | Rules | | | | | |
		1	2	3	4	5	6
Conditions	Internal Distribution	Y	Y	Y			
	External Distribution				Y	Y	Y
	Less than 10 copies	Y			Y		
	Between 10 and 100 copies		Y			Y	
	More than 100 copies			Y			Y
Actions	Xerox	X			X	X	
	Thermofax Ditto		X				
	Print in print shop			X			X

Y = yes (condition exists)
X = action taken

Reading vertically, we have:

1. If item is to have Internal Distribution and Less than 10 Copies, perform XEROX (move 'XEROX' to output message)
2. If item is to have Internal Distribution and between 10 and 100 Copies, perform THERMOFAX (move 'THERMOFAX' to output message), and so on.

Cards are entered as follows:

1–20 Client's Name
  21 Distribution
      1 = Internal
      2 = External
  22 No. of Copies
      1 = Less than 10 copies
      2 = Between 10 and 100 copies
      3 = More than 100 copies

If any input is incorrect, print an error message. For each card, print the following:
  Client's Name
  Action to be taken: (print one of the following)
    Xerox
    Thermofax Ditto
    Print in print shop
See Figure 16.1 on page 324 for the solution.

REVIEW QUESTIONS

True False

I. True-False Questions

1. The nested IF is another term for the compound conditional.
2. The last ELSE in a nested conditional is executed if none of the conditions specified is met.
3. The STOP statement may be used to cause a pause in execution as well as a final termination.
4. GO TO . . . DEPENDING ON can test a maximum of ten conditions.
5. The first paragraph-name mentioned in a GO TO . . . DEPENDING ON statement will be executed if the field specified has a value of 0.
6. The number of conditions that may be tested in a nested conditional is limited to 120.
7. Consider the following:
   IF NY IF URBAN ADD 1 TO TOT1 ELSE IF NJ ADD 1 TO TOT2 ELSE ADD1 TO TOT3 results in 1 being added to TOT3 if NY and not URBAN.
8. In the above, 1 is added to TOT2 if NJ and URBAN.
9. In a GO TO . . . DEPENDING ON statement, if the data-name specified is not equal to 1 through 10, an error occurs.
10. The STOP statement may be used to print a nonnumeric literal.

II. General Questions

1. Use a GO TO . . . DEPENDING ON statement to perform the following:
   branch to: BEGIN if A = 18
   RTN-X if A = 19
   RTN-Y if A = 20
   RTN-Z if A = 21
   ERR-RTN otherwise
2. Use a GO TO . . . DEPENDING ON statement to perform the following:
   branch to: PARA1 if B = −20
   PARA2 if B = −15
   PARA3 if B = −10
   PARA4 if B = −5
   ERR-RTN otherwise
3. GO TO RTNA, RTNB, RTNC, RTND DEPENDING ON FIELDX. GO TO RTNE.
   Using the above statement, indicate the branches that will occur if:
   (a) FIELDX = 0
   (b) FIELDX = 4
   (c) FIELDX = −2
   (d) FIELDX = 5
   (e) FIELDX = 1
4. Write a single statement to cause the computer to halt and to print the error code 999.
5. Write a single statement to cause the computer to halt and to print the error message 'INVALID CARD CODE'.
6. (T or F) All STOP statements cause irreversible halts; that is, the computer may not be made to restart.
7. (T or F) PERFORM statements cause the same sequence of instructions to be executed as GO TO commands.

8. Use a nested IF statement to perform the following:

A	B	Operation
Not = 7	Not = 3	PERFORM RTNC.
Not = 7	= 3	PERFORM RTND.
= 7	Anything	PERFORM RTNE.

Rewrite the routine with a series of simple conditionals.

PROBLEMS

1. An attorney wishes to obtain a computerized billing procedure. We will assume that fees are fixed so a computer can easily be used to calculate the required fees for each client. Cards are read in with the following format:

Card Columns	Type of Data
1–20	Name of Client
21	Type of Fee
22–27	Amount Recovered 9(6)

Print Name of Client and Amount of Fee (with appropriate headings and editing).

Instructions

If Type of Fee = 1, Amount of Fee = ⅓ Amount Recovered
If Type of Fee = 2, this indicates a sliding scale, Amount of Fee Equals:
  50% of first $1,000 recovered
  40% of the next $2,000 recovered
  35% of the next $22,000 recovered
  25% of any amount recovered over $25,000
If Type of Fee is not a 1 or 2, print 'INCORRECT DATA' and stop.

2. Read in Cards with the following format:

1–20	Passenger Name
21	Ticket Request
	1 = First Class
	2 = Tourist
22	Availability
	1 = First Class open
	2 = Tourist open
23	Is Alternative Class Acceptable?
	1 = Yes
	0 = No

Print an error message if any input is erroneously coded. Print, as output, the following:
  Passenger Name
  Action to be Taken
The action to be taken is indicated by the chart in Table 16.1. Note that the chart is read vertically:

Rule

1) If First Class request and
   First Class open

Action to be taken: 'ISSUE FIRST CLASS TICKET'

2) If First Class request and
   First Class not available and
   Tourist open and
   Alternate Class acceptable

Action to be taken: 'ISSUE TOURIST TICKET' and so on.

Table 16.1

						Rules				
			1	2	3	4	5	6	7	8
Conditions	1	First Class request	Y	Y	Y	Y				
	2	Tourist request					Y	Y	Y	Y
	3	First class open	Y	N	N	N		Y	N	
	4	Tourist open		Y	N		Y	N	N	N
	5	Alternate class acceptable		Y	Y	N		Y	Y	N
Actions	1	Issue first class ticket	X					X		
	2	Issue tourist ticket		X			X			
	3	Place on tourist wait list			X				X	X
	4	Place on first class wait list			X	X			X	

17 OCCURS CLAUSES— SINGLE LEVEL

To indicate the **repeated occurrence** of an item having the same format, we use an OCCURS clause in COBOL.

Consider the following example. Each input data card has ten eight-position amount fields. Each card will be read, the amount fields summed, and a total printed. Since no shortcut methods are known at this time, we must define our card with ten independent fields:

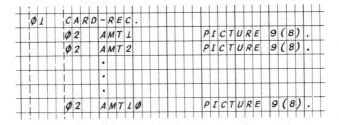

To perform the necessary addition, we write:

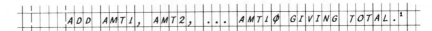

Since each amount field is an eight-position integer field, they are said to have the same format. To indicate the repeated occurrence of amount fields with the same format, we may use an OCCURS clause. Using this clause, the ten fields may be defined as follows:

[1]The series of dots indicates that each AMT must be repeated.

In this way, we have defined ten, eight-position numeric fields. All ten fields are called AMT. Thus we have described the 80-position card record with a single 02-level entry. The OCCURS clause is used to indicate the repeated occurrence of items. AMT defines 10 items, each with a PICTURE of 9(8).

There are ten items called AMT. To access any one of these entries in the PROCEDURE DIVISION, we must use identifying numbers called **subscripts.**

SUMMARY OF OCCURS
1. To denote the repeated occurrence of items with the same format, an OCCURS clause is used in the DATA DIVISION.
2. To access any of these items, a **subscript** is used in the PROCEDURE DIVISION.

A subscript is enclosed in parentheses and refers to the data-name directly preceding it. To move the **first** eight-position amount field to a print area called EDIT1, for example, we say

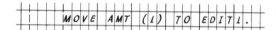

```
MOVE AMT (1) TO EDIT1.
```

AMT contains ten eight-position fields. We are moving the **first** eight-position field to EDIT1.

We may operate on any of the ten amount fields by using the corresponding subscript. Since AMT contains ten fields, the subscript used may vary from 1 to 10. The following are, however, invalid:

Invalid

```
MOVE AMT (Ø) TO EDIT2.
MOVE AMT (11) TO EDIT3.
```

The subscript can refer only to one of the ten amount fields. There is no eleventh amount nor is there a zeroeth amount. The subscript can refer only to one of the ten amount fields.

The data-name, which is specified with an OCCURS clause, will be accessed in the PROCEDURE DIVISION with a subscript. The data-name will be followed by a **space** and the corresponding subscript. The following serves to illustrate the proper spacing:

```
ADD   DATA-NAME-1   (3)   TO   TOTAL.
```

Thus far, we have discussed subscripts that are numeric literals. A subscript, however, may also be a data-name with a numeric PICTURE clause. If N were defined in the WORKING-STORAGE SECTION as follows:

```
 7 8       12      16      20      24      28      32      36
Ø1    WORK-AREAS.
       Ø2   N    PIC  99   VALUE  1.
```

the first amount field may be moved to EDIT1 as follows:

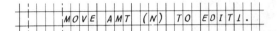

Subscripts, then, may be integers or data-names. If a data-name is used as a subscript, it must have a numeric PICTURE clause with an integer value. We use data-names as subscripts when we wish to access different items at different times.

Thus, to accumulate all ten amount fields, we may write

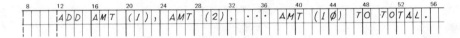

which is not any less tedious than the original method. Or we may use data-names as subscripts in conjunction with a PERFORM statement:

```
CALC-RTN.
    MOVE 1 TO CTR.
    MOVE ZEROS TO TOTAL.
    PERFORM ADD-RTN 10 TIMES.
    PERFORM WRITE-RTN.
    READ CARD-FILE AT END MOVE 1 TO EOF.
ADD-RTN.
    ADD AMT (CTR) TO TOTAL.
    ADD 1 TO CTR.
```

LOOP ROUTINE

1. Ten amount fields are to be added together.
2. CTR is the subscript; it is initialized at one.
3. First, AMT (CTR), which is initially the same as AMT (1) is added to TOTAL.
4. CTR is then incremented by one.
5. AMT (CTR) or the second amount field is then added to TOTAL.
6. This routine is performed ten times, until all ten amounts are added to TOTAL.

The TIMES option of the PERFORM statement was used in the above example. As indicated in Chapter 15, the UNTIL option may also be used to execute looping routines:

```
CALC-RTN.
    MOVE 1 TO CTR.
    MOVE ZEROS TO TOTAL.
    PERFORM ADD-RTN UNTIL CTR = 11.
    PERFORM WRITE-RTN.
    READ CARD-FILE AT END MOVE 1 TO EOF.
ADD-RTN.
    ADD AMT (CTR) TO TOTAL.
    ADD 1 TO CTR.
```

The VARYING option of the PERFORM statement provides the most direct method for coding loops:

```
CALC-RTN.
    MOVE ZEROS TO TOTAL.
    PERFORM ADD-RTN VARYING CTR FROM 1 BY 1
        UNTIL CTR > 10.
    PERFORM WRITE-RTN.
    READ CARD-FILE AT END MOVE 1 TO EOF.
ADD-RTN.
    ADD AMT (CTR) TO TOTAL.
```

OCCURS clauses are used in the DATA DIVISION to denote the repeated occurrence of items with the same format. Subscripts are identifying numbers used in the PROCEDURE DIVISION to access fields specified with OCCURS clauses. Both are very often utilized in conjunction with PERFORM statements to code program loops. The PERFORM statement, or loop, executes the same series of operations repeatedly.

The format for an OCCURS clause is:

> (level-number) (data-name) OCCURS (integer) TIMES

SPECIFICATIONS OF OCCURS CLAUSES

An OCCURS clause may be written on any level **except** 01, 77, or 88. That is, it may occur on levels 02–49. This implies that an item specified with an OCCURS clause must be part of a record. It may **not** be an independent item.

Items may occur **integer** times only. We will use integers, not data-names, preceding the word TIMES in an OCCURS clause.

The data-name used with an OCCURS clause may be an elementary item, with a PICTURE clause, or it may be a group item, which is further subdivided:

```
02  DATES    OCCURS  20  TIMES.
    03  MONTH         PICTURE X(12).
    03  YEAR          PICTURE 9(4).
```

The above OCCURS clause reserves 320 positions of storage. DATES refers to 20 groupings, **each** divided into a 12-position MONTH field and a four-position YEAR field. To say MOVE DATES (3) TO HOLD-IT will result in a **16**-position move operation. The third MONTH and the third YEAR will be moved. We may also move each individually:

```
MOVE MONTH (3) TO HOLD1.
MOVE YEAR (3) TO HOLD2.
```

Thus any item subordinate to an OCCURS clause must also be referred to with a subscript. MONTH and YEAR, as fields subordinate to DATES, must be accessed with the use of a subscript.

Example

Every input data card has five amount fields, each ten positions long. Print each amount and the total of all five amounts for each card on one line.

The input record has five amount fields:

```
01   CARD-REC.
     02   AMOUNT     OCCURS  5  TIMES,  PIC  9(10).
     02   FILLER                       PIC  X(30).
```

The output area has **six** numeric amount fields. We will consider the TOTAL field to be the sixth amount. We will **not,** however, define these fields as follows:

```
01   PRINT-REC.
     02   FILLER              PICTURE  X.
     02   AMOUNT2  OCCURS  6  TIMES,  PICTURE  9(10).
     02   FILLER              PICTURE  X(72).
```

This would place all amount fields next to one another, with no spaces between them. For readability of reports, we wish to have a number of spaces between each output amount field:

```
01   PRINT-REC.
     02   FILLER              PICTURE  X.
     02   AMTS  OCCURS  6  TIMES.
          03   AMOUNT2  PICTURE  9(10).
          03   FILLER   PICTURE  X(5).
     02   FILLER              PICTURE  X(42).
```

In this way, each amount field has a five-position filler separating it from the next field. To perform the necessary operations, a data-name, to be used as a subscript, is defined in the WORKING-STORAGE SECTION:

```
01   WORK-AREAS.
     02   SUB1      PICTURE  9,  VALUE  1.
```

Subscripts are generally initialized at 1 rather than zero. The PROCEDURE DIVISION entries, then, for the above routine, are as follows:

```
PROCEDURE DIVISION.
    OPEN INPUT CARD-FILE, OUTPUT PRINT-FILE.
    READ CARD-FILE AT END MOVE 1 TO EOF.
    PERFORM CALC-RTN UNTIL EOF = 1.
    CLOSE CARD-FILE, PRINT-FILE.
    STOP RUN.
CALC-RTN.
    MOVE SPACES TO PRINT-REC.
    MOVE ZEROS TO AMOUNT2 (6).
    PERFORM ADD-RTN 5 TIMES.
    WRITE PRINT-REC AFTER ADVANCING 2 LINES.
    MOVE 1 TO SUB1.
    READ CARD-FILE AT END MOVE 1 TO EOF.
ADD-RTN.
    ADD AMOUNT (SUB1) TO AMOUNT2 (6).
    MOVE AMOUNT (SUB1) TO AMOUNT2 (SUB1).
    ADD 1 TO SUB1.
```

A subscript may be an integer or a data-name. Integers are used as subscripts when the specific item is known and remains constant. AMOUNT2 (6) refers to the last output amount field, which is the TOTAL. Since all amounts from the card are to be added to the TOTAL, the receiving field in the addition is AMOUNT2 (6).

When the subscripts are meant to be variable, data-names are used. The data-name must be defined in the DATA DIVISION, have a numeric PICTURE clause, and contain only integers. We initialize the subscript at 1. In the above example, the subscript should only vary from 1 to 5, since the input area consists of five amount fields only.

OCCURS CLAUSES AND TABLES

OCCURS clauses denote the repeated occurrence of items with the same format. A widely used application of OCCURS clauses is in the defining of tables. A table is a series of stored items that is called on to provide pertinent data necessary for the execution of the program. A TAX-TABLE and a DISCOUNT-RATE-TABLE are examples of items stored during execution of a program.

Such table data is read into the computer. Since it is called on at various points in the program, the data is usually stored in the WORKING-STORAGE SECTION. An area is **reserved** in WORKING-STORAGE; the data is then **read** and moved to this area.

Suppose a POPULATION TABLE, consisting of 50 state population figures, has been read into some area of WORKING-STORAGE. The table may be defined in WORKING-STORAGE as follows:

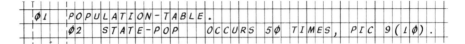

```
01   POPULATION-TABLE.
     02   STATE-POP    OCCURS 50 TIMES, PIC 9(10).
```

Note that the OCCURS clause may not be used on the 01 level. OCCURS clauses may be written only on the 02–49 levels, subordinate to a record level.

The above table, in the WORKING-STORAGE SECTION, defines 50 ten-position numeric fields. Five hundred storage positions are reserved for this table.

To access any of the 50 figures, a subscript must be used in conjunction with the data-name STATE-POP. Since STATE-POP is a data-name defined by an OCCURS clause, it must **always** be accessed with a subscript.

Note that POPULATION-TABLE is the **record name** for these 50 fields; POPULATION-TABLE may **not** be accessed in the PROCEDURE DIVISION. Only the item containing the OCCURS clause or items subordinate to the OCCURS clause, if they exist, may be accessed in the PROCEDURE DIVISION. STATE-POP or any 03-level item subordinate to STATE-POP, if one existed, may be used.

The above entry defines the storage area for the table. Data must be **read** from an input device and **moved** into this area. Later in this section, we will discuss the routines necessary for reading and accumulating the table data. Let us assume, at this point, that data is already stored in POPULATION-TABLE; that is, the information has been read and moved to this area. Thus, 50 figures have been stored in this table and are now available for processing.

Problem 1

Write a routine to find the total population of all 50 states. The total population will be placed in a field called USA-POP. Assume CTR, a WORKING-STORAGE item, is the subscript. The main module of the program will simply say: PERFORM TOTAL-USA-RTN.

We wish to add STATE-POP (1), STATE-POP (2), . . . STATE-POP (50) to USA-POP. The most efficient method to accomplish this is to use some variation of the PERFORM statement:

(a)
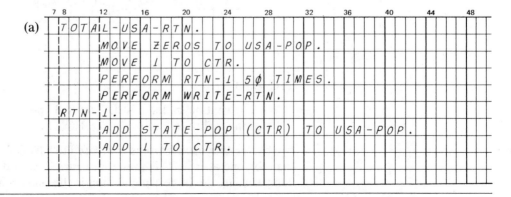

```
TOTAL-USA-RTN.
     MOVE ZEROS TO USA-POP.
     MOVE 1 TO CTR.
     PERFORM RTN-1 50 TIMES.
     PERFORM WRITE-RTN.
RTN-1.
     ADD STATE-POP (CTR) TO USA-POP.
     ADD 1 TO CTR.
```

(b)
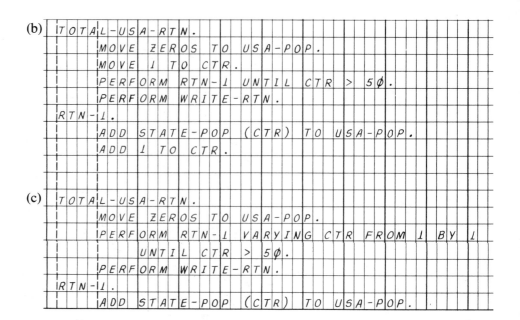

```
TOTAL-USA-RTN.
        MOVE  ZEROS  TO  USA-POP.
        MOVE  1  TO  CTR.
        PERFORM  RTN-1  UNTIL  CTR  >  50.
        PERFORM  WRITE-RTN.
RTN-1.
        ADD  STATE-POP  (CTR)  TO  USA-POP.
        ADD  1  TO  CTR.

(c)
TOTAL-USA-RTN.
        MOVE  ZEROS  TO  USA-POP.
        PERFORM  RTN-1  VARYING  CTR  FROM  1  BY  1
              UNTIL  CTR  >  50.
        PERFORM  WRITE-RTN.
RTN-1.
        ADD  STATE-POP  (CTR)  TO  USA-POP.
```

In all cases, CTR is a numeric item defined in the WORKING-STORAGE SEC-
TION. MOVE 1 TO CTR in routines a and b could be replaced by a VALUE
clause, where CTR is set equal to 1.

Problem 2

Suppose the population figures are in alphabetic order; that is, STATE-POP
(1), the first entry in the table, refers to the population of ALABAMA. STATE-
POP (2) corresponds to the population for ALASKA, . . . STATE-POP (50)
corresponds to WYOMING's population. Write a routine to move CALIFOR-
NIA's population to an output area called POP1. (CALIFORNIA is the fifth
state in alphabetic order):

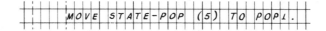

```
        MOVE  STATE-POP  (5)  TO  POP1.
```

Problem 3

Write a routine called LARGE to find the largest state population figure.
Place this figure in an area called HOLD-IT.

Observe that each figure is compared to HOLD-IT. If the population is greater
than the one at HOLD-IT, then that figure is placed in HOLD-IT. Thus, after 50
comparisons, the largest population is the one accumulated at HOLD-IT. CTR,

the subscript, may be initialized in the WORKING-STORAGE SECTION by a VALUE clause. If, however, the same subscript is used repeatedly throughout the program, it must be initialized at every routine.

```
            .
            .
            .
            PERFORM LARGE.
            .
            .
            .
LARGE.
            MOVE 1 TO CTR.
            MOVE ZEROS TO HOLD-IT.
            PERFORM RTN-2 50 TIMES.
RTN-2.
            IF STATE-POP (CTR) > HOLD-IT
                MOVE STATE-POP (CTR) TO HOLD-IT.
            ADD 1 TO CTR.
```

Problem 4

Find the **number** of the state with the largest population, and place this integer in HOLDX. If the 30th state has the largest population, for example, then 30 must be placed in HOLDX.

This is only a minor variation of Problem 3. In addition to storing the largest population, we must also store the **number of the state** with the largest population. The number of the state is the value of CTR:

```
            MOVE 1 TO CTR.
            MOVE ZEROS TO HELD.
            PERFORM TEST1 UNTIL CTR = 51.
TEST1.
            IF STATE-POP (CTR) > HELD
                MOVE STATE-POP (CTR) TO HELD
                MOVE CTR TO HOLDX.
            ADD 1 TO CTR.
```

Note that in the above, the statement PERFORM TEST1 UNTIL CTR = 51 may be replaced by:

```
            PERFORM TEST1 50 TIMES.
```

Problem 5

Find the number of states that have population figures in excess of 1,000,000. Place this number in TOTAL.

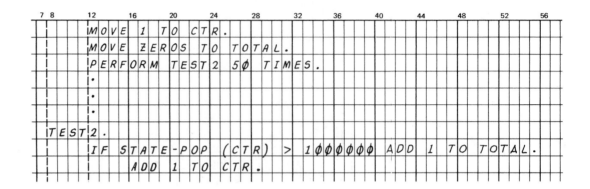

```
        MOVE 1 TO CTR.
        MOVE ZEROS TO TOTAL.
        PERFORM TEST2 50 TIMES.
        .
        .
        .
TEST2.
        IF STATE-POP (CTR) > 1000000 ADD 1 TO TOTAL.
              ADD 1 TO CTR.
```

STORING TABLE DATA   In the five examples above, we have assumed that our population table has been read and accumulated in storage. Let us now consider the routine to perform the reading and accumulating of the data into the table.

Suppose there are 50 table cards, each having a ten-position population figure. We wish to accumulate these 50 figures in WORKING-STORAGE for future processing. Note that the table data is not read and immediately processed, as is the convention with other forms of input, but is read and **stored** for future processing.

Our card format is as follows:

```
01  CARD-REC.
    02  POP       PICTURE 9(10).
    02  FILLER    PICTURE X(70).
```

We will read 50 such cards and accumulate the data in the following WORKING-STORAGE area:

```
01  POPULATION-TABLE.
    02  STATE-POP    OCCURS 50 TIMES, PIC 9(10).
```

Note that the card record does **not** have an OCCURS clause associated with it. Fields or items **within records** that have repeated occurrences are specified with OCCURS clauses. To indicate that the card record itself is read 50 times, we issue 50 READ instructions in the PROCEDURE DIVISION:

```
 7 8     12      16      20      24      28      32      36      40      44      48
PROCEDURE DIVISION.
       OPEN INPUT CARD-FILE.
       MOVE 1 TO X.
       PERFORM STORE-TABLE 50 TIMES.
       .
       .
       .
STORE-TABLE.
       READ CARD-FILE AT END MOVE 1 TO EOF.
       MOVE POP TO STATE-POP (X).
       ADD 1 TO X.
```

The routine reads 50 cards and places the population figure of each card in the table. The only item to be subscripted is STATE-POP, since this is the only item defined by an OCCURS clause.

Let us elaborate upon the read routine, slightly, by altering the card format. Suppose **each** card has five population figures instead of one. The first 50 positions of the card contain five population figures, each ten positions long. Thus only **ten** READ instructions will be performed, since each card has five figures. The card format contains an OCCURS clause for the five figures on **each** card:

```
 7 8     12      16      20      24      28      32      36      40      44      48
01  CARD-REC.
    02   POP      OCCURS 5 TIMES, PIC 9(10).
    02   FILLER   PIC X(30).
```

The routine to accumulate this data in the WORKING-STORAGE area, POPULATION-TABLE, is as follows:

```
 7 8     12      16      20      24      28      32      36      40      44      48
PROCEDURE DIVISION.
       OPEN INPUT CARD-FILE.
       MOVE 1 TO X2.
       PERFORM READ-TABLE 10 TIMES.
       .
       .
       .
READ-TABLE.
       READ CARD-FILE AT END MOVE 1 TO EOF.
       MOVE 1 TO X1.
       PERFORM STORE-TABLE 5 TIMES.
STORE-TABLE.
       MOVE POP (X1) TO STATE-POP (X2).
       ADD 1 TO X1.
       ADD 1 TO X2.
```

X1 and X2 are subscripts that are both initialized at 1. X2, the subscript used with STATE-POP, is incremented from 1 to 51. X1, however, ranges from 1 to 5, since POP of the card file has only **five** figures associated with it.

Two other PERFORM statements, one contained within the other, may be used to accomplish the same operations as above:

```
          PERFORM READ-RTN UNTIL X2 = 51.
          .
          .
          .
READ-RTN.
          READ CARD-FILE AT END MOVE 1 TO EOF.
          MOVE 1 TO X1.
          PERFORM STORE-TABLE UNTIL X1 = 6.
STORE-TABLE.
          MOVE POP (X1) TO STATE-POP (X2).
          ADD 1 TO X1.
          ADD 1 TO X2.
```

Let us look at another problem. We wish to accumulate Table 17-1 in storage.

NO-OF-YRS-EMPLOYED will **not** be an entry in the table. That is, the fifth grouping in the table, for example, will refer to five years of employment. The X's indicated below denote the number of positions in the field. WEEKS-VACATION, for example, is a two-position field.

TABLE 17-1 BENEFITS TABLE

NO OF YRS EMPLOYED	NO OF EMPLOYEES	WEEKS VACATION	EXCUSED DAYS
1	XXXX	XX	XXX
2	XXXX	.	.
3	.	.	.
.	.	.	.
.	.	.	.
50	XXXX	XX	XXX

The table is denoted in the WORKING-STORAGE SECTION as follows:

```
01  BENEFITS-TABLE.
    02  ITEMX OCCURS 50 TIMES.
        03  NO-OF-EMPLOYEES
        03  WEEKS-VACATION
        03  NO-OF-EXCUSED-DAYS
```

Let us assume that data for the table will be read in on cards with the following format:

```
Ø1   CARD-REC.
     Ø2   MAJOR.
          Ø3   NO-OF-EMPLOYEES-IN      PIC 9(4).
          Ø3   WEEKS-VACATION-IN       PIC 99.
          Ø3   NO-OF-EXCUSED-DAYS-IN   PIC 999.
     Ø2   FILLER                       PIC X(71).
```

To read 50 cards and accumulate the data in BENEFITS-TABLE, the following routine may be used, where SUB1 is a numeric item in WORKING-STORAGE initialized at 1:

```
          PERFORM READ-RTN 5Ø TIMES.
          :
READ-RTN.
          READ CARD-FILE AT END CLOSE CARD-FILE STOP RUN.
          MOVE NO-OF-EXCUSED-DAYS-IN TO NO-OF-EXCUSED-DAYS (SUB1).
          MOVE WEEKS-VACATION-IN TO WEEKS-VACATION (SUB1).
          MOVE NO-OF-EMPLOYEES-IN TO NO-OF-EMPLOYEES (SUB1).
          ADD 1 TO SUB1.
```

With the use of a group MOVE operation, we may simplify the above:

```
          PERFORM READ-RTN 5Ø TIMES.
          :
READ-RTN.
          READ CARD-FILE AT END CLOSE CARD-FILE STOP RUN.
          MOVE MAJOR TO ITEMX (SUB1).
          ADD 1 TO SUB1.
```

Problem 1

Find the number of weeks vacation to which an employee with eight years of service is entitled. Place the result in a field called HELD:

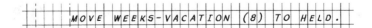

```
          MOVE WEEKS-VACATION (8) TO HELD.
```

Since the eighth entry in the table refers to eight years of service, the MOVE operation above will produce the desired results.

Problem 2

Find the total number of employees. Place the result in a field called TOTAL.

```
        MOVE ZEROS TO TOTAL.
        MOVE 1 TO SUB1.
        PERFORM ADD-RTN 50 TIMES.
        .
        .
        .
ADD-RTN.
        ADD NO-OF-EMPLOYEES (SUB1) TO TOTAL.
        ADD 1 TO SUB1.
```

Problem 3

Find the average number of excused days to which any employee is entitled. Place the result in AVERAGE.

```
        MOVE ZEROS TO AVERAGE.
        MOVE 1 TO SUB1.
        PERFORM AVG-RTN 50 TIMES.
        DIVIDE 50 INTO AVERAGE.
        PERFORM WRITE-RTN.
        .
        .
        .
AVG-RTN.
        ADD NO-OF-EXCUSED-DAYS (SUB1) TO AVERAGE.
        ADD 1 TO SUB1.
```

Problem 4

Find the number of years an employee must be employed to accumulate more than 100 excused days. Place the result in WORK. Assume that the excused days' entries increment with each year of employment; that is, an employee with X number of years employment is entitled to less excused days than an employee with X + 1 years of service:

```
        MOVE 1 TO SUB1.
        PERFORM LOOK-UP UNTIL
            NO-OF-EXCUSED-DAYS (SUB1) > 100.
        PERFORM WRITE-RTN.
LOOK-UP.
        ADD 1 TO SUB1.
```

The coding for Problem 4 represents one way of performing a **table look-up,** which is a routine for finding a specified value in a table. To ensure that a table look-up does not result in an error, it is wise to include one additional step. Since it is possible, in the previous routine, that no entry in the table has NO-OF-EXCUSED-DAYS in excess of 100, we should test for this possibility. If not, then the above routine would cause the computer to hang up, once SUB1 exceeded 50. Hence, the following would result in more complete coding.

```
    MOVE 1 TO SUB1.
    PERFORM LOOK-UP UNTIL
        NO-OF-EXCUSED-DAYS (SUB1) > 100
        OR SUB1 > 50.
    IF SUB1 > 50
        PERFORM ERR-RTN
    ELSE
        PERFORM WRITE-RTN.
LOOK-UP.
    ADD 1 TO SUB1.
```

Note that once an entry has been defined by an OCCURS clause, it may **not** be redefined. Thus the following is invalid:

Invalid:

```
02  ITEM-X OCCURS 4 TIMES   PIC S999.
02  ITEM-Y REDEFINES ITEM-X   PIC X(12).
```

Similarly, an item defined with an OCCURS clause may not have a VALUE associated with it.

It is, however, valid to define an entry **and then** redefine it with an OCCURS clause. In addition, the first entry may have a VALUE clause if it is in the WORKING-STORAGE SECTION.

The following example will illustrate the usefulness of defining an entry and then redefining it with an OCCURS clause:

Example

```
02  ITEM-Z          PIC X(36) VALUE
        'JANFEBMARAPRMAYJUNJULAUGSEPOCTNOVDEC'.
02  MONTH REDEFINES ITEM-Z OCCURS 12 TIMES PIC XXX.
```

The first 02 field, ITEM-Z, establishes the appropriate constant. MONTH then redefines ITEM-Z and allows each three-position abbreviation for months 1 to 12 to be accessed independently using a subscript. Thus moving MONTH (4), for example, would result in APR, an abbreviation for the fourth month. In this way, each abbreviation for a month can be accessed by using the corresponding subscript.

To print the appropriate three-character month, we may use the following routine:

```
           .
           .
           .
      PERFORM PRINT-TABLE VARYING SUB FROM 1 BY 1 UNTIL SUB > 12.
           .
           .
           .
  PRINT-TABLE.
      MOVE MONTH (SUB) TO MONTH-OUT.
           .
           .
           .
      WRITE PRINT-OUT AFTER ADVANCING 2 LINES.
```

SUMMARY OF OCCURS CLAUSE

1. OCCURS clauses are used in the DATA DIVISION to denote the repeated occurrence of items with the same format.
2. The format for an OCCURS clause is:

   (level number) (data-name) OCCURS (integer) TIMES

3. OCCURS clauses may be written on any level except 01, 77, 88.
4. The data-name used with an OCCURS clause may signify an elementary or group item.
5. An entry defined by an OCCURS clause may not be redefined.

SUMMARY OF SUBSCRIPTS

1. Every item defined by an OCCURS clause in the DATA DIVISION must be accessed in the PROCEDURE DIVISION with a subscript.
2. A subscript may be a numeric literal with an integer value.
3. A subscript may be a numeric field with an integer value.
4. Subscripts are enclosed in parentheses.
5. Example: ADD TAX (5) TO TOTAL.
   5 is the subscript.
   The statement adds the fifth entry in the TAX table to TOTAL.

SELF-EVALUATING QUIZ

1. An OCCURS clause is used to denote _____.
   *****
   the repeated occurrence of an item

2. An OCCURS clause is only used in the _____ DIVISION.
   *****
   DATA

3. (T or F) An OCCURS clause may be used in either the FILE SECTION or the WORKING-STORAGE SECTION of the DATA DIVISION.
   *****
   T

4. An OCCURS clause may not be used on the _____, _____, or _____ levels.
   *****
   01
   77
   88

5. An item defined by an OCCURS clause or subordinate to another item defined by an OCCURS clause may be accessed in the PROCEDURE DIVISION with the use of a _____.
   *****
   subscript

6. Subscripts may be _____ or _____.
   *****
   integers
   data-names

7. If a subscript is a data-name, its PICTURE clause must indicate a _____ field.
   *****
   numeric (integer)

8. (T or F) MOVE ITEM1 (A) TO HELD, where A has a value of zero, is a valid statement.
   *****
   F

9. 01   TABLE-X.
        02   ITEM-A OCCURS 120 TIMES.
             03 ITEM-A1 PICTURE 99.
             03 ITEM-A2 PICTURE XXX.

   The above entry reserves _____ positions of storage. MOVE ITEM-A (6) TO HELD is a (no.)-position MOVE.
   *****
   600
   5

10. Write a routine, using a PERFORM . . . UNTIL statement, to read ten cards with the following format into the table below:

    1–5   Salary
    6–8   Tax
    9–80   Not Used

    01   TABLE-X.
         02   RATE OCCURS 10 TIMES.
              03   SALX PICTURE 9(5).
              03   TAXX PICTURE 9(3).
    *****

```
        MOVE 1 TO CTR.
        PERFORM STORE-1 UNTIL CTR = 11.
        .
        .
        .
    STORE-1.
        READ CARD-FILE AT END CLOSE CARD-FILE STOP RUN.
        MOVE SALARY TO SALX (CTR).
        MOVE TAX TO TAXX (CTR).
        ADD 1 TO CTR.
```

11. Write a routine for the above using a PERFORM . . . TIMES statement.
    *****

```
        MOVE 1 TO CTR.
        PERFORM STORE-1 10 TIMES.
        .
        .
        .
    STORE-1.
        READ CARD-FILE AT END CLOSE CARD-FILE STOP RUN.
        MOVE SALARY TO SALX (CTR).
        MOVE TAX TO TAXX (CTR).
        ADD 1 TO CTR.
```

12. Is the following routine the same as the routines in Questions 10 and 11?

```
        PERFORM STORE-1 VARYING CTR FROM 1 BY 1 UNTIL CTR > 10.
    STORE-1.
        READ CARD-FILE AT END CLOSE CARD-FILE STOP RUN.
        MOVE SALARY TO SALX (CTR). MOVE TAX TO TAXX (CTR).
```

    *****
    Yes.

PRACTICE PROBLEM—
WITH SOLUTION

Write a program to build a benefit table from the following input card format:

    1   Code
    2–3 Number of years of service
    4–5 Number of weeks vacation
    6–12 Life insurance policy xxxxx.xx
    13–14 Excused days
    15–80 Not used

All input cards should have a 1 in Column 1. If any input card does **not** have a 1, stop the run.

The program checks to see that the input cards are in sequence by number of years in service, with no missing numbers or duplicates, starting with 1 and ending with 50. If any record is out of sequence, stop the run.

The benefits table should have 50 records consisting of number of weeks' vacation, life insurance policy, and excused days—number of years of service is not part of the table.

Punch three output cards, the first indicating the average number of weeks' vacation, the second the average life insurance policy, and the third indicating the average number of excused days.

See Figure 17.1 for the solution.

```
IDENTIFICATION DIVISION.
PROGRAM-ID. CHAPT17.
ENVIRONMENT DIVISION.
CONFIGURATION SECTION.
SOURCE-COMPUTER. IBM-370.
OBJECT-COMPUTER. IBM-370.
INPUT-OUTPUT SECTION.
FILE-CONTROL.
     SELECT TABLE-FILE ASSIGN TO UR-S-SYSIN.
     SELECT PUNCH-FILE ASSIGN TO UR-S-SYSPCH.
DATA DIVISION.
FILE SECTION.
FD  TABLE-FILE
    LABEL RECORDS ARE OMITTED
    RECORD CONTAINS 80 CHARACTERS
    DATA RECORD IS REC-IN.
01  REC-IN.
    02  CODEX               PIC X.
    02  YRS-SERVICE         PIC 99.
    02  MAJOR.
        03  WKS-VACATION    PIC 99.
        03  LIFE-INSUR      PIC 9(5)V99.
        03  EXCUSED-DAYS    PIC 99.
    02  FILLER              PIC X(66).
FD  PUNCH-FILE
    LABEL RECORDS ARE OMITTED
    RECORD CONTAINS 80 CHARACTERS
    DATA RECORD IS REC-OUT.
01  REC-OUT.
    02  MESSAGE-1           PIC X(30).
    02  AVERAGE             PIC 999.99.
    02  FILLER              PIC X(44).
WORKING-STORAGE SECTION.
01  WORK-AREAS.
    02  CTR                 PIC 999 VALUE ZEROS.
    02  EOF                 PIC 9 VALUE 0.
    02  AVERAGE-A           PIC 999V99 VALUE ZEROS.
01  TABLE-1.
    02  ITEMX OCCURS 50 TIMES.
        03  VACATION        PIC 99.
        03  INSURANCE       PIC 9(5)V99.
        03  DAYS            PIC 99.
PROCEDURE DIVISION.
    OPEN INPUT TABLE-FILE, OUTPUT PUNCH-FILE.
    READ TABLE-FILE AT END MOVE 1 TO EOF.
    PERFORM TABLE-ENTRY 50 TIMES.
    PERFORM TOTAL-RTN.
    CLOSE TABLE-FILE, PUNCH-FILE.
    STOP RUN.
TABLE-ENTRY.
    ADD 1 TO CTR.
    IF CTR > 50 DISPLAY 'ERROR IN TABLE ENTRY'
            STOP RUN.
    IF CTR NOT EQUAL TO YRS-SERVICE
            DISPLAY 'ERROR IN TABLE ENTRY' STOP RUN.
    IF CODEX NOT EQUAL TO 1 DISPLAY 'ERROR IN TABLE ENTRY'
            STOP RUN.
    MOVE MAJOR TO ITEMX (CTR).
    READ TABLE-FILE AT END MOVE 1 TO EOF.
TOTAL-RTN.
    MOVE ZEROS TO CTR.
    PERFORM VACATION-RTN 50 TIMES.
    MOVE 'AVERAGE NO. OF WEEKS VACATION' TO MESSAGE-1.
    PERFORM PUNCH-RTN.
    PERFORM INSURANCE-RTN 50 TIMES.
    MOVE 'AVERAGE AMT OF INSURANCE' TO MESSAGE-1.
    PERFORM PUNCH-RTN.
    PERFORM DAYS-RTN 50 TIMES.
    MOVE 'AVERAGE NO. OF EXCUSED DAYS' TO MESSAGE-1.
    PERFORM PUNCH-RTN.
PUNCH-RTN.
    DIVIDE 50 INTO AVERAGE-A.
    MOVE AVERAGE-A TO AVERAGE.
    WRITE REC-OUT.
    MOVE ZEROS TO CTR.
    MOVE ZEROS TO AVERAGE-A.
VACATION-RTN.
    ADD 1 TO CTR.
    ADD VACATION (CTR) TO AVERAGE-A.
INSURANCE-RTN.
    ADD 1 TO CTR.
    ADD INSURANCE (CTR) TO AVERAGE-A.
DAYS-RTN.
    ADD 1 TO CTR.
    ADD DAYS (CTR) TO AVERAGE-A.
```

Figure 17.1

REVIEW QUESTIONS

True False

True	False	
☒	☐	
☒	☐	
☐	☒	
☒	☐	
☒	☐	
☒	☐	
☒	☐	
☐	☒	
☒	☐	

I. True-False Questions

1. OCCURS clauses may be used in both the FILE SECTION and the WORK-ING-STORAGE SECTION.
2. The OCCURS clause may be used on the 02 level.
3. Subscripts may be zero, in which case the table entry is not looked up.
4. Tables that will contain totals should be initialized before processing.
5. A table look-up is usually executed with the use of a PERFORM statement.
6. A REDEFINES statement must not follow an OCCURS clause.
7. Each parenthesis used to contain a subscript must be preceded and followed by at least one space.
8. OCCURS clauses may be used to define either group or elementary items.
9. Only one elementary item may follow a group item described with an OCCURS clause.
10. Table data is usually read into the computer prior to normal detail input.

II. General Questions

Correct the errors, if any, in each of the following (1–6):

```
1. 01   ITEM-X OCCURS 100 TIMES.
        02 ITEM-1X PICTURE S99.
2. 01   ITEM-T.
        02 ITEM-T1 OCCURS 150 TIMES, PICTURE S999.
3. 77   ITEM-W OCCURS 20 TIMES, PICTURE 9999.
4. MOVE ITEM-XX (3) TO HOLD-1.
   MOVE ITEM-XX (0) TO HOLD-2.
5. 01   ITEM-Z.
        02 ITEM-ZZ OCCURS 10 TIMES, PICTURE S99.
            .
            .
            .
        MOVE ITEM-Z (X1) TO HELD.
6. 02   X5 PICTURE XX VALUE '01'.
            .
            .
   MOVE ITEM-Z (X5) TO HELD.
```

7. Using the following table in storage, write a routine to print the state with the smallest population. Also print the smallest population figure.
```
01   POPULATION-TABLE.
     02 STATE OCCURS 50 TIMES, PICTURE S9(10).
```

8. Using the table entry above, write a routine to print the number of states that have populations smaller than 250,000. Also print the number of each of these states.

9. Using the BENEFITS-TABLE described in the chapter, find the total number of employees who have been with the company more than 20 years.

10. Using the BENEFITS-TABLE in this chapter, write a routine to print the number of employees who have been with the company an odd number of years and the number of employees who have been with the company an even number of years.

PROBLEMS   1. Monthly take-home pay is to be computed for each employee of Company ABC.

(a) A tax table must be read into main storage from 20 input cards:

    1–5   Low bound salary
    6–10 High bound salary
    11–13 State tax percentage (.xxx)
    14–16 Federal tax percentage (.xxx)
    17–80 Not used

Low bound	High bound	State tax	Federal tax
Example 06700	09800	020	100

denotes that state tax is 2% and federal tax is 10% for the salary range 6700–9800.

(b) Following the tax cards are detail employee cards containing the following information:

    1–20 Employee name
    21–25 Annual salary
       26 Number of dependents
    27–80 Not used

(c) Monthly take-home pay is computed as follows:

(1) Standard deduction = 10% of the first $10,000 of annual salary
(2) Dependent deduction = 750 × number of dependents
(3) FICA (social security tax) = 6.7% of the first $32,400 of salary
(4) Taxable income = Annual salary − standard deduction − dependent deduction
(5) Find tax of taxable income in tax table
(6) Annual take home pay = Annual salary − (state tax % × Taxable income) − (federal tax % × Taxable income) − FICA
(7) Monthly take home pay = Annual take home pay / 12

(d) Print employee name and monthly take home pay (edited).

2. Input table entries have the following format:

1–3   Warehouse number
4–6   Product number
7–11 Unit price xxx.xx

The above input is entered on tape, the blocking factor is 50, and labels are standard. There are 250 of these table entries.
The detail card file is as follows:

1–3   Product number
4–7   Quantity
8–20 Customer name
21–80 Not used

Create an output tape containing product number, unit price, quantity, total amount, and customer name for each detail card. Total amount is equal to unit price multiplied by quantity.

Note that, for each detail card, the product number must be found on the table file to obtain the corresponding unit price.

3. There are 20 salespeople in Company XYZ. Each sale that they have made is punched into a card with the following format:

1–2   Salesperson's No. (from 1 to 20)
3–17 Salesperson's name
18–22 Amount of sale xxx.xx
23–80 Not used

The number of input cards is unknown. Salesperson X may have ten sales, Salesperson Y may have five sales, etc. The cards are **not** in sequence.

Write a program to print the total amount of sales for each salesperson. Note that x number of input cards will be read and that 20 total amounts are to be printed, one for each salesperson. All figures must be edited.
Print:

Salesperson	Total Amount
1	xxxxx.xx
.	.
.	.
20	xxxxx.xx

4. Write a program to print 12 transaction amounts, one for each month of the year and, in addition, a grand yearly total. The input is as follows:

1–5   Transaction amount xxx.xx
6–30 Not used
31–32 Month number
33–80 Not used

Note that an undetermined number of cards will serve as input, but only 12 totals are to be printed. All figures must be edited. **Note:** The cards are **not** in sequence.

5. Each input card will have the following format:

1–5   Amount of sales − day x   xxx.xx
6–10 Amount of sales − day x + 1 xxx.xx
11–80 Not used

Twenty cards will serve as input, representing 40 daily figures. The first card will have sales amount for day 1 in columns 1-5, the sales amount for day 2 in columns 6-10. The second card will contain amount of sales for day 3 in columns 1-5 and the amount of sales for day 4 in columns 6-10, and so on.

Write a program to create one block of 40 tape records, each five positions long. The first tape record should contain sales amount for day 40, the second for day 39, and so on. Labels are standard.

18 TABLE HANDLING ROUTINES USING THE SEARCH STATEMENT

TABLE LOOK-UPS AND THE SEARCH STATEMENT

As already noted, a table look-up is a procedure used to find a specific entry in a table. Suppose, for example, that each customer is entitled to a discount that is dependent on the amount of purchase. That is, a 2% discount is allowed for purchases from $1 (inclusive) to $101 (exclusive) which, in this instance, is the same as $100 (inclusive); a 5% discount may be allowed for purchases from $101 (inclusive) to $200; a 6% discount for purchases from $201 to $300; and so on. The table could be stored in the computer with the following data:

DISCOUNT-TABLE		
AMT-OF-PURCHASE		DISCOUNT
LOWER-LIMIT	UPPER-LIMIT	PERCENT
0001	0101	2.0%
0101	0201	5.0
0201	0301	6.0
.	.	.
.	.	.
.	.	.

Thus, if a specific amount is = LOWER-LIMIT or (> LOWER-LIMIT and < UPPER-LIMIT) the discount percent applies.

The OCCURS clause would be used to store these table entries. If there were 50 such discount entries, we would have:

```
WORKING-STORAGE SECTION.
01   WORK-AREAS.
     02   SUB1          PIC   99.
01   TABLE-1.
     02   DISCOUNT-TABLE OCCURS 50 TIMES.
          03   LOWER-LIMIT    PIC 9(4).
          03   UPPER-LIMIT    PIC 9(4).
          03   DISCOUNT-PCT   PIC V999.
```

SUB1 would be used as a subscript or index. Note that a discount of 6.0% = .060. Suppose AMT-OF-PURCHASE is an entry read in from each customer record. To find the appropriate discount to which the customer is entitled, we would code:

```
CALC-DISCT.
    MOVE 1 TO SUB1.
    PERFORM TABLE-LOOK-UP UNTIL
        (AMT-OF-PURCHASE = LOWER-LIMIT (SUB1)
            OR AMT-OF-PURCHASE > LOWER-LIMIT (SUB1)
            AND AMT-OF-PURCHASE < UPPER-LIMIT (SUB1))
        OR SUB1 = 51.
    IF SUB1 = 51 PERFORM ERR-RTN ELSE
        MULTIPLY DISCOUNT-PCT (SUB1) BY AMT-OF-PURCHASE
        GIVING DISCOUNT-AMT.
    .
    .
    .
TABLE-LOOK-UP.
    ADD 1 TO SUB1.
```

The test for SUB1 = 51 is necessary to avoid any errors. If it happens that an AMT-OF-PURCHASE does not fall within the limits of the table, SUB1 will keep incrementing until it exceeds 50. An effort to compare LOWER-LIMIT (SUB1) to AMT-OF-PURCHASE where SUB1 > 50 will cause the computer to abort the run. To avoid such errors we should build into the program an error routine that will indicate when the AMT-OF-PURCHASE does not fall within the range.

Note that when the lower limit of each table entry (after the first) is precisely the same as the previous upper limit, the lower limit entry need not be tested at all. That is, the following PERFORM statement could be substituted for the previous entry if, and only if, the table entries are entered sequentially as illustrated above:

```
PERFORM TABLE-LOOK-UP UNTIL
    AMT-OF-PURCHASE < UPPER-LIMIT (SUB1) OR SUB1 = 51.
```

SEARCH

Another method of performing a table look-up, one that enables the programmer to perform more sophisticated indexing, is associated with the use of the SEARCH verb.

Indexed By   To use the SEARCH instruction, the OCCURS clause must be modified so that the index, which functions like a subscript, is defined in the same sentence:

```
01  TABLE-1.
    02  DISCOUNT-TABLE OCCURS 50 TIMES INDEXED BY SUB1.
        03  LOWER-LIMIT    PIC 9(4).
        03  UPPER-LIMIT    PIC 9(4).
        03  DISCOUNT-PCT   PIC V999.
```

Using the INDEXED BY format, SUB1 is defined within the OCCURS clause. SUB1 is **not** specified by any other WORKING-STORAGE entry.

The SEARCH statement has the following format:

```
SEARCH (table)

    [AT END imperative-statement-1]

    WHEN   condition-1   { imperative-statement-2 }
                         { NEXT SENTENCE          }

    [WHEN  condition-2   { imperative-statement-3 } ] . . .
                         { NEXT SENTENCE          }
```

The AT END clause is optional and is used to specify what is to be done if the table has been completely searched and the required entry not found. Only one WHEN clause must be included; others are optional. The WHEN clause indicates the condition(s) on which the SEARCH is to be terminated. This clause would normally test if a table entry, which is specified with an index, meets some condition.

Example

The following SEARCH may be used in place of the table look-up routine discussed previously:

```
SEARCH DISCOUNT-TABLE AT END PERFORM ERR-RTN
    WHEN AMT-OF-PURCHASE < UPPER-LIMIT (SUB1)
        MULTIPLY AMT-OF-PURCHASE BY DISCOUNT-PCT (SUB1)
        GIVING DISCOUNT-AMT.
```

The SEARCH statement will result in a table look-up procedure. The table will be searched and the index automatically incremented until either the AT END condition is met or the condition specified in the WHEN clause is satisfied.

SET   The above routine requires SUB1 to be initialized before each SEARCH is executed. When SUB1 was defined as a subscript in WORK-AREAS, as in the last chapter, and the table look-up executed with a PERFORM statement, then SUB1 was initialized by coding:

MOVE 1 TO SUB1.

When an index is defined by an INDEXED BY clause in an OCCURS sentence and is to be accessed by a SEARCH, it must be initialized by a SET statement:

Format

```
SET (index-name) TO (integer)
```

Example

SET SUB1 TO 1.

Usually an index is set to one prior to the SEARCH statement. Hence the full routine for a table look-up using the SEARCH would be as follows:

```
SET SUB1 TO 1.
SEARCH DISCOUNT-TABLE AT END PERFORM ERR-RTN
    WHEN AMT-OF-PURCHASE < UPPER-LIMIT (SUB1) NEXT SENTENCE.
MULTIPLY AMT-OF-PURCHASE BY DISCOUNT-PCT (SUB1)
    GIVING DISCOUNT-AMT.
```

LOADING A TABLE INTO STORAGE

You will recall that before we can SEARCH a table we must load it into storage. Consider again the following table:

```
01  TABLE-1.
    02  DISCOUNT-TABLE OCCURS 50 TIMES INDEXED BY SUB1.
        03  LOWER-LIMIT    PIC 9(4).
        03  UPPER-LIMIT    PIC 9(4).
        03  DISCOUNT-PCT   PIC V999.
```

Suppose TABLE-1 will contain data from 50 cards with the following format:

```
01  CARD-REC.
    02  MAJOR.
        03  C-LOWER-LIMIT    PIC 9(4).
        03  C-UPPER-LIMIT    PIC 9(4).
        03  C-DISCOUNT-PCT   PIC V999.
    02  FILLER              PIC X(69).
```

To load these 50 cards into storage we would begin with the following:

```
READ CARD-FILE AT END MOVE 1 TO EOF.
SET SUB1 TO 1.
PERFORM TABLE-ENTRY-RTN 50 TIMES.
```

At TABLE-ENTRY-RTN we move the card data to the indexed table entry and increment the index. Note, however, that SUB1, our index, is defined not as a subscript within WORK-AREAS, but by an INDEXED BY clause. This means that it cannot be operated on in the usual way. We have already seen that to initialize SUB1 we must use a SET statement. Similarly, to increment SUB1, we must use a SET . . . UP statement:

```
TABLE-ENTRY-RTN.
    MOVE MAJOR TO DISCOUNT-TABLE (SUB1).
    SET SUB1 UP BY 1.
    READ CARD-FILE AT END MOVE 1 TO EOF.
```

In summary, to operate on any entry defined with an INDEXED BY clause, we must use the SET statement. The full format for the SET is:

The following table provides a comparison of subscripts and indexes:

COMPARISON OF SUBSCRIPTS AND INDEXES	
SUBSCRIPT	**INDEX**
1. Set up as a separate item in WORKING-STORAGE	Established in an INDEXED BY clause along with the OCCURS
2. Initialized by MOVE statement	Initialized by SET statement
3. Incremented by ADD statement	Incremented by SET . . . UP statement
4. Used in table look-ups with PERFORM loops	Used in table look-ups with SEARCH statement

VARYING OPTION OF SEARCH

It is sometimes useful to increment indexes from other tables while performing a SEARCH on one specific table. This is particularly useful when two or more tables have entries that correlate. For example, two tables contain the same PART-NO entries, one table includes number-on-hand for one warehouse and the other includes number-on-hand for another warehouse. Suppose we wish to determine the total number-on-hand of a particular PART-NO **from both warehouses.** The following table entries might be coded:

```
01   TABLE-1.
     02   WH-1 OCCURS 500 TIMES INDEXED BY X1.
          03   PART-NO1     PIC 9(5).
          03   NO-ON-HAND1  PIC 9(4).


01   TABLE-2.
     02   WH-2 OCCURS 500 TIMES INDEXED BY X2.
          03   PART-NO2     PIC 9(5).
          03   NO-ON-HAND   PIC 9(4).
```

We can search TABLE-1 to find the appropriate PART-NO1 (X1). Instead of searching TABLE-2 to find the same PART-NO2 (X2), we can include an option in the first SEARCH that will transfer the contents of X1 to X2, thereby eliminating the second search. We do this with the VARYING option of the SEARCH statement, as discussed below.

FULL FORMAT FOR SEARCH

SEARCH (table) [VARYING (index)]

[AT END imperative-statement-1]

WHEN   condition-1   { imperative-statement-2 / NEXT SENTENCE }

[WHEN   condition-2   { imperative-statement-3 / NEXT SENTENCE }]

. . .

Note that the index specified in the VARYING clause is **not** the index used in the SEARCH since the specified table index is automatically incremented. Rather, the index used in the VARYING clause refers to some other index that could therefore be initialized with a MOVE statement:

Example

```
SET X2 TO 1.
SET X1 TO 1.
SEARCH WH-1 VARYING X2
   WHEN PART-NO OF DETAIL-REC = PART-NO1 (X1)
      ADD PART-NO1 (X1), PART-NO2 (X2) GIVING TOTAL-OUT.
```

If the AT END clause is **not** specified in a SEARCH statement and the condition tested is not met, then control would pass to the next sentence. In the previous examples, as in most examples, this would produce erroneous results. In general, one should always make certain that the condition tested can be met using the entries in the table. If the possibility for error exists (and it usually does), include an AT END clause where an error routine would be executed.

FLOWCHART OF SEARCH

Figure 18.1 illustrates a flowchart of the SEARCH procedure.

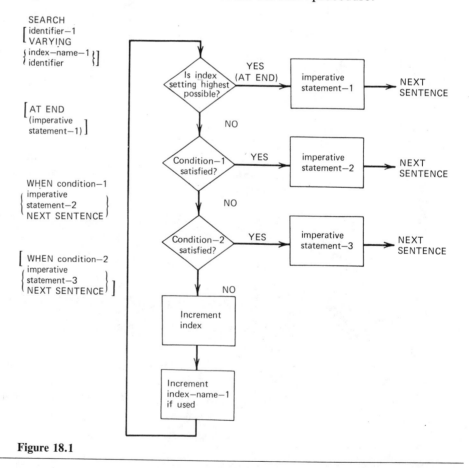

Figure 18.1

1. Suppose an entire table has been searched and the specific condition being tested has not been reached. What will happen?
   *****
   The statement following the AT END clause will be executed if it has been included; if not, the next sentence will be executed.

2. (T or F) A SEARCH statement is required for table look-ups.
   *****
   F—the PERFORM statement may be used instead

3. If a SEARCH statement is used in the PROCEDURE DIVISION, then the OCCURS clause entry must also include a(n) _____ clause.
   *****
   INDEXED BY

4. Suppose the following entry has been coded:

```
01   TABLE-X.
        02   CTRS OCCURS 100 TIMES INDEXED BY X1.
           03   FLD1   PIC 999.
```

   Write a statement to initialize the subscript.
   *****
   SET X1 TO 1.

5. Write a SEARCH statement to look up the entries of DIM-1 until FLD1 within the table = 123.
   *****

```
SEARCH DIM-1 AT END
     PERFORM ERR-RTN
        WHEN FLD1 = 123 NEXT SENTENCE.
```

6. (T or F) A condition must always follow the WHEN entry in a SEARCH statement.
   *****
   T

7. (T or F) The condition coded in a WHEN clause should test a table entry for a particular condition.
   *****
   T

SEARCH ALL Statement

DEFINITION OF A SERIAL SEARCH

Thus far, we have discussed two techniques for performing a table look-up. One method requires a PERFORM statement and the other uses a SEARCH statement. Both methods perform the look-up in the following serial manner:

SERIAL SEARCH
1. The first entry in the table is searched.
2. If the condition is met, the look-up is completed.
3. If the condition is not met, the index or subscript is incremented and the next entry is searched.

.
.
.

A sequential or serial search is best used when the entries in a table are arranged randomly. Random organization of a table means that the table contains entries that do not have any sequence. In such a case, the best method for searching the table is to begin with the first entry, continue with the next, and so on.

In many instances, however, the table entries are arranged in some sequence. In our DISCOUNT-TABLE discussed in the last section, for example, the LOWER-LIMIT, UPPER-LIMIT, and DISCOUNT-PCT are all arranged within the table in ascending sequence:

DISCOUNT-TABLE		
AMT-OF PURCHASE		DISCOUNT
LOWER-LIMIT	UPPER-LIMIT	PERCENT
0001	0101	2.0%
0101	0201	5.0%
0201	0301	6.0%
.	.	.
.	.	.
.	.	.

```
01   TABLE-1.
     02   DISCOUNT-TABLE OCCURS 50 TIMES.
          03   LOWER-LIMIT     PIC 9(4).
          03   UPPER-LIMIT     PIC 9(4).
          03   DISCOUNT-PCT    PIC V999.
```

That is, the entries in the LOWER-LIMIT fields increase in value so that LOWER-LIMIT (1) < LOWER-LIMIT (2) . . . . Similarly, UPPER-LIMIT (1) < UPPER-LIMIT (2) < . . . . Also, DISCOUNT-PCT (1) < DISCOUNT-PCT (2) < . . . .

In cases where one or more entries of a table are in sequence, a serial search is really inefficient. For example, it would be inefficient to begin at the first entry when searching for DISCOUNT-PCT for an AMT-OF-PURCHASE of $9500. Since the table is in sequence, we know that 9500 is somewhere near the end of the table; hence beginning with the first entry would waste time.

BINARY SEARCH

When table entries are arranged in sequence by some field, such as UPPER-LIMIT in our illustration, the most efficient look-up is performed in the following manner:

> **ALTERNATIVE METHOD FOR TABLE LOOK-UP: BINARY SEARCH**
>
> 1. Compare AMT-OF-PURCHASE of the customer record to the middle table entry for UPPER-LIMIT.
> 2. If AMT-OF-PURCHASE > UPPER-LIMIT (25) (which is the middle entry in our table) we have eliminated the need for searching the first half of the table.
>
>   In such a case, we compare AMT-OF-PURCHASE to UPPER-LIMIT (37), the middle entry of the second half of the table and continue our comparison in this way.
> 3. If AMT-OF-PURCHASE < UPPER-LIMIT (25), we compare AMT-OF-PURCHASE to UPPER-LIMIT (12), that is, we divide the top half of the table into two segments and continue our comparison in this way.

Example

Suppose AMT-OF-PURCHASE = 5000

		TABLE ENTRIES		
		LOWER-LIMIT	UPPER-LIMIT	DISCOUNT-PCT
	1.	0001	0101	2.0%
	2.	0101	0201	5.0%
	3.	0201	0301	6.0%
	4.	0301	0350	6.1%
	.			
	.			
	.			
	.			
1st compare	25.	4301	4325	8.3% (>)
	.			
	.			
3rd compare	31.	4891	4925	8.4 (>)
	.			
	.			
4th compare	34.	4985	5080	8.6
	.			
	.			
2nd compare	37.	5315	5400	9.4 (<)
	.			
	.			
	50.	9941	9999	11.1

An AMT-OF-PURCHASE of $5000 was within the range of the 34th entry. If a serial search were used, 34 comparisons would be required. Using the alternative method, however, only 4 comparisons were required.

This alternative method is called a **binary search** because each comparison eliminates one half the entries under consideration; that is, each comparison reduces the entries to be considered by a factor of 2.

A binary search is more efficient than a serial search in the following instances:

USES OF A BINARY SEARCH
1. When table entries are arranged in some sequence—either ascending or descending.
2. When tables with a large number of sequential entries are to be looked up or searched.

For small tables or those in which entries are **not** arranged in a sequence, the standard look-up methods previously described are to be used. For large tables in which entries are arranged in a specific sequence, the binary search is most efficient. It is hard to explicitly define a "large" table, but let us say that any table containing more than 50 or 60 entries and with the entries in some sequence could benefit from the use of the binary search method.

SEARCH ALL

In order to have the computer **automatically** perform a binary search, we use the SEARCH ALL statement.

The format of the SEARCH ALL is similar to that of the SEARCH.

Format

SEARCH ALL (table)
   [AT END imperative-statement-1]
      WHEN condition-1 $\left\{ \begin{array}{l} \text{imperative-statement-2} \\ \text{NEXT SENTENCE} \end{array} \right\}$

Note that the SEARCH ALL permits only one WHEN clause, but this clause can contain a compound conditional. In order for the SEARCH ALL to be meaningful, the WHEN statement must test the indexed table entry to see if it meets a specified condition.

Example

```
SET SUB1 TO 1.
SEARCH ALL DISCOUNT-TABLE AT END PERFORM ERR-RTN
    WHEN (AMT-OF-PURCHASE = LOWER-LIMIT (SUB1) OR
        AMT-OF-PURCHASE > LOWER-LIMIT (SUB1) AND
        AMT-OF-PURCHASE < UPPER-LIMIT (SUB1))
    NEXT SENTENCE.
MULTIPLY AMT-OF-PURCHASE BY DISCOUNT-PCT (SUB1)
    GIVING DISCOUNT-AMT.
```

Ascending or Descending Key To use the SEARCH ALL statement, we must indicate the entry in the table that will serve as the KEY field. That is, we must specify which table entry appears in sequence so that the binary search can be used to compare against that field. Moreover, we must indicate whether that KEY is ASCENDING or DESCENDING:

KEY FIELD

ASCENDING KEY—entries are in sequence and increasing in value.

DESCENDING KEY—entries are in sequence and decreasing in value.

The ASCENDING or DESCENDING KEY is specified along with the OCCURS and INDEXED BY clauses of a table entry when a SEARCH ALL is to be used.

Format

(level-number)   (table-name)

  OCCURS (integer) TIMES

    INDEXED BY (index-name)

$\begin{bmatrix} \text{ASCENDING} \\ \text{DESCENDING} \end{bmatrix}$ KEY IS (data-name)

Example

```
01   TABLE-1.
     02   DISCOUNT-TABLE OCCURS 50 TIMES INDEXED BY SUB1
          ASCENDING KEY LOWER-LIMIT, UPPER-LIMIT.
          03   LOWER-LIMIT    PIC 9(4).
          03   UPPER-LIMIT    PIC 9(4).
          03   DISCOUNT-PCT   PIC V999.
```

The data name used in the ASCENDING KEY clause must be an entry within the table. If entries in the table decrease in value then DESCENDING KEY would be used.

In the above illustration all three fields LOWER-LIMIT, UPPER-LIMIT, DIS-COUNT-PCT increase in value as we move through the table; hence, any one of the fields could have been used in the ASCENDING KEY clause. Since both LOWER-LIMIT and UPPER-LIMIT are used in the WHEN clause, they are both used as KEY fields.

For best results, the KEY entries in the table should be unique; that is, there should be no duplicate KEYS for any entry. If it happens, however, that two KEY entries in the table have identical values and one of them is to be accessed, we cannot predict which one the computer will look up.

SUMMARY

Statement:	SEARCH ALL
Purpose:	To perform binary search
Limitations:	Some table entry must be in sequence to use a binary search; should have 50 or more table entries.
Requirements:	ASCENDING or DESCENDING KEY must be used as part of table entry. All specifications for the SEARCH are maintained.

SELF-EVALUATING QUIZ

1. The SEARCH statement is used for a _____ search and the SEARCH ALL statement for a _____ search.
*****
serial
binary

2. A binary search is used for (large, small) tables that are _____.
*****
large
arranged in some sequence

3. Each look-up in a binary search reduces the number of entries to be searched by a factor of (no.).
*****
2

4. When entries are not arranged in any specific sequence, then the (SEARCH, SEARCH ALL) statement may be used.
*****
SEARCH

5. The SEARCH ALL statement requires the programmer to use the _____ and _____ clauses with the OCCURS entry.
*****
INDEXED BY
KEY

6. (T or F) The KEY field specifies an entry within the table.
*****
T

7. If the entries are arranged so that they increase in value, then _____ KEY is used with the OCCURS clause.
*****
ASCENDING

8. A _____ statement is used to initialize an index or subscript before a _____ statement is executed.
*****
SET
SEARCH or SEARCH ALL

PRACTICE PROBLEM— WITH SOLUTION

Write a program that will read in 500 inventory tape records with the following data:

PART-NO   1-5   (Blocking factor = 50)
NO-ON-HAND   6-10

These records will serve as a table. The detail cards contain the following data:

CUSTOMER-NAME   1-20
PART-NO   21-25
NO-ORDERED   26-30

These cards are **not** in sequence. For each customer card read, subtract the NO-ORDERED from the NO-ON-HAND. If the NO-ON-HAND for any PART-NO falls below zero, print a message and the corresponding PART-NO.

At the end, create a new tape with the updated inventory data.

Note: Use the SEARCH.

See Figure 18.2 for the solution.

```
IDENTIFICATION DIVISION.
PROGRAM-ID. CHAPT18.
ENVIRONMENT DIVISION.
CONFIGURATION SECTION.
SOURCE-COMPUTER. IBM-370.
OBJECT-COMPUTER. IBM-370.
INPUT-OUTPUT SECTION.
FILE-CONTROL.
    SELECT INV-TAPE-IN ASSIGN TO UT-S-SYS001.
    SELECT DETAIL-CARDS ASSIGN TO UR-S-SYSIN.
    SELECT INV-TAPE-OUT ASSIGN TO UT-S-SYS002.
DATA DIVISION.
FILE SECTION.
FD  INV-TAPE-IN
    LABEL RECORDS ARE STANDARD
    RECORD CONTAINS 10 CHARACTERS
    BLOCK CONTAINS 50 RECORDS
    DATA RECORD IS INV-REC-IN.
01  INV-REC-IN.
    02  T-PART-NO              PIC 9(5).
    02  T-NO-ON-HAND           PIC S9(5).
FD  DETAIL-CARDS
    LABEL RECORDS ARE OMITTED
    RECORD CONTAINS 80 CHARACTERS
    DATA RECORD IS DETAIL-REC.
01  DETAIL-REC.
    02  CUST-NAME              PIC X(20).
    02  C-PART-NO              PIC 9(5).
    02  C-NO-ORDERED           PIC 9(5).
    02  FILLER                 PIC X(50).
FD  INV-TAPE-OUT
    LABEL RECORDS ARE OMITTED
    RECORD CONTAINS 10 CHARACTERS
    DATA RECORD IS INV-REC-OUT.
01  INV-REC-OUT.
    02  O-PART-NO              PIC 9(5).
    02  O-NO-ORDERED           PIC S9(5).
WORKING-STORAGE SECTION.
01  WORK-AREAS.
    02  EOF                    PIC 9 VALUE 0.
01  INV-TABLE.
    02 TABLE-ENTRIES OCCURS 500 TIMES INDEXED BY X1.
        03  PART-NO            PIC 9(5).
        03  NO-ON-HAND         PIC S9(5).
PROCEDURE DIVISION.
    OPEN INPUT INV-TAPE-IN, DETAIL-CARDS
              OUTPUT INV-TAPE-OUT.
    READ INV-TAPE-IN AT END DISPLAY 'ERROR IN TAPE'.
    SET X1 TO 1.
    PERFORM TABLE-ENTRY-RTN 500 TIMES.
    READ DETAIL-CARDS AT END MOVE 1 TO EOF.
    PERFORM CALC-RTN THRU CALC-RTN-EXIT UNTIL EOF = 1.
    SET X1 TO 1.
    PERFORM WRITE-TAPE 500 TIMES.
    CLOSE INV-TAPE-IN, DETAIL-CARDS, INV-TAPE-OUT.
    STOP RUN.
TABLE-ENTRY-RTN.
    MOVE T-PART-NO TO PART-NO (X1).
    MOVE T-NO-ON-HAND TO NO-ON-HAND (X1).
    SET X1 UP BY 1.
    READ INV-TAPE-IN AT END DISPLAY 'NO MORE TAPE'.
CALC-RTN.
    SET X1 TO 1.
    SEARCH TABLE-ENTRIES AT END
            GO TO CALC-RTN-EXIT
    WHEN C-PART-NO = PART-NO (X1) NEXT SENTENCE.
    SUBTRACT C-NO-ORDERED FROM NO-ON-HAND (X1).
    IF NO-ON-HAND (X1) IS NEGATIVE
            DISPLAY 'PART NO', PART-NO (X1), 'BELOW ZERO'.
CALC-RTN-EXIT.
    READ DETAIL-CARDS AT END MOVE 1 TO EOF.
WRITE-TAPE.
    WRITE INV-REC-OUT FROM TABLE-ENTRIES (X1).
    SET X1 UP BY 1.
```

Figure 18.2

True False

True	False	
☒	☐	
☐	☒	
☒	☐	
☐	☒	
☒	☐	
☐	☒	
☐	☒	
☒	☐	
☒	☐	
☒	☐	

I. True-False Exercises

1. After a WHEN condition has been satisfied in a SEARCH, the index contains the subscript of the element found.
2. The KEY option of the OCCURS clause is used with **both** the SEARCH and the SEARCH ALL statements.
3. When the SEARCH ALL statement is used, the table must be in ASCENDING or DESCENDING sequence.
4. The WHEN clause is an optional part of the SEARCH and SEARCH ALL statements.
5. SEARCH ALL is used for a binary search.
6. An index used in a SEARCH is initialized by a MOVE statement.
7. A subscript of zero is permissible.
8. The SEARCH ALL statement can test for a compound or simple condition.
9. The second WHEN clause is an optional part of both SEARCH statements.
10. The SET statement must be used with indexes.

II. General Questions

1. Indicate the uses of the following clauses or statements:
   ASCENDING KEY
   WHEN clause
   SET
   INDEXED BY
2. Indicate when a SEARCH statement would normally be used and when a SEARCH ALL would normally be used.
3. A _____ statement must be used to initialize an index before a _____ can be executed.
4. Indicate the main differences between a binary and a serial search.
5. Consider the following table in storage:
   01   POPULATION-TABLE.
       02   STATE OCCURS 50 TIMES, PIC S9(10).

   Modify the table and use a SEARCH statement to find both the largest and the smallest state population figures.
6. Using the table above, write a routine (with the SEARCH) to print the total number of states that have populations smaller than 250,000.
7. For Problem 6 above, also print the number of each of these states.

PROBLEMS   Using the SEARCH statement, do Problems 1 and 2 from the previous chapter.

19 OCCURS CLAUSES— DOUBLE AND TRIPLE LEVELS

A. DOUBLE LEVEL OCCURS CLAUSE

When describing an area of storage, more than one level of OCCURS clauses may be used. Consider the following illustration. A population table for each state contains six population figures, one for each decade from 1900 to 1959. That is, each state contains six figures, one for 1900–1909, one for 1910–1919, and so on. Here is a pictorial representation of this table:

	1900–1909	1910–1919	1920–1929	1930–1939	1940–1949	1950–1959
Alabama						
Alaska						
. . .	. . .	. . .	. . .	. . .	. . .	. . .
Wyoming						

We may define this table in the WORKING-STORAGE SECTION with a **single** level OCCURS clause:

```
Ø1    POPULATION-TABLE.
      Ø2    STATE OCCURS 5Ø TIMES.
            Ø3    DECADE1    PIC 9(1Ø).
            Ø3    DECADE2    PIC 9(1Ø).
            Ø3    DECADE3    PIC 9(1Ø).
            Ø3    DECADE4    PIC 9(1Ø).
            Ø3    DECADE5    PIC 9(1Ø).
            Ø3    DECADE6    PIC 9(1Ø).
```

Each state is subdivided into six figures. To access the population for the first state, Alabama, for 1910–1919, we use DECADE2 (1).

You will recall that an OCCURS clause may be used to denote the repeated occurrence of an item. Since each state is subdivided into six identical decade formats, the decades may also be defined by an OCCURS clause.

Example 1

```
01    POPULATION-TABLE.
      02    STATE OCCURS 50 TIMES.
            03    DECADE OCCURS 6 TIMES, PIC 9(10).
```

In this way, **each** state is subdivided into six decade figures. There are 300 decade fields in POPULATION-TABLE, each ten positions long.

To access any of these areas, the **lowest** level data-name must be used. We use the data-name DECADE, not STATE, to access any of the above areas.

DECADE is defined by **two** OCCURS clauses. Thus two subscripts must be used to access any of the decades within a state. The **first** subscript refers to the **major** level OCCURS clause, defining STATE. The **second** subscript refers to the **minor** level, defining the DECADE. Thus DECADE (5,2) is a population figure for STATE 5, California, and DECADE 2, 1910–1919. To access the population figure for Arizona, the third state, for 1940–1949, we use DECADE (3,5). The first subscript, 3, refers to the major level item, STATE. The second subscript, 5, refers to the minor level item, DECADE.

The first subscript, then, may vary from 1 to 50 since there are 50 STATE figures. The second subscript may vary from 1 to 6, since there are six DECADE figures within each state. To say MOVE DECADE (5, 51) is **not** valid, since the second subscript may not exceed 6. This is a pictorial representation of the table, with the appropriate subscripts:

	1900–1909	1910–1919	1920–1929	1930–1939	1940–1949	1950–1959
Alabama	(1, 1)	(1, 2)	(1, 3)	(1, 4)	(1, 5)	(1, 6)
Alaska	(2, 1)	(2, 2)	(2, 3)	(2, 4)	(2, 5)	(2, 6)
.	.	.	.	.	.	.
.	.	.	.	.	.	.
.	.	.	.	.	.	.
Wyoming	(50, 1)	(50, 2)	(50, 3)	(50, 4)	(50, 5)	(50, 6)

Note that we may **not** access six decade figures for Alabama, for example, by using STATE (1). Only the lowest level item may be accessed. The data-name STATE may **not** be used in the PROCEDURE DIVISION. The data-name

DECADE, or any item subordinate to DECADE (if one exists), must be employed.

Note the following rules for double level OCCURS clauses:

RULES FOR USING DOUBLE LEVEL OCCURS CLAUSES

1. If an item is defined by a double level OCCURS clause, it must be accessed by using **two** subscripts.
2. The subscripts used must be enclosed in parentheses.
3. The left parenthesis must be preceded by one space; the right parenthesis must be followed by one space.
4. The first subscript within the parentheses is followed by a comma and a space.
5. Subscripts may be integers or data-names with integer contents.

Example

| D | E | C | A | D | E | | (| 4 | 7 | , | | 6 |) | |

or

| D | E | C | A | D | E | | (| C | T | R | 1 | , | | C | T | R | 2 |) |

where CTR1 has contents of 47 and CTR2 has contents of 6.

Let us consider the following illustration of double level OCCURS clauses. Assume a table has been established in the WORKING-STORAGE SECTION and data has been read into the table. The WORKING-STORAGE entry is

```
01  TABLE1.
    02  STATE OCCURS 50 TIMES.
        03  COUNTY OCCURS 10 TIMES, PIC 9(10).
```

The above table defines 500 fields of data: each of 50 states is subdivided into 10 counties.

COUNTY / STATE	1	2	3	4	5	6	7	8	9	10
Alabama										
Alaska										
. . .	. . .	. . .	. . .	. . .	. . .	. . .	. . .	. . .	. . .	. . .
Wyoming										

Let us write a routine to find the sum of all 500 fields. That is, we wish to accumulate a total USA population. We will add all ten counties for each of 50 states. In addition, let us use subscripts with PERFORM statements.

We must access a field by using the lowest level item, COUNTY. COUNTY must be described by **two** subscripts. The first will define the major level, STATE, and the second will define the minor level, COUNTY. COUNTY (5, 10) refers to STATE 5, COUNTY 10. The first subscript may vary from 1 to 50; the second may vary from 1 to 10.

To perform the required addition, we first accumulate all county figures for State 1. Thus the second subscript will vary from 1 to 10. After ten additions are performed, the ten county figures for State 2 must be accumulated. Thus we will add COUNTY (2, 1), COUNTY (2, 2), . . . COUNTY (2, 10) before we add the figures for State 3.

Note that **two** loops are implicit in this routine. The minor loop will increment the minor subscript from 1 to 10. The major loop will increment the major subscript from 1 to 50. A PERFORM statement within a PERFORM statement may be used to accumulate the TOTAL population:

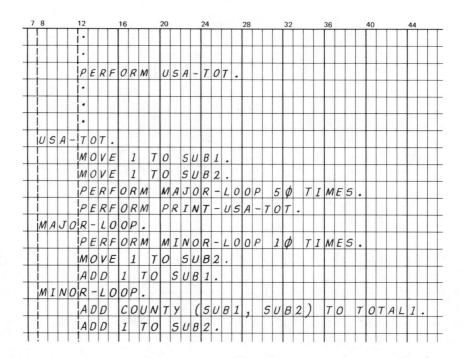

Using the above routine, the following sequence of ADD statements is performed: COUNTY (1, 1), COUNTY (1, 2), . . . COUNTY (1, 10), COUNTY (2, 1), COUNTY (2, 2), . . . COUNTY (2, 10), . . . COUNTY (50, 1), . . . COUNTY (50, 10). The routine may also be performed with other PERFORM options:

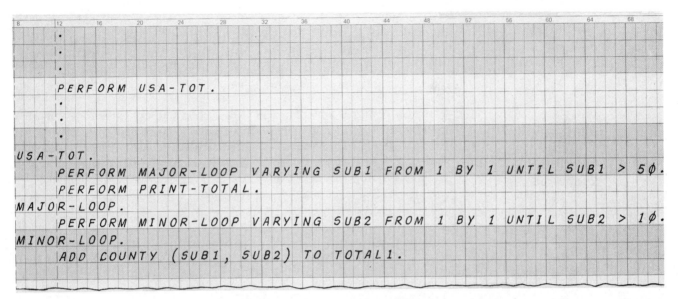

```
          .
          .
          .
     PERFORM  USA-TOT.
          .
          .
          .
USA-TOT.
     PERFORM  MAJOR-LOOP  VARYING  SUB1  FROM  1  BY  1  UNTIL  SUB1  >  5Ø.
     PERFORM  PRINT-TOTAL.
MAJOR-LOOP.
     PERFORM  MINOR-LOOP  VARYING  SUB2  FROM  1  BY  1  UNTIL  SUB2  >  1Ø.
MINOR-LOOP.
     ADD  COUNTY  (SUB1,  SUB2)  TO  TOTAL1.
```

Using either of the routines above, we vary the minor subscript first, holding the major subscript constant. That is, when the major subscript is equal to 1, denoting State 1, all counties within that State are summed. We set SUB1 equal to 1 and increment SUB2 from 1 to 10. SUB1 is then set to 2, and we again increment SUB2 from 1 to 10, and so on.

Note that the sequence of additions may also be performed as follows: COUNTY (1, 1), COUNTY (2, 1), . . . COUNTY (50, 1), COUNTY (1, 2), COUNTY (2, 2), . . . COUNTY (50, 2), . . . COUNTY (50, 10). That is, we first add the population figures for all 50 states, first county. We vary the major subscript, holding the minor subscript constant. We set SUB2 equal to 1 and increment SUB1 from 1 to 50; we then set SUB2 equal to 2 and increment SUB1 again from 1 to 50 and so on. Using a PERFORM . . . VARYING, we have:

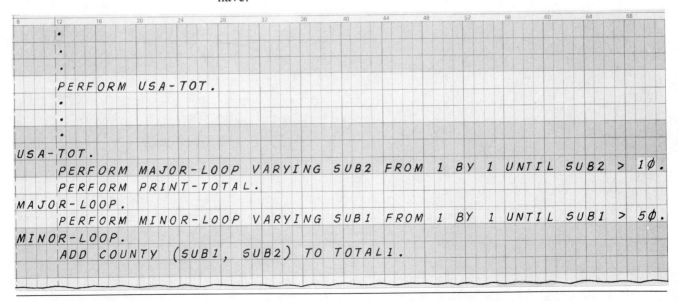

```
          .
          .
          .
     PERFORM  USA-TOT.
          .
          .
          .
USA-TOT.
     PERFORM  MAJOR-LOOP  VARYING  SUB2  FROM  1  BY  1  UNTIL  SUB2  >  1Ø.
     PERFORM  PRINT-TOTAL.
MAJOR-LOOP.
     PERFORM  MINOR-LOOP  VARYING  SUB1  FROM  1  BY  1  UNTIL  SUB1  >  5Ø.
MINOR-LOOP.
     ADD  COUNTY  (SUB1,  SUB2)  TO  TOTAL1.
```

Both sequences of operations result in the same accumulated population figure.

Example 2

We wish to store a table that will contain 12 monthly figures for each salesman in Company X. Each figure denotes the monthly sales amount credited to the salesman. Thus the first figure will be the sales amount for January, the second for February, and so on. Company X has 25 salesmen, each having 12 monthly sales figures.

The WORKING-STORAGE SECTION entry to store this table is:

```
Ø1   COMPANY-SALES-TABLE.
     Ø2   SALESMAN OCCURS 25 TIMES.
          Ø3   MONTH-AMT OCCURS 12 TIMES, PIC 9999
```

The major level of OCCURS clause denotes that 25 salesmen are represented in the table. **Each** of the 25 has 12 monthly figures. Thus there are 300 fields, each four positions long, in the table.

The WORKING-STORAGE entry merely reserves storage for the table. Data must be read into storage before any processing may begin. Suppose 25 cards, each having 12 monthly figures, are to be read. We wish to perform several operations on the sales figures only after all the data has been accumulated in the WORKING-STORAGE SECTION.

The FD for the sales cards is:

```
FD   CARD-FILE
     LABEL RECORDS ARE OMITTED
     RECORD CONTAINS 80 CHARACTERS
     DATA RECORD IS SALES-RECORD.
Ø1   SALES-RECORD.
     Ø2   AMOUNT OCCURS 12 TIMES, PIC 9999.
     Ø2   FILLER PIC X(32).
```

Since each card contains 12 monthly figures, we use an OCCURS clause in the FILE SECTION to denote the repeated occurrence of the amount field. Note that the FD contains **no** indication that 25 sales cards will be read. This is indicated in the PROCEDURE DIVISION, by performing the READ operation 25 times.

The PROCEDURE DIVISION routines necessary to read data from the cards and store it in the table are:

```
7 8     12      16      20      24      28      32      36      40      44      48
        MOVE 1 TO X1.
        MOVE 1 TO X2.
        PERFORM READ-RTN 25 TIMES.
        :
READ-RTN.
        READ CARD-FILE AT END MOVE 1 TO EOF.
        PERFORM STORE-RTN 12 TIMES.
        MOVE 1 TO X2.
        ADD 1 TO X1.
STORE-RTN.
        MOVE AMOUNT (X2) TO MONTH-AMT (X1, X2).
        ADD 1 TO X2.
```

AMOUNT, a field within the card record, is described by a single level OCCURS clause. Thus it must be qualified by a single subscript in the PROCEDURE DIVISION. MONTH-AMT, an entry in the WORKING-STORAGE SECTION, is described by a double level OCCURS clause and must then be qualified by two subscripts in the PROCEDURE DIVISION. The subscript used to qualify AMOUNT is the same as the minor level subscript used to qualify MONTH-AMT. Since there are 12 AMOUNT figures, one for each month, and there are 12 MONTH-AMT figures for each salesman, the subscript will be the same for both items.

Using the above table now stored in the WORKING-STORAGE SECTION, we wish to print 12 lines of monthly data. Each line will contain 25 figures, one for each salesman. Line 1 will denote January data and contain 25 sales figures for January; line 2 will contain February data and have 25 sales figures; and so on.

The print record is described this way:

```
7 8     12      16      20      24      28      32      36      40
  FD  PRINT-FILE
      LABEL RECORDS ARE OMITTED
      RECORD CONTAINS 133 CHARACTERS
      DATA RECORD IS PRINT-REC.
  01  PRINT-REC.
      02  FILLER          PIC X.
      02  ITEMX OCCURS 25 TIMES.
          03  SALES-ITEM      PIC 9999.
          03  FILLER          PIC X.
      02  FILLER              PIC X(7).
```

Note that we use a **single** level OCCURS clause to describe the print entry. Each line will contain 25 figures. Thus, only one level OCCURS clause is necessary. The fact that there will be 12 lines is **not** denoted by an OCCURS clause, but by repeating the print routine 12 times. As defined in the above illustration, we say ITEMX OCCURS 25 TIMES. **Each** of these 25 items consists of **two** fields, SALES-ITEM and a FILLER. That is, a one-position filler will separate each amount field to make the line more "readable." If each sales item appeared next to another, it would be difficult to read the line.

The PROCEDURE DIVISION routine necessary to perform the required operation is:

```
            MOVE SPACES TO PRINT-REC.
            MOVE 1 TO X1.
            MOVE 1 TO X2.
            PERFORM WRITE-RTN 12 TIMES.
            PERFORM EOJ-RTN.
        WRITE-RTN.
            PERFORM MOVE-RTN 25 TIMES.
            WRITE PRINT-REC AFTER ADVANCING 2 LINES.
            MOVE 1 TO X1.
            ADD 1 TO X2.
        MOVE-RTN.
            MOVE MONTH-AMT (X1, X2) TO SALES-ITEM (X1).
            ADD 1 TO X1.
```

DOUBLE LEVEL OCCURS AND THE SEARCH STATEMENT

Assume that the following table has been loaded into storage:

```
01  INVENTORY-TABLE.
    02  WAREHOUSE OCCURS 50 TIMES INDEXED BY X1.
        03  ITEM-X OCCURS 100 TIMES INDEXED BY X2.
            04  PART-NO      PIC 9(4).
            04  UNIT-PRICE   PIC 999V99.
```

Each warehouse stores 100 items. Moreover, these 100 items are unique to each warehouse, so that a specific PART-NO will appear **only once** in the table.

Suppose that input detail cards have the following format:

1–4   PART-NO-IN
5–6   QTY-ORDERED

For each PART-NO-IN on a detail card, we need to look up the corresponding PART-NO in the table and find its UNIT-PRICE. The output will be a printed report listing the PART-NO and the TOTAL-AMT where TOTAL-AMT = QTY-ORDERED (from the detail card) × UNIT-PRICE (from the table).

We could use a double-level PERFORM to obtain the results required, but a SEARCH would be more efficient. To use a SEARCH, the table described above includes the appropriate INDEXED BY clauses. The following routine is used:

```
CALC-RTN.
    SET X1, X2 TO 1.
    PERFORM SEARCH-RTN UNTIL X1 > 3 OR
        FLAG = 1.
    IF X1 > 3 PERFORM ERR-RTN.
    MOVE 0 TO FLAG.
    READ CARD-FILE AT END MOVE 1 TO EOF.
SEARCH-RTN.
    SEARCH ITEM-X
        AT END SET X1 UP BY 1, SET X2 TO 1
    WHEN PART-NO-IN = PART-NO (X1, X2)
        MULTIPLY UNIT-PRICE (X1, X2) BY QTY-ORDERED
            GIVING TOTAL-AMT
        MOVE 1 TO FLAG
        DISPLAY PART-NO-IN, '        ', TOTAL-AMT.
ERR-RTN.
    DISPLAY PART-NO-IN, ' *** INVALID'.
```

Note that each SEARCH varies the index associated with the identifier specified.

B. TRIPLE LEVEL OCCURS CLAUSE

We have seen that OCCURS clauses may be written on one or two levels. We may also employ **triple** level OCCURS clauses. A **maximum** of three levels of OCCURS clauses may be used in a COBOL program.

Suppose we have a population table consisting of 50 state breakdowns. Each state is further subdivided into ten counties. Each county has five district figures. The following table may be established in the WORKING-STORAGE SECTION:

```
01  POPULATION-TABLE.
    02  STATE OCCURS 50 TIMES.
        03  COUNTY OCCURS 10 TIMES.
            04  DISTRICT OCCURS 5 TIMES, PIC 9(10).
```

In this way, we have defined 2500 fields (50 × 10 × 5) in storage, each ten positions long. To access any field defined by several OCCURS clauses, we use the **lowest** level data-name. In the illustration above, the data-name DISTRICT must be used to access any of the 2500 fields of data.

Since DISTRICT is defined by a triple level OCCURS clause, **three** subscripts must be used to access the specific field desired. The **first** subscript refers to the **major** level item, STATE. The **second** subscript refers to the **intermediate** level item, COUNTY. The **third** subscript refers to the **minor** level, DISTRICT. Subscripts are always enclosed within parentheses. Each subscript is separated from the next by a comma and a space. Thus

```
DISTRICT (5, 4, 3)
```

refers to the population figure for:

STATE 5
COUNTY 4
DISTRICT 3

An item defined by a triple level OCCURS clause is accessed by utilizing three subscripts. Since no more than three levels of OCCURS clauses may be used to describe an item, we cannot have more than a triple level subscript.

Example 1

Write a routine to find the smallest population figure in the above table. (We are assuming that data has already been placed in the table.) Place this smallest figure in HELD.

Using three PERFORM statements, we have:

```
        MOVE 1 TO SUB1.
        MOVE 1 TO SUB2.
        MOVE 1 TO SUB3.
        MOVE DISTRICT (1, 1, 1) TO HELD.
        PERFORM RTN-1 50 TIMES.
        ...
RTN-1.
        PERFORM RTN-2 10 TIMES.
        MOVE 1 TO SUB2. ADD 1 TO SUB1.
RTN-2.
        PERFORM RTN-3 5 TIMES.
        MOVE 1 TO SUB3. ADD 1 TO SUB2.
RTN-3.
        IF DISTRICT (SUB1, SUB2, SUB3) IS LESS THAN HELD
            MOVE DISTRICT (SUB1, SUB2, SUB3) TO HELD.
        ADD 1 TO SUB3.
```

Using PERFORM . . . VARYING statements to execute the above looping, we have:

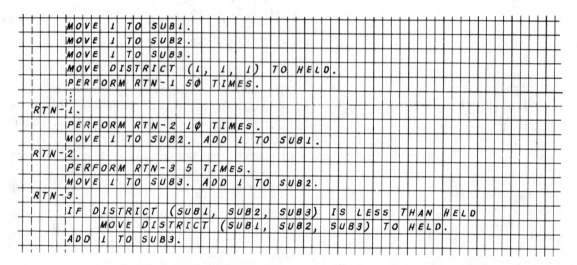

```
        MOVE DISTRICT (1, 1, 1) TO HELD.
        PERFORM RTN-1 VARYING SUB1 FROM 1 BY 1 UNTIL SUB1 > 50.
        PERFORM NEXT-RTN.
        PERFORM EOJ-RTN.
RTN-1.
        PERFORM RTN-2 VARYING SUB2 FROM 1 BY 1 UNTIL SUB2 > 10.
RTN-2.
        PERFORM RTN-3 VARYING SUB3 FROM 1 BY 1 UNTIL SUB3 > 5.
RTN-3.
        IF DISTRICT (SUB1, SUB2, SUB3) IS LESS THAN HELD
            MOVE DISTRICT (SUB1, SUB2, SUB3) TO HELD.
```

Some restrictions when using OCCURS clauses should be reviewed. VALUE clauses may **not** be used in conjunction with OCCURS clauses. Consider the following total areas:

```
 7 8      12     16     20     24     28     32     36     40     44
Ø1    TOTALS.
      Ø2    SUMX  OCCURS  2Ø  TIMES,      PIC  999.
```

It is necessary to initialize each of the twenty SUMX areas before any accumulations are performed. We may not, however, use a VALUE clause. Instead, each SUMX must be set to zero in an initializing routine in the PROCEDURE DIVISION.

```
 7 8      12     16     20     24     28     32     36
      MOVE  1  TO  X1.
      PERFORM  CLEAR  2Ø  TIMES.
      .
      .
      .
CLEAR.
      MOVE  ZEROS  TO  SUMX  (X1).
      ADD  1  TO  X1.
```

We may also say MOVE ZEROS TO TOTALS, the 01-level item.

A VALUE clause may not be used in conjunction with an OCCURS clause in the DATA DIVISION. We may **not** say:

Invalid:

```
01   TOTALS VALUE ZEROS.
     02 SUMX OCCURS 20 TIMES,
        PICTURE 999.
```

since only elementary items may contain VALUE statements and TOTALS is a group item, which is further subdivided. Similarly, we may **not** say:

Invalid:

```
01   TOTALS.
     02 SUMX OCCURS 20 TIMES,
        PICTURE 999 VALUE ZEROS.
```

since the computer is not able to determine **which** of the 20 occurrences of SUMX is to be set to zero. Thus any attempt to initialize an area defined by an OCCURS clause must be performed in the PROCEDURE DIVISION in an initializing routine and not by a VALUE clause.

Areas defined by an OCCURS clause may not be redefined; that is, a RE-

DEFINES clause may **not** follow an OCCURS clause. The following is **not** permissible:

Invalid:

```
01   TABLE-X.
     02 ITEM-A OCCURS 10 TIMES,
        PICTURE 99.
     02 ITEM-B REDEFINES ITEM-A
        PICTURE X(20).
```

Once an entry has been defined by an OCCURS clause, it may not be redefined. The converse, however, is acceptable. An item with an OCCURS clause may redefine another entry. The following **is** permissible:

Valid:

```
01   TABLE-X.
     02 ITEM-B PICTURE X(20).
     02 ITEM-AA REDEFINES ITEM-B.
        03 ITEM-A OCCURS 10 TIMES,
           PICTURE 99.
```

A REDEFINES clause may precede an OCCURS clause or the two may be used in conjunction:

```
Ø1   TABLE-X.
     Ø2   ITEM-B   PIC  X(2Ø).
     Ø2   ITEM-A   REDEFINES  ITEM-B  OCCURS  1Ø  TIMES,  PIC  99.
```

The point to remember when using an OCCURS clause in conjunction with a REDEFINES clause is that the **last** clause that may be used to describe an entry is an OCCURS clause.

The concept of OCCURS clauses, although complex, is a crucial part of COBOL programming. The use of OCCURS clauses requires precise, logical thinking on the part of the programmer. Most intermediate and high-level COBOL programs require knowledge of this concept.

SELF-EVALUATING QUIZ

1. To access areas defined by double or triple level OCCURS clauses, we must use the _____ level item defined by an OCCURS clause.
   *****
   lowest

2. If MOVE ITEMX (SUB1, SUB2) TO HELD is a statement in the PROCEDURE DIVISION, then SUB1 refers to the _____ level OCCURS clause and SUB2 refers to the _____ level OCCURS clause.
   *****
   major
   minor

3. Consider the following DATA DIVISION entry:

    ```
    01   HELD.
         02 FIELDX OCCURS 20 TIMES.
            03 FIELDXX OCCURS 50 TIMES.
               04 ITEMX PICTURE S99.
    ```

    The number of storage positions reserved for this area is _____. The data-name that may be accessed in the PROCEDURE DIVISION is _____. If ITEMX (CTRA, CTRB) is used in the PROCEDURE DIVISION, then CTRA may vary from _____ to _____ and CTRB may vary from _____ to _____.
    *****
    2000
    ITEMX (or FIELDXX)
    1 to 20
    1 to 50

4. A maximum of _____ levels of OCCURS clauses may be used in the DATA DIVISION.
    *****
    three

5. If three levels of OCCURS clauses are used, then (no.) subscripts must be used to access the specific field desired.
    *****
    three

6. If three subscripts are used to access an item, the first refers to the _____ level, the second to the _____ level, and the third to the _____ level.
    *****
    major
    intermediate
    minor

7. Each subscript within the parentheses is separated from the next by a _____ and a _____.
    *****
    comma
    space

8. A _____ clause may not be used in conjunction with an OCCURS clause in the DATA DIVISION.
    *****
    VALUE

9. Areas defined by an OCCURS clause may not be _____.
    *****
    redefined

10. An item with an OCCURS clause (may, may not) redefine another entry.
    *****
    may

PRACTICE PROBLEM—
WITH SOLUTION

Write a program to tabulate the number of employees by area within department. The input card record has the following format:

  1–20 Employee name (not used)
21–22 Department number
23–24 Area number
25–80 Not used

NOTES:

(a) There are 10 areas within each department; there are 50 departments.
(b) Cards are not in sequence.
(c) Output is a report with the following format:

TOTAL NUMBER OF EMPLOYEES BY AREA WITHIN DEPARTMENT			
DEPARTMENT—01			
AREA 1	AREA 2	. . .	AREA 10
xxx	xxx		xxx
DEPARTMENT—02			
AREA 1	AREA 2	. . .	AREA 10
xxx	xxx		xxx
.			
.			
.			
DEPARTMENT—50			
AREA 1	AREA 2	. . .	AREA 10
xxx	xxx		xxx

All totals should be edited to suppress high-order zeros.
Allow for page overflow.
See Figure 19.1 for solution.

```
IDENTIFICATION DIVISION.
PROGRAM-ID. CHAPT19.
ENVIRONMENT DIVISION.
CONFIGURATION SECTION.
SOURCE-COMPUTER. IBM-370.
OBJECT-COMPUTER. IBM-370.
SPECIAL-NAMES. C01 IS NEXT-PAGE.
INPUT-OUTPUT SECTION.
FILE-CONTROL.
    SELECT CARD-FILE ASSIGN TO UR-S-SYSIN.
    SELECT PRINT-FILE ASSIGN TO UR-S-SYSOUT
        RESERVE NO ALTERNATE AREAS.
DATA DIVISION.
FILE SECTION.
FD  CARD-FILE
    LABEL RECORDS ARE OMITTED
    RECORD CONTAINS 80 CHARACTERS
    DATA RECORD IS CARD-REC.
01  CARD-REC.
    02  FILLER              PIC X(20).
    02  DEPT                PIC 99.
    02  AREA1               PIC 99.
    02  FILLER              PIC X(56).
FD  PRINT-FILE
    LABEL RECORDS ARE OMITTED
    RECORD CONTAINS 133 CHARACTERS
    DATA RECORD IS PRINT-REC.
01  PRINT-REC               PIC X(133).
WORKING-STORAGE SECTION.
01  WORK-AREAS.
    02  EOF         PIC 9 VALUE 0.
    02  CTR1        PIC 99 VALUE 1.
    02  CTR2        PIC 99 VALUE 1.
01  TOTALS.
    02  DEPTX OCCURS 50 TIMES.
        03  AREAX OCCURS 10 TIMES        PIC 9(3).
```

```
01  HEADER-1.
    02  FILLER                    PIC X(91)
        VALUE 'TOTAL NO OF EMPLOYEES BY AREA WITHIN DEPARTMENT'
            JUSTIFIED RIGHT.
    02  FILLER                    PIC X(42) VALUE SPACES.
01  HEADER-2.
    02  FILLER                    PIC X(25)
                VALUE 'DEPARTMENT-' JUSTIFIED RIGHT.
    02  DEPT-NO                   PIC 99 VALUE 00.
    02  FILLER                    PIC X(106) VALUE SPACES.
01  HEADER-3.
    02  FILLER                    PIC X(30) VALUE SPACES.
    02  FILLER                    PIC X(103)
        VALUE '   AREA 1    AREA 2    AREA 3    AREA 4    AREA 5
        'AREA 6    AREA 7    AREA 8    AREA 9    AREA 10'.
01  DETAIL-LINE.
    02  FILLER                    PIC X(30) VALUE SPACES.
    02  ITEMX OCCURS 10 TIMES.
        03  FILLER  PIC XX.
        03  AREAY   PIC 999.
        03  FILLER  PIC X(5).
    02  FILLER                    PIC XXX VALUE SPACES.
PROCEDURE DIVISION.
    OPEN INPUT CARD-FILE, OUTPUT PRINT-FILE.
    MOVE SPACES TO DETAIL-LINE.
    PERFORM INITIALIZE-RTN 500 TIMES.
    READ CARD-FILE AT END MOVE 1 TO EOF.
    PERFORM READ-RTN UNTIL EOF = 1.
    PERFORM EOJ-RTN.
    CLOSE CARD-FILE, PRINT-FILE.
    STOP RUN.
INITIALIZE-RTN.
    MOVE ZEROS TO AREAX (CTR1, CTR2).
    ADD 1 TO CTR2.
    IF CTR2 = 11 ADD 1 TO CTR1
            MOVE 1 TO CTR2.
READ-RTN.
    ADD 1 TO AREAX (DEPT, AREA1).
    READ CARD-FILE AT END MOVE 1 TO EOF.
EOJ-RTN.
    PERFORM HEADER-RTN.
    PERFORM TOTAL-UP VARYING CTR1 FROM 1 BY 1 UNTIL CT.
TOTAL-UP.
    MOVE CTR1 TO DEPT-NO.
    WRITE PRINT-REC FROM HEADER-2 AFTER ADVANCING 2 LINES
            AT EOP PERFORM HEADER-RTN.
    PERFORM RTN2 VARYING CTR2 FROM 1 BY 1 UNTIL CTR2 > 10.
    WRITE PRINT-REC FROM DETAIL-LINE AFTER ADVANCING 2 LINES
            AT EOP PERFORM HEADER-RTN.
RTN2.
    MOVE AREAX (CTR1, CTR2) TO AREAY (CTR2).
HEADER-RTN.
    WRITE PRINT-REC FROM HEADER-1 AFTER ADVANCING NEXT-PAGE.
```

Figure 19.1

REVIEW QUESTIONS

True False

I. True-False Questions

1. In a subscript referencing a double level OCCURS clause, the first entry refers to the lower level subscript.
2. Triple level subscripting is the maximum that may be coded.
3. To initialize entries referenced by a double level OCCURS clause we usually use a PERFORM within a PERFORM.
4. Subscripts must always be numeric.
5. The following entries define 5000 positions of storage:
   01   TABLE-1.
       02   ITEM-1 OCCURS 50 TIMES.
           03   ITEM-2 OCCURS 10 TIMES PIC S9(10).
6. The above entry can be referenced by using either ITEM-1 or ITEM-2 in the PROCEDURE DIVISION.
7. For the above, a reference to ITEM-2 (9, 43) is permissible.

8. For the above, a reference to ITEM-2 (43, 9) is permissible. ☒

9. Data may be entered into table areas in sequence only. ☐

10. Total fields defined by double or triple level OCCURS clauses need not be initialized. ☒

II. General Questions

1. There are 50 classes in College X. Each class has exactly 40 students. Each student has taken six exams. Write a **double** level OCCURS clause to define an area of storage that will hold these scores.

2. Write a **triple** level OCCURS clause for Question 1.

3. How many storage positions are reserved for the above OCCURS clause?

4. Write the File Description for a file of cards that will contain the students' test scores. Each card will contain six scores in the first 18 columns. The first card is for the first student in class 1, . . . the 40th card is for the 40th student in class 1, the 41st card is for the first student in class 2, and so on.

5. Using the solutions to Questions 2 and 4, write the PROCEDURE DIVISION routines to read the test cards and to accumulate the data in the table area.

6. Write a routine to find the class with the highest class average.

7. Write a routine to find the student with the highest average.

8. If the following is a WORKING-STORAGE entry, write a routine to initialize the fields. Note that all areas to be used in arithmetic operations must first be cleared or set to zero:

```
01  TOTALS.
    02 MAJOR-TOTAL OCCURS 100 TIMES.
       03 INTERMEDIATE-TOTAL OCCURS 45 TIMES.
          04 MINOR-TOTAL OCCURS 25 TIMES, PICTURE S9(5).
```

Make necessary corrections to each of the following (9–10).

9.
```
01  ITEMX OCCURS 20 TIMES, VALUE ZEROS.
    02 MINOR-ITEM OCCURS 15 TIMES, PICTURE S9.
```

10.
```
01  TABLE-A.
    02 FIELDX OCCURS 10 TIMES, PICTURE S99.
    02 FIELDY REDEFINES FIELDX PICTURE X(20).
```

PROBLEMS 1. Input tape records have the following format:

    1–2 Day number (01-07)
    3–5 Salesman number (001-025)
    6–10 Amount of transaction xxx.xx
    11–25 Not used

Labels are standard; blocking factor = 30.

Write a program to print **two** reports:

(a) The first report is a daily report giving seven daily figures, edited:

DAY	SALES-AMOUNT
1	$xx,xxx.xx
2	
.	.
.	.
.	.
7	$xx,xxx.xx

(b) The second report is a salesman report giving 25 salesmen figures, edited:

SALESMAN NUMBER	SALES-AMOUNT
001	$xx,xxx.xx
.	.
.	.
025	$xx,xxx.xx

For report (a), each daily figure consists of the addition of 25 salesmen figures for the corresponding day.

For report (b), each salesman figure consists of the addition of 7 daily figures for the corresponding salesman.

NOTE: Records are not in sequence.

2. Write a program to tabulate the number of employees by territory within area within department. The input tape record has the following format:

1–2 Territory number
3–4 Area number
5–6 Department number
7–50 Not used

Labels are standard; blocking factor = 10.

NOTES:

(a) There are three territories within each area; there are three areas within each department; there are ten departments.
(b) Tape records are **not** in sequence.
(c) Output is a report with the following format:

```
 _____
|          TOTAL NUMBER OF EMPLOYEES BY TERRITORY WITHIN AREA           |
|                           WITHIN DEPT                                 |
|                                                                       |
| DEPARTMENT—01                                                         |
|     -----AREA 1-----        -----AREA 2-----        -----AREA 3-----  |
| TERR-A TERR-B TERR-C    TERR-A TERR-B TERR-C    TERR-A TERR-B TERR-C  |
|  xxx    xxx    xxx       xxx    xxx    xxx       xxx    xxx    xxx     |
| .                                                                     |
| .                                                                     |
| .                                                                     |
| DEPARTMENT—10                                                         |
|     -----AREA 1-----        -----AREA 2-----        -----AREA 3-----  |
| TERR-A TERR-B TERR-C    TERR-A TERR-B TERR-C    TERR-A TERR-B TERR-C  |
|  xxx    xxx    xxx       xxx    xxx    xxx       xxx    xxx    xxx     |
|_____|
```

3. Rewrite the program for Problem 2, assuming that tape records are in sequence by territory within area within department. This means that each line could be printed as the data is read. There is no need to accumulate all of the data in a table prior to printing.

4. The following card records are used to create a table in storage:

   1–5 Product number
   6–10 Unit number
   11–15 Price xxx.xx
   16–80 Not used

   There are 10 units for each product. There are 25 product numbers. The table, then, consists of 250 unit-prices.

   The following is the format for the detail tape records:

   1–20 Customer name
   21–25 Product number
   26–30 Unit number
   31–33 Quantity sold

   Labels are standard; blocking factor = 35.

   Create output tape records with the following format:

   1–20 Customer name
   21–28 Amount xxxxxx.xx
   29–30 Not used

   Labels are standard; blocking factor = 50.

   For each detail tape record, perform a table look-up of the price for the product number and unit number given. Amount of the output record = Quantity × Price. Note that Price is in the accumulated table.

5. Redo Problem 1(a) assuming records are in sequence by day number.

6. Write a program to tabulate the number of employees by area within department. The input card record has the following format:

   1–20 Employee name (not used)
   21–22 Department number
   23–24 Area number
   25–80 Not used

   NOTES:

   (a) There are 10 areas within each department; there are 50 departments.
   (b) Cards are in sequence by area within department.

(c) Output is a report with the following format:

```
TOTAL NUMBER OF EMPLOYEES BY AREA WITHIN DEPARTMENT

DEPARTMENT—01
        AREA 1              AREA 2         . . .      AREA 10
         xxx                 xxx                        xxx
DEPARTMENT—02
        AREA 1              AREA 2         . . .      AREA 10
         xxx                 xxx                        xxx
   .
   .
   .
DEPARTMENT—50
        AREA 1              AREA 2         . . .      AREA 10
         xxx                 xxx                        xxx
```

All totals should be edited to suppress high-order zeros.
Allow for page overflow.

NOTE: Since cards are entered in sequence, this program can be coded using a "control break sequence." See the next chapter for a full discussion of the procedures involved.

5 TAPE AND DISK PROCESSING

CHAPTER

20 SEQUENTIAL FILE PROCESSING

A. UPDATING SEQUENTIAL FILES

Throughout this text a number of our illustrations have used tapes as input or output or both. For those students with no prior experience with tapes, consult Appendix B, which contains a review of the technical features of tape processing.

As already noted, tapes have the following advantages:

ADVANTAGES OF TAPE PROCESSING
1. Tape is a high-speed medium.
2. Records can be any length.
3. A single tape can store millions of characters.

SEQUENTIAL PROCESSING OF TAPE

In addition, a main feature of tape processing is that tapes must be accessed in sequence. That is, to access the 55,000th record on a tape file, for example, the computer first reads 54,999 records in sequence. There is no convenient, short-cut method of moving directly to the middle of the tape or to some point near the end of the tape.

Hence, files that need to be accessed quickly and directly for inquiry purposes would not be stored on tape, since access time would be too slow. An airline reservation system, for example, would store its data on a direct-access device, not on tape. Since flight information has to be made available very quickly, sequential searches through a file would be inappropriate.

Tapes are ideal for large-volume files that are usually processed in one or perhaps two fixed sequences and which are **not** generally used for direct inquiry. Payroll, Inventory, and Accounts Receivable files are examples of files commonly stored on tape.

I/O FEATURES OF TAPE

Since tapes need to be processed sequentially, it is not convenient to make changes to an existing tape file. Tape files that need to be updated, or made current, require a procedure where the existing file is read, the changes are read, and a new, updated tape file is created as output.

This chapter considers the ways in which master tape files are updated. A master file is the main file type for a particular application: it is the file containing the primary or major information. For most applications it is essential that these master files be current and relatively error-free. Hence, updating of master files is a major function of many COBOL programs.

An updating procedure is the process of making a file of data **current**. A tape update program typically consists of three files.

INPUT MASTER FILE

The input master file has all the data except that which is most current; that is, it contains master information current only up to the previous updating cycle. We will call this file OLD-MASTER.

INPUT DETAIL FILE

The input detail file contains data for the present updating cycle **only.** We will call this file DETAIL-FILE.

OUTPUT MASTER FILE[1]

The output master file incorporates the current detail data and the previous master information. That is, the output master file will combine data from OLD-MASTER and DETAIL-FILE. We will call this file NEW-MASTER.

For purposes of illustration, we will assume that the input and output master files are on tape and that the detail information is on cards.

The following **systems** flowchart indicates the operations to be performed.

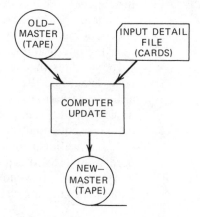

---

[1]One of the advantages of disk processing is that updated master information may "overlay" or replace input data **on the same file.** This is discussed in detail in Chapter 22.

To update files, data must be read into the computer in a specific sequence. Since we wish to update a master record with each detail record, we must ensure that each file is in the same sequence.

Let us assume that we are updating a master transaction file with detail transaction records. That is, OLD-MASTER contains all transaction data current through the previous updating cycle; DETAIL-FILE contains transactions of the current period; and NEW-MASTER will incorporate both files of information.

Let us assume, in addition, that both input files are in sequence by account number. Consider both input files to have records with the following formats:

OLD-MASTER-REC	DETAIL-REC
1-5 ACCT-NO	1-5 ACCT-NO
6-11 AMOUNT-DUE xxxx.xx	6-10 AMT-TRANS-IN-CURRENT-PER xxx.xx
12-50 FILLER	11-80 FILLER

Since NEW-MASTER will be created to update and replace the OLD-MASTER, it will have the same format as OLD-MASTER.

The update program will read data from cards and tape, both of which are in ACCT-NO sequence.

One of the following three procedures will be performed for each record read:

1. REGULAR-UPDATE
   For each ACCT-NO that is on **both** the DETAIL-FILE and the OLD-MASTER file, AMT-TRANS-IN-CURRENT-PER will be added to AMOUNT-DUE to obtain the current balance.
2. NO-UPDATE
   For each ACCT-NO that is on the OLD-MASTER file but not on the DETAIL-FILE, a record will be created on NEW-MASTER that merely duplicates the information of OLD-MASTER. In this case, we say that no updating of the record is necessary.
3. NEW-ACCT
   For each ACCT-NO that is on the DETAIL-FILE but not on the OLD-MASTER file, a record is created on NEW-MASTER that is taken directly from the DETAIL-FILE. When this occurs, we say that a new account is created.

Thus the control field on all files is ACCT-NO. The detail cards and the input master tape will both be in sequence by ACCT-NO. After reading a single card record and a tape record, we will test for three possible conditions:

(a) ACCT-NO OF DETAIL-REC = ACCT-NO OF OLD-MASTER-REC

When the account numbers are equal, the input master record is to be updated; that is, the card amount is added to the input tape amount to obtain the output AMOUNT-DUE. When the new master record is created, new card and tape records are read and processing continues.

(b) ACCT-NO OF DETAIL-REC IS GREATER THAN ACCT-NO OF
                        OLD-MASTER-REC

In this case, a master record exists with no corresponding card record. Since both files are in sequence, we may assume that no business has been transacted for the specific master record. Thus the new master record is created directly from OLD-MASTER-REC and a new input tape record is read. Note that another card is **not** read at this point. We have not yet processed the card that is in the input area. If, for example, a detail record has account number 00035 and the master record has account number 00034, we process the master record and read the next master; account number 00035 of the card file remains to be processed.

(c) ACCT-NO OF DETAIL-REC IS LESS THAN ACCT-NO OF OLD MASTER-REC

In this case, a detail card record exists for which there is no corresponding master record. The new master tape record will be created directly from the detail card. After it is created, another card is read. Note that we do not read a tape record at this point, since the previous record has not been processed.

Figure 20.1 illustrates the entries for this update program. Examine them **carefully.**

```
IDENTIFICATION DIVISION.
PROGRAM-ID. UPDATE.
ENVIRONMENT DIVISION.
INPUT-OUTPUT SECTION.
FILE-CONTROL.
    SELECT OLD-MASTER ASSIGN TO UT-S-SYS004.
    SELECT DETAIL-FILE ASSIGN TO UR-S-SYSIN.
    SELECT NEW-MASTER ASSIGN TO UT-S-SYS005.
DATA DIVISION.
FILE SECTION.
FD  OLD-MASTER
    LABEL RECORDS ARE STANDARD
    RECORD CONTAINS 100 CHARACTERS
    BLOCK CONTAINS 20 RECORDS
    DATA RECORD IS OLD-MASTER-REC.
01  OLD-MASTER-REC.
    02  ACCT-NO              PIC X(5).
    02  AMOUNT-DUE           PIC 9(4)V99.
    02  FILLER               PIC X(89).
FD  DETAIL-FILE
    LABEL RECORDS ARE OMITTED
    RECORD CONTAINS 80 CHARACTERS
    DATA RECORD IS DETAIL-REC.
01  DETAIL-REC.
    02  ACCT-NO                      PIC X(5).
    02  AMT-TRANS-IN-CURRENT-PER     PIC 9(4)V99.
    02  FILLER                       PIC X(69).
FD  NEW-MASTER
    LABEL RECORDS ARE STANDARD
    RECORD CONTAINS 100 CHARACTERS
    BLOCK CONTAINS 20 RECORDS
    DATA RECORD IS NEW-MASTER-REC.
01  NEW-MASTER-REC.
    02  ACCT-NO              PIC X(5).
    02  AMOUNT-DUE           PIC 9(4)V99.
    02  FILLER               PIC X(89).
PROCEDURE DIVISION.
    OPEN INPUT OLD-MASTER, DETAIL-FILE,
         OUTPUT NEW-MASTER.
    PERFORM READ-MASTER.
    PERFORM READ-DETAIL.
    PERFORM UPDATE-RTN UNTIL
         ACCT-NO OF OLD-MASTER-REC = HIGH-VALUES
    AND
         ACCT-NO OF DETAIL-REC = HIGH-VALUES.
    CLOSE OLD-MASTER, DETAIL-FILE, NEW-MASTER.
    STOP RUN.
```

```
UPDATE-RTN.
    IF ACCT-NO OF DETAIL-REC = ACCT-NO OF OLD-MASTER-REC
            PERFORM REGULAR-UPDATE
    ELSE
            IF ACCT-NO OF DETAIL-REC < ACCT-NO OF OLD-MASTER-REC
                    PERFORM NEW-ACCT
            ELSE
            PERFORM NO-UPDATE.
REGULAR-UPDATE.
    MOVE ACCT-NO OF OLD-MASTER-REC TO ACCT-NO OF NEW-MASTER-REC.
    ADD AMT-TRANS-IN-CURRENT-PER, AMOUNT-DUE OF OLD-MASTER-REC
            GIVING AMOUNT-DUE OF NEW-MASTER-REC.
    WRITE NEW-MASTER-REC.
    PERFORM READ-MASTER.
    PERFORM READ-DETAIL.
NEW-ACCT.
    MOVE AMT-TRANS-IN-CURRENT-PER TO AMOUNT-DUE OF
            NEW-MASTER-REC.
    MOVE ACCT-NO OF DETAIL-REC TO ACCT-NO OF NEW-MASTER-REC.
    WRITE NEW-MASTER-REC.
    PERFORM READ-DETAIL.
NO-UPDATE.
    MOVE ACCT-NO OF OLD-MASTER-REC TO ACCT-NO OF NEW-MASTER-REC.
    MOVE AMOUNT-DUE OF OLD-MASTER-REC TO AMOUNT-DUE OF
            NEW-MASTER-REC.
    WRITE NEW-MASTER-REC.
    PERFORM READ-MASTER.
READ-MASTER.
    READ OLD-MASTER AT END
            MOVE HIGH-VALUES TO ACCT-NO OF OLD-MASTER-REC.
READ-DETAIL.
    READ DETAIL-FILE AT END
            MOVE HIGH-VALUES TO ACCT-NO OF DETAIL-REC.
```

Figure 20.1

Two items in the program require further clarification.

NESTED CONDITIONALS   The use of the nested conditionals, the IF . . . ELSE IF . . . format, is particularly useful in an update procedure where we essentially have three conditions to test. You will recall from Chapter 16 that nested conditionals function as follows:

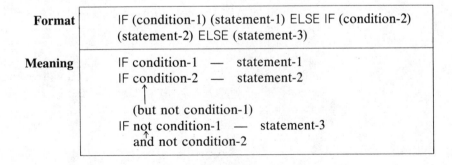

Format	IF (condition-1) (statement-1) ELSE IF (condition-2) (statement-2) ELSE (statement-3)
Meaning	IF condition-1 — statement-1 IF condition-2 — statement-2 ↑ (but not condition-1) IF not condition-1 — statement-3 ↑ and not condition-2

In our program, the following was coded:

	Condition	**Result**
A.	IF ACCT-NO OF DETAIL-REC = ACCT-NO OF OLD-MASTER-REC	PERFORM REGULAR-UPDATE

B.   IF ACCT-NO OF DETAIL-REC   PERFORM
      < ACCT-NO OF OLD-MASTER-REC   NEW-ACCT

not (A or B) implies:
      IF ACCT-NO OF DETAIL-REC   PERFORM
      > ACCT-NO OF OLD-MASTER-REC   NO-UPDATE

We use the nested conditional because we need a **single** statement to perform the test on ACCT-NO.

END-OF-JOB   HIGH-VALUES
ROUTINES   With update routines, it is possible for all records in the DETAIL-FILE to be processed before we have reached the end of the OLD-MASTER file. It is, however, also possible to run out of OLD-MASTER records before we reach the end of the DETAIL-FILE. For the sake of completeness we must program for both possibilities.

Note the use of the COBOL reserved word HIGH-VALUES in READ-MASTER and READ-DETAIL. HIGH-VALUES is the expression used for the largest data value in the specific computer's collating sequence. When the OLD-MASTER file has reached the end, there may be additional detail records to process. Hence we would not want to automatically terminate processing at an OLD-MASTER end-of-file condition. To accomplish this, we place HIGH-VALUES in ACCT-NO of OLD-MASTER-REC. In this way subsequent attempts to compare the ACCT-NO of new detail records against the ACCT-NO of OLD-MASTER-REC will always result in a '<' or 'less than' condition. That is, the NEW-ACCT routine will be executed until there are no more detail records.

Similarly, an AT END condition for DETAIL-FILE may mean there are still OLD-MASTER records left to process. Hence, at READ-DETAIL an AT END condition moves HIGH-VALUES, a kind of "dummy" ACCT-NO, which will always compare high, or '>', to ACCT-NO of OLD-MASTER-REC. In this way UPDATE-RTN will be performed. Any remaining OLD-MASTER records will be read and processed using the NO-UPDATE sequence. This procedure will continue until an AT END condition at OLD-MASTER is reached.

Only when **both** AT END conditions have been reached does control return to the first paragraph (main module) where the program is terminated.

Note that HIGH-VALUES may only be used with fields that are defined as alphanumeric. If ACCT-NO had been defined with a PIC of 9's, we could have moved 99999 to the ACCT-NO fields of the respective input files to achieve the same results.

B. CHECKING FOR VALIDITY IN TRANSACTIONS

Checking for
New Records

There are two ways of handling the case where an ACCT-NO OF DETAIL-REC is less than an ACCT-NO OF OLD-MASTER-REC. On the one hand, we may have a procedure where **all** detail records are supposed to have corresponding master records. If ACCT-NO OF DETAIL-REC has no match with ACCT-NO OF OLD-MASTER-REC, this means that an error has occurred. Or, where ACCT-NO OF DETAIL-REC is less than ACCT-NO OF OLD-MASTER-REC, this may mean that a new ACCT-NO must be added to the master file. In the latter case, it is usually advisable to build into the update program a routine ascertaining that this detail ACCT-NO is, indeed, a new record and not an erroneously coded field. To provide this check, new accounts usually include a coded entry, frequently in column 80 of a card, which will contain a specified character for new accounts.

Example

A DETAIL-REC may have the following format:
1–5   ACCT-NO
6–11 AMT-TRANS-IN-CURRENT-PER
12–79 FILLER
80   CODE-1 [N = NEW-ACCT]

The routine at NEW-ACCT would include the following:

```
NEW-ACCT.
    IF CODE-1 NOT EQUAL TO 'N'
        PERFORM ERR-RTN
    ELSE
        MOVE AMT-TRANS-IN-CURRENT-PER TO AMOUNT-DUE OF NEW-MASTER-REC
        MOVE ACCT-NO OF DETAIL-REC TO ACCT-NO OF NEW-MASTER-REC
        WRITE-NEW-MASTER-REC.
    PERFORM READ-DETAIL.
```

This coded field may also be used to double-check normal update records as well. CODE-1 of DETAIL-REC may contain the following:

```
80 CODE-1
       N = NEW-ACCT
       D = DELETION
       U = UPDATE
```

REGULAR-UPDATE would then be modified as follows:

```
REGULAR-UPDATE.
    IF CODE-1 = 'D'
        NEXT SENTENCE
    ELSE
        IF CODE-1 = 'U'
            MOVE ACCT-NO OF OLD-MASTER-REC TO ACCT-NO OF NEW-MASTER-REC
            ADD AMT-TRANS-IN-CURRENT-PER, AMOUNT-DUE OF OLD-MASTER-REC
                GIVING AMOUNT-DUE OF NEW-MASTER-REC
            WRITE NEW-MASTER-REC
        ELSE
            PERFORM ERR-RTN.
    PERFORM READ-MASTER.
    PERFORM READ-DETAIL.
```

Checking for
Sequence Errors

Note that the sequence of the records in the files to be updated is critical. If one or more records on a detail or master file has been sequenced incorrectly, the entire production run could be erroneous. Hence it is necessary to attempt to detect such errors while processing. Consider the following:

	DETAIL-FILE	OLD-MASTER	
	ACCT-NO	ACCT-NO	
	0006	0006	
	0009	0009	
all these	⌐ 0118	0014 ⌐	all these
records would	0015	0015	records would
be incorrectly	0016	0016	be incorrectly
processed	.	.	processed
	.	.	
	.	.	
	.	.	
	.	0108 ⌐	

A sequence error in DETAIL-FILE causes the above files to be processed incorrectly.

If the possibility for a sequence error exists, it is advisable to include a sequence check in your program:

```
01    CHECK-SEQ            PIC  9(4)  VALUE  ZERO.
      .
      .
      .
      PERFORM  READ-DETAIL.
      .
      .
      .
READ-DETAIL.
      READ  DETAIL-FILE  AT  END
            MOVE  HIGH-VALUES  TO  ACCT-NO  OF  DETAIL-REC.
      IF  ACCT-NO  OF  DETAIL-REC  <  CHECK-SEQ
            PERFORM  ERR-RTN
      ELSE  MOVE  ACCT-NO  OF  DETAIL-REC  TO  CHECK-SEQ.
```

At ERR-RTN, you may want to (1) simply print a message indicating that a sequence error has occurred; (2) stop the run; or (3) count the number of such errors and abort the run if the count exceeds a predetermined limit.

ALTERNATIVE METHOD FOR SEQUENCE CHECKING

Aborting a run, resequencing detail records, and then updating the master file again would usually be a lengthy and costly procedure. A better alternative is to create the DETAIL-FILE on tape, if it is not already there, and issue a SORT command, which is described in the next chapter. With a computer-generated SORT, we can be relatively certain that the file is properly sequenced.

MERGE PROGRAMS

The routines described above for updating files are applicable for merging files as well. We may, for example, have two files:

UPSTATE   DOWNSTATE

ACCT-NO Sequence   ACCT-NO Sequence

We may want to merge them by some sequenced field such as ACCT-NO into a single sequenced file under one of the following circumstances:

1. There should be no duplicates. If a record with an ACCT-NO appears on one file we should not have the same ACCT-NO on the other.
   [IF ACCT-NO OF UPSTATE = ACCT-NO OF DOWNSTATE PERFORM ERROR-RTN.]

2. There may be duplication, in which case the UPSTATE record appears first.
   IF ACCT-NO OF UPSTATE = ACCT-NO OF DOWNSTATE
       MOVE UPSTATE TO NEW-REC
           WRITE NEW-REC
       MOVE DOWNSTATE TO NEW-REC
           WRITE NEW-REC

3. There **must** be duplication. There should be **exactly** the same ACCT-NOs on both files.
   IF ACCT-NO OF UPSTATE NOT EQUAL TO ACCT-NO OF DOWNSTATE PERFORM ERROR-RTN.

OTHER APPLICATIONS OF SEQUENTIAL FILE PROCESSING

In summary, update and merge programs make use of the following techniques:

TECHNIQUES USED IN UPDATE AND MERGE PROGRAMS

1. All files to be processed must be in sequence by one specified field—that is, ACCT-NO, SOC-SEC-NO, and so on.
2. A record is read from each file and specified routines are performed depending on whether or not there are matching records.
3. A nested conditional is usually used to perform these specified routines. One of the following conditions must be met:
   a. = or matching condition
      (Record from first file = record from second file.)
      Actions:
      Process both records.
      Read from both files.
   b. < condition
      (Record from first file is less than record from second file.)
      Actions:
      Process record from the first file.
      Read a record from the first file.
   c. > condition
      (Record from first file is greater than record from second file.)
      Actions:
      Process record from the second file.
      Read a record from the second file.
4. End-of-job test for each file must be processed individually. By moving HIGH-VALUES to the sort field (assuming that this field is not numeric), we can be assured that the other file will always compare low and hence will continue to be processed. The job is terminated only after **all** files have been processed.

Numerous variations of these procedures are used in a wide variety of sequential file processing routines. Consider the following examples:

Example 1: Matching Records

A company has two warehouses, each storing precisely the same inventory. The inventory file at each warehouse is in PART-NO sequence.

At the end of each month, a report is printed indicating the total quantity on hand for each part. This total is the sum of the QTY-ON-HAND field for each part from both warehouses.

If there is an erroneous PART-NO that appears in the file for warehouse 1 (WH-1) but not in the file for warehouse 2 (WH-2), the total for this part should **not** be included in the report. It should instead be displayed as an error, on the console. The same procedure should be followed if a PART-NO exists for the WH-2 file but does not exist for the WH-1 file.

The PROCEDURE DIVISION entries for this program appear in Figure 20.2

```
PROCEDURE DIVISION.
    OPEN INPUT WH-1, WH-2, OUTPUT PRINT-REPORT-FILE.
    PERFORM READ-WH-1-RTN.
    PERFORM READ-WH-2-RTN.
    PERFORM MATCH-IT UNTIL PART-NO OF WH-1-REC = HIGH-VALUES
            AND PART-NO OF WH-2-REC = HIGH-VALUES.
    CLOSE WH-1, WH-2, PRINT-REPORT-FILE.
    STOP RUN.
MATCH-IT.
    IF PART-NO OF WH-1-REC = PART-NO OF WH-2-REC
            PERFORM REPORT-RTN
            PERFORM READ-WH-1-RTN
            PERFORM READ-WH-2-RTN
    ELSE
        IF PART-NO OF WH-1-REC < PART-NO OF WH-2-REC
            DISPLAY WH-1-REC,
            'WAREHOUSE 1 RECORD -- NO MATCHING WAREHOUSE 2 RECORD'
                UPON CONSOLE
            PERFORM READ-WH-1-RTN
    ELSE
            DISPLAY WH-2-REC
            'WAREHOUSE 2 RECORD -- NO MATCHING WAREHOUSE 1 RECORD'
                UPON CONSOLE
            PERFORM READ-WH-2-RTN.
REPORT-RTN.
    ADD QTY-ON-HAND OF WH-1-REC,
        QTY-ON-HAND OF WH-2-REC GIVING TOTAL.
    MOVE CORR WH-1-REC TO PRINT-REC.
    WRITE PRINT-REC AFTER ADVANCING 2 LINES.
READ-WH-1-RTN.
    READ WH-1 AT END MOVE HIGH-VALUES TO PART-NO OF WH-1-REC.
READ-WH-2-RTN.
    READ WH-2 AT END MOVE HIGH-VALUES TO PART-NO OF WH-2-REC.
```

Figure 20.2 PROCEDURE DIVISION entries for Example 1.

Example 2: Matching Records—With A Variation

a. FILE-1 is a master tape of all customers who have bank accounts with Bank ABC. This file is in sequence by ACCT-NO.

b. FILE-2 is a detail tape of all deposits and withdrawals made during the previous week. This file is also in sequence by ACCT-NO.

Write an edit program to make certain that all transactions on the detail tape, FILE-2, refer to existing customers, those with an ACCT-NO on FILE-1.

That is,

1. Every ACCT-NO on FILE-2 **must** have a matching ACCT-NO on FILE-1. If there is an ACCT-NO on FILE-2 with no matching ACCT-NO on FILE-1, print the record from FILE-2 as an error.
2. There may be records on FILE-1 that have no corresponding records on FILE-2. These would be customers who have not made any transactions—deposits or withdrawals—during the previous week.
3. There may be **more than one** record on FILE-2 with the **same** ACCT-NO. This is because it is possible to make several transactions—deposits or withdrawals—in any given week.

The PROCEDURE DIVISION entries for this program appear in Figure 20.3.

```
PROCEDURE DIVISION.
    OPEN INPUT FILE-1, FILE-2.
    PERFORM READ-FILE-1-RTN.
    PERFORM READ-FILE-2-RTN.
    PERFORM MATCH-CHECK UNTIL ACCT-NO OF REC-1 = HIGH-VALUES AND
            ACCT-NO OF REC-2 = HIGH-VALUES.
    CLOSE FILE-1, FILE-2.
    STOP RUN.
MATCH-CHECK.
    IF ACCT-NO OF REC-1 < ACCT-NO OF REC-2
            PERFORM READ-FILE-1-RTN
    ELSE
        IF ACCT-NO OF REC-1 > ACCT-NO OF REC-2
            DISPLAY REC-2, 'NO MATCHING ACCT-NO FROM FILE-1'
            PERFORM READ-FILE-2-RTN
    ELSE
            PERFORM READ-FILE-2-RTN UNTIL ACCT-NO OF REC-1
                NOT EQUAL TO ACCT-NO OF REC-2
            PERFORM READ-FILE-1-RTN.
READ-FILE-1-RTN.
    READ FILE-1 AT END MOVE HIGH-VALUES TO ACCT-NO OF REC-1.
    READ-FILE-2-RTN.
    READ FILE-2 AT END MOVE HIGH-VALUES TO ACCT-NO OF REC-2.
```

Figure 20.3 PROCEDURE DIVISION entries for Example 2.

SELF-EVALUATING QUIZ

1. The process of making a file of data current is called a(n) _____.
   *****
   update
2. (T or F) A tape file may be processed sequentially or randomly.
   *****
   F—tapes may only be processed sequentially.
3. (T or F) It is easy to update an existing tape file by simply adding records to it.
   *****
   F—a new file must be created.
4. (T or F) Files must be in some sequence in order to perform an update.
   *****
   T
5. The three files necessary to perform a sequential update are _____, _____, and _____.
   *****
   detail file
   old master
   new master

6. Suppose EMPLOYEE-NO is a field in a payroll record. Write a routine to make certain that the payroll file is in EMPLOYEE-NO sequence.
*****

```
02   EMPLOYEE-NO-HOLD          PIC 9(5), VALUE ZERO.
 .

 .

 .

READ PAYROLL-FILE AT END MOVE 1 TO EOF.
IF EMPLOYEE-NO < EMPLOYEE-NO-HOLD
    PERFORM ERR-RTN
ELSE
    MOVE EMPLOYEE-NO TO EMPLOYEE-N0-HOLD.
```

7. The COBOL reserved word HIGH-VALUES means _____.
*****

the largest data value for the specific computer

8. If the statement:

```
MOVE HIGH-VALUES TO TRANS-NO OF DETAIL-REC
```

is executed and a later instruction

```
IF TRANS-NO OF MASTER-REC < TRANS-NO OF DETAIL-REC
    PERFORM MASTER-RTN
ELSE
        PERFORM UPDATE.
```

is executed, then the computer will always perform _____.
*****

MASTER-RTN—The comparison will always result in a '<' condition.

9. A merge program is one that _____.
*****

takes two or more files and combines them into a single file

10. (T or F) Files should be in sequence for a merge program.
*****

T

C. CONTROL BREAKS

Sequential files are those that have been sorted into a specific sequence. Reports prepared from sequential files may require:

TYPES OF REPORT PRINTING

Detail printing—containing information on each specific record.
Group printing—containing information that summarizes specific records.

We have discussed an aspect of control breaks in Chapter 13.

Consider the report in Figure 20.4. This report contains both detail printing and group printing as specified in the figure. Lines 10, 12, 16, 18, 24, and 28 represent detail printing; lines 14, 20, 22, 26, 30, 32, and 34 represent group printing.

The customer names are printed within department within territory. Hence,

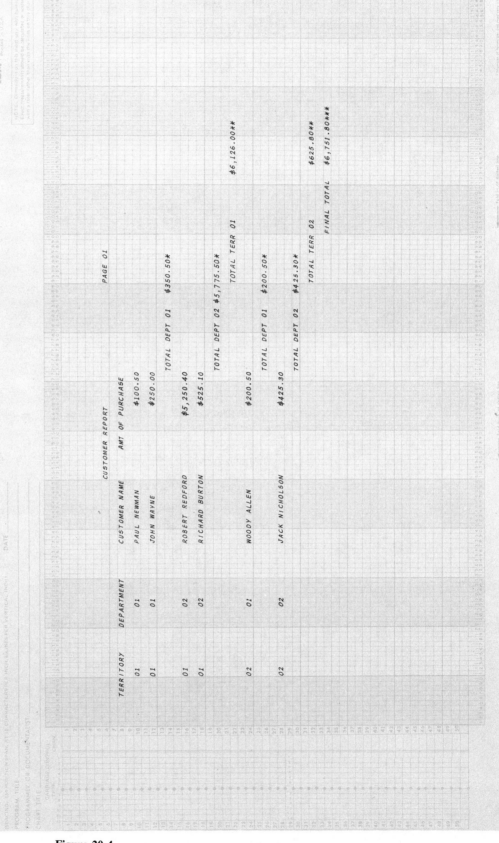

Figure 20.4

```
                                                              CUSTOMER REPORT                    PAGE 01
TERRITORY    DEPARTMENT    CUSTOMER NAME      AMT OF PURCHASE

   01           01         PAUL NEWMAN            $100.50
   01           01         JOHN WAYNE             $250.00
                                      TOTAL DEPT 01   $350.50*

   01           02         ROBERT REDFORD      $5,250.40
   01           02         RICHARD BURTON        $525.10
                                      TOTAL DEPT 02 $5,775.50*

                                             TOTAL TERR 01    $6,126.00**

   02           01         WOODY ALLEN           $200.50
                                      TOTAL DEPT 01   $200.50*

   02           02         JACK NICHOLSON        $425.30
                                      TOTAL DEPT 02   $425.30*

                                             TOTAL TERR 02      $625.80**

                                             FINAL TOTAL    $6,751.80***
```

Figure 20.5

the sort fields are as follows:

> **SORT FIELDS**
> Major sort field—territory ·
> Minor sort field—department

Customer records are read and then printed. When a change in department occurs, a **control break** routine is performed. This control break results in the printing of a total amount for the entire department. The total is printed with a single asterisk (*), which is usually used to denote the lowest level of control.

When a change in territory occurs, **two** control breaks must be performed:

1. The minor control break that prints the department total (*).
2. The major control break that prints the territory total—with two asterisks (**).

At the end of the job, **three** control breaks must be performed:

1. A control break that prints the department total (*).
2. A control break that prints the territory total (**).
3. A control break that prints the final total (***).
   (See Figure 20.5 for sample output.)

To determine when a control break occurs, we must:

1. Store the territory and department from the first record in a WORKING-STORAGE area.
2. Compare subsequent records to this area—if a change occurs, we must perform a control break.
3. If no change occurs, simply add the AMT-OF-PURCHASE from the existing record into a DEPT-CTR, a TERR-CTR, and a FINAL-CTR.

The program could be coded as indicated in Figure 20.6.

All programs with control breaks follow the pattern described above. Note that the major level test for TERR is performed **before** the minor level test for DEPT. This is because a TERR break is used to force a DEPT break as well. A change in TERR means that we want to print the previous DEPT totals as well as the previous TERR totals.

CONTROL BREAKS AND OCCURS CLAUSES

Suppose that for the previous program we wish to print the group or total lines **only.** The program may be written as indicated **without** any detail printing. Note, however, that such control break programs can only be coded **if the** input data is in the appropriate sequence. If the input data were **not** in sequence, then the totals would need to be stored using OCCURS clauses:

```
01  TOTALS.
    02  TERR  OCCURS  20  TIMES.
        03  DEPT  OCCURS  30  TIMES.
            04  TOTAL    PIC  9(4)V99.
```

```
                    IDENTIFICATION DIVISION.
                    PROGRAM-ID. CONTROL1.
                    ENVIRONMENT DIVISION.
                    INPUT-OUTPUT SECTION.
                    FILE-CONTROL.
                        SELECT IN-FILE ASSIGN TO UR-S-SYS010.
                        SELECT PRINT-FILE ASSIGN TO UR-S-SYSOUT.
                    DATA DIVISION.
                    FILE SECTION.
                    FD  IN-FILE
                        LABEL RECORDS ARE OMITTED
                        RECORD CONTAINS 80 CHARACTERS
                        BLOCK CONTAINS 10 RECORDS
                        DATA RECORD IS IN-REC.
                    01  IN-REC.
                        02  TERR                PIC 99.
                        02  DEPT                PIC 99.
                        02  NAME                PIC X(20).
                        02  AMT-OF-PURCHASE     PIC 9(4)V99.
                        02  FILLER              PIC X(50).
                    FD  PRINT-FILE
                        LABEL RECORDS ARE OMITTED
                        RECORD CONTAINS 133 CHARACTERS
                        DATA RECORD IS PRINT-REC.
                    01  PRINT-REC       PIC X(133).
                    WORKING-STORAGE SECTION.
                    01  WORK-AREAS.
                        02  HOLD-TERR   PIC 99.
                        02  HOLD-DEPT   PIC 99.
                        02  TERR-TOT    PIC 9(5)V99 VALUE ZERO.
                        02  DEPT-TOT    PIC 9(5)V99 VALUE ZERO.
                        02  FINAL-TOT   PIC 9(6)V99 VALUE ZERO.
                        02  LINE-CT     PIC 99 VALUE 1.
                        02  EOF         PIC 9 VALUE ZERO.
                    01  HDR-REC1.
                        02  FILLER      PIC X(66) VALUE 'CUSTOMER REPORT'
                                JUSTIFIED RIGHT.
                        02  FILLER      PIC X(30) VALUE 'PAGE '
                                JUSTIFIED RIGHT.
                        02  PAGE-CT     PIC 99 VALUE 01.
                        02  FILLER      PIC X(35) VALUE SPACES.
                    01  HDR-REC2.
                        02  FILLER      PIC X(31) VALUE
                            '          TERRITORY      DEPARTMENT'.
                        02  FILLER              PIC X(26) VALUE
                            '          CUSTOMER NAME          '.
                        02  FILLER              PIC X(76) VALUE
                            'AMT OF PURCHASE'.
                    01  DETAIL-REC.
                        02  FILLER      PIC X(11) VALUE SPACES.
                        02  TERR        PIC 99.
                        02  FILLER      PIC X(12) VALUE SPACES.
                        02  DEPT        PIC 99.
                        02  FILLER      PIC X(11) VALUE SPACES.
                        02  NAME        PIC X(20).
                        02  FILLER      PIC X(6) VALUE SPACES.
                        02  AMT-OF-PURCHASE   PIC $$,$$$.99.
                        02  FILLER      PIC X(61) VALUE SPACES.
                    01  DEPT-TOT-REC.
                        02  FILLER              PIC X(84) VALUE 'TOTAL DEPT '
                                JUSTIFIED RIGHT.
                        02  DEPT-OUT            PIC 99.
                        02  FILLER              PIC X(4).
```

Figure 20.6

```
            02  TOT-DEPT-OUT         PIC $$$,$$$.99.
            02  FILLER               PIC X(33) VALUE '*'.
        01  TERR-TOT-REC.
            02  FILLER               PIC X(102) VALUE 'TOTAL TERR '
                    JUSTIFIED RIGHT.
            02  TERR-OUT             PIC 99.
            02  FILLER               PIC X(7) VALUE SPACES.
            02  TOT-TERR-OUT         PIC $$$,$$$.99.
            02  FILLER               PIC X(12) VALUE '**'.
        01  FINAL-REC.
            02  FILLER               PIC X(112) VALUE 'FINAL TOTAL'
                    JUSTIFIED RIGHT.
            02  TOT-FINAL-OUT        PIC $$$$,$$$.99.
            02  FILLER               PIC X(10) VALUE '***'.
    PROCEDURE DIVISION.
        OPEN INPUT IN-FILE, OUTPUT PRINT-FILE.
        PERFORM HDR-RTN.
        READ IN-FILE AT END MOVE 1 TO EOF.
        MOVE TERR OF IN-REC TO HOLD-TERR.
        MOVE DEPT OF IN-REC TO HOLD-DEPT.
        PERFORM CALC-RTN UNTIL EOF = 1.
        PERFORM TERR-BREAK.
        PERFORM FINAL-BREAK.
        CLOSE IN-FILE, PRINT-FILE.
        STOP RUN.
    CALC-RTN.
        IF TERR OF IN-REC NOT EQUAL TO HOLD-TERR
                PERFORM TERR-BREAK.
        IF DEPT OF IN-REC NOT EQUAL TO HOLD-DEPT
                PERFORM DEPT-BREAK.
        ADD AMT-OF-PURCHASE OF IN-REC TO DEPT-TOT, TERR-TOT,
                FINAL-TOT.
        MOVE CORR IN-REC TO DETAIL-REC.
        WRITE PRINT-REC FROM DETAIL-REC AFTER ADVANCING 2 LINES.
        ADD 1 TO LINE-CT.
        IF LINE-CT > 25 PERFORM HDR-RTN.
        READ IN-FILE AT END MOVE 1 TO EOF.
    TERR-BREAK.
        PERFORM DEPT-BREAK.
        MOVE HOLD-TERR TO TERR-OUT.
        MOVE TERR-TOT TO TOT-TERR-OUT.
        WRITE PRINT-REC FROM TERR-TOT-REC AFTER ADVANCING 2 LINES.
        ADD 1 TO LINE-CT.
        MOVE TERR OF IN-REC TO HOLD-TERR.
        MOVE ZEROS TO TERR-TOT.
    DEPT-BREAK.
        MOVE HOLD-DEPT TO DEPT-OUT.
        MOVE DEPT-TOT TO TOT-DEPT-OUT.
        WRITE PRINT-REC FROM DEPT-TOT-REC AFTER ADVANCING 2 LINES.
        ADD 1 TO LINE-CT.
        MOVE DEPT OF IN-REC TO HOLD-DEPT.
        MOVE ZEROS TO DEPT-TOT.
    HDR-RTN.
        WRITE PRINT-REC FROM HDR-REC1 AFTER ADVANCING 0 LINES.
        ADD 1 TO PAGE-CT.
        MOVE ZEROS TO LINE-CT.
        WRITE PRINT-REC FROM HDR-REC2 AFTER ADVANCING 2 LINES.
    FINAL-BREAK.
        MOVE FINAL-TOT TO TOT-FINAL-OUT.
        WRITE PRINT-REC FROM FINAL-REC AFTER ADVANCING 2 LINES.
```

As the data is read it is added to the appropriate TOTAL. After all the data has been read, then the information is printed and totalled.

SELF-EVALUATING QUIZ

1. (T or F) In order to code a program that includes control breaks, the files must be in some sequence.
   *****
   T
2. (T or F) Control break programs can include both detail and group printing.
   *****
   T
3. (T or F) Major control break routines usually force minor and intermediate control breaks.
   *****
   T
4. (T or F) Totals printed with two asterisks would usually be considered minor totals while totals printed with a single asterisk would usually be considered major totals.
   *****
   F—usually the more asterisks used, the more comprehensive the total.
5. (T or F) Control breaks are limited to three within a single program.
   *****
   F—any number may be used.
6. _____ printing is used for the printing of individual lines of data whereas _____ printing is used for summary information.
   *****
   Detail
   group

PRACTICE PROBLEM— WITH SOLUTION

Write a merge program using the following input files:

Detail Tape File

1–5 Transaction Number
6–10 Transaction Amount xxx.xx
11–70 Not used

Master Tape File

1–5 Transaction Number
6–10 Transaction Amount xxx.xx

All files are blocked 50 and have standard labels.

NOTES:

(a) Output file has the same format as the master tape file.
(b) Output file is to combine both input files into one file in transaction number sequence (both input files are in transaction number sequence).
(c) Transaction numbers for each file must be unique; that is, detail transaction number must **not** match master transaction numbers. If a match occurs, print an error message.

See Figure 20.7 for the solution.

```
            IDENTIFICATION DIVISION.
            PROGRAM-ID. CHAPT20.
            ENVIRONMENT DIVISION.
            CONFIGURATION SECTION.
            SOURCE-COMPUTER. IBM-370.
            OBJECT-COMPUTER. IBM-370.
            INPUT-OUTPUT SECTION.
            FILE-CONTROL.
                SELECT DETAIL-TAPE ASSIGN TO UT-S-SYS001.
                SELECT MASTER-TAPE-IN ASSIGN TO UT-S-SYS002.
                SELECT MASTER-TAPE-OUT ASSIGN TO UT-S-SYS003.
            DATA DIVISION.
            FILE SECTION.
            FD  DETAIL-TAPE
                LABEL RECORDS ARE STANDARD
                RECORD CONTAINS 70 CHARACTERS
                BLOCK CONTAINS 50 RECORDS
                DATA RECORD IS REC-IN1.
            01  REC-IN1.
                02   D-TRANS-NO          PIC X(5).
                02   D-AMT               PIC 999V99.
                02   FILLER              PIC X(60).
            FD  MASTER-TAPE-IN
                LABEL RECORDS ARE STANDARD
                RECORD CONTAINS 10 CHARACTERS
                BLOCK CONTAINS 50 RECORDS
                DATA RECORD IS REC-IN2.
            01  REC-IN2.
                02   M-TRANS-NO          PIC X(5).
                02   M-AMT               PIC 999V99.
            FD  MASTER-TAPE-OUT
                LABEL RECORDS ARE STANDARD
                RECORD CONTAINS 10 CHARACTERS
                BLOCK CONTAINS 50 RECORDS
                DATA RECORD IS REC-OUT.
            01  REC-OUT.
                02   TRANS-NO-OUT        PIC X(5).
                02   AMT-OUT             PIC 999V99.
            WORKING-STORAGE SECTION.
            01  WORK-AREAS.
                02  EOF1        PIC 9 VALUE 0.
                02  EOF2        PIC 9 VALUE 0.
            PROCEDURE DIVISION.
                OPEN INPUT DETAIL-TAPE, MASTER-TAPE-IN
                        OUTPUT MASTER-TAPE-OUT.
                READ DETAIL-TAPE AT END MOVE 1 TO EOF1.
                READ MASTER-TAPE-IN AT END MOVE 1 TO EOF2.
                PERFORM MERGE-RTN UNTIL EOF1 = 1 AND EOF2 = 1.
                CLOSE DETAIL-TAPE, MASTER-TAPE-IN, MASTER-TAPE-OUT.
                STOP RUN.
            MERGE-RTN.
                IF D-TRANS-NO < M-TRANS-NO
                        PERFORM DETAIL-IN
                ELSE IF D-TRANS-NO > M-TRANS-NO
                        PERFORM MASTER-IN
                ELSE PERFORM ERR-RTN.
            DETAIL-IN.
                MOVE D-TRANS-NO TO TRANS-NO-OUT.
                MOVE D-AMT TO AMT-OUT.
                WRITE REC-OUT.
                READ DETAIL-TAPE AT END
                        MOVE 1 TO EOF1
                        MOVE HIGH-VALUES TO D-TRANS-NO.
            MASTER-IN.
                WRITE REC-OUT FROM REC-IN2.
                READ MASTER-TAPE-IN AT END
                        MOVE 1 TO EOF2
                        MOVE HIGH-VALUES TO M-TRANS-NO.
            ERR-RTN.
                DISPLAY 'ERROR CONDITION', D-TRANS-NO, D-AMT.
                READ DETAIL-TAPE AT END
                        MOVE 1 TO EOF1
                        MOVE HIGH-VALUES TO D-TRANS-NO.
                READ MASTER-TAPE-IN AT END
                        MOVE 1 TO EOF2
                        MOVE HIGH-VALUES TO M-TRANS-NO.
```

Figure 20.7

REVIEW QUESTIONS

True False   **I. True-False Questions**

☐ ☐   1. Tape updating is the process of making a file current.

☐ ☐   2. Exactly two files are required for tape updating.

☐ ☐   3. Records on a tape can be any length.

☐ ☐   4. Tapes may be processed randomly or sequentially.

☐ ☐   5. The nested conditional is used in a typical tape update routine because it makes it possible to test three separate conditions in a single sentence.

☐ ☐   6. When any input file is completed during a tape update, the program should be terminated.

☐ ☐   7. A detail record with no corresponding master record always means an error.

☐ ☐   8. HIGH-VALUES is a COBOL reserved word meaning the highest value in the collating sequence.

☐ ☐   9. It is not necessary to perform a sequence check on detail or master files.

☐ ☐   10. A merge program uses routines similar to those used in tape updates.

II. General Questions

1. Provide program flowcharts for the following routines:
   a. update
   b. sequence-check
   c. merge

2. In an update, describe three different ways that a detail record **might** be processed if it is '<' a master record.

3. In a merge, describe three different ways to process the routine in which one tape record's sort field is '<' another tape record's.

4. Indicate the major advantages of tape processing.

5. Indicate the major disadvantages of tape processing.

Define the following terms (6–8):

6. control break

7. detail printing

8. group printing

9. If a file is arranged in DEPT within AREA sequence, would we need to establish OCCURS clauses to print the data out in that sequence?

PROBLEMS   1. Write an update program using the following input files:

Detail Card File	**Master Tape File**
1-5 Employee no.	1-5 Employee no.
6-20 Employee name	6-20 Employee name
21-25 Annual salary	21-25 Annual salary
26-80 Not used	26-50 Other data
	(Standard labels; blocking factor = 25)

Both files are in sequence by Employee no.

NOTES:

(a) The output file has the same format as input master file.

(b) For master tape records with no corresponding detail records (no match on employee no.) create an output record from the input tape.

(c) For detail records with no corresponding tape records, create an output record from the input card.

(d) For master tape records with corresponding card records, take annual salary from card and all other data from tape.

2. Write a program to read the following input tape records: (Blocking factor = 20)

STATE NO	COUNTY NO	DISTRICT NO	POPULATION
1 2	3 4	5 6	7 12

All records are in sequence by DISTRICT within COUNTY within STATE. Print a report that indicates group totals in the following manner:

```
STATE NO xx   COUNTY  POPULATION
              xx      xxx,xxx
              xx      xxx,xxx
              .       .
              .       .
              xx      xxx,xxx
                                  TOTAL FOR STATE xx,xxx,xxx*
STATE NO xx   COUNTY  POPULATION
              .       .
              .       .

                                  TOTAL FOR STATE xx,xxx,xxx*
                                  FINAL TOTAL xxx,xxx,xxx**
```

NOTE: Do not use OCCURS clause to store the data. Assume that the input is in the correct sequence.

3. Write a merge program using the following input tape files:

Detail File
1–5 Account Number
6–10 Transaction Amount
11–80 Not used

Master File
1–5 Account Number
6–80 Other identifying data

(a) Merge the two files—both are in sequence by account number.

(b) Both files should have exactly the same account numbers. Hence the new file should contain a master followed by one or more detail records with the same Account Number.

(c) There may be master records for which there are no corresponding detail records—simply put the master records on the new file.

(d) If there are detail records with no corresponding master record, do not put them on the new file—simply display them.

4. There are two input files, one called MASTER-DEPOSITORS-FILE and the other called WEEKLY-TRANSACTION-FILE, each in sequence by ACCT-NO and both with the same format.

```
FD   MASTER-DEPOSITORS-FILE
        .
        .
        .
01   MASTER-REC.
     02 ACCT-NO1 PIC X (5).
        .
        .
        .
FD   WEEKLY-TRANSACTION-FILE
        .
        .
        .
01   TRANS-REC.
     02 ACCT-NO2 PIC X(5).
        .
        .
        .
```

Each record from the WEEKLY-TRANSACTION-FILE must match a record on the MASTER-DEPOSITORS-FILE, although there may be MASTER-REC records with no corresponding TRANS-REC records. Moreover, there may be more than one TRANS-REC record for a given MASTER-REC record.

The output is to be a merged file that has records from both files in sequence by account number. For an account number with matching records from both files, the MASTER-REC record is to be followed by all TRANS-REC records with the same number:

Example

MASTER-REC	TRANS-REC
00120	00120
00124	00120
00125	00125
00127	00126

```
            MASTER-OUT-REC
            00120 M
            00120 T
            00120 T
            00124 M
            00125 M
            00125 T
            00127 M  [00126 T is to be printed as an error]
```

M = MASTER-REC record
T = TRANS-REC record

21 THE SORT FEATURE

INTRODUCTION

When processsng high-speed tapes and disks, it is sometimes necessary to access these media in a sequence other than the one in which they were created. A payroll file, for example, may be created in social security number sequence for ease of editing, but the creation of checks from that payroll file may require an alphabetic sort or a sort by office location.

There are prepackaged programs that can sort files. The user need only supply some specifications about the type of sort desired. Thus a programmer can call in a separate program that is maintained by most computer installations. COBOL programmers, however, can include as **part of their program** an initializing routine that sorts a file just prior to, or in conjunction with, the actual processing required.

A simplified format for the SORT statement in COBOL is as follows:

SORT (sort-file-name)

ON $\left\{ \begin{array}{l} \underline{DESCENDING} \\ \underline{ASCENDING} \end{array} \right\}$ KEY (data-name-1)

$\left[ON \left\{ \begin{array}{l} \underline{DESCENDING} \\ \underline{ASCENDING} \end{array} \right\} KEY (data-name-2) \right]$ . . .

$\left\{ \underline{USING} \text{ file-name-2} \underline{GIVING} \text{ file-name-3} \right\}$

ASCENDING OR DESCENDING KEY

It is possible to sort a file in two ways:

SORT OPTIONS
1. ASCENDING—from lowest to highest.
2. DESCENDING—from highest to lowest.

The SORT option may be used to sort a numeric or alphanumeric field. Ascending sequence used with an alphabetic field will cause data to be sorted in alphabetic order. Descending sequence will cause data to be sorted in reverse alphabetic order, from Z to A.

The EBCDIC collating sequence for the COBOL character set (letters and digits) is as follows:[1]

Lowest	ƀ
	A
	B
	.
	.
	.
	.
	Z
	0
	1
	.
	.
	.
	.
Highest	9

Note that the SORT may be used to sequence records with more than one SORT key. Suppose, for example, we wish to sort a payroll file so that it is alphabetic (by name), within each level, for each office. That is:

Office number is the major sort field.

Level number is the intermediate sort field.

Name is the minor sort field.

Thus for Office 1, we want

OFFICE-NO	LEVEL-NO	NAME
1	1	ADAMS, J. R.
1	1	BROCK, P. T.
1	1	CALVIN, S.
1	2	ARTHUR, Q. C.
1	2	EVANS, J.
1	3	DRAPER, A. P.
.	.	.
.	.	.
.	.	.

For Office Number 1, Level 1, all entries are alphabetic. These are followed by Office Number 1, Level 2, entries, in alphabetic order, and so on.

We may use a SORT option to perform this procedure. The first entry indicated is the **major** field to be sorted, the next entries represent intermediate sort fields, followed by minor sort fields.

[1]If the reader is using an ASCII computer, the collating sequence is ƀ 0–9 A–Z.

The following is an excerpt of the SORT option that would be appropriate for the above entry:

```
SORT PAYROLL-FILE
     ON ASCENDING KEY OFFICE-NO,
     ON ASCENDING KEY LEVEL-NO,
     ON ASCENDING KEY NAME.
```

Note that all keys are independent. Hence, one key can be sorted in AS-CENDING sequence and others in DESCENDING sequence. Note too that the word ON is optional.

FILES USED IN A SORT   There are three major file types used in a sort:

FILES USED IN A SORT
1. Input file—file on which unsorted records are entered.
2. Work file or sort file—used for accumulating records in the correct sequence.
3. Output file—file on which sorted records appear.

FD is used to define input and output as usual. SD is used to define a work or sort file. The only distinction between SD and FD entries is that sort files do not contain a LABEL RECORDS clause.

Example

```
FD      IN-FILE

  .

  .

  .

FD      OUT-FILE

  .

  .

  .

SD      SORT-FILE
```

All three files are defined in the ENVIRONMENT DIVISION in the usual way:

```
SELECT      IN-FILE ASSIGN TO SYS001-UT-2400-S.
SELECT      OUT-FILE ASSIGN TO SYS002-UT-2400-S.
SELECT      SORT-FILE ASSIGN TO SYS003-UT-2400-S.
```

The KEY fields are part of the **sort** file:

```
FD      IN-FILE

  .

  .

  .

FD      OUT-FILE

  .

  .

  .
```

```
SD      SORT-FILE
                .
                .
                .
01      SORT-REC.
        02 DEPT-NO
                .
                .
                .
```

DEPT-NO may be used as a KEY field:

7 8		12		16		20		24		28		32		36		40		44		48
		SORT	SORT-FILE	ASCENDING	KEY	DEPT-NO				
		USING	IN-FILE							
		GIVING	OUT-FILE.							
	STOP	RUN.								

The file specified in the USING clause is the input file and the file specified in the GIVING clause is the output file.

SELF-EVALUATING
QUIZ

1. If we want to sort a file so that it is in territory number sequence with Territory 10 appearing first followed by Territory 9, and so on, we call this a (DESCENDING/ASCENDING) sort.
   *****
   DESCENDING
   *****

2. Suppose we want records in alphabetic order by NAME within DISTRICT within TERRITORY, all in ascending sequence. Complete the key descriptions:
   SORT   FILE-X _____
   *****
   ASCENDING KEY TERRITORY, ASCENDING KEY DISTRICT
   ASCENDING KEY NAME USING IN-FILE
   GIVING OUT-FILE.

3. At least (no.) files must be used in a SORT routine. Describe these files.
   *****
   three
   input—unsorted
   work file
   output—sorted

4. The work file is defined as _____ in the DATA DIVISION.
   *****
   SD

5. Suppose we have the following DATA DIVISION entries:

```
SD      NET-FILE
        .
        .
        .

FD      NET-FILE-IN
        .
        .
        .

FD      NET-FILE-OUT
```

We want the file sorted into ascending department number sequence. Code the PROCEDURE DIVISION entry.

*****

```
SORT    NET-FILE
        ASCENDING KEY DEPT-NO
        USING NET-FILE-IN
        GIVING NET-FILE-OUT
        STOP RUN.
```

6. DEPT-NO must be a field defined in the record associated with an (SD/FD) level.

*****

```
SD
```

INPUT PROCEDURE

A file may be sorted into a specified sequence using the above routine. It is, however, also possible to process records **before** they are sorted. We may wish, for example, to edit the records before they are sorted, to count them, display them, and so on.

To perform an INPUT procedure, we must alter our SORT format:

$$\text{SORT (sort or work file-name) ON} \begin{Bmatrix} \underline{\text{ASCENDING}} \\ \underline{\text{DESCENDING}} \end{Bmatrix}$$

$$\underline{\text{KEY}} \text{ (data-name-1) } \ldots$$

$$\begin{Bmatrix} \underline{\text{INPUT}} \ \underline{\text{PROCEDURE}} \text{ IS section-name-1 } [\underline{\text{THRU}} \text{ section-name}] \\ \underline{\text{USING}} \begin{Bmatrix} \text{input-file} \\ \text{file-name-2} \end{Bmatrix} \end{Bmatrix}$$

$$\underline{\text{GIVING}} \begin{Bmatrix} \text{output-file} \\ \text{file-name-3} \end{Bmatrix}$$

The INPUT PROCEDURE may be used **in place of the** USING (input-file) clause.

To use the INPUT PROCEDURE, a section-name must be defined.

Example

```
SORT FILE-1 ASCENDING KEY DEPT
     INPUT PROCEDURE TEST-IT GIVING OUT-FILE.
STOP RUN.
TEST-IT SECTION.
   .
   .
   .
```

The section-name used with the INPUT PROCEDURE must have the following entries:

INPUT PROCEDURE ENTRIES
1. OPEN INPUT (name of input-file).
2. Standard processing using READ statement.
3. Move processed record to sort record.
4. Sort records are **not** written in an INPUT PROCEDURE. Instead, when a record has been permanently processed, a RELEASE statement is issued, in place of a WRITE, which then releases the record for sorting. The record name associated with the RELEASE is the sort record.
5. After processing has been completed, CLOSE the input file.
6. After the INPUT PROCEDURE has been completed, an EXIT statement is usually coded to indicate the end of the section. This is because the last statement coded in the SECTION must be the last one executed.

Suppose, for example, we wish to sort a file but first we want to eliminate all records from the sort that have a zero balance. The following indicates the correct coding:

```
PROCEDURE DIVISION.
    SORT SORT-FILE ASCENDING KEY DEPT
            INPUT PROCEDURE ELIMINATE-0-BAL
            GIVING NEW-FILE-WITHOUT-0-BAL.
    STOP RUN.
ELIMINATE-0-BAL SECTION.
MAIN-PARA.
    OPEN INPUT REG-FILE.
    READ REG-FILE AT END MOVE 1 TO EOF.
    PERFORM BAL-0 UNTIL EOF = 1.
    GO TO FINISH-UP.
BAL-0.
    IF BAL NOT = ZERO
            MOVE REG-REC-IN TO REC-TO-BE-SORTED
            RELEASE REC-TO-BE-SORTED.
    READ REG-FILE AT END MOVE 1 TO EOF.
FINISH-UP.
    CLOSE REG-FILE.
ELIMINATE-0-BAL-EXIT.
    EXIT.
```

NOTE: Each SECTION in a COBOL program must begin with a paragraph-name.

SUMMARY OF INPUT PROCEDURE
1. Begin with section name.
2. Input file is opened.
3. READ input records and process them.
4. When records have been processed, RELEASE them (instead of writing).
5. CLOSE the input file after processing.
6. The last statement in the PROCEDURE should be an exit.

OUTPUT PROCEDURE   After each record is sorted, it is available for further processing. To perform such processing, we may use an OUTPUT PROCEDURE option in place of the GIVING OPTION in a SORT statement.

The format for the OUTPUT PROCEDURE is as follows:

FULL FORMAT OF SORT STATEMENT

SORT   (sort-file-name) ON $\left\{ \begin{array}{l} \underline{DESCENDING} \\ \underline{ASCENDING} \end{array} \right\}$ KEY (data-name-1) . . .

$\left\{ \begin{array}{l} \underline{INPUT}\ \underline{PROCEDURE}\ IS\ section\text{-}name\text{-}1\ [\underline{THRU}\ section\text{-}name\text{-}2] \\ \underline{USING}\ file\text{-}name\text{-}2 \end{array} \right\}$

$\left\{ \begin{array}{l} \underline{OUTPUT}\ \underline{PROCEDURE}\ IS\ section\text{-}name\text{-}3\ [\underline{THRU}\ section\text{-}name\text{-}4] \\ \underline{GIVING}\ file\text{-}name\text{-}3 \end{array} \right\}$

In the SECTION specified in an OUTPUT PROCEDURE, the following must be included:

OUTPUT PROCEDURE ENTRIES

1. OPEN OUTPUT (file-name).
2. Instead of reading from the sort file, the RETURN (sort-file) AT END . . . is used.
3. Sort-file records are processed and written.
4. At the end of the section, the output file is closed and an exit paragraph ends the routine.

INPUT and OUTPUT procedures may be used together or may be used separately.

Example

After a file has been processed, MOVE .02 TO DISCOUNT for all records with AMT-OF-PURCHASE in excess of $500. The following indicates the correct coding:

```
PROCEDURE DIVISION.
    SORT SORT-FILE ASCENDING KEY TRANS-NO
            USING INPUT-FILE
            OUTPUT PROCEDURE CALC-DISCOUNT.
    STOP RUN.
CALC-DISCOUNT SECTION.
MAIN-PARAGRAPH.
    OPEN OUTPUT OUTPUT-FILE.
    RETURN SORT-FILE AT END MOVE 1 TO EOF.
    PERFORM DISC-RTN UNTIL EOF = 1.
    GO TO FINISH-UP.
DISC-RTN.
    IF AMT-OF-PURCHASE > 500
            MOVE .02 TO DISCOUNT
            WRITE OUT-REC.
    RETURN SORT-FILE AT END MOVE 1 TO EOF.
FINISH-UP.
    CLOSE OUTPUT-FILE.
CALC-DISCOUNT-EXIT.
    EXIT.
```

Figure 21.1 provides a schematic of the SORT feature and its options.

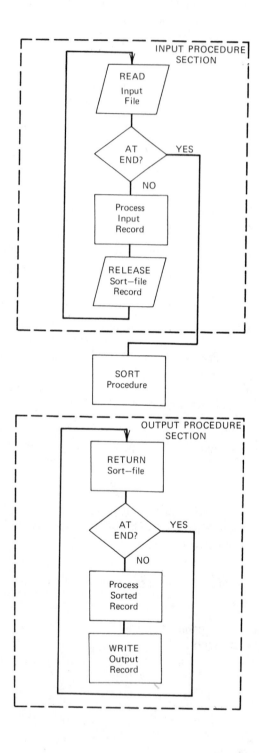

Figure 21.1 Schematic of INPUT and OUTPUT PROCEDURE with a SORT.

1. Code a simple SORT to read in a tape-file called IN-TAPE, sort it into ascending NAME sequence, and create an output disk called OUT-DISK in the required sequence.
   *****
   SORT   SORT-FILE ON ASCENDING NAME USING IN-TAPE
             GIVING OUT-DISK

2. It is possible to process records before they are sorted by using the _____ option in place of the _____ option.
   *****
   INPUT PROCEDURE
   USING

3. (T or F) A sort file is opened in an INPUT PROCEDURE.
   *****
   F—the input file is opened.

4. (T or F) A sort or work file is opened in an OUTPUT PROCEDURE.
   *****
   F—sort files are not opened.

5. A(n) _____ file is opened in an INPUT PROCEDURE and a(n) _____ file is opened in an OUTPUT PROCEDURE.
   *****
   unsorted input (FD)
   sorted output (FD)

6. In place of a WRITE statement in an INPUT PROCEDURE, the _____ verb is used.
   *****
   RELEASE

7. In place of a READ statement in an OUTPUT PROCEDURE, the _____ verb is used.
   *****
   RETURN

8. Indicate the format of a RETURN statement.
   *****
   RETURN (sort-file) AT END (imperative statement)

9. (T or F) The file name used with the RELEASE statement would normally be the same file name used with the RETURN statement.
   *****
   T—the sort file

10. If the clause INPUT PROCEDURE TEST-RTN is coded with the sort statement, then code the first statement of the TEST-RTN entry.
    *****
    TEST-RTN SECTION.

Sort a tape file into ascending territory (TERR), area (AREAX), and department (DEPT) sequence (major, intermediate, minor):

```
 1–2  TERR
 3–5  AREAX
 6–8  DEPT
 9–20 LAST-NAME
21–28 FIRST-NAME
29–50 Additional Data     (Blocking factor = 30)
```

See Figure 21.2 for the solution.

```
IDENTIFICATION DIVISION.
PROGRAM-ID. CHAPT21.
ENVIRONMENT DIVISION.
CONFIGURATION SECTION.
SOURCE-COMPUTER. IBM-370.
OBJECT-COMPUTER. IBM-370.
INPUT-OUTPUT SECTION.
FILE-CONTROL.
    SELECT IN-FILE ASSIGN TO UT-S-SYS001.
    SELECT SORT-FILE ASSIGN TO UT-S-SYS002.
    SELECT OUT-FILE ASSIGN TO UT-S-SYS003.
DATA DIVISION.
FILE SECTION.
FD  IN-FILE
    LABEL RECORDS ARE STANDARD
    RECORD CONTAINS 50 CHARACTERS
    DATA RECORD IS IN-REC.
01  IN-REC            PIC X(50).
SD  SORT-FILE
    RECORD CONTAINS 50 CHARACTERS
    DATA RECORD IS SORT-REC.
01  SORT-REC.
    02  TERR                 PIC XX.
    02  AREAX                PIC X(3).
    02  DEPT                 PIC X(3).
    02  LAST-NAME            PIC X(12).
    02  FIRST-NAME           PIC X(8).
    02  FILLER               PIC X(22).
FD  OUT-FILE
    LABEL RECORDS ARE STANDARD
    RECORD CONTAINS 50 CHARACTERS
    DATA RECORD IS OUT-REC.
01  OUT-REC          PIC X(50).
PROCEDURE DIVISION.
    SORT SORT-FILE
    ASCENDING KEY TERR
            ASCENDING KEY AREAX
            ASCENDING KEY DEPT
    USING IN-FILE
    GIVING OUT-FILE.
    STOP RUN.
```

Figure 21.2

REVIEW QUESTIONS

True False

I. True-False Questions

1. If the OUTPUT PROCEDURE is specified with the SORT verb, then the INPUT PROCEDURE is required.
2. RELEASE must be used in an INPUT PROCEDURE.
3. RETURN must be used in an OUTPUT PROCEDURE.
4. The RELEASE statement is used in place of the WRITE statement.
5. A maximum of three SORT fields are permitted in a single SORT statement.
6. The only method for sorting a file is with the use of the SORT statement.
7. Data may be sorted in either ascending or descending sequence.
8. The EXIT statement is usually coded at the end of an INPUT PROCEDURE.
9. If a file is described by an SD statement, it is not defined in a SELECT clause.
10. In the collating sequence described in this book, a blank is the character with lowest value.

II. General Questions

1. What is the purpose of the SORT statement?
2. Indicate the ways in which a SORT may be performed.
3. Indicate the meaning of SD and state how it is used.
4. If we code SORT S-1 ASCENDING DEPT DESCENDING AREA-X, _____ is the major field to be sorted, _____ is the minor field to be sorted, and both these fields must be described in the _____ record.
5. Indicate how an INPUT PROCEDURE is used and the specifications for it.
6. Indicate how an OUTPUT PROCEDURE is used and the specifications for it.

PROBLEMS

1. Sort a tape file into ascending LOCATION, LEVEL, and SSNO sequence (major, intermediate, minor):

1–2	LOCATION
3	LEVEL
4–12	SSNO
13–17	SALARY
18–100	Additional data (Blocking factor = 20)

2. Sort the above file eliminating all employees with a blank LOCATION, LEVEL, or SSNO.
3. Sort the above file, eliminating records with the blank fields, and add one to the level number of any employee who earns more than $25,000.
4. After the above sort, print the SSNO for all employees at LOCATION 14 who earn more than $75,000.

22 DISK PROCESSING

INTRODUCTION The magnetic disk is another high-speed medium that can serve as either input to, or output from a computer system. Like tape, it has an iron oxide coating that is used to store millions of characters of data, typically 6 to 10 million, but can store as many as 70 million characters. The magnetic disk drive (Figure 22.1) is used to record information onto the disk and to read information from it.

Figure 22.1 Disk drive. (Courtesy NCR Corporation.)

Figure 22.2 Disk pack. (Courtesy Burroughs.)

PHYSICAL
CHARACTERISTICS

Figure 22.2 illustrates a typical disk pack. The pack resembles a series of concentric disks similar to phonograph records that rotate on a vertical shaft.

Each surface of the disk consists of numbered concentric tracks and each track is used to store information. A read/write head is used to read information from, and record information onto, any of the tracks.

Disks have many of the same advantages as tapes. They can store large numbers of records in a condensed area. The disk drive, like the tape drive, reads and records information electronically and thus is a high-speed device. Records on a disk can essentially be any length. They are not fixed, as is the case with 80-column cards, for example.

Disk processing, however, has some additional features that are not available with tape processing. A disk may be used for either **random or sequential** processing.

In addition to handling records in sequence, a disk has the facility to access records in some order other than the one in which they were originally recorded. The processing of records on disk is similar to the accessing of phonograph records from a juke box. By indicating that phonograph record 106 is required, for example, the mechanism is capable of accessing 106 **directly** without first reading records 1 to 105, as is required with tape processing.

DISK FILE ORGANIZATION

The most common method for accessing magnetic disk records randomly is with the use of an **index.** During the creation of records, the computer establishes an index on the disk itself. The index essentially indicates where each record is located. We will see that this is similar in concept to the index found at the end of a textbook, which specifies the page where each item of information can be located.

The disk index indicates the "address" or location of records that are stored on the disk. The address, in basic terms, refers to the surface number, sector, and track where a particular record can be found. Some disks use **sectors** in addition to tracks and cylinders to define a location. A sector is a wedge or segment of the disk pack. A **key data field** in each record is established by the programmer and is used by the computer as the basis for storing address information in the index. As an example, if a Payroll file is stored on disk, a key field would probably be Social Security Number or Employee Number. Because key fields uniquely define a record, they are frequently used as a means of identification.

To access any disk record, the user need only supply a particular key data field, such as Employee Number 17537. The computer then "looks up" the corresponding disk address for this record from the index and seeks that record directly.

A disk can also be accessed using the **direct method.** A key field is established which, through some calculation, can be used to compute an address. This is the fastest access method but it requires additional programming for calculating an address.

It is also possible to access a disk using the **relative method,** where each record is identified by an integer that specifies its record number and its address. Thus the fifth record on the file is addressed by record number 5 and is placed in the fifth recording area.

Thus there are four methods that may be used to access a disk: (1) sequential; (2) indexed; (3) direct; (4) relative. We will discuss these methods later in the chapter. The last three methods utilize the direct-access capability of the disk as discussed below.

UPDATING RECORDS

Disks can also permit updates or changes to existing records **on the same disk.** In this way, a new disk need not be created to incorporate changes, as in tape processing. That is, the same disk may be used for **both** input and output. We can read a record from a disk and make changes to that record on the same disk. Moreover, we can add records to the disk and we can delete records from it.

DIRECT (RANDOM)-ACCESS FEATURE

This type of processing is extremely advantageous for specific applications. Suppose, for example, a police department wishes to obtain information on three known criminals immediately. Suppose too that the department maintains a 100,000 record criminal file. If the criminal file were on tape (a sequential medium) each tape record would be read, in sequence, until the appropriate ones were found.

To read 100,000 data records would require some time. If, however, the file were on a disk pack, then each of the three records could be accessed directly, in a much shorter time period. We merely supply the key data field, which may be Man Number or Prison Record Number. Where time is critical and random processing is frequently required, disks are far more suitable than tapes. For **online** updating where immediate processing of data is performed, a disk file is usually used, since individual detail records can update the disk file quickly and easily.

Direct-access files are used with increasing frequency for business applications. Large Accounts Receivable Systems that may have master files with 50,000 customers may utilize a disk so that daily changes to a small number of these customer records can be performed quickly in an online environment (or even in a batch-processing environment). The detail records, with the changes, need not be sorted. They can be used to look up the disk record, by providing the key field such as Customer Number. Changes can then be made to existing accounts; new accounts can be added and accounts with no balance or no activity in recent months can be deleted. All this can be performed on a single master disk; no re-creation is necessary.

Notice that this type of random processing is timesaving only if a relatively small number of records need be altered on a relatively large file. If most of the records have some activity, then it is just as efficient to sort the detail file and use a magnetic tape for the master file in a batch-processing environment. In this way, the reading of the tape file will result in most of the records being processed. Thus excessive read commands for bypassing records would not be a factor. Note, however, that tape processing would require a **new** output tape for each run.

It should be noted that a sequential file can also be established on disk, **without** any key fields. In such a case, the disk is essentially being used as a high-speed tape.

In short, a disk is extremely advantageous for processing records randomly (or directly), as well as sequentially. Disks do, however, possess some inherent limitations.

(a) The disk drives are relatively expensive devices compared to others, such as tape drives.
(b) The identification of disk files, just as with tapes, often results in some problems. Disk files, like tape files, cannot be visibly read; hence labels, both external (physically glued to the pack) or internal (programmed data labels), are required.
(c) Tape update procedures usually result in a new master file that is created from the previous master file and a series of change records; the previous master can always be used as backup, should the new master be defective and a re-creation process deemed necessary. Since update procedures on a master disk file add to or delete from the one master, re-creation, if it becomes necessary, is very difficult unless some duplicate file is created.

Table 22.1 reviews the basic advantages and disadvantages of disk processing.

TABLE 22.1 ADVANTAGES AND DISADVANTAGES OF DISK PROCESSSNG

Advantages

Same ⎡ 1. Can store millions of characters
as   ⎨ 2. Suitable for high-speed processing
tape ⎣ 3. Any size record length
      4. Direct access capability
      5. May be used for **both** I-O during a single run

Disadvantages

      1. Disk drives are relatively expensive
      2. Identification is a problem
      3. Since disk updates are performed directly on master disks, recreation, if it becomes necessary, is somewhat difficult unless a duplicate file is created.

Disk files are created as computer output or by key-to-disk devices. Like key-to-tape encoders, there are two types of key-to-disk encoders: stand-alone and key-to-disk preparation systems. The latter type, with the use of a small processor, formats, edits, and verifies disk data in addition to recording it. The key-to-disk preparation system is far more prevalent in business today.

Because of the cost of these devices, many businesses still utilize other input media and then record data onto a disk via a normal updating procedure.

RECORDING DATA ON A DISK

A typical disk storage unit consists of a series of platters or disks resembling phonograph records. These are arranged in a vertical stack called a **disk pack,** as shown in Figure 22.3. Depending on the manufacturer, the disk pack can contain a varying number of disks. Figure 22.3, for example, illustrates an 11-platter disk pack.

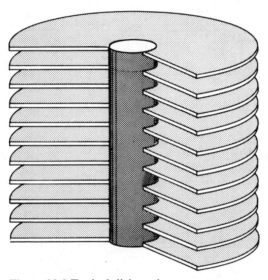

Figure 22.3 Typical disk pack.

Data may be recorded on both sides of the disk. The upper surface of the top disk and the lower surface of the bottom disk cannot be utilized for recording data since they tend to gather dust. Hence, in an 11-platter disk pack there are 20 recording surfaces.

Each of the recording surfaces may be accessed by its own individual read/write head, which is capable of both retrieving and writing information. The read/write heads are on access arms that function like the arm of a record player. See Figure 22.4.

Data is recorded on the disk's recording surfaces. Each surface consists of a series of numbered concentric tracks, as shown in Figure 22.5. Here, again, the number of tracks depends on the specific disk pack, but 200 to 400 tracks per disk is not uncommon. Each track can store information in the form of magnetized bits. Although it may appear as if track number 398, for example, would contain far less data than track number 1, all tracks store exactly the same amount of data. That is, data is stored more compactly or densely in higher track numbers that have smaller surface areas. We say that the **recording density** varies from one track to another.

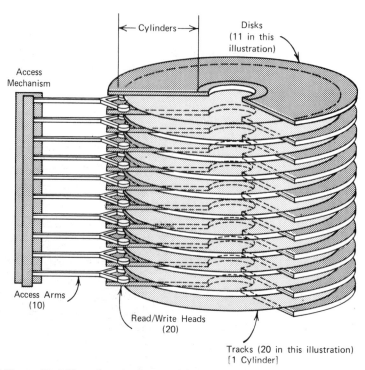

Figure 22.4 How data is accessed from a disk pack. Each read/write head accesses a specific surface. The read/write heads move in and out together as a function of the access mechanism.

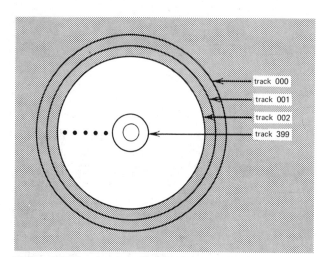

Figure 22.5 Tracks on a disk surface.

The amount of data that can be stored on a track also varies from manufacturer to manufacturer. Typically, each track can store thousands and even tens of thousands of characters or bytes. The storage capacity of a disk pack is equal to the number of bytes per track multiplied by the number of tracks multiplied by the number of recording surfaces. This is usually in the millions of bytes, or megabyte, range. Thus, a disk that can store 10,000 bytes per track, that has 200 tracks per surface, and that has 20 recording surfaces has a 40 megabyte (written 40 MB) capacity.

An important feature of the disk pack is the **cylinder** concept. One way of understanding this concept is to visualize, for example, all the tracks numbered 050 **on the entire pack,** as shown in Figure 22.6.

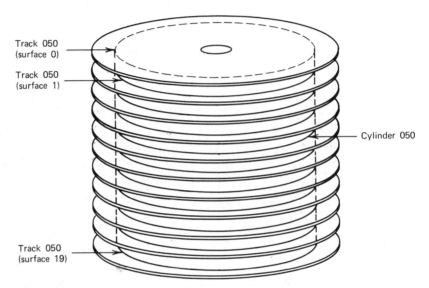

Track 050
(surface 0)

Track 050
(surface 1)

Cylinder 050

Track 050
(surface 19)

Figure 22.6 The cylinder concept on a magnetic disk.

The stack of vertical tracks can then be thought of as forming a hypothetical cylinder. There are, therefore, 203 cylinders on a 203-track disk pack, numbered 000 to 202.

Note that disk files may be blocked and may contain standard labels just as with tape processing.

A. ORGANIZATION OF FILES ON DISK

You will recall that the term **file** refers to a collection of related records. We speak of an Accounts Receivable file, for example, as being the collection of all records of customers who owe money to the company. We will now discuss the various ways in which files can be stored on a disk storage unit. With an understanding of how disk files can be organized, business and data processing students will be able to see the advantages of utilizing disk storage for meeting the requirements of information processing today.

There are generally four different ways in which information can be organized on a magnetic disk: **standard sequential, indexed sequential, direct,** and **relative.** We will now discuss each of these types of file organization in greater depth.

STANDARD SEQUENTIAL FILE ORGANIZATION

The simplest type of disk file organization is standard sequential. This type of file is identical in concept to the way in which information is stored on magnetic tape. Typically, the records to be stored on a standard sequential file are first sorted into some sequence such as customer number, part number, employee number, and so on. When this sorted file is stored on disk, it is then relatively easy to locate a given record. The record with employee number 00986, for example, would be physically located between records with employee numbers 00985 and 00987.

The main disadvantage with this type of processing, however, is that if we want to access **only** the 986th record in a standard sequential disk file, the read/write heads must first read past 985 records in order to be in the proper position. This process of reading past records can consume valuable time. Thus this type of file is identical to a sequential tape file as shown in Figure 22.7. Note that the part of the disk file illustrated appears in cylinder 000, the outermost cylinder. In effect, a standard sequential disk file utilizes the disk as if it were a high-speed tape.

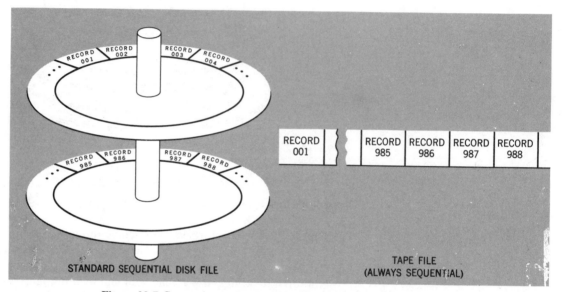

Figure 22.7 Comparison of sequential disk and tape files.

This type of file organization on disk is efficient only when there is a large number of records, such as in a major company's Payroll file and when most or all of these would be required for processing. In that case, little time would be wasted in locating a particular record, since the read/write heads would be passing over the previous records anyway to process them. However, if all or most of the records in a file are **not** ordinarily required during processing for a given run, then the access time of sequential processing can sometimes be excessive. For example, suppose a company has an Inventory file with 10,000 records stored on a disk, with each record pertaining to a different part that is required by the sales department of the company. Suppose that most of the time the file is used to process only a small number of records. As an example, each day only those records pertaining to merchandise sold are updated to reflect the new stock status. If, on the average, only 1200 different items are sold daily, of the total 10,000 items, then much processing time would be wasted if a standard sequential file were used.

Standard sequential file organization, therefore, is not an efficient method when only small numbers of records are required for processing from a relatively large file. Standard sequential file organization is also not an efficient method when records required for processing must be accessed in some sequence other than the one in which the file is organized. That is, when input is entered randomly to update or make inquiries about a sequential disk file, then this access method is extremely inefficient. Suppose, for example, that inquiries about an Accounts Receivable disk file are made periodically throughout the day. If such inquiries represent a significant volume and if they are entered randomly, then access time could be excessive, unless another method of file organization were selected.

The three other commonly used methods of file organization for disk, indexed sequential, direct, and relative, offer alternatives to this processing problem. These methods of organization can utilize the disk's direct-access ability more effectively.

INDEXED SEQUENTIAL
(ISAM) FILE ORGANIZATION

An indexed sequential file is a method of organization that facilitates random processing of disk files. The term ISAM stands for Indexed Sequential Access Method. An index, or reference table, is maintained as information is recorded on the disk. This index essentially references a **key field** within each record of the file and indicates the corresponding address of that record. The key field, such as employee number, part number, and so on, within the disk record must be designated by the programmer as a unique field. Therefore, when a specific record is required for processing, the computer can check the reference table or index to determine the address or location of that record once the key field is supplied. The address for a disk record consists of the cylinder and track numbers. It should be noted that the index is stored on the same disk pack as the file that it references.

Once the address has been obtained from the index, the access mechanism can move directly to the appropriate cylinder without requiring the read/write heads to read past all the previous records in the file until the desired one is found. This concept is analogous to a book's index that has unique subjects (keys) and their corresponding page numbers (addresses). Thus a specific topic can be accessed from the index without having to read the book from the beginning until that topic is found.

The programmer states, for example, that the social security number of each record within the employee file is to serve as a key field. This is appropriate, since all social security numbers are unique. The computer then establishes the index on the disk with references to the addresses of employee records, based on their social security numbers. To access a specific record, the social security number of the desired record is supplied, and the computer "looks up" its address on the index and then moves the access mechanism accordingly. Thus, when records must be accessed in a random manner, indexed sequential file organization can result in a substantial amount of time saved as compared to standard sequential organization. Suppose, for example, that the manager of a company wants to retrieve information pertaining to 1000 employees from a 75,000-employee file. The requested employee data is not sequenced. With an indexed sequential file, it is a relatively simple matter to read and extract these records randomly. Thus the term random-access implies that records are to be processed or accessed in some order other than the one in which they were written on the disk.

DIRECT FILE
ORGANIZATION

Another method of disk organization is called direct organization. In this type of file, records are accessed by a key field that, through some arithmetic calculations, reduces to the actual address (cylinder and track numbers) of the record, without the necessity to first seek the record and its address from an index. Suppose, for example, that the value of a specific key field, such as Part Number, can be multiplied by 85 and then subtracted from 23115 to yield the cylinder number where the record is located. In addition, suppose that if that part number is divided by 63, the result is the track number. Thus, no table is required from which the actual address is searched; instead, some mathematical calculations are performed by the computer according to programmer-supplied formulas to yield the address.

Although direct organization can result in extremely fast access of specific records, in practice there are several factors that must be considered before this type of organization is adopted. More programming effort is required with direct files, since it is necessary for the programmer to supply the formula for converting the key fields into actual addresses. It should be noted that the example above used extremely simple formulas to determine the address. In reality, very complex formulas are often necessary. This is usually the case since programmers can only use specified areas of the disk for their files; the remaining areas may be either filled with other data or have a "dedicated" use. As a consequence, the task of finding the appropriate formulas to refer to only certain available addresses can become very difficult. In addition to this difficulty, complex formulas may result in increased access time as compared to indexed sequential organization. It might require more time for the computer to perform the calculation to find the address than to look up the address in the index. Because of the aforementioned considerations, direct files are not as commonly used in business applications as indexed sequential files.

RELATIVE FILE ORGANIZATION

You will recall that the relative method may also be used for directly accessing a disk file. With this method, each record is identified by an integer that specifies its record number and its address.

B. PROCESSING SEQUENTIAL DISK FILES

For processing standard sequential disk files, we typically use the following SELECT statement:

PROCESSING A SEQUENTIAL DISK FILE

SELECT file name ASSIGN TO

$\begin{cases} \text{DA-S[-(external name)]} \\ \text{SYSnnn-DA-(device no.)-S[-(external name)]} \end{cases}$

[ORGANIZATION IS SEQUENTIAL]

In the ASSIGN clause, the entries have the following meaning:

1. DA-S-(external name)

   DA—Direct Access
   S—sequential
   external name—programmer-supplied name; 1–8 characters

2. SYSnnn-DA-(device no.)-(external name)

   SYSnnn—system number; nnn = 001-256
   DA—Direct Access
   device no.—manufacturer-supplied number
   external name—programmer-supplied; 1–8 characters

Examples

SELECT DISK1-OUT ASSIGN TO DA-S-MASTER.
SELECT DISK2-IN ASSIGN TO SYS007-DA-3340-S-DETAIL.

The ORGANIZATION clause in the SELECT statement is required for some computers. As the name implies, it indicates how the file will be established or organized.

For standard sequential disk processing, the only entry that requires unique coding is this SELECT statement. That is, processing disk files sequentially is performed in **exactly** the same manner as was discussed previously for tape processing. Even label records and blocking are the same.

C. PROCESSING INDEXED SEQUENTIAL (ISAM) DISK FILES

1. CREATING AN ISAM FILE

All disk files that are to be randomly accessed—ISAM, direct, or relative—are usually created in sequence. That is, the file is created by reading each input record, in sequence, and writing the output disk records in the same sequence.

For ISAM files, an index is created that stores the key field for each record along with the corresponding disk address for that record. Thus, even though we are creating a file in sequence, we must indicate what the KEY field for each record is so that the index may be created. The index will be used for accessing the disk file randomly at some later date. The key field is usually numeric and must be unique for each record. Fields such as ACCT-NO, SOCSEC-NO, PART-NO, and so on are all acceptable key fields. The key field is the first data field on each disk record.

The SELECT statement for an ISAM file that is to be created sequentially would be as follows:

CREATING AN ISAM FILE

SELECT (file name) ASSIGN TO

$$\begin{cases} \text{DA-I[-(external name)]} \\ \text{SYSnnn-DA-(device no.)-I[-(external name)]} \end{cases}$$

[ORGANIZATION IS INDEXED]

ACCESS IS SEQUENTIAL

RECORD KEY IS (data name)

The device assignment in the ASSIGN clause is **exactly** the same as for standard sequential disk files except that an ⟦I⟧ appears in the entry to denote Indexed.

The clause ORGANIZATION IS INDEXED is required on some computers to indicate that the file is to be created with an index. Note that even though we are creating the file sequentially, we must instruct the computer to establish an index for future random accessing.

Since ISAM files may be accessed either sequentially or randomly, the ACCESS clause must be used to denote which method will be used.

The RECORD KEY is used to name the key field that will be used to form the index. This field will normally be the first data field defined within the disk file. It must have a unique value for each record and it must be numeric.

Creating the ISAM file is performed in exactly the same manner as creating a tape or a standard sequential disk file, with some minor exceptions. See Figure 22.8 for an illustration of a program that creates an ISAM file sequentially.

```
IDENTIFICATION DIVISION.
PROGRAM-ID. CREATISAM.
***************************************************
*      THIS PROGRAM CREATES AN INDEXED
*        SEQUENTIAL DISK FILE FROM AN
*               INPUT CARD FILE.
***************************************************
ENVIRONMENT DIVISION.
INPUT-OUTPUT SECTION.
FILE-CONTROL.
    SELECT PAYROLL-FILE ASSIGN TO UR-S-SYSIN.
    SELECT MASTER-FILE ASSIGN TO DA-I-MASTER
            ACCESS IS SEQUENTIAL
            RECORD KEY IS ISAM-SSNO.
DATA DIVISION.
FILE SECTION.
FD  PAYROLL-FILE
    LABEL RECORDS ARE OMITTED
    RECORD CONTAINS 80 CHARACTERS
    DATA RECORD IS PAYROLL-REC.
01  PAYROLL-REC.
    02   SSNO-IN            PIC 9(9).
    02   NAME-IN            PIC X(20).
    02   SALARY-IN          PIC 9(5).
    02   ADDTL-DATA-IN      PIC X(46).
FD  MASTER-FILE
    LABEL RECORDS ARE STANDARD
    RECORD CONTAINS 100 CHARACTERS
    BLOCK CONTAINS 20 RECORDS
    DATA RECORD IS MASTER-REC.
01  MASTER-REC.
    02   ISAM-DELETE-CODE   PIC X.            ──── to be explained
    02   ISAM-SSNO          PIC 9(9).              under DELETE CODE
    02   ISAM-NAME          PIC X(20).
    02   ISAM-SALARY        PIC 9(5).
    02   ADDTL-DATA         PIC X(65).
WORKING-STORAGE SECTION.
01  WORK-AREAS.
    02   EOF                PIC 9 VALUE 0.
PROCEDURE DIVISION.
    OPEN INPUT PAYROLL-FILE OUTPUT MASTER-FILE.
    READ PAYROLL-FILE AT END MOVE 1 TO EOF.
    PERFORM CREATE-RTN UNTIL EOF = 1.
    CLOSE PAYROLL-FILE, MASTER-FILE.
    STOP RUN.
CREATE-RTN.
    MOVE LOW-VALUES TO ISAM-DELETE-CODE.
    MOVE SSNO-IN TO ISAM-SSNO.
    MOVE NAME-IN TO ISAM-NAME.
    MOVE SALARY-IN TO ISAM-SALARY.
    MOVE ADDTL-DATA-IN TO ADDTL-DATA.
    WRITE MASTER-REC INVALID KEY              to be explained
            DISPLAY 'INVALID RECORD', MASTER-REC.   under INVALID KEY
    READ PAYROLL-FILE AT END MOVE 1 TO EOF.
```

Figure 22.8

DELETE CODE

Note in Figure 22.8 that prior to the key field, ISAM-SSNO, there is a one-position field called ISAM-DELETE-CODE. That field must have LOW-VALUES or blank as its contents for all active records. The value of that field changes only when we want to delete the record, as will be discussed later in the chapter. Hence, prior to the key field, establish a one-position field and move LOW-VALUES (or SPACES) into it before writing a disk record.

INVALID KEY

Examine the WRITE statement in Figure 22.8. Note that it includes an IN-VALID KEY clause. The INVALID KEY clause tests to see if there are any records that have the same or duplicate keys or that have blank keys. If, for example, two records have the same SSNO or if a record has a blank SSNO, the index would not be able to associate the record with a disk address. In that case, we say that the record has an INVALID KEY.

An INVALID KEY option may accompany a WRITE statement. The computer will execute the clauses following INVALID KEY if the disk record being created contains a blank key or if the key duplicates one already on the disk file. The format for using the INVALID KEY is:

$$\underline{\text{WRITE}} \text{ (record name)} \left[\underline{\text{INVALID}} \text{ KEY} \left(\begin{array}{c} \text{imperative} \\ \text{statement(s)} \end{array} \right) \right]$$

You will see shortly, that when reading from an ISAM file, we can use the INVALID KEY test as well:

$$\underline{\text{READ}} \text{ (file name)} \left[\underline{\text{INVALID}} \text{ KEY} \left(\begin{array}{c} \text{imperative} \\ \text{statement(s)} \end{array} \right) \right]$$

2. ACCESSING AN ISAM FILE

An ISAM file may be read from, or accessed, sequentially or randomly. Suppose, for example, that we have an inventory disk file that is in PART-NO sequence and contains the quantity on hand for each part.

a. Sequential access—we may print a weekly status report that is also in PART-NO sequence, which means that we would read or access the disk sequentially.

b. Random access—on the other hand, when a purchase is made, we may want to access the disk's PART-NO directly to make certain that a sufficient quantity is on hand. In this case, we would be accessing the disk file randomly. Since purchase orders are **not** entered in PART-NO order, the method of accessing the disk is random.

The SELECT statement for accessing an ISAM disk file would include the following:

```
                   ACCESSING AN ISAM FILE
SELECT (file name) ASSIGN TO

{ DA-I[-(external name)]                    }
{ SYSnnn-DA-(device no.)-I[-(external name)]}

[ORGANIZATION IS INDEXED]

               { SEQUENTIAL }
ACCESS IS      { RANDOM     }

RECORD KEY IS (data name)
```

Assuming that the ORGANIZATION clause is optional and omitting the RE-CORD KEY for a moment, consider the following illustrations.

Example 1

Suppose we wish to read from a tax table file on disk. Detail employee card records have salary amount as a data field. For each of these records, we wish to find the corresponding tax amount from the table. The SELECT clauses in the ENVIRONMENT DIVISION would contain the following entries:

Since the detail data cards are not in sequence by salary, the tax table file must be accessed randomly. In the above case, the tax table file is used only for input and is so defined in the PROCEDURE DIVISION.

Example 2

A group of input transaction tape records is used to create an indexed sequential disk file. The ENVIRONMENT DIVISION SELECT clause entries are as follows:

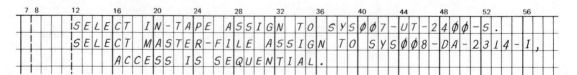

Keep in mind that the device specification is computer dependent.

Example 3

An update program will use detail cards to update every record on a master disk file. The detail cards are in the same sequence as the master disk file.

The ENVIRONMENT DIVISION SELECT clause entries are as follows:

```
SELECT CARD-FILE ASSIGN TO SYS009-UR-2540R-S.
SELECT MASTER-FILE ASSIGN TO SYS002-DA-2314-I,
       ACCESS IS SEQUENTIAL.
```

Since the card data is in the same order as the disk records, each disk record will be accessed in sequence. Thus the access method of the disk file is sequential.

Table 22.2 reviews the ACCESS clause for the file organizations discussed thus far.

TABLE 22.2

File Type / Clause	Sequential files (tape or disk)	Output ISAM files	Input ISAM files
ACCESS IS	SEQUENTIAL (or omitted)	SEQUENTIAL	RANDOM or SEQUENTIAL

For accessing indexed sequential files **sequentially,** we include the RECORD KEY entry along with the SELECT statement as above:

RECORD KEY IS (data name)

The data name specified in the RECORD KEY is the first data field in the disk record (following a one-position blank). To actually read from the disk, in sequence, we code the program in exactly the same manner as for tape or standard sequential disk.

For accessing ISAM files **randomly,** we need to have an additional detail file, frequently on cards or tape, that will indicate which disk records we want to read or access. This detail file will contain, for each record, the field corresponding to RECORD KEY on the disk. That is, suppose we wish to access records that have PART-NO as the key field on an ISAM file. We must read in detail records containing the actual PART-NOs we want accessed. If the detail file is on cards, let us call the part number fields CD-PT-NO. We must instruct the computer that CD-PT-NO will be supplying the key field entry we wish to access. To do this we must perform the following:

1. Read the detail record
   (each record contains CD-PT-NO)
2. Move CD-PT-NO to WS-PT-NO
   (move the field to a WORKING-STORAGE entry)
3. Instruct the computer to look up or access the disk record that has a key field equal to WS-PT-NO

When the card's part number, CD-PT-NO, is moved to a WORKING-STORAGE entry, it becomes a NOMINAL KEY—the field whose contents must equal the RECORD KEY on the ISAM file for look-up purposes.

On some computers, this field is indicated by specifying NOMINAL KEY in the SELECT statement:

```
          ACCESSING AN ISAM FILE RANDOMLY
SELECT (file name) ASSIGN TO

 ⎰ DA-I[-(external name)]                              ⎱
 ⎱ SYSnnn-DA-(device no.)-I[-(external name)] ⎰

[ORGANIZATION IS INDEXED]

ACCESS IS RANDOM

RECORD KEY IS (data name)

[NOMINAL KEY IS (data name)]
```

Example

```
SELECT ISAM-FILE ASSIGN TO DA-I-MASTER
    ORGANIZATION INDEXED
    ACCESS RANDOM
    RECORD KEY IS PART-NO
    NOMINAL KEY IS WS-PT-NO.
```

To access the disk record, we must read in the detail record, move its CD-PT-NO to WS-PT-NO, and then read the disk:

```
READ DETAIL-FILE AT END MOVE 1 TO EOF.
MOVE CD-PT-NO TO WS-PT-NO.
READ ISAM-FILE INVALID KEY STOP RUN.
```

The record from ISAM-FILE will have a RECORD KEY equal to WS-PT-NO.

Note that when reading a disk file randomly, it is not necessary to test for an AT END condition; instead, we can include an INVALID KEY test.

On some computers, the NOMINAL KEY is **not** coded in the SELECT statement. Rather, it is specified in the READ itself:

```
READ  ISAM-FILE  KEY IS WS-PT-NO  ←——————— Used in place
                                              of NOMINAL KEY
            INVALID KEY STOP RUN          on some computers.
```

Note that the computer executes the INVALID KEY option if the WS-PT-NO does not match any of the disk records.

Example

Suppose we read a disk TABLE-FILE as input that has as its key field CITY. This file contains each city and its corresponding sales tax. We also read an indexed sequential disk file that is in transaction-number sequence. The program will read the transaction file, process it, look up the CITY of each transaction record on the TABLE-FILE to obtain CITY-TAX, and print a report.

The SELECT clauses for the two disk input files are:

Note that a NOMINAL KEY is not necessary when reading records **sequentially** from an indexed sequential file. In that case, we need not indicate to the computer which record we are seeking, since we are reading them in the order in which they appear.

3. UPDATING AN ISAM FILE

You will recall that updating a tape required **three** files, each in sequence by a specific key field:

DETAIL-FILE—contains change records

PREVIOUS-MASTER—contains master file information current through the previous updating cycle

NEW-MASTER—combines DETAIL-FILE data and PREVIOUS-MASTER data to form one updated file

A main advantage of disk processing is that master records can be updated directly without having to create a new file.

To accomplish this, the master disk must be opened as an I-O file—it is used as input (I) because we must read or access the disk, and it is used as output (O) because we will write onto it. The master disk has its records stored by RECORD KEY and the detail file accesses each record to be updated using the NOMINAL KEY. Data from the detail file is moved to the master file and we issue a REWRITE to add the additional data. Thus for updating an ISAM file, we have:

UPDATING AN ISAM FILE

1) OPEN the ISAM file as I-O
2) Read a detail record
   Read a master record, where NOMINAL KEY is obtained from the detail record
3) At this point, we have a detail record and corresponding master record that needs to be updated
4) Make the changes to the disk record directly
5) REWRITE the disk record

Example

Assume that cards are entered as detail records with a transaction number and an amount of transaction. The amount from the card is to be added to the corresponding disk record, where the KEY field for the disk is its transaction number. STORE-TRAN is the NOMINAL KEY—the WORKING-STORAGE entry that will indicate the record we want to access from the disk:

```
      OPEN INPUT CARD-IN, I-O DISK-FILE.
      READ CARD-IN AT END MOVE 1 TO EOF.
      PERFORM CALC-RTN UNTIL EOF = 1.
      CLOSE CARD-IN, DISK-FILE.
      STOP RUN.
CALC-RTN.
      MOVE TRAN OF CARD-REC TO STORE-TRAN.
      READ DISK-FILE INVALID KEY PERFORM ERR-RTN.
      ADD AMT OF CARD-REC TO TOTAL OF DISK-REC.
      REWRITE DISK-REC INVALID KEY PERFORM ERR-RTN.
      READ CARD-FILE AT END MOVE 1 TO EOF.
```

When defining a disk as an I-O file, it is possible to perform all three of the following update procedures:

1. Creation of new records—new hires must be added to a payroll file. A simple WRITE command may be used to create new records.
2. Deletion of some old records—resignations must be deleted from a payroll file. Special delete codes must be placed in the key.
3. Changes to specific records—promotions, raises, and transfers must be incorporated in existing records. The REWRITE verb may be used to alter existing records.

4. DELETING RECORDS FROM AN ISAM FILE

Note that records are not usually physically removed from an ISAM file during updating; instead, they are deactivated. A one-byte field is established as the first item of an ISAM record. For normal processing, that field will contain LOW-VALUES, the lowest character in the collating sequence for the specific compiler. To deactivate (or delete) a record, we simply code the following:

```
01  DISK-REC.
    02   DELETE-CODE   PIC X.
    02   RECORD-KEY    PIC 9(5).
        .
        .
        .
PROCEDURE DIVISION.
        .
        .
        .
    MOVE HIGH-VALUES TO DELETE-CODE.
    REWRITE DISK-REC.
```

Examples

1. Consider an update program where card data will be used to change existing records or to create new records. The cards are **not** in the same sequence as the disk. The card format is as follows:

1–9   Social security number
10–79 Payroll data
   80 Code (1-new employee, 2-update, 3-separation from company)

The disk format is as follows:

1   Delete code
2–10 Social security number
11–80 Payroll data

See Figure 22.9 for solution.

The IDENTIFICATION DIVISION of programs utilizing disk is the same as previously described. The ENVIRONMENT DIVISION merely incorporates the specified disk options. Since the disk file is indexed sequential and the records are not accessed in sequence, ACCESS IS RANDOM. Both NOMINAL KEY and RECORD KEY are required for randomly accessed indexed sequential files.

The DATA DIVISION is basically the same as when describing standard sequential files. Note that the NOMINAL KEY, NOM-KEY, is described in WORKING-STORAGE. Note also that disk records generally utilize standard labels unless programmers wish to supply their own labels. The first data field within the disk file is the RECORD KEY.

The PROCEDURE DIVISION entries indicate the format of an update routine. Note, however, that SOC-SEC-NO must be moved to the NOMINAL KEY, NOM-KEY, before a disk record may be accessed. NOMINAL KEY and RECORD KEY must be the same for such records.

  2. See Figure 22.10 for an illustration of a program that accesses an ISAM file sequentially and makes use of the delete code as well.

SELF-EVALUATING
QUIZ

1. A disk may be opened as _____, _____, or _____.
   *****
   INPUT
   OUTPUT
   I-O
2. If OPEN I-O FILE-X is a coded statement, then FILE-X must be a _____ file.
   *****
   disk
3. (T or F) If one record is to be added to a tape file, it can be added to the same tape.
   *****
   F
4. (T or F) If one record is to be added to a disk file, it can be added to the same disk.
   *****
   T
5. A unique field within an indexed sequential file that is used to locate records on a disk pack is called a _____ _____.
   *****
   RECORD KEY

```
IDENTIFICATION DIVISION.
PROGRAM-ID. DISKUP.
ENVIRONMENT DIVISION.
INPUT-OUTPUT SECTION.
FILE-CONTROL.
    SELECT CARDS ASSIGN TO UR-S-SYSIN.
    SELECT DISK-A ASSIGN TO DA-I-SYS005
            ACCESS IS RANDOM
            NOMINAL KEY IS NOM-KEY
            RECORD KEY IS DISK-SSNO.
DATA DIVISION.
FILE SECTION.
FD  CARDS
    LABEL RECORDS ARE OMITTED
    RECORD CONTAINS 80 CHARACTERS
    DATA RECORD IS IN-REC.
01  IN-REC.
    02  SOC-SEC-NO          PIC X(9).
    02  PAYROLL-DATA         PIC X(70).
    02  CODE-FIELD           PIC X.
            88  NEW-EMPLOYEE                   VALUE '1'.
            88  SEPARATION                     VALUE '3'.
FD  DISK-A
    LABEL RECORDS ARE STANDARD
    RECORD CONTAINS 80 CHARACTERS
    BLOCK CONTAINS 50 RECORDS
    DATA RECORD IS DISK-REC.
01  DISK-REC.
    02  DELETE-CODE          PIC X.
    02  DISK-SSNO            PIC X(9).
    02  DISK-DATA            PIC X(70).
WORKING-STORAGE SECTION.
01  WORK-AREAS.
    02  EOF        PIC 9 VALUE 0.
    02  NOM-KEY    PIC X(9).
PROCEDURE DIVISION.
    OPEN INPUT CARDS, I-O DISK-A.        ◄── When disks are updated
    READ CARDS AT END MOVE 1 TO EOF.          they are opened as I-O
    PERFORM CALC-RTN UNTIL EOF = 1.
    CLOSE CARDS, DISK-A.
    STOP RUN.
CALC-RTN.
    IF NEW-EMPLOYEE PERFORM NEW-RTN
            ELSE IF SEPARATION PERFORM DELETE-RTN
    ELSE PERFORM UPDATE.
    READ CARDS AT END MOVE 1 TO EOF.
NEW-RTN.
    MOVE SOC-SEC-NO TO DISK-SSNO.
    MOVE PAYROLL-DATA TO DISK-DATA
    WRITE DISK-REC.
UPDATE.
    MOVE SOC-SEC-NO TO NOM-KEY.
    READ DISK-A INVALID KEY STOP RUN.    ◄── Accesses disk record that
                                             corresponds to card record
    MOVE PAYROLL-DATA TO DISK-DATA.
    MOVE SOC-SEC-NO TO DISK-SSNO.
    REWRITE DISK-REC INVALID KEY STOP RUN.  ◄── Disk record is updated with
                                                 card information
DELETE-RTN.
    MOVE SOC-SEC-NO TO NOM-KEY.
    READ DISK-A INVALID KEY STOP RUN.
    MOVE HIGH-VALUES TO DELETE-CODE.
    REWRITE DISK-REC INVALID KEY STOP RUN.
    MOVE LOW-VALUES TO DELETE-CODE.
```

Figure 22.9

```
        IDENTIFICATION DIVISION.
        PROGRAM-ID. SEQISAM.
        **********************************************
        *     THIS PROGRAM ACCESSES AN INDEXED
        *       SEQUENTIAL FILE SEQUENTIALLY.
        *       DATA IS PRINTED FROM THE FILE IN THE
        *       SAME MANNER AS IF THE FILE WAS ON TAPE.
        **********************************************
        ENVIRONMENT DIVISION.
        INPUT-OUTPUT SECTION.
        FILE-CONTROL.
            SELECT MASTER-FILE ASSIGN TO DA-I-SYS004          SELECT Statement
                    ACCESS IS SEQUENTIAL                      for ISAM file,
                    RECORD KEY IS ISAM-SSNO.                  which is to be
            SELECT PRINT-OUT ASSIGN TO UR-S-SYSOUT.           accessed sequentially
        DATA DIVISION.
        FILE SECTION.
        FD  MASTER-FILE
            LABEL RECORDS ARE STANDARD
            BLOCK CONTAINS 20 RECORDS
            RECORD CONTAINS 100 CHARACTERS
            DATA RECORD IS MASTER-REC.
        01  MASTER-REC.                              Will contain HIGH-VALUES
            02  ISAM-DELETE-CODE      PIC X.         if record is to be deleted
            02  ISAM-SSNO             PIC 9(9).      RECORD KEY field
            02  ISAM-NAME             PIC X(20).
            02  ISAM-SALARY           PIC 9(5).
            02  FILLER                PIC X(65).
        FD  PRINT-OUT
            LABEL RECORDS ARE OMITTED
            RECORD CONTAINS 133 CHARACTERS
            DATA RECORD IS PRINT-REC.
        01  PRINT-REC               PIC X(133).
        WORKING-STORAGE SECTION.
        01  WORK-AREAS.
            02  EOF        PIC 9 VALUE 0.
            02  LINE-CT    PIC 99 VALUE ZEROS.
            02  PAGE-CT    PIC 999 VALUE ZEROS.
        01  HDG.
            02  FILLER              PIC X(78)
                    VALUE 'PAYROLL SUMMARY REPORT'
                    JUSTIFIED RIGHT.
            02  FILLER              PIC X(25) VALUE 'PAGE '
                    JUSTIFIED RIGHT.
            02  PAGE-OUT            PIC ZZ9.
            02  FILLER              PIC X(27)  VALUE SPACES.
        01  DETAIL-REC.
            02  FILLER              PIC X(10) VALUE SPACES.
            02  SSNO-OUT            PIC 9(9).
            02  FILLER              PIC X(10) VALUE SPACES.
            02  NAME-OUT            PIC X(20).
            02  FILLER              PIC X(10) VALUE SPACES.
            02  SALARY-OUT          PIC $ZZ,ZZZ.ZZ.
            02  FILLER              PIC X(64) VALUE SPACES.
        PROCEDURE DIVISION.
            OPEN INPUT MASTER-FILE, OUTPUT PRINT-OUT.     Note that an AT END clause
            PERFORM HDG-RTN.                              is used with ISAM file when
            READ MASTER-FILE                              file is accessed sequentially
                AT END MOVE 1 TO EOF.
            PERFORM CALC-RTN THRU CALC-RTN-EXIT UNTIL EOF = 1.
            CLOSE MASTER-FILE, PRINT-OUT.
            STOP RUN.
        CALC-RTN.                                                         Tests for
            IF ISAM-DELETE-CODE = HIGH-VALUES GO TO CALC-RTN-EXIT.        inactive
            MOVE ISAM-SSNO TO SSNO-OUT.                                   record
            MOVE ISAM-NAME TO NAME-OUT.
            MOVE ISAM-SALARY TO SALARY-OUT.
            WRITE PRINT-REC FROM DETAIL-REC AFTER ADVANCING 2 LINES.
            ADD 1 TO LINE-CT.
            IF LINE-CT > 25 PERFORM HDG-RTN.
        CALC-RTN-EXIT.
            READ MASTER-FILE AT END MOVE 1 TO EOF.
        HDG-RTN.
            ADD 1 TO PAGE-CT.
            MOVE PAGE-CT TO PAGE-OUT.
            WRITE PRINT-REC FROM HDG AFTER ADVANCING 0 LINES.
            MOVE ZEROS TO LINE-CT.
```

Figure 22.10

6. A unique field not part of an indexed sequential file that is used to locate records on that file is called a _____ _____.
*****
NOMINAL KEY

7. The first character in an ISAM record is used as a _____. This one-position field will contain _____ for active records. When a record is to be deleted from a file, we move _____ to this one-position field.
*****
delete code
LOW-VALUES
HIGH-VALUES

8. A key field, when specified, must be _____ and _____.
*****
unique
nonblank

9. A PROCEDURE DIVISION test for the duplication of a KEY field is called the _____ _____ option.
*****
INVALID KEY

10. The INVALID KEY option is part of a _____ or _____ statement for disk files.
*****
READ
WRITE (REWRITE)

11. The INVALID KEY option tests the validity of the _____ KEY.
*****
RECORD

12. If READ FILE-X INVALID KEY PERFORM ERROR-1 is executed, ERROR-1 will be performed if _____.
*****
two records on the file have the same KEY

13. The specific key used to locate a record is specified in the _____ DIVISION.
*****
ENVIRONMENT [or in the PROCEDURE DIVISION as READ . . . KEY IS (   ), depending on the computer.]

14. A REWRITE statement is used to _____.
*****
alter previously existing disk records

15. If a record is to be added to a disk file, a (WRITE, REWRITE) statement is used.
*****
WRITE

16. If REWRITE REC-X is executed, and REC-X is part of FILE-X, then FILE-X must have been opened as _____ and a _____ command must have preceded the REWRITE.
*****
I-O
READ

17. The REWRITE statement is most often used as part of _____ programs.
   *****
   update

18. An update is _____.
   *****
   the process of making a file current with new detail data

19. The three steps generally necessary to update a file are _____,
   _____, and _____.
   *****
   creation of new records
   deletion of some old records
   additions to some existing records

20. To change or add to an existing record requires the use of the _____
   verb for disk files.
   *****
   REWRITE

21. Consider the following input card record:

   cc1–   Code (1-new account; 2-update of old account; 3-deletion)
      2–5   Transaction No.
      6–80 Transaction data

   Consider the following master disk record:

      1–   Deletion Code
      2–5   Transaction No.
      6–80 Transaction data

   Write a PROCEDURE DIVISION routine to update the master file with input
   data.
   *****

```
PROCEDURE DIVISION.
    OPEN INPUT TRANS-CARDS, I-O DISK-FILE.
    READ TRANS-CARDS AT END MOVE 1 TO EOF.
    PERFORM CALC-RTN UNTIL EOF = 1.
    CLOSE TRANS-CARDS, DISK-FILE.
    STOP RUN.
CALC-RTN.
    MOVE TRANS-REC TO DISK-REC.
    IF CODE-X = 1 PERFORM NEW-ACCT
         ELSE IF CODE-X = 2 PERFORM UPDATE-RTN
              ELSE PERFORM DELETE-RTN.
    READ TRANS-CARDS AT END MOVE 1 TO EOF.
NEW-ACCT.
    MOVE LOW-VALUES TO DELETE-CODE.
    WRITE DISK-REC
         INVALID KEY STOP RUN.
UPDATE-RTN.
    MOVE LOW-VALUES TO DELETE-CODE.
    REWRITE DISK-REC
         INVALID KEY STOP RUN.
DELETE-RTN.
    MOVE HIGH-VALUES TO DELETE-CODE.
    REWRITE DISK-REC
         INVALID KEY STOP RUN.
```

D. PROCESSING DIRECT FILES

A direct file has a key field that is actually used to compute the disk address. For example, suppose a direct file has a field of TRANS-NO, where TRANS-NO is three digits. We can establish the first digit as equal to the disk's track number and the other digits as equal to the record number within that track. Therefore, a record with TRANS-NO 123 would be placed on track 1, record number 23. This is a rather simplified example, but such a direct conversion from key to address can be made. In this way, there is no need to establish any index and records may be accessed directly, simply by supplying the conversion formula.

As with indexed sequential files, direct files are usually

    a. created sequentially

    b. accessed sequentially or randomly

Hence the SELECT statement for a direct file may be coded as follows:

```
        SELECT STATEMENT FOR DIRECT FILE

 SELECT (file name) ASSIGN TO

 { DA-D[-(external name)]                    }
 { SYSnnn-DA-(device no.)-D[-(external name)]}

 [ORGANIZATION IS DIRECT]

              { RANDOM     }
 ACCESS IS    { SEQUENTIAL }

 ACTUAL KEY IS (data name)
```

The ACTUAL KEY is computed from the direct file's key field. The ACTUAL KEY is usually a WORKING-STORAGE entry that contains the actual disk address. It must be unique, numeric, and nonblank; like the NOMINAL KEY, it is stored in WORKING-STORAGE.

When creating a direct file, the only novel programming entry is the mathematical routine used for calculating the disk record's location. See Figure 22.11 for an illustration of a program that creates a direct file. Note the arithmetic routine for calculating TRACK-NO.

Accessing the direct file can be performed either sequentially or randomly. Sequential access means that disk records are read and processed as with tape and standard sequential disks. Random access means that another input file, a detail file, indicates which disk records are to be accessed.

Suppose that a master criminal file has been created with SSNO used to calculate the ACTUAL KEY—the field used for computing each disk record's address. To access any record on this file, we read in a field called IN-SSNO, perform the calculations necessary for obtaining the address, and store that address in a field called SSNO-CONVERTED. If we define the ACTUAL KEY as SSNO-CONVERTED when we say READ DIRECT-FILE, the computer will locate the record whose address is indicated at SSNO-CONVERTED. (See Figure 22.11 again).

All the PROCEDURE DIVISION entries that apply to ISAM files apply here as well:

```
              CLAUSES USED TO UPDATE RANDOM-ACCESS FILES
 OPEN I-O      —use when a direct file is being updated
 REWRITE       —to write back onto a direct file (can only use REWRITE
                 when file is opened as I-O)
 INVALID KEY   —may be used with READ or WRITE; computer will perform
                 statements within INVALID KEY if record cannot be found
                 or if ACTUAL KEY is blank or not numeric on direct files
```

```
IDENTIFICATION DIVISION.
PROGRAM-ID. CREATEDIR.
*******************************
** THIS PROGRAM CREATES A DIRECT**
** FILE FROM CARD INPUT.         **
*******************************
ENVIRONMENT DIVISION.
INPUT-OUTPUT SECTION.
FILE-CONTROL.
    SELECT CARD-IN ASSIGN TO UR-S-SYSIN.
    SELECT DIRECT-FILE ASSIGN TO DA-D-MASTER
        ACCESS IS RANDOM
        ACTUAL KEY IS ACTUAL-KEY-STORE.
DATA DIVISION.
FILE SECTION.
FD  CARD-IN
    LABEL RECORDS ARE OMITTED
    RECORD CONTAINS 80 CHARACTERS
    DATA RECORD IS IN-REC.
01  IN-REC.
    02  PART-NO              PIC 9(5).
    02  QTY-ON-HAND          PIC 9(4).
    02  TOTAL-PRICE          PIC 9(5)V99.
    02  FILLER               PIC X(64).
FD  DIRECT-FILE
    LABEL RECORDS ARE STANDARD
    RECORD CONTAINS 81 CHARACTERS
    DATA RECORD IS DISK-REC-OUT.
01  DISK-REC-OUT.
    02  DELETE-CODE          PIC X.
    02  DISK-REC-DATA.
        03  D-PART-NO        PIC 9(5).
        03  D-QTY-ON-HAND    PIC 9(4).
        03  D-TOTAL-PRICE    PIC 9(5)V99.
        03  FILLER           PIC X(64).
WORKING-STORAGE SECTION.
01  WORK-AREAS.
    02  EOF                      PIC 9 VALUE 0.
    02  STORE1                   PIC S9(8).
    02  STORE2                   PIC S9(8).
01  ACTUAL-KEY-STORE.
    02  TRACK-NO             PIC S9(5).
    02  RECORD-KEY           PIC 9(5).
PROCEDURE DIVISION.
    OPEN INPUT CARD-IN. OUTPUT DIRECT-FILE.

    READ CARD-IN AT END MOVE 1 TO EOF.
    PERFORM WRITE-RTN UNTIL EOF = 1.
    CLOSE CARD-IN, DIRECT-FILE.
    STOP RUN.
WRITE-RTN.
    MOVE SPACES TO DELETE-CODE.
*****NOTE THAT DELETE-CODE = HIGH-VALUES ONLY WHEN ****
**** A RECORD IS TO BE DELETED.                    ****
    MOVE IN-REC TO DISK-REC-DATA.
    MOVE PART-NO TO STORE1, RECORD-KEY.
    DIVIDE STORE1 BY 97 GIVING STORE2
        REMAINDER TRACK-NO.
****************************************
*****THE ABOVE INSTRUCTION IS ONE METHOD*
*****FOR CALCULATING TRACK NO.***********
****************************************
    WRITE DISK-REC-OUT INVALID KEY
        DISPLAY TRACK-NO, RECORD-KEY.
    READ CARD-IN AT END MOVE 1 TO EOF.
```

Figure 22.11

The main difference, then, between using a direct file and using an ISAM file is that direct files require the coding of a calculation for computing the actual address.

E. PROCESSING RELATIVE DISK FILES

You will recall that this method uses a key field that specifically reflects an actual disk address. We will simply outline this method briefly. Suppose, for example, that Accounts Receivable records are entered in sequence by ACCT-NO. If the ACCT-NOs vary from 0001-9999, then ACCT-NO 1 can be placed in the first disk location, ACCT-NO 2 can be placed in the next and so on. This type of file organization is best used where each record contains a kind of built-in record number. Since not all files lend themselves to this type of processing, relative files are not often used.

The field that supplies the key information, such as ACCT-NO above, is called the RELATIVE KEY. Thus the full format for the SELECT statement for disk files is as follows:

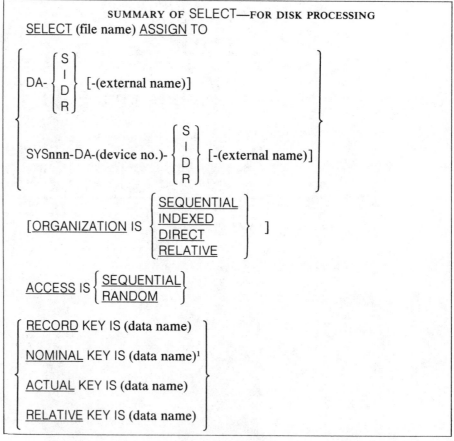

SUMMARY OF SELECT—FOR DISK PROCESSING

[1]Note that the NOMINAL KEY is replaced by the {READ . . . . KEY IS (data name)} on some computers.

Table 22.3 summarizes the use of KEY fields with the different types of file organization.

TABLE 22.3

	ORGANIZATION	ACCESS	KEY
OUTPUT	INDEXED (I) DIRECT (D) RELATIVE (R)	SEQUENTIAL SEQUENTIAL SEQUENTIAL	RECORD KEY ACTUAL KEY RELATIVE KEY
INPUT	INDEXED (I)	SEQUENTIAL	RECORD KEY (NOMINAL KEY optional)[a]
		RANDOM	RECORD KEY NOMINAL KEY
	DIRECT (D)	SEQUENTIAL	ACTUAL KEY
		RANDOM	ACTUAL KEY NOMINAL KEY
	RELATIVE (R)	SEQUENTIAL	no key
		RANDOM	RELATIVE KEY

[a]Where an optional NOMINAL KEY is noted, the programmer may include it to check for INVALID KEY. The INVALID KEY test is performed in the PROCEDURE DIVISION and requires a key field different from RECORD KEY. Note that for 1974 ANS COBOL users, the NOMINAL KEY is replaced by the KEY IS clause, which accompanies the READ statement.

   All coding of PROCEDURE DIVISION entries for random or sequential processing of relative files is similar to the coding of ISAM or direct programs.

SELF-EVALUATING QUIZ

1. To use a direct-access device sequentially is the same as using a _____.
   *****
   high-speed tape

2. When using indexed sequential files, we say that the organization of the file is _____.
   *****
   indexed

3. The initial creation of an indexed sequential file is performed _____.
   *****
   sequentially

4. Addressing of records in indexed sequential files is performed by _____ while addressing of direct files is performed by _____.
   *****
   the input-output control system
   the programmer

5. When **creating** an indexed sequential file ACCESS IS _____. When using an indexed sequential file as input, ACCESS IS either _____ or _____.
   *****
   SEQUENTIAL
   SEQUENTIAL
   RANDOM

6. ACTUAL KEY may not be used with _____ files.
   *****
   indexed sequential (or sequential)
7. (T or F) If ACCT-NO is used to calculate an address for records on a direct
   file then ACCT-NO is the ACTUAL KEY.
   *****
   F—ACCT-NO is used in the calculation and the resulting address is the
   ACTUAL KEY.
8. (T or F) An ACTUAL KEY need not be unique.
   *****
   F—it must be unique.
9. (T or F) Relative file organization is the most popular method for organizing
   a disk file.
   *****
   F—it is the least popular method.

PRACTICE PROBLEM—
WITH SOLUTION

1. Write a program to update a master transaction disk file. The format of the
   disk file is as follows:

   1   Delete code
   2–6   Transaction number
   7–11 Amount xxx.xx
   Labels are standard; blocking factor is 50.
   Transaction number is key field.

   The disk file is to be updated with tape records having the following format:

   1–5   Transaction number
   6–10 Amount xxx.xx
   11–25 Not used
   Labels are standard; blocking factor is 12.

   NOTES:
   (1) Tape records are to update amount fields on disk file. If a tape record
       has the same transaction number as a disk record, process; if not, dis-
       play the tape record as an error.
   (2) Disk records are indexed sequential; tape records are not in sequence
       by transaction number.

   See Figure 22.12 for the solution.

REVIEW QUESTIONS

True False

☐ ☐
☐ ☐

I. True-False Questions
1. Indexed sequential files are frequently referred to as ISAM files.
2. An indexed sequential file is usually created with ACCESS IS RANDOM
   but read with ACCESS IS SEQUENTIAL.

```
IDENTIFICATION DIVISION.
PROGRAM-ID. CHAPT22.
ENVIRONMENT DIVISION.
INPUT-OUTPUT SECTION.
FILE-CONTROL.
    SELECT MASTER-DISK ASSIGN TO DA-I-MASTER
            ACCESS IS RANDOM
            RECORD KEY IS TRAN-NO-DISK
            NOMINAL KEY IS KEY-A.
    SELECT DETAIL-TAPE ASSIGN TO UT-S-SYS004.
DATA DIVISION.
FILE SECTION.
FD  MASTER-DISK
    LABEL RECORDS ARE STANDARD
    BLOCK CONTAINS 50 RECORDS
    DATA RECORD IS DISK-REC.
01  DISK-REC.
    02   DELETE-CODE          PIC X.
    02   TRAN-NO-DISK         PIC 9(5).
    02   AMT                  PIC 999V99.
FD  DETAIL-TAPE
    LABEL RECORDS ARE STANDARD
    RECORD CONTAINS 25 CHARACTERS
    BLOCK CONTAINS 12 RECORDS
    DATA RECORD IS TAPE-REC.
01  TAPE-REC.
    02   TRAN-NO-TAPE         PIC 9(5).
    02   AMT                  PIC 999V99.
    02   FILLER               PIC X(15).
WORKING-STORAGE SECTION.
01  WORK-AREAS.
    02   EOF                  PIC 9 VALUE 0.
    02   KEY-A                PIC 9(5).
PROCEDURE DIVISION.
    OPEN INPUT DETAIL-TAPE, I-O MASTER-DISK.
    READ DETAIL-TAPE AT END MOVE 1 TO EOF.
    PERFORM CALC-RTN THRU CALC-RTN-EXIT UNTIL EOF = 1.
    CLOSE DETAIL-TAPE, MASTER-DISK.
    STOP RUN.
CALC-RTN.
    MOVE TRAN-NO-TAPE TO KEY-A.
    READ MASTER-DISK INVALID KEY
                DISPLAY 'INVALID TAPE RECORD'
                TAPE-REC
                GO TO CALC-RTN-EXIT.
    MOVE AMT OF TAPE-REC TO AMT OF DISK-REC.
    REWRITE DISK-REC.
CALC-RTN-EXIT.
    READ DETAIL-TAPE AT END MOVE 1 TO EOF.
```

Figure 22.12

☐ ☐   3. If the ACCESS IS SEQUENTIAL clause is included in the SELECT statement, then the file may later be accessed randomly if a KEY field is specified.

☐ ☐   4. An ACTUAL KEY would not be used with the following ASSIGN clause: DA-2314-S-OPT

☐ ☐   5. The REWRITE clause may only be used with a file that has been opened as I-O.

☐ ☐   6. The INVALID KEY clause may be used with READ or WRITE statements.

☐ ☐   7. LOW-VALUES is placed in a delete code of an I-O disk record if the record is to be deactivated.

☐ ☐   8. The NOMINAL KEY entry must be a WORKING-STORAGE item.

☐ ☐   9. The ACTUAL KEY entry is only used for direct files.

☐ ☐   10. Disk files are never accessed sequentially.

II. General Questions

1. Write the ENVIRONMENT DIVISION entries for the creation of an indexed sequential file called DISK-FILE.
2. Write the ENVIRONMENT DIVISION entries for an indexed sequential file called IN-FILE that is in transaction number sequence but will be accessed by invoice number.
3. Explain the purpose of the REWRITE statement in a COBOL program.
4. Explain the use of the INVALID KEY option.
5. When is a file opened as I-O?

PROBLEMS 1. Write a program to update a master disk file. The format of the disk file is:

    1   Delete code
    2–5   Customer no.
    6–21 Customer name
    22–26 Mailing address
    27–30 Date of last purchase—month/year
    31–36 Amount owed xxxx.xx
    Labels are standard; blocking factor is 75.
    Customer name is key field.

The disk file is to be updated with card records with the following format:

    1–4   Customer no.
    5–20 Customer name
    21–24 Date of purchase—month/year
    25–29 Amount of purchase xxx.xx
    30–80 Not used

NOTES:

(1) Create a disk record for any card that does not have a corresponding master record (compare on customer no.)
(2) For all cards with corresponding master records (these are master records to be updated), add amount of purchase from card to amount owed on disk and update the date of last purchase.
(3) There need not be a card record for each master record.
(4) Master file is indexed sequential; cards are not in sequence.

2. A table is to be created in storage from the following card records:

    1–5   Product number
    6–10 Unit price xxx.xx
    11–80 Not used
    Product number is key field.

There are 150 product numbers with independent unit prices. Create an indexed sequential disk file from the following tape records:

    1–5   Customer number
    6–20 Customer name
    21–23 Quantity sold
    24–28 Product number
    29–30 Not used
    Labels are standard; blocking factor is 100.

The disk file is to have the following format:

1   Delete code
2–6   Customer number
7–14 Amount owed xxxxxx.xx
15–19 Product number
20–21 Not used
Labels are standard; blocking factor is 100.
Customer number is key field.

Amount owed = Quantity sold × Unit price (from table).

Perform a table lookup using the product number from tape to find the unit price in the table.

3. Three disk files contain the following table records:

File 1   **File 2**
1   Delete code   1   Delete code
2–4   Employee number   2–4   Title number
5–21 Employee name   5–7   Job number
                                     8–21 Job name

File 3
1   Delete code
2   Level number
3–9   Salary xxxxx.xx
10–21 Not used

Labels are standard; blocking factor is 100 for each file.
First field after the delete code of each file represents the key field.

Write a program to create an indexed sequential disk file from the following card records:

1–3   Employee number
4–6   Title number
7–9   Job number
10   Level number
11–80 Not used

The format for the output disk records is as follows:

1   Delete code
2–4   Employee number
5–21 Employee name
22–24 Title number
25–27 Job number
28–41 Job name
42   Level number
43–49 Salary
50–51 Not used
Labels are standard; blocking factor is 75.

Employee name, Job name, and Salary are obtained from the three table files on disk.

(**Hint:** Define three input disk files. Use employee number on card for NOM-INAL KEY to look up employee name, and so on.)

4. A disk file contains the following table records:

   1   Delete code
   2–3 State number
   4–5 County number
   6–8 Tax rate .xxx
   9–11 Not used

   Labels are standard; blocking factor is 100.
   State number is key field.

   Write a program to create an indexed sequential disk file from the following tape records:

   1–20 Customer name
   21–25 Quantity
   26–30 Price/unit xxx.xx
   31–32 State number
   33–34 County number
   35   Not used

   Labels are standard; blocking factor is 50.

   The format for the output disk records is as follows:

   1   Delete code
   2–35 (Same as tape positions 1–34)
   36–45 Amount owed
   46   Not used

   Labels are standard; blocking factor is 75.

   Amount Owed = Quantity × Price/Unit + Tax Rate × (Quantity × Price)
   Tax Rate is obtained from the table.

ADDITION COBOL OPTIONS

CHAPTER 23
ADDITIONAL ENTRIES FOR EDITING AND MAXIMIZING PROGRAM EFFICIENCY

A. INSPECT STATEMENT

The INSPECT statement may be used for replacing a specific character in a data record with another character. Replacing blanks (SPACES) with zeros is a common application of the INSPECT statement. Blanks are invalid in a numeric field but are often erroneously included to imply a zero balance or amount. If an arithmetic operation were performed on such a field, the computer would abort the run. Before performing an arithmetic operation on such a data field, therefore, an INSPECT statement is often executed to replace all blanks with zeros.

The use of the INSPECT verb to substitute one character for another is considered part of a validity checking routine. Validity checking operations are performed on data prior to any file maintenance to ensure, insofar as possible, the accuracy of the data.

Another use of the INSPECT statement is for counting the number of occurrences of a specific character within a record or a field. Hence, the two applications of the INSPECT are:

APPLICATIONS OF INSPECT STATEMENT
1. To count the number of occurrences of specific characters in a data item.
2. To replace specific occurrences of a given character with another character.

There are two formats of the INSPECT statement. Format 1 may be used to perform the first function specified above; that is, count the number of times specific characters occur.

Format 1

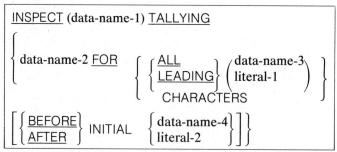

INSPECT (data-name-1) TALLYING

$$\left\{ \begin{array}{l} \text{data-name-2 } \underline{\text{FOR}} \quad \left\{ \begin{array}{l} \left\{ \begin{array}{l} \underline{\text{ALL}} \\ \underline{\text{LEADING}} \end{array} \right\} \left(\begin{array}{l} \text{data-name-3} \\ \text{literal-1} \end{array} \right) \\ \text{CHARACTERS} \end{array} \right\} \\ \left[\left\{ \begin{array}{l} \underline{\text{BEFORE}} \\ \underline{\text{AFTER}} \end{array} \right\} \text{INITIAL} \left\{ \begin{array}{l} \text{data-name-4} \\ \text{literal-2} \end{array} \right\} \right] \end{array} \right\}$$

Examples

```
    7 8   12      16      20      24      28      32      36      40      44      48      52      56
1.         INSPECT ITEM-1 TALLYING CTR1 FOR ALL SPACES.
2.         INSPECT ITEM-2 TALLYING CTR2 FOR CHARACTERS
                   BEFORE INITIAL SPACE.
3.         INSPECT ITEM-3 TALLYING CTR3 FOR LEADING ZEROS.
```

Items	Resulting Contents
ITEM-1 = ƀƀƀ67ƀ	CTR1 = 4
ITEM-2 = 01787ƀ	CTR2 = 5
ITEM-3 = 007800	CTR3 = 2

This format of the INSPECT statement will **always** count specified occurrences of data-name-3 or literal-1. Literal-1 must be a single character or a figurative constant. ZERO, SPACE, and 'X' are all valid entries for literal-1. The tallied count is placed in data-name-2, which is usually established as an independent item in the WORKING-STORAGE SECTION.

Example 4

```
    7 8   12      16      20      24      28      32      36      40      44      48      52      56
           INSPECT ITEM-A TALLYING CTRA FOR ALL SPACES.
           IF CTRA > Ø PERFORM ERR-RTN.
```

The above routine will perform an error routine if there are **any** spaces in ITEM-A.

The BEFORE or AFTER INITIAL clause in Format 1 is an optional entry. If included, a count will be taken depending on the condition specified:

Statement	Meaning
INSPECT ITEM-B TALLYING CTRB FOR ALL '5' BEFORE INITIAL SPACE	Count the number of occurrences of the digit 5 until the first space is encountered.
INSPECT ITEM-C TALLYING CTRC FOR ALL '5' AFTER INITIAL SPACE	Count the number of occurrences of the digit 5 after encountering the first space.

One of the following three COBOL expressions is required when using Format 1:

CLAUSES FOLLOWING FOR IN INSPECT STATEMENT

(a) ALL $\begin{bmatrix} \text{data-name-3} \\ \text{literal-1} \end{bmatrix}$

(b) LEADING $\begin{bmatrix} \text{data-name-3} \\ \text{literal-1} \end{bmatrix}$

(c) CHARACTERS

(a) If ALL is specified, **every** occurrence of literal-1 in the data field will be counted.

Examples

```
12   16    20    24    28    32    36    40    44    48    52
INSPECT  ITEM-F  TALLYING  CTRF  FOR  ALL  ZEROS .
INSPECT  ITEM-F  TALLYING  CTRG  FOR  ALL  ZEROS
         BEFORE  INITIAL  2 .
```

	ITEM-F		Resulting Value
	Before	**After**	
	102050	102050	CTRF = 3
	102050	102050	CTRG = 1

(b) If LEADING is specified, all occurrences of literal-1 **preceding any other character** will be tallied.

Examples

```
12   16    20    24    28    32    36    40    44    48    52    56
INSPECT  ITEM-C  TALLYING  CTRH  FOR  LEADING  9 .
INSPECT  ITEM-C  TALLYING  CTRH  FOR  LEADING  SPACE
         BEFORE  INITIAL  2 .
```

	ITEM-C		Resulting Value of CTRH
	Before	**After**	
	99129	99129	2
	ƀƀ12ƀ	ƀƀ12ƀ	2

(c) If CHARACTERS is specified, **all characters** will be tallied.

Examples

```
INSPECT  ITEM-D  TALLYING  CTRQ  FOR  CHARACTERS .
INSPECT  ITEM-D  TALLYING  CTRQ  FOR  CHARACTERS
         AFTER  INITIAL  2 .
```

	ITEM-D		Resulting Value of CTRQ
	Before	**After**	
	12300	12300	5
	12349	12349	3

Format 2 of the INSPECT statement will replace specified occurrences of a given character with another character. It will **not** tally the occurrences of any character.

Format 2

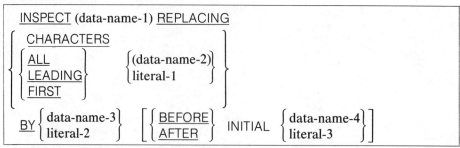

As in Format 1, literals must be single characters or figurative constants consistent with the type of field being examined.

ALL, LEADING, and CHARACTERS have the same meaning as previously noted. If FIRST is specified in Format 2, then the first occurrence of literal-1 will be replaced by literal-2. That is, a single character replacement will occur if literal-1 is present in the data field.

Examples

		ITEM—E	
		Before	After
`INSPECT ITEM-E REPLACING ALL 'I' BY '2'.`		112111	222222
`INSPECT ITEM-E REPLACING LEADING 'I' BY '2'.`		112111	222111
`INSPECT ITEM-E REPLACING CHARACTERS BY '3'`		112111	332111
`      BEFORE INITIAL '2'.`			
`INSPECT ITEM-E REPLACING FIRST 'X' BY 'Y'.`		ABCXYZ	ABCYYZ

No counting operation is performed with Format 2.

Note that when using Format 2, rules for inserting characters in data fields apply. We cannot, for example, replace an 'A' in an alphabetic data field that has a PICTURE of A's with a '1' because a '1' is not a valid alphabetic character.

SELF-EVALUATING
QUIZ

1. The two major functions of the INSPECT statement are _____ and _____.

   *****

   to replace certain characters with other characters
   to count the number of occurrences of a given character in a data item

2. (T or F) Literals in an INSPECT statement must be single characters or figurative constants.

   *****

   T

In the following statements, fill in the missing columns, where applicable.

	Statement	FLDX Before	After	Value of CTR1
3.	INSPECT FLDX TALLYING CTR1 FOR ALL ZEROS.	10050		
4.	INSPECT FLDX REPLACING ALL ZEROS BY SPACES.	10050		
5.	INSPECT FLDX TALLYING CTR1 FOR LEADING ZEROS.	00057		
6.	INSPECT FLDX TALLYING CTR1 FOR CHARACTERS BEFORE INITIAL '9'.	00579		

*****

3. 10050   3
4. 1   5
5. 00057   3
6. 00579   4

B. LIBRARY FACILITY

INTRODUCTION

It is assumed that the student, at this point, has debugged and successfully run a number of COBOL programs. During the course of running several programs, it might have become apparent that the preparation by each student of standard or uniform sections within an assigned program is redundant and perhaps unnecessary.

It is possible to establish a library containing, for example, the FD and record description entries for a complex tape file. In this way, each programmer can simply call in the required entries from the library rather than code extensive file description entries.

Similarly, a complex arithmetic routine may be included in a library. This routine may then be simply "called in" by any COBOL program.

The use of library statements serves two major purposes.

PURPOSE OF LIBRARY STATEMENTS
1. It results in **standard** data-names and other programmer-supplied words that may then be used by all programmers.
2. It facilitates programming since redundant and cumbersome coding is eliminated.

CREATION OF A LIBRARY

Most COBOL compilers are stored on a disk or other direct-access device. The computer's supervisor or monitor program calls in this compiler when a COBOL program requires a compilation. The device on which the COBOL compiler is stored also contains other compilers and software aids that can be called in by the computer system, as required. This device can also store a **library** of FD entries, procedure names, routines, and so on, that can be accessed by any COBOL program, as needed.

The creation of the entries on this library is a function of Job Control. Appendix D illustrates some Job Control specifications.

COPY STATEMENT   The COPY statement permits the COBOL programmer to include prewritten
ENVIRONMENT, DATA, or PROCEDURE DIVISION entries in his or her source
program. That is, the COPY statement permits the programmer to extract entries from a library. The general areas where the COPY statement may be used
are as follows:

<u>ENVIRONMENT DIVISION</u>

Option 1 (within CONFIGURATION SECTION):

> SOURCE-COMPUTER. <u>COPY</u> (library-name).
> OBJECT-COMPUTER. <u>COPY</u> (library-name).
> SPECIAL-NAMES. <u>COPY</u> (library-name).

Option 2 (within INPUT-OUTPUT SECTION):

> FILE-CONTROL. <u>COPY</u> (library-name).
> I-O-CONTROL. <u>COPY</u> (library-name).

<u>DATA DIVISION</u>

Option 1 (within FILE SECTION):

> FD file-name <u>COPY</u> (library-name)

Option 2 (within a File Description entry):

> 01 data-name <u>COPY</u> (library-name).

<u>PROCEDURE DIVISION</u>

> paragraph-name. <u>COPY</u> (library-name).

Note that there are a great variety of entries that may be copied from a
library. Most medium and large-scale companies with well organized data management personnel have many files and routines on a library. In such companies, the programmer often extracts entries from the library to be included in
his or her program, as needed.

Examples

> 1. 01   DATA-REC COPY PAYROLL.
> 2. FD   FILE-4 COPY INVFILE.
> 3. PARA-1. COPY LOGRTN.

In Example 1, the library entries for the record called PAYROLL, including
all its subordinate record description entries, are called into the program.

In Example 2, the FD for INVFILE, which is in the library along with all
INVFILE's record description entries, is called into the program.

In Example 3, LOGRTN and its corresponding statements are called into the program.

No other statement or clause may appear in the same entry as the COPY statement.

On the COBOL listing, all entries associated with the library-name are copied and **directly** follow the COPY statement.

Suppose we code the following DATA DIVISION entry:

01 PAYROLL COPY PAYLIB.

where PAYLIB has the following entries on the library:

```
01   PAYLIB.
     02   A    PIC S99.
     02   B    PIC S9(5)V99.
     02   C    OCCURS 40 TIMES  PIC 99.
```

The following will print on the computer listing:

```
01   PAYROLL COPY PAYLIB.
01   PAYLIB.
     02   A    PIC S99.
     02   B    PIC S9(5)V99.
     02   C    OCCURS 40 TIMES  PIC 99.
```

The library entries remain unchanged.

Suppose we wish to copy a library function but must make some minor changes. The following COPY format includes this option:

Format

```
COPY (library-name) [REPLACING word-1 BY word-2
                     word-3 BY word-4 . . . . . .]
```

Example (using preceding illustration.)

01 PAYROLL COPY PAYLIB REPLACING A BY AMT, B BY PAY-CODE.

The output listing would appear as follows:

```
01   PAYLIB.
     02   AMT      PIC S99.
     02   PAY-CODE PIC S9(5)V99.
     02   C        OCCURS 40 TIMES  PIC 99.
```

The above format including the REPLACING option does not alter library functions or routines in the library itself but changes their specifications within the calling program.

SELF-EVALUATING
QUIZ

1. A single File Description or COBOL routine may be utilized in many programs by placing it in a _____ and _____ for it when needed.
*****
library
calling

2. The _____ clause permits the COBOL programmer to include prewritten entries in his or her program.
*****
COPY
3. The format for copying files is _____.
*****
FD (file-name) COPY (library-name).
4. The library-name must conform to the rules for forming _____.
*****
external names
5. (T or F) It is possible to alter library routines for the source program.
*****
True
6. (T or F) Using the REPLACING option of the COPY statement, it is possible to alter the routines in the library itself.
*****
False—this option only alters library functions **for the source program.**
7. The purposes for using library functions are to _____ and to _____.
*****
facilitate coding
enhance standardization of programmer-supplied words

C. USAGE CLAUSE

The manner in which data is stored internally within the computer is significant because it can determine the type of processing performed on the data and can optimize the program's efficiency.

The USAGE clause specifies the form in which data is stored within the computer. It is a clause associated with either a group or elementary item in any section of the DATA DIVISION.

The format for the USAGE clause is:

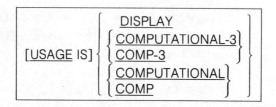

Note that the above format does not represent all the options that can be associated with a USAGE clause, but it includes the most commonly used ones. Note also that the COMPUTATIONAL-3 and COMP-3 options are not available with all compilers. Consult your specifications manual for a complete list of options available with this clause.

Examples

```
1. 01  TABLE-X USAGE IS COMPUTATIONAL.
       02  ITEM-X OCCURS 40 TIMES  PIC S9(10).
       02  ITEM-Y OCCURS 40 TIMES  PIC S9(5).

2. 02  LISTX PIC X(5) USAGE IS DISPLAY.
```

```
3. 02  LISTY PIC XXX USAGE DISPLAY.
```

The USAGE clause may be associated with a group item or an elementary item. If it is used with a group item then it refers to **all** elements within the group.

To fully understand the USAGE options, we must consider the method employed by the computer for storing characters of data. Although the method discussed is not universal, it is applicable to most computers.

USAGE IS DISPLAY | REPRESENTATION OF EXTERNAL OR ZONED DECIMAL CHARACTERS IN STORAGE
The computer utilizes its own code for representing data in storage. This code is called EBCDIC, or Extended Binary Coded Decimal Interchange Code. Each **byte** or position of storage is used to store one character of data in external or zoned decimal format.[1] As with Hollerith code representation, each storage position contains a zone and digit portion.

The EBCDIC representation is referred to as External or Zoned Decimal Representation. If a USAGE clause is omitted from a data description entry, the standard EBCDIC representation is assumed.

Similarly, the clause USAGE IS DISPLAY calls for an external or zoned decimal format.

Thus the DISPLAY option can be either **explicit,** when specified, or **implicit,** when omitted. It indicates that data is stored in character form, one character per single byte of storage. This representation corresponds to the form in which card input, using the Hollerith code, is entered, and the form in which printed output is produced. Each character is represented by a zone and digit portion.

USAGE IS
COMPUTATIONAL-3
OR COMP-3 | REPRESENTATION OF DATA IN PACKED FORM
Thus far, we have seen that data may be represented in zoned decimal format using one byte of storage for each character.

This is an inefficient method for storing numeric items since the zone portion, representing a sign, should **not** be required for every digit within the field.

That is, instead of representing a five-position numeric field, for example, in 5 bytes, it is possible to utilize a zone for each **field** rather than for each **digit.** In this way, each storage position can hold two digits rather than a single digit.

Thus, it is really unnecessary to include a zone for each digit within a number. One zone for the entire field, indicating a positive or negative sign would suffice. There is a method that the computer can use to eliminate or strip the zone of all digits except one, which would represent the sign. In this way, the zone portion of each byte can be employed to represent another digit. That is, **two** digits can be represented within a single byte. This technique is called **packing.**[2]

Note that the number in zoned decimal format occupies more bytes than in

---

[1]For a thorough discussion of data representation, see Stern and Stern, *Principles of Data Processing,* John Wiley and Sons, Inc., 2nd ed., 1979.
[2]For a thorough discussion of packing, see any introductory data processing textbook.

packed format. A major advantage of packing numbers, then, is to conserve storage. Thus the data elements represented by:

```
01   TABLE-X.
     02   ITEM-X OCCURS 40 TIMES PIC S9(10).'
     02   ITEM-Y OCCURS 40 TIMES PIC S9(5).
```

occupy 600 storage positions. To reduce this area by approximately 50% (two digits/byte) we use the COMPUTATIONAL-3 clause, which packs the data.

```
01   TABLE-X USAGE IS COMPUTATIONAL-3.
     02   ITEM-X OCCURS 40 TIMES PIC S9(10).
     02   ITEM-Y OCCURS 40 TIMES PIC S9(5).
```

The COMPUTATIONAL-3 or COMP-3 option that results in packing should be used for numeric fields only. As in the above example, it can also be used on the group level, if the corresponding elementary items are numeric.

The COMPUTATIONAL-3, or COMP-3 option should **not** be used for printing output because the data is not readable, since each byte does **not** contain a zone and digit as in normal EBCDIC coding.

Thus, for numeric fields we can save considerable storage space by using the packed format. In addition, the computer **requires** numeric fields to be packed for it to perform arithmetic operations.

Consider the following field:

02   AMT   PIC 99.

The usage of the above entry is implicity zoned decimal since no USAGE clause is specified. To perform an arithmetic operation on AMT requires the computer to automatically:

1. Pack AMT.
2. Perform operation.
3. Unpack AMT.

If AMT were specified as a packed field, two of the above three operations would be unnecessary. Thus the revised coding of:

```
02 AMT PIC 99 COMPUTATIONAL-3.
or
02 AMT PIC 99 COMP-3.
```

is more efficient, since its compilation eliminates compiler-generated instructions that would be required if the numeric fields were not packed.

As a general rule, numeric WORKING-STORAGE items to be used in arithmetic operations should be specified with USAGE COMP-3 or COMPUTATIONAL-3. Input is usually not entered in packed format, and output is usually not produced in packed format; thus, this option of the USAGE clause would usually be inappropriate in the FILE SECTION.

The computer automatically handles conversions from packed to unpacked form and vice versa. To move a packed numeric field in WORKING-STORAGE to an unpacked numeric field, for example, requires no additional programming effort.

USAGE IS
COMPUTATIONAL OR
COMP

REPRESENTATION OF DATA IN BINARY FORM

Instead of representing numeric data in zoned decimal format, it is possible to represent data in binary form. When numeric data is to be entered, operated upon, or produced as output in **binary** form, the clause USAGE IS COMPUTATIONAL or USAGE IS COMP must be specified.

The COMPUTATIONAL or COMP usage is used for numeric items only, to represent data strictly in binary form. For some mathematical purposes, binary arithmetic is more efficient. That is, the binary format is desirable when many repetitive computations must be performed. Similarly, for some operations, it is more efficient to produce binary output, so that when the data is read in again at a later date, conversion to binary is not necessary.

SELF-EVALUATING QUIZ

1. The USAGE clause is used to specify _____.
   *****
   the form in which data is stored
2. The USAGE clause is used with a _____.
   *****
   record description entry—either group or elementary level item
3. (T or F) The USAGE clause may be used in any section of the DATA DIVISION.
   *****
   True
4. (T or F) The USAGE clause may precede or follow the PICTURE clause of an elementary item.
   *****
   False—it must follow the PICTURE clause.
5. Input is usually entered in _____ format.
   *****
   External or Zoned Decimal
6. Zoned Decimal Format means that a single _____ of data is represented in one byte of storage.
   *****
   character
7. In Zoned Decimal Format, each character is represented by a _____ portion and a _____ portion. The entire character represents one _____ of storage.
   *****
   zone
   digit
   byte or position
8. Zoned Decimal Format for storage of data is obtained by specifying USAGE IS _____ or by _____.
   *****
   DISPLAY
   omitting the USAGE clause
9. The purpose of packing data is to _____ and _____.
   *****
   conserve storage
   make more efficient use of the computer

10. Only _____ items can be packed.
    *****
    numeric

11. In general, packing numbers saves approximately _____ percent storage.
    *****
    50% (Packing actually requires one byte more than 50% of the bytes used for zoned decimal representation.)

12. In addition to saving storage space, packing of fields results in _____ when arithmetic operations are to be performed.
    *****
    fewer compiler-generated instructions (computer does not have to pack field before operation and then unpack it after the operation)

13. (T or F) Any storage field may be packed.
    *****
    False—only numeric fields.

14. (T or F) If an output field is specified as COMP-3, it will be readable when produced.
    *****
    False

15. To specify fields strictly in binary form the _____ or _____ option of the USAGE clause is used.
    *****
    COMPUTATIONAL
    COMP

PRACTICE PROBLEM—
WITH SOLUTION

Write an edit program using the following format for card input:

    1–20 Name
    21–35 Address
    36–40 Quantity purchased
    41–47 Amount owed xxxxx.xx
    48–51 Date of purchase Mo/Yr
    52–55 Transaction number
    56–80 Not used

Output is a tape file with the following format:

    1–4   Transaction number
    5–9   Quantity purchased
    10–16 Amount owed
    17–36 Name
    37–51 Address
    52–55 Date

Labels are standard; blocking factor = 40.

NOTE: For all numeric fields (quantity, amount owed, date of purchase, transaction number), replace blanks with zeros.

See Figure 23.1 for the solution.

```
IDENTIFICATION DIVISION.
PROGRAM-ID. CHAPT24.
ENVIRONMENT DIVISION.
CONFIGURATION SECTION.
SOURCE-COMPUTER. IBM-370.
OBJECT-COMPUTER. IBM-370.
INPUT-OUTPUT SECTION.
FILE-CONTROL.
    SELECT CARD-FILE ASSIGN TO UR-S-SYSIN.
    SELECT TAPE-OUT ASSIGN TO UT-S-SYS001.
DATA DIVISION.
FILE SECTION.
FD  CARD-FILE
    LABEL RECORDS ARE OMITTED
    RECORD CONTAINS 80 CHARACTERS
    DATA RECORD IS CARD-REC.
01  CARD-REC.
    02  NAME                    PIC X(20).
    02  ADDRESSX                PIC X(15).
    02  NUMERIC-FIELDS.
        03  QTY             PIC 9(5).
        03  AMT             PIC 9(5)V99.
        03  DATE1           PIC 9(4).
        03  TRANS-NO        PIC 9(4).
    02  FILLER                  PIC X(25).
FD  TAPE-OUT
    LABEL RECORDS ARE STANDARD
    RECORD CONTAINS 55 CHARACTERS
    BLOCK CONTAINS 40 RECORDS
    DATA RECORD IS TAPE-REC.
01  TAPE-REC.
    02  TRANS-NO                PIC 9(4).
    02  QTY                     PIC 9(5).
    02  AMT                     PIC 9(5)V99.
    02  NAME                    PIC X(20).
    02  ADDRESSX                PIC X(15).
    02  DATE1                   PIC 9(4).
WORKING-STORAGE SECTION.
01  WORK-AREAS.
    02  EOF                             PIC 9 VALUE 0.
PROCEDURE DIVISION.
    OPEN INPUT CARD-FILE, OUTPUT TAPE-OUT.
    READ CARD-FILE AT END MOVE 1 TO EOF.
    PERFORM CALC-RTN UNTIL EOF = 1.
    CLOSE CARD-FILE, TAPE-OUT.
    STOP RUN.
CALC-RTN.
    EXAMINE NUMERIC-FIELDS REPLACING ALL ' ' BY ZEROS.
    MOVE CORRESPONDING CARD-REC TO TAPE-REC.
    WRITE TAPE-REC.
    READ CARD-FILE AT END MOVE 1 TO EOF.
```

Figure 23.1

REVIEW QUESTIONS

True False

I. True-False Questions

□ □ 1. The INSPECT statement may be used with numeric fields only.

□ □ 2. Figurative constants cannot be used in an INSPECT statement.

□ □ 3. The INSPECT statement allows the programmer to replace invalid characters with valid ones.

□ □ 4. One version of the INSPECT statement allows the programmer to count the invalid occurrences of a given character without replacing them.

□ □ 5. The COPY statement may be used to include sections that have been catalogued into one's program.

□ □ 6. Structured programming facilitates the use of the COPY statement for PROCEDURE DIVISION entries.

□ □ 7. A major advantage of the COPY statement is that it enables programmers to use data definitions that are standard for the company where the programmers are employed.

☐ ☐ 8. A USAGE clause describes the way in which data is represented by the computer.

☐ ☐ 9. The phrase USAGE COMP-3 means that data will be represented in binary form.

☐ ☐ 10. If the USAGE clause is omitted, USAGE IS DISPLAY is assumed.

II. General Questions

1. Write an INSPECT statement to determine the number of J's in a data field, called ITEM-A. If the number of J's exceed ten, branch to ERR-RTN.
2. Write an INSPECT statement to determine the number of characters that precede the first nine in a field called AMOUNT.
3. Explain the use of the COPY statement.
4. Explain the use of the following entries:
   a. USAGE IS DISPLAY
   b. USAGE IS COMP-3
   c. USAGE IS COMP

PROBLEMS

1. Economic order quantity is used in inventory control to determine the most economical quantity of a product for the company to produce. Data cards with the following format will serve as input:

   1–5   Product number
   6–20   Product name
   21–26 Total yearly production requirement   R
   27–31 Inventory carrying cost/unit   I   xxx.xx
   32–36 Setup cost/order   S   xxx.xx

   The economic order quantity Q may be determined from the formula

   $$Q = \sqrt{\frac{2RS}{I}}$$

   Make certain there are no blank numeric fields. Print the product name and the economic order quantity for each item. Also indicate the product with the **least** economic order quantity.

2. Write a program to create utility bills.

   Charges: First 100 kilowatt hours (kwh) $.05/kwh
   Next 200 kwh   .04/kwh
   All other   .03/kwh

   The input consists of a master tape and a detail card file.

Master Tape File	Detail Card File
1–20 Customer name	1–20 Customer name
21–25 Previous balance xxx.xx	21–40 Address
26 Credit rating	41–44 Kwh used
	45–80 Not used

   Labels are standard; blocking factor = 10.

The two input files are used to create a utility punched card bill with the following format:

  1–20 Name
21–40 Address
41–45 Amount owed
46–80 Message (if applicable)

Make certain there are no blank numeric fields.

NOTES:

There is one detail card for each tape record. For all matching tape and card records:

(a) Calculate current charge from kwh on card.
(b) Add to previous balance to obtain amount owed.
(c) If credit rating is A, person may owe up to $50. If over $50, print REMINDER in message field.
(d) If credit rating is B, person may owe up to $20.
    If person owes from $20-50, print REMINDER.
    If person owes over $50, print WARNING.
(e) If credit rating is C, print REMINDER if person owes from $0-20 and WARNING if person owes over $20.

3. Write a cost-of-item program using the following input tape format:

  1–20 Item description
21–24 Date purchased
25–29 Invoice number
30–34 Number of units bought
35–39 Cost of each item xxx.xx
40–44 Labor   xxx.xx
45–49 Freight charges xxx.xx
50–54 Sales tax   xxx.xx
55   Not used

Labels are standard; blocking factor = 50.

Print item description and unit price for each tape record.

$$\text{Unit price} = \text{Cost of item} + \frac{\text{Freight}}{\text{No. Units}} + \text{Labor} + \text{Overhead}$$

Overhead is equal to 20% of Labor.

Make certain there are no blank numeric fields.

24 DEBUGGING COBOL PROGRAMS

Our discussion is divided into two phases: Debugging a Program—Compilation Phase; and Debugging a Program—Execution Phase.

A. DEBUGGING A PROGRAM— COMPILATION PHASE

UNDERSTANDING AND CORRECTING DIAGNOSTICS

Once you understand the basic rules of a COBOL program, you can code and run your own programs. You will recall that a coded program must be converted to a machine-readable form. Let us assume that the coded program is converted to punched cards. These cards, representing the source deck, are used as input in a compilation or translation process.

In attempting to translate or compile your program into machine language so that it can be executed, the computer requires that specified coding rules be followed. If any violations appear in your program, the computer will print out diagnostic messages during the compilation phase. This list of diagnostics will appear together at the end of the COBOL listing or individually, preceding or following each erroneous statement. Note that logic errors are **not** detected during this phase, but may only be determined during actual execution of the program. A rule violation may be, for example:

SAMPLE RULE VIOLATIONS
1. Attempting to add two operands using the verb AD instead of ADD.
2. Attempting to subtract from a nonnumeric field.
3. Using a field in the PROCEDURE DIVISION that has not been defined.

If the above examples seem trite, leaving you incredulous that people actually make such mistakes, the results of your first compilation should be an eye-opening experience. In reality, both experienced and novice programmers make numerous ''simple'' errors that result in many diagnostics.

Do not become unnecessarily discouraged or distraught if numerous diagnostics accompany your source program listings. The important point is to be able to understand these messages and to correct the source errors with minimum difficulty.

Each compiler has its own file of diagnostic messages. Consult your computer's specifications manual for a listing of applicable diagnostics. Note, however, that while the messages illustrated in this section may not conform exactly to those for your machine, the general format is the same. Thus, knowledge of, and experience with, diagnostics of one compiler greatly facilitates the understanding of diagnostics of another compiler.

Most diagnostic messages have the following format:

Card No.	Error Code	Error Message

Card No. refers to the sequence number assigned by the compiler to each source program card. This card number is referenced in the source program listing. To find the item in error, simply cross-reference the sequence number in the source program listing.

Error Code is the code assigned to the specific message in the Specifications Manual. That is, you can cross-reference the specific diagnostic in the manual by using the Error Code. When the Error Message is not clear, it is sometimes beneficial to look up the Error Code in the manual for clarification.

Error Message is a concise description of the rule violation. In a short time, the novice programmer becomes familiar enough with error messages so that he or she can spot the problem with minimum effort.

The following represents sample diagnostics:

SAMPLE DIAGNOSTICS		
Card No.	Error Code	Error Message
18	IKF204I-C	NO OPEN CLAUSE FOUND FOR FILE
25	IKF065I-W	PERIOD MISSING IN PRECEDING STATEMENT
28	IKF001I-C	LITERAL EXCEEDS 120 CHARACTERS
29	IKF553I-E	FIGURATIVE CONSTANT IS NOT ALLOWED AS RECEIVING FIELD
30	IKF401I-C	SYNTAX REQUIRES A DATA-NAME FOUND 'DATA'.

Note that when a corresponding card number is supplied with any of the above diagnostics during a compilation, it is a relatively simple task to find the error. If the error message is not clear enough, the COBOL Specifications Manual references each code with a more explicit error message.

It is simply not feasible to undertake a discussion of **all** possible diagnostics. The student will, however, be able to understand most messages from the beginning, once the format is clear.

Note that sometimes a single error results in several diagnostics. Similarly, the error detected by the machine may have been triggered by a mistake several entries earlier. Thus, if the error is not readily found, examine other lines in the general vicinity of the error message.

The Error Code accompanying all diagnostics contains, as the last character, usually a W, C, or E (or, correspondingly, a 0, 1, 2). These letters or numbers indicate the severity of the error and indicate whether the job must be terminated.

(a) W- or 0-LEVEL ERRORS

Minor level errors, sometimes called observation, W-level, or Level-0 messages, will **not** cause termination of the program. They are merely warnings to the programmer. To attempt to place a five-position alphanumeric field into a three-position alphanumeric field, for example, may result in the following warning message:

> DESTINATION FIELD DOES NOT ACCEPT THE
> WHOLE SENDING FIELD IN MOVE

To perform the above operation is **not** incorrect. The compiler is merely indicating that truncation will occur. If truncation occurs as a result of a programming oversight, it should be corrected. If, however, the programmer **chooses** to truncate a field, no changes are necessary. That is, the program will execute with such diagnostics.

(b) C- or LEVEL 2 ERRORS

Intermediate level errors are **conditional** errors, usually called C-level, where the compiler makes an adjustment for the error. If the correction is what the programmer intended to do, execution will proceed normally. If, however, the correction is **not** the desired one, execution must be terminated and the error corrected. Consider the following C-level diagnostic:

> 007020 C-QUALIFICATION—NAME REQUIRES MORE QUALIFICATION
> FIRST NAME DEFINED IS ASSUMED

which applies to the following statement (007020 refers to page 007, line 020):

> 007020 MOVE NAME TO NAME OF REC-OUT.

The first NAME field in the statement is not properly qualified. The diagnostic indicates that the first NAME field encountered in the DATA DIVISION is considered the desired one. If, in fact, the first NAME field designated in the DATA DIVISION is the required one, the statement need not be corrected for execution to continue properly. If, however, the NAME field required is **not** the first one, then the program must be corrected before execution can begin. In any case, all C-level diagnostics should eventually be corrected.

(c) E- or LEVEL 3 ERRORS

Major level errors, called **execution**-level, or **fatal**, diagnostics by some compilers, will terminate execution. The compiler deems these errors of such magnitude that it will not permit execution to occur. The following are examples of major level errors:

```
              MAJOR LEVEL ERRORS
FILE SECTION OUT OF SEQUENCE
ENVIRONMENT DIVISION MISSING
UNDEFINED DATA-NAME
INVALID LITERAL: $100.00
INVALID DATA-NAME: DISCOUNT-%
```

Consider the following COBOL listing:

```
001      IDENTIFICATION DIVISION.
002      PROGRAM-ID. SAMPLE.
003      ENVIRONMENT DIVISION.
004      FILE-CONTROL. SELECT EMPLOYEE-CARDS ASSIGN TO UR-S-SYSIN.
005          SELECT PAYROLL-FILE ASSIGN TO UT-S-SYS005.
006      DATA DIVISION.
007      FD  EMPLOYEE-CARDS
008      01  EMPLOYEE-RECORD.
009          02      EMPLOYEE-NAME   PIC A(20).
010          02      HOURS-WORKED    PIC 99.
011          02      HOURLY-RATE     PIC 9V99.
012      FD  PAYROLL-FILE
013      01  PAYROLL-RECORD.
014          02      NAME-OUT        PIC A(20).
015          02      HOURS-OUT       PIC 99.
016          02      RATE-OUT        PIC 9V99.
017          02      WEEKLY-WAGES    PIC 999V99.
018      WORKING-STORAGE SECTION.
019      01  EOF     PIC 9 VALUE 0.
020      PROCEDURE DIVISION.
021      START.
022          READ EMPLOYEE-CARDS AT END MOVE 1 TO EOF.
023          PERFORM CALC-RTN UNTIL EOF = 1.
024          STOP RUN.
025      CALC-RTN.
026          MOVE EMPLOYEE-NAME TO NAME-OUT.
027          MOVE HOURS-WORKED TO HOURS-OUT.
028          MOVE HOURLY-RATE TO RATE-OUT.
029          MULTIPLY HOURS-WORKED BY HOURLY-RATE GIVING WEEKLY-WAGES.
030          WRITE PAYROLL-RECORD.
031          READ EMPLOYEE-CARDS AT END MOVE 1 TO EOF.
```

The errors associated with this listing are shown in Figure 24.1

Notice that since there is at least one E-level diagnostic, the program must be corrected before it can be executed. A program can be executed with W- or C-level diagnostics but E-level errors automatically abort the run.

1. 4   IKF1002I-W   INPUT-OUTPUT SECTION HEADER MISSING. ASSUMED PRESENT.

This error indicates that card number 4 should have specified the INPUT-OUTPUT SECTION. The computer automatically assumes that the entry is present. Hence, this is considered a W or Warning level error only.

2. 7   IKF1002I-W   FILE SECTION HEADER MISSING. ASSUMED PRESENT.

```
CARD    ERROR MESSAGE


4       IKF1002I-W      INPUT-OUTPUT SECTION HEADER MISSING. ASSUMED PRESENT.

7       IKF1002I-W      FILE SECTION HEADER MISSING. ASSUMED PRESENT.

4       IKF2049I-C      NO OPEN CLAUSE FOUND FOR FILE.

4       IKF2133I-W      LABEL RECORDS CLAUSE MISSING. DD CARD OPTION WILL BE TAKEN.

8       IKF1043I-W      END OF SENTENCE SHOULD PRECEDE 01 . ASSUMED PRESENT.

5       IKF2049I-C      NO OPEN CLAUSE FOUND FOR FILE.

5       IKF2133I-W      LABEL RECORDS CLAUSE MISSING. DD CARD OPTION WILL BE TAKEN.

13      IKF1043I-W      END OF SENTENCE SHOULD PRECEDE 01 . ASSUMED PRESENT.

21      IKF1087I-W      ' START ' SHOULD NOT BEGIN A-MARGIN.

21      IKF4050I-E      SYNTAX REQUIRES QISAM-FILE WITH NOMINAL KEY . FOUND END-OF-SENT . STATEMENT

                        DISCARDED.
```

Figure 24.1

This error states that card number 7 should have specified the FILE SEC-
TION. Note, however, that this is a W-level error or warning. It is not
critical since the compiler automatically assumes that the FILE SECTION
entry is present.

3. 4   IKF2049I-C   NO OPEN CLAUSE FOUND FOR FILE.

   4   IKF2133I-W   LABEL RECORDS CLAUSE MISSING. DD CARD OPTION WILL BE TAKEN.

The file defined on card number 4, EMPLOYEE-CARDS, is not properly
opened in the PROCEDURE DIVISION nor does it contain a label records
clause. Since no label records clause exists, the compiler assumes that labels
are omitted.

4. 8   IKF1043I-W   END OF SENTENCE SHOULD PRECEDE 01 . ASSUMED PRESENT.

All file description entries should end with a period. This is only a W-level
error, since the compiler assumes the presence of the period.

5. 5   IKF2049I-C   NO OPEN CLAUSE FOUND FOR FILE.

   5   IKF2133I-W   LABEL RECORDS CLAUSE MISSING. DD CARD OPTION WILL BE TAKEN.

The file defined on card number 5, PAYROLL-FILE, is not properly opened
in the PROCEDURE DIVISION nor does it contain a label records clause.

6. 13   IKF1043I-W   END OF SENTENCE SHOULD PRECEDE 01 . ASSUMED PRESENT.

All file description entries should end with a period.

7. 21   IKF1087I-W   ' START ' SHOULD NOT BEGIN A-MARGIN.

   21   IKF4050I-E   SYNTAX REQUIRES QISAM-FILE WITH NOMINAL KEY . FOUND END-OF-SENT . STATEMENT

                        DISCARDED.

Here is an example of a single error causing two diagnostics. START is an invalid paragraph-name because it is a reserved word for the COBOL compiler used here. Thus line 21 is in error, since START is defined there as a paragraph-name. The diagnostics refer to the reserved meaning of the word START.

B. DEBUGGING A COBOL PROGRAM— EXECUTION PHASE

You will recall that it is not sufficient to simply code a COBOL program, compile it, eliminate the diagnostics and then consider the program complete. All programs must be tested with either:

DESIGN OF TEST DATA

(a) Test or ''dummy'' data, which is carefully designed to test all conditions in the program.

(b) ''Live'' data, which is used for the specific application under normal processing conditions.

The programmer must make certain that any data used to test the program contains appropriate information that will test every possible condition or alternative. If this is not adequately performed, the programmer may very well be embarrassed and besieged by late night calls from computer operators because his or her program failed to operate properly.

Programmers must provide for every conceivable alternative by using comprehensive test data to ensure that programs contain no bugs. An extremely important facet of the programmer's responsibility is to ensure that the program operates properly under any condition.

Once test data has been adequately designed, the programmer can execute or test the program. Usually, programs contain minor logic errors that cause the computer to abort the run or to produce erroneous results. We direct our discussion to the methods used to find these logic errors. Because of the nature of COBOL, the process of discovering the cause of logic errors is sometimes difficult.

FINDING LOGIC ERRORS

The COBOL language is considered a very high-level programming language. That is, it is different from machine language. It is a language that is relatively easy for a programmer to code but one that requires a rather complex compilation process, since the translation to machine language is very intricate.

Because COBOL is a high-level language, so different from machine language, it is somewhat difficult for the programmer to pinpoint **logic errors or machine interrupts.**

In previous computer generations, program errors were debugged by taking a ''core dump'' and determining what was actually in memory at the time the error or interrupt occurred. At that time, when most programmers were experts at assembler language, it was a relatively simple task to seek out instructions in storage and determine error points. In COBOL, however, when the computer aborts the run because of a program error, it displays a machine address that usually has little or no significance to the COBOL programmer.

Since determining the machine language equivalent of a COBOL program is, at best, a cumbersome task, the computer's display of a machine address, by itself, is of little value to most programmers.

In this section, we consider debugging aids that can be incorporated directly in the program and can assist the programmer in pinpointing logic errors or machine interrupt points, where errors are of such a magnitude that the computer aborts the run.

Since these debugging aids are used within the program itself, the necessity for memory dumps and external displays of machine addresses is reduced. After a program has been successfully compiled with no major diagnostic messages, and then fully tested, these debugging aids may be removed from the program. The program is then turned over to the operations staff for execution on a regular basis.

DEBUGGING TOOLS

There are three major tools that may be incorporated as **part of** a COBOL program during the test phase to facilitate program control. These tools can then be eliminated once the program is operable. These aids are:

```
┌─────────────────────────────┐
│     DEBUGGING TOOLS         │
│ 1. TRACE                    │
│ 2. EXHIBIT or DISPLAY       │
│ 3. ON                       │
└─────────────────────────────┘
```

a. TRACE
The TRACE option is used for indicating the actual paragraphs that the program executes during a specific run.

Example

The following program converts any 4-digit binary number to its decimal equivalent. The program was coded in such a way that all paragraph-names executed are printed (as a result of the READY TRACE) and clearly indicate the sequence of operations performed by the program (Figure 24.2).

Using several binary numbers as input, the programmer manually determines which paragraph-names the program should be printing. Then he or she checks the list with the paragraph-names actually printed out as a result of the READY TRACE. If there are any discrepancies, then a logic error exists and can easily be found in the paragraph listed **prior to** the discrepancy. That is, if the programmer's hand computation and the computer's automatic computation lead to two different routines, then the paragraph prior to this deviation contains an error.

Depending on the specific input, the program may take several different branches. To determine that the correct paths are taken for specified input conditions, we insert a READY TRACE statement prior to the normal processing flow.

This READY TRACE causes all paragraphs encountered during the run to be printed on the system's logical output device, usually the printer. Thus, for the above program, if the input were as follows:

```
1001
1100
0100
```

the listing shown in Figure 24.2a would print.

```
IDENTIFICATION DIVISION.
PROGRAM-ID. BINARY.
********************************************************
**** NOTE THAT THIS PROGRAM HAS MANY MORE PARAGRAPH   ****
**** NAMES THAN ARE ACTUALLY NEEDED. THESE ARE USED TO****
**** ILLUSTRATE THE   READY TRACE.                    ****
********************************************************
ENVIRONMENT DIVISION.
CONFIGURATION SECTION.
SOURCE-COMPUTER. IBM-370.
OBJECT-COMPUTER. IBM-370.
DATA DIVISION.
WORKING-STORAGE SECTION.
01   WORK-AREAS.
        02   DEC-NO              PIC 99.
01   BITS.
        02   BIT8                PIC 9.
        02   BIT4                PIC 9.
        02   BIT2                PIC 9.
        02   BIT1                PIC 9.
PROCEDURE DIVISION.
    READY TRACE.
    ACCEPT BITS FROM SYSIN.
    PERFORM BEGIN THRU WRITE-ROUTINE UNTIL BITS = 9999.
    STOP RUN.
BEGIN.
    MOVE ZEROS TO DEC-NO.
BIT8-TEST.
    IF BIT8 = 1 PERFORM ADD-8 ELSE PERFORM NO-ADD.
BIT4-TEST.
    IF BIT4 = 1 PERFORM ADD-4 ELSE PERFORM NO-ADD.
BIT2-TEST.
    IF BIT2 = 1 PERFORM ADD-2 ELSE PERFORM NO-ADD.
BIT1-TEST.
    IF BIT1 = 1 PERFORM ADD-1 ELSE PERFORM NO-ADD.
WRITE-ROUTINE.
    DISPLAY DEC-NO.
    ACCEPT BITS FROM SYSIN.
ADD-8.
    ADD 8 TO DEC-NO.
ADD-4.
    ADD 4 TO DEC-NO.
ADD-2.
    ADD 2 TO DEC-NO.
ADD-1.
    ADD 1 TO DEC-NO.
NO-ADD.
    ADD ZERO TO DEC-NO.
```

Figure 24.2 Illustration of READY TRACE.

```
BEGIN
BIT8-TEST
ADD-8
BIT4-TEST
NO-ADD
BIT2-TEST
NO-ADD
BIT1-TEST
ADD-1
WRITE-ROUTINE
09
BEGIN
BIT8-TEST
ADD-8
BIT4-TEST
ADD-4
BIT2-TEST
NO-ADD
BIT1-TEST
NO-ADD
WRITE-ROUTINE
12
BEGIN
BIT8-TEST
NO-ADD
BIT4-TEST
ADD-4
BIT2-TEST
NO-ADD
BIT1-TEST
NO-ADD
WRITE-ROUTINE
04
```

Figure 24.2a

The listing for 1001 is explained as follows:

> BEGIN: the first paragraph encountered
> BIT8-TEST: tests the first bit for 1
> ADD-8: since the first bit is 1, we must add 8 to the DEC-NO
> BIT4-TEST: tests the second bit for 1
> NO-ADD: since the second bit is 0, no add is performed
> BIT2-TEST: tests the third bit for 1
> NO-ADD: since the third bit is 0
> BIT1-TEST: fourth bit is tested for 1
> ADD-1: since the fourth bit is 1, we must add 1 to DEC-NO
> WRITE-ROUTINE: the decimal number 09 is displayed
>   This is the display of the decimal equivalent of 1001.

Once the READY TRACE is removed from the source deck, only the 09, the decimal equivalent of 1001, will print.

You may follow the logic flow for the remaining two numbers.

Note that the READY TRACE option specifies all paragraph-names encountered during the run. In this way, if an error exists in the logic of the program, it could be easily detected. Thus if BIT4-TEST were erroneously coded with a GO TO as follows:

IF BIT4 = 1 GO TO ADD-4 ELSE PERFORM NO-ADD.

the READY TRACE would pinpoint the error immediately, since, when ADD-4 was executed, it would be followed by ADD-2, and so on.

Thus if a programmer inserts a READY TRACE card in his or her source deck when debugging a program, logic errors can be more easily identified and thus corrected. Once all logic errors have been debugged, the READY TRACE card must be removed from the source deck. Most regularly scheduled runs would not require the printing of each paragraph-name as it is encountered.

It is sometimes advantageous to incorporate a READY TRACE in specified facets of a program run. That is, when the logic of separate modules is functioning properly, we may want to use the READY TRACE until a particular condition occurs and then "turn it off" so that superfluous paragraph-names are not repeatedly printed unnecessarily. We can use a RESET TRACE to "turn off" a previously defined READY TRACE. Consider the following illustration, where a 10-bit binary number is converted to its decimal equivalent, using subscripting (Figure 24.3):

```
IDENTIFICATION DIVISION.
PROGRAM-ID. DECIMAL.
ENVIRONMENT DIVISION.
CONFIGURATION SECTION.
SOURCE-COMPUTER. IBM-370.
OBJECT-COMPUTER. IBM-370.
DATA DIVISION.
WORKING-STORAGE SECTION.
01  WORK-AREAS.
      02  X1              PIC 99.
      02  DEC-NO          PIC 999.
      02  BIT-CONFIG      PIC 999.
01  BIN-NO.
      02  BIT  OCCURS 10 TIMES PIC 9.
PROCEDURE DIVISION.
      READY TRACE.
      ACCEPT BIN-NO FROM SYSIN.
      PERFORM BEGIN THRU COMPUTE-RTN UNTIL BIN-NO = 9999999999.
      STOP RUN.
BEGIN.
      MOVE 10 TO X1.
      MOVE 1 TO BIT-CONFIG.
      MOVE ZEROS TO DEC-NO.
COMPUTE-RTN.
      PERFORM BIT-TEST 10 TIMES.
      DISPLAY DEC-NO.
      ACCEPT BIN-NO FROM SYSIN.
BIT-TEST.
      IF BIT (X1) = 1 PERFORM ADD-RTN.
      COMPUTE BIT-CONFIG = 2 ** (11 - X1)
      SUBTRACT 1 FROM X1.
      IF X1 = 5 RESET TRACE.
ADD-RTN.
      ADD BIT-CONFIG TO DEC-NO.
```

Figure 24.3 Illustration of READY TRACE and RESET TRACE.

In the figure, the listing of paragraph-names is deemed necessary for only 5 bits rather than all 10. Once these 5 bits are operated upon correctly the programmer has decided that the READY TRACE is unnecessary. That is, if the program works for 5 bits, the programmer assumes that it will work for 10. Thus, a RESET TRACE is issued that terminates the listing of paragraph-names encountered.

Note that READY TRACE and RESET TRACE are debugging tools and are only used during the **testing** of a program. Prior to a "live" program run, the READY TRACE and RESET TRACE instructions must be removed from the source deck.

b. EXHIBIT OR DISPLAY

During the testing of a program, the printing of specified data fields at key points in the logic flow can greatly facilitate debugging.

Beginning programmers often find that the end results of their programs contain erroneous data. Without the use of debugging tools, it is a cumbersome task to find the error point or points. To make debugging easier, it is possible to print key data fields at various check points in the program, usually after they have been altered. In this way, the programmer can spot a logic error easily by simply manually performing the necessary operations on the data and comparing the results with the displayed fields. When a discrepancy exists the logic error must have occurred after the previous check point.

The EXHIBIT statement prints the required data fields on the printer. A simplified format of the EXHIBIT statement is as follows:

$$\underline{\text{EXHIBIT}} \quad \left(\begin{array}{l} \text{data-name-1} \\ \text{nonnumeric-literal-1} \end{array} \right), \quad \left(\begin{array}{l} \text{data-name-2} \\ \text{nonnumeric-literal-2} \end{array} \right), \dots$$

Examples

```
EXHIBIT FLD1.
EXHIBIT 'TEST FLD2', FLD2.
EXHIBIT FLD3, FLD4.
```

The EXHIBIT statements should be placed at key locations or "check points" in the program to test the outcome of specified arithmetic or logic instructions. During the run, the execution of the EXHIBIT statements will cause the printing of the specified data fields.

Example

Using our 10-bit binary number problem, we can eliminate the READY TRACE and just test the DEC-NO after each phase to ensure that it is incrementing properly (Figure 24.4):

TOF:

```
            IDENTIFICATION DIVISION.
            PROGRAM-ID. DECIMAL.
            ENVIRONMENT DIVISION.
            CONFIGURATION SECTION.
            SOURCE-COMPUTER. IBM-370.
            OBJECT-COMPUTER. IBM-370.
            DATA DIVISION.
            WORKING-STORAGE SECTION.
            77  X1              PIC 99.
            77  DEC-NO                  PIC 999.
            77  BIT-CONFIG              PIC 999.
            01  BIN-NO.
                02  BIT   OCCURS 10 TIMES PIC 9.
            PROCEDURE DIVISION.
                ACCEPT BIN-NO FROM SYSIN.
                PERFORM BEGIN THRU COMPUTE-RTN UNTIL BIN-NO = 9999999999.
                STOP RUN.
            BEGIN.
                MOVE 10 TO X1.
                MOVE 1 TO BIT-CONFIG.
                MOVE ZEROS TO DEC-NO.
            COMPUTE-RTN.
                PERFORM BIT-TEST 10 TIMES.
                DISPLAY DEC-NO.
                ACCEPT BIN-NO FROM SYSIN.
            BIT-TEST.
                IF BIT (X1) = 1 PERFORM ADD-RTN.
                COMPUTE BIT-CONFIG = 2 ** (11 - X1)
                EXHIBIT BIT-CONFIG.
                EXHIBIT X1.
                SUBTRACT 1 FROM X1.
            ADD-RTN.
                ADD BIT-CONFIG TO DEC-NO.
                EXHIBIT DEC-NO.
```

EOF:

Figure 24.4 Illustration of EXHIBIT statements.

The result would then be as shown in Figure 24.5.

```
001
002
10
003
004
09
008
08
016
07
019
032
06
051
064
05
128
04
256
03
512
02
024
01
THE DECIMAL NO IS 051
002
10
002
004
09
006
008
08
016
07
032
06
038
064
05
128
04
256
03
512
02
024
01
THE DECIMAL NO IS 038
002
10
002
004
```

Figure 24.5

By stepping through the program manually, you can compare your intermediate results with the exhibited items to ensure proper execution.

From the above example, we have seen that the use of the EXHIBIT statement greatly facilitates debugging by printing intermediate results at crucial check points in the program. Note, however, that the printing of the above results would be difficult to locate in a normal **print** program. That is, the EXHIBIT statement could cause the printing of these fields in the middle of a report that is being produced by the program. To facilitate the reading of an exhibited field, we can have its name print:

$$\text{\underline{EXHIBIT} \underline{NAMED}} \left(\begin{array}{c} \text{data-name-1} \\ \text{nonnumeric-literal-1} \end{array} \right), \left(\begin{array}{c} \text{data-name-2} \\ \text{nonnumeric-literal-2} \end{array} \right), \ldots$$

Consider the previous example, but with the EXHIBIT statements changed to EXHIBIT NAMED statements as shown in Figure 24.6.

```
IDENTIFICATION DIVISION.
PROGRAM-ID. DECIMAL.
ENVIRONMENT DIVISION.
CONFIGURATION SECTION.
SOURCE-COMPUTER. IBM-370.
OBJECT-COMPUTER. IBM-370.
DATA DIVISION.
WORKING-STORAGE SECTION.
01   WORK-AREAS.
     02   X1              PIC 99.
     02   DEC-NO          PIC 999.
     02   BIT-CONFIG      PIC 999.
01   BIN-NO.
     02   BIT   OCCURS 10 TIMES PIC 9.
PROCEDURE DIVISION.
     ACCEPT BIN-NO FROM SYSIN.
     PERFORM BEGIN THRU COMPUTE-RTN UNTIL BIN-NO = 9999999999.
     STOP RUN.
BEGIN.
     MOVE 10 TO X1.
     MOVE 1 TO BIT-CONFIG.
     MOVE ZEROS TO DEC-NO.
COMPUTE-RTN.
     PERFORM BIT-TEST 10 TIMES.
     DISPLAY 'THE DECIMAL NO IS ', DEC-NO.
     ACCEPT BIN-NO FROM SYSIN.
BIT-TEST.
     IF BIT (X1) = 1 PERFORM ADD-RTN.
     COMPUTE BIT-CONFIG = 2 ** (11 - X1)
     EXHIBIT NAMED BIT-CONFIG.
     EXHIBIT NAMED X1.
     SUBTRACT 1 FROM X1.
ADD-RTN.
     ADD BIT-CONFIG TO DEC-NO.
     EXHIBIT NAMED DEC-NO.
```

Figure 24.6 Illustration of EXHIBIT NAMED statements.

The use of EXHIBIT NAMED DEC-NO, BIT-CONFIG, X1, will cause the results in Figure 24.7 to print.

```
DEC-NO  =  001
BIT-CONFIG  =  002
X1 = 10
DEC-NO  =  003
BIT-CONFIG  =  004
X1 = 09
BIT-CONFIG  =  008
X1 = 08
BIT-CONFIG  =  016
X1 = 07
DEC-NO  =  019
BIT-CONFIG  =  032
X1 = 06
DEC-NO  =  051
BIT-CONFIG  =  064
X1 = 05
BIT-CONFIG  =  128
X1 = 04
BIT-CONFIG  =  256
X1 = 03
BIT-CONFIG  =  512
X1 = 02
BIT-CONFIG  =  024
X1 = 01
THE DECIMAL NO IS 051
BIT-CONFIG  =  002
X1 = 10
DEC-NO  =  002
BIT-CONFIG  =  004
X1 = 09
DEC-NO  =  006
BIT-CONFIG  =  008
X1 = 08
BIT-CONFIG  =  016
X1 = 07
BIT-CONFIG  =  032
X1 = 06
DEC-NO  =  038
BIT-CONFIG  =  064
X1 = 05
BIT-CONFIG  =  128
X1 = 04
BIT-CONFIG  =  256
X1 = 03
BIT-CONFIG  =  512
X1 = 02
BIT-CONFIG  =  024
X1 = 01
THE DECIMAL NO IS 038
BIT-CONFIG  =  002
X1 = 10
DEC-NO  =  002
BIT-CONFIG  =  004
X1 = 09
DEC-NO  =  006
BIT-CONFIG  =  008
```

Figure 24.7

We sometimes want an EXHIBIT to be executed only in the event that the contents of a data field actually changes. That is, if a data field is altered only in given circumstances, we may wish to EXHIBIT that field only when it changes. We can use the following options of the EXHIBIT statement for this purpose.

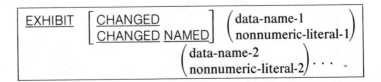

Examples

    EXHIBIT CHANGED DEC-NO.
    EXHIBIT CHANGED NAMED BIT-CONFIG.

Thus the complete format of an EXHIBIT statement is:

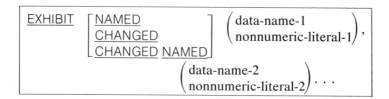

Note that the use of a nonnumeric literal with any of the three options NAMED, CHANGED, or CHANGED NAMED just causes the literal to print. For a CHANGED option, that literal will print only when the contents in the data-name has been altered.

Use of a Display in Place of an Exhibit   You will recall that a DISPLAY statement follows many of the same rules indicated above for an EXHIBIT statement. In fact, a DISPLAY statement may be used in place of an EXHIBIT statement to print out values of key fields at given check points **only when** the program does **not** use the printer as an output device. That is, it is permissible to DISPLAY on the printer only if it is not designated as a device used in the program.

Although the DISPLAY statement may be used with the UPON CONSOLE option as a debugging aid for **any** program, this is **not** a recommended procedure. Using the console in debugging programs makes it difficult for computer operators to control program handling.

Thus the EXHIBIT statement may always be used to print key fields at check points. The DISPLAY statement is an alternate debugging aid when the printer is not used by the program.

C. ON STATEMENT

The ON statement has the following simplified format:

    ON (integer) (imperative statement)

Example

                    ON 100 EXHIBIT NAMED COUNT.

The ON statement enables the programmer to perform some debugging operation when a set of procedures has been executed a specified number of times. That is, in the above, COUNT will be exhibited when the statement has been executed 100 times.

Some programmers automatically incorporate one or more of the above debugging tools in all their programs. Others use them more discriminately. That is, when errors or bugs become evident and the programmer cannot easily locate the problem, he or she then incorporates one or more of the above options. The precise manner in which these tools are used is determined by the programmer. He or she must be familiar with these options so that they can be used if necessary.

FINDING AN ERROR POINT WHEN AN INTERRUPT OCCURS

As indicated, we can use a READY TRACE to list all paragraphs encountered in a program. If a program interrupt occurs, the last paragraph listed is the one that contains the error.

Under most operating systems, the use of a Job Control card can result in the computer printing the **actual instruction** that caused the error to occur.

Consult your computer's job control specifications manual or ask the computer room supervisor for the required entries to print error points.

VALIDITY OF INPUT DATA

A final word on ensuring program integrity. **Never** assume that input data is necessarily valid. Numerous programming errors result from programmers assuming the validity of input data. Always **check** input fields for valid data, insofar as possible, before processing. A numeric input field that is blank, for example, can cause the computer to abort the run if an ADD is performed. A space is not a valid numeric character, and when used inadvertently in numeric fields can cause program interruptions.

REVIEW QUESTIONS

True False

True-False Questions

1. A READY TRACE is used to list all the paragraphs that have been coded in a program.
2. If the program is in an infinite loop, the READY TRACE will list the same paragraph-name over and over again.
3. A RESET TRACE is used to list the paragraphs executed in reverse order.
4. EXHIBIT (data-name) differs from EXHIBIT CHANGED (data-name) because EXHIBIT always prints the field while EXHIBIT CHANGED only prints it when the contents have changed.
5. Most logic errors are detected during the compilation process.
6. If a program has been compiled without any errors, it will generally run properly.
7. Warning-level diagnostics do not usually interfere with the execution of the program.
8. Sometimes conditional errors are corrected by the computer in such a manner that the program will run properly.
9. A single error in a COBOL program sometimes generates numerous error messages.
10. One or two input records are normally sufficient for test data.

A CHARACTERS IN THE COBOL CHARACTER SET

Letters—A–Z

Digits—0–9

and the following special characters:

Name	Symbol
Blank or space	(written ᚦ in the text)
Plus sign	+
Minus sign or hyphen	−
Asterisk or multiplication sign	*
Slash or division sign	/
Equal sign	=
Period or decimal point	.
Semicolon	;
Comma	,
Quotation mark	'
Left parenthesis	(
Right parenthesis	)
Dollar sign	$
"Greater than" symbol	>
"Less than" symbol	<

COBOL RESERVED WORDS

Each COBOL compiler has a list of reserved words that:

1. Include most entries of the ANS COBOL standard.
2. Omit some ANS entries not used by the specific compiler.
3. Include additional entries not part of the standard but which the specific compiler accepts.

Hence no list of COBOL reserved words will be complete. The following is based on the 1974 American National Standard. You may find that your computer has additional reserved words. Diagnostic messages will print if you are using a reserved word incorrectly.

ACCEPT	CORRESPONDING	EXTEND	LESS
ACCESS	COUNT		LIMIT
ADD	CURRENCY	FD	LIMITS
ADVANCING		FILE	LINAGE
AFTER	DATA	FILE-CONTROL	LINAGE-COUNTER
ALL	DATE	FILLER	LINE
ALPHABETIC	DATE-COMPILED	FINAL	LINE-COUNTER
ALSO	DATE-WRITTEN	FIRST	LINES
ALTER	DAY	FOOTING	LINKAGE
ALTERNATE	DE	FOR	LOCK
AND	DEBUG-CONTENTS	FROM	LOW-VALUE
ARE	DEBUG-ITEM		LOW-VALUES
AREA	DEBUG-LINE	GENERATE	
AREAS	DEBUG-NAME	GIVING	MEMORY
ASCENDING	DEBUG-SUB-1	GO	MERGE
ASSIGN	DEBUG-SUB-2	GREATER	MESSAGE
AT	DEBUG-SUB-3	GROUP	MODE
AUTHOR	DEBUGGING		MODULES
	DECIMAL-POINT	HEADING	MOVE
BEFORE	DECLARATIVES	HIGH-VALUE	MULTIPLE
BLANK	DELETE	HIGH-VALUES	MULTIPLY
BLOCK	DELIMITED		
BOTTOM	DELIMITER	I-O	NATIVE
BY	DEPENDING	I-O-CONTROL	NEGATIVE
	DESCENDING	IDENTIFICATION	NEXT
CALL	DESTINATION	IF	NO
CANCEL	DETAIL	IN	NOT
CD	DISABLE	INDEX	NUMBER
CF	DISPLAY	INDEXED	NUMERIC
CH	DIVIDE	INDICATE	
CHARACTER	DIVISION	INITIAL	OBJECT-COMPUTER
CHARACTERS	DOWN	INITIATE	OCCURS
CLOCK-UNITS	DUPLICATES	INPUT	OF
CLOSE	DYNAMIC	INPUT-OUTPUT	OFF
COBOL		INSPECT	OMITTED
CODE	EGI	INSTALLATION	ON
CODE-SET	ELSE	INTO	OPEN
COLLATING	EMI	INVALID	OPTIONAL
COLUMN	ENABLE	IS	OR
COMMA	END		ORGANIZATION
COMMUNICATION	END-OF-PAGE	JUST	OUTPUT
COMP	ENTER	JUSTIFIED	OVERFLOW
COMPUTATIONAL	ENVIRONMENT		
COMPUTE	EOP	KEY	PAGE
CONFIGURATION	EQUAL		PAGE-COUNTER
CONTAINS	ERROR	LABEL	PERFORM
CONTROL	ESI	LAST	PF
CONTROLS	EVERY	LEADING	PH
COPY	EXCEPTION	LEFT	PIC
CORR	EXIT	LENGTH	PICTURE

PLUS	RERUN	SPACE	TYPE
POINTER	RESERVE	SPACES	
POSITION	RESET	SPECIAL-NAMES	UNIT
POSITIVE	RETURN	STANDARD	UNSTRING
PRINTING	REVERSED	STANDARD-1	UNTIL
PROCEDURE	REWIND	START	UP
PROCEDURES	REWRITE	STATUS	UPON
PROCEED	RF	STOP	USAGE
PROGRAM	RH	STRING	USE
PROGRAM-ID	RIGHT	SUB-QUEUE-1	USING
	ROUNDED	SUB-QUEUE-2	
QUEUE	RUN	SUB-QUEUE-3	VALUE
QUOTE		SUBTRACT	VALUES
QUOTES	SAME	SUM	VARYING
	SD	SUPPRESS	
RANDOM	SEARCH	SYMBOLIC	WHEN
RD	SECTION	SYNC	WITH
READ	SECURITY	SYNCHRONZIED	WORDS
RECEIVE	SEGMENT		WORKING-STORAGE
RECORD	SEGMENT-LIMIT	TABLE	WRITE
RECORDS	SELECT	TALLYING	
REDEFINES	SEND	TAPE	ZERO
REEL	SENTENCE	TERMINAL	ZEROES
REFERENCES	SEPARATE	TERMINATE	ZEROS
RELATIVE	SEQUENCE	TEXT	
RELEASE	SEQUENTIAL	THAN	
REMAINDER	SET	THROUGH	
REMOVAL	SIGN	THRU	
RENAMES	SIZE	TIME	
REPLACING	SORT	TIMES	
REPORT	SORT-MERGE	TO	
REPORTING	SOURCE	TOP	
REPORTS	SOURCE-COMPUTER	TRAILING	

APPENDIX
B MAGNETIC TAPE FEATURES

A magnetic tape is a **high-speed** medium that can serve as input to, or output from, a computer. It is the most common file type for medium- or large-scale processing.

A magnetic tape drive (Figure B.1) is the device that can either read a tape

(a)

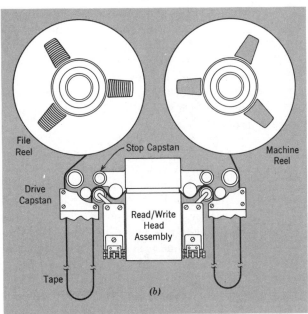

File Reel

Stop Capstan

Machine Reel

Drive Capstan

Read/Write Head Assembly

Tape

(b)

Figure B.1. (a) Magnetic tape drive. (Courtesy Burroughs.) (b) Read/write head for tape. (Courtesy IBM.)

or write onto a tape. It has a read/write head that is accessed by the computer for either reading or writing.

Magnetic tape drives function like home tape recorders. Data can be recorded, or written, onto a tape and "played back," or read, from the same tape at a later date. If data is written on a tape, previous data is written over or destroyed. For this reason, computer centers must take precautions to protect important tapes that should not inadvertently be "written over."

A typical magnetic tape is generally 2400 to 3600 feet long and ½ inch wide. The tape is made of plastic with an iron oxide coating that can be magnetized to represent data. Since the magnetized spots or **bits** are extremely small and not visible to the human eye, large volumes of data can be condensed into a relatively small area of tape. Information from an entire 80-column card, for example, can typically be stored in one tenth of an inch of magnetic tape, or less. The average tape, which costs approximately $25, can store approximately 20 million characters. After a tape file has been processed and is no longer needed, the same tape may be reused repeatedly to store other information.

Because tape drives read data **electronically** by sensing magnetized areas, and write data electronically by magnetizing areas, tapes may be processed at very high speeds. Data can be read or written at speeds averaging 100,000 to 300,000 characters **per second.**

Thus tape files are frequently used for large volumes of data. One tape can store hundreds of thousands of records, transmit and receive data at very high speeds, and store the data in a compact form. In many medium- or large-scale companies, **master files** for Payroll, Accounts Receivable, Accounts Payable, Inventory, and so on are stored on tape. A master file is the main data file that holds all current information for a specific department or system.

A record on a tape may be any size, as long as it is physically consistent with the size of memory. That is, it is not feasible to create 5000-position records using a 4000-position computer, since the output area (5000 positions) must be located in storage. Aside from this limitation, tape records may usually be any size. Keep in mind, however, that extremely large record sizes are more difficult to process.

Because of a tape's capacity to handle large volumes of data in a relatively short time, it is ideally suited for **batch processing,** or processing in cumulative groups.

TAPE FILES MAY BE CREATED BY

1. **A tape drive of a computer system.**

   In such a case, the tape serves as output, the product of a computer run. The data is initially entered from some other device, such as a card reader, and then converted, by the computer, to magnetic tape.

2. **A key-to-tape encoder or converter** (Figure B.2)

   This device is similar to a keypunch machine. It requires an operator to code data from a source document to a magnetic tape via a typewriter-like keyboard. The operator depresses a specific character key and the device converts it to the appropriate magnetized coding. Tapes encoded in this manner may be verified by the same device to ensure their accuracy. It should be noted that key-to-tape encoders are also used for creating tape cassettes, "mini"-tapes, or cartridges for eventual use in a data communications environment.

Figure B.2 Keytape encoder. Simple keyboard—operating ease is one of the many advantages of Honeywell's Keytape devices. The units bypass conventional punched card preparation by transcribing information directly onto magnetic tape from the keyboard. Typing and control functions are similar to those on a keypunch machine, easing the task of keypunch operators in learning to use the devices. (Courtesy Honeywell.)

The key-to-tape equipment in use today can be divided into two basic categories:

KEY-TO-TAPE EQUIPMENT

1. Stand-alone encoders are used to convert source documents to a magnetic tape.
2. Key-to-tape preparation systems, which include a small computer with a main storage capacity of 8K (8000) to 16K, a tape drive, and from 6 to 64 key entry stations. Using this processor, data keyed in by an operator may be formatted, verified, edited, and then placed on a tape for use by the standard computer at the installation.

In short, tape is a very common file medium for high-speed, voluminous processing. It does, however, have several inherent disadvantages.

DISADVANTAGES OF
TAPE PROCESSING

Data recorded on a tape may only be processed **sequentially.** That is, to access a record with Transaction Number 254 from a tape file that is maintained in Transaction Number sequence, we must read past the first 253 records. We instruct the computer to read a record, test if it contains Transaction Number 254, and, if it does not, to read the next record. Thus, 254 records are read. There is no convenient method to instruct the tape drive to skip the first few inches of tape or to go directly to the middle of the tape.

Thus, unless all or most records from a tape file are required for processing **most of the time,** this method could become inefficient and costly.

If an Inventory File is created on tape with 100,000 records and only a handful of these are required to print a report, then tapes may not provide the most efficient file type. Processing time, and thus cost, would be excessive, since most of the file must be read even to process only a small number of records. Sequential processing is beneficial only when **most** records on the file are required for normal processing in sequence. Master Payroll, Accounts Receivable and Accounts Payable files are ideally suited to magnetic tape, since most records are required for processing during normal runs. We must read and process an entire Payroll file, for example, to print checks; thus, a tape file is suitable.

Another disadvantage of tape processing is that a given tape can usually be used **either** as input or output during a single run, but cannot serve as both an input/output medium. That is, an **updating** application, or the process of making a master file of data current, generally requires the master file as input and the creation of a new physical tape. Consider the update illustration in Figure B.3.

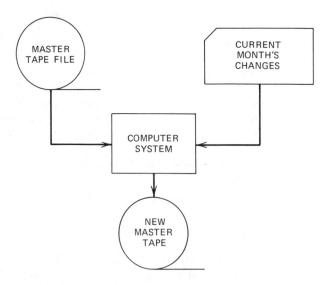

Figure B.3 Illustration of an update procedure.

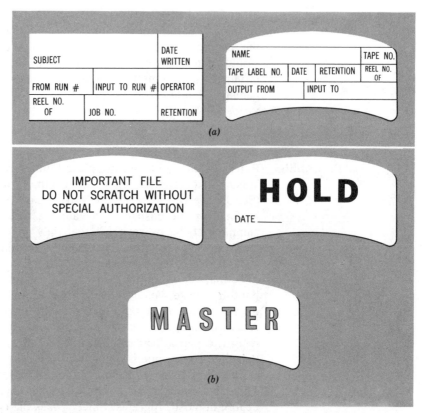

Figure B.4 External tape labels: (a) Two commonly used external labels. (b) Three commonly used special-purpose tape labels.

A new tape must be created that, in effect, rewrites the information from the previous master tape and adds the current month's changes. The input master tape cannot be conveniently processed to add new records, delete some records, and make changes to existing records. A **new** tape must be created that incorporates master information along with the current changes.

This inability of the tape to be conveniently processed as **both** input and output during a single computer run results in several limitations. Since two tapes are required for such runs, **two** tape drives are necessary to process them. The necessity of having to read many master records that have **not** changed during the present month, and to recreate them without alteration on an output tape drive, results in increased processing time. That is, if only 30 payroll changes, for example, are needed to amend a 1000-record Master Tape, then 970 master records that do not require revisions must be read and rewritten onto the new tape. Keep in mind that although this inability results in increased processing time, the increased time is not always excessive, since tape records are written very quickly. We would require tapes with many thousands of inactive records in order to substantially affect the processing time.

A third disadvantage of tape processing is the identification problem. Most medium- and large-scale computer installations have hundreds or even thousands of magnetic tapes, each utilized for a specific application. Because data recorded on these tapes are not ''readable'' or visible to the naked eye, it is often difficult to identify them. If a Master Accounts Receivable tape is inadvertently "written over," or used as **output** for some other job, for example, the result could be an expensive recreation process, since the writing of output would destroy the existing information. Several steps have been implemented at most installations to prevent such occurrences, or to reduce the extent of damage, should errors occur.

TAPE LABELS
External gummed labels are placed on the face of each tape, identifying it and indicating its **retention cycle** (the length of time the tape should be maintained). (See Figure B.4.) These labels are clearly visible to anyone, so that chances for inadvertent misuse of a valuable tape are reduced. The problem with gummed labels, however, is that they sometimes become unglued. Their effectiveness is also directly related to the effort and training of the computer staff. If operators are negligent, then the labels will not be used properly.

To make the identification of tapes more reliable, most programs include a built-in routine which creates a **tape label record** on output tapes that is produced as any other tape record, with magnetized bits. The label is the first record on the tape. When the tape is later used as input, then this first label record, called a **header label,** is checked as part of the program, to ascertain that the correct tape is being used.

Thus header labels are created on output tapes and checked on input tapes. This label creation for output and label checking for input is a standard procedure in most programs. Since it uses the computer to verify that the correct tapes are being used, there is less danger of human error.

TAPE LIBRARIAN
Most medium- and large-scale companies have numerous tapes that must be filed or stored, and released for reuse when no longer required. Such companies employ a tape librarian to maintain the proper usage of tape files. If he or she performs the job properly, there will be less misuse or misplacing of tapes.

FILE PROTECTION RING
(Fig. B.5)
Those available tapes that may be written on, or used as output, have a **file protection ring** inserted in the back. The tape drive is electronically sensitized so that it **will not** create an output record unless this ring is in its proper place. For those tapes that are to be maintained and not "written over" the ring has been removed. Thus if an operator inadvertently uses such a tape for an output operation, the computer prints a message that states, in effect **"NO RING— NO WRITE."** If operators are cautious, they will examine the external label and, it is hoped, will realize that the wrong tape is being used. If they are persistent they will merely place a ring on the tape (any file protection ring fits all tapes) and restart the job. Thus this method, alone, deters the misuse of tape but does not totally alleviate the problem.

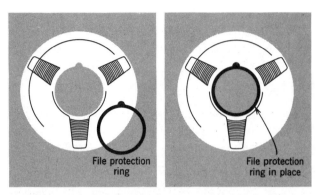

Figure B.5 The file protection ring is a plastic ring that fits into the groove in the tape reel. When the ring is in place, both writing and reading of tape records can occur. When the ring is removed, only reading can occur. In this way, the file is protected from accidental erasure.

BACK-UP TAPES   Since tapes can sometimes be written over or become physically damaged, it is necessary to maintain backup tapes so that the re-creation process, should it become necessary, does not become enormously costly and cumbersome.

Suppose the update procedure shown in Figure B.3 is performed each month. After processing, it is best to store the old master tape and the detail records **along with** the new master tape. In this way, if some mishap should befall the new master tape, it is a simple task to recreate it from the two forms of input. Normally, we maintain **two** previous tapes as backup, in addition to the present one, in order to prevent any serious problem. Hence, the three generations of tapes maintained for important files are called the **grandfather-father-son** tapes. (See Figure B.6.)

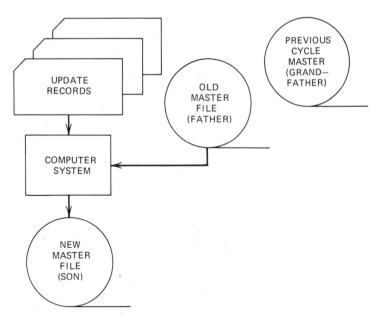

Figure B.6 Grandfather-father-son method of file backup.

REPRESENTATION OF DATA ON MAGNETIC TAPE

A. MAGNETIC TAPE CODE

You will recall that data is recorded on magnetic tape on a thin film of iron-oxide coating. Many third-generation tapes have 9-tracks in which to record data (see Figure B.7), although 7-track tapes are still widely used.[1] We shall discuss 9-track tapes in detail.

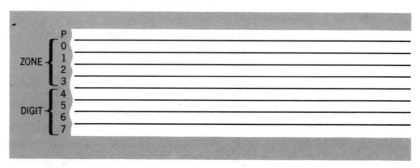

Figure B.7 A 9-track tape.

Each of these tracks can be magnetized or demagnetized depending on the data represented. The coded representation of data on these 9 tracks, labeled P and 0 to 7, is the **same** code used by the computer for the internal representation known as EBCDIC, or Extended Binary Coded Decimal Interchange Code. The Hollerith code, on a punched card that uses a combination of a single zone and a single digit, can be converted to this **9-bit** machine code. We will present EBCDIC concepts briefly (See Figure B.8.)

Disregarding the P-bit momentarily, we may represent any character using this combination of 4 zone and 4 digit bits. The letter A, a combination of a 12-zone and a 1-digit in Hollerith code, would be represented as indicated on tape in Figure B.9.

A typical way to represent any **integer** on magnetic tape would be to use 1111 in the zone positions, in addition to the corresponding digit representation. Thus the number 172 in a numeric field will be represented as indicated in Figure B.9.

Note that the illustrated code is the **same** one as the computer uses for internal representation of data. In essence, the 1's denote magnetized positions or current "on." The 0's denote demagnetized positions or current "off." Magnetic tape can be processed quickly by computer because no code conversion is required. Data is represented on tape in 9-track form, with each track having current "on" and "off" in the same manner as is represented internally in the computer by 9 bits for each character, using current "on" or "off." Thus, for the computer to read from or write onto magnetic tape is a high-speed process.

---

[1]The 7-track tape uses the BCD code.

ZONE \ BITS	0	1	2	3
12 (for letters A–I)	1	1	0	0
11 (for letters J–R)	1	1	0	1
0 (for letters S–Z)	1	1	1	0
DIGITS	1	1	1	1

ZONE PORTION

DIGIT \ BITS	4	5	6	7
0	0	0	0	0
1	0	0	0	1
2	0	0	1	0
3	0	0	1	1
4	0	1	0	0
5	0	1	0	1
6	0	1	1	0
7	0	1	1	1
8	1	0	0	0
9	1	0	0	1

DIGIT PORTION

Figure B.8 Typical representation of data on a 9-track tape. Note: Digit Bits: 4 5 6 7 correspond to binary values 8 4 2 1.

PARITY The P-bit corresponds to a **P**arity or check bit and is used to check the coded representation of data. When data is coded, both internally in the computer and on magnetic tape, there is a remote possibility that a single bit position can sometimes become demagnetized, or an ''off'' position can become magnetized. The Parity or P-bit is used to determine if this error has occurred.

Odd Parity is the utilization of an odd number of on-bits to represent any character. Thus Figure B.10 illustrates how the digit 5 is represented on tape.

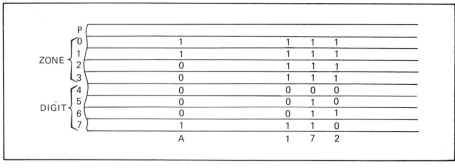

A: 12 Zone: 1100 Zone Bits   172: Zone Bits: 1111 for each byte
1 Digit: 0001 Digit Bits   Digit Bits:

```
        8 4 2 1                              8 4 2 1 | 8 4 2 1 | 8 4 2 1
        0 0 0 1                              0 0 0 1 | 0 1 1 1 | 0 0 1 0
                                                1         7         2
```

Figure B.9 Representation of sample characters on a 9-track tape. (P-bit is subsequently discussed.)

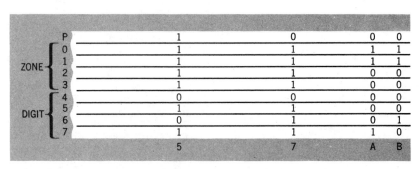

Figure B.10 Representation of characters: 5, 7, A, B, on a 9-track tape.

Note that there are **six** bits on, not counting the P-bit. Using the concept of odd parity, the machine would automatically magnetize or "turn on" the P-bit.

Thus, the complete codes for the number 7 and the letters A and B are denoted also in Figure B.10. The P-bit is used to ensure that an odd number of bits is always on for the computer that uses odd-parity checking.

For **even**-parity computers, the P-bit is used to ensure that an even number of bits is always on.

In short, the number of bits on must always be **odd** for odd-parity computers. Thus magnetic tapes typically utilize an odd number of bits for each character. During the reading of a magnetic tape, the number of bits on is checked to determine if, in fact, an odd number exists. If a single bit were inadvertently demagnetized or the current turned "off," or similarly an extra bit were magnetized, this would result in a parity error. The computer would not continue processing this tape until the problem was located.

Notice that this technique of parity checking only works when a **single** bit for a specific character is erroneously transmitted. If two bits are demagnetized, an odd number would still exist and no parity error would occur. Keep in mind, however, that the loss or gain of a single bit during processing is a remote possibility, but one that must nonetheless be properly handled; the loss of two bits, however, has almost no probability of occurring during processing and thus is simply not handled by most computers.

B. DENSITY

We have seen in this Appendix that millions of characters can be recorded on a single magnetic tape. Different tapes, however, have different storage capabilities. The **density** of a tape denotes the number of characters that can be represented in a given area of tape. Usually we indicate tape density as the **number of bits (characters) per inch.** The most frequently used densities are

556 bpi
800 bpi
1600 bpi
3200 bpi
6250 bpi

Bpi is an abbreviation for bits per inch. In effect, this indicates the number of characters per inch. Thus the most frequently used tape densities are from 556 to 6250 characters per inch.

Obviously, the larger tape densities enable the tape to store more characters. As noted, some magnetic tapes have densities of up to 6000 or more characters per inch.

C. BLOCKING

We have seen that tapes, unlike cards, can utilize any record size. The size of tape records is only restricted by the physical limitations of the computer.

Thus we may have 100-position tape records or 500-position tape records. When all records on a single tape file are the same size, we say that the file employs **fixed-length** records. When records on a single tape file have different sizes depending on the format of each record, we say that the file employs **variable-length** records.

Programming effort is simplified by using fixed-length records on a tape. Variable-length tape records require far more sophisticated programming and thus are not usually employed unless processing is optimized by utilizing records of different sizes as in some database systems.

We will, therefore, restrict our discussion to fixed-length tape records, where each record is the same size. The specific size of each record, however, is determined for each application by the Systems and Programming Staff.

Many applications use, for example, 100 characters per record. We shall now see, however, that small records such as these can, if not handled properly, lead to inefficient processing.

Between tape records the computer automatically reserves a fraction of an inch of blank tape called an Interblock Gap (IBG). Thus when a tape is created as computer output, it is created as noted in Figure B.11.

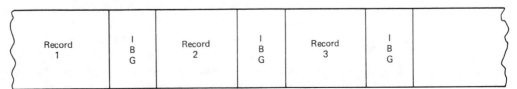

Figure B.11 Physical records separated by interblock gaps on a tape.

For some tape drives, this interblock gap between records is ¾ inch, for others it is 3/5 inch. The smaller the IBG, the less wasted tape there is.

This blank area of tape called an IBG is a necessary part of tape processing. When a computer reads from a tape, it reads an entire record at the average rate of more than 100 inches per second. This is an extremely fast rate. Once a record has been read, and the computer senses its end, it requires a fraction of a second for the equipment to physically stop and cease reading because of the speed with which it functions. This concept is called **inertia.** It is similar to the automobile traveling 60 miles per hour which, after the brake has been applied, requires numerous feet before it actually comes to a full stop.

Thus a magnetic tape that is read or written at tremendous speeds needs a fraction of a second to physically stop after the end of a record has been reached. In this fraction of a second, a fraction of an inch of tape has been bypassed. That is, in the time it takes the read/write head of a tape drive to stop, an extra fraction of an inch of tape has been passed.

To accommodate for this inertia, each record, upon creation, is automatically written with a blank area of tape next to it. This blank area called an IBG is the exact size necessary to accommodate for inertia, so that when the fraction of an inch of tape has been bypassed, no significant data will be lost.

Thus each record has a blank area of tape called an IBG adjacent to it. Let us consider the size of the IBG to be 0.6 inches, which it is for some tape drives. If each tape record were 100 characters long, and the tape has a density of 800 bpi, we would have data represented on tape as indicated in Figure B.12.

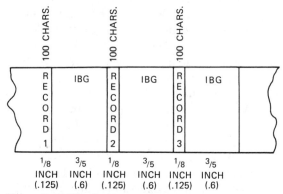

Figure B.12 Physical representation of data on a tape—without blocking.

You will note that while each record occupies ⅛ (0.125) of an inch, each IBG adjacent to it uses 3/5 (0.6) inches. In effect, we would have more blank tape than recorded areas.

To alleviate this problem, the computer systems allow us to "**block**" or group tape records to make maximum use of the tape area. The Systems and Programming Staff determines the size of the block, or the blocking factor, as indicated in Figure B.13, where the blocking factor is 8.

In this example, the computer processes 8 records as a group. If each record contained 100 characters, the physical record or block would contain 800 characters. At 800 bpi, that would be 1 inch of tape. Thus we would have our 0.6 inch IBG between each inch of data. This is a distinct improvement over our

BLOCKING OF TAPE RECORDS

blocking factor: 8
8 records = 1 block

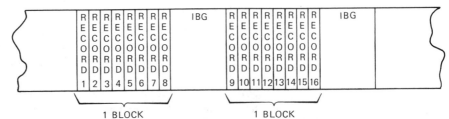

Figure B.13 Blocking of tape records. Blocking factor: 8; 8 records = 1 block.

previous example where we had substantially more blank area than recorded data.

The blocking of data on tape does **not** represent very much increase of programming effort. Most modern computers have advanced Input and Output Control Systems that facilitate programming effort using magnetic tape or disk. The programmer is merely required to supply the blocking factor and the record size and the computer itself will perform the specific input/output functions. When a computer is instructed to read from a tape, for example, it reads a **physical record** or **block** into storage (See Figure B.14).

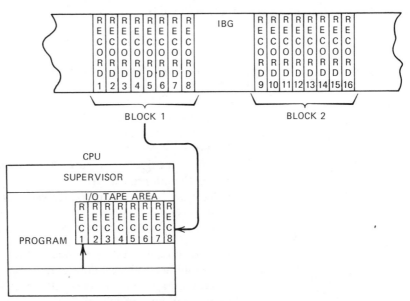

Figure B.14 How blocked records are processed by a program.

The computer then makes the first **logical record,** Record 1, available for processing. When it is instructed to read a second record, it does **not** go to the tape again, but makes Record 2 **from storage** available for processing. Thus for the first 8 READ TAPE commands, the computer accesses the tape only once. It then makes each of the logical records available **from storage** as they are called on by a READ TAPE Command. On the ninth READ TAPE command, the computer must physically access the next block of 8 records, and place it in storage overlaying the previous 8 records.

The creation of output tape records operates similarly. If the blocking factor is again 8, the computer will accumulate 8 logical records in storage before it physically writes a block. Thus the first 8 WRITE TAPE commands merely result in the accumulation of 8 logical records **in storage.** The ninth WRITE TAPE command causes the previous block of 8 records to be created on tape and the ninth logical record placed in storage. Here, again, the computer accesses the tape only after every 8 records have been processed.

In summary, tape records are blocked in an effort to make maximum use of the tape area. The blocking factor is determined by the Systems and Programming Staff and is subject again to the physical limitations of the computer. A record size of 1000 and a blocking factor of 50, for example, would simply be too cumbersome or too large to be effectively handled by most computers. In addition, the larger the physical block, the more chance there is for transmission errors.

The programming effort required for blocking records is not very great, since the computer's Input/Output Control System is capable of handling many of the details. The programmer is required to supply the record size and the blocking factor and the computer can perform much of the internal processing. The programmer need only supply READ and WRITE commands and blocking and deblocking is automatically handled.

The complex coding of the following can usually be eliminated when coding a program in COBOL.

---

1. Tape labels
   (header labels for identification, trailer labels for summary or total information)
2. Creation of IBGs
3. Blocking of records
4. End-of-file conditions
5. End-of-reel conditions
   (where a specific file requires more than one physical tape reel)
6. Wrong length record errors
   (where programming or transmission errors result in a record that is not of the specified length).

The programmer need only specify the length of a logical record, and the COBOL compiler will incorporate in the program a wrong length record check. Similarly, the programmer need only specify the blocking factor, and blocking techniques will also be included.

SELF-EVALUATING QUIZ

1. Data is recorded on magnetic tape on a thin film of _____.
   * * * * *
   iron-oxide coating
2. Most computer centers use (no.) or (no.) track tapes.

   * * * * *
   7 or 9

3. The tracks of a 9-track tape are labeled _____ to _____ and _____.

* * * * *

0; 7; P

4. Four bits are used to represent the _____ and four bits are used to represent the _____.

* * * * *

zone; digit

5. To represent any integer on magnetic tape we typically use _____ in the zone positions.

* * * * *

1111

6. The digit positions of bits 4 to 7 represent the integers _____, _____, _____, and _____, respectively.

* * * * *

8, 4, 2, 1

7. The P-bit corresponds to a _____ or _____ bit.

* * * * *

parity; check

8. _____ is the term used to represent the utilization of an odd number of on-bits for any character.

* * * * *

Odd parity

9. The number of characters per inch of tape is called _____.

* * * * *

density

10. The most frequently used densities range from (no.) to (no.), although some tapes have densities in excess of _____.

* * * * *

556; 3200; 6000

11. When records on a single tape file have different sizes depending on the format of each record, then the file uses _____ records.

* * * * *

variable-length

12. Between tape records the computer automatically reserves a fraction of an inch of blank tape called an _____.

* * * * *

interblock gap (IBG)

13. This fraction of an inch is necessary to provide for the physical concept of _____.

* * * * *

inertia

14. To make maximum use of the tape area so that less tape is wasted, logical records are often grouped or _____.

* * * * *

blocked

15. (T or F) Suppose an input file is blocked 8. The computer physically reads from the tape after every READ command.

* * * * *

F

16. (T or F) If an input file is blocked 8, after every eight READ commands a physical record is read into storage.
    * * * * *
    T

17. (T or F) The programmer is required to handle most of the sophisticated tape routines in a program.
    * * * * *
    F

C FLOWCHARTS AND PSEUDOCODES

A. FLOWCHARTS

A useful tool for analyzing the logic necessary in a program is called a **flowchart.** A flowchart is a diagram, or pictorial representation, of the logic flow of a program; it is drawn **before** the problem is coded. It is like the blueprint an architect prepares before a house is built. Through the use of a flowchart, the programmer can organize and verify the logic that must be employed.

This section is designed to illustrate the **elements** of program flowcharting; it does not teach the beginner how to draw such diagrams. It will, however, indicate the method used to **read** flowcharts since they are employed throughout the book to denote program logic. It is hoped that the ability to write flowcharts will come with constant exposure to their use.

Those students already familiar with flowcharting will note that the illustrations in this chapter vary slightly from those used in introductory textbooks. The examples in this appendix illustrate the **structured** approach to programming. Using the method of flowcharting presented here will enable the reader to code a structured COBOL program directly from a flowchart.

Consider the flowchart in Figure C.1. This is a simple chart that reads punched cards and prints the data contained on them.

FLOWCHART RULES
1. A logic flow is read from top to bottom unless a specific condition alters the path.
2. Different symbols are used to denote different functions.
3. All symbols have explanatory notes indicating the specific operations. Since a symbol denotes a major class of functions such as input-output or processing, a note is required within the symbol to describe the specific operations to be performed.

You will note that there are two separate sequences or **routines** indicated in this flowchart. The main routine, which begins with a symbol labeled START, performs the following operations.

1. Files are opened or prepared for processing.
2. A 0 (zero) is moved to EOF.
   EOF is a special end-of-file indicator that is initialized at 0 and changed to 1 only **after** the last input record has been read and processed. Thus, EOF is zero throughout the entire sequence except when there are no more cards to process.
3. A card is read. If there are no more cards, an AT END condition is denoted, and 1 is moved to EOF.
4. A separate routine called CALC-RTN is executed repeatedly until EOF = 1; that is, until there are no more cards.
5. CALC-RTN will be executed until all input cards have been processed; then the files are deactivated by closing them.
6. The job is terminated by a STOP RUN command.

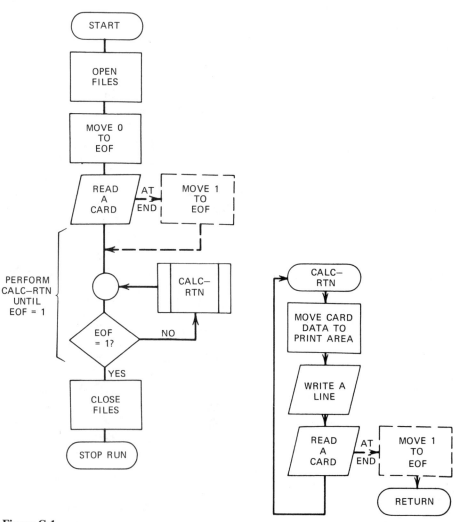

Figure C.1

CALC-RTN is the sequence or set of steps that performs the required operation on each card. When CALC-RTN is executed **for the first time** a card has already been read. See the previous sequence. At CALC-RTN, we have the following:

---

1. The card data is moved from the input area, in which it was read, to the print area.
2. A line is written.
3. A new card is read.
4. The sequence of steps at CALC-RTN is repeated until an AT END condition occurs. When an AT END condition occurs, a 1 is moved to EOF, the sequence is terminated and control returns to the first sequence where files are closed and the job is terminated.

Note that the flowchart indicated in Figure C.2 shows the very same logic. In Figure C.2, however, CALC-RTN is coded as part of the main flow.

Consider now the program flowchart indicated in Figure C.3.

This flowchart depicts the logic flow used to print salary checks for all salespeople in a company. If a salesperson has made over $100 in sales, the commission is 10% of sales, which is added to the salesperson's salary. If a salesperson has made $100 or less in sales, then the commission is only 5% or .05 of sales.

Here, again, there are two sequences: one beginning with START and the other with CALC-RTN. Note that the START sequence has the very same set of instructions as the previous illustrations. The main difference in this chart is the actual operations to be performed on input cards. This is indicated at CALC-RTN.

If sales are greater than $100, 10% of sales is used to determine the commission; otherwise 5% is used. After the commission has been determined, the amount of each check is calculated, and a check is written with name and amount. Another salesperson's card is read and CALC-RTN is repeated until an AT END condition exists. When an AT END condition exists, a 1 is moved to EOF and control is returned to the main sequence where files are closed and the run is terminated.

The following symbols are the ones most frequently used in program flowcharts.

Symbol	**Name**	**Use**
	Input-Output	Used for all I-O operations. For example, the reading of a card, the writing of a line, and the writing of a magnetic tape are considered I-O functions.
	Processing	Used for all arithmetic and data transfer operations. For example, moving of data from one area of storage (input) to another area (output), and multiplying percentage by total sales are processing functions.

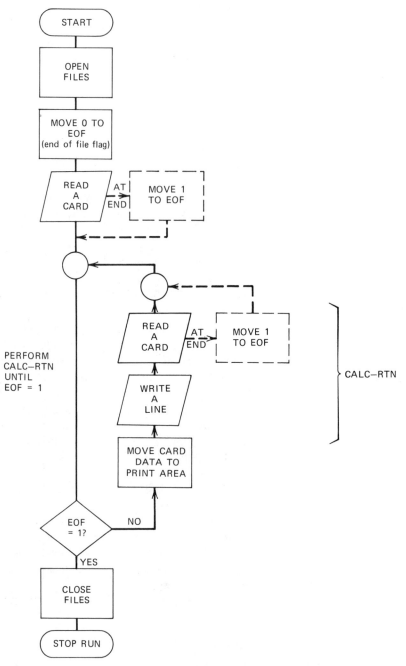

Figure C.2

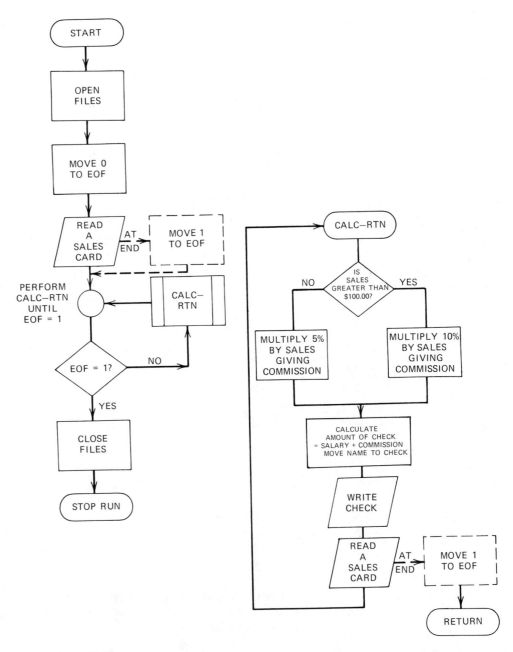

Figure C.3

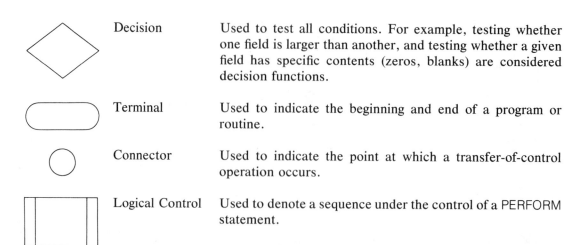

| Decision | Used to test all conditions. For example, testing whether one field is larger than another, and testing whether a given field has specific contents (zeros, blanks) are considered decision functions. |

Terminal — Used to indicate the beginning and end of a program or routine.

Connector — Used to indicate the point at which a transfer-of-control operation occurs.

Logical Control — Used to denote a sequence under the control of a PERFORM statement.

Note that the Processing symbol cut off by two parallel bars is used to denote a sequence under the control of a PERFORM statement. That is, control is passed to the sequence of steps and is then returned to the point directly following the PERFORM. The PERFORM . . . UNTIL sequence can therefore be flowcharted as follows:

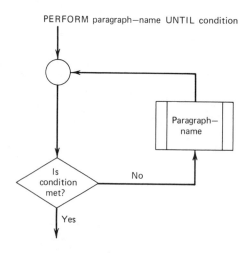

Let us consider another illustration. From the following card format, we wish to print the names of all blue-eyed, blonde males and all brown-eyed, brunette females.

Card format

Card cols:
1–20 Name
21   Sex (M-male, F-female)
22   Color of eyes
         (1-Blue, 2-Brown, 3-Other)
23   Color of hair
         (1-Brunette, 2-Blonde, 3-Other)
24–80 Not used

The flowchart for this problem is illustrated in Figure C.4.

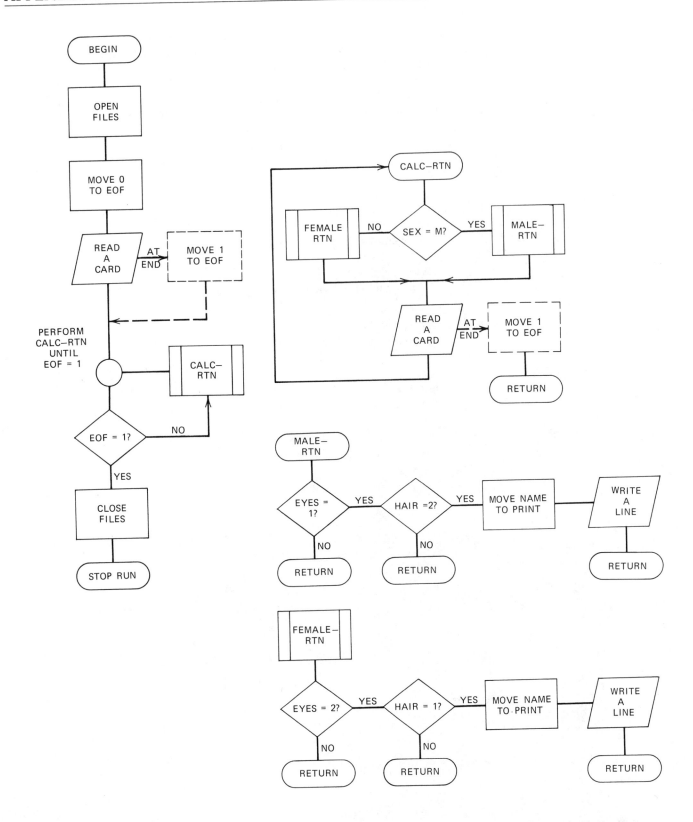

Figure C.4

Note that the writing of flowcharts is a difficult task for the beginner in data processing. One advantage of COBOL is that the elementary level programs are relatively simple to code and a flowchart is therefore unnecessary. For intermediate level programs, where the logic flow is often complex, a flowchart can be quite helpful. At this stage, however, it is hoped that the student will be familiar enough with data processing to be able to write adequate flowcharts. We do suggest that even when the logic is not complex, flowcharts should be written for documentation purposes.

SELF-EVALUATING
QUIZ

1. A flowchart is used for analyzing the _____ necessary in a program.
   * * * * *
   logic

2. A flowchart is drawn (before, after) the problem is coded.
   * * * * *
   before

3. A program flowchart is read from _____ to _____.
   * * * * *
   top
   bottom

4. Different _____ are used to denote different functions.
   * * * * *
   symbols

5. The input-output symbol is coded as _____.
   * * * * *

6. A processing symbol is coded as _____.
   * * * * *

7. is called a _____ symbol.

   * * * * *
   decision

8. The is used to denote a _____.

   * * * * *
   transfer of control

9. After a transfer of control is executed, the logic flow continues with
_____.
* * * * *
the next sequential statement (after the transfer)
10. All symbols have _____ indicating the specific operations to be performed.
* * * * *
explanatory notes

B. PSEUDOCODE

In the previous section, we demonstrated how flowcharts may be used for depicting the logic flow coded in programs. Such flowcharts have been the traditional tool of the programmer for planning the sequence of necessary steps.

In recent years, however, flowcharts have been widely criticized for being cumbersome and difficult to follow. Moreover, the techniques of structured programming do not entirely lend themselves to simplified representation by flowcharts. An alternative method for depicting the logic flow in a program has, therefore, been developed and is called **pseudocode.** The name implies that the representation is a **code,** like that used in a program; the term **'pseudo'** implies that while this code is similar to that used in a program, it is merely a representation, not a language itself.

Pseudocode has been designed to easily represent a structured approach. Each processing or input-output step is denoted by a line of pseudocode. Just as with flowcharts, the pseudocode need not indicate all the processing details; abbreviations are permissible.

The logical control instructions are indicated by:
1. PERFORM statements
2. IFTHENELSE specifications—to test specific conditions

PERFORM STATEMENTS

The structure of a PERFORM is as follows:

PERFORM

```
___
___       }  instructions to be performed
___
___
```

ENDPERFORM

The indented statements would be those under the control of a PERFORM. We can also use a PERFORM . . . UNTIL this way. See the pseudocode for Flowchart C.1 (Figure C.5), which illustrates the use of a PERFORM.

> **Pseudocode for Flowchart C.1**
>   Housekeeping Operations
>   Read a Card Record; At End Move 1 to EOF
>   PERFORM . . . UNTIL EOF = 1
>   Move Card Data to Print Area
>   Write a Line
>   Read a Card Record; At End Move 1 to EOF
>   ENDPERFORM
>   End-of-Job Functions
>   Stop Run

Figure C.5

NOTE: (1) Only the transfer-of-control functions are capitalized.
      (2) Operations under the control of PERFORM or other transfer instructions are indented.

IFTHENELSE SPECIFICATIONS

To indicate the testing of conditions, the following format is used:

IF	(condition)
THEN	(operation to be performed)
ELSE	(operation to be performed if condition is not met)
ENDIF	

See the pseudocode for Flowchart C.3 (Figure C.6) for an illustration.

> **Pseudocode for Flowchart C.3**
>   Open Files
>   Move 0 to EOF
>   Read a Sales Card; At End Move 1 to EOF
>   PERFORM CALC-RTN UNTIL EOF = 1
>   IF Sales Greater Than 100.00
>   THEN
>   Multiply 10% (.10) by Sales Giving Commission
>   ELSE
>   Multiply 5% (.05) by Sales Giving Commission
>   ENDIF
>   Calculate Amount of Check = Salary + Commission
>   Move Name to Check
>   Write Check
>   Read a Sales Card; At End Move 1 to EOF
>   ENDPERFORM
>   Close Files
>   Stop Run

Figure C.6

Pseudocodes are being used for structured programs with increasing frequency both for documentation and for assisting the programmer in providing the most efficient and accurate logic flow necessary.

SELF-EVALUATING QUIZ

1. Pseudocodes have been used with increasing frequency in place of _____.

   * * * * *

   flowcharts

2. Pseudocodes are used for depicting the _____ of a program.

   * * * * *

   logic

3. The transfer of control or decision specifications are denoted by a _____ and _____ respectively.

   * * * * *

   PERFORM
   IFTHENELSE

4. The last step in a PERFORM sequence is _____.

   * * * * *

   ENDPERFORM

5. The last step in an IF sequence is _____.

   * * * * *

   ENDIF

REVIEW QUESTIONS

1. Give four examples of input-output functions.
2. Give four examples of processing functions.
3. Give two examples of decision functions.
4. (T or F) A program flowchart is required before any programs are written.
5. What is the purpose of EOF?

PROBLEMS

1. Consider the following flowchart.
   With the following input cards, what will be the contents of TOTAL at the end of all operations?

Card No.	Contents of Column 18	Contents of Column 19
1	1	2
2	1	3
3	1	2
4	1	0
5	(blank)	(blank)
6	(blank)	1
7	1	(blank)
8	1	2
9	1	2
10	(blank)	2

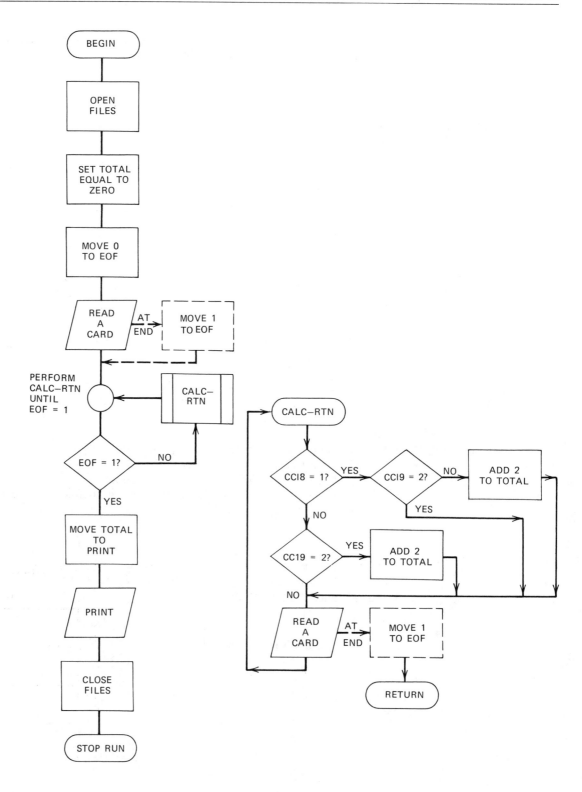

Use the following flowchart (continued on the next page) to answer Questions 2(a)-2(c) on page 524.

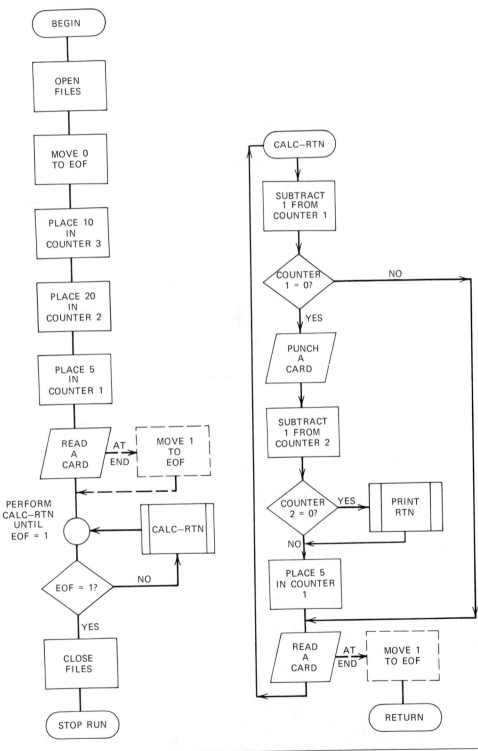

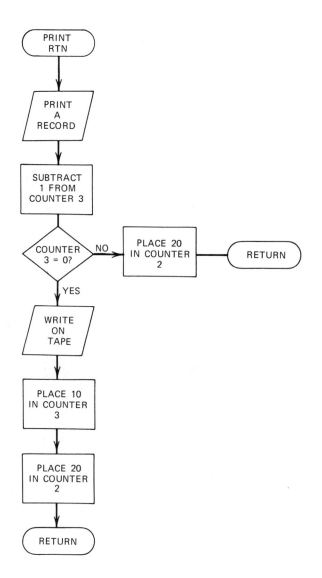

Use this flowchart to answer Questions 3(a)-3(d) on page 524.

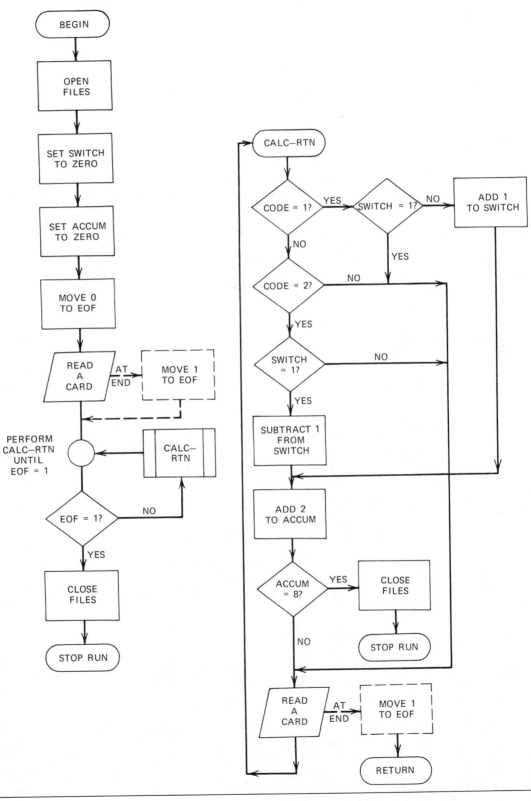

2. (a) In the above system, a record is punched after reading how many cards? Explain.
   (b) The system is printing a record after reading how many cards? Explain.
   (c) The system is writing on tape after reading how many cards? Explain.

3. Questions a-d refer to the flowchart on page 523.
   Input used is on 15 cards.
   Codes on 15 cards (in Column 1) are:

   1, 2, 3, 2, 1, 1, 2, 2, 3, 3, 1, 2, 3, 1, 2

   (a) How many cards will be read?
   (b) What is the value of SWITCH when a STOP RUN occurs?
   (c) What is the value of ACCUM when STOP RUN occurs?
   (d) How many cards would have been read if ACCUM were originally set to 1 instead of 0?

4. Write a Pseudocode for Problems 1–3 above.

D JOB CONTROL LANGUAGE

A. THE CONTROL SYSTEM

THE SUPERVISOR (FIG. D.1)

The **supervisor,** sometimes called a **monitor,** is a special program usually supplied by the manufacturer, which is always stored within the CPU, in modern computers. That is, a supervisor resides in memory for the purpose of controlling the operations of the computer. The supervisor is part of a larger control system typically stored on a high-speed input/output device such as a tape or disk. This control system is part of the software supplied by the manufacturer. The supervisor must be **loaded** into main memory each day prior to any processing. It then calls in each program and extracts items, as needed, from the control system. That is, if a program needs to be compiled, the supervisor calls in the corresponding compiler. If a complex input/output function is required for the program, the supervisor accesses the control system and calls the appropriate routines into memory. Thus the supervisor controls the operations of the computer. When the end of a program is reached, for example, the supervisor calls in the next one.

CENTRAL PROCESSING UNIT

SUPERVISOR
PROGRAM

Figure D.1 The supervisor and the program within the CPU.

THE OPERATING SYSTEM

The control system that is typically stored on a high-speed device such as tape or disk for accessibility, is sometimes referred to as an **operating system.** For many computer systems, where a modified operating system is stored on disk, it is referred to as DOS (**D**isk **O**perating **S**ystem), and when a full operating system exists, it is referred to as OS.

The supervisor permits the computer to operate essentially without manual intervention in OS systems. A brief discussion of the major functions of the supervisor should help reassure the student that the computer is rigorously controlled. It is only a remote possibility that the computer itself would malfunction and cause errors to go undetected. There are special circuits within the CPU that check to see if data put into the computer is inadvertently altered or destroyed by a machine malfunction. If data has been so destroyed, the supervisor will automatically interrupt operations. The manufacturer must then send its engineers to fix the equipment. When errors in final output do occur, they are usually traceable to data processing personnel and/or businesspeople who have in some way misunderstood or improperly communicated all requirements of the particular problem that was programmed.

Up to this point, we have seen that the major steps involved in writing and running a program generally include keypunching the program, and then putting the source deck into the computer to be translated by a special program called a compiler or an assembler, depending on the language of the source program. Several points should be made here so that the student is fully aware of computer capabilities.

First, most commercial computers are capable of handling source programs written in several different languages. It is quite common, for example, to have a computer that can process source programs written in COBOL, FORTRAN, PL/1, Assembler Language, and RPG. Some of the smaller business computers can process only a few languages, often simply Assembler language, RPG, and perhaps BASIC. Regardless of the specific combination of languages available, each machine must have a translator, either a compiler or an assembler, for each language to be translated into machine language.

The compilers and assemblers are typically located on a high-speed input/output medium such as a disk. When a source program is read into the computer, to be translated, the supervisor will bring into the CPU the appropriate compiler or assembler to perform the translation. (The specific manner in which the supervisor recognizes which compiler or assembler is required is discussed later.) The diagram in Figure D.2 will clarify the points just made for a COBOL source program entered into a system capable of handling many languages. The illustration shows what typically happens if the program is successfully translated.

The supervisor must be provided with instructions that may indicate, for example:

SUPERVISOR IS PROVIDED WITH THE FOLLOWING INFORMATION
1. The options used with the program.
2. The language the program is written in.
3. Whether a program is to be compiled only or compiled and executed.
4. The labels to be included with tape and disk files.
5. The specifications for the tapes and disks used.

One way that the programmer can inform the supervisor of the above type of information is to use certain **job control cards** in conjunction with the source deck, as shown in the diagram in Figure D.3.

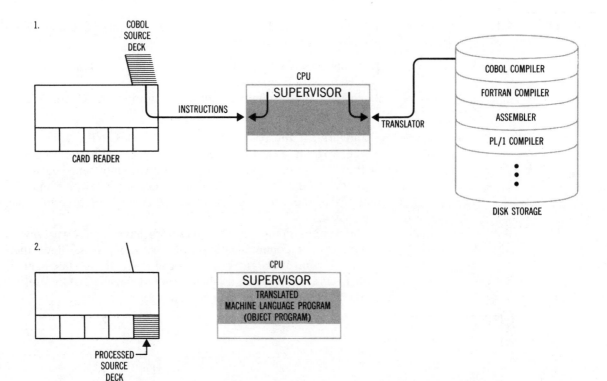

Figure D.2 The process of obtaining an object (translated) program.

Note that the job control cards in Figure D.3 indicate to the supervisor what operations the programmer wants the computer to perform on the COBOL source deck. The illustrated job control applies to a specific computer (IBM S/370). Note that although job control on all computers can accomplish similar tasks, the specifications may be slightly different.

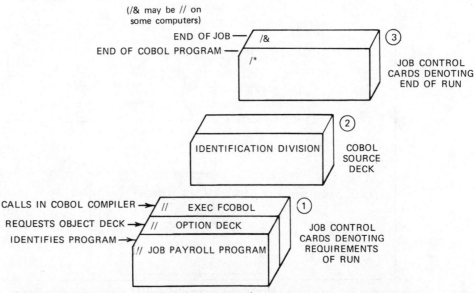

Figure D.3 Example of IBM S/370 DOS job control cards used with a COBOL source deck to compile a program and produce an object deck.

B. DOS JCL

The illustration in Figure D.4 indicates how a programmer can direct the supervisor in a DOS system to:

1. Translate a COBOL Accounts Receivable program, and, if the translation is successfully achieved,
2. Execute the resultant object program in the CPU, running it with test data supplied by the programmer.

Similarly, if the programmer wants to direct the computer to use a sort/ merge program, a card-to-tape utility program, or a user program that is already in the library, the appropriate job control statements must be read into the computer to direct the supervisor. Thus, any operation that the programmer requires of the computer must be indicated by job control messages to the supervisor.

The various computer manufacturers have their own types of job control statements for communicating with the supervisor. Since there are usually many job control statements to choose from, these statements are commonly thought of as comprising a **job control language** (JCL) by itself. JCL cards are an integral part of all computer runs.

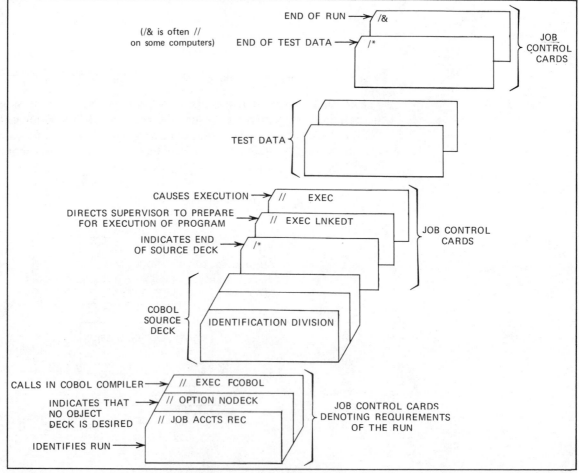

Figure D.4 Example of IBM S/370 DOS job control cards used with a COBOL source deck to direct supervisor to translate and run program.

SUMMARY OF
BASIC DOS JCL

Columns 1 and 2	Begin in Column 3	Leave 1 space after last entry
//	JOB	Job name 1–8 characters First character is alphabetic (comments to 72)
//	OPTION	(See Figure D.5 for entries)
//	EXEC	FCOBOL
	[source program]	
/*		
//	EXEC	LNKEDT
//	EXEC	
	[any data cards]	
/*		
/& (or //)		

	PARTIAL LIST OF DOS OPTION ENTRIES
DUMP	Prints a dump of main storage in case of abnormal program termination
NODUMP	Suppresses the DUMP option
LINK	Must be used if program is to be link-edited and executed
NOLINK	Suppresses the LINK option
DECK	Punches an object deck
NODECK	Suppresses the DECK option
LISTX	Prints a PROCEDURE DIVISION map
NOLISTX	Suppresses the LISTX option
XREF	Prints a cross-reference list
NOXREF	Suppresses the XREF option
SYM	Prints a DATA DIVISION map
NOSYM	Suppresses the SYM option
ERRS	Prints compiler diagnostic messages
NOERRS	Suppresses the ERRS option
CATAL	Catalogs the program

Check your installation's JCL to determine which of these options are
defaults.

Figure D.5

C. OS JCL

The following is a summary of the more frequently used OS JCL entries. For
a complete description of all entries, check your OS Specifications Manual.

We will consider in detail the following JCL for OS systems:

SUMMARY OF OS JCL CARDS	
Statement	**Meaning**
JOB	This statement signals the beginning of a job. It must be the first JCL card for every job. It indicates important information relevant to job requirements.
EXEC	This statement indicates each job step and informs the operating system which program or procedures to execute. It may also indicate options that are to be used with the program.
DD	Each Data Definition statement identifies and describes each file used for the job.

JOB STATEMENT Let us first review the format statement specifications:

GENERAL REVIEW OF FORMAT ENTRIES
1. Lowercase entries are programmer supplied.
2. Uppercase entries are reserved words.
3. [ ] indicate optional entries.
4. { } indicates that one of the enclosed entries must be used.
5. Punctuation must be followed **precisely.**

The following is the format for the JOB card:

Format
// job name   JOB   [(accounting information)]
                      [, programmer name]
                      [, MSGLEVEL = a,b]
                      [, CLASS = job class]
                      [, PRTY = nn]
                      [, REGION = nnnk]

Examples

```
//TESTRUN3 JOB (TEST, 3), STERN, CLASS E, REGION=200K
//TESTRUN2 JOB (TEST, 2), STERN, MSGLEVEL=1, 2, CLASS A, PRTY=10
//TESTRUN1 JOB (TEST, 1), STERN, MSGLVEL=1, 2
```

REQUIRED JOB CARD ENTRIES

1. // in columns 1 and 2.
2. Job name beginning in column 3.
   Job name: 1–8 characters; must begin with alphabetic character or $, #, or @.
3. JOB must be preceded and followed by at least one space.
4. Most installations require (or highly recommend) programmer name entry: 1–20 characters. This is not required for all systems.

OPTIONAL ENTRIES

1. (accounting information)—coded in parentheses—provided by installation
2. MSGLEVEL = a,b

   Meaning = message level
   Entries:
   a = 0 if only JOB card of JCL is to print
   a = 1 if all JCL is to print
   b = 0 if no system messages are to print (except for abnormal termination)
   b = 1 if all system messages are to print

3. CLASS = job class

   Meaning: Indicates classification of job, which determines what partition or region the job is to be run in. This in turn determines job priority.
   Entries:
   Usually letters A–F
   A is used for the most common job types.

4. PRTY = nn

   Meaning: Region to be used by program.
   Normally this is included if the region required for processing is larger than that established by default.
   Entries:
   nnn = even number of bytes
   For example, 90K = 90,000 bytes

EXEC STATEMENT This card indicates the program or procedures to be executed.

There are many options available with the EXEC Statement. Among the more common are the following:

$$
\text{// [step name] EXEC} \quad \left\{ PGM = \begin{bmatrix} \text{program name} \\ \text{procedure name} \end{bmatrix} \right\}
$$

$$
\begin{bmatrix} PARM.COB = \text{'values'}, \\ TIME = \text{(minutes, seconds)} \end{bmatrix}
$$

Examples

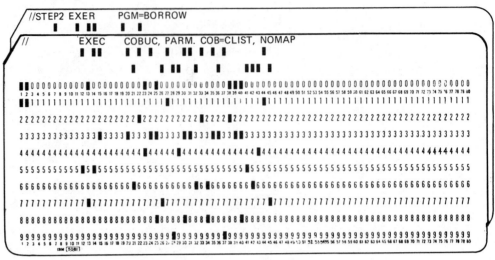

REQUIRED ENTRIES

1. // in columns 1 and 2.
2. EXEC preceded and followed by at least one space.
3. For COBOL programs:

    COBUG—for compiling a program **only**

    COBUCLG—for compiling, linking and executing (go)

OPTIONAL ENTRIES

1. stepname	**Meaning:** Name assigned to EXEC statement.
	 Entries:
	 1. Must begin in column 3
	 2. Same rules as **job name:**
	     1–8 characters
	     must begin with a letter, \$, #, or @

2. PARM.COB = 'values'	**Meaning:** There are a series of options called defaults that are standard for each specific installation. The (PARM.COB =) is used to override these defaults. **Entries:** Keep in mind that each installation establishes its own defaults, those options best suited to its own processing needs. Figure D.6 indicates all the possible entries that may be included with the PARM. The entries that are standard for your installation need not be coded.
3. TIME = (minutes, seconds)	**Meaning:** Indicates a limit in terms of CPU time to be placed on program execution.

PARM OPTIONS

Parameter	Meaning
$\begin{bmatrix} \text{CLIST} \\ \text{NOCLIST} \end{bmatrix}$	CLIST prints a condensed PROCEDURE DIVISION map—not used when PMAP is used
$\begin{bmatrix} \text{DECK} \\ \text{NODECK} \end{bmatrix}$	DECK punches object deck
$\begin{bmatrix} \text{DMAP} \\ \text{NODMAP} \end{bmatrix}$	DMAP prints a DATA DIVISION Map
$\begin{bmatrix} \text{FLAGW} \\ \text{FLAGE} \end{bmatrix}$	FLAGW prints all diagnostic messages; FLAGE omits W-level diagnostics
$\begin{bmatrix} \text{LIB} \\ \text{NOLIB} \end{bmatrix}$	LIB is used when COPY statements are included in the program
$[\text{LINECNT} = nn]$	Indicates the number of lines to be printed on source listing; if omitted, 60 is assumed
$\begin{bmatrix} \text{LOAD} \\ \text{NOLOAD} \end{bmatrix}$	LOAD stores the object program on a direct access device
$\begin{bmatrix} \text{PMAP} \\ \text{NOPMAP} \end{bmatrix}$	Prints a complete PROCEDURE DIVISION Map
$\begin{bmatrix} \text{QUOTE} \\ \text{APOST} \end{bmatrix}$	Indicates whether quotation marks (") or apostrophe (') is used to denote nonnumeric literals
$\begin{bmatrix} \text{SEQ} \\ \text{NOSEQ} \end{bmatrix}$	SEQ checks the sequence of source statements
$\begin{bmatrix} \text{SOURCE} \\ \text{NOSOURCE} \end{bmatrix}$	SOURCE prints a source listing
$\begin{bmatrix} \text{SUPMAP} \\ \text{NOSUPMAP} \end{bmatrix}$	SUPMAP suppresses PROCEDURE DIVISION map if an E-level diagnostic appears
$\begin{bmatrix} \text{XREF} \\ \text{NOXREF} \end{bmatrix}$	XREF prints a cross-reference listing

Figure D.6

DD STATEMENT The DD or Data Definition statement is used to define and describe each file identified in a SELECT statement.

The general format for DD statements is

```
// DD-name        DD  operands
```

Examples

Consider the following SELECT statements:
SELECT   FILE-IN ASSIGN TO UR-2540R-S-SYSIN.
SELECT   FILE-OUT ASSIGN TO UR-1403-S-PRINTOUT.

The DD statements might read:

```
//              GO.SYSIN          DD        *
//              GO.PRINTOUT       DD        SYSOUT = A
```

The DD entries for card and print files are relatively simple. The DD entries for tape and disk files are somewhat more complex.

The word GO is used to indicate that the data defined is to be used during the execution phase. The entry COB. would be used in place of GO for all Data Definitions required for the compile phase.

DD ENTRIES FOR CARDS ARE:

// GO. ‿‿‿‿ DD *
external name defined in SELECT
    * indicates that card data will follow this entry

DD ENTRIES FOR PRINT FILES ARE:

// GO. ‿‿‿‿ DD SYSOUT = value
external name defined in SELECT
  The value is defined by the installation.
  SYSOUT = A is common.

DD entries for Tape and Disk include

// GO. ‿‿‿‿‿‿ DD ‿‿‿‿
  external-name   DISP =
  defined in SELECT   UNIT =
                     VOL =
                     DCB =
                     SPACE =
                     LABEL =
                     DSN =

1. DISP = (status, normal-action, abnormal action)

Meaning: Disposition—This entry tells the operating system the current status of the file and what to do in case of an abnormal or successful job termination.

Entries:

Status = NEW or OLD (for new or old file)

$\left. \begin{matrix} \text{Normal action} \\ \text{Abnormal action} \end{matrix} \right\}$ = KEEP or DELETE

                KEEP—retain file
                DELETE—release file

status, normal-action and abnormal action usually used for disks;

status and normal-action usually used for tapes

Examples

DISP = (NEW, DELETE)
DISP = (NEW, KEEP, DELETE)

2. UNIT = $\begin{Bmatrix} \text{device type} \\ \text{group name} \end{Bmatrix}$

Meaning: This entry indicates the physical I/O device on which the data set or file is to be processed.
Entries:
Device type—2400 for S/360 tapes
                    3420 for S/370 tapes
                    $\left.\begin{array}{l} 3300 \\ 2314 \end{array}\right]$ for disks
Group name—TAPE
                      SYSDA—for either 3300 or 2314

Examples

UNIT = 2400
UNIT = SYSDA

3. VOL = SER = xxxxxx

Meaning: This entry indicates the tape volume that contains the data set.
Entries:
VOL = SER = xxxxxx where xxxxxx indicates the number assigned to the specific tape or disk.

Example

VOL = SER = 123456

causes a message to be printed telling the operator to mount tape 123456

4. DCB = ([RECFM = xxxx,] [LRECL = xxxx,] [BLKSIZE = xxxx])

Meaning: This entry describes the data in the Data Control Block. It is used to indicate record format (RECFM), logical record length (LRECL), and blocking factor (BLKSIZE). It overrides specifications indicated in the FD, thereby allowing changes without the necessity of recompiling. It is required for all tape and disk files.
Entries:
RECFM indicates record format:
   FB = fixed blocked
   F = fixed
LRECL indicates logical record length—length of each specific record
BLKSIZE indicates block size

Examples

DCB = (RECFM = FB,LRECL = 500,BLKSIZE = 2500)

5. SPACE $= (\begin{Bmatrix} TRK \\ CYL \end{Bmatrix}, X [,RLSE])$

Meaning: This entry is used for disks to indicate the size of the disk data set.

Entries:
TRK—track or
CYL—cylinder specifications
X—how many primary areas
RLSE—releases any unused portion of disk

Examples:
SPACE = (TRK, 400)
 400 tracks required
SPACE = (CYL, 100)
 100 cylinders required

6. LABEL $= (\{n\}, \begin{Bmatrix} SL \\ NL \end{Bmatrix})$

Meaning: This entry indicates the type of label and the location of a file on a volume.

Entries:
n is coded **for tapes** if the file is not the first one on a reel
SL—standard label
NL—no label

7. DSN = name

Meaning: This entry specifies the data set name. This is required if the data set is to be catalogued.

Entries: Name must be 1–8 characters, begin with a letter, $, #, or @.

These entries may be coded in any sequence. A DD statement for one file may exceed an individual card's limitations. You may proceed with additional cards, remembering to code // in columns 1–2 of each card used.

Example—represents one DD

```
// GO.OLDTAPE   DD   DSN=OLDMAST, UNIT=TAPE
// VOL=SER=001234, (DISP=OLD,KEEP)
```

Figure D.7 illustrates OS JCL for a simple COBOL Program that uses card input.

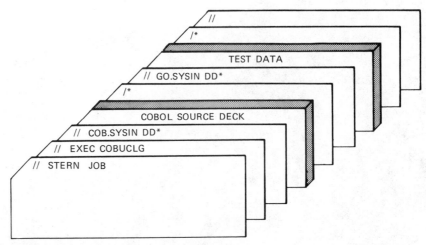

Figure D.7 OS JCL for a Simple COBOL Program.

APPENDIX E
IBM Full American COBOL Format National Standard Summary[1]

IDENTIFICATION DIVISION — BASIC FORMATS

$$\left\{ \begin{array}{l} \underline{\text{IDENTIFICATION DIVISION}.} \\ \boxed{\underline{\text{ID DIVISION}}.} \end{array} \right\}$$

<u>PROGRAM-ID</u>. *program-name*.

<u>AUTHOR</u>. [*comment-entry*] . . .

<u>INSTALLATION</u>. [*comment-entry*] . . .

<u>DATE-WRITTEN</u>. [*comment-entry*] . . .

<u>DATE-COMPILED</u>. [*comment-entry*] . . .

<u>SECURITY</u>. [*comment-entry*] . . .

<u>REMARKS</u>. [*comment-entry*] . . .

ENVIRONMENT DIVISION — BASIC FORMATS

<u>ENVIRONMENT DIVISION</u>.

<u>CONFIGURATION SECTION</u>.

<u>SOURCE-COMPUTER</u>. *computer-name*.

<u>OBJECT-COMPUTER</u>. *computer-name* [<u>MEMORY</u> SIZE *integer* $\left\{ \begin{array}{l} \underline{\text{WORDS}} \\ \underline{\text{CHARACTERS}} \\ \underline{\text{MODULES}} \end{array} \right\}$]

    [<u>SEGMENT-LIMIT</u> IS *priority-number*].

<u>SPECIAL-NAMES</u>. [*function-name* IS *mnemonic-name*] . . .

    [<u>CURRENCY</u> SIGN <u>IS</u> *literal*]

    [<u>DECIMAL-POINT</u> <u>IS</u> <u>COMMA</u>].

---

[1]Reprinted by permission of International Business Machines Corporation. Items printed on a shaded background are IBM's extensions to ANS COBOL.

INPUT-OUTPUT SECTION.

FILE-CONTROL.

{SELECT [OPTIONAL] *file name*

ASSIGN TO [*integer-1*] *system-name-1* [*system-name-2*] . . .

[FOR MULTIPLE $\left\{ \begin{array}{c} \text{REEL} \\ \text{UNIT} \end{array} \right\}$]

RESERVE $\left\{ \begin{array}{c} \text{NO} \\ \textit{integer-1} \end{array} \right\}$ ALTERNATE $\left[\begin{array}{c} \text{AREA} \\ \text{AREAS} \end{array} \right]$

$\left\{ \begin{array}{l} \text{FILE-LIMIT IS} \\ \text{FILE-LIMITS ARE} \end{array} \right\}$ $\left\{ \begin{array}{l} \textit{data-name-1} \\ \textit{literal-1} \end{array} \right\}$ THRU $\left\{ \begin{array}{l} \textit{data-name-2} \\ \textit{literal-2} \end{array} \right\}$

[$\left\{ \begin{array}{l} \textit{data-name-3} \\ \textit{literal-3} \end{array} \right\}$ THRU $\left\{ \begin{array}{l} \textit{data-name-4} \\ \textit{literal-4} \end{array} \right\}$] . . .

ACCESS MODE IS $\left\{ \begin{array}{l} \text{SEQUENTIAL} \\ \text{RANDOM} \end{array} \right\}$

PROCESSING MODE IS SEQUENTIAL

ACTUAL KEY IS *data-name*

NOMINAL KEY IS *data-name*

RECORD KEY IS *data-name*

TRACK-AREA IS $\left\{ \begin{array}{l} \textit{data-name} \\ \textit{integer} \end{array} \right\}$ CHARACTERS

TRACK-LIMIT IS *integer* $\left[\begin{array}{l} \text{TRACK} \\ \text{TRACKS} \end{array} \right]$.} . . .

I-O-CONTROL.

RERUN ON *system-name* EVERY $\left[\begin{array}{l} \textit{integer} \text{ RECORDS} \\ \text{[END OF]} \left\{ \begin{array}{l} \text{REEL} \\ \text{UNIT} \end{array} \right\} \end{array} \right]$ OF *file-name*

SAME $\left[\begin{array}{l} \text{RECORD} \\ \text{SORT} \end{array} \right]$ AREA FOR *file-name-1* {*file-name-2*} . . .

MULTIPLE FILE TAPE CONTAINS *file-name-1* [POSITION *integer-1*]

[*file-name-2* [POSITION *integer-2*]] . . .

APPLY WRITE-ONLY ON *file-name-1* [*file-name-2*] . . .

APPLY CORE-INDEX ON *file-name-1* [*file-name-2*] . . .

APPLY RECORD-OVERFLOW ON *file-name-1* [*file-name-2*] . . .

APPLY REORG-CRITERIA TO *data-name* ON *file-name* . . .

NOTE: Format 2 of the RERUN Clause (for Sort Files) is included with Formats for the SORT feature.

DATA DIVISION — BASIC FORMATS

DATA DIVISION.

FILE SECTION.

FD *file-name*

BLOCK CONTAINS [*integer-1* TO] *integer-2* $\left\{ \begin{array}{l} \text{CHARACTERS} \\ \underline{\text{RECORDS}} \end{array} \right\}$

RECORD CONTAINS [*integer-1* TO] *integer-2* CHARACTERS

RECORDING MODE IS *mode*

LABEL $\left\{ \begin{array}{l} \underline{\text{RECORD}} \text{ IS} \\ \underline{\text{RECORDS}} \text{ ARE} \end{array} \right\}$ $\left\{ \begin{array}{l} \underline{\text{OMITTED}} \\ \underline{\text{STANDARD}} \\ \textit{data-name-1} \text{ [\textit{data-name-2}]} \ldots \text{ [\underline{TOTALING} AREA IS} \\ \qquad \textit{data-name-3} \text{ \underline{TOTALED} AREA IS \textit{data-name-4}]} \end{array} \right\}$

VALUE OF *data-name-1* IS $\left\{ \begin{array}{l} \textit{literal-1} \\ \textit{data-name-2} \end{array} \right\}$ [*data-name-3* IS $\left\{ \begin{array}{l} \textit{literal-2} \\ \textit{data-name-4} \end{array} \right\}$] . . .

DATA $\left\{ \begin{array}{l} \underline{\text{RECORD}} \text{ IS} \\ \underline{\text{RECORDS}} \text{ ARE} \end{array} \right\}$ *data-name-1* [*data-name-2*] . . . .

NOTE: Format for the REPORT Clause is included with Formats for the REPORT WRITER feature.

01-49 $\left\{ \begin{array}{l} \textit{data-name-1} \\ \underline{\text{FILLER}} \end{array} \right\}$

REDEFINES *data-name-2*

BLANK WHEN ZERO

$\left\{ \begin{array}{l} \underline{\text{JUSTIFIED}} \\ \underline{\text{JUST}} \end{array} \right\}$ RIGHT

$\left\{ \begin{array}{l} \underline{\text{PICTURE}} \\ \underline{\text{PIC}} \end{array} \right\}$ IS *character string*

[SIGN IS] $\left\{ \begin{array}{l} \underline{\text{LEADING}} \\ \underline{\text{TRAILING}} \end{array} \right\}$ [SEPARATE CHARACTER] (Version 3 & 4)

$\left\{ \begin{array}{l} \underline{\text{SYNCHRONIZED}} \\ \underline{\text{SYNC}} \end{array} \right\}$ $\left[\begin{array}{l} \underline{\text{LEFT}} \\ \underline{\text{RIGHT}} \end{array} \right]$

[USAGE IS] $\left\{ \begin{array}{l} \underline{\text{INDEX}} \\ \underline{\text{DISPLAY}} \\ \left\{ \begin{array}{l} \underline{\text{COMPUTATIONAL}} \\ \underline{\text{COMP}} \end{array} \right\} \\ \left\{ \begin{array}{l} \underline{\text{COMPUTATIONAL-1}} \\ \underline{\text{COMP-1}} \end{array} \right\} \\ \left\{ \begin{array}{l} \underline{\text{COMPUTATIONAL-2}} \\ \underline{\text{COMP-2}} \end{array} \right\} \\ \left\{ \begin{array}{l} \underline{\text{COMPUTATIONAL-3}} \\ \underline{\text{COMP-3}} \end{array} \right\} \\ \left\{ \begin{array}{l} \underline{\text{COMPUTATIONAL-4}} \\ \underline{\text{COMP-4}} \end{array} \right\} \\ \underline{\text{DISPLAY-ST}} \end{array} \right\}$ (Version 3 & 4)

88 *condition-name* $\left\{ \begin{array}{l} \underline{\text{VALUE}} \text{ IS} \\ \underline{\text{VALUES}} \text{ ARE} \end{array} \right\}$ *literal-1* [THRU *literal-2*]

[*literal-2* [THRU *literal-4*]] . . .

66 *data-name-1* <u>RENAMES</u> *data-name-2* [<u>THRU</u> *data-name-3*].

NOTE: Formats for the OCCURS Clause are included with Formats for the
TABLE HANDLING feature.

<u>WORKING-STORAGE</u> <u>SECTION</u>.

77 *data-name-1*

01-49 { *data-name-1* }
      { <u>FILLER</u>   }

    <u>REDEFINES</u> *data-name-2*

    <u>BLANK</u> WHEN <u>ZERO</u>

    { <u>JUSTIFIED</u> } RIGHT
    { <u>JUST</u>   }

    { <u>PICTURE</u> } IS *character string*
    { <u>PIC</u>   }

    [<u>SIGN</u> IS] { <u>LEADING</u> } [<u>SEPARATE</u> CHARACTER] (version 3 & 4)
           { <u>TRAILING</u> }

    { <u>SYNCHRONIZED</u> } [<u>LEFT</u>]
    { <u>SYNC</u>   } [<u>RIGHT</u>]

                (<u>INDEX</u>
                 <u>DISPLAY</u>

                 { <u>COMPUTATIONAL</u> }
                 { <u>COMP</u>   }

                 { <u>COMPUTATIONAL-1</u> }
                 { <u>COMP-1</u>   }

[<u>USAGE</u> IS] { <u>COMPUTATIONAL-2</u> }
                 { <u>COMP-2</u>   }

                 { <u>COMPUTATIONAL-3</u> }
                 { <u>COMP-3</u>   }

                 { <u>COMPUTATIONAL-4</u> } (Version 3 & 4)
                 { <u>COMP-4</u>   }
                 <u>DISPLAY-ST</u>

    <u>VALUE</u> IS *literal*

88 *condition-name* { <u>VALUE</u> IS   } *literal-1* [<u>THRU</u> *literal-2*]
               { <u>VALUES</u> ARE }

    [*literal-3* [<u>THRU</u> *literal-4*]]. . .

66 *data-name-1* <u>RENAMES</u> *data-name-2* [<u>THRU</u> *data-name-3*].

NOTE: Formats for the OCCURS Clause are included with Formats for the
TABLE HANDLING feature.

<u>LINKAGE</u> <u>SECTION</u>.

77 *data-name-1*

01-49 { *data-name-1* }
      { <u>FILLER</u>   }

    <u>REDEFINES</u> *data-name-2*

BLANK WHEN ZERO

$$\left\{ \begin{array}{l} \underline{\text{JUSTIFIED}} \\ \underline{\text{JUST}} \end{array} \right\} \text{RIGHT}$$

$$\left\{ \begin{array}{l} \underline{\text{PICTURE}} \\ \underline{\text{PIC}} \end{array} \right\} \text{IS } character\ string$$

$$[\underline{\text{SIGN}} \text{ IS}] \left\{ \begin{array}{l} \underline{\text{LEADING}} \\ \underline{\text{TRAILING}} \end{array} \right\} [\underline{\text{SEPARATE}} \text{ CHARACTER}] \text{ (Version 3 \& 4)}$$

$$\left\{ \begin{array}{l} \underline{\text{SYNCHRONIZED}} \\ \underline{\text{SYNC}} \end{array} \right\} \left[\begin{array}{l} \underline{\text{LEFT}} \\ \underline{\text{RIGHT}} \end{array} \right]$$

$$[\underline{\text{USAGE}} \text{ IS}] \left\{ \begin{array}{l} \underline{\text{INDEX}} \\ \underline{\text{DISPLAY}} \\ \left\{ \begin{array}{l} \underline{\text{COMPUTATIONAL}} \\ \underline{\text{COMP}} \end{array} \right\} \\ \left\{ \begin{array}{l} \underline{\text{COMPUTATIONAL-1}} \\ \underline{\text{COMP-1}} \end{array} \right\} \\ \left\{ \begin{array}{l} \underline{\text{COMPUTATIONAL-2}} \\ \underline{\text{COMP-2}} \end{array} \right\} \\ \left\{ \begin{array}{l} \underline{\text{COMPUTATIONAL-3}} \\ \underline{\text{COMP-3}} \end{array} \right\} \\ \left\{ \begin{array}{l} \underline{\text{COMPUTATIONAL-4}} \\ \underline{\text{COMP-4}} \end{array} \right\} \text{ (Version 3 \& 4)} \\ \underline{\text{DISPLAY-ST}} \end{array} \right\}$$

88 *condition-name* $\left\{ \begin{array}{l} \underline{\text{VALUE}} \text{ IS} \\ \underline{\text{VALUES}} \text{ ARE} \end{array} \right\}$ *literal-1* [$\underline{\text{THRU}}$ *literal-2*]

[*literal-3* [$\underline{\text{THRU}}$ *literal-4*]] . . .

66 *data-name-1* $\underline{\text{RENAMES}}$ *data-name-2* [$\underline{\text{THRU}}$ *data-name-3*].

NOTE: Formats for the OCCURS Clause are included with Formats for the TABLE HANDLING feature.

PROCEDURE DIVISION — BASIC FORMATS

$$\left\{ \begin{array}{l} \underline{\text{PROCEDURE}} \ \underline{\text{DIVISION}}. \\ \underline{\text{PROCEDURE}} \ \underline{\text{DIVISION}} \ \underline{\text{USING}} \ identifer\text{-}1 \ [identifier\text{-}2] \ . \ . \ . \quad . \end{array} \right\}$$

ACCEPT Statement

FORMAT 1

$$\underline{\text{ACCEPT}} \ identifier \ \left[\underline{\text{FROM}} \left\{ \begin{array}{l} \underline{\text{SYSIN}} \\ \underline{\text{CONSOLE}} \\ mnemonic\text{-}name \end{array} \right\} \right]$$

FORMAT 2 (Version 4)

$$\underline{\text{ACCEPT}} \ identifier \ \underline{\text{FROM}} \left\{ \begin{array}{l} \underline{\text{DATE}} \\ \underline{\text{DAY}} \\ \underline{\text{TIME}} \end{array} \right\}$$

ADD Statement

FORMAT 1

ADD $\begin{Bmatrix} identifier\text{-}1 \\ literal\text{-}1 \end{Bmatrix}$ $\begin{bmatrix} identifier\text{-}2 \\ literal\text{-}2 \end{bmatrix}$ . . . TO identifier-m [ROUNDED]

[identifier-n [ROUNDED]] . . . [ON SIZE ERROR imperative-statemer

FORMAT 2

ADD $\begin{Bmatrix} identifier\text{-}1 \\ literal\text{-}1 \end{Bmatrix}$ $\begin{Bmatrix} identifier\text{-}2 \\ literal\text{-}2 \end{Bmatrix}$ $\begin{bmatrix} identifier\text{-}3 \\ literal\text{-}3 \end{bmatrix}$ . . . GIVING

identifier-m [ROUNDED] [ON SIZE ERROR imperative-statement]

FORMAT 3

ADD $\begin{Bmatrix} \text{CORRESPONDING} \\ \text{CORR} \end{Bmatrix}$ identifier-1 TO identifier-2 [ROUNDED]

[ON SIZE ERROR imperative-statement]

ALTER Statement

ALTER procedure-name-1 TO [PROCEED TO] procedure-name-2

[procedure-name-3 TO [PROCEED TO] procedure-name-4] . . .

CALL Statement

FORMAT 1

CALL literal-1 [USING identifier-1 [identifier-2] . . .]

FORMAT 2 (Version 4)

CALL identifier-1 [USING identifier-2 [identifier-3] . . .]

CANCEL Statement (Version 4)

CANCEL $\begin{Bmatrix} literal\text{-}1 \\ identifier\text{-}1 \end{Bmatrix}$ $\begin{bmatrix} literal\text{-}2 \\ identifier\text{-}2 \end{bmatrix}$ . . .

CLOSE Statement

FORMAT 1

CLOSE file-name-1 $\begin{bmatrix} \text{REEL} \\ \text{UNIT} \end{bmatrix}$ [WITH $\begin{Bmatrix} \text{NO REWIND} \\ \text{LOCK} \end{Bmatrix}$]

[file-name-2 $\begin{bmatrix} \text{REEL} \\ \text{UNIT} \end{bmatrix}$ [WITH $\begin{Bmatrix} \text{NO REWIND} \\ \text{LOCK} \end{Bmatrix}$]] . . .

FORMAT 2

CLOSE file-name-1 [WITH $\begin{Bmatrix} \text{NO REWIND} \\ \text{LOCK} \\ \text{DISP} \end{Bmatrix}$]

[file-name-2 [WITH $\begin{Bmatrix} \text{NO REWIND} \\ \text{LOCK} \\ \text{DISP} \end{Bmatrix}$]] . . .

FORMAT 3

$$\underline{\text{CLOSE}} \textit{ file-name-1} \begin{Bmatrix} \underline{\text{REEL}} \\ \underline{\text{UNIT}} \end{Bmatrix} \left[\text{WITH} \begin{Bmatrix} \underline{\text{NO REWIND}} \\ \underline{\text{LOCK}} \\ \boxed{\underline{\text{POSITIONING}}} \end{Bmatrix} \right]$$

$$\left[\textit{file-name-2} \begin{Bmatrix} \underline{\text{REEL}} \\ \underline{\text{UNIT}} \end{Bmatrix} \left[\text{WITH} \begin{Bmatrix} \underline{\text{NO REWIND}} \\ \underline{\text{LOCK}} \\ \boxed{\underline{\text{POSITIONING}}} \end{Bmatrix} \right] \right] \ldots$$

COMPUTE Statement

$$\underline{\text{COMPUTE}} \textit{ identifier-1} \text{ } [\underline{\text{ROUNDED}}] = \begin{Bmatrix} \textit{identifier-2} \\ \textit{literal-1} \\ \textit{arithmetic-expression} \end{Bmatrix}$$

$$[\text{ON } \underline{\text{SIZE}} \text{ } \underline{\text{ERROR}} \textit{ imperative-statement}]$$

DECLARATIVE Section

<u>PROCEDURE</u> <u>DIVISION</u>.

<u>DECLARATIVES</u>.

{*section-name* <u>SECTION</u>. <u>USE</u> *sentence*.

{*paragraph-name*. {*sentence*} . . .} . . .} . . .
<u>END</u> <u>DECLARATIVES</u>.

DISPLAY Statement

$$\underline{\text{DISPLAY}} \begin{Bmatrix} \textit{literal-1} \\ \textit{identifier-1} \end{Bmatrix} \begin{bmatrix} \textit{literal-2} \\ \textit{identifier-2} \end{bmatrix} \ldots [\underline{\text{UPON}} \begin{Bmatrix} \boxed{\begin{matrix} \underline{\text{CONSOLE}} \\ \underline{\text{SYSPUNCH}} \\ \underline{\text{SYSOUT}} \end{matrix}} \\ \textit{mnemonic-name} \end{Bmatrix}]$$

DIVIDE Statement

FORMAT 1

$$\underline{\text{DIVIDE}} \begin{Bmatrix} \textit{identifier-1} \\ \textit{literal-1} \end{Bmatrix} \underline{\text{INTO}} \textit{ identifier-2} \text{ } [\underline{\text{ROUNDED}}]$$

$$[\text{ON } \underline{\text{SIZE}} \text{ } \underline{\text{ERROR}} \textit{ imperative-statement}]$$

FORMAT 2

$$\underline{\text{DIVIDE}} \begin{Bmatrix} \textit{identifier-1} \\ \textit{literal-1} \end{Bmatrix} \begin{Bmatrix} \underline{\text{INTO}} \\ \underline{\text{BY}} \end{Bmatrix} \begin{Bmatrix} \textit{identifier-2} \\ \textit{literal-2} \end{Bmatrix} \underline{\text{GIVING}} \textit{ identifier-3}$$

$$[\underline{\text{ROUNDED}}] \text{ } [\underline{\text{REMAINDER}} \textit{ identifier-4}] \text{ } [\text{ON } \underline{\text{SIZE}} \text{ } \underline{\text{ERROR}} \textit{ imperative-statement}]$$

ENTER Statement

$$\underline{\text{ENTER}} \textit{ language-name} \text{ } [\textit{routine-name}].$$

ENTRY Statement
$$\underline{\text{ENTRY}} \textit{ literal-1} \text{ } [\underline{\text{USING}} \textit{ identifier-1} \text{ } [\textit{identifier-2}] \ldots]$$

EXAMINE Statement

FORMAT 1

EXAMINE *identifier* TALLYING $\left\{\begin{array}{l}\underline{UNTIL}\ \underline{FIRST}\\ \underline{ALL}\\ \underline{LEADING}\end{array}\right\}$ *literal-1*

[REPLACING BY *literal-2*]

FORMAT 2

EXAMINE *identifier* REPLACING $\left\{\begin{array}{l}\underline{ALL}\\ \underline{LEADING}\\ \underline{FIRST}\\ \underline{UNTIL}\ \underline{FIRST}\end{array}\right\}$ *literal-1* BY *literal-2*

EXIT Statement

paragraph-name. EXIT [PROGRAM].

GOBACK Statement

GOBACK.

GO TO Statement

FORMAT 1

GO TO procedure-name-1

FORMAT 2

GO TO *procedure-name-1* [*procedure-name-2*] . . . DEPENDING ON *identifier*

FORMAT 3

GO TO.

IF Statement

IF *condition* THEN $\left\{\begin{array}{l}statement\text{-}1\\ \underline{NEXT}\ \underline{SENTENCE}\end{array}\right\}\left\{\begin{array}{l}\underline{ELSE}\\ \underline{OTHERWISE}\end{array}\right\}\left\{\begin{array}{l}statement\text{-}2\\ \underline{NEXT}\ \underline{SENTENCE}\end{array}\right\}$

MOVE Statement

FORMAT 1

MOVE $\left\{\begin{array}{l}identifier\text{-}1\\ literal\text{-}1\end{array}\right\}$ TO *identifier-2* [*identifier-3*] . . .

FORMAT 2

MOVE $\left\{\begin{array}{l}\underline{CORRESPONDING}\\ \underline{CORR}\end{array}\right\}$ *identifier-1* TO *identifier-2*

MULTIPLY Statement

FORMAT 1

$$\text{\underline{MULTIPLY}} \begin{Bmatrix} \textit{identifier-1} \\ \textit{literal-1} \end{Bmatrix} \text{\underline{BY}} \textit{identifier-2} \; [\text{\underline{ROUNDED}}]$$
$$[\text{ON \underline{SIZE} \underline{ERROR}} \textit{imperative-statement}]$$

FORMAT 2

$$\text{\underline{MULTIPLY}} \begin{Bmatrix} \textit{identifier-1} \\ \textit{literal-1} \end{Bmatrix} \text{\underline{BY}} \begin{Bmatrix} \textit{identifier-2} \\ \textit{literal-2} \end{Bmatrix} \text{\underline{GIVING}} \textit{identifier-3}$$
$$[\text{\underline{ROUNDED}}] \; [\text{ON \underline{SIZE} \underline{ERROR}} \textit{imperative-statement}]$$

NOTE Statement

$$\text{\underline{NOTE}} \textit{character string}$$

OPEN Statement

FORMAT 1

$$\text{\underline{OPEN}} \; [\text{\underline{INPUT}} \; \{ \textit{file-name} \begin{bmatrix} \text{\underline{REVERSED}} \\ \text{WITH \underline{NO} \underline{REWIND}} \end{bmatrix} \} \ldots]$$
$$[\text{\underline{OUTPUT}} \; \{ \textit{file-name} \; [\text{WITH \underline{NO} \underline{REWIND}}] \} \ldots]$$
$$[\text{\underline{I-O}} \; \{ \textit{file-name} \} \ldots]$$

FORMAT 2

$$\text{\underline{OPEN}} \; [\text{\underline{INPUT}} \; \{ \textit{file-name} \begin{bmatrix} \text{\underline{REVERSED}} \\ \text{WITH \underline{NO} \underline{REWIND}} \end{bmatrix} \begin{bmatrix} \text{\underline{LEAVE}} \\ \text{\underline{REREAD}} \\ \text{\underline{DISP}} \end{bmatrix} \} \ldots]$$

$$[\text{\underline{OUTPUT}} \; \{ \textit{file-name} \; [\text{WITH \underline{NO} \underline{REWIND}}] \begin{bmatrix} \text{\underline{LEAVE}} \\ \text{\underline{REREAD}} \\ \text{\underline{DISP}} \end{bmatrix} \} \ldots]$$

$$[\text{\underline{I-O}} \; \{ \textit{file-name} \} \ldots]$$

PERFORM Statement

FORMAT 1

$$\text{\underline{PERFORM}} \textit{procedure-name-1} \; [\text{\underline{THRU}} \textit{procedure-name-2}]$$

FORMAT 2

$$\text{\underline{PERFORM}} \textit{procedure-name-1} \; [\text{\underline{THRU}} \textit{procedure-name-2}] \begin{Bmatrix} \textit{identifier-1} \\ \textit{integer-1} \end{Bmatrix} \text{\underline{TIMES}}$$

FORMAT 3

$$\text{\underline{PERFORM}} \textit{procedure-name-1} \; [\text{\underline{THRU}} \textit{procedure-name-2}] \text{\underline{UNTIL}} \textit{condition-1}$$

FORMAT 4

PERFORM *procedure-name-1* [THRU *procedure-name-2*]

VARYING $\begin{Bmatrix} \textit{index-name-1} \\ \textit{identifier-1} \end{Bmatrix}$ FROM $\begin{Bmatrix} \textit{index-name-2} \\ \textit{literal-2} \\ \textit{identifier-2} \end{Bmatrix}$ BY $\begin{Bmatrix} \textit{literal-3} \\ \textit{identifier-3} \end{Bmatrix}$ UNTIL *condition-1*

[AFTER $\begin{Bmatrix} \textit{index-name-4} \\ \textit{identifier-4} \end{Bmatrix}$ FROM $\begin{Bmatrix} \textit{index-name-5} \\ \textit{literal-5} \\ \textit{identifier-5} \end{Bmatrix}$ BY $\begin{Bmatrix} \textit{literal-6} \\ \textit{identifier-6} \end{Bmatrix}$ UNTIL *condition-2*

[AFTER $\begin{Bmatrix} \textit{index-name-7} \\ \textit{identifier-7} \end{Bmatrix}$ FROM $\begin{Bmatrix} \textit{index-name-8} \\ \textit{literal-8} \\ \textit{identifier-8} \end{Bmatrix}$ BY $\begin{Bmatrix} \textit{literal-9} \\ \textit{identifier-9} \end{Bmatrix}$ UNTIL *condition-3*]]

READ Statement

READ *file-name* RECORD [INTO *identifier*]

$\begin{Bmatrix} \text{AT END} \\ \text{INVALID KEY} \end{Bmatrix}$ *imperative-statement*

REWRITE Statement

REWRITE *record-name* [FROM *identifier*] [INVALID KEY *imperative-statement*]

SEEK Statement

SEEK *file-name* RECORD

START Statement

FORMAT 1

START *file-name* [INVALID KEY *imperative-statement*]

FORMAT 2 (Version 3 & 4)

START *file-name*

USING KEY *data-name* $\begin{Bmatrix} \text{EQUAL TO} \\ = \end{Bmatrix}$ *identifier*

[INVALID KEY *imperative-statement*]

STOP Statement

STOP $\begin{Bmatrix} \text{RUN} \\ \textit{literal} \end{Bmatrix}$

SUBTRACT Statement

FORMAT 1

SUBTRACT $\begin{Bmatrix} \textit{identifier-1} \\ \textit{literal-1} \end{Bmatrix}$ $\begin{bmatrix} \textit{identifier-2} \\ \textit{literal-2} \end{bmatrix}$ . . . FROM *identifier-m* [ROUNDED]

[*identifier-n* [ROUNDED]] . . . [ON SIZE ERROR *imperative-statement*]

FORMAT 2

$$\underline{\text{SUBTRACT}} \begin{Bmatrix} identifier\text{-}1 \\ literal\text{-}1 \end{Bmatrix} \begin{bmatrix} identifier\text{-}2 \\ literal\text{-}2 \end{bmatrix} \ldots \underline{\text{FROM}} \begin{Bmatrix} identifier\text{-}m \\ literal\text{-}m \end{Bmatrix} \underline{\text{GIVING}} \, identifier\text{-}n$$

$$[\underline{\text{ROUNDED}}] \, [\text{ON} \, \underline{\text{SIZE}} \, \underline{\text{ERROR}} \, imperative\text{-}statement]$$

FORMAT 3

$$\underline{\text{SUBTRACT}} \begin{Bmatrix} \underline{\text{CORRESPONDING}} \\ \underline{\text{CORR}} \end{Bmatrix} identifier\text{-}1 \, \underline{\text{FROM}} \, identifier\text{-}2 \, [\underline{\text{ROUNDED}}]$$

$$[\text{ON} \, \underline{\text{SIZE}} \, \underline{\text{ERROR}} \, imperative\text{-}statement]$$

TRANSFORM Statement

$$\underline{\text{TRANSFORM}} \, identifier\text{-}3 \, \text{CHARACTERS} \, \underline{\text{FROM}} \begin{Bmatrix} figurative\text{-}constant\text{-}1 \\ nonnumeric\text{-}literal\text{-}1 \\ identifier\text{-}1 \end{Bmatrix}$$

$$\underline{\text{TO}} \begin{Bmatrix} figurative\text{-}constant\text{-}2 \\ nonnumeric\text{-}literal\text{-}2 \\ identifier\text{-}2 \end{Bmatrix}$$

USE Sentence

FORMAT 1

Option 1:

$$\underline{\text{USE}} \begin{Bmatrix} \underline{\text{BEFORE}} \\ \underline{\text{AFTER}} \end{Bmatrix} \text{STANDARD} \, [\underline{\text{BEGINNING}}] \begin{bmatrix} \underline{\text{REEL}} \\ \underline{\text{FILE}} \\ \underline{\text{UNIT}} \end{bmatrix}$$

$$\underline{\text{LABEL}} \, \underline{\text{PROCEDURE}} \, \text{ON} \begin{Bmatrix} \{file\text{-}name\} \ldots \\ \underline{\text{OUTPUT}} \\ \underline{\text{INPUT}} \\ \underline{\text{I-O}} \end{Bmatrix}$$

Option 2:

$$\underline{\text{USE}} \begin{Bmatrix} \underline{\text{BEFORE}} \\ \underline{\text{AFTER}} \end{Bmatrix} \text{STANDARD} \, [\underline{\text{ENDING}}] \begin{bmatrix} \underline{\text{REEL}} \\ \underline{\text{FILE}} \\ \underline{\text{UNIT}} \end{bmatrix}$$

$$\underline{\text{LABEL}} \, \underline{\text{PROCEDURE}} \, \text{ON} \begin{Bmatrix} \{file\text{-}name\} \ldots \\ \underline{\text{OUTPUT}} \\ \underline{\text{INPUT}} \\ \underline{\text{I-O}} \end{Bmatrix}$$

FORMAT 2

$$\underline{\text{USE}} \, \underline{\text{AFTER}} \, \text{STANDARD} \, \underline{\text{ERROR}} \, \underline{\text{PROCEDURE}}$$

$$\text{ON} \begin{Bmatrix} \{file\text{-}name\text{-}1\} \, [file\text{-}name\text{-}2] \ldots \\ \underline{\text{INPUT}} \\ \underline{\text{OUTPUT}} \\ \underline{\text{I-O}} \end{Bmatrix}$$

$$[\underline{\text{GIVING}} \, data\text{-}name\text{-}1 \, [data\text{-}name\text{-}2]].$$

NOTE: Format 3 of the USE Sentence is included in Formats for the REPORT WRITER feature.

WRITE Statement

FORMAT 1

$\underline{\text{WRITE}}$ *record-name* [$\underline{\text{FROM}}$ *identifier-1*] [$\left\{ \begin{array}{l} \underline{\text{BEFORE}} \\ \underline{\text{AFTER}} \end{array} \right\}$ ADVANCING

$\left\{ \begin{array}{l} \textit{identifier-2 } \text{LINES} \\ \textit{integer } \text{LINES} \\ \textit{mnemonic-name} \end{array} \right\}$] [AT $\left\{ \begin{array}{l} \underline{\text{END-OF-PAGE}} \\ \underline{\text{EOP}} \end{array} \right\}$ *imperative-statement*]

FORMAT 2

$\underline{\text{WRITE}}$ *record-name* [$\underline{\text{FROM}}$ *identifier-1*] $\underline{\text{AFTER}}$ $\underline{\text{POSITIONING}}$ $\left\{ \begin{array}{l} \textit{identifier-2} \\ \textit{integer} \end{array} \right\}$ LINES

[AT $\left\{ \begin{array}{l} \underline{\text{END-OF-PAGE}} \\ \underline{\text{EOP}} \end{array} \right\}$ *imperative-statement*]

FORMAT 3

$\underline{\text{WRITE}}$ *record-name* [$\underline{\text{FROM}}$ *identifier-1*] $\underline{\text{INVALID}}$ $\underline{\text{KEY}}$ *imperative-statement*

SORT — BASIC FORMATS

Environment Division Sort Formats

FILE-CONTROL PARAGRAPH — SELECT SENTENCE
SELECT Sentence (for GIVING option only)
   $\underline{\text{SELECT}}$ *file-name*

   $\underline{\text{ASSIGN}}$ TO [*integer-1*] *system-name-1* [*system-name-2*] . . .

   $\underline{\text{OR}}$ *system-name-3* [FOR $\underline{\text{MULTIPLE}}$ $\left\{ \begin{array}{l} \underline{\text{REEL}} \\ \underline{\text{UNIT}} \end{array} \right\}$]

   [$\underline{\text{RESERVE}}$ $\left\{ \begin{array}{l} \textit{integer-2} \\ \underline{\text{NO}} \end{array} \right\}$ ALTERNATE $\left[\begin{array}{l} \text{AREA} \\ \text{AREAS} \end{array} \right]$].

SELECT Sentence (for Sort Work Files)

   $\underline{\text{SELECT}}$ *sort-file-name*

   $\underline{\text{ASSIGN}}$ TO [*integer*] *system-name-1* [*system-name-2*] . . .

I-O-CONTROL PARAGRAPH

RERUN Clause

   $\underline{\text{RERUN}}$ $\underline{\text{ON}}$ *system-name*

SAME RECORD/SORT AREA Clause

   $\underline{\text{SAME}}$ $\left\{ \begin{array}{l} \underline{\text{RECORD}} \\ \underline{\text{SORT}} \end{array} \right\}$ AREA FOR *file-name-1* {*file-name-2* } . . .

Data Division Sort Formats

SORT-FILE DESCRIPTION

<u>SD</u> *sort-file-name*

<u>RECORDING</u> MODE IS *mode*

<u>DATA</u> $\left\{ \begin{array}{l} \underline{RECORD} \text{ IS} \\ \underline{RECORDS} \text{ ARE} \end{array} \right\}$ *data-name-1* [*data-name-2*] . . .

<u>RECORD</u> CONTAINS [*integer-1* <u>TO</u>] *integer-2* CHARACTERS

[<u>LABEL</u> $\left\{ \begin{array}{l} \underline{RECORD} \text{ IS} \\ \underline{RECORDS} \text{ ARE} \end{array} \right\}$ $\left\{ \begin{array}{l} \underline{STANDARD} \\ \underline{OMITTED} \end{array} \right\}$] .   (Version 4)

Procedure Division Sort Formats

RELEASE Statement

<u>RELEASE</u> *sort-record-name* [<u>FROM</u> *identifier*]

RETURN Statement

<u>RETURN</u> *sort-file-name* RECORD [<u>INTO</u> *identifier*]

AT <u>END</u> *imperative-statement*

SORT Statement

<u>SORT</u> *file-name-1* ON $\left\{ \begin{array}{l} \underline{DESCENDING} \\ \underline{ASCENDING} \end{array} \right\}$ KEY {*data-name-1*} . . .

[ON $\left\{ \begin{array}{l} \underline{DESCENDING} \\ \underline{ASCENDING} \end{array} \right\}$ KEY {*data-name-2*} . . .] . . .

$\left\{ \begin{array}{l} \underline{INPUT} \ \underline{PROCEDURE} \text{ IS } section\text{-}name\text{-}1 \ [\underline{THRU} \ section\text{-}name\text{-}2] \\ \underline{USING} \ file\text{-}name\text{-}2 \end{array} \right\}$

$\left\{ \begin{array}{l} \underline{OUTPUT} \ \underline{PROCEDURE} \text{ IS } section\text{-}name\text{-}2 \ [\underline{THRU} \ section\text{-}name\text{-}4] \\ \underline{GIVING} \ file\text{-}name\text{-}3 \end{array} \right\}$

REPORT WRITER — BASIC FORMATS

Data Division Report Writer Formats

NOTE: Formats that appear as Basic Formats within the general description of the Data Division are illustrated there.

FILE SECTION — REPORT Clause

$\left\{ \begin{array}{l} \underline{REPORT} \text{ IS} \\ \underline{REPORTS} \text{ ARE} \end{array} \right\}$ *report-name-1* [*report-name-2*] . . .

REPORT SECTION
 <u>REPORT</u> <u>SECTION</u>.

<u>RD</u> *report-name*

  WITH <u>CODE</u> *mnemonic-name*

$$\left\{ \begin{array}{l} \underline{\text{CONTROL}} \text{ IS} \\ \underline{\text{CONTROLS}} \text{ ARE} \end{array} \right\} \left\{ \begin{array}{l} \underline{\text{FINAL}} \\ \textit{identifier-1} \ [\textit{identifier-2}\ ] \ \dots \\ \underline{\text{FINAL}}\ \textit{identifier-1}\ [\textit{identifier-2}\ ]\ \dots \end{array} \right\}$$

$$\underline{\text{PAGE}} \left[\begin{array}{l} \text{LIMIT IS} \\ \text{LIMITS ARE} \end{array} \right] \textit{integer-1} \left\{ \begin{array}{l} \underline{\text{LINE}} \\ \underline{\text{LINES}} \end{array} \right\}$$

    [<u>HEADING</u> *integer-2*]

    [<u>FIRST</u> <u>DETAIL</u> *integer-3*]

    [<u>LAST</u> <u>DETAIL</u> *integer-4*]

    [<u>FOOTING</u> *integer-5*].

REPORT GROUP DESCRIPTION ENTRY

FORMAT 1

01 [*data-name-1*]

$$\underline{\text{LINE}} \text{ NUMBER IS} \left\{ \begin{array}{l} \textit{integer-1} \\ \underline{\text{PLUS}}\ \textit{integer-2} \\ \underline{\text{NEXT}}\ \underline{\text{PAGE}} \end{array} \right\}$$

$$\underline{\text{NEXT}}\ \underline{\text{GROUP}} \text{ IS} \left\{ \begin{array}{l} \textit{integer-1} \\ \underline{\text{PLUS}}\ \textit{integer-2} \\ \underline{\text{NEXT}}\ \underline{\text{PAGE}} \end{array} \right\}$$

$$\underline{\text{TYPE}} \text{ IS} \left\{ \begin{array}{ll} \left\{ \begin{array}{l} \underline{\text{REPORT}}\ \underline{\text{HEADING}} \\ \underline{\text{RH}} \end{array} \right\} \\ \left\{ \begin{array}{l} \underline{\text{PAGE}}\ \underline{\text{HEADING}} \\ \underline{\text{PH}} \end{array} \right\} \\ \left\{ \begin{array}{l} \underline{\text{CONTROL}}\ \underline{\text{HEADING}} \\ \underline{\text{CH}} \end{array} \right\} & \left\{ \begin{array}{l} \textit{identifier-n} \\ \underline{\text{FINAL}} \end{array} \right\} \\ \left\{ \begin{array}{l} \underline{\text{DETAIL}} \\ \underline{\text{DE}} \end{array} \right\} \\ \left\{ \begin{array}{l} \underline{\text{CONTROL}}\ \underline{\text{FOOTING}} \\ \underline{\text{CF}} \end{array} \right\} & \left\{ \begin{array}{l} \textit{identifier-n} \\ \underline{\text{FINAL}} \end{array} \right\} \\ \left\{ \begin{array}{l} \underline{\text{PAGE}}\ \underline{\text{FOOTING}} \\ \underline{\text{PF}} \end{array} \right\} \\ \left\{ \begin{array}{l} \underline{\text{REPORT}}\ \underline{\text{FOOTING}} \\ \underline{\text{RF}} \end{array} \right\} \end{array} \right\}$$

  USAGE Clause.

FORMAT 2

nn [*data-name-1*]
   LINE Clause — See Format 1
   USAGE Clause.

FORMAT 3

nn   [*data-name-1*]
  COLUMN NUMBER IS *integer-1*

  GROUP INDICATE

  JUSTIFIED Clause
  LINE Clause — See Format 1
  PICTURE Clause
  RESET ON $\begin{Bmatrix} identifier\text{-}1 \\ FINAL \end{Bmatrix}$

  BLANK WHEN ZERO Clause
  SOURCE IS $\begin{Bmatrix} \text{TALLY} \\ identifier\text{-}2 \end{Bmatrix}$
  SUM $\begin{Bmatrix} \text{TALLY} \\ identifier\text{-}3 \end{Bmatrix}$ $\begin{bmatrix} \text{TALLY} \\ identifier\text{-}4 \end{bmatrix}$ . . . [UPON *data-name*]
  VALUE IS *literal-1*

  USAGE Clause.

FORMAT 4

01   *data-name-1*
  BLANK WHEN ZERO Clause
  COLUMN Clause — See Format 3
  GROUP Clause — See Format 3
  JUSTIFIED Clause
  LINE Clause — See Format 1
  NEXT GROUP Clause — See Format 1
  PICTURE Clause
  RESET Clause — See Format 3
  $\begin{Bmatrix} \text{SOURCE Clause} \\ \text{SUM Clause} \\ \text{VALUE Clause} \end{Bmatrix}$ See Format 3
  TYPE Clause — See Format 1
  USAGE Clause.

Procedure Division Report Writer Formats

GENERATE Statement
  GENERATE *identifier*

INITIATE Statement
  INITIATE *report-name-1* [*report-name-2*] . . .

TERMINATE Statement
  TERMINATE *report-name-1* [*report-name-2*] . . .

USE Sentence
  USE BEFORE REPORTING *data-name*.

TABLE HANDLING — BASIC FORMATS

Data Division Table Handling Formats

OCCURS Clause

FORMAT 1

OCCURS *integer-2* TIMES

$\left[\begin{array}{l} \underline{\text{ASCENDING}} \\ \underline{\text{DESCENDING}} \end{array} \right\}$ KEY IS *data-name-2* [*data-name-3* . . .] . . .

[INDEXED BY *index-name-1* [*index-name-2*] . . .]

FORMAT 2

OCCURS *integer-1* TO *integer-2* TIMES [DEPENDING ON *data-name-1*]

$\left[\begin{array}{l} \underline{\text{ASCENDING}} \\ \underline{\text{DESCENDING}} \end{array} \right\}$ KEY IS *data-name-2* [*data-name-3*] . . .] . . .

[INDEXED BY *index-name-1* [*index-name-2*] . . .]

FORMAT 3

OCCURS *integer-2* TIMES [DEPENDING ON *data-name-1*]

$\left[\begin{array}{l} \underline{\text{ASENDING}} \\ \underline{\text{DESCENDING}} \end{array} \right\}$ KEY IS *data-name-2* [*data-name-3*] . . .] . . .

[INDEXED BY *index-name-1* [*index-name-2*] . . .]

USAGE Clause
[USAGE IS] INDEX

Procedure Division Table Handling Formats

SEARCH Statement

FORMAT 1

SEARCH *identifier-1* [VARYING $\left\{ \begin{array}{l} \textit{index-name-1} \\ \textit{identifier-2} \end{array} \right\}$]

    [AT END *imperative-statement-1*]

      WHEN *condition-1* $\left\{ \begin{array}{l} \textit{imperative-statement-2} \\ \underline{\text{NEXT}}\ \underline{\text{SENTENCE}} \end{array} \right\}$

      [WHEN *condition-2* $\left\{ \begin{array}{l} \textit{imperative-statement-3} \\ \underline{\text{NEXT}}\ \underline{\text{SENTENCE}} \end{array} \right\}$] . . .

FORMAT 2

SEARCH ALL *identifier-1* [AT END *imperative-statement-1*]

      WHEN *condition-1* $\left\{ \begin{array}{l} \textit{imperative-statement-2} \\ \underline{\text{NEXT}}\ \underline{\text{SENTENCE}} \end{array} \right\}$

SET Statement

FORMAT 1

$$\underline{\text{SET}} \begin{Bmatrix} \textit{index-name-1} \; [\textit{index-name-2}] \; \ldots \\ \textit{identifier-1} \quad\; [\textit{identifier-2} \quad] \ldots \end{Bmatrix} \underline{\text{TO}} \begin{Bmatrix} \textit{index-name-3} \\ \textit{identifier-3} \\ \textit{literal-1} \end{Bmatrix}$$

FORMAT 2

$$\underline{\text{SET}} \; \textit{index-name-4} \; [\textit{index-name-5}] \; \ldots \begin{Bmatrix} \underline{\text{UP}} \; \underline{\text{BY}} \\ \underline{\text{DOWN}} \; \underline{\text{BY}} \end{Bmatrix} \begin{Bmatrix} \textit{identifier-4} \\ \textit{literal-2} \end{Bmatrix}$$

SEGMENTATION — BASIC FORMATS

Environment Division Segmentation Formats

OBJECT-COMPUTER PARAGRAPH
SEGMENT-LIMIT Clause
    $\underline{\text{SEGMENT-LIMIT}}$ IS *priority-number*

Procedure Division Segmentation Formats

Priority Numbers
section-name $\underline{\text{SECTION}}$ [*priority-number*].

SOURCE PROGRAM LIBRARY FACILITY

COPY Statement
    $\underline{\text{COPY}}$ *library-name* [SUPPRESS]

$$\left[\underline{\text{REPLACING}} \; \textit{word-1} \; \underline{\text{BY}} \begin{Bmatrix} \textit{word-2} \\ \textit{literal-1} \\ \textit{identifier-1} \end{Bmatrix} \left[\textit{word-3} \; \underline{\text{BY}} \begin{Bmatrix} \textit{word-4} \\ \textit{literal-2} \\ \textit{identifier-2} \end{Bmatrix} \right] \ldots \right] .$$

Extended Source Program Library Facility

BASIS Card

$\underline{\text{BASIS}}$ *library-name*

INSERT Card

$\underline{\text{INSERT}}$ *sequence-number-field*

DELETE Card
$\underline{\text{DELETE}}$ *sequence-number-filed*

DEBUGGING LANGUAGE — BASIC FORMATS

Procedure Division Debugging Formats

EXHIBIT Statement

$$\underline{\text{EXHIBIT}} \begin{Bmatrix} \underline{\text{NAMED}} \\ \underline{\text{CHANGED}} \; \underline{\text{NAMED}} \\ \underline{\text{CHANGED}} \end{Bmatrix} \begin{Bmatrix} \textit{identifier-1} \\ \textit{nonnumeric-literal-1} \end{Bmatrix} \left[\begin{matrix} \textit{identifier-2} \\ \textit{nonnumeric-literal-2} \end{matrix} \right] \ldots$$

ON (Count-Conditional) Statement

FORMAT 1

ON *integer-1* [AND EVERY *integer-2*] [UNTIL *integer-3*]

$$\left\{ \begin{matrix} imperative\text{-}statement \\ \underline{NEXT}\ \underline{SENTENCE} \end{matrix} \right\} \left\{ \begin{matrix} \underline{ELSE} \\ \underline{OTHERWISE} \end{matrix} \right\} \left\{ \begin{matrix} statement \ldots \\ \underline{NEXT}\ \underline{SENTENCE} \end{matrix} \right\}$$

FORMAT 2 (Version 3 & 4)

ON $\left\{ \begin{matrix} integer\text{-}1 \\ identifier\text{-}1 \end{matrix} \right\}$ [AND EVERY $\left\{ \begin{matrix} integer\text{-}2 \\ identifier\text{-}2 \end{matrix} \right\}$] [UNTIL $\left\{ \begin{matrix} integer\text{-}3 \\ identifier\text{-}3 \end{matrix} \right\}$]

$$\left\{ \begin{matrix} imperative\text{-}statement \\ \underline{NEXT}\ \underline{SENTENCE} \end{matrix} \right\} \left\{ \begin{matrix} \underline{ELSE} \\ \underline{OTHERWISE} \end{matrix} \right\} \left\{ \begin{matrix} statement \ldots \\ \underline{NEXT}\ \underline{SENTENCE} \end{matrix} \right\}$$

TRACE Statement

$\left\{ \begin{matrix} \underline{READY} \\ \underline{RESET} \end{matrix} \right\}$ TRACE

Compile-Time Debugging Packet

DEBUG Card

DEBUG *location*

FORMAT CONTROL — BASIC FORMATS

EJECT Statement

1	Area B
	EJECT

SKIP1, SKIP2, SKIP3 Statements

1	Area B
	$\left\{ \begin{matrix} SKIP1 \\ SKIP2 \\ SKIP3 \end{matrix} \right\}$

STERLING CURRENCY — BASIC FORMATS

Data Division Sterling Formats
Nonreport PICTURE Clause

$\left\{ \begin{matrix} \underline{PICTURE} \\ \underline{PIC} \end{matrix} \right\}$ IS 9 [(*n*)] D [8] 8D $\left\{ \begin{matrix} 6[6] \\ 7[7] \end{matrix} \right\}$ [[V] 9 [(*n*)]] [USAGE IS] DISPLAY-ST

Report PICTURE Clause

$\left\{ \begin{matrix} \underline{PICTURE} \\ \underline{PIC} \end{matrix} \right\}$ IS

[*pound-report-string*] [*pound-separator-string*] *delimiter shilling-report-string* [*shilling-separator-string*] *delimiter pence-report-string* [*pence-separator-string*] [*sign-string*] [USAGE IS] DISPLAY-ST

PROGRAM PRODUCT INFORMATION — VERSION 4

TELEPROCESSING — BASIC FORMATS
Data Division Teleprocessing Formats

CD Entry

FORMAT 1

<u>CD</u> *cd-name* FOR <u>INPUT</u>

    [[[SYMBOLIC <u>QUEUE</u>   IS *data-name-1*]

        [SYMBOLIC <u>SUB-QUEUE-1</u>   IS *data-name-2*]

        [SYMBOLIC <u>SUB-QUEUE-2</u>   IS *data-name-3*]

        [SYMBOLIC <u>SUB-QUEUE-3</u>   IS *data-name-4*]

        [<u>MESSAGE</u> <u>DATE</u>   IS *data-name-5*]

        [<u>MESSAGE</u> <u>TIME</u>   IS *data-name-6*]

        [SYMBOLIC <u>SOURCE</u>   IS *data-name-7*]

        [<u>TEXT</u> <u>LENGTH</u>   IS *data-name-8*]

        [<u>END</u> <u>KEY</u>   IS *data-name-9*]

        [<u>STATUS</u> <u>KEY</u>   IS *data-name-10*]

        [<u>QUEUE</u> <u>DEPTH</u>   IS *data-name-11*]]

        [*data-name-1 data-name-2 . . . data-name-11*]].

FORMAT 2

    <u>CD</u> *cd-name* FOR <u>OUTPUT</u>

        [<u>DESTINATION</u> <u>COUNT</u>   IS *data-name-1*]

        [<u>TEXT</u> <u>LENGTH</u>   IS *data-name-2*]

        [<u>STATUS</u> <u>KEY</u>   IS *data-name-3*]

        [<u>ERROR</u> <u>KEY</u>   IS *data-name-4*]

        [SYMBOLIC <u>DESTINATION</u>   IS *data-name-5*].

Procedure Division Teleprocessing Formats

Message Condition
    [<u>NOT</u>] <u>MESSAGE</u> FOR *cd-name*

RECEIVE Statement

    <u>RECEIVE</u> *cd-name* $\begin{Bmatrix} \underline{MESSAGE} \\ \underline{SEGMENT} \end{Bmatrix}$ <u>INTO</u> *identifier-1*

      [<u>NO</u> DATA *imperative-statement*]

SEND Statement

FORMAT 1
    <u>SEND</u> *cd-name* <u>FROM</u> *identifier-1*

FORMAT 2

$$\underline{\text{SEND}}\ cd\text{-}name\ [\underline{\text{FROM}}\ identifier\text{-}1]\ \begin{Bmatrix} \text{WITH}\ identifier\text{-}2 \\ \text{WITH}\ \underline{\text{ESI}} \\ \text{WITH}\ \underline{\text{EMI}} \\ \text{WITH}\ \underline{\text{EGI}} \end{Bmatrix}$$

STRING MANIPULATION — BASIC FORMATS

STRING Statement

$$\underline{\text{STRING}}\ \begin{Bmatrix} identifier\text{-}1 \\ literal\text{-}1 \end{Bmatrix}\ \begin{bmatrix} identifier\text{-}2 \\ literal\text{-}2 \end{bmatrix}\ \ldots\ \underline{\text{DELIMITED}}\ \text{BY}\ \begin{Bmatrix} identifier\text{-}3 \\ literal\text{-}3 \\ \underline{\text{SIZE}} \end{Bmatrix}$$

$$\left[\begin{Bmatrix} identifier\text{-}4 \\ literal\text{-}4 \end{Bmatrix}\ \begin{bmatrix} identifier\text{-}5 \\ literal\text{-}5 \end{bmatrix}\ \ldots\ \underline{\text{DELIMITED}}\ \text{BY}\ \begin{Bmatrix} identifier\text{-}6 \\ literal\text{-}6 \\ \underline{\text{SIZE}} \end{Bmatrix}\right]\ldots$$

$$\underline{\text{INTO}}\ identifier\text{-}7\ [\text{WITH}\ \underline{\text{POINTER}}\ identifier\text{-}8]$$

$$[\text{ON}\ \underline{\text{OVERFLOW}}\ imperative\text{-}statement]$$

UNSTRING Statement

$$\underline{\text{UNSTRING}}\ identifier\text{-}1$$

$$\left[\underline{\text{DELIMITED}}\ \text{BY}\ [\underline{\text{ALL}}]\ \begin{Bmatrix} identifier\text{-}2 \\ literal\text{-}2 \end{Bmatrix}\ [\text{OR}\ [\underline{\text{ALL}}]\ \begin{Bmatrix} identifier\text{-}3 \\ literal\text{-}3 \end{Bmatrix}\ ]\ldots\right]$$

$$\underline{\text{INTO}}\ identifier\text{-}4\ [\underline{\text{DELIMITER}}\ \text{IN}\ identifier\text{-}5]$$

$$[\underline{\text{COUNT}}\ \text{IN}\ identifier\text{-}6]$$

$$[identifier\text{-}7\ [\underline{\text{DELIMITER}}\ \text{IN}\ identifier\text{-}8]$$

$$[\underline{\text{COUNT}}\ \text{IN}\ identifier\text{-}9]]\ldots$$

$$[\text{WITH}\ \underline{\text{POINTER}}\ identifier\text{-}10]$$

$$[\underline{\text{TALLYING}}\ \text{IN}\ identifier\text{-}11]$$

$$[\text{ON}\ \underline{\text{OVERFLOW}}\ imperative\text{-}statement]$$

VSAM FORMATS (OS/VS COBOL Only)

Environment Division — File-Control Entry

FORMAT 1 — Sequential VSAM Files

$$\underline{\text{FILE-CONTROL}}.$$

$$\{\underline{\text{SELECT}}\ [\underline{\text{OPTIONAL}}]\ file\text{-}name$$

$$\underline{\text{ASSIGN}}\ \text{TO}\ system\text{-}name\text{-}1\ [system\text{-}name\text{-}2]\ldots$$

$$[\underline{\text{RESERVE}}\ integer\ \begin{bmatrix} \text{AREA} \\ \text{AREAS} \end{bmatrix}\ ]$$

$$[\underline{\text{ORGANIZATION}}\ \text{IS}\ \underline{\text{SEQUENTIAL}}]$$

$$[\underline{\text{ACCESS}}\ \text{MODE}\ \text{IS}\ \underline{\text{SEQUENTIAL}}]$$

$$[\underline{\text{PASSWORD}}\ \text{IS}\ data\text{-}name\text{-}1]$$

$$[\text{FILE}\ \underline{\text{STATUS}}\ \text{IS}\ data\text{-}name\text{-}2]\ .\}\ldots$$

FORMAT 2 — Indexed VSAM Files

<u>FILE-CONTROL</u>.

{<u>SELECT</u> *file-name*

<u>ASSIGN</u> TO *system-name-1* [*system-name-2*] . . .

[<u>RESERVE</u> *integer* $\begin{bmatrix} \text{AREA} \\ \text{AREAS} \end{bmatrix}$]

<u>ORGANIZATION</u> IS <u>INDEXED</u>

[<u>ACCESS</u> MODE IS $\left\{ \begin{matrix} \underline{\text{SEQUENTIAL}} \\ \underline{\text{RANDOM}} \\ \underline{\text{DYNAMIC}} \end{matrix} \right\}$]

<u>RECORD</u> KEY IS *data-name-3*

[<u>PASSWORD</u> IS *data-name-1*]

[FILE <u>STATUS</u> IS *data-name-2*] . } . . .

Environment Division — I-O-Control Entry

<u>I-O-CONTROL</u>.

[<u>RERUN</u> <u>ON</u> *system-name* <u>EVERY</u> *integer* <u>RECORDS</u>

OF *file-name-1*] . . .

[<u>SAME</u> [<u>RECORD</u>] AREA

FOR *file-name-2* [*file-name-3*] . . .] . . .

Data Division

LABEL RECORDS Clause

LABEL $\left\{ \begin{matrix} \underline{\text{RECORD}} \text{ IS} \\ \underline{\text{RECORDS}} \text{ ARE} \end{matrix} \right\}$ $\left\{ \begin{matrix} \underline{\text{STANDARD}} \\ \underline{\text{OMITTED}} \end{matrix} \right\}$

NOTE: Other Data Division clauses have the same syntax for VSAM files that they have for other files.

Procedure Division

CLOSE Statement

<u>CLOSE</u> *file-name-1* [WITH <u>LOCK</u>]

[*file-name-2* [WITH <u>LOCK</u>]] . . .

DELETE Statement

<u>DELETE</u> *file-name* RECORD

[<u>INVALID</u> KEY *imperative-statement*]

OPEN Statement

<u>OPEN</u> $\left\{ \begin{matrix} \underline{\text{INPUT}} & \textit{file-name-1} \; [\textit{file-name-2}] \ldots \\ \underline{\text{OUTPUT}} \; \textit{file-name-1} \; [\textit{file-name-2}] \ldots \\ \underline{\text{I-O}} & \textit{file-name-1} \; [\textit{file-name-2}] \ldots \\ \underline{\text{EXTEND}} \; \textit{file-name-1} \; [\textit{file-name-2}] \ldots \end{matrix} \right\}$ . . .

READ Statement

FORMAT 1
READ *file-name* [NEXT] RECORD [INTO *identifier*]

[AT END *imperative-statement*]

FORMAT 2
READ *file-name* RECORD [INTO *identifier*]

[INVALID KEY *imperative-statement*]

REWRITE Statement
REWRITE *record-name* [FROM *identifier*]

[INVALID KEY *imperative-statement*]

START Statement

START *file-name* [KEY IS $\left\{ \begin{array}{l} \underline{\text{EQUAL}} \text{ TO} \\ = \\ \underline{\text{GREATER}} \text{ THAN} \\ > \\ \underline{\text{NOT}} \underline{\text{LESS}} \text{ THAN} \\ \underline{\text{NOT}} < \end{array} \right\}$]

[INVALID KEY *imperative-statement*]

USE Sentence

USE AFTER STANDARD $\left\{ \begin{array}{l} \underline{\text{EXCEPTION}} \\ \underline{\text{ERROR}} \end{array} \right\}$ PROCEDURE

ON $\left\{ \begin{array}{l} \textit{file-name-1} \text{ [}\textit{file-name-2}\text{] } \ldots \\ \underline{\text{INPUT}} \\ \underline{\text{OUTPUT}} \\ \underline{\text{I-O}} \\ \underline{\text{EXTEND}} \end{array} \right\}$

WRITE Statement
WRITE *record-name* [FROM *identifier*]

[INVALID KEY *imperative-statement*]

MERGE FACILITY FORMATS (OS/VS COBOL Only)

Environment Division — Input-Output Section

FILE-CONTROL Entry

FILE-CONTROL.

{SELECT *file-name*

ASSIGN TO *system-name-1* [*system-name-2*] . . . ,} . . .

I-O-CONTROL Entry
I-O-CONTROL.

SAME $\left\{ \begin{array}{l} \underline{\text{SORT}} \\ \underline{\text{SORT-MERGE}} \\ \underline{\text{RECORD}} \end{array} \right\}$ AREA FOR *file-name-1* [*file-name-2*] . . .

Data Division — merge File Description Entry

SD *merge-file-name*

[RECORD CONTAINS [*integer-1* TO] *integer-2* CHARACTERS]

[DATA $\begin{Bmatrix} \underline{RECORD} \text{ IS} \\ \underline{RECORDS} \text{ ARE} \end{Bmatrix}$ *data-name-1* [*data-name-2*] ...] .

Procedure Division — Merge Statement

MERGE *file-name-1*

ON $\begin{Bmatrix} \underline{ASCENDING} \\ \underline{DESCENDING} \end{Bmatrix}$ KEY *data-name-1* [*data-name-2*] ...

[ON $\begin{Bmatrix} \underline{ASCENDING} \\ \underline{DESCENDING} \end{Bmatrix}$ KEY *data-name-3* [*data-name-4*] ...] ...

USING *file-name-2* *file-name-3* [*file-name-4*] ...

$\begin{Bmatrix} \underline{GIVING} \text{ *file-name-5*} \\ \underline{OUTPUT} \ \underline{PROCEDURE} \text{ IS *section-name-1*} \ [\underline{THRU} \text{ *section-name-2*}] \end{Bmatrix}$

APPENDIX F

DIFFERENCES BETWEEN THE 1968 AND 1974 ANS COBOL FEATURES AS OUTLINED IN THIS BOOK

The following summary gives the main differences between the 1968 and 1974 ANS COBOL features that have been discussed in this book. Note that this is not a complete list. For a description of all the differences between the 1968 and 1974 versions, see the Federal Information Processing Standard Publication 43, ''Aids for COBOL Program Conversion.'' This is available from the Superintendent of Documents, Washington, D.C. 20402 (SD catalog number 13.52:43).

1968 ANS COBOL

1. Comments
   a. The REMARKS paragraph may be coded as the last paragraph in the IDENTIFICATION DIVISION for providing comments.
   b. NOTE as the first word in a statement may be used to designate an entire statement as a comment. NOTE as a paragraph-name designates the entire paragraph as a comment.

2. Level 77 items as used in the WORKING-STORAGE SECTION
   a. Level 77 items must precede level 01 entries.

3. REDEFINES Statement
   a. When using the REDEFINES statement, lower-level items **may appear** between the redefined entry and the redefining entry.

4. Asterisk (*) as a Check Protection Symbol
   a. The asterisk **may appear** as part of a report-item with the BLANK WHEN ZERO option.

1974 ANS COBOL

a. An * in column 7 designates an entire line as a comment.

a. There is no restriction on the placement of 77-level items.

a. When using the REDEFINES statement, lower-level items **may not appear** between the redefined entry and the redefining entry.

a. The asterisk **may not appear** as part of a report-item with the BLANK WHEN ZERO option.

563

1968 ANS COBOL	**1974 ANS COBOL**

5. Mnemonic-Names (as used in the SPECIAL-NAMES and other paragraphs)

   a. Mnemonic-names may consist of all numbers.

           a. Mnemonic-names must contain at least one alphabetic character.

6. B in PICTURE clause

   a. Alphabetic items **may not** be edited into report-items that contain a B in the PICTURE clause.

           a. Alphabetic items **may** be edited into report-items that contain a B in the PICTURE clause.

7. Size of numeric fields

   a. No restriction

           a. A maximum of 18 digits may be designated in a numeric PICTURE clause.

8. Slash (/) as an edit symbol

   a. Slash is not permitted.

           a. Slash may be used as an edit symbol in a report item.

9. ACCEPT statement

   a. The following formats are permitted:

   ACCEPT (data-name)

   ACCEPT (data-name) FROM $\left\{ \begin{array}{l} \text{CONSOLE} \\ \text{mnemonic-name} \end{array} \right\}$

           a. The following formats are permitted:

           ACCEPT (data-name)

           ACCEPT (data-name) FROM $\left\{ \begin{array}{l} \text{CONSOLE} \\ \text{mnemonic-name} \end{array} \right\}$

           ACCEPT (data-name) FROM $\left\{ \begin{array}{l} \text{DATE} \\ \text{DAY} \\ \text{TIME} \end{array} \right\}$

           where DATE, DAY and TIME are internal specifications that are automatically updated by the supervisor or by a timer.

10. Use of the word TO

    a. The word TO is required in:
    EQUAL TO
    GO TO

            a. The word TO is optional in:
    EQUAL TO
    GO TO

11. Comparing numeric operands to nonnumeric operands

    a. The comparison of numeric to nonnumeric operands is not permitted—it can cause a program interrupt.

            a. The numeric operand is treated as if it were moved to an alphanumeric entry of the same size and then the comparison is made.

12. REMAINDER option with the DIVIDE statement

    a. REMAINDER must specify a data-name that is numeric.

            a. REMAINDER may specify a data-name that is either numeric or a report-item.

13. Checking for specific values within a record

    a. Use EXAMINE statement

            a. Use INSPECT statement

14. ADVANCING option

    a. LINES must be used with the ADVANCING option—LINE is not permitted. To obtain single spacing, we write

    WRITE (record name) AFTER ADVANCING 1 LINES.

            a. LINE or LINES may be used with the ADVANCING option.

15. Punctuation

a. A space may not precede a comma, period, or semicolon, or follow a left parenthesis.

a. A space following a left parenthesis or preceding a comma, period, or semicolon is optional.

LINAGE Clause   Chapter 13 illustrates how page control may be accomplished by using a line counter. A new technique added to the 1974 COBOL standard provides an alternate method for performing line counting. The LINAGE clause enables programmers to uniquely define the format of the printed page to be generated by the program. This clause is used as part of the FD entry. The format for the LINAGE clause is as follows:

$$\left[\underline{\text{LINAGE}} \text{ IS} \begin{Bmatrix} \text{data-name-1} \\ \text{integer-1} \end{Bmatrix} \text{LINES} \right.$$
$$\left[\text{WITH } \underline{\text{FOOTING}} \text{ AT} \begin{Bmatrix} \text{data-name-2} \\ \text{integer-2} \end{Bmatrix} \right]$$
$$\left[\text{LINES AT } \underline{\text{TOP}} \begin{Bmatrix} \text{data-name-3} \\ \text{integer-3} \end{Bmatrix} \right]$$
$$\left. \left[\text{LINES AT } \underline{\text{BOTTOM}} \begin{Bmatrix} \text{data-name-4} \\ \text{integer-4} \end{Bmatrix} \right] \right]$$

Example

```
FD   PRINT-FILE
     LABEL RECORDS ARE OMITTED
     DATA RECORD IS PRINT-REC
     LINAGE IS 60 LINES
         WITH FOOTING AT 57
         LINES AT TOP 3
         LINES AT BOTTOM 3.
```

The meaning of the LINAGE clause in the above is as follows:

Clause	Meaning
LINAGE IS 60 LINES	60 lines to the page
WITH FOOTING AT 57	the last print line is line 57
LINES AT TOP 3	3 blank lines at the top of each page
LINES AT BOTTOM 3	3 blank lines at the bottom of each page

Note that the clause WITH FOOTING AT 57 will cause an EOP (end of page) condition to be met at line 57 of each page.

The three clauses accompanying the LINAGE statement are all optional. The integers indicated in the example may be replaced by data-names with integer values which can be established in the DATA DIVISION.

INDEX